Baseball America's

1998
Directory

**Major And Minor League
Names, Addresses, Schedules,
Phone and FAX Numbers**

**Detailed Information
On International, College and
Amateur Baseball**

**PUBLISHED BY
BASEBALL AMERICA**

Published By Baseball America

EDITOR
Allan Simpson

ASSOCIATE EDITOR
Stephen Borelli

ASSISTANT EDITORS
Mark Derewicz
John Royster

PRODUCTION
Valerie Holbert
Casey Mansfield Thomas

BASEBALL AMERICA, INC.

PUBLISHER
Dave Chase

EDITOR
Allan Simpson

MANAGING EDITOR
Will Lingo

PRODUCTION COORDINATOR
Jeff Brunk

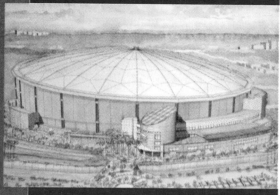

TABLE**OF**CONTENTS

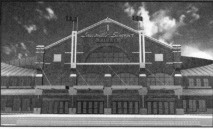

1998-1999 CALENDAR

March, 1998

Sun	Mon	Tues	Wed	Thur	Fri	Sat
1	2	3	4	5	6	7
8	9	10	11	12	13	14
15	16	17	18	19	20	21
22	23	24	25	26	27	28
29	30	31				

April, 1998

Sun	Mon	Tues	Wed	Thur	Fri	Sat
			1	2	3	4
5	6	7	8	9	10	11
12	13	14	15	16	17	18
19	20	21	22	23	24	25
26	27	28	29	30		

May, 1998

Sun	Mon	Tues	Wed	Thur	Fri	Sat
					1	2
3	4	5	6	7	8	9
10	11	12	13	14	15	16
17	18	19	20	21	22	23
24	25	26	27	28	29	30
31						

June, 1998

Sun	Mon	Tues	Wed	Thur	Fri	Sat
	1	2	3	4	5	6
7	8	9	10	11	12	13
14	15	16	17	18	19	20
21	22	23	24	25	26	27
28	29	30				

July, 1998

Sun	Mon	Tues	Wed	Thur	Fri	Sat
			1	2	3	4
5	6	7	8	9	10	11
12	13	14	15	16	17	18
19	20	21	22	23	24	25
26	27	28	29	30	31	

August, 1998

Sun	Mon	Tues	Wed	Thur	Fri	Sat
						1
2	3	4	5	6	7	8
9	10	11	12	13	14	15
16	17	18	19	20	21	22
23	24	25	26	27	28	29
30	31					

September, 1998

Sun	Mon	Tues	Wed	Thur	Fri	Sat
		1	2	3	4	5
6	7	8	9	10	11	12
13	14	15	16	17	18	19
20	21	22	23	24	25	26
27	28	29	30			

October, 1998

Sun	Mon	Tues	Wed	Thur	Fri	Sat
				1	2	3
4	5	6	7	8	9	10
11	12	13	14	15	16	17
18	19	20	21	22	23	24
25	26	27	28	29	30	31

November, 1998

Sun	Mon	Tues	Wed	Thur	Fri	Sat
1	2	3	4	5	6	7
8	9	10	11	12	13	14
15	16	17	18	19	20	21
22	23	24	25	26	27	28
29	30					

December, 1998

Sun	Mon	Tues	Wed	Thur	Fri	Sat
		1	2	3	4	5
6	7	8	9	10	11	12
13	14	15	16	17	18	19
20	21	22	23	24	25	26
27	28	29	30	31		

January, 1999

Sun	Mon	Tues	Wed	Thur	Fri	Sat
					1	2
3	4	5	6	7	8	9
10	11	12	13	14	15	16
17	18	19	20	21	22	23
24	25	26	27	28	29	30
31						

February, 1999

Sun	Mon	Tues	Wed	Thur	Fri	Sat
	1	2	3	4	5	6
7	8	9	10	11	12	13
14	15	16	17	18	19	20
21	22	23	24	25	26	27
28						

March, 1999

Sun	Mon	Tues	Wed	Thur	Fri	Sat
	1	2	3	4	5	6
7	8	9	10	11	12	13
14	15	16	17	18	19	20
21	22	23	24	25	26	27
28	29	30	31			

April, 1999

Sun	Mon	Tues	Wed	Thur	Fri	Sat
				1	2	3
4	5	6	7	8	9	10
11	12	13	14	15	16	17
18	19	20	21	22	23	24
25	26	27	28	29	30	

EVENTS CALENDAR

March 1998-February 1999

March

18—Opening Day: Mexican League.
31—Opening Day: American League (Detroit at Tampa Bay, Kansas City at Baltimore, Cleveland at Seattle, Chicago at Texas).
31—Opening Day: National League (Philadelphia at New York, Milwaukee at Atlanta, Chicago at Florida, San Diego at Cincinnati, Colorado at Arizona, Los Angeles at St. Louis, San Francisco at Houston).

April

1—Opening Day: American League (Minnesota at Toronto, New York at Anaheim, Boston at Oakland).
1—Opening Day: National League (Pittsburgh at Montreal).
2—Opening Day: Southern League, Texas League, California League, South Atlantic League.
3—Opening Day: Japan Central League.
4—Opening Day: Japan Pacific League
7—Opening Day: Pacific Coast League.
8—Opening Day: Eastern League, Florida State League.
9—Opening Day: International League, Midwest League.
10—Opening Day: Carolina League.
13—National Classic High School Tournament at Orange County, Calif. (through April 16)

May

14—NCAA play-in series at campus sites (through May 16)
16—Junior College Division III World Series at Batavia, N.Y. (through May 22)
18—NAIA World Series at Tulsa, Okla. (through May 23)
20—Opening Day: Atlantic League
21—NCAA Division I Regionals at campus sites (through May 24)
21—Opening Day: Texas-Louisiana League
22—Opening Day: Western League
23—NCAA Division III World Series at Salem, Va. (through May 27)
23—NCAA Division II World Series at Montgomery, Ala. (through May 30)
23—Junior College Division II World Series at Millington, Tenn. (through May 29)
23—Junior College World Series at Grand Junction, Colo. (through May 30)
28—Opening Day: Northern League
29—College World Series at Omaha (through June 6)
29—Opening Day: Heartland League
29—Opening Day: Northeast League
29—Opening Day: Shenandoah Valley League
29—Opening Day: Jayhawk League
29—Opening Day: Coastal Plain League

June

1—Mexican League all-star game at Merida, Yucatan.
1—Opening Day: Dominican Summer League, Venezuelan Summer League.
2—Amateur free agent draft (through June 4)
3—Opening Day: Atlantic Collegiate League
4—Opening Day: New England Collegiate League
4—Opening Day: Frontier League
4—Opening Day: Central Illinois Collegiate League
5—Opening Day: Northwoods League
5—Opening Day: Interleague games (EAST—Montreal at Tampa Bay, Mets at Boston, Philadelphia at Toronto, Atlanta at Baltimore, Florida at Yankees. CENTRAL—Minnesota at Pittsburgh, Cleveland at Cincinnati, White Sox at Cubs, Detroit at Milwaukee, Kansas City at Houston, Kansas City at Houston. WEST—Anaheim at Colorado, Los Angeles at Seattle, Arizona at Oakland, San Diego at Texas).
6—Opening Day: Northeastern League
7—Opening Day: Alaska League
10—Opening Day: Great Lakes League
11—Opening Day: Cape Cod League
16—Opening Day: New York-Penn League, Northwest League, Pioneer League.
16—California League all-star game at Lancaster, Calif.
16—South Atlantic League all-star game at Charleston, S.C.
17—Opening Day: Appalachian League.
19—Opening Day: Gulf Coast League.

19—USA Junior Olympic Championship at Tucson, Ariz. (through June 28).
20—Florida State League all-star game at Fort Myers, Fla.
22—Southern League all-star game at Mobile, Ala.
23—Carolina League all-star game at Wilmington, Del.
23—Midwest League all-star game at Clinton, Iowa.
23—Sunbelt Classic Baseball Series at Shawnee/Tecumseh, Okla. (through June 27)
24—Opening Day: Arizona League.

July

7—69th Major League all-star game at Coors Field, Denver
8—Triple-A all-star game at Norfolk, Va.
8—Double-A all-star game at New Haven, Conn.
8—AA Youth World Championship at Fairview Heights, Ill. (through July 19).
10—Team One National Showcase at St. Petersburg, Fla. (through July 12)
13—Texas-Louisiana League all-star game at Fort Worth, Texas.
13—Western League all-star game at Chico, Calif.
19—Goodwill Games at New York (through Aug. 2).
21—World Senior Baseball Cup at Italy (through Aug. 2).
22—Japan major league all-star game at Nagoya Dome.
23—Japan major league all-star game at Chiba Marine Stadium.
26—Hall of Fame induction ceremonies, Cooperstown.
27—Hall of Fame Game, Baltimore vs. Toronto at Cooperstown.
28—Texas League all-star game at Little Rock, Ark.
31—National Baseball Congress World Series at Wichita, Kan. (through Aug. 14).

August

1—End of major league trading period without waivers.
1—Cape Cod League all-star game at Chatham, Mass.
3—Northern League all-star game at Sioux City, Iowa.
5—Eastern Professional Baseball Showcase at Wilmington, N.C. (through Aug. 8).
7—Connie Mack World Series at Farmington, N.M. (through Aug. 13).
15—Babe Ruth 16-18 World Series at Dare County, N.C. (through Aug. 22).
15—Pony League World Series at Washington, Pa. (through Aug. 22).
15—Babe Ruth 13-15 World Series at Pine Bluff, Ark. (through Aug. 22).
16—Area Code Games at Long Beach (through Aug. 15).
23—Little League World Series at Williamsport, Pa. (through Aug. 29).
21—American Legion World Series at Las Vegas (through Aug. 25).
31—Postseason major league roster eligibility frozen.

September

1—Major league roster limits expanded from 25 to 40.
27—Major league season ends.
28—Beginning of major league trading period without waivers.
29—Major league Division Series begin.
30—Opening Day: Arizona Fall League.

October

6—Major League Championship Series begin.
17—World Series begins at home of American League champion.
17—Japan Series begins at home of Central League champion.

November

20—Forty-man major league winter rosters must be filed.

December

4—National High School Baseball Coaches Association convention at Tulsa (through Dec. 6).
11—96th annual Winter Meetings at Nashville (through Dec. 15).
14—Rule 5 major league/minor league drafts.
18—Goodwill Series X at Adelaide, Australia (through Dec. 31).

January 1999

7—American Baseball Coaches Association convention at Atlanta (through Jan. 10).

February 1999

4—Caribbean World Series at San Juan, Puerto Rico (through Feb. 9).

BASEBALL AMERICA

ESTABLISHED 1981

PUBLISHER: Dave Chase

EDITOR: Allan Simpson

MANAGING EDITOR: Will Lingo

SENIOR ASSOCIATE EDITOR: John Royster

ASSOCIATE EDITOR: Lacy Lusk

ASSISTANT EDITOR: Stephen Borelli

ASSISTANT EDITOR: John Manuel

NATIONAL CORRESPONDENTS: David Rawnsley, Alan Schwarz

EDITORIAL INTERN: Mark Derewicz

PRODUCTION SUPERVISOR: Jeff Brunk

PRODUCTION MANAGER: Valerie Holbert

PRODUCTION ASSISTANT: Casey Mansfield Thomas

CUSTOMER SERVICE: Ronnie McCabe, Maxine Tillman

ADVERTISING SALES
Kris Howard, Advertising Manager
Carole Budd, Marketplace Manager
P.O. Box 2089, Durham, NC 27702
Phone (800) 845-2726; FAX: 919-682-2880

Michael Applegate, Southeast Representative
3132 Paces Station Ridge, Atlanta, GA 30339
Phone (770) 805-0949

NATIONAL NEWSSTAND CONSULTANT
John Blassingame, Linden, NJ

BASEBALL AMERICA, Inc.
PRESIDENT: Miles Wolff
P.O. Box 2089, Durham, NC 27702
Street Address: 600 S. Duke St., Durham, NC 27701
Phone: (919) 682-9635 • Toll-Free: (800) 845-2726
FAX: (919) 682-2880
E-Mail Address: ba@interpath.com
Website: www.fanlink.com/ba

BASEBALL AMERICA, the nation's most complete all-baseball
newspaper, publishes 26 issues a year. Subscription rates
are $48.95 for one year, payable in U.S. funds.

BASEBALL AMERICA PUBLICATIONS

1998 Almanac: A comprehensive look at the 1997 season, featuring major and minor league statistics and commentary. **$12.95**

1998 Directory: Names, addresses, phone numbers, major and minor league schedules—vital to baseball insiders and fans. **$12.95**

1998 Super Register: A complete record, with biographical information, of every player who played professional baseball in 1997. **$24.95**

1998 Great Minor League Ballparks Calendar: $10.95

Encyclopedia of Minor League Baseball: The first total compilation of the teams and standings in the 90-year history of minor league baseball. The ultimate research tool. **$48.95 hardcover, $39.95 softcover**

The Minor League Register: An updated compilation of SABR's The Minor League Stars with more than 200 new entries, minor league milestones. **$39.95 softcover**

BASEBALL AMERICA

1997 AWARD WINNERS

AMERICAN LEAGUE

Player of the Year
Ken Griffey, of, Seattle

Pitcher of the Year
Roger Clemens, rhp, Toronto

Rookie of the Year
Nomar Garciaparra, ss, Boston

Manager of the Year
Phil Garner, Milwaukee

Executive of the Year
Randy Smith, Detroit

NATIONAL LEAGUE

Player of the Year
Larry Walker, of, Colorado

Pitcher of the Year
Pedro Martinez, rhp, Montreal

Rookie of the Year
Scott Rolen, 3b, Philadelphia

Manager of the Year
Dusty Baker, San Francisco

Executive of the Year
Brian Sabean, San Francisco

MINOR LEAGUES

Organization of the Year
Detroit Tigers

Player of the Year (overall)
Paul Konerko, 3b, Albuquerque Dukes (Pacific Coast)

Manager of the Year
Gary Jones, Edmonton Trappers (Pacific Coast)

Team of the Year
West Michigan Whitecaps (Midwest)

Players of the Year
Triple-A: Paul Konerko, 3b, Albuquerque
Double-A: Ben Grieve, of, Huntsville
Class A: Adrian Beltre, 3b, Vero Beach
Short Season: Dermal Brown, of, Spokane

Freitas Awards
Triple-A: Rochester (International)
Double-A: Bowie (Eastern)
Class A: Rancho Cucamonga (California)
Short Season: Oneonta (New York-Penn)

INDEPENDENT BASEBALL

Player of the Year
Mike Meggers, of, Duluth-Superior (Northern)

WINTER BASEBALL

Player of the Year
Jose Hernandez, ss, Mayaguez (Puerto Rico)

COLLEGE BASEBALL

Player of the Year
J.D. Drew, of, Florida State

Coach of the Year
Jim Wells, Alabama

Freshman of the Year
Brian Roberts, ss, North Carolina

AMATEUR BASEBALL

Player of the Year
Pat Burrell, 3b, Team USA

HIGH SCHOOL BASEBALL

Player of the Year
Darnell McDonald, of, Cherry Creek HS, Englewood, Colo.

TOLLFREENUMBERS

Airlines

Aeromexico	800-237-6639
Air Canada	800-776-3000
Alaska Airlines	800-426-0333
Aloha Airlines	800-227-4900
America West	800-235-9292
American Airlines	800-433-7300
Continental Airlines	800-525-0280
Delta Airlines	800-221-1212
Northwest Airlines	800-225-2525
Olympic Airways	800-223-1226
Qantas Airways	800-227-4500
Southwest Airlines	800-435-9792
Trans World Airlines	800-221-2000
United Airlines	800-631-1500
U.S. Airways	800-428-4322

Car Rentals

Alamo (except Florida)	800-327-9633
Alamo (Florida only)	800-732-3232
Avis	800-331-1212
Avis International	800-331-1084
Budget	800-527-0700
Dollar	800-800-4000
Enterprise	800-325-8007
Hertz	800-654-3131
Hertz International	800-654-3001
National	800-227-7368
Thrifty	800-367-2277

Hotels/Motels

Best Western	800-528-1234
Choice Hotels	800-424-6423
Courtyard by Marriott	800-321-2211
Days Inn	800-325-2525
Doubletree Hotels/Guest Suites	800-424-2900
Embassy Suites	800-362-2779
Hampton Inns	800-426-7866
Hilton Hotels	800-445-8667
Holiday Inns	800-465-4329
Howard Johnsons Motor Lodges	800-654-2000
Hyatt Hotels	800-228-9000
La Quinta	800-531-5900
Marriott Hotels	800-228-9290
Omni Hotels	800-843-6664
Radisson Hotels	800-333-3333
Ramada Inns	800-228-2828
Red Roof Inns	800-843-7663
Sheraton Hotels	800-325-3535
Renaissance Hotels/Resorts	800-468-3571
TraveLodge	800-578-7878
Westin Hotels	800-228-3000

Rail

Amtrak	800-872-7245

WHAT'S NEW IN '98

MAJOR LEAGUE BASEBALL

TEAMS
- Arizona Diamondbacks begin play in National League (Western Division)
- Tampa Bay Devil Rays begin play in American League (Eastern Division)
- Milwaukee relocated from American League to National League (Central Division)
- Detroit relocated from American League Eastern Division to AL Central Division

BALLPARKS
- Anaheim: Edison International Field
- Arizona: Bank One Ballpark
- Tampa Bay: Tropicana Field

SPRING TRAINING
- Atlanta relocated to Orlando, Fla., from West Palm Beach
- Chicago White Sox relocated to Tucson, Ariz., from Sarasota, Fla.
- Cincinnati relocated to Sarasota from Plant City, Fla.
- Milwaukee relocated to Maryvale, Ariz., from Chandler
- Montreal relocated to Jupiter, Fla., from West Palm Beach
- St. Louis relocated to Jupiter from St. Petersburg

MINOR LEAGUES

Triple-A
- American Association disbanded
- Iowa, Nashville, New Orleans, Omaha and Oklahoma (formerly Oklahoma City) absorbed by Pacific Coast League from American Association
- Buffalo, Indianapolis and Louisville absorbed by International League from American Association
- Phoenix (Pacific Coast) relocated to Fresno
- Expansion franchises granted to Durham (International) and Memphis (Pacific Coast)
- AFFILIATION CHANGES:
  Arizona to Tucson (Pacific Coast)
  Chicago (AL) from Nashville to Calgary
  Milwaukee from Tucson to Louisville
  Pittsburgh from Calgary to Nashville
  St. Louis from Louisville to Memphis
  Tampa Bay to Durham

Double-A
- Memphis (Southern) relocated to West Tenn (Jackson, Tenn.)
- AFFILIATION CHANGES:
  Chicago (NL) from Orlando to West Tenn
  Seattle from Memphis to Orlando

Class A
- Durham (Carolina) relocated to Danville, Va. (franchise will relocate to Myrtle Beach, S.C., in 1999)
- West Palm Beach (Florida State) relocated to Jupiter
- AFFILIATION CHANGES:
  Los Angeles drops Savannah
  Texas adds Savannah

Short-Season
  White Sox relocated to Arizona League from Gulf Coast League

BALLPARKS
- Jupiter: Roger Dean Stadium
- Lowell: Edward Lacheur Park
- Oklahoma: Southwestern Bell Stadium
- Tucson: Tucson Electric Park
- West Tenn: Pringles Park

NICKNAMES
- Tucson from Toros to Sidewinders
- Batavia from Trojans to Muckdogs
- Oklahoma from 89ers to Redhawks

INDEPENDENT LEAGUES
- Atlantic League begins operations
- Big South League, Prairie League disbanded

The C405™Plus outer wall *has been thinned 7%, giving you more pop.*

The Air Pressurized Chamber *runs the length of the 10% longer barrel, giving you the largest sweet spot in the game.*

The new solid sound and feel *come from the Air Pressurized Chamber, which also gives you optimum performance on contact.*

The new Air Attack is already a pressure performer *at these schools: Miami, Auburn, Rice, Florida, USC, Ohio State, Arizona State, Oklahoma State, Cal State Fullerton, Georgia Tech.*

HIT BETTER UNDER PRESSURE.

Introducing the new TPX Air Attack maximum performance bat with exclusive Air Pressurized Chamber technology.* It's been specifically designed to turn every at bat into a pressure situation. For your opposition.

You want to be a better hitter? No pressure. Get the new TPX Air Attack from Louisville Slugger.

www.slugger.com

MAJOR LEAGUE BASEBALL

Mailing Address: 350 Park Ave., 17th Floor, New York, NY 10022. **Telephone:** (212) 339-7800. **FAX:** (212) 355-0007.

Commissioner: Vacant.

Chairman, Executive Council: Allan H. "Bud" Selig.

President, Chief Operating Officer: Paul Beeston.

Bud Selig

Officers and Directors

Vice President, Chief Information Officer: James Masterson.

Executive Director, Baseball Operations: Bill Murray. **Director, Baseball Operations:** Roy Krasik. **Administrator, Baseball Operations:** Jeff Pfeifer. **Records Coordinator:** George Moreira. **Administrative Assistant:** Jean Coen.

Executive Director, Minor League Operations: Jimmie Lee Solomon.

Executive Director, Public Relations: Richard Levin. **Managers, Public Relations:** Carole Coleman, Pat Courtney. **Baseball Information Systems:** Rob Doelger. **Supervisor, Public Relations:** Kathleen Fineout. **Administrator, Media Relations:** Denise Michaels. **Assistant, Public Relations:** Matt Gould. **Administrative Assistant:** Blakely Blum.

Executive Director, Security/Facility Management: Kevin Hallinan.

Chief Financial Officer: Jeffrey White. **Controller:** Robert Clark.

General Counsel: Thomas Ostertag.

Executive Director, Market Development and MLB Charities: Kathleen Francis.

Director of Human Resources: Wendy Lewis.

Vice President, Broadcasting/New Media Development: Leslie Sullivan. **Director, Broadcast Operations:** Bernadette McDonald.

Director, Special Events: Carolyn Taylor.

Events

1998 Major League All-Star Game: July 7 at Coors Field, Colorado.

1998 World Series: Begins Oct. 17 at home of American League champion.

MAJOR LEAGUE BASEBALL
PLAYER RELATIONS COMMITTEE

Mailing Address: 350 Park Ave., New York, NY 10022. **Telephone:** (212) 339-7400. **FAX:** (212) 371-2242.

Chief Labor Negotiator: Randy Levine.

Associate Counsel: John Westhoff, Louis Melendez.

Director, Contract Administration: John Ricco.

MAJOR LEAGUE BASEBALL
PROPERTIES

Mailing Address: 350 Park Ave., New York, NY 10022. **Telephone:** (212) 339-7900. **FAX:** (212) 339-7628

President: Bob Gamgort.

Vice President, Business Development and New Ventures: Unavailable. **Vice President, Creative Design and Marketing Services:** Anne Occi. **Vice President, Finance and Royalty Administration:** Tom Duffy.

MAJOR LEAGUE BASEBALL
INTERNATIONAL

Mailing Address: 350 Park Ave., 22nd Floor, New York, NY 10022. **Telephone:** (212) 350-8300. **FAX:** (212) 826-2230.

Chief Operating Officer: Tim Brosnan.

Vice President, International Licensing: Sharon Dennis. **Vice President, Production and Television Operations:** Russell Gabay. **Vice President, Corporate Sponsorship:** Paul Archey.

Director, European Operations: Clive Russell.

Director, Southeast Asia/Australia/New Zealand: Peter Carton.

Associate Director, Game Development: Julie Croteau. **Associate Director, Broadcasting:** Margaret O'Neill. **Associate Director, Client Services:** Sara Loarte. **Administrator, International Licensing:** Michael Luscher.

American League

AMERICAN LEAGUE

Mailing Address: 350 Park Ave., 18th Floor, New York, NY 10022. **Telephone:** (212) 339-7600. **FAX:** (212) 593-7138.

Years League Active: 1901-.

President: Gene Budig.

Vice President: Gene Autry (Anaheim).

Board of Directors: Anaheim, Baltimore, Boston, Chicago, New York, Texas.

Executive Director, Umpiring: Marty Springstead. **Coordinator, Umpire Operations:** Philip Janssen. **Administrator, Umpire Travel:** Tess Basta.

Senior Vice President: Phyllis Merhige.

Vice President, Finance: Derek Irwin.

Director of Waiver and Player Records: Kim Ng.

Administrative Assistant, Secretary to the President: Carolyn Coen.

Gene Budig

Receptionist: Nancy Perez.

1998 Opening Date: March 31. **Closing Date:** Sept. 27.

Regular Season: 162 games.

Division Structure: East—Baltimore, Boston, New York, Tampa Bay, Toronto. **Central**—Chicago, Cleveland, Detroit, Kansas City, Minnesota. **West**—Anaheim, Oakland, Seattle, Texas.

Playoff Format: Three division champions and second-place team with best record play in best-of-5 Division Series. Winners meet in best-of-7 League Championship Series.

All Star-Game: July 7 at Denver, CO (American League vs. National League).

Roster Limit: 25, through Aug. 31 when rosters expand to 40.

Brand of Baseball: Rawlings.

Statistician: Elias Sports Bureau, 500 Fifth Ave., New York, NY 10110.

Umpires: Larry Barnett (Prospect, OH), Joe Brinkman (Cocoa, FL), Gary Cedarstrom (Minot, ND), Al Clark (Williamsburg, VA), Drew Coble (Graham, NC), Derryl Cousins (Hermosa Beach, CA), Terry Craft (Sarasota, FL), Don Denkinger (Waterloo, IA), Jim Evans (Castle Rock, CO), Dale Ford (Jonesboro, TN), Rich Garcia (Clearwater, FL), Ted Hendry (Scottsdale, AZ), John Hirschbeck (Poland, OH), Mark Johnson (Honolulu, HI), Jim Joyce (Beaverton, OR), Ken Kaiser (Pompano Beach, FL), Greg Kosc (Medina, OH), Tim McClelland (West Des Moines, IA), Larry McCoy (Greenway, AR), Jim McKean (St. Petersburg, FL), Chuck Meriwether (Nashville, TN), Durwood Merrill (Hooks, TX), Dan Morrison (Largo, FL), Dave Phillips (Lake St. Louis, MO), Rick Reed (Rochester Hills, MI), Mike Reilly (Battle Creek, MI), Rocky Roe (Milford, MI), Dale Scott (Portland, OR), John Shulock (Vero Beach, FL), Tim Tschida (Turtle Lake, WI), Tim Welke (Kalamazoo, MI), Larry Young (Roscoe, IL).

Stadium Information

City	Stadium	Dimensions			Capacity	'97 Att.
		LF	CF	RF		
Anaheim	Edison International	365	406	365	45,050	1,767,324
Baltimore	Camden Yards	333	410	318	48,876	3,711,132
Boston	Fenway Park	310	390	302	33,871	2,226,136
Chicago	Comiskey Park	347	400	347	44,321	1,865,222
Cleveland	Jacobs Field	325	405	325	42,865	3,404,750
Detroit	Tiger Stadium	340	440	325	46,945	1,365,157
Kansas City	Kauffman Stadium	330	400	330	40,625	1,517,638
Minnesota	Humphrey Metrodome	343	408	327	48,678	1,411,064
New York	Yankee Stadium	318	408	314	57,545	2,580,445
Oakland	Alameda County	330	400	330	43,012	1,261,219
Seattle	Kingdome	331	405	312	58,801	3,198,995
Tampa Bay*	Tropicana Field	315	407	322	45,200	—
Texas	Ballpark in Arlington	334	400	325	49,166	2,945,228
Toronto	SkyDome	328	400	328	50,516	2,589,297

*Expansion team

ANAHEIM

Telephone, Address
Office Address: Edison International Field of Anaheim, 2000 Gene Autry Way, Anaheim, CA 92806. **Mailing Address:** P.O. Box 2000, Anaheim, CA 92803. **Telephone:** (714) 940-2000. **FAX:** (714) 940-2205.

Ownership
Operated by: Anaheim Sports, Inc.
Principal Owners: Gene Autry, Anaheim Sports, Inc.
Chairman/Chief Excecutive Officer: Michael Eisner. **President:** Tony Tavares. **Administrative Assistant to the President:** Jennifer Mitchell.

Michael Eisner

BUSINESS OPERATIONS
Vice President, Finance/Administration: Andy Roundtree.
Vice President, Business Affairs: Kevin Gilmore. **Administrative Assistant, Business Affairs:** Tia Wood. **Manager, Business Operations:** Larry Cohen.
Manager, Human Resources: Jenny Price. **Administrative Assistant, Human Resources:** Cindy Williams. **Manager, Information Services:** Andy Roe.

Finance
Director, Sales: Martin Greenspun. **Assistant Controllers:** Cristina Fisher, Melody Martin.

Marketing, Sales
Director, Sales: Bob Gobrecht. **Director, Advertising and Broadcast Sales:** Bob Wagner. **Manager, Promotions and Sponsorship Services:** Sue O'Shea. **Manager, Group Sales:** Andy Silverman. **Manager, Marketing:** Lisa Manning.
Sales Managers, Advertising and Broadcasting: John Covarrubias, Richard McClemmy, Dave Severson. **Sponsorship Services Representative:** Tony Reagins. **Director, Entertainment:** Marty Berg.

Public Relations, Communications
Telephone: (714) 940-2000. **FAX:** (714) 940-2205.
Director, Communications: Unavailable.
Manager, Media Services: Larry Babcock. **Manager, Publications:** Doug Ward. **Community Relations:** Jennifer Guran. **Coordinator, Media Relations:** Luis Garcia. **Assistant, Media Relations:** Cynthia Jacobs.
Speakers Bureau: Clyde Wright.

Stadium Operations
Director, Stadium Operations: Kevin Uhlich. **Administrative Assistant:** Leslie Flammini. **Manager, Facility Services:** Mike McKay. **Event Supervisor:** John Drum.
Manager, Field/Ground Maintenance: Barney Lopas.
PA Announcer: David Courtney. **Official Scorer:** Ed Munson.

Ticketing
Manager, Ticket Operations: Don Boudreau. **Assistant Ticket Manager:** Susan Weiss.

Travel, Clubhouse
Equipment Manager: Ken Higdon. **Visiting Clubhouse:** Brian Harkins. **Senior Video Coordinator:** Diego Lopez.

General Information
Hometown Dugout: Third Base. **Playing Surface:** Grass.
Stadium Location: Highway 57 (Orange Freeway) to Katella Ave. exit, west on Katella, stadium on west side of Orange Freeway. **Standard Game Times:** 7:05 p.m., Wed. 7:35, Sun. 5:05.
Player Representative: Tim Salmon.

ANGELS

BASEBALL OPERATIONS

Vice President/General Manager: Bill Bavasi.
Assistant General Manager: Ken Forsch. Special Assistants to General Manager: Preston Gomez, Bob Harrison. Adminsistrative Assistant to President: Jennifer Mitchell. Administrative Assistant to General Manager: Cathy Carey.

Legal Counsel/Contract Negotiations: Mark Rosenthal.

Major League Staff

Manager: Terry Collins.
Coaches: Bench—Joe Maddon; Pitching—Marcel Lachemann; Batting—Rod Carew; First Base—George Hendrick; Third Base—Larry Bowa; Bullpen—Joe Coleman; Bullpen Coordinator—Mick Billmeyer.

Bill Bavasi

Medical, Training

Medical Director: Dr. Lewis Yocum. Team Physician: Dr. Craig Milhouse.
Trainers: Ned Bergert, Rick Smith. Strength and Conditioning: Tom Wilson. Sports Psychologist: Ken Ravizza. Physical Therapy Consultant: Bick Harmon.

Minor Leagues

Telephone: (714) 740-2031. FAX: (714) 940-2203. Director, Player Development: Jeff Parker. Administrative Assistants: Janet Castillo, Laura Fazioli. Roving Instructors: Bob Clear (special assignment), Mike Couchee (pitching), Brian Grapes (strength and conditioning), Bruce Hines (defense), John McNamara (catching), Gene Richards (hitting).

Terry Collins

Farm System

Class	Farm Team	Manager	Coach	Pitching Coach
AAA	Vancouver	Mitch Seoane	Leon Durham	Greg Minton
AA	Midland	Don Long	Todd Claus	Rick Wise
A	Lake Elsinore	Mario Mendoza	Joe Urso	Kernan Ronan
A	Cedar Rapids	Garry Templeton	Tyrone Boykin	Jim Bennett
A	Boise	Tom Kotchman	Charlie Romero	Howie Gershberg
R	Butte	Bill Lachemann	Orlando Mercado	Zeke Zimmerman
R	DSL	Unavailable	Unavailable	Unavailable

Scouting

Director, Scouting: Bob Fontaine. Administrative Assistant, Scouting: Janet Castillo.

Advance Scout: Matt Keough (Cota de Caza, CA).
Major League Scouts: Dave Garcia (El Cajon, CA), Jay Hankins (Greenwood, MO), Bob Harrison (Long Beach, CA), Nick Kamzic (Evergreen Park, IL), Joe McDonald (Lakeland, FL), Tom Romenesko (Santee, CA), Moose Stubing (Villa Park, CA).

National Crosscheckers: Rick Ingalls (Anaheim Hills, CA), Hal Keller (Issaquah, WA), Rich Schlenker (Walnut Creek, CA).

Free-Agent Supervisors: John Burden (Fairfield, OH), Tom Burns (Harrisburg, PA), Pete Coachman (Cottonwood, AL), Steve Gruwell (West Covina, CA), Tim Kelly (Carlsbad, CA), Kris Kline (Arlington, TX), Tom Kotchman (Seminole, FL), Ron Marigny (Lake Charles, LA), Jim McLaughlin (Yonkers, NY), Darrell

Bob Fontaine

Miller (Yorba Linda, CA), Tom Osowski (Milwaukee, WI), Rick Schroeder (San Jose, CA), Jerry Streeter (Modesto, CA), Dale Sutherland (La Crescenta, CA), Jack Uhey (Vancouver, WA), Dick Wilson (Sun Valley, NV).

International Scouts: Pompeyo Davalillo (Venezuela), Jose Gomez (Dominican Republic), Felipe Gutierrez (Mexico), Ta Honda (Japan), George Lauzerique (Latin America), Mario Mendoza (Mexico).

BALTIMORE

Telephone, Address
Office Address: 333 West Camden St., Baltimore, MD 21201. Telephone: (410) 685-9800. FAX: (410) 547-6272. Website: theorioles.com.

Ownership
Operated by: The Home Team Limited Partnership.

Chairman, Chief Executive Officer: Peter Angelos. Vice Chairman/Community Projects and Public Affairs: Tom Clancy.

Peter Angelos

BUSINESS OPERATIONS
Vice Chairman, Business and Finance: Joe Foss. General Counsel: Russell Smouse.

Director, Human Resources: Martena Clinton.

Benefits Coordinator: Lisa Tolson. Director, Computer Services: James Kline. Purchasing Agent: Angela Knight.

Finance
Chief Financial Officer: Robert Ames. Controller: Edward Kabernagel. Assistant Controller: Michael Hoppes. Accountant: Chris Voxakis.

Marketing, Sales
Executive Director, Marketing and Broadcasting: Mike Lehr. Director, Marketing and Advertising: Scott Nickle. Manager, Advertising and Promotions: Jim Brylewski. Managers, Corporate Marketing: Michelle Bereau, Jim Hawes. Administrative Assistant, Marketing and Broadcasting: Kristen Kepple.

Director, Sales: Matthew Dryer. Director, Fan Services: Donald Grove. Assistant Director, Fan Services: Vernon Burk.

Public Relations, Communications
Telephone: (410) 547-6150. FAX: (410) 547-6272.

Director, Public Relations: John Maroon. Assistant Director, Public Relations: Bill Stetka. Administrative Assistant, Public Relations: Heather Tilles.

Director, Publications: Stephanie Parrillo. Assistant, Publications: Monica Windley.

Director, Community Relations: Julie Wagner. Assistant Director, Community Relations: Stacey Beckwith. Administrative Assistant, Community Relations: Jennifer Steier.

Director, Ballpark Entertainment and On-Line Services: Spiro Alafassos.

Stadium Operations
Director, Ballpark Operations: Ken Bullough. Administrative Assistant, Ballpark Operations: Ileen Wagner.

Head Groundskeeper: Paul Zwaska.

PA Announcer: Unavailable. Official Scorers: Jim Henneman, Marc Jacobson, Jim Oremland.

Ticketing
Telephone: (410) 547-6600. FAX: (410) 547-6270.

Manager, Ticket Office: Audrey Brown. Assistant Ticket Manager: Denise Addicks. Operations Manager: Steve Kowalski. Vault Supervisor: Stephanie Crockett. Box Office Supervisor: Joe Vacek. Coordinator, Mail Order Service: Cynthia Dumas. Group Ticket Coordinator: Tom Heyerdahl.

Travel, Clubhouse
Traveling Secretary: Phil Itzoe.

Equipment Manager, Home: Jim Tyler. Equipment Manager, Visitors: Fred Tyler.

General Information
Hometown Dugout: First Base. Playing Surface: Grass.
Stadium Location: I-95 to exit 395, downtown to Russell Street.
Standard Games Times: 7:35 p.m., Sat. 1:35 and 7:05, Sun. 1:35.
Player Representative: Mike Mussina.

ORIOLES

BASEBALL OPERATIONS

Telephone: (410) 547-6122. **FAX:** (410) 547-6271.
General Manager: Pat Gillick.
Assistant General Manager: Kevin Malone.
Administrative Assistant, Baseball Operations:
Ellen Harrigan.

Major League Staff

Manager: Ray Miller.
Coaches: Dugout—Eddie Murray; Pitching—
Mike Flanagan; Batting—Rick Down; First Base—
Carlos Bernhardt; Third Base—Sam Perlozzo;
Bullpen—Elrod Hendricks.

Pat Gillick

Medical, Training

Club Physicians: Dr. William Goldiner, Dr.
Michael Jacobs.
Head Trainer: Richie Bancells. **Assistant Trainer:** Brian Ebel. **Strength
and Conditioning Coach:** Tim Bishop.

Minor Leagues

Telephone: (410) 547-6120. **FAX:** (410) 547-6298.
Director, Player Development: Syd Thrift.
Assistant Director, Player Development: Don
Buford. **Administrative Assistant, Player Development:** Ann Lange.
Coordinator, Instruction: Tom Trebelhorn.
Camp Coordinator: Lenny Johnston. **Roving
Instructors:** Moe Drabowsky (pitching), John
Stearns (catching), David Stockstill (hitting), Joe
Tanner (bunting/baserunning).
Medical Coordinator: Guido Van Ryssegem.
Strength and Conditioning: Pat Hedge.

Ray Miller

Farm System

Class	Farm Team	Manager	Coach	Pitching Coach
AAA	Rochester	Marv Foley	Dave Cash	Larry McCall
AA	Bowie	Joe Ferguson	Bien Figueroa	Bo McLaughlin
A	Frederick	Tommy Shields	Todd Brown	Larry Jaster
A	Delmarva	David Machemer	Bobby Rodriguez	Dave Schmidt
R	Bluefield	Andy Etchebarren	Jerry Greeley	Charlie Puleo
R	Sarasota	Butch Davis	Jesus Alfaro	John O'Donoghue
R	DSL	Salvador Ramirez	Miguel Tavalara	Unavailable

Scouting

Telephone: (410) 547-6133. **FAX:** (410) 547-6298.
Director, Scouting: Gary Nickels.
Administrator, Scouting: Matt Slater. **Assistant, Computer Services:** Marcy Zerhusen.
Advance Scout: Fred Uhlman Sr. (Baltimore, MD).
Major League Scouts: Curt Motton (Woodstock, MD), Deacon Jones (Sugar Land, TX), Don
Welke (Louisville, KY).
National Crosschecker: Mike Ledna (Arlington
Heights, IL).
Regional Supervisors: West—Logan White
(Phoenix, AZ); Midwest—Earl Winn (Bowling
Green, KY); East—John Green (Conowingo, MD).

Gary Nickels

Full-Time Scouts: Dean Decillis (Tamarac, FL), Lane Decker (Piedmont,
OK), John Gillette (Kirkland, WA), Jim Howard (Clifton Park, NY), Ray
Krawczyk (Laguna Niguel, CA), Gil Kubski (Huntington Beach, CA), Jeff
Morris (Tucson, AZ), Lamar North (Rossville, GA), Fred Petersen (Lisle, IL),
Jim Robinson (Mansfield, TX), Harry Shelton (Ocoee, FL), Ed Sprague
(Lodi, CA), Marc Tramuta (Germantown, MD), Mike Tullier (New Orleans,
LA), Marc Ziegler (Canal Winchester, OH).
International Supervisor: Manny Estrada (Brandon, FL).
International Scouts: Patrick Guerrero (Dominican Republic), Chu
Halabi (Aruba), Ubaldo Heredia (Venezuela), Salvador Ramirez (Dominican
Republic), Arturo Sanchez (Venezuela), Brett Ward (Australia).

BOSTON

Telephone, Address
Office Address: Fenway Park, 4 Yawkey Way, Boston, MA 02215. Telephone: (617) 267-9440. FAX: (617) 375-0944. Internet Address: www.redsox.com.

Ownership
Operated by: Boston Red Sox Baseball Club.
General Partner: Jean R. Yawkey Trust (Trustees: John Harrington, William Gutfarb). Limited Partners: ARAMARK Corporation (Chairman: Joseph Neubauer); Dexter Group (Principal: Harold Alfond); Jean R. Yawkey Trust; Dr. Arthur Pappas; Samuel Tamposi Trust; Thomas DiBenedetto; John Harrington; John Kaneb.

John Harrington

Chief Executive Officer: John Harrington.

BUSINESS OPERATIONS
Executive Vice President, Administration: John Buckley.

Finance
Vice President, Chief Financial Officer: Robert Furbush.
Controller: Stanley Tran. Staff Accountant: Robin Yeingst.

Marketing, Sales
Vice President, Marketing/Sales: Larry Cancro.
Director, Advertising and Sponsorship: Jeffrey Goldenberg. Director, Food Services: Patricia Flanagan. Director, Sales: Rob Capilli.
Manager, Promotions/Special Events: Susan Salerno.
Vice President, Broadcasting/Technology: Jim Healey. Manager, Information Technology: Clay Rendon. Broadcasting Manager: James Shannahan.

Public Affairs, Community Relations
Vice President, Public Affairs: Dick Bresciani.
Community Relations Manager: Ron Burton. Customer Relations Manager: Ann Marie Starzyk. Publications Manager: Debra Matson. Public Affairs Administrator: Mary Jane Ryan. Executive Consultant, Public Affairs: Lou Gorman.
Director, Communications/Baseball Information: Kevin Shea. Credentials Administrator: Kate Gordon.

Stadium Operations
Vice President, Stadium Operations: Joe McDermott.
Director, Facilities Management: Tom Queenan. Superintendent, Grounds and Maintenance: Joe Mooney. Ground Crew Manager: Casey Erven. Property Maintenance Manager: John Caron.
PA Announcer: Unavailable. Official Scorer: Charlie Scoggins.

Ticketing
Telephone: (617) 267-1700. FAX: (617) 236-6640.
Director, Ticket Operations: Joe Helyar. Group Sales Manager: Tim Dalton. Season Ticket Manager: Joe Matthews. Box Office Manager: Dick Beaton. Telephone Sales Manager: Jeff Connors.

Travel, Clubhouse
Traveling Secretary: John McCormick.
Equipment Manager/Clubhouse Operations: Joe Cochran. Visiting Clubhouse: Tom McLaughlin.

General Information
Hometown Dugout: First Base. Playing Surface: Grass.
Standard Games Times: 7:05 p.m.; Sat. 1:05, 5:05, Sun. 1:05.
Directions to Stadium: Massachusetts Turnpike (I-90) to Prudential exit (stay left), right at first set of lights, right on Dalton Street, left on Boylston Street, right on Ipswich Street.
Player Representative: Tim Wakefield.

RED SOX

BASEBALL OPERATIONS

Telephone: (617) 267-9440. FAX: (617) 236-6649.
Executive Vice President, General Manager:
Dan Duquette.

Vice President, Baseball Operations: Mike
Port. Assistant General Manager/Legal Counsel:
Elaine Steward. Special Assistant to General
Manager: Lee Thomas. Director, Major League
Administration: Steve August. Coordinator, Baseball Development/Administration: Kent Qualls.
Assistant, Baseball Operations: Tom Moore.

Major League Staff

Dan Duquette

Manager: Jimy Williams.
Coaches: Dugout—
Grady Little; Pitching—Joe Kerrigan; Batting—Jim
Rice; First Base—Dave Jauss; Third Base—
Wendell Kim; Bullpen—Dick Pole.

Medical, Training

Medical Director: Dr. Arthur Pappas.
Head Trainer: Jim Rowe. Strength/Conditioning Coordinator: B.J. Baker. Physical Therapist:
Rich Zawacki.

Minor Leagues

Jimy Williams

Telephone: (617) 267-9440. FAX: (617) 236-6695.
Director, Player Development: Bob Schaefer.
Director, Affiliate Operations: Ed Kenney. Special Assistant, Player Development: Johnny Pesky.

Assistant Field Coordinator: Dick Berardino. Roving Instructors:
Buddy Bailey (catching), Tommy Barrett (infield), Steve Braun (hitting),
Sammy Ellis (pitching), Bobby Mitchell (outfield, baserunning). Rehab
Coordinator: Chris Correnti.

Special Instructors: Eddie Popowski, Charlie Wagner, Ted Williams,
Carl Yastrzemski.

Coordinator, Latin American Instruction: Felix Maldonado.

Farm System

Class	Farm Team	Manager	Coach	Pitching Coach
AAA	Pawtucket	Ken Macha	Gerald Perry	John Cumberland
AA	Trenton	DeMarlo Hale	Dave Gallagher	Ralph Treuel
A	Sarasota	Bob Geren	Victor Rodriguez	Jeff Gray
A	Michigan	Billy Gardner Jr.	Bill Madlock	Larry Pierson
A	Lowell	Dick Berardino	Unavailable	Dennis Rasmussen
R	Fort Myers	Luis Aguayo	Gomer Hodge	Dave Hodge
R	DSL	Nelson Norman	Ino Guerrero	Milciades Olivo

Scouting

Telephone: (617) 267-9440. FAX: (617) 236-6695.
Director, Scouting: Wayne Britton (Staunton,
VA). Administrative Assistant, Scouting: Andrae
Wyatt.

Advance Scout: Jerry Stephenson (Fullerton,
CA). Special Assignment Scouts: Eddie Haas
(Paducah, KY), Frank Malzone (Needham, MA),
Eddie Robinson (Fort Worth, TX).

Scouts: Ray Blanco (Miami, FL), Buzz Bowers
(Wayland, MA), Kevin Burrell (Sharpsburg, GA),
Ray Crone (Cedar Hill, TX), Luis Delgado (Hatillo,
PR), Ray Fagnant (Manchester, CT), Butch Hobson
(Fairhope, AL), Ernie Jacobs (Wichita, KS), Wally
Komatsubara (Aiea, HI), Joe Mason (Millbrook, AL)

Wayne Britton

Steve McAllister (Chillicothe, IL), Gary Rajsich (Lake Oswego, OR), Mike
Rizzo (Rolling Meadows, IL), Matt Sczesny (Deer Park, NY), Harry Smith
(Oceanside, CA), Fay Thompson (Vallejo, CA), Luke Wrenn (Lakeland, FL),
Jeff Zona (Mechanicsville, VA).

Director, International Scouting: Ray Poitevint (Shadow Hills, CA).
Director, Latin America Scouting: Levy Ochoa (Cabimas, Venezuela).

CHICAGO

Telephone, Address
Office Address: 333 W. 35th St., Chicago, IL 60616. Telephone: (312) 674-1000. FAX: (312) 674-5116. Website: www.chisox.com.

Ownership
Operated by: Chicago White Sox, Ltd.
Chairman: Jerry Reinsdorf. Vice Chairman: Eddie Einhorn.
Board of Directors: Fred Brzozowski, Jack Gould, Robert Judelson, Judd Malkin, Robert Mazer, Allan Muchin, Jay Pinsky, Larry Pogofsky, Lee Stern, Sanford Takiff, Burton Ury, Charles Walsh.
General Counsel: Allan Muchin.

Jerry Reinsdorf

BUSINESS OPERATIONS
Executive Vice President: Howard Pizer.
Director, Information Services: Don Brown. Director, Human Resources: Moira Foy.
Assistant to the Chairman: Anita Fasano.

Finance
Vice President, Finance: Tim Buzard.
Controller: Bill Waters. Accounting Manager: Julie O'Shea.

Marketing, Sales
Senior Vice President, Marketing and Broadcasting: Rob Gallas.
Director, Marketing and Broadcasting: Bob Grim. Manager, Promotions/Marketing Services: Sharon Sreniawski.
Director, Sales: Jim Muno. Manager, Sponsorship Sales: Dave Eck. Manager, Advertising: Amy Kress. Manager, Scoreboard Operations/Production: Jeff Szynal. Manager, Marketing Communications and Services: Dan Polvere. Marketing Account Executives: Jim Biegalski, Ty Harvey, Pam Walsh. Coordinator, Promotions and Marketing Services: Jo Simmons.

Public Relations, Communications
Telephone: (312) 674-5300. FAX: (312) 674-5116.
Director, Public Relations: Scott Reifert. Manager, Public Relations: Bob Beghtol. Coordinator, Public Relations: Jennifer Sloan.
Manager, Publications: Suzanne Reichart. Coordinator, Publications: Kyle White.
Director, Community Relations: Christine Makowski. Coordinator, Community Relations: Amber Simons. Coordinator, Charitable Programs: Dionne Smith.

Stadium Operations
Vice President, Stadium Operations: Terry Savarise.
Director, Park Operations: David Schaffer. Director, Guest Services/Diamond Suite Operations: Julie Taylor.
Head Groundskeeper: Roger Bossard.
PA Announcer: Gene Honda. Official Scorer: Bob Rosenberg.

Ticketing
Telephone: (312) 674-1000. FAX: (312) 674-5102.
Director, Ticket Sales: Carola Ross.
Director, Ticket Operations: Bob Devoy. Manager, Ticket Sales: Carola Ross. Ticket Manager: Ed Cassin.

Travel, Clubhouse
Traveling Secretary: Glen Rosenbaum.
Equipment Manager/Clubhouse Operations: Willie Thompson. Visiting Clubhouse: Gabe Morell. Umpires Clubhouse: Vince Fresso.

General Information
Hometown Dugout: Third Base. Playing Surface: Grass.
Standard Game Times: 7:05 p.m., Sat. 6:05, Sun. 1:05.
Stadium Location: 35th Street exit off Dan Ryan Expressway (I-90/94).
Player Representative: Unavailable.

WHITE SOX

BASEBALL OPERATIONS

Senior Vice President, Major League Operations: Ron Schueler. **Senior Vice President, Baseball:** Jack Gould.

Director, Baseball Operations: Dan Evans. **Assistant, Baseball Operations:** Brian Porter. **Computer Scouting Analyst:** Mike Gellinger.

Major League Staff

Manager: Jerry Manuel.

Coaches: Dugout—Joe Nossek; Pitching—Mike Pazik; Batting—Bill Buckner; First Base—Bryan Little; Third Base—Wallace Johnson; Bullpen—Art Kusnyer.

Ron Schueler

Medical, Training

Senior Team Physician: Dr. James Boscardin.

Head Trainer: Herm Schneider. **Assistant Trainer:** Mark Anderson. **Director, Conditioning:** Steve Odgers.

Jerry Manuel

Minor Leagues

Telephone: (312) 674-1000. **FAX:** (312) 674-5105.

Vice President, Player Development: Ken Williams. **Director, Minor League Administration:** Steve Noworyta. **Coordinator, Cultural Development/Minor League Administration:** Sal Artiaga. **Clubhouse and Equipment Manager:** Mark Brown.

Director, Instruction: Jim Snyder. **Roving Instructors:** Don Cooper (pitching), Mike Gellinger (infield), Mike Lum (hitting), Gary Pettis (outfield/baserunning), Jerry Terrell (infield), Tommy Thompson (catching).

Farm System

Class	Farm Team	Manager	Coach	Pitching Coach
AAA	Calgary	Tom Spencer	Von Joshua	Kirk Champion
AA	Birmingham	Dave Huppert	Steve Whitaker	Steve Renko
A	Winston-Salem	Chris Cron	Dallas Williams	Curt Hasler
A	Hickory	Mark Haley	Gregg Ritchie	Sean Snedeker
R	Bristol	Nick Capra	Darryl Boston	J.R. Perdew
R	Tucson	Tony Pena	Orsino Hill	Unavailable

Scouting

Vice President, Free Agent and Major League Scouting: Larry Monroe.

Director, Scouting: Duane Shaffer.

Assistant to Director, Scouting/Minor League Administration: Grace Guerrero Zwit. **Assistant to Director, Scouting/Minor League Operations:** Dan Fabian.

Advance Scout: Mark Weidemaier (Tierra Verde, FL). **Special Assignment Scouts:** Ed Brinkman (Cincinnati, OH), Dave Yoakum (Orlando, FL).

National Crosschecker: Doug Laumann (Florence, KY).

Regional Supervisors: West—Ed Pebley (Half Moon Bay, CA), Midwest—Ken Stauffer (Katy, TX), East Coast—George Bradley (Tampa, FL).

Full-Time Scouts: Joseph Butler (East Rancho Dominguez, CA), Scott Cerny (Davis, CA), Rico Cortes (Tampa, FL), Alex Cosmidis (Raleigh, NC), Ed Crosby (Garden Grove, CA), Nathan Durst (Elmhurst, IL), Larry Grefer (Park Hills, KY), Warren Hughes (Mobile, AL), Joe Karp (Bothell, WA), John Kazanas (Phoenix, AZ), Jose Ortega (Hialeah, FL), Gary Pellant (Chandler, AZ), Paul Provas (Shawnee Mission, KS), Mike Sgobba (Yorba Linda, CA), John Tumminia (Newburgh, NY), Emmanuel Upton (Chesapeake, VA).

Duane Shaffer

CLEVELAND

Telephone, Address
Office Address: Jacobs Field, 2401 Ontario St., Cleveland, OH 44115. **Telephone:** (216) 420-4200. **FAX:** (216) 420-4396. **Website:** www.indians.com.

Ownership
Operated by: Richard E. Jacobs Group.
Board of Directors: Richard Jacobs, Martin Cleary, Gary Bryenton.
Chairman/Chief Executive Officer: Richard Jacobs. **Vice President:** Martin Cleary.

BUSINESS OPERATIONS
Executive Vice President, Business: Dennis Lehman.

Richard Jacobs

Manager, Spring Training: Jerry Crabb. **Manager, Human Resources/Benefits:** Sara Lehrke.

Finance
Vice President, Finance: Ken Stefanov.
Controller: Ron McQuate. **Director, Information Systems:** Dave Powell. **Manager, Compensation/Compliance:** Lisa Ostry. **Senior Accountant:** Karen Menzing. **Senior Systems Analyst:** Matt Tagliaferri.

Marketing, Sales
Vice President, Marketing and Communications: Jeff Overton.
Director, Corporate Marketing/Broadcasting: Jon Starrett. **Manager, Corporate Marketing:** Chris Previte.
Director, Advertising/Publications: Valerie Arcuri. **Manager, Advertising/Publications:** Bernadette Repko.
Director, Merchandising/Licensing: Jayne Churchmack. **Manager, Merchandise:** Michael Thom. **Manager, Concessions:** Keith Miller.

Public Relations, Communications
Telephone: (216) 420-4350. **FAX:** (216) 420-4396.
Vice President, Public Relations: Bob DiBiasio.
Manager, Media Relations: Bart Swain. **Manager, Media Relations:** Joel Gunderson. **Manager, Media Relations/Administration, Credentials:** Susie Giuliano. **Administrative Assistant, Public Relations:** Angela Brdar.
Manager, Broadcasting/Special Events: Nadine Glinski. **Coordinator, Broadcasting/Special Events:** Dan Foust.
Director, Community Relations: Allen Davis. **Manager, Community Relations:** Melissa Zapanta.

Stadium Operations
Director, Ballpark Operations: Jim Folk. **Manager, Field Maintenance:** Brandon Koehnke. **Manager, Building Maintenance:** Chris Donahoe. **Assistant Manager, Field Maintenance:** Tony Walley.
PA Announcer: Mark Tromba. **Official Scorers:** Hank Kosloski, Bill Nichols, Rick Rembielak.

Ticketing
Telephone: (216) 420-4240. **FAX:** (216) 420-4481.
Director, Ticket Services: John Schulze. **Manager, Box Office:** Gail Leibenguth. **Controller, Box Office:** Carolyne Villao.
Director, Ticket Sales: Scott Sterneckert. **Manager, Ticket Sales:** Larry Abel. **Senior Account Executive:** Dick Sapara.

Travel, Clubhouse
Director, Team Travel: Mike Seghi.
Home Clubhouse/Equipment Manager: Ted Walsh. **Visiting Clubhouse Manager:** Cy Buynak.

General Information
Hometown Dugout: Third Base. **Playing Surface:** Grass.
Standard Game Times: 7:05 p.m., Sat-Sun. 1:05.
Stadium Location: From south, I-77 North to East 9th Street exit, to Ontario Street; From east, I-90/Route 2 west to downtown, remain on Route 2 to East 9th Street, left to stadium.
Player Representative: Chad Ogea.

INDIANS

BASEBALL OPERATIONS

Telephone: (216) 420-4305. FAX: (216) 420-4321.
Executive Vice President, General Manager: John Hart.

Director, Baseball Operations/Assistant General Manager: Dan O'Dowd. Administrator, Player Personnel: Wendy Hoppel. Executive Administrative Assistant, Baseball Operations: Ethel LaRue. Assistant, Baseball Operations: Paul DePodesta. Administative Assistant, Baseball Operations: Barbara Lessman.

John Hart

Major League Staff

Manager: Mike Hargrove.
Coaches: Dugout—John Goryl; Pitching—Mark Wiley; Batting—Charlie Manuel; First Base—Al Bumbry; Third Base—Jeff Newman; Bullpen—Luis Isaac.

Medical, Training

Medical Director: Dr. William Wilder.
Head Trainer: Paul Spicuzza. Assistant Trainer: Jim Warfield. Strength and Conditioning Coach: Fernando Montes.

Minor Leagues

Telephone: (216) 420-4200. FAX: (216) 420-4321.
Director, Minor League Operations: Mark Shapiro. Assistant Director, Minor League Operations: Neal Huntington. Administrative Assistant: Joan Pachinger.

Mike Hargrove

Coordinator, Instruction: Boyd Coffie. Roving Instructors: Mike Brown (pitching), Erik Pence (strength and conditioning), Brian Graham (defense), Gordie MacKenzie (hitting), Ted Kubiak (general), Dr. Charles Maher (sports psychologist).

Farm System

Class	Farm Team	Manager	Coach	Pitching Coach
AAA	Buffalo	Jeff Datz	Dave Keller	Bud Black
AA	Akron	Joel Skinner	Billy Williams	Tony Arnold
A	Kinston	Mako Oliveras	Mike Sarbaugh	Dave Miller
A	Columbus	Eric Wedge	Eric Fox	Ken Rowe
A	Watertown	Ted Kubiak	Willie Aviles	Steve Lyons
R	Burlington	Joe Mikulik	Jack Mull	Carl Willis
R	DSL	Felix Fermin	Virgilio Veras	Juan Jimenez

Scouting

Telephone: (216) 420-4309. FAX: (216) 420-4321.
Director, Scouting: Lee MacPhail.
Assistant Director, Scouting: Josh Byrnes.
Assistant, Scouting: Brad Grant.

Major League/Special Assignment Scouts: Dan Carnevale (Buffalo, NY), Dom Chiti (Bartlett, TN), Bob Gardner (Oviedo, FL), Tom Giordano (Amityville, NY), Tom McDevitt (Charleston, IL), Jay Robertson (Citrus Heights, CA), Ted Simmons (Chesterfield, MO), Bill Werle (San Mateo, CA).

National Crosschecker: Bill Schmidt (Yorba Linda, CA). Regional Supervisors: West—Jesse

Lee MacPhail

Flores (Sacramento, CA), East—Jerry Jordan (Wise, VA), Midwest—Bob Mayer (Somerset, PA).

Full-Time Area Scouts: Steve Abney (Lawrence, KS), Steve Avila (Olympia, WA), Doug Baker (Carlsbad, CA), Keith Boeck (Chandler, AZ), Ted Brzenk (Waukesha, WI), Paul Cogan (Rocklin, CA), Henry Cruz (Fajardo, PR), Jim Gabella (Deltona, FL), Rene Gayo (Galveston, TX), Mark Germann (Chattanooga, TN), Chris Jefts (Redondo Beach, CA), Guy Mader (Tewksbury, MA), Kasey McKeon (Burlington, NC), Chuck Ricci (Germantown, MD), Bill Schudlich (Dearborn, MI), Max Semler (Spanish Fort, AL), Rob Walton (Dallas, TX).

DETROIT

Telephone, Address
Office Address: Tiger Stadium, 2121 Trumbull Ave., Detroit, MI 48216. Telephone: (313) 962-4000. FAX: (313) 965-2138. Website: www.detroit-tigers.com.

Ownership
Operated by: Detroit Tigers, Inc.
Principal Owner: Mike Ilitch.
Chairman of the Board: Mike Ilitch. President, Chief Executive Officer: John McHale Jr. Assistant to the President: Margaret Gramlich.

John McHale Jr.

BUSINESS OPERATIONS
Vice President, Business Operations: David Glazier. Assistant to the Vice President, Business Operations: Andrea Dohring.

Finance
Senior Director, Finance: Steve Quinn. Controller: Jennifer Marroso. Manager, Payroll Administration: Maureen Kraatz. Corporate Accountant: Steve Dady. Supervisor, Accounts Payable: Christine Edwards.

Marketing, Sales, Merchandising
Director, Marketing and Broadcasting: Michael Dietz. Administrative Assistant: Stephanie Mulrine. Manager, Marketing: Howard Krugal. Coordinator, Marketing: Jodi Brewer. Coordinator, Promotions: Joel Scott.
Senior Director, Corporate Sales: Gary Vitto. Director, Corporate Sales: Martin Pawlusiak. Senior Account Executives: Earle Fisher, Bob Raymond, Bob Sinagoga. Coordinator, Advertising Sales: Andrea Petty.
Director, Merchandise: Kayla French. Coordinators, Merchandising: DeAndre Berry, Amukhoye Lieutsi.

Media, Community Relations
Telephone: (313) 965-2114. FAX: (313) 965-2138.
Director, Public Relations: Tyler Barnes. Assistant Director, Public Relations: David Matheson. Manager, Community Relations: Celia Bobrowsky. Coordinator, Public Relations: Giovanni Loria. Administrative Assistant, Public Relations: Erikka Cullum. Coordinators, Community Relations: Christina Branham, Herman Jenkins.

Stadium Operations
Director, Stadium Operations: Tom Folk. Administrative Assistant: Mary Bodie.
Head Groundskeeper: Frank Feneck. Supervisor, Stadium Services: Ed Goward. Manager, Guest Services: Jodi Engler. Coordinator, Stadium Operations: Derrick Ross.
PA Announcer: Jimmy Barrett. Official Scorers: Chuck Klonke, Rich Shook.

Ticketing
Telephone: (313) 963-2050. FAX: (313) 965-2179.
Director, Ticket Services: Ken Marchetti. Assistant Director, Ticket Services: James Cleary.

Travel, Clubhouse
Traveling Secretary: Bill Brown.
Manager, Tiger Clubhouse: Jim Schmakel. Assistant Manager, Visitors Clubhouse: John Nelson. Baseball Video Operations: Tom Progar.

General Information
Hometown Dugout: Third Base. Playing Surface: Grass.
Standard Game Times: Day—1:05 p.m. Night—7:05.
Stadium Directions: From north, I-75 South to exit 49A, or I-96 East to Lodge Freeway (US 10), to Rosa Parks Blvd. exit; From south, I-75 North to exit 49A; From east, I-94 West to exit 215A, to Lodge Freeway (US 10), to I-75 South, to Trumbull Ave. exit; From west, I-94 East to exit 213B, to Lodge Freeway (US 10), to Rosa Parks Blvd.
Player Representative: Unavailable.

TIGERS

BASEBALL OPERATIONS
Telephone: (313) 965-2098. **FAX:** (313) 965-2099.
Vice President, Baseball Operations/General Manager: Randy Smith.
Assistant General Manager: Steve Lubratich. **Assistant, Baseball Operations:** Ricky Bennett. **Special Assistants to General Manager:** Al Hargesheimer, Randy Johnson. **Assistant to General Manager:** Gwen Keating.

Major League Staff
Manager: Buddy Bell.
Coaches: Dugout—Larry Parrish; Pitching—Rick Adair; Batting—Larry Herndon; First Base—Jerry White; Third Base—Perry Hill; Bullpen—Fred Kendall.

Randy Smith

Medical, Training
Team Physicians: Dr. David Collon, Dr. Clarence Livingood, Dr. Terry Lock.
Head Trainer: Russ Miller. **Assistant Trainer:** Steve Carter. **Strength and Conditioning Coach:** Brad Andress.

Minor Leagues
Telephone: (941) 686-8075. **FAX:** (941) 688-9589.
Director, Minor League Operations: David Miller. **Administrative Assistant, Minor Leagues:** Audrey Zielinski.
Coordinator, Instruction: Steve Boros.
Roving Instructors: Glenn Ezell (catching), Toby Harrah (hitting), Mike Humphreys (outfield/baserunning), Marty Martinez (infield), Jon Matlack (pitching).

Buddy Bell

Farm System

Class	Farm Team	Manager	Coach	Pitching Coach
AAA	Toledo	Gene Roof	Brad Komminsk	Jeff Jones
AA	Jacksonville	Dave Anderson	Matt Martin	Rich Bombard
A	Lakeland	Mark Meleski	Gary Green	Joe Georger
A	West Mich.	Bruce Fields	Skeeter Barnes	Steve McCatty
A	Jamestown	Tim Torricelli	Unavailable	Dan Warthen
R	Lakeland	Kevin Bradshaw	Basilio Cabrera	Greg Sabat
R	DSL	Liliano Castro	Felix Nivar	Jose Tapia

Scouting
Telephone: (313) 965-2098. **FAX:** (313) 965-2099.
Director, Scouting: Greg Smith. **Administrative Assistant, Scouting:** Gwen Keating.
Advance Scout: Tom Runnells (Sylvania, OH).
Major League Scouts: Larry Bearnarth (Seminole, FL), Dan Warthen (Portland, OR).
National Crosschecker: John Mirabelli (Cary, NC).
Regional Supervisors: Midwest—Dave Owen (Arlington, TX); Northeast—Rob Guzik (Latrobe, PA); Southeast—Jeff Wetherby (Tampa, FL); West—Jeff Malinoff (Lopez, WA).

Greg Smith

Scouts: Bill Buck (Manassas, VA), Louis Eljaua (Pembroke Pines, FL), Jack Hays (Portland, OR), Ray Hayward (Oklahoma City, OK), Lou Laslo (Pemberville, OH), Steve Lemke (Lincolnshire, IL), Dennis Lieberthal (Westlake, CA), James Merriweather (West Covina, CA), Mark Monahan (Ann Arbor, MI), Jim Olander (Tucson, AZ), Ramon Pena (New York, NY), Rusty Pendergrass (Sugar Land, TX), Dave Roberts (Portland, OR), Clyde Weir (Mt. Pleasant, MI), Rob Wilfong (West Covina, CA), Gary York (Rome, GA).
Latin American Coordinator: Ramon Pena (New York, NY).

Telephone, Address

Office Address: One Royal Way, Kansas City, MO 64129. **Mailing Address:** P.O. Box 419969, Kansas City, MO 64141. **Telephone:** (816) 921-8000. **FAX:** (816) 921-5775. **Website:** www.kcroyals.com.

Ownership

David Glass

Operated by: Kansas City Royals Baseball Club, Inc.

Principal Owner: Greater Kansas City Community Foundation.

Chairman, Chief Executive Officer: David Glass.

Board of Directors: David Glass, Richard Green, Michael Herman, Larry Kauffman, Janice Kreamer, Joe McGuff, Louis Smith.

BUSINESS OPERATIONS

Senior Vice President, Business Operations/Administration: Art Chaudry.

General Counsel: Jay Newcom.

Director, Administration: John Johnson. **Director, Human Resources:** Lauris Hawthorne. **Secretary, Human Resouces:** Lynne Elder. **Administrative Assistant, Administration:** Cindy Hamilton.

Finance

Vice President, Finance: Dale Rohr.

Director, Information Systems: Jim Edwards. **Director, Compensation:** Tom Pfannenstiel.

Marketing, Sales

Vice President, Marketing/Communications: Mike Levy.

Director, Marketing/Sales: Mike Behymer. **Manager, Marketing:** Tonya Mangels. **Coordinator, Marketing:** Chasni Briggans. **Secretary, Marketing:** Patty Bowen.

Director, Special Markets: Vernice Givens. **Director, Season Ticket Sales:** Chris Muehlbach. **Manager, Group Sales:** Michele Kammerer. **Manager, Corporate Sponsorships:** Jeff Foster.

Public Relations, Communications

Telephone: (816) 504-4362. **FAX:** (816) 921-5775.

Director, Media Relations: Steve Fink. **Administrative Assistant, Media Relations:** Chris Stathos.

Director, Community Relations: Jim Lachimia. **Manager, Community Relations:** Christy Frank. **Secretary, Community Relations:** Melinda Hix.

Stadium Operations

Manager, Stadium Operations: Rodney Lewallen. **Assistant Director, Stadium Operations:** Rey Chavez. **Stadium Engineer:** Wes Earring.

Head Groundskeeper: Trevor Vance.

PA Announcer: Dan Hurst. **Official Scorers:** Del Black, Sid Bordman.

Ticketing

Telephone: (816) 921-8000.

Director, Ticket Operations: John Walker. **Manager, Ticket Office:** Christine Burgeson. **Director, Season Ticket Services:** Joe Grigoli. **Associate, Ticket Sales:** Betty Bax. **Coordinator, Group Sales:** Jacque Tschirhart.

Travel, Clubhouse

Director, Team Travel: David Witty.

Equipment Manager: Mike Burkhalter. **Visiting Clubhouse Manager:** Chuck Hawke.

General Information

Hometown Dugout: First Base. **Playing Surface:** Grass.

Standard Game Times: 7:05; Sat., Sun. 1:05.

Stadium Location: From north or south, take I-435 to stadium exits. From east or west, take I-70 to stadium exits.

Player Representative: Johnny Damon.

ROYALS

BASEBALL OPERATIONS
Telephone: (816) 921-8000. **FAX:** (816) 924-0347.
Executive Vice President/General Manager: Herk Robinson. **Vice President, Baseball Operations:** George Brett.
Assistant General Manager: Jay Hinrichs. **Senior Special Assistant to General Manager:** Art Stewart. **Special Assistant to General Manager:** Allard Baird.
Vice President, Player Personnel: Larry Doughty. **Assistant Director, Player Personnel:** Dan Glass.

Herk Robinson

Major League Staff
Manager: Tony Muser.
Coaches: Dugout—Jamie Quirk; Pitching—Bruce Kison; Batting—Tom Poquette; First Base—Frank White; Third Base—Rich Dauer; Bullpen—Tom Burgmeier.

Medical, Training
Team Physician: Dr. Steve Joyce. **Club Physicians:** Dr. Mark Bernhardt, Dr. Dan Gurba, Dr. Thomas Phillips, Dr. Charles Rhoades.

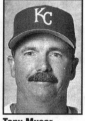

Head Trainer: Nick Swartz. **Assistant Trainer:** Steve Morrow. **Coordinator, Strength and Conditioning:** Kevin Barr.

Minor Leagues
Telephone: (816) 921-2200. **FAX:** (816) 924-0347.
Director, Minor League Operations: Bob Hegman. **Assistant to Director, Minor League Operations:** Jeff Wood. **Secretary:** Mindy Walker.
Coordinator, Instruction: Jimmy Johnson.

Tony Muser

Roving Instructors: Juan Agosto (pitching), Mike Jirschele (infield), Sixto Lezcano (outfield), Mark Littell (pitching), Brian Poldberg (catching).

Farm System

Class	Farm Team	Manager	Coach	Pitching Coach
AAA	Omaha	Ron Johnson	U.L. Washington	Gary Lance
AA	Wichita	John Mizerock	Phil Stephenson	Mike Mason
A	Wilmington	Darrell Evans	Kevin Long	Steve Crawford
A	Lansing	Bob Herold	Rodney McCray	Larry Carter
A	Spokane	Jeff Garber	Steve Balboni	Rick Mahler
R	Fort Myers	Andre David	Jose Tartabull	Hal Dyer
R	DSL	Oscar Martinez	Fausto Sosa	Unavailable

Scouting
Director, Scouting: Terry Wetzel.
Assistant to Director, Scouting: Phil Huttmann. **Secretary, Scouting:** Karol Kyte.
Advance Scout: Ron Clark (Largo, FL).
Major League Scouts: Gail Henley (La Verne, CA), Dick Wiencek (Rancho Mirage, CA).
National Crosscheckers: Carl Blando (Overland Park, KS), Steve Flores (Temecula, CA), Pat Jones (Davie, FL), Jeff McKay (Walterville, OR).
Area Scouts: Frank Baez (Los Angeles, CA), Paul Baretta (Kensington, CT), Bob Bishop (San Dimas, CA), Monte Bothwell (Phoenix, AZ), Jason Bryans (Detroit, MI), Balos Davis (Charlotte, NC), Albert Gonzalez (Pembroke Pines, FL), Dave Herrera (Danville, CA), Keith Hughes (Berwyn, PA),

Terry Wetzel

Gary Johnson (Costa Mesa, CA), Mike Lee (Bald Knob, AR), Cliff Pastornicky (Venice, FL) Bill Price (Austin, TX), Johnny Ramos (Carolina, PR), Wil Rutenschroer (Cincinnati, OH), Chet Sergo (Madison, WI), Greg Smith (Harrington, WA), Theo Shaw (Lee's Summit, MO), Gerald Turner (Euless, TX), Dennis Woody (Mobile, AL).
Latin American Coordinator: Luis Silverio (Dominican Republic).

MINNESOTA

Telephone, Address
Office Address: 34 Kirby Puckett Place, Minneapolis, MN 55415. **Telephone:** (612) 375-1366. **Website:** www.mntwins.com.

Ownership
Operated by: The Minnesota Twins.
Owner: Carl Pohlad. **Chairman, Executive Committee:** Howard Fox.
Executive Board: Jerry Bell, Chris Clouser, Carl Pohlad, Eloise Pohlad, James Pohlad, Robert Pohlad, William Pohlad, Kirby Puckett.
President: Jerry Bell.

Carl Pohlad

BUSINESS OPERATIONS
Vice President, Operations: Matt Hoy. **Administrative Assistant to President/Office Manager:** Joan Boeser.

Finance
Director, Human Resources: Raenell Dorn. **Controller:** Kip Elliott. **Administrative Assistant, Human Resources:** Lori Beasley. **Accountant:** Jerry McLaughlin. **Accounts Payable:** Marlys Keeney. **Coordinator, Human Resources/Accounting:** Lisa Johnson. **Director, Information Systems:** Wade Navratil. **Programmer/Operations:** John Avenson.

Marketing, Promotions
Director, Sales: Phil Huebner. **Manager, Sales:** Jon Arends. **Senior Account Sales Executive:** Scott O'Connell. **Account Sales Executives:** Jack Blesi, Stacey Bjorklund, Chris Malek, John Neppl, Mike Roslansky. **Coordinator, Sales:** Beth Vail. **Manager, Telemarketing:** Jim Pounian. **Assistant Manager, Telemarketing:** Skip Harman.
Director, Corporate Marketing: Laura Day. **Corporate Sales Executives:** Jeff Jurgella, Dick Schultz. **Director, Communications:** Dave St. Peter. **Assistant Manager, Community Affairs:** Darrell Cunningham. **Special Projects Manager:** Dan Endy. **Manager, Advertising:** Wayne Petersen. **Manager, Promotions:** Julie Arndt. **Coordinator, Marketing:** Chad Jackson.

Media Relations
Telephone: (612) 375-1366. **FAX:** (612) 375-7473.
Manager, Media Relations: Sean Harlin. **Assistant Manager, Media Relations:** Brad Smith. **Media Relations Coordinator:** Wendie Erickson.

Stadium Operations
Manager, Stadium Operations: Ric Johnson. **Assistant Manager, Stadium Operations:** Dave Horsman. **Coordinator, Operations:** Heidi Sammon.
Manager, Security: Doug Wills. **Managers, Pro Shop:** Mike Pitzen, Dave Strobel.
Head Groundskeeper: Steve Maki.
PA Announcer: Bob Casey. **Official Scorers:** Tom Mee, Barry Fritz.

Ticketing
Telephone: (612) 33TWINS. **FAX:** (612) 375-7464.
Manager, Tickets: Paul Froehle. **Assistant Manager, Tickets:** Mike Stiles. **Supervisor, Ticket Office:** Sue Szulczewski. **Coordinator, Ticket Office Operations:** Dan Lamey.

Travel, Clubhouse
Traveling Secretary: Remzi Kiratli.
Equipment Manager: Jim Dunn. **Visitors Clubhouse:** Troy Matchan. **Internal Video Specialist:** Nyal Peterson.

General Information
Hometown Dugout: Third Base. **Playing Surface:** Astroturf.
Standard Game Times: 7:05 p.m., Sun. 1:05.
Stadium Directions: I-35W south to Washington Ave. exit or I-35W north to 3rd Street exit. I-94 East to I-35W north to 3rd Street exit or I-94 West to 5th Street exit.
Player Representative: Frank Rodriguez.

TWINS

BASEBALL OPERATIONS
Telephone: (612) 375-1366. **FAX:** (612) 375-7417.

Vice President, General Manager: Terry Ryan.

Executive Vice President, Baseball: Kirby Puckett. **Vice President, Assistant General Manager:** Bill Smith. **Special Assistant to General Manager:** Joe McIlvaine (Tuckahoe, NY).

Director, Baseball Operations: Rob Antony. **Administrative Assistant, Major League Operations:** Ann Waara.

Major League Staff
Manager: Tom Kelly.

Coaches: Pitching—Dick Such; Batting—Terry Crowley; First Base—Ron Gardenhire; Third Base—Scott Ullger; Bullpen—Rick Stelmaszek.

Terry Ryan

Medical, Training
Club Physicians: Dr. L.J. Michienzi, Dr. John Steubs.

Head Trainer: Dick Martin. **Assistant Trainer:** Jim Kahmann. **Strength and Conditioning Coach:** Randy Popple.

Minor Leagues
Telephone: (612) 375-7486. **FAX:** (612) 375-7417.

Director, Minor Leagues: Jim Rantz. **Administrative Assistant, Minor Leagues:** Colleen Schroeder.

Field Coordinator: Larry Corrigan. **Roving Instructors:** Jim Dwyer (hitting), Tony Oliva (hitting), Rick Knapp (pitching).

Tom Kelly

Farm System

Class	Farm Team	Manager	Coach	Pitching Coach
AAA	Salt Lake	Phil Roof	Bill Springman	Rick Anderson
AA	New Britain	John Russell	Rob Ellis	Eric Rasmussen
A	Fort Myers	Mike Boulanger	Jeff Carter	Stu Cliburn
A	Fort Wayne	Jose Marzan	Riccardo Ingram	David Perez
R	Elizabethton	Jon Mathews	Ray Smith	Jim Shellenback
R	Fort Myers	Steve Liddle	Jose Baez	Kevin O'Sullivan

Scouting
Telephone: (612) 375-7474. **FAX:** (612) 375-7417.

Director, Scouting: Mike Radcliff.

Administrative Assistant, Scouting: Alison Walk.

Advance Scouts: Ray Coley (Gold Canyon, AZ), Wayne Krivsky (Arlington, TX).

Special Assignment Scouts: Cal Ermer (Chattanooga, TN), Bill Harford (Chicago, IL), Eddie Robinson (Fort Worth, TX).

Scouting Supervisors: West Coast—Vern Followell (Buena Park, CA); Midwest—Mike Ruth (Lee's Summit, MO); East—Earl Frishman (Tampa, FL).

Mike Radcliff

Full-Time Scouts: Ellsworth Brown (Beason, IL), Gene DeBoer (Brandon, WI), Marty Esposito (Hewitt, TX), Scott Groot (Mission Viejo, CA), Deron Johnson (Antioch, CA), John Leavitt (Garden Grove, CA), Joel Lepel (Plato, MN), Bill Lohr (Centralia, WA), Bill Milos (South Holland, IL), Kevin Murphy (Studio City, CA), Tim O'Neil (Lexington, KY), Hector Otero (Carolina, PR), Mark Quimuyog (Lynn Haven, FL), Clair Rierson (Gilbert, AZ), Ricky Taylor (Hickory, NC), Brad Weitzel (Haines City, FL), John Wilson (West Paterson, NJ).

International Scouts: Enrique Brito (Venezuela), Howard Norsetter (Australia, Canada), Johnny Sierra (Dominican Republic).

NEW YORK

Telephone, Address
Office Address: Yankee Stadium, 161st Street and River Avenue, Bronx, NY 10451. Telephone: (718) 293-4300. FAX: (718) 293-8431. Website: www.yankees.com.

Ownership
Operated by: New York Yankees.

Principal Owner: George Steinbrenner. General Partners: Stephen Swindal, Harold Steinbrenner.

George Steinbrenner

Limited Partners: Daniel Crown, James Crown, Lester Crown, Michael Friedman, Marvin Goldklang, Barry Halper, John Henry, Daniel McCarthy, Jessica Molloy, Harry Nederlander, James Nederlander, Robert Nederlander, William Rose Jr., Edward Rosenthal, Jack Satter, Henry Steinbrenner, Joan Steinbrenner, Jennifer Swindal, Charlotte Witkind, Richard Witkind.

BUSINESS OPERATIONS
Executive Vice President, General Counsel: Lonn Trost. Vice President, Business Development: Joseph Perello.

Director, Office Administration: Harvey Winston.

Finance
Vice President, Chief Financial Officer: Mike Macaluso.

Controller: Robert Brown.

Marketing, Public Relations
Director, Marketing: Deborah Tymon.

Director, Community Relations: Brian Smith. Director, Yankee Alumni Association: Jim Ogle. Director, Entertainment: Stanley Kay. Special Assistant: Joe Pepitone.

Media Relations, Publications
Telephone: (718) 293-4300. FAX: (718) 293-8414.

Special Advisor/Consultant: Arthur Richman.

Director, Media Relations/Publicity: Rick Cerrone. Assistant Director, Media Relations: John Thursby.

Director, Publications/Multimedia: Tim Wood. Assistant Director, Publications: Kara McGovern.

Director, Television/Video Productions: Joe Violone.

Stadium Operations
Director, Stadium Operations: Sonny Hight. Manager, Stadium Operations: Kirk Randazzo. Assistant, Stadium Operations: Bob Pelegrino. Stadium Superintendant: Bob Wilkinson. Head Groundskeeper: Dan Cunningham.

Director, Customer Services: Joel White.

Manager, Broadcasting and Video Operations: Doyal Martin. Assistant Director, Broadcasting and Video Operations: Joe Pullia.

PA Announcer: Bob Sheppard. Official Scorers: Bill Shannon, Red Foley.

Ticketing
Telephone: (718) 293-6000. FAX: (718) 293-4841.

Vice President, Ticket Operations: Frank Swaine. Executive Director, Ticket Operations: Jeff Kline. Ticket Director: Ken Skrypek.

Travel, Clubhouse
Traveling Secretary: David Szen.

Equipment Manager: Rob Cucuzza. Visiting Clubhouse: Lou Cucuzza.

General Information
Hometown Dugout: First Base. Playing Surface: Grass.

Standard Game Times: 7:35 p.m., Weekends 1:35.

Stadium Directions: From I-95 North, George Washington Bridge to Cross Bronx Expressway to exit 1C, Major Deegan South (I-87) to exit G (161st Street); I-87 North to 149th or 155th Streets; I-87 South to 161st Street.

Player Representative: David Cone.

YANKEES

BASEBALL OPERATIONS

Vice President, General Manager: Brian Cashman.

Administrator, Major Leagues: Tom May. **Special Advisory Group:** Reggie Jackson, Clyde King, Dick Williams.

Major League Staff

Manager: Joe Torre.

Coaches: Dugout—Don Zimmer; Pitching—Mel Stottlemyre; Batting—Chris Chambliss; First Base /Outfield—Jose Cardenal; Third Base/Infield—Willie Randolph; Bullpen—Tony Cloninger.

Joe Torre

Medical, Training

Team Physician: Dr. Stuart Hershon.

Head Trainer: Gene Monahan. **Assistant Trainer:** Steve Donohue. **Strength and Conditioning Coach:** Jeff Mangold.

Minor Leagues

Florida Complex: 3102 N. Himes Ave., Tampa, FL 33607. **Telephone:** (813) 875-7569. **FAX:** (813) 877-2302.

Vice President, Player Development: Mark Newman.

Director, Player Personnel: Gordon Blakeley. **Assistant Director, Player Development:** Rigo Garcia. **Administrative Assistant, Player Development:** Dan Matheson.

Coordinator/Latin America Player Development: Ken Dominguez. **Special Advisor, Latin America Affairs:** Ray Negron.

Coordinator, Instruction: Rob Thomson. **Pitching Coordinator:** Billy Connors. **Roving Instructors:** Greg Pavlick (pitching), Gary Denbo (hitting), Mick Kelleher (defense).

Farm System

Class	Farm Team	Manager	Coach	Pitching Coach
AAA	Columbus	Stump Merrill	Tony Perezchica	Oscar Acosta
AA	Norwich	Trey Hillman	Arnie Beyeler	Rick Tomlin
A	Tampa	Lee Mazzilli	Fred Langiotti	Mark Shiflett
A	Greensboro	Tom Nieto	Jason Garcia	Tom Filer
A	Oneonta	Joe Arnold	Bobby DeJardin	Steve Webber
R	Tampa	Ken Dominguez	Hector Lopez	Rich Monteleone
R	DSL	Unavailable	Unavailable	Unavailable

Scouting

Telephone: (813) 875-7569. **FAX:** (813) 348-9198.

Director, Scouting: Lin Garrett. **Assistant Director, Scouting:** Joe Caro. **Scouting Secretary:** Tom Larson.

Advance Scout: Bob Didier (Seattle, WA).

Special Assignment Scouts: Ket Barber (Ocala, FL), Bill Emslie (Safety Harbor, FL), Bobby DeJardin (Hidden Hills, CA).

National Crosscheckers: West Coast—John Cox (Redlands, CA); Midwest—Damon Oppenheimer (Phoenix, AZ); East Coast—Don Rowland (Orlando, FL).

Mark Newman

Scouts: Rich Arena (Fort Lauderdale, FL), Joe Arnold (Lakeland, FL), Mike Baker (Cave Creek, AZ), Mark Batchko (Arlington, TX), Lee Elder (Martinez, GA), Mick Kelleher (Solvang, CA), Tim Kelly (New Lenox, IL), Greg Orr (Sacramento, CA), Les Parker (Tampa, FL), Scott Pleis (Lake St. Louis, MO), Cesar Presbott (Bronx, NY), Joe Robison (Dayton, TX), Phil Rossi (Archbald, PA), Steve Webber (Watkinsville, GA), Roy White (Oradell, NJ), Leon Wurth (Nashville, TN), Bill Young (Long Beach, CA).

Director, International Operations: Gordon Blakeley (Safety Harbor, FL). **Coordinator, Canadian Scouting:** Dick Groch (Marysville, MI).

OAKLAND

Telephone, Address
Office Address: 7677 Oakport St., Second Floor, Oakland, CA 94621. **Telephone:** (510) 638-4900. **FAX:** (510) 568-3770. **E-Mail Address/Website:** www.oaklandathletics.com.

Ownership
Operated by: Athletics Investment Group LLC (1996).

Co-Owner/Managing Partner: Steve Schott. **Partner/Owner:** Ken Hofman.

President: Sandy Alderson. **Executive Assistant to the President:** Betty Shinoda.

Steve Schott

BUSINESS OPERATIONS
Director, Human Resources: Eleanor Yee.

Finance
Chief Financial Officer: Michael Crowley. **Controller:** Paul Wong. **Manager, Accounting:** Linda Rease.

Marketing, Sales
Senior Director, Sales and Marketing: David Alioto.

Director of Customer, Ticket and Information Services: David Lozow. **Director, Merchandising:** Drew Bruno. **Director, Corporate Advertising Sales:** Franklin Lowe.

Director, Promotions and Special Events: Susan Bress. **Director, Marketing Communications:** Jim Bloom.

Manager, Special Projects and Publications: Audrey Minagawa.

Manager, Spring Training Marketing Operations: Travis Dray. **Manager, Promotions and Special Events:** Ross Hatamiya. **Manager, Multi-Cultural Marketing:** Cindy Carrasquilla.

Manager, Client Services: Kathy Barrett. **Manager, Box Office and Customer Service:** Steve Fanelli.

Public Relations, Communications
Telephone: (510) 563-2207. **FAX:** (510) 562-1633.

Senior Director, Broadcasting and Communications: Ken Pries.

Manager, Baseball Information: Mike Selleck. **Manager, Public Relations:** Eric Carrington. **Manager, Broadcasting:** Robert Buan. **Manager, Community Relations:** Shannon Severson.

Director, Stadium Entertainment: Troy Smith. **Director, Multimedia Services:** David Don. **Coordinator, Diamond Vision:** David Martindale.

Stadium Operations
Senior Director, Stadium Operations: David Rinetti.

Manager, Stadium Operations/Facility and Special Events: Matt Fucile. **Director, Game Day Services:** Martha Hutchinson.

Ticketing
Director, Ticket Sales: Paul Solby. **Manager, Ticket/Customer Service:** Michael Ono. **Manager, Ticket Operations:** Gary Phillips. **Manager, Ticket Projects:** Jennie Costa. **Manager, Ticket Sales:** Dennis Murphy.

Travel, Clubhouse
Director, Team Travel: Mickey Morabito.

Equipment Manager: Steve Vucinich. **Visitors Clubhouse:** Mike Thalblum. **Assistant Equipment Manager:** Brian Davis. **Head Groundskeeper:** Clay Wood.

General Information

Hometown Dugout: Third Base. **Playing Surface:** Grass.

Standard Game Times: Weekday—12:15 p.m., 1:05, 7:05, 7:35. Weekend—1:05.

Stadium Location: From San Jose—north on I-880 to Oakland, exit at 66th Ave.; From San Francisco—east on Bay Bridge to I-580 toward Hayward, to downtown Oakland and I-880 south, exit at 66th Avenue; From Sacramento—I-80 west to Oakland, I-580 toward Hayward and I-980 to downtown Oakland, then I-880 South, exit at 66th Avenue.

Player Representative: Willie Adams.

ATHLETICS

BASEBALL OPERATIONS

General Manager: Billy Beane.
Special Assistants to the General Manager: Bob Johnson, J.P. Ricciardi, Bill Rigney.
Director, Baseball Administration: Pamela Pitts. **Administrative Assistant, Baseball Operations:** Raki Bogan.

Major League Staff

Manager: Art Howe.
Coaches: Dugout—Duffy Dyer; Pitching—Bob Cluck; Batting—Denny Walling; First Base—Gary Jones; Third Base—Ron Washington; Bullpen—Brad Fischer.

Billy Beane

Medical, Training

Team Physician: Dr. Allan Pont. **Team Orthopedist:** Dr. Jerrald Goldman. **Consulting Orthopedists:** Dr. John Frazier, Dr. Lewis Yocum.

Trainers: Larry Davis, Steve Sayles. **Strength and Conditioning Coach:** Bob Alejo.

Minor Leagues

Telephone, Oakland: (510) 638-4900. **FAX:** (510) 563-2376.
Arizona Complex: Papago Park Baseball Complex, 1802 North 64th St., Phoenix, AZ 85008. **Telephone:** (602) 949-5951. **FAX:** (602) 945-0557.
Director, Player Development: Keith Lieppman. **Assistant Director, Player Development:** Dave Hudgens.
Director, Arizona Operations: Ted Polakowski.
Roving Instructors: Dave Hudgens (fielding), Rick Peterson (hitting), Ron Plaza (infield).

Art Howe

Farm System

Class	Farm Team	Manager	Coach	Pitching Coach
AAA	Edmonton	Mike Quade	Orv Franchuk	Pete Richert
AA	Huntsville	Jeffrey Leonard	Dave Joppie	Bert Bradley
A	Modesto	Juan Navarrete	Brian McArn	Rick Rodriguez
A	Visalia	Tony DeFrancesco	David Robb	Glenn Abbott
A	So. Oregon	Greg Sparks	Jim Pransky	Gil Lopez
R	Scottsdale	John Kuehl	Ruben Escalera	Curt Young
R	DSL I	Evaristo Lantigua	Luis Martinez	Leandro Mejia
R	DSL II	Luis Gomez	Tomas Silverio	Nasusel Cabrera

Scouting

Telephone: (510) 638-4900, ext. 2369. **FAX:** (510) 563-2376.
Director, Scouting: Grady Fuson.
Assistant Director, Scouting: David Seifert.
Special Assignment Scout: Dick Bogard (La Palma, CA). **Advance/Major League Scout:** Bob Johnson (Rockaway, NJ).
National Crosscheckers: Ron Hopkins (Seattle, WA), Chris Pittaro (Hamilton, NJ).
Scouts: Steve Bowden (Houston, TX), Tom Clark (Worcester, MA), Ron Elam (Henderson, NC), Ruben Escalera (Villa Carolina, PR), Tim Holt (Dallas, TX), John Kuehl (Fountain Hills, AZ), Rick

Grady Fuson

Magnante (Van Nuys, CA), Gary McGraw (Newberg, OR), John Poloni (Tarpon Springs, FL), Jim Pransky (Davenport, IA), Will Schock (Oakland, CA), Mike Soper (Tampa, FL), Rich Sparks (Sterling Heights, MI), Ron Vaughn (Corona, CA).
Latin American Supervisor: Karl Kuehl (Fountain Hills, AZ). **Pacific Rim Coordinator:** Eric Kubota (Oakland, CA).
International Scouts: Heberto Andrade (Venezuela), Rafael Espinal (Dominican Republic), Angel Eusebio (Dominican Republic), Julio Franco (Venezuela), Gerardo Santana (Dominican Republic).

SEATTLE

Telephone, Address
Office Address: 83 South King St., Seattle, WA 98104. **Mailing Address:** P.O. Box 4100, Seattle, WA 98104. **Telephone:** (206) 346-4000. **FAX:** (206) 346-4050. **E-Mail Address:** mariners@mariners.org. **Website:** www.mariners.org.

Chuck Armstrong

Ownership
Operated by: Baseball Club of Seattle, LP.

Board of Directors: Minoru Arakawa, John Ellis, Chris Larson, Howard Lincoln, John McCaw, Frank Shrontz, Craig Watjen.

Chairman, Chief Executive Officer: John Ellis. **President, Chief Operating Officer:** Chuck Armstrong.

BUSINESS OPERATIONS
Vice President, Business Development: Paul Isaki. **Vice President, Ballpark Planning and Development:** John Palmer.

Director, Human Resources: Katherine Kummerow.

Finance
Vice President, Finance and Administration: Kevin Mather.

Controller: Tim Kornegay. **Assistant Controller:** Michelle Shelley.

Director, Merchanding: Todd Vecchio. **Manager, Merchandising:** Tracy Stirrett.

Marketing, Sales
Vice President, Business/Sales: Bob Aylward.

Director, Corporate Business: Joe Chard. **Director, Corporate Marketing:** Gail Hunter. **Director, Marketing:** Kevin Martinez. **Manager, Marketing:** Jon Schuller. **Director, Regional Marketing:** David Venneri. **Assistant Director, Ticket Sales:** Ron Babes. **New Ballpark Suite Sales:** Moose Clausen. **Senior Account Executive/Ticket Sales:** Bob Hellinger.

Public Relations, Communications
Telephone: (206) 346-4000. **FAX:** (206) 346-4400.

Vice President, Communications: Randy Adamack.

Director, Public Relations: Dave Aust. **Assistant Director, Public Relations:** Tim Hevly. **Administrative Assistant, Public Relations:** Sara Weisinger.

Coordinator, Community Projects: Sean Grindley. **Coordinator, Community Relations:** Gina Hasson. **Coordinator, Promotions/Special Events:** Gina Short.

Manager, Graphic Design: Carl Morton.

Ticketing
Telephone: (206) 346-4001. **FAX:** (206) 346-4100.

Director, Ticket Services: Kristin Fortier. **Manager, Ticket Services:** Rob Brautigam. **Manager, Ticket Operations:** Connie McKay. **Coordinator, Group Tickets:** Jennifer Sweigert. **Coordinator, Ticket Sales:** Kasey Marolich. **Coordinator, Suite Sales:** Tristan Baird.

Stadium Operations
Vice President, Ballpark Operations: Neil Campbell. **Director, Ballpark Operations:** Tony Pereira. **Assistant Director, Ballpark Operations:** Kameron Durham. **Manager, Ballpark Engineering/Maintenance:** Mike Allison. **Coordinator, Ballpark Operations:** Sylvia Gonzales.

PA Announcer: Tom Hutyler. **Official Scorer:** Unavailable.

Travel, Clubhouse
Director, Team Travel: Ron Spellecy.

Clubhouse Manager: Scott Gilbert. **Visiting Clubhouse Manager:** Henry Genzale. **Video Coordinator:** Carl Hamilton.

General Information
Hometown Dugout: Third Base. **Playing Surface:** Artificial turf.
Standard Game Times: 7:05 p.m., Sun. 1:35.
Stadium Location: I-5 or I-90 to Fourth Ave. South exit.
Player Representative: Dan Wilson.

MARINERS

BASEBALL OPERATIONS

Vice President, Baseball Operations: Woody Woodward.

Vice President, Baseball Administration: Lee Pelekoudas. **Assistants to Vice President, Baseball Operations:** Larry Beinfest, George Zuraw. **Administrator, Baseball Operations:** Debbie Larsen.

Major League Staff

Manager: Lou Piniella.

Coaches: Dugout—Steve Smith; Pitching—Nardi Contreras; Batting—Jesse Barfield; First Base—Sam Mejias; Third Base—John McLaren; Bullpen—Matt Sinatro.

Woody Woodward

Lou Piniella

Medical, Training

Club Physicians: Dr. Larry Pedegana, Dr. Mitch Storey.

Head Trainer: Rick Griffin. **Assistant Trainer:** Tom Newberg. **Strength and Conditioning Coach:** Allen Wirtala.

Minor Leagues

Telephone: (206) 346-4313. **FAX:** (206) 346-4300.

Vice President, Scouting and Player Development: Roger Jongewaard.

Director, Player Development: Benny Looper. **Assistant Director, Player Development:** Greg Hunter. **Administrative Assistant, Player Development:** Jan Plein.

Coordinator, Instruction: Mike Goff. **Roving Instructors:** Roger Hansen (catching), Bryan Price (pitching).

Farm System

Class	Farm Team	Manager	Coach	Pitching Coach
AAA	Tacoma	Dave Myers	Dave Brundage	Ron Romanick
AA	Orlando	Dan Rohn	Henry Cotto	Pat Rice
A	Lancaster	Rick Burleson	Unavailable	Jim Slaton
A	Wisconsin	Gary Varsho	Omer Munoz	Steve Peck
A	Everett	Terry Pollreisz	Tommy Cruz	Gary Wheelock
R	Peoria	Darrin Garner	Dana Williams	Rafael Chavez

Scouting

Telephone: (206) 346-4000. **FAX:** (206) 346-4300.

Director, Scouting: Frank Mattox (Long Beach, CA). **Administrator, Scouting:** Hallie Larson.

Director, Professional Scouting: Ken Compton (Cypress, CA).

Major League/Special Assignment Scouts: Bill Kearns (Milton, MA), George Zuraw (Englewood, FL).

Advance Scout: Stan Williams (Lakewood, CA).

National Crosschecker: Carroll Sembera (Shiner, TX).

Scouting Supervisors: West—Curtis Dishman (San Juan Capistrano, CA); East—Steve Pope (Asheville, NC).

Frank Mattox

Area Scouts: Dave Alexander (Lafayette, IN), Fernando Arguelles (Miami, FL), Rodney Davis (Glendale, AZ), Ed Gustafson (Portland, OR), Des Hamilton (Tulsa, OK), Larry Harper (San Francisco, CA), Steve Jongewaard (Manhattan Beach, CA), Ken Madeja (Novi, MI), John McMichen (Treasure Island, FL), Tom McNamara (Haverstraw, NY), Billy Merkel (Columbia, TN), Don Poplin (Norwood, NC), Steve Rath (Buena Park, CA), Alex Smith (Bel Air, MD), Chris Smith (The Woodlands, TX).

Director, Pacific Rim Scouting: Jim Colborn (Ventura, CA). **Supervisor, Latin America Scouting:** Fernando Arguelles (Miami, FL). **International Scout:** Ramon de los Santos (Dominican Republic).

TAMPA BAY

Telephone, Address
Office Address: Tropicana Field, One Tropicana Dr., St. Petersburg, FL 33705. **Telephone:** (813) 825-3137. **FAX:** (813) 825-3111. **Website:** www.devilray.com.

Ownership
Operated by: Tampa Bay Devil Rays, Ltd.
Managing General Partner/Chief Executive Officer: Vincent Naimoli. **Executive Assistant to Managaing General Partner:** Cass Halpin.

BUSINESS OPERATIONS
Senior Vice President/General Counsel: John Higgins.

Vince Naimoli

Finance
Senior Vice President, Chief Financial Officer: Raymond Naimoli.
Controller/Chief Financial Officer: Patrick Smith. **Accountant:** Sheryl Evans. **Payroll Supervisor:** Joy Benjamin. **Administrative Assistant:** Jennifer Thayer.

Marketing, Sales
Vice President, Sales and Marketing: David Auker.
Directors, Corporate Sales: John Browne, Larry McCabe. **Account Executive:** Noel Beaulieu. **Managers, Sponsorship Coordination:** Tammy Atmore, Jennifer Pajerski, Chris Trautmann.
Director, Merchandise: Robert Katz. **Director, Ticket Sales:** David Barry. **Director, Sales Operations:** James Cook. **Manager, Group Sales:** Robert Saunders. **Group Sales Representative:** Rhett Cecil. **Account Executives:** Chris Bertolli, Ray Johnson, Drew Cloud, Todd Rutledge, Joe Andrade.
Devil Ray Express Coordinator: Robert Caskey.

Public Relations, Communications
Telephone: (813) 825-3242. **FAX:** (813) 825-3111.
Vice President, Public Relations: Rick Vaughn.
Manager, Media Relations: Andrew Maraniss. **Assistant, Media Relations:** Steve Matesich. **Director, Publications:** Mike Flanagan. **Assistant Director, Publications:** Raul Alsina. **Director, Photography:** Robert Rogers.
Director, Community Development: Orestes Destrade. **Director, Community Relations:** Julie Williamson. **Assistant Director, Community Relations:** Liz Lauck.
Director, Event Productions and Entertainment: John Franzone. **Event Producer, Public Address Announcer:** Eric Rannebarger. **Director, Video Production:** David Berggren. **Director, Audio Visual Services:** Todd Schirmer. **Administrative Assistant, Public Relations:** Carmen Molina.

Stadium Operations
Vice President, Stadia Operations and Facilities: Rick Nafe. **Director, Business Administration and Purchasing:** Bill Wiener Jr. **Director, Event Services and Bookings:** Robert Rose. **Director, Operations:** James Duffy.
Head Groundskeeper: Mike Williams. **Official Scorers:** Jim Ferguson, Allen Lewis, Ken Nigro.

Ticketing
Telephone: (813) 825-3250. **FAX:** (813) 825-3111.
Director, Ticket Operations: Robert Bennett. **Assistant Director, Ticket Operations:** Ken Mallory.

Travel, Clubhouse
Traveling Seceretary: Ken Lehner. **Equipment Manager/Home Clubhouse:** Carlos Ledezma. **Visitor Clubhouse Operations:** Guy Gallagher.

General Information
Hometown Dugout: First Base. **Playing Surface:** Artificial Turf.
Standard Games Times: 7:05 p.m., Sat. 6:35, Sun. 1:05.
Directions to Stadium: Route 275 South to St. Petersburg, exit 11, left onto Fifth Ave., right onto 16th Street.
Player Representative: Unavailable.

DEVIL RAYS

BASEBALL OPERATIONS
Telephone: (813) 825-3170. **FAX:** (813) 825-3365.
Senior Vice President, Baseball Operations/General Manager: Chuck LaMar.
Assistant General Managers: Bart Braun (baseball operations), Scott Proefrock (administration). **Special Assistants to the General Manager:** Bill Geivett, Bart Johnson, Mickey White.
Administrative Assistant, Baseball Operations: Sandy Dengler.

Major League Staff
Manager: Larry Rothschild.
Coaches: Dugout—Frank Howard; Pitching—Rick Williams; Batting—Steve Henderson; First Base—Billy Hatcher; Third Base—Greg Riddoch; Bullpen—Orlando Gomez.

Chuck LaMar

Medical, Training
Medical Director: Dr. James Andrews. **Club Physicians:** Dr. William Carson, Dr. Michael Reilly, Dr. Koco Eaton.
Head Trainer: Jamie Reed. **Assistant Trainer:** Ken Crenshaw. **Coordinator, Conditioning and Rehabilitation:** Kevin Harmon.

Minor Leagues
Telephone: (813) 384-5604. **FAX:** (813) 343-5479.
Director, Player Personnel: Bill Livesey. **Assistant, Player Development:** Mitch Lukevics. **Administrative Assistant, Player Development:** Denise Vega.
Director, Minor League Operations: Tom Foley.
Roving Instructors: Buddy Biancalana (infield), Chuck Hernandez (pitching), John Pierson (hitting).

Larry Rothschild

Farm System

Class	Farm Team	Manager	Coach	Pitching Coach
AAA	Durham	Bill Evers	Dave Hilton	Pete Filson
A	St. Petersburg	Roy Silver	Steve Livesey	Greg Harris
A	Charleston, S.C.	Greg Mahlberg	Julio Garcia	Bryan Kelly
A	Hudson Valley	Charlie Montoyo	Brad Rippelmeyer	Ray Searage
R	Princeton	David Howard	Mike Tosar	Milt Hill
R	St. Petersburg	Bobby Ramos	Edwin Rodriguez	Steve Mumaw
R	DSL	Manny Castillo	Hector Del Pozo	Marcus Vivas

Scouting
Telephone: (813) 825-3241. **FAX:** (813) 825-3365.
Director, Scouting: Dan Jennings. **Assistant Director, Scouting:** Michael Hill. **Administrative Assistant, Scouting:** LaRonda Graham.
Major League Scouts: Jerry Gardner (Los Alamitos, CA), Al LaMacchia (San Antonio, TX), Don Lindeberg (Anaheim, CA), Don Williams (Paragould, AR).
National Crosscheckers: Jack Gillis (Sarasota, FL), Stan Meek (Norman, OK).
Regional Crosscheckers: East—Shawn Pender (Drexel Hill, PA). West—R.J. Harrison (Phoenix, AZ).

Dan Jennings

Area Scouts: Fernando Arango (Oklahoma City, OK), Skip Bundy (Birmingham, AL), Tim Corcoran (La Verne, CA), Matt Dodd (Boston, MA), Kevin Elfering (Wesley Chapel, FL), Paul Faulk (Raleigh, NC), Doug Gassaway (Blum, TX), Matt Kinzer (Fort Wayne, IN), Paul Kirsch (Tigard, OR), Blaise Kozeniewski (Somerdale, NJ), Mark McKnight (Atlanta, GA), Pat O'Neil (Covington, IN), Edwin Rodriguez (Mayaguez, PR), Nelson Rood (Scottsdale, AZ), Charles Scott (San Rafael, CA), Craig Weissmann (LaCosta, CA).
Director, Latin American Scouting: Rudy Santin (Miami, FL).

TEXAS

Telephone, Address
Office Address: 1000 Ballpark Way, Arlington, TX 76011. **Mailing Address:** P.O. Box 90111, Arlington, TX 76004. **Telephone:** (817) 273-5222. **FAX:** (817) 273-5206. **E-Mail Address:** www.texas rangers.com.

Ownership
Operated by: Texas Rangers, Ltd.
General Partners: Edward "Rusty" Rose, J. Thomas Schieffer.
President: J. Thomas Schieffer. **Assistant to the President:** Nolan Ryan.

Thomas Schieffer

BUSINESS OPERATIONS
Vice President, Business Operations/Treasurer: John McMichael.
Vice President, Human Resources: Kimberly Smith. **Vice President, Information Technology:** Steve McNeill.
General Counsel: Gerald Haddock. **Administrative Assistant to VP, Business Operations:** Jennifer Aafedt.

Finance
Assistant Vice President/Controller: Charles Sawicki. **Assistant Controller:** Susan Capps. **Staff Accountant:** Melissa Barksdale.

Marketing, Sales
Vice President, Marketing: Charles Seraphin.
Director, Corporate Sales: Mike Phillips. **Director, In-Park Entertainment:** Chuck Morgan. **Director, Merchandising:** Nancy Hill. **Director, Sales:** Ross Scott. **Director, Special Events:** Jennifer Lumley. **Director, Camps and Clinics:** Jack Lazorko.

Public Relations, Communications
Telephone: (817) 273-5203. **FAX:** (817) 273-5206.
Vice President, Public Relations: John Blake.
Assistant Director, Public Relations: Charley Green. **Assistant Director, Public Relations/Community, Ballpark Activities:** Lydia Traina. **Administrative Assistant, Public Relations:** Amy Gunter.
Director, Publications: Eric Kolb. **Assistant Director, Publications:** Michelle Lancaster. **Director, Player Relations:** Taunee Taylor. **Assistant Director, Player Relations:** Dana Wilcox.
Coordinator, Special Projects: Dana Williams. **Coordinator, Community Relations:** Rhonda Houston.

Stadium Operations
Assistant Vice President, Facilities: Billy Ray Johnson.
Director, Ballpark Operations: Kevin Jimison. **Director, Field Operations:** Tom Burns. **Youth Ballpark Groundskeeper:** Andrew Gulley. **Director, Complex Grounds:** Gib Searight.
PA Announcer: Chuck Morgan. **Official Scorer:** Kurt Iverson.

Ticketing
Telephone: (817) 273-5100. **FAX:** (817) 273-5190.
Director, Ticket Operations: Marty Schueren. **Assistant Director, Ticket Operations:** Michael Wood. **Ticket Operations:** Ranae Lewis.
Manager, Season/Group Sales: Bob Benson. **Coordinator, Box Office:** David Larson. **Coordinator, Group Sales:** Scott Faris.

Travel, Clubhouse
Director, Travel: Chris Lyngos.
Equipment and Home Clubhouse Manager: Zack Minasian. **Visiting Clubhouse:** Joe Macko.

General Information
Hometown Dugout: First Base. **Playing Surface:** Grass.
Game Times: 7:35 p.m.; Sun. (April-May, Sept.) 2:05, (June-August) 7:05.
Directions to Stadium: From I-30, take Ballpark Way exit, south on Ballpark Way; From Route 360, take Randol Mill exit, west on Randol Mill.
Player Representative: Will Clark.

RANGERS

BASEBALL OPERATIONS
Telephone: (817) 273-5226. **FAX:** (817) 273-5285.
Executive Vice President/General Manager: Doug Melvin.
Assistant General Manager: Dan O'Brien.
Director, Major League Administration: Judy Johns.

Major League Staff
Manager: Johnny Oates.
Coaches: Dugout—Bucky Dent; Pitching—Dick Bosman; Batting—Rudy Jaramillo; First Base—Ed Napoleon; Third Base—Jerry Narron; Bullpen— Larry Hardy.

Doug Melvin

Medical, Training
Medical Director: Dr. John Conway. **Team Internist:** Dr. Scott Hunter.
Head Trainer: Danny Wheat. **Assistant Trainer:** Ray Ramirez. **Director, Strength and Conditioning:** Tim Lang.

Minor Leagues
Telephone: (817) 273-5228. **FAX:** (817) 273-5285.
Director, Player Development: Reid Nichols. **Assistant Director, Player Development:** Alex Smith.
Field Coordinator: Bob Miscik. **Roving Instructors:** Mike Arndt (conditioning), Julio Cruz (baserunning/infield), Bob Dernier (outfield), Al Nipper (pitching), Don Reynolds (hitting), Butch Wynegar (catching).

Johnny Oates

Farm System

Class	Farm Team	Manager	Coach	Pitching Coach
AAA	Oklahoma	Greg Biagini	None	Tom Brown
AA	Tulsa	Bobby Jones	None	Brad Arnsberg
A	Charlotte	James Byrd	None	Lee Tunnell
A	Savannah	Paul Carey	None	Dan Gakeler
R	Pulaski	Unavailable	None	Aris Tirado
R	Port Charlotte	Darryl Kennedy	Vince Roman	Jamie Garcia
R	DSL	Unavailable	None	Unavailable

Scouting
Telephone: (817) 273-5277. **FAX:** (817) 273-5285.
Director, Scouting: Chuck McMichael. **Assistant to Director, Scouting:** Debbie Bent.
Assistant Director, Professional/International Scouting: Monty Clegg.
Advance Scout: Mike Paul (Tucson, AZ).
Professional Scouts: Larry D'Amato (Tualatin, OR), Toney Howell (Country Club Hills, IL), Bryan Lambe (North Massapequa, NY), Bob Reasonover (Smyrna, TN), Rudy Terrassas (Pasadena, TX).
National Crosscheckers: Tim Hallgren (Clarkston, WA), Dave Klipstein (Eupora, MS), Jeff Taylor (Newark, DE).

Chuck McMichael

Full-Time Area Scouts: Dave Birecki (Peoriz, AZ), Mike Cadahia (Miami, FL), Mike Daughtry (St. Charles, IL), Jay Eddings (Sperry, OK), Kip Fagg (Manteca, CA), Jim Fairey (Clemson, SC), Mark Giegler (Fenton, MI), Joel Grampietro (Shrewsbury, MA), Mike Grouse (Arlington, TX), Todd Guggiana (Garden Grove, CA), Doug Harris (Carlisle, PA), Bobby Heck (Tallahassee, FL), Larry Izzo (Deer Park, NY), Jim Lentine (Rancho San Clemente, CA), Randy Taylor (Katy, TX), Greg Whitworth (Dillon, MT).
Latin Coordinator: Manny Batista (Vega Alta, PR).
International Scouts: Hector Acevedo (Dominican Republic), Roney Calderon (Venezuela), Pedro Gonzalez (Dominican Republic), Graciano Ravelo (Venezuela), Richard Seko (Pacific Rim), Danilo Troncoso (Dominican Republic).

Telephone, Address

Office/Mailing Address: 1 Blue Jays Way, Suite 3200, Toronto, Ontario M5V 1J1. **Telephone:** (416) 341-1000. **FAX:** (416) 341-1250. **E-Mail Address:** bluejays@bluejays.ca. **Website:** www.bluejays.ca.

Ownership

Operated by: Toronto Blue Jays Baseball Club. **Principal Owner:** Interbrew SA.

Board of Directors: Allan Chapin, Luc Missorten, Hugo Powell, George Radford, George Taylor.

Chairman/Chief Executive Officer: Sam Pollock.

Sam Pollock

BUSINESS OPERATIONS

Vice President, Business: Bob Nicholson.

Finance

Director, Finance: Susan Quigley. **Manager, Accounting:** Cathy McNamara-Mackay. **Manager, Employee Compensation:** Perry Nicoletta.

Marketing, Sales

Coordinator, Community Relations: Laurel Lindsay.
Manager, Promotions and Advertising: Rick Amos.

Public Relations, Communications

Telephone: (416) 341-1301/1303. **FAX:** (416) 341-1250.

Director, Public Relations: Howard Starkman. **Assistant Director, Public Relations:** Jay Stenhouse. **Manager, Public Relations:** Janis Davidson Pressick. **Assistant, Public Relations:** Laura Ammendolia.

Stadium Operations

Director, Stadium and Ticket Operations: George Holm.

Head Groundskeeper: Tom Farrell. **PA Announcer:** Murray Eldon. **Official Scorers:** Joe Sawchuk, Doug Hobbs, Neil MacCarl, Louis Cauz.

Ticketing

Telephone: (416) 341-1280. **FAX:** (416) 341-1177.

Assistant Director, Ticket Operations/Box Office Manager: Randy Low. **Manager, Season Ticket Sales:** Doug Barr. **Manager, Group Sales:** Maureen Haffey. **Manager, Ticket Vault Services:** Paul Goodyear. **Manager, Mail Order Services:** Sandra Wilbur. **Manager, Special Ticket Services:** Sheila Cantarutti. **Manager, Telephone Order Services:** Jan Marshall.

Travel, Clubhouse

Traveling Secretary: John Brioux.

Equipment Manager: Jeff Ross. **Clubhouse Operations:** Kevin Malloy. **Visitors Clubhouse:** Len Frejlich.

General Information

Hometown Dugout: Third Base. **Playing Surface:** Artificial turf.
Standard Game Times: 7:05 p.m.; Sat. 1:05 or 4:05; Sun. 1:05.
Stadium Location: From west—take QEW/Gardiner Expressway eastbound and exit at Spadina Ave., go north on Spadina one block, right on Blue Jays Way. From east—take Gardiner Expressway westbound and exit at Spadina Ave., north on Spadina one block, right on Blue Jays Way.
Player Representative: Shawn Green.

BLUE JAYS

BASEBALL OPERATIONS

Telephone: (416) 341-1000. **FAX:** (416) 341-1245.
Vice President, General Manager: Gord Ash.
Senior Advisor, Baseball Operations: Bob Engle. **Assistant General Manager:** Tim McCleary. **Special Assistants to General Manager:** Al Widmar, Moose Johnson, Gordon Lakey.
Director, Baseball Administration: Bob Nelson. **Administrative Assistants:** Fran Brown, Heather Connolly, Trina Hiscock.

Major League Staff

Manager: Tim Johnson.
Coaches: Bench—Jim Lett; Pitching—Mel Queen; Batting—Gary Matthews; First Base—Jack Hubbard; Third Base—Eddie Rodriguez; Bullpen—Sal Butera.

Gord Ash

Medical, Training

Club Physicians: Dr. Ron Taylor, Dr. Allan Gross, Dr. Steve Mirabello, Dr. Anthony Miniaci.
Head Trainer: Tommy Craig. **Assistant Trainer:** Scott Shannon. **Director, Strength and Conditioning:** Unavailable.

Minor Leagues

Telephone: (416) 341-1228. **FAX:** (416) 341-1245.
Director, Player Development: Jim Hoff.
Administrative Assistant: Charlie Wilson.
Roving Instructors: George Bell (hitting), Randy Holland (strength and conditioning), Garth Iorg (defense), Rance Mulliniks (hitting), Hector Torres (infield), Bruce Walton (pitching), Ernie Whitt (catching).

Tim Johnson

Farm System

Class	Farm Team	Manager	Coach	Pitching Coach
AAA	Syracuse	Terry Bevington	Lloyd Moseby	Scott Breeden
AA	Knoxville	Omar Malave	J.J. Cannon	Bill Monbouquette
A	Dunedin	Rocket Wheeler	Dennis Holmberg	Rick Langford
A	Hagerstown	Marty Pevey	Paul Elliott	Hector Berrios
A	St. Catharines	Duane Larson	Hector Torres	Neil Allen
R	Medicine Hat	Rolando Pino	Randy Phillips	Lester Stryker
R	DSL	Geovany Miranda	Melvin Gomez	Mariano Alcala
R	VSL	Alexis Infante	Hedbertt Hurtado	Benito Malave

Scouting

Telephone: (416) 341-1342. **FAX:** (416) 341-1245.
Director, Scouting: Tim Wilken. **Administrative Assistant, Scouting:** Donna Kuzoff.
Advance Scout: Darren Balsley.
National Crosscheckers: Chris Buckley (Temple Terrace, FL), Duane Larson (Knoxville, TN). **Regional Supervisors:** Tom Hinkle (West), Ted Lekas (Worcester, MA), Mark Snipp (Fort Worth, TX).
Scouting Supervisors: Charles Aliano (West Hempstead, NY), Tony Arias (Miami Lakes, FL), David Blume (Elk Grove, CA), Chris Bourjos (Scottsdale, AZ), Bus Campbell (Littleton, CO), John Cole (Lake Forest, CA), Ellis Dungan (Pensacola, FL), Jim Hughes (Prosper, TX), Ben McLure (Palmyra, PA), Marty Miller (Chicago, IL), Bill Moore (Alta Loma, CA), Alvin Rittman (Memphis, TN), Jorge Rivera (Puerto Nuevo, PR), Joe Siers (Lexington, KY), Ron Tostenson (Issaquah, WA), Steve Williams (Raleigh, NC).
Scouts: Richard Cerrone (Boulder City, NV), Joe Ford (Yukon, OK), Andy Pienovi (Portland, OR), Jerry Sobeck (Milpitas, CA), Bob Warner (San Diego, CA).
Director, International Scouting: Wayne Morgan (Morgan Hill, CA).
Director, Latin American Operations: Herb Raybourn (Bradenton, FL).
Director, Canadian Scouting: Bill Byckowski.

Tim Wilken

National League

NATIONAL LEAGUE

Mailing Address: 350 Park Ave., New York, NY 10022. **Telephone:** (212) 339-7700. **FAX:** (212) 935-5069.

Years League Active: 1876-.

President: Leonard Coleman.

Executive Committee: Claude Brochu (Montreal), Bill Bartholomay (Atlanta), Peter Magowan (San Francisco).

Senior Vice President, Secretary: Katy Feeney.

Administrative Director, Umpires: Paul Runge. **Administrative Assistant, Umpires:** Cathy Davis.

Executive Director, Public Relations: Ricky Clemons.

Executive Director, Player Records: Nancy Crofts. **Assistant, Media Relations and Player Records:** Glenn Wilburn.

Leonard Coleman

Executive Secretary: Rita Aughavin.

1998 Opening Date: March 31. **Closing Date:** Sept. 27.

Regular Season: 162 games.

Division Structure: East—Atlanta, Florida, Montreal, New York, Philadelphia. **Central**—Chicago, Cincinnati, Houston, Milwaukee, Pittsburgh, St. Louis. **West**—Arizona, Colorado, Los Angeles, San Diego, San Francisco.

Playoff Format: Three division champions and second-place team with best record play in best-of-5 Division Series. Winners meet in best-of-7 League Championship Series.

All Star-Game: July 7 at Denver, CO (American League vs. National League).

Roster Limit: 25, until Aug. 31 when roster can be expanded to 40.

Brand of Baseball: Rawlings.

Statistician: Elias Sports Bureau, 500 Fifth Ave., New York, NY 10110.

Umpires: Wally Bell (Canfield, OH), Greg Bonin (Broussard, LA), Gerry Crawford (Havertown, PA), Gary Darling (Phoenix, AZ), Bob Davidson (Littleton, CO), Gerry Davis (Appleton, WI), Dana DeMuth (Gilbert, AZ), Bruce Froemming (Vero Beach, FL), Brian Gorman (Camarillo, CA), Eric Gregg (Philadelphia, PA), Tom Hallion (Louisville, KY), Angel Hernandez (Hollywood, FL), Mark Hirschbeck (Stratford, CT), Bill Hohn (Collegeville, PA), Jeff Kellogg (Ypsilanti Township, MI), Jerry Layne (Winter Haven, FL), Randy Marsh (Edgewood, KY), Ed Montague (San Mateo, CA), Larry Poncino (Tucson, AZ), Frank Pulli (Palm Harbor, FL), Jim Quick (Scottsdale, AZ), Ed Rapuano (North Haven, CT), Charlie Reliford (Tampa, FL), Rich Rieker (St. Louis, MO), Steve Rippley (Seminole, FL), Terry Tata (Cheshire, CT), Larry Vanover (Antioch, TN), Harry Wendelstedt (Ormond Beach, FL), Joe West (Kitty Hawk, NC), Charlie Williams (Chicago, IL), Mike Winters (Poway, CA).

Stadium Information

City	Stadium	Dimensions LF	CF	RF	Capacity	'97 Att.
Arizona*	Bank One Ballpark	330	407	334	48,500	—
Atlanta	Turner Field	335	401	330	50,528	3,463,988
Chicago	Wrigley Field	355	400	353	38,884	2,190,308
Cincinnati	Cinergy Field	330	404	330	52,953	1,785,788
Colorado	Coors Field	347	415	350	50,200	3,888,453
Florida	Pro Player Stadium	335	410	345	40,585	2,364,387
Houston	Astrodome	325	400	325	54,370	2,046,811
Los Angeles	Dodger	330	395	330	56,000	3,318,886
Milwaukee#	County Stadium	315	402	315	53,192	1,444,027
Montreal	Olympic Stadium	325	404	325	46,500	1,497,609
New York	Shea Stadium	338	410	338	55,777	1,766,174
Philadelphia	Veterans Stadium	330	408	330	62,363	1,490,638
Pittsburgh	Three Rivers	335	400	335	48,044	1,657,022
St. Louis	Busch Stadium	330	402	330	49,676	2,658,357
San Diego	Qualcomm Stadium	327	405	327	46,510	2,089,336
San Francisco	3Com Park	335	400	328	63,000	1,690,831

*Expansion team   #Member of American League in 1997

ARIZONA

Telephone, Address
Office Address: Bank One Ballpark, 401 East Jefferson St., Phoenix, AZ 85004. **Mailing Address:** P.O. Box 2095, Phoenix, AZ 85001. **Telephone:** (602) 462-6500. **FAX:** (602) 462-6600. **E-Mail Address:** www.azdiamondbacks.com.

Ownership
Operated by: AZPB Limited Partnership.
Chairman: Jerry Colangelo.
Advisory Committee: George Getz, Dale Jensen, David Moore, Jerry Moyes, Rich Stephan.

Jerry Colangelo

BUSINESS OPERATIONS
President: Richard Dozer. **Assistant to President:** Michelle Avella.
General Counsel: Jane Birge.
Director, Human Resources: Cheryl Naumann.

Finance
Vice President, Finance: Tom Harris.
Controller: Larry White. **Director, Management Information Systems:** Bill Bolt. **Manager, Accounting:** Barbara Ragsdale. **Administrative Assistant:** Kelly Wilson.

Marketing, Sales
Senior Vice President, Sales and Marketing: Scott Brubaker.
Vice President, Sales: Blake Edwards. **Director, Hispanic Marketing:** Richard Saenz. **Director, Public Affairs:** Craig Pletenik. **Director, Tucson Operations:** Mark Fernandez. **Director, Broadcasting:** Scott Geyer. **Manager, Broadcast Services:** Leo Gilmartin. **Manager, Marketing:** Gina Giallonardo.

Public Relations, Communications
Telephone: (602) 462-6500. **FAX:** (602) 462-6527.
Director, Public Relations: Mike Swanson. **Manager, Media Relations:** Bob Crawford. **Media Coordinator:** Brenda Morse. **Assistants, Media Relations:** David Pape, Mike McNally. **Editor, Diamondbacks Quarterly:** Joel Horn.

Stadium Operations
President/General Manager: Bob Machen.
Vice President/Assistant General Manager: Alvan Adams. **Director, Operations:** Gary Rich. **Director, Ballpark Services:** Russ Amaral. **Director, Suite Services:** Diney Mahoney.
Head Groundskeeper: Grant Trenbeath.
PA Announcer: Jeff Munn.

Ticketing
Telephone: (602) 514-8400. **FAX:** (602) 462-4141.
Vice President, Tickets and Special Services: Dianne Aguilar.
Director, Sales: Rob Kiese.

Travel, Clubhouse
Director, Team Travel: Roger Riley.
Equipment Manager/Home Clubhouse: Chris Guth. **Vistitors Clubhouse:** Bob Doty.

General Information
Hometown Dugout: Third Base. **Playing Surface:** Grass.
Standard Game Times: 7:05 p.m.
Directions to Stadium: Exit at Seventh Street from I-10 and turn south, or I-17 and turn north.
Player Representative: Brian Anderson.

DIAMONDBACKS

BASEBALL OPERATIONS

Telephone: (602) 462-6000. **FAX:** Unavailable.
Vice President, General Manager: Joe Garagiola Jr.

Senior Executive Vice President, Baseball Operations: Roland Hemond. **Director, Baseball Administration:** Ralph Nelson. **Special Assistants to General Manager:** Shooty Babitt, Ron Hassey, Sandy Johnson. **Assistant to General Manager:** Valerie Dietrich.

Director, Pacific Rim Operations: Jim Marshall.
Coordinator, Spring Training: Ethan Blackaby.

Joe Garagiola Jr.

Major League Staff

Manager: Buck Showalter.

Coaches: Bench—Carlos Tosca; Pitching—Mark Connor; Batting—Jim Presley; First Base—Dwayne Murphy; Third Base—Brian Butterfield; Bullpen—Glenn Sherlock.

Medical, Training

Club Physicians: Dr. David Zeman, Dr. Roger McCoy.

Head Trainer: Paul Lessard. **Assistant Trainer:** Dave Edwards. **Strength and Conditioning Coach:** Jeff Forney.

Minor Leagues

Telephone: (602) 462-6000. **FAX:** (602) 462-6527.
Director, Player Development: Mel Didier.
Director, Minor League Operations: Tommy Jones. **Minor League Administrator:** Tyler Agenter. **Administrative Assistant:** Suzy Hinds.

Roving Instructors: Bobby Dickerson (infield), Rafael Landestoy (outfield), Bob Mariano (hitting), Gil Patterson (pitching).

Buck Showalter

Farm System

Class	Farm Team	Manager	Coach	Pitching Coach
AAA	Tucson	Chris Speier	Mike Barnett	Chuck Kniffin
A	High Desert	Don Wakamatsu	Ty Van Burkleo	Dennis Lewallyn
A	South Bend	Roly de Armas	Rick Schu	Mike Parrott
R	Lethbridge	Joe Almaraz	Jeff Davenport	Dave Jorn
R	Peoria	Mike Brumley	George Lopez	Royal Clayton
R	DSL	Julio Paula	Gregorio Ramirez	Pablo Frias

Scouting

Telephone: (602) 462-6000. **FAX:** (602) 462-6421.
Director, Scouting: Don Mitchell. **Assistant Director, Scouting:** Edwin Hartwell. **Administrative Assistant, Scouting:** Lisa Ventresca.

Advance Scout: Dick Scott.

Coordinator, Professional Scouting: Ed Durkin. **Professional Scouts:** Brannon Bonifay (Okeechobee, FL), Julian Mock (Peachtree City, GA).

National Coordinator: Kendall Carter.

National Supervisors: Clay Daniel (Keller, TX), Howard McCullough (Greenville, NC), Steve Springer (Huntington Beach, CA).

Don Mitchell

Area Supervisors: Tony Arango (Stamford, CT), David Cassidy (Phoenix, AZ), Arnold Cochran (Ponce, PR), Ray Corbett (College Station, TX), Bill Earnhart (Point Clear, AL), Jesse Flores (Post Falls, ID), Brian Guinn (Richmond, CA), Scott Jaster (Midland, MI), James Keller (Long Beach, CA), Chris Knabenshue (Edmond, OK), Greg Lonigro (Connellsville, PA), David May (Newark, DE), Louie Medina (Phoenix, AZ), Mike Piatnik (Winter Haven, FL), Mac Seibert (Molino, FL), Steve Swail (Macon, GA), Brad Vaughn (Griffithville, AR), Harold Zonder (Louisville, KY).

International Coordinator: Clay Daniel. **Latin American Coordinator:** Junior Noboa.

ATLANTA

Telephone, Address

Office Address: 755 Hank Aaron Dr., Atlanta, GA 30315. **Mailing Address:** P.O. Box 4064, Atlanta, GA 30302. **Telephone:** (404) 522-7630. **FAX:** (404) 614-1391. **E-Mail Address:** firstname.lastgame@turner.com. **Website:** www.atlanta braves.com.

Ownership

Operated by: Atlanta National League Baseball Club, Inc.

Principal Owner: Ted Turner. **Chairman:** Bill Bartholomay.

Board of Directors: Henry Aaron, Bill Bartholomay, Bobby Cox, Stan Kasten, Rubye Lucas, Terry McGuirk, John Schuerholz, M.B. Seretean, Ted Turner.

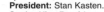

Stan Kasten

President: Stan Kasten.

Senior Vice President, Assistant to President: Hank Aaron.

BUSINESS OPERATIONS

Senior Vice President, Administration: Bob Wolfe. **Team Counsel:** David Payne. **Director, Human Resources:** Lisa Stricklin.

Finance

Controller: Chip Moore.

Marketing, Sales

Vice President, Marketing/Broadcasting: Wayne Long.

Senior Director, Promotions/Civic Affairs: Miles McRea. **Director, Ticket Sales:** Paul Adams. **Director, Advertising:** Amy Richter. **Director, Community Relations/Fan Development:** Dexter Santos. **Director, Braves Foundation:** Danny Goodwin.

Public Relations, Communications

Telephone: (404) 614-1302. **FAX:** (404) 614-1391.

Director, Public Relations: Jim Schultz.

Assistant, Media Relations: Glen Serra. **Administrative Assistants, Public Relations:** Joan Hicks, Steve Copses, Robert Gahagan, Dena Hamby.

Stadium Operations

Director, Stadium Operations/Security: Larry Bowman. **Field Director:** Ed Mangan.

PA Announcer: Bill Bowers. **Official Scorers:** Mark Frederickson, Scott McGregor. **Director, Audio-Visual Operations:** Jennifer Berger.

Ticketing

Telephone: (800) 326-4000. **FAX:** (404) 614-1391.

Director, Ticket Operations: Ed Newman.

Travel, Clubhouse

Director, Team Travel/Equipment Manager: Bill Acree. **Assistant Clubhouse Manager:** Casey Stevenson. **Visiting Clubhouse Manager:** John Holland.

General Information

Hometown Dugout: First Base. **Playing Surface:** Grass.

Standard Game Times: 7:40 p.m.; Sat. 7:10, Sun. 1:10.

Directions to Stadium: I-75/85 northbound, take exit 91 (Fulton Street); I-75/85 southbound, take exit 91 (Fulton Street); I-20 westbound, take exit 24 (Capitol Avenue); I-20 eastbound, take exit 22 (Windsor Street), right on Windsor Street, left on Fulton Street.

Player Representative: Tom Glavine.

BRAVES

BASEBALL OPERATIONS
Telephone: (404) 522-7630. **FAX:** (404) 523-3962.
Executive Vice President, General Manager: John Schuerholz.

Assistant General Manager: Dean Taylor. **Special Assistants to General Manager:** Bill Lajoie, Brian Murphy. **Special Assistants to GM/Player Development:** Jose Martinez, Willie Stargell.

Major League Staff
Manager: Bobby Cox.
Coaches: Dugout—Jim Beauchamp; Pitching—Leo Mazzone; Batting—Clarence Jones; First Base—Pat Corrales; Third Base—Bobby Dews; Bullpen—Ned Yost.

John Schuerholz

Bobby Cox

Medical, Training
Team Physician: Dr. David Watson.
Trainer: Dave Pursley. **Assistant Trainer:** Jeff Porter.
Strength and Conditioning Coach: Frank Fultz.

Minor Leagues
Telephone: (404) 614-1354. **FAX:** (404) 614-1350.
Director, Scouting/Player Development: Paul Snyder.

Director, Minor League Operations: Deric Ladnier. **Assistant, Baseball Operations:** Tyrone Brooks. **Administrative Assistants, Minor Leagues:** Lena Burney, Bobbie Cranford, Kathy Miller.

Field Coordinators: Chino Cadahia (catching).
Roving Instructors: Leon Roberts (hitting), Jerry Nyman (pitching).

Farm System

Class	Farm Team	Manager	Coach	Pitching Coach
AAA	Richmond	Jeff Cox	Max Venable	Bill Fischer
AA	Greenville	Randy Ingle	Mel Roberts	Mike Alvarez
A	Danville	Paul Runge	Bobby Moore	Bruce Dal Canton
A	Macon	Brian Snitker	Glenn Hubbard	Mark Ross
A	Eugene	Jim Saul	Dan Norman	Jerry Nyman
R	Danville	Franklin Stubbs	Ralph Henriquez	Bill Slack
R	Orlando	Rick Albert	Ed Renteria	Eddie Watt
R	DSL	Pedro Gonzalez	Unavailable	Unavailable

Scouting
Telephone: (404) 614-1354. **FAX:** (404) 614-1350.
Director, Scouting: Paul Snyder. **Assistant Director, Scouting:** Dayton Moore.

Advance Scout: Bobby Wine (Norristown, PA).

Major League Scouts: Dick Balderson (Aurora, CO), Scott Nethery (Houston, TX), Fred Shaffer (New Castle, PA), Bill Wight (Westminster, CA).

National Crosscheckers: Roy Clark (Martinsville, VA), Bob Wadsworth (Westminster, CA).

Regional Supervisors: East—Hep Cronin (Cincinnati, OH); Midwest—John Flannery (Austin, TX); West—Butch Baccala (Windsor, CA).

Paul Snyder

Area Scouts: Mike Baker (Santa Ana, CA), Stu Cann (Bradley, IL), Sherard Clinkscales (Indianapolis, IN), Bob Dunning (Phoenix, AZ), Rob English (Duluth, GA), Rene Francisco (Lake Worth, FL), Ralph Garr (Missouri City, TX), Rod Gilbreath (Lilburn, GA), John Hagemann (Staten Island, NY), Dexter Harris (Chambersburg, PA), Marcus Harrison (Sacramento, CA), Ray Jackson (Birmingham, AL), Kurt Kemp (Eugene, OR), Brian Kohlscheen (Norman, OK), Al Kubski (Carlsbad, CA), Jim Martz (Lima, OH), Marco Paddy (Palm Coast, FL), Julian Perez (Levittown, PR), John Ramey (Murrieta, CA), Charlie Smith (Austin, TX), Doug Smith (Fairfield, OH), John Stewart (Granville, NY), Junior Vizcaino (Wake Forest, NC).

International Supervisor: Bill Clark (Columbia, MO). **Pacific Rim Coordinator:** Phil Dale (Wantirna, Australia).

CHICAGO

Telephone, Address
Office Address: Wrigley Field, 1060 West Addison St., Chicago, IL 60613. **Telephone:** (773) 404-2827. **FAX:** (773) 404-4129. **Website:** www.cubs.com.

Ownership
Operated by: Chicago National League Ball Club, Inc. **Owner:** Tribune Company.

Board of Directors: James Dowdle, Andy MacPhail, Andrew McKenna.

President/Chief Executive Officer: Andy MacPhail.

BUSINESS OPERATIONS

Andy MacPhail

Executive Vice President, Business Operations: Mark McGuire.

Manager, Information Systems: Carl Rice.

Senior Legal Counsel/Corporate Secretary: Crane Kenney. **Executive Secretary, Business Operations:** Annette Hannah.

Director, Human Resources: Jenifer Surma.

Finance
Controller: Jodi Norman. **Manager, Accounting:** Terri Lynn. **Senior Accountant:** Vanessa Smith. **Staff Accountants:** Felicia Moore, Jamal Simmons.

Marketing, Sales
Vice President, Marketing and Broadcasting: John McDonough.

Director, Promotions and Advertising: Jay Blunk. **Director, Special Events and Community Relations:** Connie Kowal. **Manager, Cubs Care/Community Relations:** Rebecca Polihronis. **Coordinator, Cubs Care/Community Relations:** Mary Dosek. **Manager, Mezzanine Suites:** Louis Artiaga. **Manager, Sponsorship Sales:** Susan Otolski.

Media Relations, Publications
Telephone: (773) 404-4191. **FAX:** (773) 404-4129.

Director, Media Relations: Sharon Pannozzo. **Coordinator, Media Information:** Chuck Wasserstrom. **Assistant, Media Relations:** Wanda Taylor.

Director, Publications/Special Projects: Ernie Roth. **Publications Editorial Specialists:** Jim McArdle, Jay Rand. **Senior Graphics Designer:** Patricia Mora-Gonzalez. **Internet Coordinator:** John Davila.

Stadium Operations
Director, Stadium Operations: Tom Cooper. **Assistant Director, Stadium Operations:** Paul Rathje.

Manager, Event Operations/Security: Mike Hill. **Head Groundskeeper:** Roger Baird. **Facility Supervisor:** Bill Scott. **Coordinator, Office Services:** Randy Skocz. **Coordinator, Stadium Operations:** Danielle Alexa.

PA Announcer: Paul Friedman. **Official Scorers:** Bob Rosenberg, Don Friske.

Ticketing
Telephone: (773) 404-2827. **FAX:** (773) 404-4014.

Director, Ticket Operations: Frank Maloney. **Assistant Director, Ticket Sales:** Brian Garza. **Assistant Director, Ticket Services:** Joe Kirchen. **Vault Room Supervisor:** Cherie Blake.

Travel, Clubhouse
Traveling Secretary: Jimmy Bank.

Equipment Manager: Yosh Kawano. **Assistant Equipment Manager:** Dana Noeltner. **Visiting Clubhouse Manager:** Tom Hellmann.

General Information

Hometown Dugout: Third Base. **Playing Surface:** Grass.

Standard Game Times: 1:20 p.m., 7:05; Sat. 12:15, 1:20, 3:05; Sun. 1:20.

Stadium Location: Five miles along Addison Street East exit off I-90/I-94.

Player Representative: Scott Servais.

CUBS

BASEBALL OPERATIONS

Telephone: (773) 404-4035. FAX: (773) 404-4147.
General Manager: Ed Lynch.
Director, Baseball Administration: Scott Nelson.
Special Assistants to General Manager: Larry Himes (Mesa, AZ), Ken Kravec (Sarasota, FL).
Special Player Consultant: Hugh Alexander (Brooksville, FL).

Executive Assistant to President and General Manager: Arlene Gill. Baseball Operations Assistant: Michelle Blanco.

Major League Staff

Manager: Jim Riggleman.

Ed Lynch

Coaches: Bench—Billy Williams; Pitching—Phil Regan; Hitting—Jeff Pentland; First Base—Dan Radison; Third Base—Tom Gamboa; Bullpen—Dave Bialas.

Medical, Training

Team Physicians: Dr. John Marquardt, Dr. Michael Schafer.
Head Trainer: David Tumbas. Assistant Trainer: Steve Melendez. Strength Coordinator: Bruce Hammel.

Minor Leagues

Telephone: (773) 404-4035. FAX: (773) 404-4147.
Director, Minor Leagues: David Wilder.
Coordinator, Instruction: Alan Regier. Assistant, Minor League Operations: Patti Kargakis.
Roving Instructors: Sandy Alomar Sr. (infield), Bruce Hammel (strenth and conditioning), Jimmy Piersall (outfield), Lester Strode (pitching).

Jim Riggleman

Farm System

Class	Farm Team	Manager	Coach	Pitching Coach
AAA	Iowa	Terry Kennedy	Glenn Adams	Marty DeMerritt
AA	West Tenn	Dave Trembley	Tack Wilson	Alan Dunn
A	Daytona	Steve Roadcap	Richie Zisk	Jose Santiago
A	Rockford	Ruben Amaro	Manny Trillo	Stan Kyles
A	Williamsport	Bob Ralston	Damon Farmar	Charlie Greene
R	Mesa	Nate Oliver	Carmelo Martinez	Rick Tronerud
R	DSL	Julio Valdez	Leo Hernandez	Unavailable

Scouting

Telephone: (773) 404-4039. FAX: (773) 404-4147.
Director, Scouting: Jim Hendry.
Administrative Assistant: Patricia Honzik.
Major League Advance Scout: Keith Champion (Ballwin, MO).

Regional Supervisors: Central—John Stockstill (Lee's Summit, MO); East—Tony DeMacio (Virginia Beach, VA); West—Larry Maxie (Upland, CA).

Full-Time Scouts: Mark Adair (Fairfield, OH), Billy Blitzer (Brooklyn, NY), Tom Bourque (Cambridge, MA), Bill Capps (Arlington, TX), Jim Crawford (Chattanooga, TN), Oneri Fleita (Newnan, GA), Steve Fuller (Brea, CA), Al Geddes (Canby, OR), John Gracio (Chandler, AZ), Gene

Jim Hendry

Handley (Huntington Beach, CA), Steve Hinton (Harrisburg, PA), Joe Housey (Hollywood, FL), Sam Hughes (Bastrop, LA), Spider Jorgensen (Cucamonga, CA), Buzzy Keller (Seguin, TX), Brad Kelley (San Jose, CA), Scott May (Wonder Lake, IL), Brian Milner (Arlington, TX), Marc Russo (Columbia, SC), Mark Servais (La Crosse, WI), Billy Swoope (Norfolk, VA).

International Supervisors: Canada—Tom Bourque (Cambridge, MA); Latin America—Oneri Fleita (Newnan, GA); Pacific Rim—Leon Lee (Folsom, CA). International Scouts: Alberto Rondon (Venezuela), Jose Serra (Dominican Republic), Jose Trujillo (Puerto Rico).

CINCINNATI

Telephone, Address

Office Address: 100 Cinergy Field, Cincinnati, OH 45202. Telephone: (513) 421-4510. FAX: (513) 421-7342. Website: www.cincinnatireds.com.

Ownership

Operated by: The Cincinnati Reds, Inc.

President, Chief Executive Officer: Marge Schott.

Partners: Frisch's Restaurants, Inc.; Gannett Co., Inc.; Carl Kroch; Carl Lindner; Mrs. Louis Nippert; William Reik Jr.; George Strike.

Managing Executive: John Allen.

John Allen

BUSINESS OPERATIONS

General Counsel, Treasurer: Robert Martin.

Chief Administrative Assistant, Executive Office: Joyce Pfarr. Administrator, Business and Broadcasting: Ginny Kamp.

Finance

Controller: Anthony Ward. Supervisor, Payroll: Cathy Secor. Supervisor, Accounts Payable: Cheri White. System Administrator: Kelly Gronotte. Administrative Assistant: Lois Wingo.

Marketing, Sales

Consultant, Marketing: Cal Levy. Administrative Assistant, Marketing: Kathy Schwab. Assistant, Marketing: Nancy Marazzi.

Director, Season Ticket Sales: Pat McCaffrey. Director, Group Sales: Barbara McManus. Assistants, Group Sales: Brad Callahan, Lisa Washnock. Assistants, Season Ticket Sales: Beth Gladura, Cindi Strzynski.

Public Relations, Communications

Telephone: (513) 421-2990. FAX: (513) 421-7342.

Director, Media Relations: Rob Butcher.

Director, Public Relations and Publications: Mike Ringering. Assistant, Public Relations: Charles Henderson. Administrative Assistant, Public Relations: Kelly Lippincott.

Stadium Operations

Director, Stadium Operations: Jody Pettyjohn. Superintendent, Stadium Operations: Bob Harrison. Stadium Superintendent: Jeff Guilkey.

Head Groundskeeper: Unavailable.

PA Announcer: John Walton. Official Scorers: Glenn Sample, Ron Roth.

Ticketing

Telephone: (513) 421-4510, ext. 4300. FAX: (513) 421-7342.

Director, Ticket Department: John O'Brien. Assistant Ticket Director: Ken Ayer. Ticket Office Assistants: Hallie Kinney, Colleen Brown.

Travel, Clubhouse

Traveling Secretary: Gary Wahoff.

Equipment Manager/Clubhouse Operations: Bernie Stowe. Home Clubhouse: Rick Stowe. Visitors Clubhouse: Mark Stowe.

General Information

Hometown Dugout: First Base. Playing Surface: Artificial turf.

Standard Game Times: 7:05 p.m.; Sat., Sun. 1:15.

Stadium Location: From north, take I-75 South and exit at 1A, follow downtown signs to Pete Rose Way; From north, take I-71 South and exit at Elm Street/Third Street, right on Third Street, right on Race Street to Pete Rose Way, left to stadium. From Kentucky, take I-75/I-71 North, follow I-71 sign to Pete Rose Way.

Player Representative: Mike Remlinger.

REDS

BASEBALL OPERATIONS

Telephone: (513) 421-4510. **FAX:** (513) 421-7342.
General Manager: Jim Bowden. **Assistant General Manager:** Darrell "Doc" Rodgers.

Director of Baseball Operations: Larry Barton Jr. (Fontana, CA). **Special Assistant to General Manager:** Gene Bennett (Wheelersburg, OH). **Senior Advisor, Player Personnel:** Bob Boone (Villa Park, CA). **Senior Advisor/Baseball Operations:** Bob Zuk (Redlands, CA). **Special Consultant to General Manager:** Johnny Bench (Cincinnati, OH).

Administrative Assistant, Baseball Operations: Brad Kullman.

Executive Assistant to General Manager: Lois Schneider.

Jim Bowden

Major League Staff

Manager: Jack McKeon.

Jack McKeon

Coaches: Dugout—Denis Menke; Pitching—Don Gullett; Batting—Ken Griffey Sr.; First Base/Infield—Ron Oester. Third Base—Harry Dunlop; Bullpen—Tom Hume.

Medical, Training

Club Physician: Dr. Tim Kremcheck. **Senior Consultant/Orthopedics:** Dr. James Andrews. **Orthopedic Physician:** Dr. Robert Burger.

Head Trainer: Greg Lynn. **Assistant Trainer:** Mark Mann. **Conditioning Coordinator:** Lance Sewell.

Minor Leagues

Senior Director, Scouting and Player Development: Al Goldis. **Senior Advisor, Major League and Player Development:** Chief Bender.

Director, Player Development: Muzzy Jackson. **Administrative Assistant, Player Development:** Lois Hudson.

Field Coordinator: Donnie Scott. **Roving Instructors:** Bill Doran (baserunning/infield), George Foster (hitting/outfield), Mike Griffin (pitching), Jim Hickman (hitting), Jim Thrift (offensive), Lemmie Miller (outfield).

Farm System

Class	Farm Team	Manager	Coach	Pitching Coach
AAA	Indianapolis	Dave Miley	Russ Nixon	Grant Jackson
AA	Chattanooga	Mark Berry	Mark Wagner	Mack Jenkins
A	Burlington	Phillip Wellman	None	Derek Botelho
A	Charleston, W.Va.	Barry Lyons	Amador Arias	Andre Rabouin
R	Billings	Russ Nixon	Amador Arias	Terry Abbott
R	DSL	Unavailable	None	Unavailable

Scouting

Telephone: (513) 421-4510. **FAX:** (513) 421-7342.
Director, Scouting: DeJon Watson (Hollywood, FL).
Director, Scouting Administration: Wilma Mann.

National Crosschecker: Johnny Almaraz (Spring Branch, TX). **Regional Crosscheckers:** Central—Thomas Wilson (Tuscaloosa, AL); East, Puerto Rico—Hank Sargent (Palm Harbor, FL); West—Jeff Barton (Gilbert, AZ).

Scouts: Fred Blair (Springfield, OH), Jim Grief (Paducah, KY), Don Gust (West Jordan, UT), Fred Hayes (Battle Creek, MI), Don Hill (Kingsville, OH), Les Houser (Surprise, AZ) Fred Leone (Pelham Manor, NY), Dion Lowe (Decatur, GA), Armando Morales (Levittown, PR), Denny Nagel (Cincinnati, OH), Jerry Raddatz (Winona, MN), Glenn Serviente (Hurst, TX), Doug Stuart (Brentwood, TN), Marlon Styles (Cincinnati, OH), Lee Toole (Council Bluffs, IA), John Walsh (Windsor, CT).

DeJon Watson

International Scouts: Ismael Cruz (Colombia), Felix Delgado (Venezuela), Tomas Herrera (Mexico), Jose Moreno (Dominican Republic), Murray Zuk (Canada).

COLORADO

Telephone, Address
Office Address: 2001 Blake St., Denver, CO 80205. **Telephone:** (303) 292-0200. **FAX:** (303) 312-2319. **Website:** www.coloradorockies.com.

Ownership
Operated by: Colorado Rockies Baseball Club, Ltd.

Principal Owners: Jerry McMorris, Charles Monfort, Richard Monfort.

Chairman/Chief Executive Officer: Jerry McMorris.

BUSINESS OPERATIONS

Jerry McMorris

Senior Vice President, Business Operations: Keli McGregor. **Senior Vice President, Corporate Counsel:** Clark Weaver.

Director, Personnel and Administration: Elizabeth Stecklein.

Finance
Senior Vice President, Chief Financial Officer: Hal Roth. **Vice President, Finance:** Michael Kent.

Director, Information Systems: Mary Burns. **Director, Accounting:** Gary Lawrence. **Senior Accountant:** Phil Emerson. **Accountant:** Holly Schneider.

Marketing, Sales
Vice President, Sales and Marketing: Greg Feasel.

Director, Marketing/Sales: Marcy English. **Assistant Director, Sales/Marketing:** Dave Madsen. **Account Executives:** Carey Brandt, Dina Cooper.

Director, Promotions: Alan Bossart. **Director, Ticket Sales:** Kevin Fenton. **Assistant Director, Group Sales:** Erin Weiss. **Assistant Director, Season Ticket Sales:** Jeff Benner.

Director, Broadcasting: Eric Brummond.

Public Relations, Communications
Telephone: (303) 312-2325. **FAX:** (303) 312-2319.

Director, Public Relations: Jay Alves. **Assistant Director, Public Relations:** Brandy Lay. **Coordinator, Public Relations:** Charity Stovell. **Assistant, Public Relations:** Zak Gilbert.

Director, Publications: Jimmy Oldham.

Director, Community Affairs: Roger Kinney. **Manager, Community Affairs:** Sean McGraw. **Coordinator, Community Affairs:** Angela Keenan. **Assistant to Director, Community Affairs:** Stacy Schafer.

Stadium Operations
Senior Director, Stadium Services: Kevin Kahn. **Director, Coors Field Development:** Dave Moore. **Manager, Game Day Services:** Mike Rock.

Head Groundskeeper: Mark Razum.

PA Announcer: Kelly Burnham. **Official Scorer:** Unavailable.

Ticketing
Telephone: (303) ROCKIES. **FAX:** (303) 312-2115.

Director, Ticket Operations: Chuck Javernick. **Manager, Season Ticket Sales:** Kent Hakes. **Assistant Director, Ticket Sales:** Jill Roberts.

Travel, Clubhouse
Director, Team Travel: John Howell. **Assistant to Director, Team Travel/Coordinator, Player Relations:** Adele Armagost.

Clubhouse and Equipment Manager: Dan McGinn. **Visiting Clubhouse Manager:** Keith Schulz.

General Information
Hometown Dugout: First Base. **Playing Surface:** Grass.

Standard Game Times: 7:05 p.m., 1:05; Sun. 1:05.

Stadium Location: From I-70 to I-25 South to exit 213 (Park Avenue) or 212C (20th Street); I-25 to 20th Street.

Player Representative: Unavailable.

ROCKIES

BASEBALL OPERATIONS
Telephone: (303) 292-0200. **FAX:** (303) 312-2320.
Executive Vice President, General Manager: Bob Gebhard.
Assistant General Manager: Tony Siegle.

Major League Staff
Manager: Don Baylor.
Coaches: Dugout—Jackie Moore; Pitching—Frank Funk; Batting/First Base—Clint Hurdle; Third Base—Gene Glynn; Bullpen—Bill Hayes.

Medical, Training
Club Physicians: Dr. Wayne Gersoff, Dr. Allen Schreiber.

Bob Gebhard

Head Trainer: Dave Cilladi. **Assistant Trainer:** Tom Probst. **Strength and Conditioning Coordinator:** Mark Wilbert.

Minor Leagues
Director, Player Development: Paul Egins.
Assistant Director, Player Development: Marc Gustafson. **Administrative Assistant, Player Development:** Chris Rice.

Don Baylor

Coordinator, Instruction: Rick Mathews (pitching). **Roving Instructors:** Greg Gross (hitting), Joe Marchese (infield), Rolando Fernandez (Latin coordinator).

Farm System

Class	Farm Team	Manager	Coach	Pitching Coach
AAA	Colo. Springs	Paul Zuvella	Tony Torchia	Sonny Siebert
AA	New Haven	Tim Blackwell	Stu Cole	Jim Wright
A	Salem	Jay Loviglio	Elanis Westbrooks	Jack Lamabe
A	Asheville	Ron Gideon	Billy White	Jerry Cram
A	Portland	Jim Eppard	Al Bleser	Tom Edens
R	Tucson	P.J. Carey	Fred Ocasio	Cam Walker
R	DSL	Dario Arias	None	Herminio Toribio

Scouting
Telephone: (303) 292-0200. **FAX:** (303) 312-2320.
Vice President, Scouting: Pat Daugherty.
Assistant Director, Scouting: Coley Brannon.
Administrative Assistant, Scouting: Penny Biever.
Director, Professional and International Scouting: Jeff Schugel.
Advance Scout: Dan Gladden.
Major League Scouts: Jack Bloomfield (McAllen, TX), Jim Fanning (Pointe Claire, Quebec), Bill Harford (Chicago, IL), Larry High (Mesa, AZ), Bill Wood (Coppell, TX).
National Crosscheckers: Bill Gayton (Houston, TX), Dave Holliday (Coalgate, OK).

Pat Daugherty

Regional Crosscheckers: West—Bruce Andrew (Northridge, CA); Midwest—Jay Darnell (Plano, TX), East—Robyn Lynch (Safety Harbor, FL).
Full-Time Scouts: John Cedarburg (Fort Myers, FL), Ty Coslow (Louisville, KY), Dar Cox (Red Oak, TX), Mike Ericson (Glendale, AZ), Abe Flores (Huntington Beach, CA), Mike Garlatti (Edison, NJ), Bert Holt (Visalia, CA), Greg Hopkins (Portland, OR), Bill Hughes (Sherman Oaks, CA), Damon Iannelli (Brandon, MI), Bill MacKenzie (Ottawa, Ontario), Danny Montgomery (Charlotte, NC), Lance Nichols (Dodge City, KS), Steve Payne (Smyrna, GA), Art Pontarelli (Cranston, RI), Ed Santa (Columbus, OH), Nick Venuto (Crown Point, IN), Tom Wheeler (Pleasant Hill, CA).
Latin America Supervisor: Jorge Posada.

FLORIDA

Telephone, Address
Office Address: Pro Player Stadium, 2267 NW 199th St., Miami, FL 33056. Telephone: (305) 626-7400. FAX: (305) 626-7428. E-Mail Address: www.flamarlins.com.

Ownership
Operated by: Florida Marlins Baseball Club, Inc.
Principal Owner/Chairman: Wayne Huizenga.
Partners: Steven Berrard, Harris Hudson, Harry Huizenga, Wayne Huizenga Jr.
President: Don Smiley.

Wayne Huizenga

BUSINESS OPERATIONS

Finance
Vice President, Finance and Administration: Jonathan Mariner.
Director, Finance/Controller: Susan Jaison. Programmer, Analyst, Information Systems: David Kuan. Manager, Information Technology: Esther Fleming. Senior Staff Accountant: Nancy Hernandez. Executive Secretary, Finance and Administration: Ann Saliwanchik.

Marketing, Sales
Vice President, Sales and Marketing: James Ross.
Director, In-Game Entertainment and Marketing Coordination: Susan Julian Budd. Director, Marketing Partnerships: Ben Creed. Director, Season/Group Ticket Sales: Lou DePaoli. Assistant Director, Group Sales: Pat McNamara. Senior Manager, Season Ticket Sales: John Pierce. Sales Manager: Adrien Bouchet.

Public Relations, Communications
Telephone: (305) 626-7429. FAX: (305) 626-7302.
Director, Baseball Information and Publicity: Ron Colangelo. Assistant Director, Baseball Information and Publicity: Julio Sarmiento. Manager, Baseball Information and Publicity: Margo Malone. Coordinator, Baseball Information and Publicity: Sandra van Meek.
Director, Communications: Mark Geddis. Director, Creative Services: Leslie Riguero. Manager, Community Affairs: Nancy Olson. Manager, Foundation and Community Affairs: Alan Brown. Manager, Speakers Bureau and Player Relations: Brian Randolph.

Stadium Operations
Vice President, Stadium Operations: Bruce Schulze. Director, Event Operations: Todd Ellzey. Head Groundskeeper: Alan Sigwardt.
PA Announcer: Jay Rokeach. Official Scorers: Harvey Greene, Sonny Hirsch, Doug Pett.

Ticketing
Telephone: (305) 930-4487. FAX: (305) 626-7432.
Vice President, Ticket Operations: Bill Galante. Director, Club Level Services: Andy Major. Manager, Ticket Operations: Daniel Katz.

Travel, Clubhouse
Director, Team Travel: Bill Beck.
Equipment Manager: Mike Wallace. Assistant Equipment Manager: Javier Castro. Visitors Clubhouse: Matt Rosenthal.

General Information
Hometown Dugout: First Base. Playing Surface: Grass.
Standard Game Times: 7:05 p.m.; Sun. 1:05.
Stadium Location: From south, Florida Turnpike extension to stadium exit; From north, I-95 to I-595 West to Florida Turnpike to stadium exit; From west, I-75 to I-595 to Florida Turnpike to stadium exit; From east, Highway 826 West to NW 27th Ave., north to 199th St., right to stadium.
Player Representative: Unavailable.

MARLINS

BASEBALL OPERATIONS

Telephone: (305) 626-7434. **FAX:** (305) 626-7433.
Executive Vice President, General Manager: Dave Dombrowski. **Vice President, Assistant General Manager:** Frank Wren. **Special Assistant to General Manager:** Tony Perez.

Vice President, Player Personnel: Gary Hughes. **Senior Advisor, Player Personnel:** Whitey Lockman. **Administrative Assistant, Baseball:** Mike Carr.

Director, Latin American Operations: Al Avila.

Major League Staff

Manager: Jim Leyland.
Coaches: Dugout—Lorenzo Bundy; Pitching—Rich Dubee; Batting—Milt May; First Base—Tommy Sandt; Third Base—Rich Donnelly; Bullpen—Bruce Kimm.

Dave Dombrowski

Medical, Training

Club Physician: Dr. Dan Kanell.
Head Trainer: Larry Starr. **Assistant Trainer:** Kevin Rand. **Director, Strength and Conditioning:** Rick Slate.

Minor Leagues

Vice President, Player Development: John Boles. **Director, Minor League Administration:** Dan Lunetta. **Administrative Assistant, Player Development:** Mike Parkinson. **Administrative Assistant, Minor League Administration:** Kim-Lee Luchs.

Jim Leyland

Field Coordinator: Rob Leary. **Roving Instructors:** Joe Breeden (catching), Britt Burns (pitching), Rusty Kuntz (outfield/baserunning), Jack Maloof (hitting), Tony Taylor (infield).

Farm System

Class	Farm Team	Manager	Coach	Pitching Coach
AAA	Charlotte	Fredi Gonzalez	Adrian Garrett	Randy Hennis
AA	Portland	Lynn Jones	Sal Rende	Brian Peterson
A	Brevard County	Rick Renteria	Jose Castro	Larry Pardo
A	Kane County	Juan Bustabad	Matt Winters	Steve Luebber
A	Utica	Ken Joyce	Steve McFarland	Bill Sizemore
R	Melbourne	Jon Deeble	Manny Crespo	Euclides Rojas
R	DSL	Nelson Silverio	Carlos de la Cruz	Jose Duran

Scouting

Telephone: (305) 626-7217. **FAX:** (305) 626-7433.
Director, Scouting: Orrin Freeman.
Administrative Assistant, Scouting: Cheryl Evans.
Major League Scouts: Gary Hughes (Aptos, CA), Whitey Lockman (Scottsdale, AZ), Scott Reid (Phoeniz, AZ).

National Crosscheckers: Murray Cook (Sarasota, FL), Dick Egan (Phoenix, AZ), Jax Robertson (Cary, NC), Tim Schmidt (San Bernardino, CA), Greg Zunino (Cape Coral, FL).

Full-Time Scouts: Ed Bockman (Millbrae, CA), John Booher (Las Vegas, NV), Rich Bordi (Rohnert Park, CA), Kelvin Bowles (Rocky Mount, VA), Ty Brown (Ruther Glen, VA), Joe Campise (Bryan, TX), John Castleberry (High Point, NC), David Chadd (Wichita, KS), Whitey DeHart (Woodburn, OR), Brad Del Barba (Taylor Mill, KY), David Finley (San Diego, CA), Lou Fitzgerald (Cleveland, TN), Will George (Merchantville, NJ), Matt King (Aptos, CA), Bob Laurie (Plano, TX), Fred Long (Redlands, CA), Steve McFarland (Scottsdale, AZ), Steve Minor (Long Beach, CA), Deni Pacini (Kerman, CA), Tom Pearse (Winters, CA), Mike Russell (Gulf Breeze, FL), Stan Saleski (Dayton, OH), Bill Scherrer (Buffalo, NY), Charlie Silvera (Millbrae, CA), Keith Snider (Stockton, CA), Wally Walker (Reno, NV), Stan Zielinski (Winfield, IL).

Orrin Freeman

HOUSTON

Telephone, Address
Office Address: 8400 Kirby Dr., Houston, TX 77054. Mailing Address: P.O. Box 288, Houston, TX 77001. Telephone: (713) 799-9500. FAX: (713) 799-9794. E-Mail Address: twinspin@astros.com. Website: www.astros.com.

Drayton McLane

Ownership
Operated by: McLane Group, LP.
Principal Owner, Chairman: Drayton McLane Jr.
Board of Directors: Drayton McLane Jr., Sandy Sanford, Bob McClaren.

BUSINESS OPERATIONS
Vice President, Business Operations: Bob McClaren.
General Counsel: Frank Rynd. Director, Human Resources: Mike Anders.

Finance
Vice President, Finance: Webb Stickney.
Controller: Robert McBurnett. Director, Management Information Systems: Jeff Paschal. Accounts Receivable: Mary Ann Bell. Accounts Payable: Irene Dumenil. Manager, General Accounting: Mary Duvernay.

Marketing, Sales
Vice President, Marketing: Pam Gardner.
Director, Advertising: Chuck Pool. Director, Promotions/Broadcast Operations: Jamie Hildreth. Assistant Director, Advertising Sales/Promotions: Jim Ballweg. Coordinator, Advertising: Duone Byars.

Public Relations, Communications
Telephone: (713) 799-9600. FAX: (713) 799-9881.
Director, Media Relations: Rob Matwick. Assistant Director, Media Relations: Darrell Simon. Administrative Assistant, Media Relations: Desta Kimmel.
Director, Publications: Alyson Footer. Director, Community Relations: Marian Harper. Coordinator, Community Development: Phoenix Mak.

Stadium Operations
Director, Stadium Operations: Don Collins. Assistant Director: Greg Golightly.
Head Groundskeeper: Willie Berry.
PA Announcer: Bob Ford. Official Scorers: Ivy McLemore, Rick Blount, Fred Duckett. Scoreboard Operations: Doug Swan.

Ticketing
Telephone: (713) 799-9567. FAX: (713) 799-9812.
Director, Ticket Operations: John Sorrentino. Manager, Ticket Sales: Tina Cash. Manager, Box Office: Heather Cox. Manager, Premium Sales: Shannon Sawyer. Administrative Assistant, Group and Season Sales: Joannie Cobb. Group/Season Sales: Brent Broussard, Scott Tarrant, Scott Witherow.

Travel, Clubhouse
Traveling Secretary: Barry Waters.
Equipment Manager/Home Clubhouse: Dennis Liborio. Visiting Clubhouse: Steve Perry.

General Information
Hometown Dugout: First Base. Playing Surface: Artificial turf.
Standard Game Times: 7:05 p.m., Sun. 1:35.
Stadium Location: From I-10, exit 610 South to Kirby Drive exit, right on Kirby Drive to Murworth Gate, right to stadium. From I-45, exit 288 South to 610 West, take Kirby Drive exit to Murworth Gate.
Player Representative: Shane Reynolds.

ASTROS

BASEBALL OPERATIONS

Telephone: (713) 799-9500. **FAX:** (713) 799-9562.
General Manager: Gerry Hunsicker.
Assistant General Manager: Tim Purpura.
Special Assistant to General Manager: Andres
Reiner. **Director, Baseball Operations/Administration:** Barry Waters. **Administrative Assistant:**
Beverly Rains.

Major League Staff

Manager: Larry Dierker.
Coaches: Dugout—Matt Galante; Pitching—
Vern Ruhle; Batting—Tom McCraw; First Base—
Jose Cruz Sr.; Third Base—Mike Cubbage;
Bullpen—Dave Engle.

Gerry Hunsicker

Medical, Training

Medical Director: Dr. Bill Bryan.
Head Trainer: Dave Labossiere. **Assistant
Trainer:** Rex Jones. **Strength and Conditioning
Coach:** Dr. Gene Coleman.

Minor Leagues

Telephone: (713) 799-9500. **FAX:** (713) 799-9562.
Director, Player Development: Tim Purpura.
Administrator, Minor Leagues: Jay Edmiston.
Administrative Assistant: Carol Wogsland.
Assistant, Baseball Operations: Tomas Botas.
Coordinator, Instruction: Harry Spilman.
Roving Instructors: Ivan DeJesus (infield/
baserunning), Dewey Robinson (pitching).

Larry Dierker

Farm System

Class	Farm Team	Manager	Coach	Pitching Coach
AAA	New Orleans	John Tamargo	Al Pedrique	Jim Hickey
AA	Jackson	Jim Pankovits	Jorge Orta	Charley Taylor
A	Kissimmee	Manny Acta	Mark Bailey	Jack Billingham
A	Quad City	Mike Rojas	Sid Holland	Bill Ballou
A	Auburn	Lyle Yates	Brad Wellman	Darwin Pennye
R	Kissimmee	Julio Linares	Cesar Cedeno	Stan Boroski
R	DSL	Rolando Bell	Rafael Ramirez	Rick Aponte
R	VSL	Pablo Torrealba	Jesus Aristimuno	Oscar Padron

Scouting

Telephone: (713) 799-9500. **FAX:** (713) 799-9562.
Director, Scouting: David Lakey. **Assistant
Director, Scouting:** Pat Murphy. **Administrative
Assistant, Scouting:** Traci Dearing.

Advance Scout: Tom Wiedenbauer (Ormond
Beach, FL). **Major League Scouts:** Stan Benjamin
(Port Charlotte, FL), Fred Nelson (Richmond, TX),
Bob Skinner (San Diego, CA), Paul Weaver
(Phoenix, AZ).

Professional Scouts: Leo Labossiere (Lincoln,
RI), Tom Mooney (Pittsfield, MA), Joe Pittman
(Columbus, GA), Scipio Spinks (Houston, TX),
Lynwood Stallings (Kingsport, TN), Tim Tolman
(Tucson, AZ).

David Lakey

National Supervisor: Bill Kelso (Bedford, TX).
Regional Supervisors: West—Bob King (La Mesa, CA); East—Gerry
Craft (St. Clairsville, OH); Central—Tad Slowik (Niles, IL).
Special Assignment Scout: Walt Matthews (Texarkana, TX).
Area Scouts: Bob Blair (Commack, NY), Stan Boroski (Kissimmee, FL),
Ralph Bratton (Dripping Springs, TX), Doug Deutsch (Costa Mesa, CA), James
Farrar (Shreveport, LA), Brian Granger (Dickson, TN), David Henderson
(Oklahoma City, OK), Dan Huston (Bellevue, WA), Mark Johnson (Englewood,
CO), Brian Keegan (Charlotte, NC), Mike Maggart (Penn Yan, NY), Jerry Marik
(Chicago, IL), Mel Nelson (Highland, CA), Bob Poole (Redwood City, CA), Joe
Robinson (Burlington, IA), Deron Rombach (Escondido, CA), Steve Smith
(Marietta, GA), Frankie Thon (Guaynabo, PR), George Wellman (Danville, CA).

LOS ANGELES

Telephone, Address
Office Address: 1000 Elysian Park Ave., Los Angeles, CA 90012. Telephone: (213) 224-1500. FAX: (213) 224-1269. Website: www.dodgers.com.

Ownership
Operated by: Los Angeles Dodgers, Inc.
Principal Owner/Chairman: Peter O'Malley.
Board of Directors: Peter O'Malley, Roland Seidler, Terry Seidler.
Vice President: Tommy Lasorda. Vice President, Campo las Palmas complex (Dominican Republic): Ralph Avila.

Peter O'Malley

BUSINESS OPERATIONS
General Counsel: Sam Fernandez.
Manager, Human Resources: Gina Galasso. Supervisor, Administrative Services: Linda Cohen. Managing Director, Dodgertown: Craig Callan.

Finance
Executive Vice President: Bob Graziano.
Vice President, Accounting and Finance: Bill Foltz. Director, Management Information Services: Mike Mularky.

Marketing, Sales
Vice President, Marketing: Barry Stockhamer.
Director, Advertising and Special Events: Paul Kalil. Manager, Marketing Services: Monique LaVeau-Brennan. Manager, Corporate Account Services: Kristie Kinsella. Manager, Group Events: Steve Everett. Manager, Ticket Marketing: Jerry Stipo. Supervisor, Special Events: Melissa Akioka.

Public Relations, Communications
Telephone: (213) 224-1301. FAX: (213) 224-1459.
Vice President, Communications: Tommy Hawkins.
Director, Publicity: Derrick Hall. Assistant Director, Publicity: Shaun Rachau. Manager, Publicity: John Olguin. Administrative Assistant, Publicity: Barbara Conway. Assistant, Baseball Information: David Tuttle. Assistant, Media/International Relations: Grace Morino.
Director, Broadcast and Publications: Brent Shyer.
Director, Community Relations: Don Newcombe. Director, Community Affairs: Monique Brandon. Administrator, Community Affairs: Laura Pierson. Coordinator, Community Affairs: Matthew Bennett. Manager, Community Affairs: Lisa Sarno.

Stadium Operations
Director, Stadium Operations: Doug Duennes. Assistant Director, Stadium Operations: Chris Fighera. Manager, Stadium Operations: David Born. Head Groundskeeper: Al Myers.
PA Announcer: Mike Carlucci. Official Scorers: Larry Kahn, Ira Kaze, Dan Hardtac.

Ticketing
Telephone: (213) 224-1448. FAX: (213) 224-2609.
Director, Ticket Operations: Debra Duncan. Assistant Director, Ticket Operations: Billy Hunter. Manager, Ticket Operations: Gary Barbee.

Travel, Clubhouse
Traveling Secretary: Bill DeLury.
Equipment Manager/Dodger Clubhouse Manager: David Wright. Visiting Clubhouse Manager: Jerry Turner.

General Information
Hometown Dugout: Third Base. Playing Surface: Grass.
Stadium Location: I-5 to Stadium Way exit, left on Stadium Way, right on Academy Road, left to Stadium Way to Elysian Park Ave., left to stadium; I-110 to Dodger Stadium exit, left on Stadium Way, right on Elysian Park Ave.; U.S. 101 to Alvarado exit, right on Sunset, left on Elysian Park Ave.
Standard Game Times: 7:05 p.m., Wed. 7:35, Sun. 1:05.
Player Representative: Billy Ashley.

DODGERS

BASEBALL OPERATIONS

Telephone: (213) 224-1306. **FAX:** (213) 224-1269.
Executive Vice President, General Manager: Fred Claire.
Administrator, Baseball Operations: Robert Schweppe. **Administrative Assistant:** Rosalyn Gutierrez.

Major League Staff

Manager: Bill Russell.
Coaches: Dugout—Mike Scioscia; Pitching—Goose Gregson; Batting/Third Base—Reggie Smith; First Base—Joe Amalfitano; Bullpen—Mark Cresse.

Fred Claire

Bill Russell

Medical, Training

Team Physicians: Dr. Frank Jobe, Dr. Michael Mellman.
Head Trainer: Charlie Strasser. **Assistant Trainer:** Stan Johnston.

Minor Leagues

Telephone: (213) 224-1431. **FAX:** (213) 224-1359.
Vice President, Minor League Operations: Charlie Blaney. **Administrative Assistant, Minor Leagues:** Luchy Guerra. **Secretary:** Tana Bertaux.
Coordinator, Instruction: Glenn Hoffman.
Roving Instructors: Tom Beyers (hitting), Guy Conti (pitching), Del Crandall (catching), Chico Fernandez (infield), Dick McLaughlin (outfield/bunting), Kevin Tollefson (physical therapist), Joe Vavra (baserunning).

Farm System

Class	Farm Team	Manager	Coach	Pitching Coach
AAA	Albuquerque	Glenn Hoffman	Jon Debus	Claude Osteen
AA	San Antonio	Ron Roenicke	Lance Parrish	Edwin Correa
A	San Bernardino	Mickey Hatcher	Monte Marshall	Charlie Hough
A	Vero Beach	John Shoemaker	John Shelby	Gorman Heimueller
A	Yakima	Tony Harris	Mitch Webster	Mark Brewer
R	Great Falls	Dino Ebel	Tom Thomas	Max Leon
R	DSL I	Antonio Bautista	Algona Read	Eleodoro Arias
R	DSL II	Jose Salado	Pedro Mega	Luis Barreiro

Scouting

Telephone: (213) 224-1437. **FAX:** (213) 224-1359.
Director, Scouting: Terry Reynolds.
Advance Scout: John VanOrnum (Bass Lake, CA). **Coordinator, Professional Scouting:** Gary Sutherland (Monrovia, CA).
Major League Scout: Eddie Bane (Phoenix, AZ). **Special Assignment Scout:** Tim Thompson (Lewistown, PA).
National Crosscheckers: Gib Bodet (San Clemente, CA), Bill Singer (Costa Mesa, CA).
Regional Supervisors: West Coast—Marty Maier (Oakland, CA); Midwest—John Keenan (Great Bend, KS); East—John Barr (Palm City, FL).

Terry Reynolds

Scouts: Bill Barkley (Waco, TX), Bobby Darwin (Cerritos, CA), Joe Ferrone (Sherman Oaks, CA), Mike Hankins (Lee's Summit, MO), Dennis Haren (San Diego, CA), Hank Jones (Vancouver, WA), Lon Joyce (Spartanburg, SC), Gene Kerns (Hagerstown, MD), John Kosciak (Milford, MA), Mike Leuzinger (Grand Prairie, TX), Carl Loewenstine (Hamilton, OH), Dale McReynolds (Walworth, WI), Bill Pleis (Parrish, FL), Willie Powell (Pensacola, FL), Eddie Rodriguez (Anasco, PR), Ross Sapp (Moreno Valley, CA), Mark Sheehy (Sacramento, CA), Tom Thomas (Phoenix, AZ), Glen VanProyen (West Chicago, IL).
International Supervisor: Jim Stoeckel (Vero Beach, FL). **Supervisor, Mexico and Central America:** Mike Brito (Los Angeles, CA). **Supervisor, Venezuela and Puerto Rico:** Camilo Pascual (Miami, FL).

MILWAUKEE

Telephone, Address

Office Address: County Stadium, 201 S. 46th St., Milwaukee, WI 53214. **Mailing Address:** P.O. Box 3099, Milwaukee, WI 53201. **Telephone:** (414) 933-4114. **FAX:** (414) 933-7323. **E-Mail Address:** www.milwaukeebrewers.com.

Ownership

Operated by: Milwaukee Brewers Baseball Club.

Board of Directors: Allan "Bud" Selig, Charles Krause, Bernard Kubale, John Canning Jr., Mitchell Fromstein, Jack MacDonough.

President, Chief Executive Officer: Allan "Bud" Selig.

Bud Selig

Vice President, General Counsel: Wendy Selig-Prieb. **Assistant General Counsel:** Eugene Randolph. **Executive Assistant To President:** Lori Keck.

BUSINESS OPERATIONS

Vice President, Administration/Human Resources: Tom Gausden.

Vice President, New Ballpark Development: Michael Bucek. **Director, Suite Sales/Advertising:** Geoff Campion.

Finance

Vice President, Finance: Paul Baniel. **Director, Management Information Systems:** Dan Krautkramer.

Corporate Affairs, Marketing

Vice President, Corporate Affairs: Laurel Prieb.

Director, Corporate Sales: Dean Rennicke. **Managers, Corporate Sales:** Matt Groniger, Amy Welch. **Coordinator, Corporate Sales:** Cathy Bradley. **Associate, Corporate Sales:** Nicole Clark.

Director, Season Tickets/Group Sales: Jim Bathey. **Manager, Outbound Ticket Sales:** Scott Parsons.

Public Relations, Communications

Telephone: (414) 933-6975. **FAX:** (414) 933-3251.

Director, Media Relations: Jon Greenberg. **Assistant Director, Media Relations:** Liz Krueger. **Associate, Media Relations:** J.C. Dawkins.

Director, Publications: Mario Ziino.

Director, Community Relations: Mike Downs. **Assistant, Community Relations:** Marquette Baylor.

Director, Broadcasting: Tim Van Wagoner. **Manager, Broadcasting:** Aleta Mercer.

Stadium Operations

Vice President, Stadium Operations: Scott Jenkins.

Director, Event Services: Steve Ethier. **Director, Grounds:** Gary Vanden Berg. **Assistant Director, Grounds:** David Mellor.

PA Announcer: Bob Betts. **Official Scorers:** Tim O'Driscoll, Wayne Franke.

Ticketing

Telephone: (414) 933-9000. **FAX:** (414) 933-3547.

Vice President, Ticket Sales: Bob Voight.

Director, Ticket Operations: John Barnes. **Assistant Director, Ticket Operations:** Nancy Jorgensen. **Operations Manager, Ticketing:** Jeff Gittins.

Travel, Clubhouse

Traveling Secretary: Dan Larrea.

Director, Clubhouse Operations: Tony Migliaccio. **Home Clubhouse:** Phil Rozewicz. **Visitors Clubhouse:** Jim Ksicinski.

General Information

Hometown Dugout: First Base. **Playing Surface:** Grass.

Standard Game Times: 7:05 p.m., (April) 6:05; Day, Sun. 1:05.

Stadium Location: From airport/south, I-94 West to Madison exit, to stadium.

Player Representative: Unavailable.

BREWERS

BASEBALL OPERATIONS
Senior Vice President, Baseball Operations: Sal Bando.

Assistant General Manager/Director, Baseball Operations: Fred Stanley.

Executive Secretary To Senior Vice President: Sandy Ronback. **Administrative Assistant, Baseball Operations:** Kate Geenen. **Coordinator, Baseball Information:** Tom Flanagan.

Major League Staff
Manager: Phil Garner.

Coaches: Bench—Joel Youngblood. Pitching—Don Rowe; Batting—Lamar Johnson; First Base/Infield—Doug Mansolino; Third Base—Chris Bando; Bullpen—Bill Castro.

Sal Bando

Medical, Training
Team Physician, Orthopaedics: Dr. Angelo Mattalino. **Team Physician, Internist:** Dr. Craig Young.

Head Trainer: John Adam. **Assistant Trainer:** Roger Caplinger. **Strength and Conditioning Coach:** John Rewolinski.

Minor Leagues
Telelphone: (414) 933-4114. **FAX:** (414) 933-4655.

Director, Player Development: Cecil Cooper. **Administrator, Minor League Operations:** Barb Stark.

Field Coordinator: Ralph Dickenson. **Roving Instructors:** Bill Campbell (pitching), Larry Hisle (hitting), Javier Gonzalez (catching).

Phil Garner

Farm System
Class	Farm Team	Manager	Coach	Pitching Coach
AAA	Louisville	Gary Allenson	Luis Salazar	Mike Caldwell
AA	El Paso	Ed Romero	Jon Pont	Dwight Bernard
A	Stockton	Bernie Moncallo	John Mallee	Saul Soltero
A	Beloit	Don Money	Floyd Rayford	Randy Kramer
R	Helena	Tom Houk	Quinn Mack	R.C. Lichtenstein
R	Ogden	Ed Sedar	Carlos Ponce	Steve Cline
R	DSL	Mike Guerrero	Unavailable	Andy Araujo

Scouting
Director, Scouting: Ken Califano.

Assistant Director, Scouting: Scott Martens.

Special Assignment Scouts—Professional Coverage: Larry Haney (Orange, VA), Bob Melvin (Scottsdale, AZ), Chuck Tanner (New Castle, PA).

Special Assignment Scouts—Amateur Coverage: Felix Delgado (Rio Piedras, PR), Paul Tretiak (Hannibal, MO), Walter Youse (Sykesville, MD).

National Crosscheckers: Midwest—Fred Beene (Oakhurst, TX); Southeast—Russ Bove (Apopka, FL); West—Kevin Christman (Calabasas, CA); East—Ron Rizzi (Joppa, MD); Southwest—Ric Wilson (Chandler, AZ).

Ken Califano

Scouts: Jeff Brookens (Chambersburg, PA), Rich Chiles (Davis, CA), Steve Connelley (Durham, NC), Mike Farrell (Indianapolis, IN), Dick Foster (Otis, OR), Danny Garcia (Jericho, NY), Mike Gibbons (Pittsburgh, PA), Brian Johnson (Phoenix, AZ), Harvey Kuenn Jr. (New Berlin, WI), Demie Mainieri (Tamarac, FL), Alex Morales (Lake Worth, FL), Doug Reynolds (Tallahassee, FL), Corey Rodriguez (Hermosa Beach, CA), Bruce Seid (Hermosa Beach, CA), Bob Sloan (Amarillo, TX), Jonathan Story (Gulfport, MS), Tom Tanous (Swansea, MA), Red Whitsett (Villa Rica, GA), David Young (Kountze, TX).

Director, International Scouting: Epy Guerrero (Santo Domingo, DR).

International Scouts: Ramon Conde (Puerto Rico), Domingo Carrasquel (Venezuela), Elvio Jimenez (Dominican Republic), John Viney (Australia).

MONTREAL

Telephone, Address

Office Address: 4549 Pierre-de-Coubertin Ave., Montreal, Quebec H1V 3N7. Mailing Address: P.O. Box 500, Station M, Montreal, Quebec H1V 3P2. Telephone: (514) 253-3434. FAX: (514) 253-8282. Website: www.montrealexpos.com.

Claude Brochu

Ownership

Operated by: Montreal Baseball Club, Inc.
President/General Partner: Claude Brochu.
Chairman, Partnership Committee: Jacques Menard. Vice Chairmen, Partnership Committee: Raymond Bachand, Jocelyn Proteau, Louis Tanguay.

BUSINESS OPERATIONS

Finance

Vice President, Finance: Laurier Carpentier.
Executive Director, Finance and Treasurer: Michel Bussiere. Manager, Payroll Services: Doris Turcotte.

Marketing, Sales

Vice President, Marketing and Communications: Richard Morency.
Directors, Advertising Sales: Luigi Carola, John Di Terlizzi, Danielle La Roche. Director, Advertising: Johanne Heroux. Coordinator, Advertising: Nathalie Huot.
Coordinator, Broadcast Services: Marc Griffin. Coordinator, Special Events: Gina Hackl.

Public Relations, Communications

Director, Media Services: Monique Giroux. Director, Media Relations: P.J. Loyello. Secretary, Media: Sina Gabrielle.

Stadium Operations

Vice President, Stadium Operations: Claude Delorme. Director, Business Development: Real Sureau. Producer, Scoreboard Operations: Louis Simard.

Ticketing

Vice President, Sales: Lucien Baril.
Director, Season Ticket Sales: Gilles Beauregard.
Director, Downtown Ballpark Ticket Office: Chantal Dalpe. Director, Olympic Stadium Ticket Office: Hubert Richard. Account Executive, Season Ticket Sales: Jean-Sebastien Brault. Account Executive, Group Sales: Suzanne LeMoignan. Special Projects: Ron Piche.

Travel, Clubhouse

Traveling Secretary: Sean Cunningham.
Equipment Manager: John Silverman. Visiting Clubhouse: Bryan Greenberg.

General Information

Hometown Dugout: First Base. Playing Surface: Artificial turf.
Standard Game Times: 7:05 p.m., Sun. 1:35.
Stadium Location: From New England, take I-87 North from Vermont to Quebec Highway 15 to the Jacques Cartier Bridge, exit left, right on Sherbrooke. From upstate New York, take I-81 North to Trans Canada Highway 401, east to Quebec Highway 20, north to Highway 40 to Boulevard Pie IX exit south to stadium. Access by subway from downtown Montreal to Pie IX Metro station.
Player Representative: Unavailable.

EXPOS

BASEBALL OPERATIONS
Vice President/General Manager: Jim Beattie.
Vice President, Baseball Operations: Bill Stoneman. **Administrative Assistant:** Marcia Schnaar.

Major League Staff
Manager: Felipe Alou.
Coaches: Dugout—Jim Tracy; Pitching—Bobby Cuellar; Batting/First Base—Tommy Harper; Third Base—Pete Mackanin; Bullpen—Pierre Arsenault.

Medical, Training
Team Physician: Dr. Mike Thomassin. **Team Orthopedist:** Dr. Larry Coughlin.
Head Trainer: Ron McClain. **Assistant Trainer:** Mike Kozak. **Director, Strength and Conditioning:** Sean Cunningham.

Jim Beattie

Minor Leagues
Office Address: Roger Dean Stadium, 4751 Main St., Jupiter, FL 33458. **Telephone:** (561) 775-1818. **FAX:** (561) 630-1800.
Director, Player Development: David Littlefield. **Assistant Director, Player Development:** Chris Antonetti. **Administrative Assistant, Player Development:** Cedric Rothkegel.
Clubhouse Manager/Equipment Supervisor: Sean Wilson.
Field Coordinator: Rick Sofield (hitting).
Roving Instructors: Jim Benedict (pitching), Paul Fournier (conditioning), Alvaro Espinoza (infield).

Felipe Alou

Farm System

Class	Farm Team	Manager	Coach	Pitching Coach
AAA	Ottawa	Pat Kelly	Billy Masse	Dean Treanor
AA	Harrisburg	Rick Sweet	Tim Leiper	Brent Strom
A	Jupiter	Doug Sisson	Steve Phillips	Wayne Rosenthal
A	Cape Fear	Luis Dorante	Bert Heffeman	Randy St. Claire
A	Vermont	Unavailable	Unavailable	Unavailable
R	Jupiter	Frank Kremblas	Victor Ramirez	Tom Signore
R	DSL	Arturo DeFreites	Jose Zapata	Salomon Torres

Scouting
Office Address: Expos Minor League Development Center, 4751 Main St., Jupiter, FL 33458. **Mailing Address:** P.O. Box 8978, Jupiter, FL 33468. **Telephone:** (561) 775-1818. **FAX:** (561) 775-9935.
Director, Scouting: Jim Fleming (Purcell, OK).
Assistant Director, Scouting: Gregg Leonard.
Advance Scout: Phil Favia (Apache Junction, AZ).
National Crosschecker: Lenny Strelitz (Temple City, CA).
Regional Supervisors: East—Jim Lester (Columbus, GA), Dave Malpass (Huntington Beach, CA).
Scouts: Alex Agostino (St. Bruno, Quebec),

Jim Fleming

Matt Anderson (Raleigh, NC), Mark Baca (Tustin Ranch, CA), Mike Berger (Pittsburgh, PA), Dennis Cardoza (Denton, TX), Robby Corsaro (Adelanto, CA), Marc Delpiano (Auburn, NY), Dan Freed (Bloomington, IL), Scott Goldby (Vancouver, WA), John Hughes (Walnut Creek, CA), Joe Jordan (Blanchard, OK), Mark Leavitt (Orlando, FL), Darryl Monroe (Atlanta, GA), Bob Oldis (Iowa City, IA) Scott Stanley (Peoria, AZ), Pookie Wilson (Sylacauga, AL).
Director, International Operations: Fred Ferreira (Fort Lauderdale, FL). **International Scouts:** Carlos Acosta (Venezuela), Arturo DeFreites (Dominican Republic), Kevin Greatrex (Australia), Randy Kierce (Fort Lauderdale, FL), Juan Loyola (Puerto Rico), Carlos Moreno (Venezuela), German Obando (Panama), Rene Picota (Panama).

NEW YORK

Telephone, Address
Office Address: 123-01 Roosevelt Ave., Flushing, NY 11368. **Telephone:** (718) 507-6387. **FAX:** (718) 565-6395.

Ownership
Operated by: Sterling Doubleday.
Chairman of the Board: Nelson Doubleday.
President, Chief Executive Officer: Fred Wilpon.
Board of Directors: Nelson Doubleday, Saul Katz, Marvin Tepper, Fred Wilpon. **Special Advisor to Board of Directors:** Richard Cummins.

BUSINESS OPERATIONS

Fred Wilpon

Finance
Senior Vice President, Treasurer: Harry O'Shaughnessy.
Vice President, Business Affairs/General Counsel and Secretary: David Howard.
Senior Vice President/Consultant: Frank Cashen.
Director, Human Resources: Ray Scott. **General Counsel:** David Cohen.
Director, Administration/Data Processing: Russ Richardson.

Marketing, Sales
Vice President, Marketing/Broadcasting: Mark Bingham.
Director, Marketing: Kit Geis. **Director, Marketing Productions:** Tim Gunkel. **Director, Promotions:** James Plummer.

Public Relations, Communications
Telephone: (718) 565-4330. **FAX:** (718) 639-3619.
Director, Media Relations: Jay Horwitz.
Director, Community Outreach: Jill Knee.

Stadium Operations
Vice President, Stadium Operations: Bob Mandt.
Stadium Manager: Kevin McCarthy. **Head Groundskeeper:** Pete Flynn.
PA Announcer: Del Demontreaux. **Official Scorers:** Joe Donnelly, Red Foley, Bill Shannon.

Ticketing
Telephone: (718) 507-8499. **FAX:** (718) 507-6396.
Vice President, Ticket Sales and Services: Bill Ianniciello.
Director, Ticket Operations: Dan DeMato. **Manager, Customer Relations:** Joann Galardy.

Travel, Clubhouse
Associate Traveling Secretaries: Jay Horwitz, Charlie Samuels.
Equipment Manager: Charlie Samuels. **Assistant Equipment Manager:** Vinny Greco. **Visiting Clubhouse Manager:** Tony Carulla.

General Information
Hometown Dugout: First Base. **Playing Surface:** Grass.
Standard Game Times: Day 1:40 p.m., night 7:40, Sat. 7:10.
Stadium Location: From Bronx and Westchester, take Cross Bronx Expressway to Bronx-Whitestone Bridge, then take bridge to Whitestone Expressway to Northern Boulevard/Shea Stadium exit. From Brooklyn, take Eastbound BQE to Eastbound Grand Central Parkway. From Long Island, take either Northern State Parkway or LIE to Westbound Grand Central Parkway. From northern New Jersey, take George Washington Bridge to Cross Bronx Expressway. From Southern New Jersey, take any of bridge crossings to Verazzano Bridge, and then take either Belt Parkway or BQE to Grand Central Parkway. **By subway**—Take #7 and exit at Willets Point/Shea Stadium stop.
Player Representative: John Franco.

METS

BASEBALL OPERATIONS

Telephone: (718) 507-6387. **FAX:** (718) 507-6391.
Senior Vice President, General Manager: Steve Phillips. **Assistant General Manager:** Omar Minaya. **Secretary:** Lynne Daly-DeJoseph.
Special Assistants to General Manager: Jack Zduriencik, Dave Wallace, Harry Minor.

Major League Staff
Manager: Bobby Valentine.
Coaches: Batting—Tim Robson; Pitching—Bob Apodaca; First Base—Mookie Wilson; Third Base—Cookie Rojas; Bullpen—Randy Niemann; Catching—Bruce Benedict.

Steve Phillips

Medical, Training
Team Physician: Dr. David Altchek. **Club Psychologist:** Dr. Allan Lans.
Trainers: Fred Hina, Scott Lawrenson.

Minor Leagues
Office Address: 525 NW Peacock Blvd., Port St. Lucie, FL 34986. **Telephone:** (561) 871-2132. **FAX:** (561) 871-2181.
Director, Player Personnel: Jim Duquette. **Assistant Director, Player Personnel:** Tom Hutchinson. **Administrator:** Maureen Cooke.
Latin American Coordinator: Felix Millan.
Field Coordinator: Bob Floyd. **Roving Instructors:** Mickey Brantley (hitting), Al Jackson (pitching), Rick Miller (outfield/baserunning). **Training Coordinator:** Mike Herbst. **Strength and Conditioning:** Jason Craig.

Bobby Valentine

Farm System

Class	Farm Team	Manager	Coach	Pitching Coach
AAA	Norfolk	Rick Dempsey	Tom Lawless	Ray Rippelmeyer
AA	Binghamton	John Gibbons	Ken Berry	Rick Waits
A	St. Lucie	Howie Freiling	Gary Ward	Bob Stanley
A	Capital City	Doug Davis	Juan Lopez	Buzz Capra
A	Pittsfield	Roger LaFrancois	Tony Tijerina	Doug Simons
R	Kingsport	Unavailable	Lee May Jr.	Bill Champion
R	Port St. Lucie	John Stephenson	Felix Millan	Mickey Weston
R	DSL	Luis Natera	Unavailable	Jesus Hernaiz

Scouting
Director, Amateur Scouting: Gary LaRocque.
Assistant Director, Amateur Scouting: Fred Wright. **Administrator, Scouting:** Stephanie Morgan.
Director, Professional Scouting: Carmen Fusco. **Professional Scouts:** Dick Gernert (Reading, PA), Darrell Johnson (Suisun, CA), Howard Johnson (Lake Arrowhead, CA), Roland Johnson (Newington, CT), Buddy Kerr (Oradell, NJ), Bill Latham (Trussville, AL).
National Crosschecker: Jack Bowen (Bethel Park, PA). **Regional Supervisors:** West—Paul Fryer (Calabasas, CA), East—Paul Ricciarini (Pittsfield, MA); Midwest—Terry Tripp (Harrisburg, IL).

Gary LaRocque

Area Supervisors: Tom Allison (Phoenix, AZ), Kevin Blankenship (Roseville, CA), Quincy Boyd (Naperville, IL), Larry Chase (Pearcy, AR), Joe Delli Carri (Longwood, FL), Chuck Hensley (Bakersfield, CA), Bob Lavallee (Plaistow, NH), Dave Lottsfeldt (Garland, TX), Fred Mazuca (Tustin, CA), Marlin McPhail (Irmo, SC), Randy Milligan (Owings Mills, MD), Bob Minor (Garden Grove, CA), Joe Morlan (New Albany, OH), Joe Nigro (Staten Island, NY), Carlos Pascual (Miami, FL), Jim Reeves (Camas, WA), Junior Roman (San Sebastian, PR), Bob Rossi (Baton Rouge, LA), Joe Salermo (Fort Lauderdale, FL), Greg Tubbs (Cookeville, TN).
Director of International Scouting: Omar Minaya. **Far Eastern Scouting Supervisor:** Isao Ojimi (Japan).

PHILADELPHIA

Telephone, Address
Office Address: Veterans Stadium, 3501 South Broad St., Philadelphia, PA 19148. **Mailing Address:** Box 7575, Philadelphia, PA 19101. **Telephone:** (215) 463-6000. **FAX:** (215) 389-3050. **Website:** www.phillies.com.

Ownership
Operated by: The Phillies.

Managing General Partner: David Montgomery. **General Partner:** Bill Giles.

Partners: Claire Betz; Fitz Eugene Dixon; Double Play, Inc. (Herbert Middleton), Tri-Play Associates (Alexander Buck, Mahlon Buck, William Buck).

David Montgomery

President/Chief Executive Officer: David Montgomery. **Chairman:** Bill Giles.

BUSINESS OPERATIONS
Secretary/General Counsel: Bill Webb. **Executive Administrator:** Nancy Nolan. **Administrator:** Bettyanne Robb. **Director, Business Development:** Joseph Giles.

Finance
Senior Vice President: Jerry Clothier.

Executive Secretary/Benefits Administrator: JoAnn Marano. **Controller:** John Fusco. **Staff Accountants:** Chris Green, Reeny Samara.

Marketing, Promotions
Vice President, Marketing: Dennis Mannion. **Assistant to Vice President, Marketing/Client Services:** Debbie Nocito. **Director, Advertising Sales:** Dave Buck. **Manager, Radio Sales:** Rob MacPherson. **Director, Broadcasting/Video Services:** Rory McNeil. **Mananger, Video Operations:** Anthony Fanticola. **Manager, Fan Development:** Rob Holiday. **Director, Events:** Kurt Funk. **Manager, Promotions:** John Brazer.

Public Relations, Communications
Telephone: (215) 463-6000, 755-9321. **FAX:** (215) 389-3050.

Vice President, Public Relations: Larry Shenk.

Manager, Print/Creative Services: Tina Urban. **Manager, Publicity:** Leigh Tobin. **Manager, Media Relations:** Gene Dias.

Director, Community Relations: Regina Castellani. **Representative, Speakers' Bureau:** Maje McDonnell. **Educator, Substance Prevention:** Dickie Noles.

Stadium Operations
Director, Stadium Operations: Mike DiMuzio. **Assistant Director, Stadium Operations:** Eric Tobin. **Secretary, Stadium Operations:** Bernie Mansi. **Assistant, Stadium Operations:** Patty McKee.

PA Announcer: Dan Baker. **Official Scorers:** Bob Kenney, John McAdams, Jay Dunn.

Ticketing
Telephone: (215) 463-1000. **FAX:** (215) 463-9878.

Vice President, Ticket Operations: Richard Deats.

Director, Sales: John Weber. **Director, Ticket Operations:** Dan Goroff. **Director, Group Sales:** Kathy Killian. **Manager, Premium Seating:** Tom Mashek. **Manager, Phone Center:** Phil Feather.

Travel, Clubhouse
Traveling Secretary: Eddie Ferenz.

Manager, Equipment and Home Clubhouse: Frank Coppenbarger. **Assistant Equipment Manager:** Joe Dunn. **Manager, Visiting Clubhouse:** Kevin Steinhour. **Assistant, Home Clubhouse:** Pete Cera.

General Information
Hometown Dugout: First Base. **Playing Surface:** Astroturf.

Game Times: April, May, September 7:05 p.m.; June, July, August 7:35; Sat. 7:05; Sun. 1:35.

Stadium Location: I-95 or I-76 West to Broad Street exit.

Player Representative: Curt Schilling.

PHILLIES

BASEBALL OPERATIONS
Telephone: (215) 463-6000. **FAX:** (215) 755-9324.

Acting General Manager: Ed Wade. **Senior Advisor to General Manager:** Paul Owens. **Executive Assistant to General Manager:** Susan Ingersoll. **Computer Analysis:** Jay McLaughlin.

Major League Staff
Manager: Terry Francona.
Coaches: Dugout—Chuck Cottier; Pitching—Galen Cisco; Batting—Hal McRae; First Base—Brad Mills; Third Base—John Vukovich; Bullpen—Ramon Henderson.

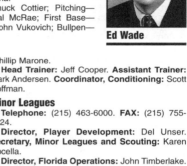

Ed Wade

Medical, Training
Team Physician: Dr. Phillip Marone.

Head Trainer: Jeff Cooper. **Assistant Trainer:** Mark Andersen. **Coordinator, Conditioning:** Scott Hoffman.

Minor Leagues
Telephone: (215) 463-6000. **FAX:** (215) 755-9324.

Director, Player Development: Del Unser. **Secretary, Minor Leagues and Scouting:** Karen Nocella.

Director, Florida Operations: John Timberlake. **Field Coordinator:** Don Blasingame. **Roving Instructors:** Ramon Aviles (infield), George Culver (pitching), Bill DeMars (hitting), Jerry Martin (hitting), Don McCormack (catching), Tony Scott (outfield).

Terry Francona

Farm System

Class	Farm Team	Manager	Coach	Pitching Coach
AAA	Scranton/W-B	Marc Bombard	Bill Robinson	Gary Ruby
AA	Reading	Al LeBoeuf	Milt Thompson	Ross Grimsley
A	Clearwater	Bill Dancy	Glenn Brummer	Darold Knowles
A	Piedmont	Ken Oberkfell	Unavailable	Ken Westray
A	Batavia	Unavailable	Albert Fana	John Martin
R	Martinsville	Greg Legg	Unavailable	Carlos Arroyo
R	DSL	Alex Taveras	Domingo Brito	Cesar Mejia

Scouting
Telephone: (215) 952-8225. **FAX:** (215) 755-9324.

Director, Scouting: Mike Arbuckle.
National Supervisor: Marti Wolever (Papillion, NE).

Professional Coverage: Lee Elia (Odessa, FL), Hank King (Limerick, PA), Dick Lawlor (Windsor, CT), Larry Rojas (Clearwater, FL), Steve Schryver (Williams Bay, WI), Jimmy Stewart (Odessa, FL).

Regional Supervisors: Central—Sonny Bowers (Waco, TX); East—Scott Trcka (Hobart, IN); West—Dean Jongewaard (Fountain Valley, CA).

Special Assignments: Jim Fregosi Jr. (Murrieta, CA).

Mike Arbuckle

Scouts: Emil Belich (West Allis, WI), Steve Gillispie (Birmingham, AL), Bill Harper (Corvallis, OR), Ken Hultzapple (Newport, PA), Jerry Lafferty (Trenton, MO), Terry Logan (Brenham, TX), Miguel Machado (Miami, FL), Lloyd Merritt (Shelbyville, TN), Venice Murray (West Covina, CA), Art Parrack (Oklahoma City, OK), Mark Ralston (Chatsworth, CA), Mitch Sokol (Phoenix, AZ), Roy Tanner (Charleston, SC).

International Supervisor: Sal Agostinelli (Nesconset, NY). **Pacific Rim Supervisor:** Doug Takargawa (Walnut Creek, CA).

International Scouts: Tomas Herrera (Mexico), Fred Manrique (Venezuela), Jesus Mendez (Venezuela), Willie Montanez (Puerto Rico), Wil Tejada (Dominican Republic).

PITTSBURGH

Telephone, Address
Office Address: 600 Stadium Circle, Pittsburgh, PA 15212. Mailing Address: P.O. Box 7000, Pittsburgh, PA 15212. Telephone: (412) 323-5000. FAX: (412) 323-9133. E-Mail Address: talkback@pirates

Ownership
Operated by: Pittsburgh Pirates Acquisition, Inc.

Board of Directors: Don Beaver, Frank Brenner, Chip Ganassi Jr., Kevin McClatchy, Thomas Murphy Jr., Ogden Nutting, William Springer.

Principal Owner: Kevin McClatchy.

GEORGE GOJKOVICH

Kevin McClatchy

BUSINESS OPERATIONS
Executive Vice President, Chief Operating Officer: Dick Freeman. Director, Human Resources: Linda Yenerall.

Finance
Vice President, Finance: James Plake.

Controller: David Bowman. Director, Finance: Patti Mistick. Director, Information Systems: Terry Zeigler.

Marketing, Sales
Vice President, Marketing/Broadcasting: Vic Gregovits.

Director, Sales: Gary Remlinger. Senior Account Executives: Jim Alexander, Chris Cronin.

Coordinator, Promotions: Rick Orienza. Coordinator, Broadcasting: Marc Garda.

Public Relations, Communications
Telephone: (412) 323-5069. FAX: (412) 323-5009.

Vice President, Communications/Ballpark Development: Steven Greenberg.

Director, Media Relations: Jim Trdinich. Assistant Director, Media Relations: Ben Bouma. Assistant, Media Relations: Mike Kennedy. Assistants, Public Relations: Sherry Rusiski, Chris Serkoch.

Director, Player Relations: Kathy Guy.

Director, Marketing Communications: Michael Gordon. Director, Corporate Affairs: Nelson Briles. Director, Community Sales: Al Gordon.

Stadium Operations
Vice President, Stadium Operations: Dennis DaPra.

Director, In-Game Entertainment: Eric Wolff. Coordinators, Operations: Patty Mihalics, J.R. Hayslip. Manager, Operations: Chris Hunter.

PA Announcer: Tim DeBacco. Official Scorers: Tony Krizmanich, Evan Pattak, Bob Webb.

Ticketing
Telephone: (412) 321-2827. FAX: (412) 323-9133.

Manager, Ticket Operations: David Wysocki. Assistant Manager, Ticket Operations: Jeff Smith.

Travel, Clubhouse
Traveling Secretary: Greg Johnson.

Equipment Manager/Home Clubhouse Operations: Roger Wilson. Visitors Clubhouse Operations: Kevin Conrad.

General Information

Hometown Dugout: First Base. Playing Surface: Artificial turf.

Standard Game Times: 7:05 p.m., Sun. 1:35.

Stadium Directions: From south—I-279 through Fort Pitt Tunnel, make left off bridge to Fort Duquesne Bridge, cross Fort Duquesne Bridge, follow signs to Three Rivers Stadium, make left to stadium parking at light. From north—I-279 to Three Rivers Stadium exit (exit 12, left lane), follow directions to parking.

Player Representative: Al Martin.

PIRATES

BASEBALL OPERATIONS
Telephone: (412) 323-5012. **FAX:** (412) 323-5024.

Senior Vice President, General Manager: Cam Bonifay.

Assistant General Manager: John Sirignano. **Senior Advisor, Player Personnel:** Lenny Yochim. **Administrative Assistant, Baseball Operations:** Jeannie Donatelli. **Special Assistants to General Manager:** Chet Montgomery, Ken Parker, Roy Smith, Willie Stargell.

Major League Staff
Manager: Gene Lamont.

Cam Bonifay

Coaches: Bench—Rich Renick; Pitching—Pete Vuckovich; Batting—Lloyd McClendon; First Base—Joe Jones; Third Base—Jack Lind; Bullpen—Spin Williams.

Medical, Training
Team Physicians: Dr. Joe Coroso, Dr. Jack Failla.

Head Trainer: Kent Biggerstaff. **Assistant Trainer:** Bill Henry. **Strength and Conditioning Coach:** Dr. Warren Sipp.

Minor Leagues
Telephone: (412) 323-5033. **FAX:** (412) 323-5024.

Director, Player Development: Paul Tinnell. **Assistant Director, Player Development:** Bill Bryk. **Administrative Assistant, Player Development:** Diane Grimaldi.

Coordinator, Instruction: Steve Demeter. **Roving Instructors:** Tom Dettore (pitching), Marc Hill (catching), Bobby Meacham (infield), Pat Roessler (hitting), Ramon Sambo (baserunning/outfield).

Gene Lamont

Farm System

Class	Farm Team	Manager	Coach	Pitching Coach
AAA	Nashville	Trent Jewett	Richie Hebner	Bruce Tanner
AA	Carolina	Jeff Banister	Curtis Wilkerson	Dave Rajsich
A	Lynchburg	Jeff Richardson	Jeff Livesey	Jim Bibby
A	Augusta	Marty Brown	Jeff Treadway	Scott Lovekamp
A	Erie	Tracy Woodson	Joe Lonnett	Chris Lein
R	Bradenton	Woody Huyke	Ben Oglivie	Doc Watson
R	DSL	Ramon Zapata	Miguel Bonilla	None

Scouting
Telephone: (412) 323-5035. **FAX:** (412) 323-5024.
Director, Scouting: Leland Maddox.

Assistant to Director, Scouting: Ron King (Sacramento, CA). **Coordinator, Scouting Systems:** Sandy Deutsch.

Special Assignment Scouts: Lenny Yochim (River Ridge, LA), Jim Guinn (Fairfield, CA), Boyd Odom (Cumming, GA).

National Coordinators: Central—Tom Barnard (Houston, TX), East—Steve Fleming (Matoaca, VA), West—Scott Littlefield (Long Beach, CA).

Area Supervisors: Jason Angel (Glen Allen, VA), Russell Bowen (Charlotte, NC), Grant Brittain (Oklahoma City, OK), Dana Brown (Somerset, NJ),

GEORGE GOJKOVICH

Leland Maddox

Dan Durst (Rockford, IL), Duane Gustavson (Schererville, IN), James House (Seattle, WA), Craig Kornfeld (Durham, NC), Greg McClain (Chandler, AZ), Jack Powell (Sweetwater, TN), Steve Riha (Houston, TX), Ed Roebuck (Lakewood, CA), Delvy Santiago (Vega Alta, PR), Rob Sidwell (Windermere, FL), George Swain (Raleigh, NC), Mike Williams (Oakland, CA).

Latin American Coordinators: Pablo Cruz (Dominican Republic), Jose Luna (Miami, FL).

ST. LOUIS

Telephone, Address
Office Address: 250 Stadium Plaza, St. Louis, MO 63102. Telephone: (314) 421-3060. FAX: (314) 425-0640. E-Mail Address: www.stlcardinals.com. Website: www.stlcardinals.com.

Ownership
General Partner/Chairman of the Board: William DeWitt Jr. Chairman: Fred Hanser. Secretary-Treasurer: Andrew Baur.

BUSINESS OPERATIONS
President: Mark Lamping. Senior Administrative Assistants: Grace Hale, Julie Laningham.

Mark Lamping

Director, Human Resources and Office Services: Marian Rhodes. Contract Coordinator and Office Services Assistant: Karen Brown.

Finance
Controller: Brad Wood. Administrative Assistant: Beverly Finger.

Director, Accounting: Deborah Pfaff. Director, Management Information Systems: Sally Lemons.

Marketing, Sales
Vice President, Corporate Sales: Dan Farrell. Administrative Assistant, Corporate Sales: Gail Ruhling. Corporate Sales Assistants: Matt Gifford, Theron Morgan, Tony Simokaitis, Kevin Stretch.

Vice President, Community Relations: Marty Hendin. Administrative Assistant, Community Relations: Mary Ellen Edmiston.

Director, Promotions: Thane van Breusegen. Director, Target Marketing: Ted Savage.

Director, Group Sales: Joe Strohm. Account Executives, Group Sales: Mary Clare Bena, Linda Burnside, Mike Hall.

Director of Merchandising: Bill DeWitt III.

Public Relations, Communications
Telephone: (314) 425-0626. FAX: (314) 982-7399.

Director, Media Relations: Brian Bartow. Webmaster, Public Relations: Terry Wells.

Manager, Publications: Steve Zesch. Assistant, Publications: Melody Yount.

Stadium Operations
Vice President, Stadium Operations: Joe Abernathy.

Director, Stadium Operations: Mike Bertani. Director, Food and Beverage: Vicki Bryant. Director, Security and Special Services: Joe Walsh. Director, Quality Assurance and Guest Services: Mike Ball. Head Groundskeeper: Steve Peeler.

Ticketing
Telephone: (314) 421-2400. FAX: (314) 425-0649.

Director, Ticket Operations: Josie Arnold. Manager, Customer Service/Telephone Operations: Patti McCormick. Customer Service Supervisor: Angie Patterson.

Group Director, Sales: Kevin Wade. Manager, Season Sales: Mark Murray. Account Executive, Ticket Sales: Dennis Dolan.

Travel, Clubhouse
Traveling Secretary: C.J. Cherre.

Equipment Manager: Buddy Bates. Assistant Equipment Manager: Rip Rowan. Visiting Clubhouse Manager: Jerry Risch. Video Coordinator: Chad Blair.

General Information

Hometown Dugout: First Base. Playing Surface: Grass.

Standard Game Times: Weekdays 7:10 p.m.; Sat. 12:15, 1:10; Sun. 1:10.

Stadium Directions: From Illinois, take I-55 South, I-64 West, I-70 West or US 40 West across the Mississippi River (Poplar Street Bridge) to Busch Stadium exit. In Missouri, take I-55 North, I-64 East, I-70 East, I-44 East or US 40 East to downtown St. Louis and Busch Stadium exit.

Player Representative: Royce Clayton.

CARDINALS

BASEBALL OPERATIONS
Telephone: (314) 425-0687. **FAX:** (314) 425-0648.

Vice President, General Manager: Walt Jocketty.

Vice President, Player Personnel: Jerry Walker. **Senior Executive Assistant to General Manager**: Judy Carpenter-Barada.

Major League Staff
Manager: Tony La Russa.

Coaches: Dugout—Carney Lansford; Pitching—Dave Duncan; Batting—Dave Parker; First Base—Dave McKay; Third Base—Rene Lachemann; Bullpen—Mark DeJohn.

Instructors: Lou Brock, Bob Gibson, Red Schoendienst.

Walt Jocketty

Medical, Training
Club Physician: Dr. Stan London.

Head Trainer: Barry Weinberg. **Assistant Trainer:** Brad Henderson.

Minor Leagues
Telephone: (314) 421-3060. **FAX:** (314) 425-0638.

Director, Player Development: Mike Jorgensen. **Manager, Business Operations/Baseball:** Scott Smulczenski. **Administrative Assistant:** Judy Francis.

Senior Field Coordinator: George Kissell. **Field Coordinator:** Joe Pettini. **Roving Instructors:** John Lewis (hitting), Dyar Miller (pitching), Dave Ricketts (catching), Mark Riggins (pitching). **Strength and Conditioning Instructor:** Pete Prinzi.

Tony La Russa

Farm System

Class	Farm Team	Manager	Coach	Pitching Coach
AAA	Louisville	Gaylen Pitts	Mitchell Page	Marty Mason
AA	Arkansas	Chris Maloney	Luis Melendez	Rich Folkers
A	Prince William	Joe Cunningham	Boots Day	Mark Grater
A	Peoria	Jeff Shireman	Tony Diggs	Gary Buckels
A	New Jersey	Jose Oquendo	None	Joe Rigoli
R	Johnson City	Steve Turco	None	Mike Snyder
R	DSL	Bobby Diaz	Manny Espinosa	Jose Sosa

Scouting
Telephone: (314) 421-3060. **FAX:** (314) 425-0638.

Director, Scouting: Ed Creech. **Assistant Director, Scouting:** John Mozeliak.

Advance Scout: Joe Sparks.

Special Assignment Scouts: Fred McAlister (Clearwater, FL), Jeff Scott (Bourbonnais, IL), Mike Squires (Kalamazoo, MI).

National Crosscheckers: West—Marty Keough (Irvine, CA); East—Mike Roberts (Kansas City, MO).

Ed Creech

Scouts: Randy Benson (Salisbury, NC), Doug Carpenter (Boca Raton, FL), Tim Conroy (Monroeville, PA), Clark Crist (Tucson, AZ), Chuck Fick (Newbury Park, CA), Ben Galante (Houston, TX), Steve Grilli (Baldwinsville, NY), Manny Guerra (Las Vegas, NV), Dave Karaff (Lee's Summit, MO), Tom McCormack (University City, MO), Scott Melvin (Quincy, IL), Scott Nichols (Richland, MS), Jay North (Vacaville, CA), Joe Rigoli (Parsippany, NJ), Roger Smith (Eastman, GA), Dane Walker (West Linn, OR).

Coordinator, International Scouting: Tim Hanser.

SAN DIEGO

Telephone, Address
Office Address: 8880 Rio San Diego Dr., Suite 400, San Diego, CA 92108. Mailing Address: P.O. Box 2000, San Diego, CA 92112. Telephone: (619) 881-6500 FAX: (619) 497-5454. Website: www.padres.com.

Larry Lucchino

Ownership
Operated by: Padres, LP.

Principal Owners: John Moores, Larry Lucchino. Board of Directors: Larry Lucchino, John Moores, Calvin Hill, Charles Noell, John Watson, Tom Werner, George Will.

Chairman: John Moores. President, Chief Executive Officer: Larry Lucchino.

BUSINESS OPERATIONS
Executive Vice President, Business Operations: Bill Adams.
Vice President, General Counsel: Alan Ostfield.
Director, Administrative Services: Lucy Freeman.

Finance
Vice President, Finance/Administration: Bob Wells.
Controller: Steve Fitch. Secretary to VP, Finance and Administration: Twila Nutter. Manager, Accounting: Duane Wright.

Marketing, Sales
Vice President, Corporate Development: Mike Dee. Vice President, Marketing: Don Johnson.
Director, Sponsorship Services: Cheryl Smith.
Director, Hispanic/Multicultural Marketing: Enrique Morones. Manager, Marketing: Darbi Gaunt. Manager, Compadres Club: Brook Govan.
Director, Sales: Louie Ruvane. Assistant Director, Sales: Ron Bumgarner. Manager, Sales Operations: Mark Tilson.

Public, Community Relations
Telephone: (619) 881-6510. FAX: (619) 497-5454.
Senior Vice President, Public Affairs: Charles Steinberg. Assistant to Vice President, Public Affairs: Dayle Boyd. Special Assistant, Public Affairs: Jennifer McLeod.
Director, Public Relations: Glenn Geffner. Director, Publications: John Schlegel. Assistant, Media Relations: John Dever. Assistant, Media Relations/Mexico: Guillermo Perez.
Director, Community Relations: Michele Anderson.
Director, Entertainment: Tim Young. Assistant Director, Entertainment/Special Events: Kate Rummer. Video Producer: Mike Howder.

Stadium Operations
Director, Stadium Operations: Mark Guglielmo. Project Manager: Jack Autry. Assistant, Stadium Operations: Ken Kawachi.

Ticketing
Telephone: (619) 283-4494. FAX: (619) 280-6239.
Director, Ticket Operations and Services: Dave Gilmore. Assistant Director, Ticket Operations: Jim Kiersnowski. Assistant Director, Ticket Services: Bill Risser. Manager, Ticket Operations: George Stieren. Manager, Ticket Services: Chandra George.

Travel, Clubhouse
Director, Team Travel/Equipment Manager: Brian Prilaman. Clubhouse Operations: David Bacharach.

General Information
Hometown Dugout: First Base. Playing Surface: Grass.
Standard Game Times: 7:05 p.m.; Wed. 7:35; Thurs. 2:05; Sun. 1:05.
Stadium Location: From downtown, Route 163 North to Friars Road, east to stadium. From north, I-15 South to Friars Road, west to stadium, or I-805 South to Route 163 South to Friars Road, west to stadium. From east, I-8 West to I-15 North to Friars Road, west to stadium. From west, I-8 East to Route 163 North to Friars Road, east to stadium.
Player Representative: Archi Cianfrocco.

PADRES

BASEBALL OPERATIONS

Telephone: (619) 881-6525 **FAX:** (619) 497-5338.
Senior Vice President/General Manager: Kevin Towers.

Assistant General Manager: Fred Uhlman Jr.
Special Assistants to General Manager: Dave Stewart, Ken Bracey. **Director, Baseball Operations:** Eddie Epstein. **Assistant, Baseball Operations:** Theo Epstein. **Video Analyst:** Mike Howder.

Major League Staff

Manager: Bruce Bochy.

Coaches: Dugout—Rob Picciolo; Pitching—Dave Stewart; Batting—Merv Rettenmund; First Base—Davey Lopes; Third Base—Tim Flannery; Bullpen—Greg Booker.

Kevin Towers

Bruce Bochy

Medical, Training

Club Physician: Scripps Clinic Medical Staff.
Head Trainer: Todd Hutcheson. **Assistant Trainer:** Jim Daniel. **Strength and Conditioning Director:** Sam Gannelli.

Minor Leagues

Telephone: (619) 881-6525. **FAX:** (619) 497-5338.

Director, Player Development: Jim Skaalen.
Director, Minor League Operations: Priscilla Oppenheimer. **Administrative Assistant, Minor Leagues:** Earleen Bender.

Coordinator of Instruction: Tye Waller. **Roving Instructors:** Jeff Andrews (pitching), Eric Bullock (outfield/baserunning), Duane Espy (hitting), Tony Franklin (infield).

Farm System

Class	Farm Team	Manager	Coach	Pitching Coach
AAA	Las Vegas	Jerry Royster	Craig Colbert	Dave Smith
AA	Mobile	Mike Ramsey	Jim Bowie	Don Alexander
A	R. Cucamonga	Mike Basso	Jason McLeod	Darrel Akerfelds
A	Clinton	Tom LeVasseur	Dan Simonds	Tony Phillips
R	Idaho Falls	Don Werner	Gary Kendall	Darryl Milne
R	Peoria	Randy Whisler	Angel Morris	Sid Monge

Scouting

Telephone: (619) 881-6500 **FAX:** (619) 497-5338.

Director, Scouting: Brad Sloan (Brimfield, IL).
Secretary, Scouting: Herta Bingham.

Major League Scouts: Ken Bracey (Morton, IL), Ray Crone (Waxahachie, TX).

Advance Scout: Jeff Gardner (Newport Beach, CA).

National Supervisor: Bob Cummings (Oaklawn, IL).

Regional Supervisors: East—Andy Hancock (Tryon, NC); West—Jim Woodward (La Mirada, CA).

Brad Sloan

Professional Scouts: Charles Bolton (San Diego, CA), Gary Roenicke (Nevada City, CA), Gene Watson (Temple, TX).

Full-Time Scouts: Joe Bochy (Plant City, FL), Howard Bowens (Tacoma, WA), Jimmy Dreyer (Euless, TX), Denny Galehouse (Doylestown, OH), Rich Hacker (Belleville, IL), Gary Kendall (Baltimore, MD), Don Lyle (Sacramento, CA), Tim McWilliam (San Diego, CA), Bill Mele (El Segundo, CA), Darryl Milne (Denver, CO), Rene Mons (Manchester, NH), Pat Murtaugh (Lafayette, IN), Steve Nichols (Mt. Dora, FL), Van Smith (Belleville, IL), Mark Wasinger (El Paso, TX).

International Scouts: Ronquito Garcia (Puerto Rico), Juan Melo (Dominican Republic), Jack Pierce (Mexico).

SAN FRANCISCO

Telephone, Address
Office Address: 3Com Park at Candlestick Point, San Francisco, CA 94124. **Telephone:** (415) 468-3700. **FAX:** (415) 467-0485. **Website:** www.sf giants.com.

Ownership
Operated by: San Francisco Baseball Associates, LP.

President, Managing General Partner: Peter Magowan. **Senior General Partner:** Harmon Burns. **Special Assistant to President:** Willie Mays.

BUSINESS OPERATIONS
Executive Vice President, Chief Operating Officer: Larry Baer. **Senior Vice President, Business Operations:** Pat Gallagher.

Peter Magowan

Vice President, General Counsel: Jack Bair.

Director, Public Affairs/Community Development: Staci Walters. **Manager, Human Resources:** Joyce Thomas.

Finance
Senior Vice President, Chief Financial Officer: John Yee.

Director, Finance: Robert J. Quinn. **Accounting Manager:** Norma Edar. **Director, Information Systems:** Jerry Drobny.

Marketing, Sales
Vice President, Marketing and Sales: Mario Alioto.

Director, Corporate Sponsorship: Jason Pearl. **Promotions Manager:** Valerie McGuire.

General Manager, Retail/Internet: Connie Kullberg. **Director, Retail Operations:** Derik Landry.

Public Relations, Communications
Telephone: (415) 330-2448. **FAX:** (415) 467-0485.

Vice President, Communications: Bob Rose.

Manager, Media Relations: Jim Moorehead. **Coordinator, Media Services/Broadcast:** Maria Jacinto. **Coordinator, Media and Player Relations:** Blake Rhodes. **Director, Publications:** Nancy Donati.

Manager, Community Development: Larry Chew.

Stadium Operations
Vice President, Stadium Operations/Security: Jorge Costa.

Director, Stadium Operations: Gene Telucci. **Director, Guest Services:** Deborah Houston. **Director, Maintenance:** Willie Guzman.

PA Announcer: Sherry Davis. **Official Scorers:** Chuck Dybdal, Dick O'Connor, Bob Stevens.

Ticketing
Telephone: (415) 467-8000. **FAX:** (415) 330-2572.

Vice President, Ticket Services: Russ Stanley. **Assistant Director, Ticket Services:** Shelley Landeros. **Manager, Ticket Services:** Bob Bisio. **Manager, Ticket Accounting:** Kem Easley. **Manager, Ticket Services:** Craig Hedrick. **Manager, Ticket Operations:** Anita Sprinkles.

Vice President, Ticket Sales: Mark Norelli. **Director, Corporate Ticket Sales:** Michael Boswell. **Manager, Group Sales:** Jeff Tucker. **Manager, Inside Sales:** Anastasia Ozegovich.

Travel, Clubhouse
Director, Travel: Reggie Younger Jr.

Equipment Manager: Mike Murphy. **Visitors Clubhouse:** Harvey Hodgerney. **Assistant Equipment Manager:** Dennis Parry.

General Information
Hometown Dugout: First Base. **Playing Surface:** Grass.

Standard Game Times: 12:35 p.m., 1:05, 7:05, 7:35; Weekends 1:05.

Stadium Location: From south, Highway 101 North to 3Com Park exit; from north, Highway 101 South to 3Com Park exit.

Player Representative: Jim Poole.

GIANTS

BASEBALL OPERATIONS
Telephone: (415) 330-2507. **FAX:** (415) 330-2691.
Senior Vice President, General Manager:
Brian Sabean.
Assistant General Manager: Ned Colletti.
Special Assistant to General Manager: Jim Fregosi.
Executive Assistant, Baseball Administration:
Jamie Gaines. **Executive Assistant, Baseball
Operations:** Karen Sweeney. **Administrative
Assistant, Baseball Operations:** Jeremy Shelley.

Major League Staff
Manager: Dusty Baker.
Coaches: Bench—Sonny Jackson; Pitching—
Ron Perranoski; Batting—Gene Clines; First

Brian Sabean

Base—Carlos Alfonso; Third Base—Ron Wotus;
Bullpen—Juan Lopez.

Medical, Training
Team Physicians: Dr. Colin Eakin, Dr. Warren
King, Dr. William Straw.
Head Trainer: Mark Letendre. **Assistant
Trainer:** Barney Nugent. **Rehabilitation Coordinator:** Stan Conte.

Minor Leagues
Director, Player Personnel: Dick Tidrow.
Director, Player Development: Jack Hiatt.
Assistant Director, Player Development: Bobby
Evans. **Assistant Director, Player Personnel:**
Matt Nerland.

Dusty Baker

Coordinator, Instruction: Keith Bodie. **Coordinator, Hitting:** Joe
Lefebvre.
Rehabilitation Coordinator: Bill Carpine. **Special Assistant, Player
Personnel:** Bobby Bonds.

Farm System

Class	Farm Team	Manager	Coach	Pitching Coach
AAA	Fresno	Jim Davenport	Joe Lefebvre	Joel Horlen
AA	Shreveport	Mike Hart	Frank Cacciatore	Todd Oakes
A	Bakersfield	Frank Reberger	None	Shawn Barton
A	San Jose	Shane Turner	None	Bryan Hickerson
A	Salem-Keizer	Carlos Lezcano	Bert Hunter	Keith Comstock
R	DSL	Ozzie Virgil Sr.	Osvaldo Oliva	None

Scouting
Telephone: (415) 330-2538. **FAX:** (415) 330-2691.
Advance Scout: Pat Dobson (Cape Coral, FL).
Major League Scout: Cal Emery (Lake Forest, CA).
Special Assignment Scouts: Joe DiCarlo
(Ringwood, NJ), Bob Hartsfield (Woodstock, GA).
National Crosschecker: Randy Waddill (Brandon, FL).
Regional Crosscheckers: West—Doug Mapson
(Phoenix, AZ); East—Paul Turco (Sarasota, FL).
Area Scouts: Dick Cole (Costa Mesa, CA), John
DiPuglia (Miami Lakes, FL), Mike Keenan
(Chicago, IL), Tom Korenek (Houston, TX), Alan
Marr (Bellmore, NY), Doug McMillan (Shingle
Springs, CA), Bobby Myrick (Colonial Heights, VA),

Dick Tidrow

Matt Nerland (Pleasant Hill, CA), Larry Osborne (Woodstock, GA), John
Shafer (Portland, OR), Joe Strain (Englewood, CO), Todd Thomas (St.
Louis, MO), Glenn Tufts (Bridgewater, MA), Darren Wittcke (Laguna Niguel,
CA), Tom Zimmer (St. Petersburg, FL).
Coordinator, International Operations: Rick Ragazzo. **Coordinator,
Pacific Rim Scouting:** Masanori Murakami.
International Scouts: Jorge Aranzamendi (Puerto Rico), Jose Cassino
(Panama), Eric Mangham (Mexico), Dan McConnon (Australia), Cesar Navarro
(Venezuela), Carlos Ramirez (Dominican Republic), Ciro Villalobos (Venezuela).

Major League Schedules

1997 Standings • Spring Training

AMERICAN LEAGUE

1997 STANDINGS

EAST	W	L	PCT	GB	Manager(s)
Baltimore Orioles	98	64	.605	—	Dave Johnson
New York Yankees*	96	66	.593	2	Joe Torre
Detroit Tigers	79	83	.488	19	Buddy Bell
Boston Red Sox	78	84	.481	20	Jimy Williams
Toronto Blue Jays	76	86	.469	22	Cito Gaston/Mel Queen
CENTRAL	W	L	PCT	GB	Manager(s)
Cleveland Indians	86	75	.534	—	Mike Hargrove
Chicago White Sox	80	81	.497	6	Terry Bevington
Milwaukee Brewers	78	83	.484	8	Phil Garner
Minnesota Twins	68	94	.420	18½	Tom Kelly
Kansas City Royals	67	94	.416	19	Bob Boone/Tony Muser
WEST	W	L	PCT	GB	Manager
Seattle Mariners	90	72	.556	—	Lou Piniella
Anaheim Angels	84	78	.519	6	Terry Collins
Texas Rangers	77	85	.475	13	Johnny Oates
Oakland Athletics	65	97	.401	25	Art Howe

PLAYOFFS: Division Series (best-of-5)—Baltimore defeated Seattle 3-1; Cleveland defeated New York 3-2. **League Championship Series** (best-of-7)— Cleveland defeated Baltimore 4-2.

NATIONAL LEAGUE

1997 STANDINGS

EAST	W	L	PCT	GB	Manager
Atlanta Braves	101	61	.623	—	Bobby Cox
Florida Marlins*	92	70	.568	9	Jim Leyland
New York Mets	88	74	.543	13	Bobby Valentine
Montreal Expos	78	84	.481	23	Felipe Alou
Philadelphia Phillies	68	94	.420	33	Terry Francona
CENTRAL	W	L	PCT	GB	Manager(s)
Houston Astros	84	78	.519	—	Larry Dierker
Pittsburgh Pirates	79	83	.488	5	Gene Lamont
Cincinnati Reds	76	86	.469	8	Ray Knight/Jack McKeon
St. Louis Cardinals	73	89	.451	11	Tony La Russa
Chicago Cubs	68	94	.420	16	Jim Riggleman
WEST	W	L	PCT	GB	Manager
San Francisco Giants	90	72	.556	—	Dusty Baker
Los Angeles Dodgers	88	74	.543	2	Bill Russell
Colorado Rockies	83	79	.512	7	Don Baylor
San Diego Padres	76	86	.469	14	Bruce Bochy

PLAYOFFS: Division Series (best-of-5)—Atlanta defeated Houston 3-0; Florida defeated San Francisco 3-0. **League Championship Series** (best-of-7)—Florida defeated Atlanta 4-2.

*Won wild-card playoff berth

WORLD SERIES
(Best-of-7)
Florida defeated Cleveland 4-3

AMERICAN LEAGUE

ANAHEIM ANGELS
Edison International Field

APRIL
1-2 .... Yankees
3-4-**5** .... Cleveland
6-7-8 .... Boston
10-11-12... at Cleveland
13-14-**15**...... at Yankees
16-17-18-**19** .... T.B.
20-21-22 .... Baltimore
24-25-**26** .... at T.B.
27-28 .... at Baltimore
29-30 .... at Boston

MAY
1-2-3-4 .... White Sox
5-6 .... Toronto
8-9-**10** .... Detroit
12-13 ...... at White Sox
14-15............ at Toronto
16-17-18......... at Detroit
19-20-21 .... Oakland
22-23-**24** ...... Minnesota
25-27 .... Kansas City
29-30-**31** ... at Minnesota

JUNE
1-2 .... at Kansas City
3-4 .... at Seattle
5-6-7............ Colorado*
9-10-11 .... at Arizona*
12-13-14-15 ..... at Texas
16-17-18 .... Seattle
19-20-**21** .... Texas
22-23....... Los Angeles*
24-25.... at Los Angeles*
26-27-**28** .... at S.D.*
30 .... San Francisco*

JULY
1-2 .... San Franciso*
3-4-5 .... Oakland
9-10-11-**12** ..... at Seattle
13-**14** .... at Oakland
15-16 .... Tampa Bay
17-18-**19** .... Baltimore
21-22-**23**... at Minnesota
24-25-26-27 ...... at K.C.
28-29-30 .... Yankees
31 .... Boston

AUGUST
1-**2**..................... Boston
3-4-**5**............. Cleveland
7-8-**9**....... at White Sox
10-11-12 .... at Detroit
13-14-**15-16** .. at Toronto
17-18 .... White Sox
19-20 .... Detroit
21-22-**23**.......... Toronto
25-26-27.... at Yankees
28-**29**-**30** ...... at Boston

SEPTEMBER
1-2.............. at Cleveland
4-5-**6** .... Kansas City
8-9 .... Minnesota
11-12-**13**.... at Baltimore
14-15...... at Tampa Bay
16-17 .... at Texas
18-19-**20** .... Seattle
21-22-23 .... Texas
24-25-**26-27**....... at Oak.

BALTIMORE ORIOLES
Oriole Park at Camden Yards

MARCH
31.............. Kansas City

APRIL
1-2 .... Kansas City
3-**4**-**5** .... Detroit
7-9 .... at Kansas City
10-**11**-**12** .... at Detroit
14-15-**16** ...... White Sox
17-18-19 .... at Texas
20-21-22 ..... at Anaheim
24-**25**-**26** .... Oakland
27-28 .... Anaheim
29-**30** .... at White Sox

MAY
1-**2**-**3** .... Minnesota
5-6............. at Cleveland
8-9-**10** ..... at Tampa Bay
11-12 ...... at Minnesota
13-14............ Cleveland
15-**16**-**17**-18 .... T.B.
19-20-21 ...... at Yankees
22-23-**24** ...... at Oakland
25-**26** .... at Seattle

28-29-**30**-31 .... Texas

JUNE
1-2...................... Seattle
3-4 .... at Boston
5-6-**7** .... Atlanta*
8-9-10 .. at Philadelphia*
12-**13**-**14**........ at Toronto
15-16-17 .... Yankees
18-19-20-**21** ...... Toronto
22-23................... Mets*
24-25 .... at Mets*
26-27-**28** .... at Montreal*
30................... Florida*

JULY
1-2 .... Florida*
3-**4**-**5** .... at Yankees
9-10-11-**12** .... Boston
13-**14** .... Toronto
15-16 .... at Texas
17-18-**19** ..... at Anaheim
21-22-23 .... Oakland
24-25-**26** .... Seattle
28-29-**30**......... at Detroit

31........... at Kansas City

AUGUST
1-2 .... at Kansas City
4-5 .... Detroit
7-8-**9**........ at Minnesota
10-11-**12**.. at Tampa Bay
13-14-**15-16** ...... at Cleve.
17-18 .... Minnesota
19-20 .... Tampa Bay
21-22-**23**........ Cleveland
25-26-27 ... at White Sox
28-29-30 ... Kansas City
31 .... White Sox

SEPTEMBER
1-2 .... White Sox
4-5-6-7 .... at Seattle
8-**9** .... at Oakland
11-12-**13**.......... Anaheim
14-15 .... Texas
16-17................. Boston
18-19-**20** .... Yankees
21-22-23.... at Toronto
24-25-**26-27** ... at Boston

NOTE: Dates in **bold** indicate afternoon games.
* Interleague Series

BOSTON RED SOX
Fenway Park

APRIL
1-**2** .... at Oakland
3-4-**5** .... at Seattle
6-7-8 .... at Anaheim
10-11-12........... Seattle
13-14-15 .... Oakland
17-**18-19-20** .. Cleveland
21-22 .... at Detroit
24-**25-26** ... at Cleveland
27-28 .... Detroit
29-30 .... Anaheim
MAY
1-**2**-3 .... Texas
5-6 .... Minnesota
7-8-9-**10** .... at K.C.
11-**12**............... at Texas
13-**14**........... Minnesota
15-**16-17** ... Kansas City
19-20 .... White Sox
22-**23-24** .... Yankees
25-26 .... Toronto
28-29-**30-31**..... at Yanks

JUNE
1-2................. at Toronto
3-4.................. Baltimore
5-**6-7** .... Mets*
8-9-10 .... at Atlanta*
12-**13-14**..... Tampa Bay
15-16-**17**.... at White Sox
18-19-20-**21**........... at T.B.
22-23 .... Philadelphia*
24-25.... at Philadelphia*
26-27-**28** ...... at Florida*
30.................... Montreal*
JULY
1-2 .... Montreal*
3-4-**5** .... White Sox
9-10-11-**12** .... at Balt.
13-**14**....... at Tampa Bay
15-16 .... Cleveland
17-18-**19**........ at Detroit
21-22........... at Cleveland
23-24-**25-26** ...... Toronto
28-29-**30** ..... at Oakland
31 .... at Anaheim

AUGUST
1-**2**................. at Anaheim
3-4 .... at Seattle
6-7-8-9 .... at Texas
11-12.......... Kansas City
13-14-**15-16**.. Minnesota
17-**18** .... Texas
19-**20** ..... at Kansas City
21-22-**23**.... at Minnesota
25-26-27 .... Oakland
28-**29-30**........ Anaheim
31 .... Seatle
SEPTEMBER
1-2................... Seattle
3-4-**5-6** .... at Toronto
7-8-9 .... Yankees
11-12-13 .... Detroit
14-15 .... at Yankees
16-17 .... at Baltimore
18-19-**20** ... at White Sox
21-22-23...... Tampa Bay
24-25-**26-27** .. Baltimore

CHICAGO WHITE SOX
Comiskey Park

MARCH
31..................... at Texas
APRIL
2...................... at Texas
3-4-**5** .... at Tampa Bay
6-8-9 .... Texas
10-**11-12**..... Tampa Bay
14-15-**16** .... at Baltimore
17-**18-19**........ at Toronto
21-22-23 .. at Cleveland
24-25-**26**........... Toronto
27-28 .... Cleveland
29-**30**............. Baltimore
MAY
1-2-**3**-4 .... at Anaheim
5-6 .... at Seattle
8-9-**10** .... at Oakland
12-13............... Anaheim
14-15................. Seattle
16-**17-18** .... Oakland
19-20 .... at Boston
22-23-**24**.......... Detroit
25-26-27 .... Yankees

JUNE
1-2 .... at Yankees
3-**4** .... at Kansas City
5-6-7 .... at Cubs*
8-9-10 .... St. Louis*
12-13-**14** ... at Minnesota
15-16-**17** .... Boston
18-19-20-**21**.. Minnesota
22-23 .... at Pittsburgh*
24-25............ Cincinnati*
26-27-**28** ..... Milwaukee*
30 .... at Houston*
JULY
1-2 .... at Houston*
3-4-**5** .... at Boston
9-10-11-**12**............. K.C.
13-14 .... Minnesota
15-**16** .... Toronto
17-18-**19**-20 .. Cleveland
21-22 .... at Toronto
24-**25-26**...... at Yankees
28-29 .... Tampa Bay

AUGUST
1-2 .... at Texas
3-4-5 .... at Tampa Bay
7-8-**9** .... Anaheim
10-11-**12** .... Oakland
14-15-**16** .... Seattle
17-18.............. at Anaheim
19-20 .... at Oakland
21-22-**23-24** ... at Seattle
25-26-27 .... Baltimore
28-29-**30** .... Texas
31 .... at Baltimore
SEPTEMBER
1-2 .... at Baltimore
4-5-**6** .... Yankees
7-8-9 .... Detroit
11-**12-13**... at Cleveland
14-15 .... at Detroit
16-17 .... Kansas City
18-19-**20** .... Boston
21-22-23 .. at Minnesota
24-25-26-**27**........... at K.C.

CLEVELAND INDIANS
Jacobs Field

MARCH
31................... at Seattle
APRIL
1..................... at Seattle
3-4-**5** .... at Anaheim
6-**8** .... at Oakland
10-11-12........... Anaheim
13-14-15 .... Seattle
17-**18-19-20** ... at Boston
21-22-23 .... White Sox
24-**25-26** .... Boston
27-28 .... at White Sox
29-30 .... Oakland
MAY
1-**2**-3........... Tampa Bay
5-6............... Baltimore
7-8-9-**10** .... at Texas
11-12....... at Tampa Bay
13-14 .... at Baltimore
15-**16-17** .... Texas
19-20-21 .... at K.C.
22-**23-24**.......... Toronto
25-26 .... Detroit

JUNE
28-29-**30-31** .. at Toronto
1-2 .... at Detroit
3-4 .... at Minnesota
5-**6-7** .... at Cincinnati*
8-9-10 .... Pittsburgh*
12-**13-14**..... at Yankees
15-16-17 .... Kansas City
18-19-20-**21**..... Yankees
22-**23**................ at Cubs*
24-25 .... St. Louis*
26-**27-28**......... Houston*
30 .... at Milwaukee*
JULY
1-2 .... at Milwaukee*
3-4-**5** .... at Kansas City
9-10-**11-12** ... Minnesota
13-14 .... Yankees
15-16 .... at Boston
17-18-**19**-20.. at Wh. Sox
21-22.................. Boston
23-24-**25-26** .... Detroit
28-29-30 .... at Seattle

AUGUST
31 .... at Oakland
1-2 .... at Oakland
3-4-**5** .... at Anaheim
7-8-**9** .... at Tampa Bay
11-12............... Texas
13-14-**15-16** .. Baltimore
17-18............ Tampa Bay
19-20 .... at Texas
21-22-**23** ... at Baltimore
25-26-27 .... Seattle
28-**29-30**-31 ..... Oakland
SEPTEMBER
1-2................... Anaheim
3-4-5-**6**........... at Detroit
7-9............. at Toronto
11-**12-13** ...... White Sox
14-15................. Toronto
16-17 .... Minnesota
18-**19-20** ... Kansas City
22-23 .... at Yankees
24-25-26-**27**....... at Minn.

DETOIT TIGERS
Tiger Stadium

MARCH
31 .... at Tampa Bay

APRIL
1-2........... at Tampa Bay
3-4-5 .... at Baltimore
7-9............. Tampa Bay
10-**11-12**........ Baltimore
13-14-15 .... at Texas
17-**18-19** ...... at Yankees
21-22................ Boston
24-**25-26** .... Yankees
27-28 .... at Boston
29-30 .... Texas

MAY
1-2-3 .... at Seattle
5-6-7 .... at Oakland
8-9-10 .... at Anaheim
12-13............... Seattle
14-15 .... Oakland
16-17-18......... Anaheim
19-20-**21** .... at Minnesota
22-23-**24** .... at Wh. Sox
25-26 .... at Cleveland

JUNE
28-29-20-**31** .. White Sox
1-2 .... Cleveland
3-4 .... at Toronto
5-6-7 .... at Milwaukee*
8-9-10 .... Houston*
12-13-**14** .... at K.C.
15-16-17 .... Minnesota
18-19-20-**21** .... K.C.
22-23 .... at St. Louis*
24-25 .... Cubs*
26-27-**28** ...... Cincinnati*
30 .... at Pittsburgh*

JULY
1-2 .... at Pittsburgh*
3-4-5 .... at Minnesota
9-10-11-**12** .... Toronto
13-14 .... Kansas City
15-16 .... Yankees
17-18-**19** .... Boston
20-21-**22** .... at Yankees
23-24-**25-26** .... at Cleve.
28-29-30 .... Baltimore

AUGUST
31 .... at Tampa Bay
1-2 .... at Tampa Bay
4-5 .... at Baltimore
6-7-8-9 .... Seattle
10-11-12 .... Anaheim
14-15-**16** .... Oakland
17-18 .... at Seattle
19-20........... at Anaheim
21-**22-23** .... at Oakland
24-25-26 .... at Texas
28-29-**30** .... T.B.
31 .... Texas

SEPTEMBER
1-2 .... Texas
3-4-5-**6** .... Cleveland
7-8-9 .... at White Sox
11-**12-13**........ at Boston
14-15 .... White Sox
16-17................ Toronto
18-**19-20** .... Minnesota
21-22-23 .... at K.C.
25-**26-27** .... at Toronto

KANSAS CITY ROYALS
Kauffman Stadium

MARCH
31 .... at Baltimore

APRIL
1-2 .... at Baltimore
3-4-**5** .... at Minnesota
7-9................ Baltimore
10-**11-12** .... Minnesota
13-14-15 .... Toronto
16-17-**18-19**... at Oak.
20-21-22 ...... at Seattle
24-25-**26** .... Texas
27-28............... Seattle
29-**30** .... at Toronto

MAY
1-2-3 .... Yankees
5-6-................ Tampa Bay
7-8-9-**10** .... Boston
11-12 .... at Yankees
13-14...... at Tampa Bay
15-16-17 .... at Boston
19-20-21....... Cleveland
22-23-**24** .... at Texas

JUNE
25-27 .... at Anaheim
29-30-**31** .... Oakland
1-2 .... Anaheim
3-4 .... White Sox
5-6-7 .... at Houston*
8-9-10 ...... Milwaukee*
12-13-**14** .... Detroit
15-16-17 ... at Cleveland
18-19-20-**21**... at Detroit
22-23 ...... at Cincinnati*
24-25 .... Pittsburgh*
26-27-**28** .... Cubs*
30 .... at St. Louis*

JULY
1-2 .... at St. Louis*
3-4-**5**.............. Cleveland
9-10-11-**12** ... at Wh. Sox
13-14 .... at Detroit
15-**16** .... at Oakland
17-18-**19** .... at Seattle
21-22-23 .... Texas
24-25-**26-27** ... Anaheim

AUGUST
1-**2** .... Baltimore
4-5-**6**......... at Minnesota
7-8-**9**........ at Yankees
11-12............. at Boston
13-14-15-**16** .... T.B.
17-18 .... Yankees
19-**20**............... Boston
21-22-**23** .... at T.B.
24-25-26-27 .. at Toronto
28-29-**30** .... at Baltimore

SEPTEMBER
1-2 .... Toronto
4-5-**6** .... at Anaheim
8-9 .... at Texas
11-**12-13**........... Seattle
14-15 .... Oakland
16-17 .... at White Sox
18-**19-20** ... at Cleveland
21-22-23 .... Detroit
24-25-26-**27**... Wh. Sox

MINNESOTA TWINS
Hubert H. Humphrey Metrodome

APRIL
1-2........... at Toronto
3-4-**5** .... Kansas City
7-8-9................. Toronto
10-**11-12**.......... at K.C.
13-14.... at Tampa Bay
16-17-**18-19** .... Seattle
20-21-**22** ...... at Oakland
24-25-**26** .... at Seattle
27-28 .... Texas
29-**30** .... Tampa Bay

MAY
1-2-3 .... at Baltimore
5-6 .... at Boston
8-9-**10** .... Yankees
11-12 .... Baltimore
13-**14**.............. Boston
15-**16-17** ..... at Yankees
19-20-21....... Detroit
22-23-**24** .... at Anaheim
25-27 .... at Texas
29-30-**31**......... Anaheim

JUNE
1-**2** .... Oakland
3-4 .... Cleveland
5-6-7 .... at Pittsburgh*
8-9-10 .... Cubs*
12-13-**14** .... White Sox
15-16-17 .... at Detroit
18-19-20-**21**... at Wh. Sox
22-**23**.......... at Houston*
24-25 .... Milwaukee*
26-27-**28** .... St. Louis*
30............. at Cincinnati*

JULY
1-2 .... at Cincinnati*
3-4-**5** .... Detroit
9-10-11-**12** ... at Cleve.
13-14 ...... at White Sox
15-16 .... at Seattle
17-**18-19** ..... at Oakland
21-22-**23**.......... Anaheim
24-25-**26** .... Texas
28-29-30 .... at K.C.
31 .... Toronto

AUGUST
1-2 .... Toronto
4-5-**6** .... Kansas City
7-8-**9** .... Baltimore
10-11-**12** ...... at Yankees
13-14-**15-16** ... at Boston
17-18 .... at Baltimore
19-20 .... Yankees
21-22-**23** .... Boston
25-26-**27** .... at T.B.
28-**29-30** .... at Toronto
31 .... Tampa Bay

SEPTEMBER
1-2-**3** .... Tampa Bay
4-5-6-**7** .... at Texas
8-9-............... at Anaheim
11-12-**13** .... Oakland
14-**15** .... Seattle
16-17......... at Cleveland
18-**19-20** .... at Detroit
21-22-23 .... Wh. Sox
24-25-26-**27** .. Cleveland

NEW YORK YANKEES
Yankee Stadium

APRIL	JUNE	31 .... at Seattle
1-2 .... at Anaheim	1-2 .... White Sox	**AUGUST**
3-4-5 .... at Oakland	3-4 .... Tampa Bay	**1-2** .... at Seattle
6-7-8 .... at Seattle	5-**6**-7 .... Florida*	3-4-5 .... at Oakland
10-11-12 .... Oakland	9-10-11 ...... at Montreal*	7-8-9 .... Kansas City
13-14-15 .... Anaheim	12-**13-14** .... Cleveland	10-11-12 .... Minnesota
17-**18-19** .... Detroit	15-16-17 ..... at Baltimore	13-14-**15-16** .... Texas
20-21-22 .... at Toronto	18-19-**20-21** .... at Cleve.	17-18 ..... at Kansas City
24-**25-26** .... at Detroit	22-23 .... Atlanta*	19-20 .... at Minnesota
27-28 .... Toronto	24-25 .... at Atlanta*	21-22-23 .... at Texas
29-30 .... Seattle	26-**27-28** .... at Mets*	25-26-27 .... Anaheim
MAY	30 .... Philadelphia*	28-**29-30** .... Seattle
1-2-**3** ...... at Kansas City	**JULY**	**SEPTEMBER**
5-6 .... at Texas	1-2 .... Philadelphia*	1-2 .... Oakland
8-9-**10** .... at Minnesota	3-**4-5** .... Baltimore	4-5-**6** .... at White Sox
11-12 .... Kansas City	9-10-11-**12** ...... at T.B.	7-8-9 .... at Boston
13-14 .... Texas	13-14 .... at Cleveland	10-11-**12-13** .... Toronto
15-**16-17** .... Minnesota	15-16 .... at Detroit	14-15 .... Boston
19-20-21 .... Baltimore	17-**18-19** .... at Toronto	16-17 ...... at Tampa Bay
22-**23-24** .... at Detroit	20-21-**22** .... Detroit	18-19-**20** ... at Baltimore
25-26-27 ... at White Sox	24-**25-26** .... White Sox	22-23 .... Cleveland
28-29-**30-31** .... Boston	28-29-30 ..... at Anaheim	24-25-**26-27** .... T.B.

OAKLAND ATHLETICS
Oakland-Alameda County Coliseum

APRIL	JUNE	31 .... Cleveland
1-**2** .... Boston	1-**2** .... at Minnesota	**AUGUST**
3-4-**5** .... Yankees	3-4 .... Texas	**1-2** .... Cleveland
6-**8** .... Cleveland	5-6-7 .... Arizona*	3-4-**5** .... Yankees
10-11-12 ...... at Yankees	8-9-10 .. at Los Angeles*	7-8-**9** .... at Toronto
13-14-**15** .... at Boston	11-12-**13-14** .... Seattle	10-11-**12** ... at White Sox
16-17-**18-19** ...... K.C.	16-17-**18** .... at Texas	14-15-**16** .... at Detroit
20-21-**22** ...... Minnesota	19-20-**21** .... at Seattle	17-**18** .... Toronto
24-**25-26** ..... at Baltimore	22-**23** .... San Francisco	**19-20** .... White Sox
27-**28** ..... at Tampa Bay	24-25 .... at S.F.*	21-22-23 .... Detroit
29-30 .... at Cleveland	26-27-**28** ...... at Colorado*	25-26-27 .... at Boston
MAY	30 .... San Diego*	28-29-**30-31** ... at Cleve.
1-2-3-**4** .... Toronto	**JULY**	**SEPTEMBER**
5-**6-7** .... Detroit	1-2 .... San Diego*	1-2 .... at Yankees
8-9-**10** .... White Sox	3-**4-5** .... at Anaheim	4-5-**6** .... Tampa Bay
12-13 .... at Toronto	**9**-10-**11-12** .... Texas	8-**9** .... Baltimore
14-15 .... at Detroit	13-**14** .... Anaheim	11-12-**13** ... at Minnesota
16-**17-18** ... at White Sox	15-**16** .... Kansas City	14-15 ..... at Kansas City
19-20-**21** .... at Anaheim	17-**18-19** .... Minnesota	16-**17** .... Seattle
22-23-**24** .... Baltimore	21-22-23 ... at Baltimore	18-19-**20** .... at Texas
25-**26** .... Tampa Bay	24-25-**26-27** ...... at T.B.	21-22-**23** .... at Seattle
29-30-**31** .... at K.C.	28-29-**30** .... Boston	24-25-**26-27** .... Anaheim

SEATTLE MARINERS
Kingdome

MARCH	28-29-30-**31** .... at T.B.	31 .... Yankees
31 .... Cleveland	**JUNE**	**AUGUST**
APRIL	1-2 .... at Baltimore	**1-2** .... Yankees
1 .... Cleveland	3-4 .... Anaheim	3-4 .... Boston
3-4-**5** .... Boston	5-6-7 .... Los Angeles*	6-7-8-**9** .... at Detroit
6-7-**8** .... New York	8-9-**10** .... at S.F.*	11-**12** .... at Toronto
10-11-12 .... at Boston	11-12-**13-14** .... at Oak.	14-15-**16** ... at White Sox
13-14-15 ... at Cleveland	16-17-18 ..... at Anaheim	17-18 .... Detroit
16-17-18-**19** .... at Minn.	19-20-**21** .... Oakland	19-20 .... Toronto
20-21-22 ...... Kansas City	22-**23** .... San Diego*	21-22-**23-24** .... White Sox
24-**25-26** .... Minnesota	24-**25** ...... at San Diego*	25-26-27 .... at Cleveland
27-28 ..... at Kansas City	26-27-**28** ...... at Arizona*	28-**29-30** .... at New York
29-30 .... at Yankees	30 .... Colorado*	31 .... at Boston
MAY	**JULY**	**SEPTEMBER**
1-2-**3** .... Detroit	1-**2** .... Colorado*	1-2 .... at Boston
5-6 .... White Sox	3-**4-5** .... at Texas	4-5-6-**7** .... Baltimore
7-8-9-**10** .... Toronto	9-10-11-**12** .... Anaheim	8-**9** .... Tampa Bay
12-13 .... at Detroit	13-14 .... Texas	11-12-**13** .... at K.C.
14-15 .... at White Sox	15-16 .... Minnesota	14-**15** .... at Minnesota
16-17-18 .... at Toronto	17-18-**19** .... Kansas City	16-17 .... at Oakland
19-20-21 .... at Texas	21-22 .... at Tampa Bay	18-19-**20** ...... at Anaheim
22-23-24 ..... Tampa Bay	24-25-**26** ..... at Baltimore	21-22-23 .... Oakland
25-**26** .... Baltimore	28-29-30 .... Cleveland	24-25-26-**27** .... Texas

AMERICAN LEAGUE 1998 SCHEDULE

TAMPA BAY DEVIL RAYS
Tropicana Field

MARCH
31 .... Detroit

APRIL
1-2 .... Detroit
3-4-5 .... White Sox
7-9 .... at Detroit
10-11-12 ... at White Sox
13-14 .... Minnesota
16-17-18-19 ...... at Ana.
21-22-23 .... at Texas
24-25-26 .... Anaheim
27-28 .... Oakland
29-30 .... at Minnesota

MAY
1-2-3 .... at Cleveland
5-6 .... at Kansas City
8-9-10 .... Baltimore
11-12 .... Cleveland
13-14 .... Kansas City
15-16-17-18 ...... at Balt.
19-20-21....... at Toronto
22-23-24 ..... at Seattle
25-26 .... at Oakland

JUNE
28-29-30-31 .... Seattle
1-2 .... Texas
3-4 .... at Yankees
5-6-7 .... Montreal*
8-9-10 .... at Mets*
12-13-14 ...... at Boston
15-16-17 ...... Toronto
18-19-20-21 ...... Boston
22-23 .... Florida*
24-25 .... at Florida*
26-27-28 .... at Phil.*
30..................... Atlanta*

JULY
1-2 .... Atlanta*
3-4-5 .... at Toronto
9-10-11-12 ...... Yankees
13-14............. Boston
15-16 .... at Anaheim
17-18-19 .... at Texas
21-22............. Seattle
24-25-26-27 ..... Oakland
28-29 .... at White Sox
31 .... Detroit

AUGUST
1-2 .... Detroit
3-4-5 .... White Sox
7-8-9............. Cleveland
10-11-12.......... Baltimore
13-14-15-16 ...... at K.C.
17-18......... at Cleveland
19-20 .... at Baltimore
21-22-23 .... Kansas City
25-26-27 ..... Minnesota
28-29-30........ at Detroit
31 .... at Minnesota

SEPTEMBER
1-2-3 .... at Minnesota
4-5-6 .... at Oakland
8-9 .... at Seattle
11-12-13.............. Texas
14-15............. Anaheim
16-17 .... Yankees
18-19-20............ Toronto
21-22-23 ...... at Boston
24-25 26-27.... at Yanks

TEXAS RANGERS
Ballpark in Arlington

MARCH
31 .... White Sox

APRIL
2 .... White Sox
3-4-5 .... at Toronto
6-8-9 .... at White Sox
10-11-12 .... Toronto
13-14-15 .... Detroit
17-18-19 .... Baltimore
21-22-23 ... Tampa Bay
24-25-26 .... at K.C.
27-28 ...... at Minnesota
29-30 .... at Detroit

MAY
1-2-3 .... at Boston
5-6 .... Yankees
7-8-9-10 .... Cleveland
11-12............... Boston
13-14 .... at Yankees
15-16-17 ... at Cleveland
19-20-21 .... Seattle
22-23-24 .... Kansas City
25-27 .... Minnesota

JUNE
28-29-30-31 ...... at Balt.
1-2 .... at Tampa Bay
3-4 .... at Oakland
5-6-7 .... San Diego*
8-9-10 .... at Colorado*
12-13-14-15 ... Anaheim
16-17-18 .... Oakland
19-20-21 ..... at Anaheim
22-23 .... Arizona*
24-25 .... at Arizona*
26-27-28 .... at S.F.*
30 .... Los Angeles*

JULY
1-2 .... Los Angeles*
3-4-5 .... Seattle
9-10-11-12 ... at Oakland
13-14 .... at Seattle
15-16 .... Baltimore
17-18-19...... Tampa Bay
21-22-23 .... at K.C.
24-25-26 ... at Minnesota
28-29-30........ at Toronto

AUGUST
31 .... White Sox
1-2 .... White Sox
4-5 .... Toronto
6-7-8-9 .... Boston
11-12 .... at Cleveland
13-14-15-16 ... at Yanks
17-18 .... at Boston
19-20 .... Cleveland
21-22-23 .... Yankees
24-25-26 .... Detroit
28-29-30 ... at White Sox
31 .... at Detroit

SEPTEMBER
1-2 .... at Detroit
4-5-6-7 .... Minnesota
8-9 .... Kansas City
11-12-13... at Tampa Bay
14-15 .... at Baltimore
16-17............. Anaheim
18-19-20 .... Oakland
21-22-23 ..... at Anaheim
24-25-26-27 ... at Seattle

TORONTO BLUE JAYS
Skydome

APRIL
1-2 .... Minnesota
3-4-5 .... Texas
7-8-9 .... at Minnesota
10-11-12 .... at K.C.
13-14-15 .... at K.C.
17-18-19 .... White Sox
20-21-22 .... Yankees
24-25-26 ... at White Sox
27-28 .... at Yankees
29-30 .... Kansas City

MAY
1-2-3-4 .... at Oakland
5-6 .... at Anaheim
7-8-9-10 .... at Seattle
12-13 .... Oakland
14-15.............. Anaheim
16-17-18 .... Seattle
19-20-21 .... Tampa Bay
22-23-24 ... at Cleveland
25-26 .... at Boston
28-29-30-31 .. Cleveland

JUNE
1-2...................... Boston
3-4 .... Detroit
5-6-7........ Philadelphia*
8-9-10 .... at Florida*
12-13-14 ...... Baltimore
15-16-17 .... at T.B.
18-19-20-21 ...... at Balt.
22-23 .... Montreal*
24-25 .... at Montreal*
26-27-28 .... at Atlanta*
30...................... Mets*

JULY
1-2 .... Mets*
3-4-5............ Tampa Bay
9-10-11-12 ...... at Detroit
13-14 .... at Baltimore
15-16 .... at White Sox
17-18-19 .... Yankees
21-22 .... White Sox
23-24-25-26 ... at Boston
28-29-30 .... Texas

AUGUST
31 .... at Minnesota
1-2 .... at Minnesota
4-5 .... at Texas
7-8-9 .... Oakland
11-12............... Seattle
13-14-15-16 .... Anaheim
17-18 .... at Oakland
19-20 .... at Seattle
21-22-23 ...... at Anaheim
24-25-26-27 .... K.C.
28-29-30........ Minnesota

SEPTEMBER
1-2 .... at Kansas City
3-4-5-6 .... Boston
7-9 .... Cleveland
10-11-12-13... at Yanks
14-15........... at Cleveland
16-17............ at Detroit
18-19-20 .... at T.B.
21-22-23 .... Baltimore
25-26-27 .... Detroit

92 • 1998 DIRECTORY

NATIONALLEAGUE

ATLANTA BRAVES
Turner Field

MARCH
31 .... Milwaukee

APRIL
2 .... Milwaukee
3-4-**5**.......... Philadelphia
7-8-9 .... at Pittsburgh
10-11-**12**-13........ at Phil.
14-15-**16** .... Pittsburgh
17-**18**-**19**-20...... at Colo.
22-23-24............ Arizona
25-**26** .... Colorado
27-28............. at Arizona
30 .... San Francisco

MAY
1-2-**3** ...... San Francisco
4-5-**6**.......... Los Angeles
7-8-9-**10** ...... San Diego
11-12 .... at Cincinnati
13-14........... at St. Louis
15-16-**17**-**18**....... at Hou.
20-21 .... Colorado
22-23-**24**-25 .... Cubs

26-27-28.......... Montreal
29-**30**-**31** ....at Cubs

JUNE
1-2-3 .... at Milwaukee
5-6-**7**........ at Baltimore*
8-9-10 .... Boston*
12-13-**14**.......... Montreal
16-17-**18**............. Florida
19-20-**21** ..... at Montreal
22-23......... at Yankees*
24-25............. Yankees*
26-27-**28** .... Toronto*
30 .... at Tampa Bay*

JULY
1-2 ...... at Tampa Bay*
3-4-**5**..................... Mets
9-10-11-**12**...... at Florida
14-**15**................ at Mets
16-17-18-**19**............. Mil.
20-21 .... Cubs
22-23 ..... at Philadelphia
24-25-**26** ... at Pittsburgh
27-28-29-**30** ....at Cin.

31 ....St. Louis

AUGUST
1-**2**...................... St. Louis
4-5-6............. Cincinnati
7-8-9 .. at San Francisco
11-12-**13**... at San Diego
14-15-16 .... at L.A.
18-19... San Francisco
20-21 .... San Diego
22-**23**-**24** .... Los Angeles
25-26 .... at Houston
27-28-29-**30**....... at St.L.
31..................... Houston

SEPTEMBER
1-2 .... Houston
4-**5**-**6** .... at Mets
8-9-10 .... at Montreal
11-12-**13**............. Florida
14-15-**16** ... Philadelphia
17-18-19-20 .. at Arizona
22-23............ at Florida
25-26-**27** .... Mets

ARIZONA DIAMONDBACKS
Bank One Ballpark

MARCH
31 .... Colorado

APRIL
1-2 .... Colorado
3-**4**-**5** ...... San Francisco
7-8-9...... at Los Angeles
10-11-**12**-**13**...... at S.D.
14-15-**16** ..... at St. Louis
17-**18**-**19**-20 .... Florida
22-23-24 .... at Atlanta
25-**26**............. at Florida
27-28................. Atlanta

MAY
1-2-**3** .... at Montreal
4-5-6................ at Mets
7-8-9-**10** .... at Phil.
11-12.................... Cubs
13-14........... Milwaukee
15-16-17-**18** .. Pittsburgh
20-**21**.............. at Florida
22-23-**24** .... Los Angeles
25-26-27 .... San Diego

28-29-**30**-**31** .... at S.F.

JUNE
1-2-3-4........ at Colorado
5-6-**7**........... at Oakland*
9-10-11 .... Anaheim*
12-13-**14** .... St. Louis
16-17-**18**.... at Cincinnati
19-**20**-**21** ..... at St. Louis
22-23............ at Texas*
24-25 .... Texas*
26-27-**28** .... Seattle*
30 .... at Cubs

JULY
1-**2** .... at Cubs
3-4-**5** .... at Houston
10-11-12 .... Cincinnati
13-14-15 .... Houston
17-18-19 .... Colorado
20-21.. at San Francisco
22-**23**........ at San Diego
24-25-26 .... at L.A.
27-28-29-**30** .... Cubs

31 .... at Milwaukee

AUGUST
1-**2**............ at Milwaukee
3-4-**5** .... at Cubs
7-8-**9** .... at Montreal
10-11-12 .... Philadelphia
14-15-16................ Mets
17-18-**19**.......... Montreal
20-21 ..... at Philadelphia
22-**23**-**24**........... at Mets
25-26............. Pittsburgh
27-28-29-30........... Mil.

SEPTEMBER
1-2-**3** .... at Pittsburgh
4-**5**-**6** .... Houston
7-8-9...... Los Angeles
11-**12**-**13**... at Cincinnati
14-15-16 .... S.F.
17-18-19-20 .... Atlanta
22-23 .... at Colorado
25-**26**-27 .... San Diego

NOTE: Dates in **bold** indicate afternoon games.
* Interleague Series

CHICAGO CUBS
Wrigley Field

MARCH
31 .... at Florida
APRIL
1-2 .... at Florida
3-4-5-6 .... Montreal
7-8-9 .... Mets
10-11-12 ...... at Montreal
14-15-16 .... at Mets
17-18-19 .... Los Angeles
21-22-23 ...... San Diego
24-25-26 .... at L.A.
27-28 ..... at San Diego
30 .... St. Louis
MAY
1-2-3 .... St. Louis
5-6 .... Houston
7-8-9-10 .... S.F.
11-12 .... at Arizona
13-14 ....at Colorado
15-16-17.... at Cincinnati
19-20-21 .... Los Angeles
22-23-24-25 ... at Atlanta

27-28 .... Philadelphia
29-30-31 .... Atlanta
JUNE
1-2-3 .... Florida
5-6-7 .... White Sox*
8-9-10 .... at Minnesota*
12-13-14 .... at Phil.
15-16-17 ...... Milwaukee
18-19-20-21 .... Phil.
22-23 .... Cleveland*
24-25 .... at Detroit*
26-27-28 .... at K.C.*
30 .... Arizona
JULY
1-2 .... Arizona
3-4-5 .... Pittsburgh
9-10-11-12 .... at Mil.
13-14-15 .. at Pittsburgh
17-18-19 ...... at Florida
20-21 .... at Atlanta
22-23 .... Montreal
24-25-26 .... Mets
27-28-29-30 .. at Arizona

31 .... Colorado
AUGUST
1-2 .... Colorado
3-4-5 .... Arizona
7-8-9 .... at St. Louis
10-11-12 .... at S.F.
14-15-16 ...... at Houston
18-19 .... St. Louis
20-21 ...... San Francisco
22-23-24 .... Houston
25-26 .... at Cincinnati
27-28-29-30 ...... at Colo.
31 .... Cincinnati
SEPTEMBER
1-2 .... Cincinnati
4-5-6 .... at Pittsburgh
7-8 .... at St. Louis
9-10 .... Pittsburgh
11-12-13 ...... Milwaukee
14-15-16-17.. at San Diego
18-19-20 .... Cincinnati
22-23 .... at Milwaukee
25-26-27 .... at Houston

CINCINNATI REDS
Cinergy Field

MARCH
31 .... San Diego
APRIL
1-2 .... San Diego
3-4-5 .... Los Angeles
7-8-9 .... at San Diego
10-11-12-13 ..... at Colo.
15-16 .... Houston
17-18-19 .... Mets
21-22-23 .... at Phil.
24-25-26 .... at Mets
27-28-29 .... Philadelphia
MAY
1-2-3 .... at Milwaukee
4-5-6 .... at Montreal
7-8-9-10 .... at Pittsburgh
11-12 .... Atlanta
13-14 .... Florida
15-16-17 .... Cubs
19-20-21 .... at Mets
22-23-24 .... Colorado
25-26-27 .... S.F.
28-29-30-31 .... at L.A.

JUNE
1-2-3 .. at San Francisco
5-6-7 .... Cleveland*
8-9-10 ...... at San Diego
12-13-14-15 ..... Houston
16-17-18 .... Arizona
19-20-21 ...... at Houston
22-23 ...... Kansas City*
24-25 ...... at White Sox*
26-27-28 ...... at Detroit*
30 .... Minnesota*
JULY
1-2 .... Minnesota*
3-4-5 .... St. Louis
10-11-12 .... at Arizona
13-14-15 ...... at St. Louis
17-18-19 ...... San Diego
20-21 ..... at Los Angeles
22-23 .... at Colorado
24-25-26 .... at S.F.
27-28-29-30 ...... Atlanta
31 .... at Florida

AUGUST
1-2 .... at Florida
4-5-6 .... at Atlanta
7-8-9 .... Milwaukee
11-12-13 .... Pittsburgh
14-15-16 .... Montreal
18-19 .... at Milwaukee
20-21 .... at Pittsburgh
22-23-24 ...... at Montreal
25-26 .... Cubs
27-28-29-30 .... Florida
31 .... at Cubs
SEPTEMBER
1-2 .... at Cubs
4-5-6 .... at St. Louis
7-8 .... at Houston
9-10 .... St. Louis
11-12-13 .... Arizona
14-15-16 ...... Milwaukee
18-19-20 .... at Cubs
21-22-23 ... Philadelphia
25-26-27 .... Pittsburgh

COLORADO ROCKIES
Coors Field

MARCH
31 .... at Arizona
APRIL
1-2 .... at Arizona
3-4-5-6 .... at Houston
7-8-9 .... St. Louis
10-11-12-13 ... Cincinnati
14-15 .... Los Angeles
17-18-19-20 ...... Atlanta
22-23-24 ...... at Florida
25-26 .... at Atlanta
27-28 .... Florida
30 .... at Mets
MAY
1-2-3 .... at Mets
4-5-6 ...... at Philadelphia
7-8-9-10 .... at Montreal
11-12 .... at Pittsburgh
13-14 .... Cubs
15-16-17-18 .... Mil.
20-21 .... at Atlanta
22-23-24 .... at Cincinnati

25-27-28 .... at St. Louis
29-30-31 .... Houston
JUNE
1-2-3-4 .... Arizona
5-6-7 .... at Anaheim*
8-9-10 .... at Texas*
12-13-14 .... at L.A.
15-16-17 .... at S.F.
18-19-20-21 .... L.A.
22-23 .... at Milwaukee
24-25 .... Houston
26-27-28 .... Oakland*
30 .... at Seattle*
JULY
1-2 .... at Seattle*
3-4-5 .... at San Diego
10-11-12 .... S.F.
13-14-15 ...... San Diego
17-18-19 ...... at Arizona
20-21 .... Houston
22-23 .... Cincinnati
24-25-26 .... St. Louis

27-28-29 .... Pittsburgh
31 .... at Cubs
AUGUST
1-2 .... at Cubs
3-4-5-6 ...... at Pittsburgh
7-8-9 .... Mets
10-11-12 .... Montreal
14-15-16 .... Philadelphia
18-19 .... at Mets
20-21 .... at Montreal
22-23-24 .... at Phil.
25-26 .... Milwaukee
27-28-29-30 .... Cubs
SEPTEMBER
1-2-3 .... at Milwaukee
4-5-6 .... San Diego
7-8-9-10 .... Florida
11-12-13 .... at S.F.
14-15-16 .... at L.A.
18-19-20 ... at San Diego
22-23 .... Arizona
25-26-27 .... S.F.

94 • 1998 DIRECTORY

FLORIDA MARLINS
Pro Player Stadium

MARCH
31 .... Cubs
APRIL
1-2 .... Cubs
3-4-5-6 .... Milwaukee
7-8-9 ...... at Philadelphia
10-11-12-13 .... at Pitt.
15-16 .... Philadelphia
17-18-19-20 .. at Arizona
22-23-24 .... Colorado
25-26 .... Arizona
27-28 .... at Colorado
30 .... San Diego
MAY
1-2-3 .... San Diego
4-5-6 ...... San Francisco
7-8-9-10 ...... Los Angeles
11-12 .... at Houston
13-14 .... at Cincinnati
15-16-17-18 .... at St.L.
20-21 .... Arizona
22-23-24 .... Pittsburgh
26-27 .... Mets

29-30-31 .. at Milwaukee
JUNE
1-2-3 .... at Cubs
5-6-7 .... at Yankees*
8-9-10 .... Toronto*
11-12-13-14 .... Mets
16-17-18 ...... at Atlanta
19-20-21 .... at Mets
22-23 ..... at Tampa Bay*
24-25 .... Tampa Bay*
26-27-28 .... Boston*
30 .... at Baltimore*
JULY
1-2 .... at Baltimore*
3-4-5 .... at Montreal
9-10-11-12 .... Atlanta
13-14-15 .... Montreal
17-18-19 .... Cubs
20-21 .... Milwaukee
22-23 .... at Pittsburgh
24-25-26 .... at Phil.
27-28-29-30 .... at Hou.
31 .... Cincinnati

AUGUST
1-2 .... Cincinnati
3-4-5 .... Houston
7-9-10 .... at San Diego
11-12-13 .... at L.A.
14-15-16 .... at S.F.
18-19 .... San Diego
20-21 ...... Los Angeles
22-23-24 .... S.F.
25-26 .... at St. Louis
27-28-29-30 .... at Cin.
31 .... St. Louis
SEPTEMBER
1-2 .... St. Louis
4-5-6 .... Montreal
7-8-9-10 ...... at Colorado
11-12-13 .... at Atlanta
14-15-16 .....at Montreal
18-19-20 .... at Mets
22-23 .... Atlanta
24-25-26-27 .... Phil.

HOUSTON ASTROS
Astrodome

MARCH
31 .... San Francisco
APRIL
1-2 .... San Francisco
3-4-5-6 .... Colorado
7-8-9 .. at San Francisco
10-11-12-13 .... at L.A.
15-16 .... at Cincinnati
17-18-19 .... Montreal
21-22-23 .... at Mets
24-25-26 ...... at Montreal
28-29 .... Mets
MAY
1-2-3 ...... at Philadelphia
5-6 .... at Cubs
8-9-10 ...... at Milwaukee
11-12 ....Florida
13-14 .... Pittsburgh
15-16-17-18 .... Atlanta
19-20-21 ...... at Montreal
22-23-24 ...... San Diego
25-26-27 ... Los Angeles

29-30-31 ..... at Colorado
JUNE
2-3-4 .... at San Diego
5-6-7 .... Kansas City*
8-9-10 .... at Detroit*
12-13-14-15 ...... at Cin.
16-17-18 .... St. Louis
19-20-21 .... Cincinnati
22-23 .... Minnesota*
24-25 .... at Colorado
26-27-28 .. at Cleveland*
30 .... White Sox*
JULY
1-2 .... White Sox*
3-4-5 .... Arizona
9-10-11-12 .. at St. Louis
13-14-15 .... at Arizona
17-18-19 .... S.F.
20-21 .... Colorado
22-23 ..... at Los Angeles
24-25-26 ..... at San Diego
27-28-29-30 .... Florida
31 .... at Pittsburgh

AUGUST
1-2 .... at Pittsburgh
3-4-5 .... at Florida
7-8-9 .... Philadelphia
10-11-12-13.. Milwaukee
14-15-16 .... Cubs
17-18-19 .... at Phil.
20-21 .... at Milwaukee
22-23-24 .... at Cubs
25-26 .... Atlanta
28-29-30 .... Pittsburgh
31 .... at Atlanta
SEPTEMBER
1-2 .... at Atlanta
4-5-6 .... at Arizona
7-8 .... Cincinnati
9-10 .... Milwaukee
11-12-13 .... St. Louis
14-15-16-17 .... Mets
18-19-20 ...... at Pittsburgh
22-23 .... at St. Louis
25-26-27 .... Cubs

LOS ANGELES DODGERS
Dodger Stadium

MARCH
31 .... at St. Louis
APRIL
2 .... at St. Louis
3-4-5 .... at Cincinnati
7-8-9 ....Arizona
10-11-12-13 ..... Houston
14-15 .... at Colorado
17-18-19 .... at Cubs
21-22-23 .. at Milwaukee
24-25-26 .... Cubs
27-28 .... Milwaukee
30 .... at Pittsburgh
MAY
1-2-3 .... at Pittsburgh
4-5-6 .... at Atlanta
7-8-9-10 .... at Florida
11-12-13-14 .... Phil.
15-16-17 .... Montreal
19-20-21 .... at Cubs
22-23-24 .... at Arizona
25-26-27 ...... at Houston

28-29-30-31 ... Cincinnati
JUNE
2-3-4 .... St. Louis
5-6-7 .... at Seattle*
8-9-10 .... Oakland*
12-13-14 .... Colorado
16-17 .... at San Diego
18-19-20-21 ...... at Colo.
22-23 .... at Anaheim*
24-25 .... Anaheim*
26-27-28 ...... Pittsburgh
30 .... at Texas*
JULY
1-2 .... at Texas*
3-4-5 .. at San Francisco
9-10-11-12 ... San Diego
13-14-15 .... S.F.
16-17-18-19 .... at St.L.
20-21 .... Cincinnati
22-23 .... Houston
24-25-26 .... Arizona
28-29-30 .... at Phil.

31 .... at Mets
AUGUST
1-2-3 .... at Mets
4-5-6 .... at Montreal
7-8-9 .... Pittsburgh
11-12-13 .... Florida
14-15-16 .... Atlanta
18-19 .... at Pittsburgh
20-21 .... at Florida
22-23-24 .... at Atlanta
25-26-27 .... Montreal
28-29-30-31 .... Mets
SEPTEMBER
1-2 .... Philadelphia
4-5-6 ...... San Francisco
7-8-9 .... at Arizona
10-11-12-13 .... at S.D.
14-15-16 .... Colorado
18-19-20 .... at S.F.
22-23 .... San Diego
24-25-26-27 .... Mil.

MILWAUKEE BREWERS
County Stadium

MARCH	
31	at Atlanta

APRIL

2	at Atlanta
3-4-**5-6**	at Florida
7-8-9	Montreal
10-**11-12**-13	Mets
14-15-**16**	at Montreal
17-**18-19**	S.F.
21-22-**23**	Los Angeles
24-**25-26**	at S.F.
27-28	at Los Angeles

MAY

1-**2-3**	Cincinnati
4-5-**6**	San Diego
8-9-**10**	Houston
11-12	at St. Louis
13-14	at Arizona
15-**16-17**-18	at Colo.
19-20-21	S.F.
22-**23-24**	at Mets
26-27	Pittsburgh

29-30-**31**	Florida

JUNE

1-2-3	Atlanta
5-6-**7**	Detroit*
8-9-10	at Kansas City*
12-13-**14**	at Pittsburgh
15-**16-17**	at Cubs
18-19-20-**21** ..	Pittsburgh
22-**23**	Colorado
24-**25**	at Minnesota*
26-**27-28**	at White Sox*
30	Cleveland*

JULY

1-2	Cleveland*
3-4-**5**	at Philadelphia
9-10-11-**12**	Cubs
13-14-**15**	Philadelphia
16-17-18-**19** ..	at Atlanta
20-21	at Florida
22-**23**	Mets
24-25-**26**	Montreal
28-29-30	at St. Louis
31	Arizona

AUGUST

1-**2**	Arizona
3-4-5	St. Louis
7-8-**9**	at Cincinnati
10-11-12-13	at Hou.
14-15-**16**...	at San Diego
18-**19**	Cincinnati
20-21	Houston
22-**23-24**	San Diego
25-26	at Colorado
27-28-29-30 ..	at Arizona

SEPTEMBER

1-2-3	Colorado
4-5-**6**	Philadelphia
7-8	at Pittsburgh
9-10	at Houston
11-12-13	at Cubs
14-15-**16**...	at Cincinnati
18-19-**20**	St. Louis
22-**23**	Cubs
24-25-26-**27**	at L.A.

MONTREAL EXPOS
Olympic Stadium

APRIL

1-**2**	Pittsburgh
3-4-5-6	at Cubs
7-8-9	at Milwaukee
10-**11-12**	Cubs
14-15-**16**	Milwaukee
17-18-19	at Cincinnati
21-22-23	St. Louis
24-25-**26**	Houston
27-28-**29**	at St. Louis

MAY

1-**2-3**	Arizona
4-5-6	Cincinnati
7-8-9-**10**	Colorado
11-12-**13-14**	at S.F.
15-16-17	at L.A.
19-20-**21**	Houston
22-23-**24-25**	Phil.
26-27-28	at Atlanta
29-30-**31** ...	at Pittsburgh

JUNE

1-2-3	at Philadelphia
5-6-**7**	at Tampa Bay*
9-10-11	Yankees*
12-13-**14**	at Atlanta
16-17-18	Mets
19-20-**21**	Atlanta
22-23	at Toronto*
24-25	Toronto*
26-27-**28**	Baltimore*
30	at Boston*

JULY

1-2	at Boston*
3-4-**5**	Florida
9-10-11-**12**	at Mets
13-14-15	at Florida
16-17-18-**19** ..	Pittsburgh
20-21	Philadelphia
22-**23**	at Cubs
24-25-**26** ..	at Milwaukee
28-29-30	S.F.

31	San Diego

AUGUST

1-**2-3**	San Diego
4-5-**6**	Los Angeles
7-8-**9**	Arizona
10-11-12	at Colorado
14-15-16	at Cincinnati
17-18-**19**	at Arizona
20-21	Colorado
22-**23-24**	Cincinnati
25-26-27	at L.A.
28-29-30-31	at S.D.

SEPTEMBER

1-**2**.....	at San Francisco
4-5-**6**	at Florida
8-9-10	Atlanta
11-12-**13**	Mets
14-15-16	Florida
18-19-**20**	at Phil.
22-23	at Mets
25-**26-27**	at St. Louis

NEW YORK METS
Shea Stadium

MARCH

31	Philadelphia

APRIL

2	Philadelphia
3-**4-5-6**	Pittsburgh
7-8-9	at Cubs
10-**11-12**-13	at Mil.
14-15-16	Cubs
17-**18-19**...	at Cincinnati
21-22-23	Houston
24-**25-26**	Cincinnati
28-29	at Houston
30	Colorado

MAY

1-**2-3**	Colorado
4-5-6	Arizona
7-8-9-**10**	St. Louis
11-12-13-**14**	at S.D.
15-**16-17**	at S.F.
19-20-21	Cincinnati
22-**23-24**	Milwaukee
26-27	at Florida

29-30-**31**	at Phil.

JUNE

1-2-3	at Pittsburgh
5-6-**7**	at Boston*
8-9-10	Tampa Bay*
11-12-13-**14**...	at Florida
16-17-18	at Montreal
19-20-**21**	Florida
22-23	at Baltimore*
24-25	Baltimore*
26-**27-28**...	Yankees*
30	at Toronto*

JULY

1-2	at Toronto*
3-4-**5**	at Atlanta
9-10-11-**12**	Montreal
14-**15**	Atlanta
16-17-18-19	Phil.
20-21	Pittsburgh
22-**23**	at Milwaukee
24-25-26	at Cubs
28-29-30	San Diego

31	Los Angeles

AUGUST

1-2-3	Los Angeles
4-5-**6**	San Francisco
7-8-**9**	at Colorado
10-11-12...	at St. Louis
14-15-16	at Arizona
18-19	Colorado
20-21	St. Louis
22-**23-24**	Arizona
25-**26-27**	at S.F.
28-29-30-31	at L.A.

SEPTEMBER

1-**2**	at San Diego
4-5-6-**7**	Atlanta
8-9-10	at Philadelphia
11-12-**13**	at Montreal
14-15-16-**17**...	at Hou.
18-**19-20**	Florida
22-23	Montreal
25-26-**27**	at Atlanta

PHILADELPHIA PHILLIES
Veterans Stadium

MARCH
31 .... at Mets

APRIL
2 .... at Mets
3-4-**5** .... at Atlanta
7-8-9................... Florida
10-11-**12-13**....... Atlanta
15-**16**.............. at Florida
17-**18-19** ... at St. Louis
21-22-23....... Cincinnati
24-25-**26** .... St. Louis
27-28-**29**.. at Cincinnati

MAY
1-2-3................ Houston
4-5-6 .... Colorado
7-8-9-**10** .... Arizona
11-12-13-14 .... at L.A.
15-16-**17**... at San Diego
19-20-21 .... St. Louis
22-23-**24**-25 ...... at Mon.
27-28 .... at Cubs
29-30-**31**................ Mets

JUNE
1-2-3................ Montreal
5-**6-7** .... at Toronto*
8-9-10 ....Baltimore*
12-13-**14** .... Cubs
15-16-**17** .... Pittsburgh
18-19-20-21 ... at Cubs
22-23 .... at Boston*
24-25 .... at Boston*
26-27-**28** .... Tampa Bay*
30............... at Yankees*

JULY
1-2.............. at Yankees*
3-4-**5**............. Milwaukee
10-11-**12**....at Pittsburgh
13-14-**15** .. at Milwaukee
16-17-18-**19** ...... at Mets
20-21 .... at Montreal
22-23-**26**............. Atlanta
24-25-**26**............ Florida
28-29-30.... Los Angeles
31 .... San Francisco

AUGUST
1-**2-3** ...... San Francisco
4-5-**6**........ at San Diego
7-8-**9**........... at Houston
10-11-12....... at Arizona
14-15-**16** ...... at Colorado
17-18-19 .... Houston
20-21................ Arizona
22-**23**-24 .... Colorado
25-26-**27**....... San Diego
28-**29-30**-31 .... at S.F.

SEPTEMBER
1-2........ at Los Angeles
4-5-6 .... at Milwaukee
8-9-10................. Mets
11-12-**13**........ Pittsburgh
14-15-16 .... at Atlanta
18-19-**20**........ Montreal
21-22-23... at Cincinnati
24-25-26-**27** ... at Florida

PITTSBURGH PIRATES
Three Rivers Stadium

APRIL
1-**2**.............. at Montreal
3-4-**5-6** .... at Mets
7-8-**9**................. Atlanta
10-**11-12**-13........ Florida
14-15-16 .... at Atlanta
17-**18-19**...... San Diego
21-22-**23** .... S.F.
24-25-**26**.... at San Diego
27-**28**.. at San Francisco
30 .... Los Angeles

MAY
1-2-**3**.......... Los Angeles
5-6................... St. Louis
7-8-9-**10**........ Cincinnati
11-**12** .... Colorado
13-14 .... at Arizona
15-16-17-**18** .. at Arizona
19-20-21...... San Diego
22-23-**24** ...... at Florida
26-27... at Milwaukee
29-30-**31**.......... Montreal

JUNE
1-2-3..................... Mets
5-**6-7**.......... Minnesota*
8-9-10 ...... at Cleveland*
12-13-**14**....... Milwaukee
15-16-**17** .... at Phil.
18-19-20-**21**....... at Mil.
22-23.......... White Sox*
24-25 ... at Kansas City*
26-27-28 .... at L.A.
30 .... Detroit*

JULY
1-2.................... Detroit*
3-4-5 .... at Cubs
10-11-**12** ... Philadelphia
13-14-15 .... Cubs
16-17-18-**19** ...... at Mon.
20-21 .... at Mets
22-23................. Florida
24-25-**26**............ Atlanta
27-28-29 ... at Colorado
31 .... Houston

AUGUST
1-**2** .... Houston
3-4-5-**6**............... Colorado
7-8-9..... at Los Angeles
11-12-13.... at Cincinnati
14-15-**16** .... at St. Louis
18-19 ...... Los Angeles
20-21 .... Cincinnati
22-**23-24** .... St. Louis
25-26............. at Arizona
28-29-30 ...... at Houston

SEPTEMBER
1-2-**3**.................. Arizona
4-5-**6** .... Cubs
7-8 .... Milwaukee
9-10 .... at Cubs
11-12-**13**............ at Phil.
14-15-16 .... at St. Louis
18-19-20 .... Houston
21-22-**23-24** .... at S.F.
25-**26-27**.... at Cincinnati

ST. LOUIS CARDINALS
Busch Stadium

MARCH
31 .... Los Angeles

APRIL
2 .... Los Angeles
3-4-**5**............... San Diego
7-8-9............. at Colorado
10-**11-12-13** .... at S.F.
14-15-**16**............ Arizona
17-**18**-19 ...... Philadelphia
21-22-23 ..... at Montreal
24-25-**26** .... at Phil.
27-28-**29**......... Montreal
30 .... at Cubs

MAY
1-2-3 .... at Cubs
5-6 .... at Pittsburgh
7-8-**9-10** .... at Mets
11-12 .... Milwaukee
13-14............... Atlanta
15-16-**17-18** .... Florida
19-20-21 .... at Phil.
22-23-**24** .... S.F.
25-27-**28** .... Colorado

29-30-**31**... at San Diego

JUNE
1 .... at San Diego
2-3-**4**....... at Los Angeles
5-6-7 ...... San Francisco
8-9-10...... at White Sox*
12-13-**14** .... at Arizona
16-17-18 ...... at Houston
19-**20-21**............ Arizona
22-23................. Detroit*
24-25 .... at Cleveland*
26-27-**28** . at Minnesota*
30 .... Kansas City*

JULY
1-2 .... Kansas City*
3-4-**5**.......... at Cincinnati
9-10-11-**12** .... Houston
13-14-15.... Cincinnati
16-17-18-**19** .... L.A.
20-21 ..... at San Diego
22-23.. at San Francisco
24-25-**26** ..... at Colorado
28-29-30....... Milwaukee

31 .... at Atlanta

AUGUST
1-**2**.................. at Atlanta
3-4-5 .... at Milwaukee
7-8-**9** .... Cubs
10-11-12................ Mets
14-15-**16** .... Pittsburgh
18-**19** .... at Cubs
20-21 .... at Mets
22-**23-24** ... at Pittsburgh
25-26................. Florida
27-28-29-**30** .... Atlanta
31 .... at Florida

SEPTEMBER
1-2....................... at Florida
4-5-**6**.............. Cincinnati
7-8 .... Cubs
9-10 ...... at Cincinnati
11-12-**13** ...... at Houston
14-15-16 ...... Pittsburgh
18-19-**20** .. at Milwaukee
22-23 .... Houston
25-**26-27**.......... Montreal

NATIONAL LEAGUE 1998 SCHEDULE

1998 DIRECTORY • 97

SAN DIEGO PADRES
Qualcomm Stadium

MARCH
31 .... at Cincinnati

APRIL
1-2 .... at Cincinnati
3-4-**5** .... at St. Louis
7-**8-9** .... Cincinnati
10-11-**12-13**....... Arizona
14-15.. at San Francisco
17-**18-19** ... at Pittsburgh
21-**22-23** .... at Cubs
24-25-**26** .... Pittsburgh
27-28 .... Cubs
30 .... at Florida

MAY
1-2-3 .... at Florida
4-5-6 .... at Milwaukee
7-8-9-**10** .... at Atlanta
11-12-13-**14** .... Mets
15-16-**17** .... Philadelphia
19-20-21 .. at Pittsburgh
22-23-**24** ...... at Houston
25-26-27 .... at Arizona

29-30-**31** .... St. Louis

JUNE
1 .... St. Louis
2-3-**4** .... Houston
5-6-**7** .... at Texas*
8-9-10............. Cincinnati
12-13-14 .... S.F.
16-17 .... Los Angeles
18-19-**20-21** .... at S.F.
22-**23** .... at Seattle*
24-**25** .... Seattle*
26-27-**28** .... Anaheim*
30 .... at Oakland*

JULY
1-2 .... at Oakland*
3-4-**5** .... Colorado
9-10-11-12 .... at L.A.
13-14-15 ..... at Colorado
17-18-**19** ... at Cincinnati
20-21 .... St. Louis
22-**23** .... Arizona
24-25-**26** .... Houston
28-29-30............ at Mets

31 .... at Montreal

AUGUST
1-**2-3** .... at Montreal
4-5-**6** .... Philadelphia
7-**9**-10................ Florida
11-12-**13** .... Atlanta
14-15-**16**....... Milwaukee
18-19................ at Florida
20-21 .... at Atlanta
22-**23**-24 .. at Milwaukee
25-26-**27** .... at Phil.
28-29-**30-31** .... Montreal

SEPTEMBER
1-2 .... Mets
4-5-**6** .... at Colorado
7-8-9 ...... San Francisco
10-11-**12-13** .... L.A.
14-15-16-**17** .... Cubs
18-19-**20** .... Colorado
22-23 ..... at Los Angeles
25-**26**-27 .... at Arizona

SAN FRANCISCO GIANTS
3Com Park at Candlestick Point

MARCH
31 .... at Houston

APRIL
1-2 .... at Houston
3-**4-5** .... at Arizona
7-8-9 .... Houston
10-**11-12-13**......St. Louis
14-15........... San Diego
17-**18-19** .. at Milwaukee
21-22-23 ... at Pittsburgh
24-**25-26**....... Milwaukee
27-**28**............. Pittsburgh
30 .... at Atlanta

MAY
1-2-**3** .... at Atlanta
4-5-6 .... at Florida
7-**8-9-10** .... at Cubs
11-12-**13-14**..... Montreal
15-**16-17** .... Mets
19-20-**21** .. at Milwaukee
22-23-**24** ..... at St. Louis
25-26-**27**.... at Cincinnati

28-29-**30-31** ...... Arizona

JUNE
1-2-3 .... Cincinnati
5-6-**7** .... at St. Louis
8-9-**10** .... Seattle*
12-13-**14**... at San Diego
15-16-**17** .... Colorado
18-19-20-**21** .... S.D.
22-**23** .... at Oakland*
24-25 .... Oakland*
26-**27-28** .... Texas*
30 .... at Anaheim*

JULY
1-2 .... at Anaheim*
3-**4-5** .... Los Angeles
10-11-**12** .... at Colorado
13-14-15 .... at L.A.
17-18-**19** ...... at Houston
20-21 .... Arizona
22-23.............. St. Louis
24-**25-26**........ Cincinnati
28-29-30 ..... at Montreal

31 .... at Philadelphia

AUGUST
1-**2-3**........ at Philadelphia
4-5-**6**.................. at Mets
7-8-9................ Atlanta
10-**11-12** .... Cubs
14-**15-16**.......... Florida
18-19.............. at Atlanta
20-21 .... at Cubs
22-**23-24** ...... at Florida
25-**26-27** .... Mets
28-**29-30**-31 .... Phil.

SEPTEMBER
1-2 .... Montreal
4-5-6...... at Los Angeles
7-8-9........ at San Diego
11-**12-13** .... Colorado
14-15-16 .... at Arizona
18-**19-20**.... Los Angeles
21-22-**23-24** .. Pittsburgh
25-**26-27** ..... at Colorado

INTERLEAGUE SCHEDULE

Philadelphia at Toronto
Montreal at Tampa Bay
Florida at Yankees
Mets at Boston
Los Angeles at Seattle
Arizona at Oakland
Colorado at Anaheim

Philadelphia at Toronto
Montreal at Tampa Bay
Florida at Yankees
Mets at Boston
Los Angeles at Seattle
Arizona at Oakland
Colorado at Anaheim

Philadelphia at Toronto
Montreal at Tampa Bay
Florida at Yankees
Mets at Boston
Los Angeles at Seattle
Arizona at Oakland
Colorado at Anaheim

Toronto at Florida
Tampa Bay at Mets
Baltimore at Philadelphia
Boston at Atlanta
Milwaukee at Kansas City

Toronto at Florida
Tampa Bay at Mets
Baltimore at Philadelphia
Boston at Atlanta
Milwaukee at Kansas City
Cubs at Minnesota

Toronto at Florida
Tampa Bay at Mets
Baltimore at Philadelphia
Boston at Atlanta
Milwaukee at Kansas City
Cubs at Minnesota

Yankees at Montreal

Montreal at Toronto
Florida at Tampa Bay
Mets at Baltimore
Atlanta at Yankees
Philadelphia at Boston
Kansas City at Cincinnati
Minnesota at Houston

Montreal at Toronto
Florida at Tampa Bay
Mets at Baltimore
Atlanta at Yankees
Philadelphia at Boston
Kansas City at Cincinnati
Minnesota at Houston

JUNE 5
San Diego at Texas
Kansas City at Houston
Minnesota at Pittsburgh
White Sox at Cubs
Detroit at Milwaukee
Cleveland at Cincinnati

JUNE 6
San Diego at Texas
Kansas City at Houston
Minnesota at Pittsburgh
White Sox at Cubs
Detroit at Milwaukee
Cleveland at Cincinnati

JUNE 7
San Diego at Texas
Kansas City at Houston
Minnesota at Pittsburgh
White Sox at Cubs
Detroit at Milwaukee
Cleveland at Cincinnati

JUNE 8
Cubs at Minnesota
St. Louis at White Sox
Houston at Detroit
Pittsburgh at Cleveland
Texas at Colorado

JUNE 9
St. Louis at White Sox
Houston at Detroit
Pittsburgh at Cleveland
Texas at Colorado
Yankees at Montreal
Anaheim at Arizona

JUNE 10
St. Louis at White Sox
Houston at Detroit
Pittsburgh at Cleveland
Texas at Colorado
Yankees at Montreal
Anaheim at Arizona

JUNE 11
Anaheim at Arizona

JUNE 22
White Sox at Pittsburgh
Detroit at St. Louis
Cleveland at Cubs
San Diego at Seattle
San Francisco at Oakland
Los Angeles at Anaheim
Arizona at Texas

JUNE 23
White Sox at Pittsburgh
Detroit at St. Louis
Cleveland at Cubs
San Diego at Seattle
San Francisco at Oakland
Los Angeles at Anaheim
Arizona at Texas

JUNE 24

Toronto at Montreal
Tampa Bay at Florida
Baltimore at Mets
Yankees at Atlanta
Boston at Philadelphia
Pittsburgh at Kansas City
Milwaukee at Minnesota

Cincinnati at White Sox
Cubs at Detroit
St. Louis at Cleveland
Seattle at San Diego
Oakland at San Francisco
Anaheim at Los Angeles
Texas at Arizona

JUNE 25

Toronto at Montreal
Tampa Bay at Florida
Baltimore at Mets
Yankees at Atlanta
Boston at Philadelphia
Pittsburgh at Kansas City
Milwaukee at Minnesota

Cincinnati at White Sox
Cubs at Detroit
St. Louis at Cleveland
Seattle at San Diego
Oakland at San Francisco
Anaheim at Los Angeles
Texas at Arizona

JUNE 26

Toronto at Atlanta
Tampa Bay at Philadelphia
Baltimore at Montreal
Yankees at Mets
Boston at Florida
Cubs at Kansas City
St. Louis at Minnesota

Milwaukee at White Sox
Cincinnati at Detroit
Houston at Cleveland
Seattle at Arizona
Oakland at Colorado
Anaheim at San Diego
Texas at San Francisco

JUNE 27

Toronto at Atlanta
Tampa Bay at Philadelphia
Baltimore at Montreal
Yankees at Mets
Boston at Florida
Cubs at Kansas City
St. Louis at Minnesota

Milwaukee at White Sox
Cincinnati at Detroit
Houston at Cleveland
Seattle at Arizona
Oakland at Colorado
Anaheim at San Diego
Texas at San Francisco

JUNE 28

Toronto at Atlanta
Tampa Bay at Philadelphia
Baltimore at Montreal
Yankees at Mets
Boston at Florida
Cubs at Kansas City
St. Louis at Minnesota

Milwaukee at White Sox
Cincinnati at Detroit
Houston at Cleveland
Seattle at Arizona
Oakland at Colorado
Anaheim at San Diego
Texas at San Francisco

JUNE 30

Mets at Toronto
Atlanta at Tampa Bay
Florida at Baltimore
Philadelphia at Yankees
Montreal at Boston
Kansas City at St. Louis
Minnesota at Cincinnati

White Sox at Houston
Detroit at Pittsburgh
Cleveland at Milwaukee
Colorado at Seattle
San Diego at Oakland
San Francisco at Anaheim
Los Angeles at Texas

JULY 1

Mets at Toronto
Atlanta at Tampa Bay
Florida at Baltimore
Philadelphia at Yankees
Montreal at Boston
Kansas City at St. Louis
Minnesota at Cincinnati

White Sox at Houston
Detroit at Pittsburgh
Cleveland at Milwaukee
Colorado at Seattle
San Diego at Oakland
San Francisco at Anaheim
Los Angeles at Texas

JULY 2

Mets at Toronto
Atlanta at Tampa Bay
Florida at Baltimore
Philadelphia at Yankees
Montreal at Boston
Kansas City at St. Louis
Minnesota at Cincinnati

White Sox at Houston
Detroit at Pittsburgh
Cleveland at Milwaukee
Colorado at Seattle
San Diego at Oakland
San Francisco at Anaheim
Los Angeles at Texas

SPRINGTRAINING

ANAHEIM ANGELS
Major League Club
Complex Address (first year): Diablo Stadium (1993), 2200 West Alameda, Tempe, AZ 85282. Telephone: (602) 438-4300. FAX: (602) 438-7950. **Seating Capacity:** 9,785.
Hotel Address: Fiesta Inn, 2100 South Priest Dr., Tempe, AZ 85282. Telephone: (602) 967-1441.

Minor League Clubs
Complex Address: Gene Autry Park, 4125 East McKellips, Mesa, AZ 85205. Telephone: (602) 830-4137. FAX: (602) 438-7950. **Hotel Address:** McKellips Garden Apartments, 2601 East McKellips, Mesa, AZ 85215.

ARIZONA DIAMONDBACKS
Major League Club
Complex Address (first year): Tucson Electric Park (1998), 2500 Ajo Way, Tucson, AZ 85713. Telphone: (520) 434-1000. **Seating Capacity:** 11,000.
Hotel Address: Viscount Suites, 4855 East Broadway, Tucson, AZ 85716. Telephone: (520) 745-6500.

Minor League Clubs
Complex Address: Kino Veterans Memorial Sportspark, 3600 South Country Club, Tucson, AZ 85713. Telephone: (520) 434-1400. (520) 434-1443. **Hotel Address:** Holiday Inn, 181 West Broadway, Tucson, AZ 85701. Telephone: (520) 624-8711. FAX: (520) 623-8121.

CHICAGO CUBS
Major League Club
Complex Address (first year): HoHoKam Park (1979), 1235 North Center St., Mesa, AZ 85201. Telephone: (602) 668-0500. FAX: (602) 668-4541. **Seating Capacity:** 8,963.
Hotel Address: Best Western Mezona Motor Hotel, 250 West Main St., Mesa, AZ 85201. Telephone: (602) 834-9233.

Minor League Clubs
Complex Address: Fitch Park, 6th and Center Streets, Mesa, AZ 85201. Telephone: (602) 668-0500. FAX: (602) 668-4545. **Hotel Address:** Motel 6, 630 West Main St., Mesa, AZ 85201. Telephone: (602) 969-8111.

CHICAGO WHITE SOX
Major League Club
Complex Address (first year): Tucson Electric Park (1998), 2500 East Ajo Way, Tucson, AZ 85713. Telephone: (520) 434-1300. **Seating Capacity:** 11,000.
Hotel Address: Best Western Inn-Airport, 7060 South Tucson Blvd., Tucson, AZ 85706 Telephone: (520) 746-0271, (800) 772-3847.

Minor League Clubs
Complex Address: Same as major league club. **Hotel Address:** Ramada Palo Verde, 5251 South Julian Drive, Tucson, AZ 85706. Telephone: (520) 294-5250.

COLORADO ROCKIES
Major League Club
Complex Address (first year): U.S. West Sports Complex at Hi Corbett Field (1993), 3400 East Camino Campestre, Tucson, AZ 85716. Telephone: (520) 322-4500. FAX: (520) 322-4545. **Seating Capacity:** 9,500.
Hotel Address: Doubletree Guest Suites, 6555 East Speedway Blvd., Tucson, AZ 85710. Telephone: (520) 721-7100.

Minor League Clubs
Complex Address: Same as major league club. **Hotel Address:** Holiday Inn-Airport, 4550 South Palo Verde Blvd., Tucson, AZ 85714. Telephone: (520) 746-1161.

MILWAUKEE BREWERS
Major League Club
Complex Address (first year): Maryvale Baseball Park (1998), 3600 North 51st Ave., Phoeniz, AZ 85031. Telephone: (602) 245-5555. FAX: (602) 247-7404.
Hotel Address: Holiday Inn, 1500 North 51st Ave., Phoenix, AZ 85043

Telephone: (602) 484-9009.

Complex Address: Maryvale Baseball Complex, 3805 North 53rd Ave., Phoenix, AZ 85031. Telephone: (602) 245-5600. FAX: (602) 849-8941. **Hotel Address:** Red Roof Inn, 5215 West Wiletta Ave., Phoenix, AZ 85043. Telephone: (602) 233-8004.

OAKLAND ATHLETICS
Major League Club
Complex Address (first year): Phoenix Municipal Stadium (1982), 5999 East Van Buren, Phoenix, AZ 85008. Telephone: (602) 225-9400. FAX: (602) 225-9473. **Seating Capacity:** 8,500.

Hotel Address: Doubletree Suites Hotel, 320 North 44th St., Phoenix, AZ 85008. Telephone: (602) 225-0500.

Minor League Clubs
Complex Address: Papago Park Baseball Complex, 1802 North 64th St., Phoenix, AZ 85008. Telephone: (602) 949-5951. FAX: (602) 945-0557. **Hotel Address:** Fairfield Inn, 5101 North Scottsdale Rd., Scottsdale, AZ 85251. Telephone: (602) 945-4392.

SAN DIEGO PADRES
Major League Club
Complex Address (first year): Peoria Sports Complex (1994), 8131 West Paradise Lane, Peoria, AZ 85382. Telephone: (602) 486-7000. FAX: (602) 486-9341. **Seating Capacity:** 10,000.

Hotel Address: Crown Plaza, 2532 West Peoria Ave., Phoenix, AZ 85025. Telephone: (602) 943-2341.

Minor League Clubs
Complex Address: Same as major league club. Telephone: (602) 412-4025. FAX: (602) 486-7154. **Hotel Address:** Premier Inn at Metro Center, 1042 Black Canyon Highway, Phoenix, AZ 85051. Telephone: (602) 943-2371.

SAN FRANCISCO GIANTS
Major League Club
Complex Address (first year): Scottsdale Stadium (1981), 7408 East Osborn Rd., Scottsdale, AZ 85251. Telephone: (602) 990-7972. FAX: (602) 990-2643. **Seating Capacity:** 10,500.

Hotel Address: Ramada Valley Ho Resort, 6850 Main St., Scottsdale, AZ 85251. Telephone: (602) 945-6321. FAX: (602) 947-5270.

Minor League Clubs
Complex Address: Indian School Park, 4415 North Hayden Road at Camelback Road, Scottsdale, AZ 85251. Telephone: (602) 990-0052. FAX: (602) 990-2349. **Hotel Address:** Days Inn, 4710 North Scottsdale Rd., Scottsdale, AZ 85351. Telephone: (602) 947-5411. FAX: (602) 946-1324.

SEATTLE MARINERS
Major League Club
Complex Address (first year): Peoria Sports Complex (1993), 15707 North 83rd Ave., Peoria, AZ 85382. Telephone: (602) 412-9000. FAX: (602) 412-7888. **Seating Capacity:** 10,000.

Hotel Address: Wyndham Metrocenter, 10220 North Metro Parkway, Phoenix, AZ 85051. Telephone: (602) 997-5900.

Minor League Clubs
Complex Address: Same as major league club. **Hotel Address:** Comfort Inn, 1711 West Bell Rd., Phoenix, AZ 85023. Telephone: (602) 866-2089.

Florida/Grapefruit League

ATLANTA BRAVES
Major League Club
Stadium Address (first year): Disney's Wide World of Sports Complex (1998), 700 South Victory Way, Kissimmee, FL 34747. Telephone: (407) 939-8600. FAX: (407) 939-8620. **Seating Capacity:** 9,100.

Hotel Address: Coronado Springs Resort, 1000 West Buena Vista Drive, Lake Buena Vista, FL 32830. Telephone: (407) 939-1000.

Minor League Clubs
Complex Address: Same as major league club. Telephone: (407) 939-8630. FAX: (407) 939-1001. **Hotel Address:** Days Inn Suites, 5820 West Irlo Bronson Memorial Hwy., Kissimmee, FL 34746. Telephone: (407) 396-7900.

BALTIMORE ORIOLES
Major League Club
Complex Address (first year): Fort Lauderdale Stadium (1996), 5301

NW 12th Ave., Fort Lauderdale, FL 33309. Telephone: (954) 776-1921. FAX: (954) 938-5758. **Seating Capacity:** 8,340.

Hotel Address: Doubletree Suites Hotel, 555 NW 62nd St., Fort Lauderdale, FL 33309. Telephone: (954) 772-5400.

Minor League Clubs
Complex Address: Twin Lakes Park, 6700 Clark Rd., Sarasota, FL 34241. Telephone: (941) 923-1996. **Hotel Address:** Ramada Inn, 1660 South Tamiami Trail, Osprey, FL 34229. Telephone: (941) 966-2121.

BOSTON RED SOX
Major League Club
Complex Address (first year): City of Palms Park (1993), 2201 Edison Ave., Fort Myers, FL 33901. Telephone: (941) 334-4799. FAX: (941) 332-8104. **Seating Capacity:** 6,850.

Hotel Address: Sheraton Harbor Place, 2500 Edwards Dr., Fort Myers, FL 33901. Telephone: (941) 337-0300.

Minor League Clubs
Complex Address: Red Sox Minor League Complex, 4301 Edison Ave., Fort Myers, FL 33916. Telephone: (941) 332-8106. FAX: (941) 332-8107. **Hotel Address:** Days Inn, 13353 North Cleveland Ave., North Fort Myers, FL 33903. Telephone: (941) 995-0535.

CINCINNATI REDS
Major League Club
Complex Address (first year): Ed Smith Stadium (1998), 12th and Tuttle, Sarasota, FL 34237. Telephone: (941) 316-1896. FAX: (941) 365-1587. **Seating Capacity:** 7,500.

Hotel Address: Marriott Residence Inn, 1040 University Pkwy., Sarasota, FL 34234. Telephone: (941) 358-1468.

Minor League Clubs
Complex Address: Same as major league club. **Hotel Address:** Quality Inn, 2303 First St. East, Bradenton, FL 34208. Telephone: (941) 747-6465.

CLEVELAND INDIANS
Major League Club
Complex Address (first year): Chain O' Lakes Park (1993), Cypress Gardens Blvd. at US 17, Winter Haven, FL 33880. Telephone: (941) 293-5405. FAX: (941) 291-5772. **Seating Capacity:** 7,000. **Hotel Address:** Holiday Inn, 1150 Third St. SW, Winter Haven, FL 33880. Telephone: (941) 294-4451.

Minor League Clubs
Complex/Hotel Address: Same as major league club.

DETROIT TIGERS
Major League Club
Complex Address (first year): Tigertown/Joker Marchant Stadium (1946), 2125 North Lake Ave., Lakeland, FL 33805. Telephone: (941) 688-9589. FAX: (941) 988-9589. **Seating Capacity:** 7,027.

Hotel Address: Holiday Inn South, 3405 South Florida Ave., Lakeland, FL 33803. Telephone: (941) 646-5731.

Minor League Clubs
Complex/Hotel Address: Same as major league club. Telephone: (941) 686-8075.

FLORIDA MARLINS
Major League Club
Complex Address (first year): Space Coast Stadium (1993), 5800 Stadium Pkwy., Viera, FL 32940. Telephone: (407) 633-9200. FAX: (407) 633-9210. **Seating Capacity:** 7,200.

Hotel Address: Melbourne Airport Hilton, 200 Rialto Place, Melbourne, FL 32901. Telephone: (407) 768-0200.

Minor League Clubs
Complex Address: Carl Barger Baseball Complex, 5600 Stadium Pkwy., Viera, FL 32940. Telephone: (407) 633-8119. FAX: (407) 633-9216. **Hotel Address:** Holiday Inn Cocoa Beach Resort, 1300 North Atlantic Ave., Cocoa Beach, FL 32931. Telephone: (407) 783-2271.

HOUSTON ASTROS
Major League Club
Complex Address (first year): Osceola County Stadium (1985), 1000 Bill Beck Blvd., Kissimmee, FL 34744. Telephone: (407) 933-6500. FAX: (407) 847-6237. **Seating Capacity:** 5,130.

Hotel Address: Renaissance Orlando Hotel Airport, 5445 Forbes Place, Orlando, FL 32812. Telephone: (407) 240-1000.

Minor League Clubs
Complex Address: Same as major league club. Telephone: (407) 933-5500. FAX: (407) 847-6237. **Hotel Address:** Holiday Inn-Kissimmee, 2009

West Vine St. (US 192), Kissimmee, FL 34741. Telephone: (407) 846-2713.

KANSAS CITY ROYALS
Major League Club
Complex Address (first year): Baseball City Stadium (1988), 300 Stadium Way, Davenport, FL 33837. Telephone: (941) 424-7211. FAX: (941) 424-5611. **Seating Capacity:** 8,000.

Hotel Address: Holiday Inn Express, 5225 U.S. Hwy. 27 North, Davenport, FL 33837. Telephone: (941) 424-2120.
Minor League Clubs
Complex/Hotel Address: Same as major league club.

LOS ANGELES DODGERS
Major League Club
Complex Address (first year): Holman Stadium (1948). **Seating Capacity:** 6,500.

Hotel Address: Dodgertown, 4001 26th St., Vero Beach, FL 32960. Telephone: (561) 569-4900. FAX: (561) 567-0819.
Minor League Clubs
Complex/Hotel Address: Same as major league club.

MINNESOTA TWINS
Major League Club
Complex Address (first year): Lee County Sports Complex/Hammond Stadium (1991), 14100 Six Mile Cypress Pkwy., Fort Myers, FL 33912. Telephone: (941) 768-4200. FAX: (941) 768-4207. **Seating Capacity:** 7,500.

Hotel Address: Radisson Inn, 12635 Cleveland Ave., Fort Myers, FL 33907. Telephone: (941) 936-4300. FAX: (941) 936-2058.
Minor League Clubs
Complex Address: Lee County Sports Complex, 14200 Six Mile Cypress Pkwy., Fort Myers, FL 33912. Telephone: (941) 768-4282. FAX: (941) 768-4211. **Hotel Address:** Same as major league club.

MONTREAL EXPOS
Major League Club
Complex Address (first year): Roger Dean Stadium (1998), 4751 Main St., Jupiter, FL 33458. Telephone: (561) 775-1818. **Seating Capacity:** 6,871.

Hotel Address: Holiday Inn-Airport, 1301 Belvedere Rd., West Palm Beach, FL 33405. **Telephone:** (561) 659-3880.
Minor League Clubs
Complex Address: Same as major league club. **Hotel Address:** Holiday Inn-Express, 13950 U.S. Hwy. 1, Juno Beach, FL 37408. Telephone: (561) 622-4366.

NEW YORK METS
Major League Club
Complex Address (first year): St. Lucie County Sports Complex (1987), 525 NW Peacock Blvd., Port St. Lucie, FL 34986. Telephone: (561) 871-2100. FAX: (561) 878-9802. **Seating Capacity:** 7,347.

Hotel Address: Holiday Inn, 10120 South Federal Hwy., Port St. Lucie, FL 34952. Telephone: (561) 337-2200. FAX: (561) 335-7872.
Minor League Clubs
Complex/Hotel Address: Same as major league club. Telephone: (561) 871-2132. FAX: (561) 871-2181.

NEW YORK YANKEES
Major League Club
Complex Address (first year): Legends Field (1996), One Steinbrenner Drive, Tampa, FL, 33614. Telephone: (813) 875-7753. FAX: (813) 673-3199. **Seating Capacity:** 10,000.

Hotel Address: Radisson Bay Harbor Inn, 770 Courtney Campbell Causeway, Tampa, FL 33607. Telephone: (813) 281-8900.
Minor League Clubs
Complex Address: Yankees Minor League Complex, 3102 North Himes Ave., Tampa, FL 33607. Telephone: (813) 875-7753. FAX: (813) 873-2302. **Hotel Address:** Holiday Inn Express, 4732 North Dale Mabry, Tampa, FL 33614.

PHILADELPHIA PHILLIES
Major League Club
Complex Address (first year): Jack Russell Memorial Stadium (1947), 800 Phillies Dr., Clearwater, FL 34615. Telephone: (813) 441-9941. FAX: (813) 461-7768. **Seating Capacity:** 6,882.

Hotel: None.

Complex Address: Carpenter Complex, 651 Old Coachman Rd., Clearwater, FL 34625. Telephone: (813) 799-0503. FAX: (813) 726-1793. **Hotel Address:** Hampton Inn, 21030 U.S. Highway 19 North, Clearwater, FL 34625. Telephone: (813) 797-8173; Econolodge, 21252 U.S. Highway 19, Clearwater, FL 34625. Telephone: (813) 799-1569.

PITTSBURGH PIRATES
Major League Club
Stadium Address (first year): McKechnie Field (1969), 17th Ave. West and 9th St. West, Bradenton, FL 34205. **Seating Capacity:** 6,562.

Complex/Hotel Address: Pirate City, Roberto Clemente Memorial Drive, 1701 27th St. East, Bradenton, FL 34208. Telephone: (941) 747-3031. FAX: (941) 747-9549.

Minor League Clubs
Complex/Hotel Address: Same as major league club.

ST. LOUIS CARDINALS
Major League Club
Complex Address (first year): Roger Dean Stadium (1998), 4751 Main St., Jupiter, FL 33458. Telephone: (561) 775-1818. **Seating Capacity:** 6,871.

Hotel Address: Sheraton Ocean Front, 3200 North Ocean Ave., Singer Island, North Palm Beach, FL 33404. Telephone: (561) 842-6171.

Minor League Clubs
Complex/Hotel: Same as major league club.

TAMPA BAY DEVIL RAYS
Major League
Complex Address (first year): Al Lang Stadium (1998), 180 2nd Ave. SE, St. Petersburg, FL 33701. Telephone: (813) 344-1306. FAX: (813) 334-1905. **Seating Capacity:** 7,227.

Hotel Address: St. Petersburg Bayfront Hilton, 333 First Ave. South, St. Petersburg, FL 33701. Telephone: (813) 894-5000.

Minor Legue Clubs
Stadium Address: Devil Rays Spring Training Complex, 7901 30th Ave. North, St. Petersburg, FL 33710. Telephone: (813) 344-1803. FAX: (813) 344-1905. **Hotel Address:** Same as major league club.

TEXAS RANGERS
Major League Club
Complex Address (first year): Charlotte County Stadium (1987), 2300 El Jobean Rd., Port Charlotte, FL 33948. Telephone: (941) 625-9500. FAX: (941) 624-5168. **Seating Capacity:** 6,026.

Hotel Address: Days Inn, 1941 Tamiami Trail, Murdock, FL 33938. Telephone: (941) 627-8900.

Minor League Clubs
Complex/Hotel Address: Same as major league club.

TORONTO BLUE JAYS
Major League Club
Stadium Address (first year): Dunedin Stadium at Grant Field (1976), 373 Douglas Ave., Dunedin, FL 34697. **Seating Capacity:** 6,218. **Complex Address:** Englebert Complex, 1700 Solon Ave., Dunedin, FL 34697. Telephone: (813) 733-3339. FAX: (813) 734-3862. **Hotel:** None.

Minor League Clubs
Complex Address: Same as major league club. **Hotel Address:** Comfort Inn, 27988 U.S. 19 North, Clearwater, FL 34621. Telephone: (813) 796-0135.

Media Information

MEDIA INFORMATION

American League

ANAHEIM ANGELS
Radio Announcer: Mario Impemba. **Flagship Station:** KRLA 1110-AM.
TV Announcers: Fox—Steve Physioc, Sparky Anderson; KCAL—Steve Physioc, Jerry Reuss. **Flagship Stations:** KCAL Channel 9, FOX Sports West (regional cable).
NEWSPAPERS, Daily Coverage: Los Angeles Times, Orange County Register, Long Beach Press-Telegram, Riverside Press Enterprise, San Bernardino Sun, La Opinion.

BALTIMORE ORIOLES
Radio Announcers: Jim Hunter, Fred Manfra. **Flagship Station:** WBAL 1090-AM.
TV Announcer: Michael Reghi. **Flagship Station:** WJZ-TV, WNUV-TV, Home Team Sports (regional cable).
NEWSPAPERS, Daily Coverage (beat writers): Baltimore Sun (Joe Strauss), Washington Post (Mark Maske), Washington Times (Kevin Seifert), York (Pa.) Daily Record (John Delcos).

BOSTON RED SOX
Radio Announcers: Joe Castiglione, Jerry Trupiano. **Flagship Station:** WEFI 590-AM.
TV Announcers: WABU—Sean McDonough, Jerry Remy. NESN—Bob Kurtz, Jerry Remy. **Flagship Stations:** WABU, New England Sports Network (regional cable).
NEWSPAPERS, Daily Coverage (beat writers): Boston Globe (Gordon Edes), Boston Herald (Tony Massarotti), Quincy Patriot Ledger (Seth Livingstone), Providence Journal (Steve Krasner), Worcester Telegram (Bill Ballou), Hartford Courant (Paul Doyle).

CHICAGO WHITE SOX
Radio Announcers: John Rooney, Ed Farmer. **Flagship Station:** WMVP 1000-AM.
TV Announcers: Ken Harrelson, Tom Paciorek. **Flagship Stations:** WGN TV-9 (national cable), FOX Sports Chicago (regional cable).
NEWSPAPERS, Daily Coverage (beat writers): Chicago Sun-Times (Joe Goddard), Chicago Tribune (Teddy Greenstein), Arlington Heights Daily Herald (Scot Gregor), Daily Southtown (Joe Crowley).

CLEVELAND INDIANS
Radio Announcers: Tom Hamilton, Mike Hegan, Dave Nelson. **Flagship Station:** Unavailable.
TV Announcers: WUAB—Jack Corrigan, Mike Hegan. FOX—Rick Manning, John Sanders. **Flagship Stations:** WUAB-TV 43, FOX Sports Ohio.
NEWSPAPERS, Daily Coverage (beat writers): Cleveland Plain Dealer (Paul Hoynes), Lake County News-Herald (Jim Ingraham), Akron Beacon-Journal (Sheldon Ocker).

DETROIT TIGERS
Radio Announcers: Frank Beckmann, Lary Sorensen. **Flagship Station:** WJR 760-AM.
TV Announcers: Al Kaline, Ernie Harwell, Jim Price, Josh Lewin. **Flagship Stations:** UPN 50, FOX Sports Detroit (regional cable).
NEWSPAPERS, Daily Coverage (beat writers): Detroit Free Press (John Lowe, Gene Guidi), Detroit News (Tom Gage), Oakland Press (Pat Caputo), Booth Newspaper Group (Danny Knobler).

KANSAS CITY ROYALS
Radio Announcers: Denny Matthews, Fred White. **Flagship Stations:** WKBZ 980-AM.
TV Announcers: Paul Splittorff, Bob Davis. **Flagship Station:** FOX Sports Rocky Mountain (regional cable).
NEWSPAPERS, Daily Coverage (beat writers): Kansas City Star (Dick Kaegel), Topeka Capital Journal (Alan Eskew).

MINNESOTA TWINS
Radio Announcers: Herb Carneal, John Gordon. **Flagship Station:** WCCO 830-AM.
TV Announcers: Bert Blyleven, Dick Bremer, Ryan Lefebvre. **Flagship Stations:** WCCO-TV, MSC (regional cable).
NEWSPAPERS, Daily Coverage: Star Tribune (LaVelle Neal), St. Paul

Pioneer Press (Scott Miller).

NEW YORK YANKEES

Radio Announcers: John Sterling, Michael Kay. **Flagship Station:** WABC 770-AM.

TV Announcers: Jim Kaat, Ken Singleton, Al Trautwig, Bobby Murcer, Suzyn Waldman, Armando Talavera (Spanish), Beto Villa (Spanish), Roberto Clemente Jr. (Spanish). **Flagship Stations:** Madison Square Garden Network (regional cable), WB-Channel 11.

NEWSPAPERS, Daily Coverage: New York Daily News, New York Post, New York Times, Newark Star-Ledger, The Bergen Record, Newsday, Hartford Courant.

OAKLAND ATHLETICS

Radio Announcers: Bill King, Ray Fosse, Ken Korach. **Flagship Station:** KNEW 910-AM.

TV Announcers: Ray Fosse, Greg Papa, Ken Wilson. **Flagship Stations:** KRON Channel 4, FOX Sports Bay Area (regional cable).

NEWSPAPERS, Daily Coverage: San Francisco Chronicle, Oakland Tribune, Contra Costa Times, Sacramento Bee, San Francisco Examiner, San Jose Mercury-News, Hayward Daily Review.

SEATTLE MARINERS

Radio Announcers: Dave Niehaus, Ron Fairly, Rick Rizzs. **Flagship Station:** KIRO 710-AM.

TV Announcers: Dave Niehaus, Ron Fairly, Rick Rizzs. **Flagship Station:** KIRO Channel 7, FOX Sports Northwest (regional cable).

NEWSPAPERS, Daily Coverage: Seattle Times, Seattle Post-Intelligencer, Tacoma News Tribune.

TAMPA BAY DEVIL RAYS

Radio Announcers: Paul Olden, Charlie Slowes. **Flagship Station:** WFLA 970-AM.

TV Announcers: Unavailable. **Flagship Stations:** WWWB-TV 32, WTSP-TV 10, SportsChannel Florida (regional cable).

NEWSPAPERS, Daily Coverage (beat writers): St. Petersburg Times (Marc Topkin), Tampa Tribune (Joe Henderson), Bradenton Herald (Jesus Ortiz), Lakeland Ledger (Pat Zier), Sarasota Herald Tribune (Chris Anderson), Orlando Sentinel (Dave Cunningham).

TEXAS RANGERS

Radio Announcers: Eric Nadel, Vince Cotroneo, Luis Mayoral (Spanish), Josue Perez (Spanish). **Flagship Station:** KRLD 1080-AM.

TV Announcers: Bill Jones, Tom Grieve. **Flagship Stations:** KXAS, KXTX, Fox Sports Southwest (regional cable).

NEWSPAPERS, Daily Coverage (beat writers): Dallas Morning News (Gerry Fraley, Evan Grant), Fort Worth Star-Telegram (Johnny Paul), Arlington Morning News (Kevin Lonnquist).

TORONTO BLUE JAYS

Radio Announcers: Tom Cheek, Jerry Howarth. **Flagship Station:** CHUM 1050-AM.

TV Announcers: TSN—Buck Martinez, Dan Shulman. CBC—Brian Williams, John Cerutti. **Flagship Stations:** CBC, The Sports Network (national cable—Canada).

NEWSPAPERS, Daily Coverage (beat writers): Toronto Sun (Mike Rutsey, Mike Ganter), Toronto Star (Jim Byers, Alan Ryan), Globe and Mail (Larry Millson), Southam News (Tom Maloney).

National League

ARIZONA DIAMONDBACKS

Radio Announcers: Thom Brennaman, Greg Schulte, Rod Allen, Ivan Lara (Spanish), Rene Boeta (Spanish). **Flagship Stations:** KTAR 620-AM, KPHX 1480-AM (Spanish).

TV Announcers: Thom Brennaman, Greg Schulte, Bob Brenly. **Flagship Stations:** KTVK-TV Channel 3, FOX Sports Arizona (regional cable). **Spanish TV Announcer:** Miguel Quintana. **Spanish Flagship Station:** KDR-TV 64.

NEWSPAPERS, Daily Coverage: Arizona Republic, Tribune Newspapers.

ATLANTA BRAVES

Radio Announcers: Skip Caray, Don Sutton, Joe Simpson, Pete Van Wieren. **Flagship Station:** WSB 750-AM.

TV Announcers: WTBS—Skip Caray, Pete Van Wieren, Don Sutton, Joe Simpson. SportSouth—Ernie Johnson, Bob Rathbun. **Flagship**

Stations: WTBS Channel 17 (national cable), Fox SportSouth (regional cable).

NEWSPAPERS, Daily Coverage (beat writers): Atlanta Journal-Constitution (Tom Stinson), Morris News Service (Bill Zack).

CHICAGO CUBS

Radio Announcers: Pat Hughes, Ron Santo. **Flagship Station:** WGN 720-AM.

TV Announcers: Steve Stone, Chip Caray. **Flagship Stations:** WGN Channel 9 (national cable), Chicagoland-TV (regional cable).

NEWSPAPERS, Daily Coverage: Chicago Tribune (Paul Sullivan), Chicago Sun-Times (Mike Kiley), Daily Southtown (Mike Deacon), Arlington Daily Herald (Bruce Miles).

CINCINNATI REDS

Radio Announcers: Marty Brennaman, Joe Nuxhall. **Flagship Station:** WLW 700-AM.

TV Announcers: George Grande, Chris Welsh. **Flagship Stations:** WKRC-TV Channel 12, FOX Sports Ohio (regional cable).

NEWSPAPERS, Daily Coverage: Cincinnati Enquirer (Scott Mac-Gregor), Cincinnati Post (Jeff Horrigan), Dayton Daily News (Hal McCoy), Columbus Dispatch (Jim Massie).

COLORADO ROCKIES

Radio Announcers: Wayne Hagin, Jeff Kingery. **Flagship Station:** KOA 850-AM.

TV Announcers: Dave Armstrong, George Frazier. **Flagship Station:** KWGN-TV Channel 2, FOX Sports Rocky Mountains (regional cable).

NEWSPAPERS, Daily Coverage (beat writers): Rocky Mountain News (Tracy Ringolsby, Jack Etkin), Denver Post (Mike Klis), Boulder Daily Camera (Barney Hutchinson).

FLORIDA MARLINS

Radio Announcers: Joe Angel, Dave O'Brien, Felo Ramirez (Spanish), Manolo Alvarez (Spanish). **Flagship Stations:** WQAM 560-AM, WQBA 1140-AM.

TV Announcers: Joe Angel, Dave O'Brien, Tommy Hutton. **Flagship Stations:** Florida Sports Channel (regional cable).

NEWSPAPERS, Daily Coverage (beat writers): Miami Herald (Mike Sheinin, Mike Phillips), Fort Lauderdale Sun-Sentinel (David O'Brien, Mike Berardino), Palm Beach Post (Dan Graziano, Cheryl Rosenberg), Florida Today (Juan Rodriguez). Spanish—El Nuevo Herald (Aurelio Moreno).

HOUSTON ASTROS

Radio Announcers: Milo Hamilton, Jim Deshaies, Alan Ashby, Francisco Ruiz (Spanish), Alex Trevino (Spanish). **Flagship Stations:** KILT 610-AM, KXYZ 1320-AM.

TV Announcers: Bill Brown, Bill Worrell, Jim Deshaies, Milo Hamilton. **Flagship Stations:** FOX Sports Southwest (regional cable).

NEWSPAPERS, Daily Coverage: Houston Chronicle (Carlton Thompson, Alan Truex), Houston Today (Jim Molony), Beaumont Enterprise (Kenton Brooks, Joe Heiling).

LOS ANGELES DODGERS

Radio Announcers: Vin Scully, Rick Monday, Ross Porter, Jaime Jarrin (Spanish), Rene Cardenas (Spanish), Pepe Yniguez (Spanish). **Flagship Stations:** KXTA 1150-AM, KWKW 1330-AM.

TV Announcers: Vin Scully, Ross Porter. **Flagship Station:** KTLA Channel 5, Fox Sports West 2 (regional cable).

NEWSPAPERS, Daily Coverage: Los Angeles Times (Jason Reid), South Bay Daily Breeze (Bill Cizek), Los Angeles Daily News (Kevin Acee), Long Beach Press-Telegram (Dave Cunningham), Pasadena Star News (Joe Haakenson), Orange County Register (Ray McNulty), San Bernardino Sun (Steve Dilbeck).

MILWAUKEE BREWERS

Radio Announcers: Bob Uecker, Jim Powell. **Flagship Station:** WTMJ 620-AM.

TV Announcers: Bill Schroeder, Matt Vasgersian. **Flagship Station:** Midwest Sports Channel, WCGV Channel 24.

NEWSPAPERS, Daily Coverage (beat writers): Milwaukee Journal (Drew Olson, Tom Haudricourt).

MONTREAL EXPOS

Radio Announcers: Dave Van Horne, Elliott Price, Joe Cannon, Jacques Doucet (French), Rodger Brulotte (French), Alain Chantelois (French). **Flagship Stations:** CIQC 600-AM, CKAC 730-AM (French).

TV Announcers: Dave Van Horne, Gary Carter. SRC/French—Rene Pothier, Claude Raymond. TQS/French—Michel Villeneuve, Marc Griffin.

RDS/French—Denis Casavant, Rodger Brulotte. **Flagship Stations:** The Sports Network (national cable); French—Societe Radio Canada.

NEWSPAPERS, Daily Coverage (beat writers): English—Montreal Gazette (Stephanie Myles). French—La Presse (Richard Milo, Michel LaJeunesse), Le Journal de Montreal (Serge Touchette).

NEW YORK METS

Radio Announcers: Bob Murphy, Gary Cohen, Ed Coleman, Billy Berroa (Spanish), Juan Alicea (Spanish). **Flagship Stations:** WFAN 660-AM, WADO 1280-AM (Spanish).

TV Announcers: WWOR—Ralph Kiner, Tim McCarver, Gary Thorne; FOX Sports—Fran Healy, Howie Rose. **Flagship Stations:** WWOR Channel 9, FOX Sports New York (regional cable).

NEWSPAPERS, Daily Coverage: New York Times, New York Daily News, New York Post, Newsday, Newark Star-Ledger, The Bergen Record, Gannett-Westchester.

PHILADELPHIA PHILLIES

Radio Announcers: Harry Kalas, Andy Musser, Chris Wheeler, Larry Andersen. **Flagship Station:** WPHT 1210-AM.

Television Announcers: Harry Kalas, Andy Musser, Larry Andersen, Chris Wheeler. **Flagship Stations:** WPHL-WB Channel 17, Comcast SportsNet (regional cable).

NEWSPAPERS, Daily Coverage: Philadelphia Inquirer, Philadelphia Daily News, Bucks County Courier-Times, Camden County Courier Post, Delaware County Daily Times, Norristown Times-Herald, Wilmington News-Journal, Trenton Times.

PITTSBURGH PIRATES

Radio Announcers: Lanny Frattare, Steve Blass, Greg Brown, Bob Walk. **Flagship Station:** KDKA 1020-AM.

TV Announcers: Steve Blass, Greg Brown, Bob Walk. **Flagship Station:** FOX Sports Pittsburgh (regional cable).

NEWSPAPERS, Daily Coverage: Pittsburgh Post-Gazette (Paul Meyer), Pittsburgh Tribune-Review (Joe Rutter), Beaver County Times (John Perrotto).

ST. LOUIS CARDINALS

Radio Announcers: Jack Buck, Joe Buck, Mike Shannon. **Flagship Station:** KMOX 1120-AM.

TV Announcers: KPLR—Bob Carpenter, Rich Gould, Bob Ramsey. FOX Sports—Bob Ramsey, Al Hrabosky. **Flagship Station:** KPLR Channel 11, FOX Sports (regional cable).

NEWSPAPER, Daily Coverage (beat writer): St. Louis Post-Dispatch (Rick Hummel).

SAN DIEGO PADRES

Radio Announcers: Jerry Coleman, Ted Leitner, Bob Chandler. **Flagship Station:** KFMB 760-AM.

TV Announcers: Mel Proctor, Rick Sutcliffe, Mark Grant. **Flagship Stations:** KUSI Channel 51 and 9, Cox Channel 4 (regional cable).

NEWSPAPERS, Daily Coverage: San Diego Union-Tribune, North County Times.

SAN FRANCISCO GIANTS

Radio Announcers: Jon Miller, Mike Krukow, Ted Robinson, Duane Kuiper, Lon Simmons, Rene de la Rosa (Spanish), Amaury Pi-Gonzalez (Spanish). **Flagship Station:** KNBR 680-AM.

TV Announcers: FOX—Jon Miller, Duane Kuiper. KTVU—Mike Krukow, Ted Robinson, Lon Simmons, Jon Miller. **Flagship Stations:** KTVU-TV, FOX Sports Bay Area (regional cable).

NEWSPAPERS, Daily Coverage (beat writers): San Francisco Chronicle, San Francisco Examiner (Henry Schulman), San Jose Mercury News (Mark Gonzales), Contra Costa Times (Joe Roderick), Sacramento Bee (Nick Peters), Oakland Tribune (John Shea), Santa Rosa Press Democrat (Jeff Fletcher).

GENERAL INFORMATION

BASEBALL STATISTICS

ELIAS SPORTS BUREAU, INC.
Official Major League Statistician

Mailing Address: 500 Fifth Ave., New York, NY 10110. **Telephone:** (212) 869-1530. **FAX:** (212) 354-0980.

General Manager: Seymour Siwoff.

HOWE SPORTSDATA INTERNATIONAL, INC.
Official Minor League Statistician

Mailing Address: Boston Fish Pier, West Bldg. #1, Suite 302, Boston, MA 02210. **Telephone:** (617) 951-0070. **Stats Service:** (617) 951-1379. **FAX:** (617) 737-9960.

President: Jay Virshbo. **Executive Vice President:** Jim Keller. **Vice President, Records and Administration:** Mike Walczak. **Vice President, Client Services:** Tom Graham. **Manager, Operations:** Chris Pollari. **Manager, Communications:** John Foley. **Manager, Data Processing:** Wally Kent. **Managing Editor:** Vin Vitro. **Manager, Special Projects:** Paul La Rocca. **Manager, Night Operations:** Brian Joura. **Assistant Manager, Night Operations:** Bob Chaban. **Statisticians:** Bob Correia, Marshall Wright.

Historical Consultant: Bill Weiss.

STATS, Inc.

Mailing Address: 8131 Monticello Ave., Skokie, IL 60076. **Telephone:** (847) 676-3322. **FAX:** (847) 676-0821. **Website:** www.stats.com.

President/Chief Executive Officer: John Dewan. **Chief Operating Officer:** Marty Gilbert. **Vice Presidents/Systems:** Susan Dewan, Arthur Ashley. **Vice President, Finance/Administration/Human Resources:** Robert Meyerhoff. **Vice President, Publications:** Don Zminda. **Vice President, Sales:** Jim Capuano. **Vice President, Marketing/Public Relations:** Stephen Byrd. **Vice President, Sports Operations:** Doug Abel. **Director, Major League Operations:** Craig Wright. **Assistant Director, Systems:** Mike Canter. **Senior Analyst, Systems:** David Pinto.

TELEVISION NETWORKS

ESPN/ESPN2

■ *Sunday Night Baseball, 1998*
■ *Wednesday Night Doubleheaders, 1998*
■ *Division Series, 1998*

Mailing Address, Connecticut Office: ESPN Plaza, Bristol, CT 06010. **Telephone:** (860) 585-2000. **FAX:** (860) 585-2213.

Mailing Address, New York Office—605 Third Ave., New York, NY 10152. **Telephone:** (212) 916-9200. **FAX:** (212) 916-9312.

President, Chief Executive Officer: Steve Bornstein. **Executive Vice President, Administration:** Ed Durso.

Executive Vice President, Production: Howard Katz. **Senior Vice President, Programming:** John Wildhack. **Senior Vice President, Managing Director—ESPN International:** David Zucker.

Senior Vice President, Executive Editor: John Walsh. **Vice President, Remote Production:** Jed Drake. **Vice President, Managing Editor/Studio Programs:** Bob Eaton. **Assistant Managing Editor, News Director/Studio Programs:** Vince Doria. **Vice President, Programming:** Steve Risser. **Senior Coordinating Producer, Baseball Tonight/Studio:** Bob Rauscher. **Coordinating Producer, Baseball Tonight/Studio:** Jeff Schneider.

Managers, Communications: Diane Lamb, Rob Tobias. **Coordinator, Communications:** Josh Krulewitz.

Sunday Night Telecasts: Play-by-play—Jon Miller. Analyst—Joe Morgan.

Studio Hosts: Chris Berman, Karl Ravech. **Studio Analysts:** Peter Gammons, Ray Knight, Harold Reynolds.

Play-by-Play Announcers: Bob Carpenter, Dan Shulman, Gary Thorne. **Analysts:** Dave Campbell, Kevin Kennedy, Joe Magrane.

FOX SPORTS

■ *Saturday Afternoon Game of the Week, 1998*
■ *Division Series, 1998*
■ *League Championship Series, 1998*
■ *World Series, 1998*

Mailing Address, Los Angeles: 10 FOX Nework Center, Building 101, 10201 West Pico Blvd., Los Angeles, CA 90035. **Telephone:** (310) 369-6000. **FAX:** (310) 969-6346.

Mailing Address, New York: 1211 Avenue of the Americas, 2nd Floor, New

York, NY 10036. **Telephone:** (212) 556-2500. **FAX:** (212) 354-6902.

President: David Hill. **Executive Producer:** Ed Goren. **Coordinating Producer, Baseball:** John Filippelli. **Senior Vice President, Media Relations:** Vince Wladika. **Vice President, Media Relations:** Lou D'Ermilio. **Publicist, Media Relations:** Dan Bell.

Play-by-Play Announcers (Analysts): Thom Brennaman (Bob Brenly), Joe Buck (Tim McCarver), John Rooney (Jeff Torborg), Josh Lewin (Ken Singleton).

FOX Sports Net

■ *Baseball Thursday (Game of the Week), 1998*
Mailing Address: 1440 South Sepulveda Blvd., Suite 286, Los Angeles, CA 90025. **Telephone:** (310) 444-8123. **FAX:** (310) 479-8856.

President/Chief Executive Officer (FOX/Liberty Network): Tony Ball.

Chief Operating Officer: Tracy Dolgin. **Executive Vice President, Programming/Production:** Arthur Smith. **Executive Vice President/Rights Acquisitions and Regional Network Operations:** Bob Thompson.

Manager, Media Relations: Denise Seomin.

FX

■ *Saturday Night Game of the Week, 1998*
Mailing Address, Los Angeles: 1440 South Sepulveda Blvd., Suite 286, Los Angeles, CA 90025. **Telephone:** (310) 444-8281. **FAX:** (310) 479-8856.

Executive Vice President: Mark Sonnenberg.

NBC SPORTS

■ *All-Star Game, 1998*
■ *Division Series, 1998*
■ *League Championship Series, 1998*
Mailing Address: 30 Rockefeller Plaza, Suite 1445, New York, NY 10112. **Telephone:** (212) 664-4444. **FAX:** (212) 664-3602.

President, NBC Sports: Dick Ebersol.

Vice President, Sports Information/Special Projects: Ed Markey.

Play-by-Play Announcer: Bob Costas. **Analysts:** Joe Morgan, Bob Uecker.

Other Television Networks

ABC SPORTS

Mailing Address: 47 West 66th St., New York, NY 10023. **Telephone:** (212) 456-7777. **FAX:** (212) 456-2877.

President, ABC Sports: Steve Bornstein. **Senior Vice President, Programming:** David Downs. **Senior Vice President, Production:** Steve Anderson. **Director, Media Relations:** Mark Mandel.

CNN/SI

Mailing Address: One CNN Center, Atlanta, GA 30303. **Telephone:** (404) 878-1600. **FAX:** (404) 878-0011.

President: Jim Walton.

Managing Editor: Steve Robinson. **Coordinating Producers:** Tony Florkowski, Bill Galum, Gus Lalone, Sandy Malcolm, Howard Sappington. **Assignment Editor:** Tony Lamb. **Coordinator, Public Relations:** Jane Tronnier.

CTV (Canada)

Mailing Address: 9 Channel Nine Court, Scarborough, Ontario M1S 4B5. **Telephone:** (416) 299-2000. **FAX:** (416) 299-2076.

Vice President, Sports: Doug Beeforth.

THE SPORTS NETWORK (Canada)

Mailing Address: 2225 Sheppard Ave. East, Suite 100, North York, Ontario M2J 5C2. **Telephone:** (416) 494-1212. **FAX:** (416) 490-7010.

Executive Vice President, General Manager: Rick Brace. **Vice President, Programming:** Keith Pelley. **Executive Producer, Baseball:** Rick Briggs-Jude. **Supervising Producer, News and Information:** Mike Day. **Manager, Public Relations:** Rosemary Pitfield.

Play-by-Play Announcers: Dan Shulman (Blue Jays), Dave Van Horne (Expos). **Analysts:** Buck Martinez (Blue Jays), Gary Carter (Expos).

Baseball Today/Tonight: Rod Smith (host), Pat Tabler (analyst).

Super Stations

WGN, Chicago (Chicago Cubs, Chicago White Sox)

Mailing Address: 2501 West Bradley Place, Chicago, IL 60618. **Telephone:** (773) 528-2311.

WTBS, Atlanta (Atlanta Braves)

Mailing Address: One CNN Center, P.O. Box 105366, Atlanta, GA 30348. **Telephone:** (404) 827-1700. **FAX:** (404) 827-1593.

Executive Producer: Glenn Diamond.

WWOR, New York (New York Mets)

Mailing Address: 9 Broadcast Plaza, Secaucus, NJ 07096. **Telephone:** (201) 330-2246. **FAX:** (201) 330-3844.

RADIO NETWORKS

ESPN SPORTS RADIO

■ *All-Star Game, 1998*
■ *All Post season games, 1998*
■ *Sunday Night Game of the Week, 1998*

Mailing Address: ESPN Plaza, Bristol, CT 06010. **Telephone:** (860) 585-2661. **FAX:** (860) 589-5523.

General Manager: Drew Hayes. **Executive Producer:** John Martin. **Program Director:** Len Weiner.

PRESS ASSOCIATIONS

ASSOCIATED PRESS

Mailing Address: 50 Rockefeller Plaza, New York, NY 10020. **Telephone:** (212) 621-1630. **FAX:** (212) 621-1639.

Sports Editor: Terry Taylor. **Deputy Sports Editor:** Brian Friedman. **Agate Editor:** Paul Montella. **Sports Photo Editor:** Brian Horton. **Baseball Writers:** Ron Blum, Ben Walker, Tom Withers.

BLOOMBERG SPORTS NEWS

Mailing Address: P.O. Box 888, Princeton, NJ 08542. **Telephone:** (609) 279-4061. **FAX:** (609) 279-5878.

Sports Editor: Jay Beberman. **National Baseball Writer:** Jerry Crasnick.

ESPN/SPORTSTICKER

Mailing Address: Harborside Financial Center, 600 Plaza Two, 8th Floor, Jersey City, NJ 07311. **Telephone:** (201) 309-1200. **FAX:** (800) 336-0383, (201) 860-9742. **E-Mail Address:** sportstick@aol.com.

Vice President, General Manager: Rick Alessandri. **Executive Director, News:** Jim Morganthaler. **General Manager, News:** John Mastroberardino. **Senior Editor, Major League Baseball:** Doug Mitler. **Director, Marketing Services:** Lou Monaco.

CANADIAN PRESS

Mailing Address: 36 King St. East, Toronto, Ontario M5C 2L9. **Telephone:** (416) 594-2154. **E-Mail Address:** sports@canpress.com.

General Sports Editor: Neil Davidson. **Baseball Writer:** Dan Ralph.

BASEBALL WRITERS ASSOCIATION OF AMERICA

Mailing Address: 78 Olive St., Lake Grove, NY 11755. **Telephone:** (516) 981-7938. **FAX:** (516) 585-4669.

President: Jim Street (Seattle Post-Intelligencer). **Vice President:** Bob Elliott (Toronto Sun).

Board of Directors: Tom Gage (Detroit News), Tom Krasovic (San Diego Union-Tribune), Hal McCoy (Dayton Daily News), Scott Miller (St. Paul Pioneer-Press).

Secretary-Treasurer: Jack O'Connell (Hartford Courant). **Assistant Secretary:** Jack Lang (SportsTicker).

NATIONAL ASSOCIATION OF BASEBALL
WRITERS AND BROADCASTERS

Mailing Address: P.O. Box A, St. Petersburg, FL 33731. **Telephone:** (813) 822-6937. **FAX:** (813) 821-5819.

Secretary-Treasurer: Jim Ferguson (National Association).

NATIONAL COLLEGIATE BASEBALL
WRITERS ASSOCIATION

Mailing Address: 35 East Wacker Dr., Suite 650, Chicago, IL 60601. **Telephone:** (312) 553-0483. **FAX:** (312) 553-0495.

Board of Directors: Bo Carter (Big 12 Conference), Bob Bradley (Clemson), Tom Price (South Carolina).

President: Alan Cannon (Texas A&M). **First Vice President:** Ken Krisolovic (St. Joseph's). **Secretary-Treasurer:** Russ Anderson (Conference USA).

Newsletter Editor: John Askins, Sports Media Group, 1255 Florida Road, Suite 5, Durango, CO 81301.

NEWSPAPERS/PERIODICALS

USA TODAY

Mailing Address: 1000 Wilson Blvd., Arlington, VA 22229. **Telephone/ Baseball Desk:** (703) 276-3731, 276-3708, 276-3725. **FAX:** (703) 558-3988.

Baseball Editors: John Porter, Rachel Shuster, Denise Tom. **Baseball Columnist:** Hal Bodley. **Major League Beat Writers:** Chuck Johnson (National Leage), Mel Antonen (American League). **Baseball Reporters:** Rod Beaton, Mike Dodd. **Agate Editor:** Matt Seaman.

USA TODAY BASEBALL WEEKLY

Mailing Address: 1000 Wilson Blvd., 21st Floor, Arlington, VA 22229. **Telephone:** (703) 558-5630. **FAX:** (703) 558-4678.

Publisher: Keith Cutler. **Executive Editor:** Lee Ivory. **Editor:** Paul White.

Manager, Classified Advertising: Lynn Busby.

ESPN MAGAZINE
Mailing Address: 19 East 34th St., New York, NY 10016. **Telephone:** (212) 515-1000. **FAX:** (212) 515-1290.

Publisher: Michael Rooney. **Editor:** John Papanek. **Executive Editor:** Steve Wulf. **Senior Editor, Baseball**: Glen Waggoner. **Associate Editor, Baseball:** Jeff Bradley. **Senior Writer:** Tim Kurkjian. **Writer/Reporter:** Brendan O'Connor.

THE SPORTING NEWS
Mailing Address: 10176 Corporate Square Dr., Suite 200, St. Louis, MO 63132. **Telephone:** (314) 997-7111. **FAX:** (314) 997-0765.

Editor: John Rawlings. **Executive Editor:** Steve Meyerhoff. **Managing Editors:** Bob Hille, Mike Nahrstedt. **Senior Writers:** Paul Attner, Michael Knisley, Steve Marantz, Dan Pompei.

SPORTS ILLUSTRATED
Mailing Address: Time & Life Building, 1271 Avenue of the Americas, New York, NY 10020. **Telephone:** (212) 522-1212. **FAX, Editorial:** (212) 522-4543. **FAX, Public Relations:** (212) 522-4832.

Managing Editor: Bill Colson. **Senior Editors:** Jay Lovinger, Greg Kelly. **Senior Writers:** Gerry Callahan, Tim Crothers, Tom Verducci.

Director, Communications: Art Berke. **Director, Publicity:** Joe Assad.

INSIDE SPORTS
Mailing Address: 990 Grove St., Evanston, IL 60201. **Telephone:** (847) 491-6440. **FAX:** (847) 491-0867.

President, Chief Executive Officer: Norman Jacobs. **Executive Vice President/Publisher:** Jerry Croft. **Editor:** Ken Leiker. **Photo Editor:** David Durochik.

SPORT MAGAZINE
Mailing Address: 6420 Wilshire Blvd., Los Angeles, CA 90048. **Telephone:** (213) 782-2828. **FAX:** (213) 782-2835.

President: Polly Perkins. **Editor:** Norb Garrett. **Editor-at-Large:** Cameron Benty. **Managing Editor:** Steve Gordon.

BASEBALL DIGEST
Mailing Address: 990 Grove St., Evanston, IL 60201. **Telephone:** (847) 491-6440. **FAX:** (847) 491-0867.

Editor: John Kuenster. **Managing Editor:** Bob Kuenster.

ATHLON'S BASEBALL
Mailing Address: 220 25th Ave. North, Suite 200, Nashville, TN 37203. **Telephone:** (615) 327-0747. **FAX:** (615) 327-1149.

Chief Executive Officer: Chuck Allen. **Managing Editor:** Charlie Miller. **Senior Editor:** Rob Doster.

STREET AND SMITH'S BASEBALL
Mailing Address: 342 Madison Ave., New York, NY 10017. **Telephone:** (212) 880-8698. **FAX:** (212) 880-4347.

Publisher: Sal Schiliro. **Editor:** Gerard Kavanagh.

SPRING TRAINING BASEBALL YEARBOOK
Mailing Address: Vanguard Sports Publications, P.O. Box 667, Chapel Hill, NC 27514. **Telephone:** (919) 967-2420. **FAX:** (919) 967-6294.

Publisher: Merle Thorpe. **Editor:** Myles Friedman.

COLLEGIATE BASEBALL
Mailing Address: P.O. Box 50566, Tucson, AZ 85703. **Telephone:** (520) 623-4530. **FAX:** (520) 624-5501. **E-Mail Address:** cbn@azstarnet.com.

Publisher: Lou Pavlovich. **Editor:** Lou Pavlovich Jr.

HIGH SCHOOL BASEBALL USA
Mailing Address: P.O. Box 8943, Cincinnati, OH 45208. **Telephone/FAX:** (606) 291-4463.

Editor: Jeff Spelman.

JUNIOR LEAGUE BASEBALL
Mailing Address: P.O. Box 9099, Canoga Park, CA 91309. **Telephone:** (818) 710-1234. **FAX:** (818) 710-1877. **Website:** www.jlbmag.com.

Publisher/Editor: Dave Destler.

BASEBALL PARENT
Mailing Address: 4437 Kingston Pike, Suite 2204, Knoxville, TN 37919. **Telephone:** (423) 523-1274. **FAX:** (423) 673-8926.

Publisher/Editor: Wayne Christensen.

INTERNATIONAL BASEBALL RUNDOWN
Mailing Address: P.O. Box 608, Glen Ellyn, IL 60138. **Telephone:** (630) 790-3087. **FAX:** (630) 790-3182.

Editor: Jeff Elijah.

TOTAL BASEBALL
Mailing Address: 445 Park Ave., 19th Floor, New York, NY 10022. **Telephone:** (212) 319-6611. **FAX:** (212) 310-3820.

Partner: Mike Gershman.

HOBBY PUBLICATIONS

BECKETT PUBLICATIONS
Mailing Address: 15850 Dallas Parkway, Dallas, TX 75248. **Telephone:** (972) 991-6657. **FAX:** (972) 991-8930.

Managing Editors: Mike McAllister, Mike Payne. **Associate Editor, Beckett Baseball Card Monthly:** Jim Thompson.

KRAUSE PUBLICATIONS
Mailing Address: 700 East State St., Iola, WI 54990. **Telephone:** (715) 445-2214. **FAX:** (715) 445-4087.

Publisher: Hugh McAloon.

Editor, Fantasy Sports/Sports Cards Magazine: Greg Ambrosius. **Editor, Sports Collectors Digest:** Tom Mortenson.

TEAM PUBLICATIONS

COMAN PUBLISHING, INC.
(Atlanta Braves, Boston Red Sox, New York Mets)
Mailing Address: P.O. Box 2331, Durham, NC 27702. **Telephone:** (800) 421-7751; (919) 688-0218. **FAX:** (919) 682-1532.

Publisher: Stuart Coman.

Editor, Tomahawk (Atlanta Braves): Bill Ballew. **Managing Editor, New York Mets Inside Pitch:** Todd McGee. **Editor, Diehard** (Boston Red Sox): George Whitney.

PHILLIES REPORT (Philadelphia Phillies)
Mailing Address: P.O. Box 0, Whitehall, PA 18052. **Telephone:** (888) 409-2200. **Editor:** Jeff Moeller.

VINE LINE (Chicago Cubs)
Mailing Address: Chicago Cubs Publications, 1060 West Addison St., Chicago, IL 60613. **Telephone:** (773) 404-2827. **Managing Editor:** Ernie Roth. **Editor:** Jay Rand.

YANKEES MAGAZINE (New York Yankees)
Mailing Address: Yankee Stadium, Bronx, NY 10451. **Telephone:** (718) 579-4495. **Publisher:** Tim Wood. **Editor:** Pat McEvoy.

JET MEDIA (Indians Ink)
Mailing Address: P.O. Box 539, Mentor, OH 44061. **Telephone:** (216) 953-2200. **FAX:** (216) 953-2202. **Editor:** Frank Derry.

OUTSIDE PITCH (Baltimore Orioles)
Mailing Address: P.O. Box 27143, Baltimore, MD 21230. **Telephone:** (410) 234-8888. **FAX:** (410) 234-1029. **Publisher:** David Simone. **Editor:** David Hill.

REDS REPORT (Cincinnati Reds)
Mailing Address: Columbus Sports Publications, P.O. Box 12453, Columbus, OH 43212. **Telephone:** (614) 486-2202. **FAX:** (614) 486-3650. **Publisher:** Frank Moskowitz. **Editor:** Steve Helwagen.

BASEBALL CARD MANUFACTURERS

SCORE BOARD
Mailing Address: 1951 Old Cuthbert Rd., Cherry Hill, NJ 08034. **Telephone:** (609) 354-9000. **FAX:** (609) 354-9671.

DONRUSS TRADING CARD CO.
Mailing Address: 907 Avenue R, Grand Prairie, TX 75050. **Telephone:** (972) 975-0022. **FAX:** (972) 975-0077.

FLEER/SKYBOX INTERNATIONAL
Mailing Address: Executive Plaza, 1120 Route 73, Suite 300, Mt. Laurel, NJ 08054. **Telephone:** (609) 231-6200. **FAX:** (609) 727-9460.

PINNACLE BRANDS
Mailing Address: 1845 Wooddall Rodgers Freeway, Suite 1300, Dallas, TX 75201. **Telephone:** (214) 981-8100. **FAX:** (214) 981-8200.

TOPPS
Mailing Address: One Whitehall St., New York, NY 10004. **Telephone:** (212) 376-0300. **FAX:** (212) 376-0573.

UPPER DECK
Mailing Address: 5909 Sea Otter Place, Carlsbad, CA 92008. **Telephone:** (760) 929-6500. **FAX:** (760) 929-6548.

GRANDSTAND CARDS
Mailing Address: 22647 Ventura Blvd., #192, Woodland Hills, CA, 91364. **Telephone:** (818) 992-5642. **FAX:** (818) 348-9122.

Majors-Other Information

GENERAL INFORMATION

MAJOR LEAGUE BASEBALL PLAYERS ASSOCIATION

Mailing Address: 12 East 49th St., 24th Floor, New York, NY 10017. **Telephone:** (212) 826-0808. **FAX:** (212) 752-4378. **Website:** bigleaguers.com.

Year Founded: 1966.

Executive Director, General Counsel: Donald Fehr.

Special Assistants: Mark Belanger, Tony Bernazard.

Associate General Counsel: Eugene Orza. **Assistant General Counsel:** Lauren Rich, Doyle Pryor, Michael Weiner. **Counsel:** Robert Lenaghan, Arthur Schack.

Director, Licensing: Judy Heeter. **General Manager:** Richard White. **Manager, Marketing Services:** Allyne Price. **Category Director, Publishing and New Products:** Scott Barrett. **Account Manager:** Jennifer Cooney. **Category Manager/Apparel and Novelties:** Richard Fullerton. **Administrative Manager:** Tina Morris. **Coordinator, Licensing:** Evan Kaplan. **Editor, Website:** Chris Dahl.

Director, Communications: Richard Weiss.

Executive Board: Player representatives of the 30 major league clubs.

League Representatives: American League—David Cone; **National League**—Tom Glavine.

MAJOR LEAGUE BASEBALL PRODUCTIONS
THE PHOENIX COMMUNICATIONS GROUP, INC.

Mailing Address: 3 Empire Blvd., South Hackensack, NJ 07606. **Telephone:** (201) 807-0888. **FAX:** (201) 807-0272.

Chairman: Joe Podesta. **President:** James Holland. **Senior Vice President, Executive Producer:** Geoff Belinfante. **Vice President, Sales and Marketing:** Rich Domich. **Vice President, Program Development:** Jim Scott. **Director, Marketing and Home Video:** Chris Brande.

SCOUTING

MAJOR LEAGUE SCOUTING BUREAU

Mailing Address: 23712 Birtcher Dr., Suite A, Lake Forest, CA 92630. **Telephone:** (714) 458-7600. **FAX:** (714) 458-9454.

Year Founded: 1974.

Director: Frank Marcos. **Consultant:** Don Pries.

Administrator: RoseMary Durgin. **Secretary:** Rease Leverenz.

Board of Directors: Bill Murray, chairman; Bill Bavasi (Angels), Dave Dombrowski (Marlins), Dan Duquette (Red Sox), Bob Gebhard (Rockies), Roland Hemond (Diamondbacks), Frank Marcos, Randy Smith (Tigers), Art Stewart (Royals).

Scouts: Mike Childers (Lexington, KY), Dick Colpaert (Utica, MI), Jeff Cornell (Lee's Summit, MO), Dan Dixon (Temecula, CA), J.D. Elliby (Richmond, VA), Art Gardner (Walnut Grove, MS), Rusty Gerhardt (New London, TX), Mike Hamilton (Arlington, TX), Doug Horning (Schereville, IN), Don Jacoby (Winter Haven, FL), Brad Kohler (Bethlehem, PA), Don Kohler (Asbury, NJ), Mike Larson (Waseca, MN), Jethro McIntyre (Pittsburg, CA), Bob Meisner (Golden, CO), Lenny Merullo (Reading, MA), Paul Mirocke (Lutz, FL), Carl Moesche (Gresham, OR), Rick Oliver (La Verne, CA), Tim Osborne (Woodstock, GA), Buddy Pritchard (Fullerton, CA), Gary Randall (Rock Hill, SC), Al Ronning (Sunnyvale, CA), Kevin Saucier (Pensacola, FL), Kirk Shrider (Lakewood, CA), Pat Shortt (Rockville Centre, NY), Craig Smajstrla (Pearland, TX), Ed Sukla (Irvine, CA), Marv Thompson (Glendale, AZ), Tom Valcke (Fresno, CA), Jim Walton (Shattuck, OK).

Canadian Scouts: Walt Burrows (Brentwood Bay, B.C.), supervisor; Jim Baba (Saskatoon, Saskatchewan), Curtis Bailey (Red Deer, Alberta), Kevin Bly (North York, Ontario), Robert Davidson (Peterborough, Ontario), Gerry Falk (Carman, Manitoba), Bill Green (Vancouver, B.C.), Sean Gulliver (St. John's, Newfoundland), Lowell Hodges (North Saanich, B.C.), Ian Jordan (Pointe-Claire, Quebec), Jay Lapp (London, Ontario), Ken Lenihan (Bedford, N.S.), Dave McConnell (Kelowna, B.C.), Jean Marc Mercier (Charlesbourg, Quebec).

Puerto Rican Scout: Pepito Centeno (Bayamon), supervisor.

UMPIRES

MAJOR LEAGUE
UMPIRES ASSOCIATION
Mailing Address: 1735 Market St., Suite 3420, Philadelphia, PA 19103. **Telephone:** (215) 979-3200. **FAX:** (215) 979-3201.

Year Founded: 1967.

General Counsel: Richie Phillips. **Associate General Counsel:** Pat Campbell.

UMPIRE DEVELOPMENT SCHOOLS
Harry Wendelstedt Umpire School
Mailing Address: 88 South St. Andrews Drive, Ormond Beach, FL 32174. **Telephone:** (904) 672-4879.

Operator: Harry Wendelstedt.

Brinkman-Froemming Umpiring School
Mailing Address: 1021 Indian River Drive, Cocoa, FL 32922. **Telephone:** (407) 639-1515. **FAX:** (407) 633-7018.

Owner/Director: Joe Brinkman.

Academy of Professional Umpiring
Mailing Address: 12885 Research Blvd., Suite 107, Austin, TX 78750. **Telephone:** (512) 335-5959. **FAX:** (512) 335-5411.

Operator: Jim Evans.

TRAINERS

PROFESSIONAL BASEBALL
ATHLETIC TRAINERS SOCIETY
Mailing Address: 400 Colony Square, Suite 1750, 1201 Peachtree St., Atlanta, GA 30361. **Telephone:** (404) 875-4000. **FAX:** (404) 892-8560.

Year Founded: 1983.

President: Kent Biggerstaff (Pittsburgh Pirates). **American League Representative:** Paul Spicuzza (Cleveland Indians). **National League Representative:** Charlie Strasser (Los Angeles Dodgers) **Secretary:** Dave Labossiere (Houston Astros).

General Counsel: Rollin Mallernee.

MUSEUMS

NATIONAL BASEBALL
HALL OF FAME AND MUSEUM
Office Address: 25 Main St., Cooperstown, NY 13326. **Mailing Address:** P.O. Box 590, Cooperstown, NY 13326. **Telephone:** (607) 547-7200. **FAX:** (607) 547-2044. **Website:** www.baseballhalloffame.org.

Year Founded: 1939.

Chairman: Ed Stack. **President:** Don Marr. **Vice President:** Frank Simio. **Controller:** Fran Althiser. **Registrar:** Peter Clark. **Executive Director, Communications:** Jeff Idelson. **Director, Communications:** John Ralph. **Executive Director, Retail Marketing:** Barbara Shinn. **Curator:** Ted Spencer. **Librarian:** Jim Gates.

Museum Hours: Oct. 1-April 30—9 a.m.-5 p.m.; May 1-Sept. 30—9 a.m.-9 p.m. Open every day except Thanksgiving, Christmas Day, New Year's Day.

1998 Hall of Fame Induction Ceremonies: July 26, 2:30 p.m., Cooperstown, NY. **Hall of Fame Game:** July 27, 2 p.m., Baltimore vs. Toronto.

NEGRO LEAGUES
BASEBALL MUSEUM
Office Address: 1616 East 18th St., Kansas City, MO 64108. **Mailing Address:** P.O. Box 414897, Kansas City, MO 64141. **Telephone:** (816) 221-1920. **FAX:** (816) 221-8424. **Website:** www.nlbm.com.

Year Founded: 1990.

Chairman: Buck O'Neil. **President:** Randall Ferguson.

Executive Director: Don Motley.

RESEARCH

SOCIETY FOR
AMERICAN BASEBALL RESEARCH
Mailing Address: P.O. Box 93183, Cleveland, OH 44101. **Telephone:** (216) 575-0500. **FAX:** (216) 575-0502.

Year Founded: 1971.

President: Larry Gerlach (Salt Lake City, UT). **Vice President:** Dick Beverage (Placentia, CA). **Secretary:** David Pietrusza (Scotia, NY). **Treasurer:** Paul Andresen (Corvallis, OR). **Directors:** Steve Gietschier, Jim Riley, Rick Salamon, Tom Shieber.

Executive Director: Morris Eckhouse. **Manager, Membership Services:** John Zajc. **Director, Publications:** Mark Alvarez.

ALUMNI ASSOCIATIONS

MLB PLAYERS ALUMNI ASSOCIATION

Mailing Address, National Headquarters: 1631 Mesa Ave., Suite C, Colorado Springs, CO 80906. **Telephone:** (719) 477-1870. **FAX:** (719) 477-1875.

Mailing Address, Florida Operations Center: 33 6th St. South, St. Petersburg, FL 33701. **Telephone:** (813) 892-6744. **FAX:** (813) 892-6771.

Year Founded: 1982.

President: Brooks Robinson.

Vice Presidents: Bob Boone, George Brett, Carl Erskine, Al Kaline, Rusty Staub, Robin Yount.

Treasurer: Fred Valentine.

Board of Directors: Nelson Briles, Darrel Chaney, Denny Doyle, Jim "Mudcat" Grant, Rich Hand, Jim Hannan (chairman), Jerry Moses, Ken Sanders, Fred Valentine.

Legal Counsel: Sam Moore. **Executive Vice President:** Dan Foster. **Director, Communications:** Robert Stirewalt. **Director, Special Events:** Chris Torgusen. **Coordinators, Special Events:** Geoff Hixson, Mike Morey. **Coordinator, Youth Baseball:** Lance James. **Office Manager:** Chandra Von Nostrand.

ASSOCIATION OF PROFESSIONAL BASEBALL PLAYERS OF AMERICA

Mailing Address: 12062 Valley View St., Suite 211, Garden Grove, CA 92845. **Telephone:** (714) 892-9900. **FAX:** (714) 897-0233.

Year Founded: 1924.

President: John McHale.

1st Vice President: Joe DiMaggio. **2nd Vice President:** Arthur Richman. **3rd Vice President:** Bob Kennedy.

Advisory Council: Calvin Griffith, Eddie Sawyer.

Secretary-Treasurer: Chuck Stevens.

BASEBALL ASSISTANCE TEAM (BAT)

Mailing Address: 350 Park Ave., New York, NY 10022. **Telephone:** (212) 339-7880. **FAX:** (212) 888-8632.

Year Founded: 1986.

Chairman: Ralph Branca. **President:** Joe Garagiola. **Vice Presidents:** Joe Black, Earl Wilson. **Secretary:** Thomas Ostertag. **Treasurer:** Jeffrey White.

Executive Director: James Martin. **Administrator:** Eleanor Mieszerski. **Consultant:** Sam McDowell.

CHAPEL

BASEBALL CHAPEL

Mailing Address: 21755 West Ravine Rd., Forest Lake, IL 60047. **Telephone:** (847) 438-0978. **FAX:** (847) 438-6554. **E-Mail Address:** baseballchapel@juno.com.

Year Founded: 1972.

President: Gary Carter. **Vice President:** Tim Burke.

Executive Director: Vince Nauss.

ATHLETES IN ACTION

Mailing Address: 3802 Ehrlich Rd., Suite 110, Tampa, FL 33624. **Telephone:** (813) 968-7400. **FAX:** (813) 968-7515.

Staff: Jason Lester, Scott Lothery, Brian Dembowczyk.

TRADE, EMPLOYMENT

THE BASEBALL TRADE SHOW

Mailing Address: P.O. Box A, St. Petersburg, FL 33731. **Telephone:** (813) 822-6937. **FAX:** (813) 821-5819.

Show Director: Kecia Tillman.

1998 Convention: Dec. 11-14 at Nashville, TN.

PROFESSIONAL BASEBALL EMPLOYMENT OPPORTUNITIES

Mailing Address: P.O. Box 310, Old Fort, NC 28762. **Telephone:** (800) 842-5618. **FAX:** (704) 668-4762.

Director: Ann Perkins.

MEN'S SENIOR BASEBALL LEAGUE
(30 and Over, 40 and Over)

Mailing Address: One Huntington Quadrangle, Suite 3N07, Mellville, NY 11747. **Telephone:** (516) 753-6725. **FAX:** (516) 753-4031.

President: Steve Sigler. **Vice President:** Gary D'Ambrisi.

1998 World Series: Oct. 26-Nov. 7, Phoenix, AZ; Nov. 2-7, St. Petersburg, FL.

MEN'S ADULT BASEBALL LEAGUE
(18 and Over)

Mailing Address: One Huntington Quadrangle, Suite 3N07, Mellville, NY 11747. **Telephone:** (516) 753-6725. **FAX:** (516) 753-4031.

President: Steve Sigler. **Vice President:** Gary D'Ambrisi.

1998 World Series: Oct. 22-25, Phoenix, AZ; Oct. 30-Nov. 1, St. Petersburg, FL.

NATIONAL ADULT BASEBALL ASSOCIATION
(18-65)

Mailing Address: 3900 East Mexico Ave., Suite 330, Denver, CO 80210. **Telephone:** (303) 639-9955. **FAX:** (303) 753-6804. **E-Mail Address:** nabanatl@aol.com.

President: Brad Coldiron. **Vice President/Chief Operating Officer:** Shane Fugita.

1998 National Championship: 18 and Over—Oct. 18-21, Phoenix, AZ. **Senior** (30 and over, 40 and over)—Oct. 21-26, Phoenix, AZ.

ROY HOBBS BASEBALL
(Open, 30 and Over, 40 and Over, 48 and Over)

Mailing Address: 2224 Akron Peninsula Rd., Akron, OH 44313. **Telephone:** (888) 484-7422. **FAX:** (330) 923-1967. **E-Mail Address:** tom@royhobbs.com. **Website:** www.royhobbs.com.

President: Tom Giffen. **Vice President:** Ellen Giffen. **Director, Operations:** Todd Windhorst.

1998 National Championship: 30 and Over (AAA, AA and A divisions)—Nov. 1-8, Fort Myers, FL; 40 and Over (AAA, AA and A divisions)—Nov. 8-14, Fort Myers, FL; 48 and Over (AAA and AA divisions)—Nov. 15-21, Fort Myers, FL

COLORADO SILVER BULLETS

Mailing Address: 1575 Sheridan Rd. NE, Suite 200, Atlanta, GA 30324. **Telephone:** (404) 636-8200. **FAX:** (404) 636-0530.

Operated by: Hope-Beckham, Inc.

President: Bob Hope. **Chairman:** Paul Beckham.

Director, Marketing: Kimberly Sacco. **Director, Merchandise:** Michael King. **Director, Business Development:** Jeff Lamkin. **Publicist:** Jeremy Friedman. **Assistant, Public Relations:** Allison Overton. **Administrator:** Molly Leonard.

Manager/Director, Player Development: Bruce Crabbe. **General Manager:** Phil Niekro. **Coaches:** John Niekro, Joe Szekely.

Minor Leagues

NATIONALASSOCIATION

NATIONAL ASSOCIATION OF PROFESSIONAL BASEBALL LEAGUES

Office Address: 201 Bayshore Dr. SE, St. Petersburg, FL 33701. **Mailing Address:** P.O. Box A, St. Petersburg, FL 33731. **Telephone:** (813) 822-6937. **FAX:** (813) 821-5819.

Year Founded: 1965.
President: Mike Moore.
Vice President: Stan Brand (Washington, DC).
Treasurer/Vice President, Administration: Pat O'Conner. **Assistant to President/Vice President, Administration:** Carolyn Ashe.
Chief Operating Officer: Rob Dlugozima.
Secretary/General Counsel: Ben Hayes. **Assistant to General Counsel:** Debbie Carlisle.

Mike Moore

Director, Operations: Tim Brunswick. **Director, Media Relations:** Jim Ferguson. **Assistant to Director, Media Relations:** Sandi Dean. **Director, Business and Finance:** Eric Krupa. **Bookkeeper:** Lillian Patterson. **Manager, Information Services:** Corey Leong. **Receptionist:** Mary Wooters.

Official Statistician: Howe Sportsdata International, Inc., Boston Fish Pier #1, Suite 302, Boston, MA 02210. Telephone: (617) 951-0070.

1998 WINTER MEETINGS: Dec. 11-14, Nashville, TN.

Affiliated Members/Council of League Presidents

Class AAA

League	President	Telephone	FAX Number
International	Randy Mobley	(614) 791-9300	(614) 791-9009
Mexican	Pedro Treto Cisneros	(525) 557-1007	(525) 395-2454
Pacific Coast	Branch Rickey	(719) 636-3399	(719) 636-1199

Class AA

League	President	Telephone	FAX Number
Eastern	Bill Troubh	(207) 761-2700	(207) 761-7064
Southern	Arnold Fielkow	(770) 428-4749	(770) 428-4849
Texas	Tom Kayser	(210) 545-5297	(210) 545-5298

Class A Advanced

League	President	Telephone	FAX Number
California	Joe Gagliardi	(408) 369-8038	(408) 369-1409
Carolina	John Hopkins	(336) 691-9030	(336) 691-9070
Florida State	Chuck Murphy	(904) 252-7479	(904) 252-7495

Class A

League	President	Telephone	FAX Number
Midwest	George Spelius	(608) 364-1188	(608) 364-1913
South Atlantic	John Moss	(704) 739-3466	(704) 739-1974

Short-Season Class A

League	President	Telephone	FAX Number
New York-Penn	Bob Julian	(315) 733-8036	(315) 797-7403
Northwest	Bob Richmond	(541) 686-5412	(541) 484-7672

Rookie Advanced

League	President	Telephone	FAX Number
Appalachian	Lee Landers	(704) 873-5300	(704) 873-4333
Pioneer	Jim McCurdy	(509) 456-7615	(509) 456-0136

Rookie

League	President	Telephone	FAX Number
Arizona	Bob Richmond	(602) 483-8224	(602) 443-3450
Dominican Summer	Freddy Jana	(809) 563-3233	(809) 563-2455
Gulf Coast	Tom Saffell	(941) 966-6407	(941) 966-6872

National Association Board of Trustees

Class AAA (at-large)—Dan Ulmer, chairman (Louisville). **International League**—Ken Young (Norfolk). **Pacific Coast League**—Richard Holtzman (Tucson). **Eastern League**—Joe Finley (Trenton). **Southern League**—Steve Bryant (Carolina). **Texas League**—Miles Prentice, vice chairman (Midland). **California League**—Hank Stickney (Rancho Cucamonga).

Carolina League—Calvin Falwell (Lynchburg). **Florida State League—** Ken Carson, secretary (Dunedin). **Midwest League—**Dave Walker (Burlington). **South Atlantic League—**Winston Blenckstone (Hagerstown). **New York-Penn League—**Sam Nader (Oneonta). **Northwest League—** Bob Beban (Eugene). **Appalachian League—**Bill Smith (Elizabethton). **Pioneer League—**Bob Wilson (Billings). **Gulf Coast League—**Cam Bonifay (Pirates).

PROFESSIONAL BASEBALL
PROMOTION CORPORATION

Office Address: 201 Bayshore Dr. SE, St. Petersburg, FL 33701. **Mailing Address:** P.O. Box A, St. Petersburg, FL 33731. **Telephone:** (813) 822-6937. **FAX/Marketing:** (813) 894-4227. **FAX/Licensing:** (813) 825-3785.

President: Mike Moore.

Treasurer/Vice President, Administration: Pat O'Connor. **Chief Operating Officer:** Rob Dlugozima. **Assistant to Chief Operating Officer:** Kelly Butler.

Director, Licensing: Misann Ellmaker. **Assistant Director, Licensing:** Brian Earle. **Assistant to Director, Licensing:** Steve Densa.

Director, Marketing: Ron Meadows. **Assistant Directors, Marketing:** Michelle Montgomery, Dale Stickney.

Director, Professional Baseball Employment Opportunities: Ann Perkins (Old Fort, NC). **Manager, Trade Show:** Kecia Tillman. **Manager, Trademarks and Contracts:** Derek Johnson.

PROFESSIONAL BASEBALL
UMPIRE CORPORATION

Office Address: 201 Bayshore Dr. SE, St. Petersburg, FL 33701. **Mailing Address:** P.O. Box A, St. Petersburg, FL 33731. **Telephone:** (813) 822-6937. **FAX:** (813) 821-5819.

President: Mike Moore.

Treasurer/Vice President, Administration: Pat O'Connor. **Secretary/ General Counsel:** Ben Hayes.

Administrator: Eric Krupa. **Bookkeeper:** Lillian Patterson.

General Supervisor: Mike Fitzpatrick (Kalamazoo, MI).

Field Evaluators/Instructors: Dennis Cregg (Webster, MA), Mike Felt (Lansing, MI), Cris Jones (Wheat Ridge, CO). **Area Observer:** George Maloney (Pembroke Pines, FL).

MINORLEAGUES

1997 STANDINGS

Parent club in parentheses. *Split-season champion.

AMERICAN ASSOCIATION   AAA

EAST	W	L	PCT	GB	Manager
Buffalo (Indians)	87	57	.604	—	Brian Graham
Indianapolis (Reds)	85	59	.590	2	Dave Miley
Nashville (White Sox)	74	69	.517	12½	Tom Spencer
Louisville (Cardinals)	58	85	.406	28½	Gaylen Pitts

WEST	W	L	PCT	GB	Manager
Iowa (Cubs)	74	69	.517	—	Tim Johnson
New Orleans (Astros)	74	70	.514	½	Steve Swisher/Matt Galante
Oklahoma City (Rangers)	61	82	.427	13	Greg Biagini
Omaha (Royals)	61	83	.424	13½	Mike Jirschele

PLAYOFFS: Semifinals (best-of-5)—Iowa defeated New Orleans 3-0; Buffalo defeated Indianapolis 3-2. **Finals** (best-of-5)—Buffalo defeated Iowa 3-0.

INTERNATIONAL LEAGUE   AAA

EAST	W	L	PCT	GB	Manager
Rochester (Orioles)	83	58	.589	—	Marv Foley
Pawtucket (Red Sox)	81	60	.574	2	Ken Macha
Scranton/W-B (Phillies)	66	76	.465	17½	Marc Bombard
Syracuse (Blue Jays)	55	87	.387	28½	Garth Iorg
Ottawa (Expos)	54	86	.386	28½	Pat Kelly

WEST	W	L	PCT	GB	Manager
Columbus (Yankees)	79	63	.556	—	Stump Merrill
Charlotte (Marlins)	76	65	.539	2½	Carlos Tosca
Norfolk (Mets)	75	67	.528	4	Rick Dempsey
Richmond (Braves)	70	72	.493	9	Bill Dancy
Toledo (Tigers)	68	73	.482	10½	Glenn Ezell/Gene Roof

PLAYOFFS: Semifinals (best-of-5)—Rochester defeated Pawtucket 3-1; Columbus defeated Charlotte 3-1. **Finals** (best-of-5)—Rochester defeated Columbus 3-2.

PACIFIC COAST LEAGUE   AAA

NORTH	W	L	PCT	GB	Manager
*Edmonton (Athletics)	80	64	.556	—	Gary Jones
Tacoma (Mariners)	75	66	.532	3½	Dave Myers
*Vancouver (Angels)	75	68	.524	4½	Bruce Hines
Salt Lake (Twins)	72	71	.503	7½	Phil Roof
Calgary (Pirates)	60	78	.435	17	Trent Jewett

SOUTH	W	L	PCT	GB	Manager
*Phoenix (Giants)	88	55	.615	—	Ron Wotus
*Colorado Spr. (Rockies)	76	64	.543	10½	Paul Zuvella
Tucson (Brewers)	64	78	.451	23½	Tim Ireland/Bob Mariano
Albuquerque (Dodgers)	62	79	.440	25	Glenn Hoffman
Las Vegas (Padres)	56	85	.397	31	Jerry Royster

PLAYOFFS: Semifinals (best-of-5)—Edmonton defeated Vancouver 3-0; Phoenix defeated Colorado Springs 3-0. **Finals** (best-of-5)—Edmonton defeated Phoenix 3-1.

EASTERN LEAGUE   AA

NORTH	W	L	PCT	GB	Manager
Portland (Marlins)	79	63	.556	—	Fredi Gonzalez
Norwich (Yankees)	73	69	.514	6	Trey Hillman
New Britain (Twins)	70	72	.493	9	Al Newman
Binghamton (Mets)	66	76	.465	13	Rick Sweet
New Haven (Rockies)	64	78	.451	15	Bill Hayes

SOUTH	W	L	PCT	GB	Manager
Harrisburg (Expos)	86	56	.606	—	Rick Sofield
Bowie (Orioles)	75	67	.528	11	Joe Ferguson
Reading (Phillies)	74	68	.521	12	Al LeBoeuf
Trenton (Red Sox)	71	70	.504	14½	DeMarlo Hale
Akron (Indians)	51	90	.362	34½	Jeff Datz

PLAYOFFS: Semifinals (best-of-5)—Portland defeated Norwich 3-2; Harrisburg defeated Bowie 3-2. **Finals** (best-of-5)—Harrisburg defeated Portland 3-1.

SOUTHERN LEAGUE   AA

EAST	W	L	PCT	GB	Manager
*Knoxville (Blue Jays)	75	63	.543	—	Omar Malave

	W	L	PCT	GB	
*Greenville (Braves)	74	66	.529	2	Randy Ingle
Jacksonville (Tigers)	66	73	.475	9½	Dave Anderson
Orlando (Cubs)	63	75	.457	12	Dave Trembley
Carolina (Pirates)	55	82	.401	19½	Marc Hill/Jeff Banister
WEST	**W**	**L**	**PCT**	**GB**	**Manager**
*Huntsville (Athletics)	77	62	.554	—	Mike Quade
Birmingham (White Sox)	76	62	.551	½	Dave Huppert
*Mobile (Padres)	69	68	.504	7	Mike Ramsey
Chattanooga (Reds)	70	69	.504	7	Mark Berry
Memphis (Mariners)	67	72	.482	10	Dave Brundage

PLAYOFFS: Semifinals (best-of-5)—Greenville defeated Knoxville 3-1; Huntsville defeated Mobile 3-2. **Finals** (best-of-5)—Greenville defeated Huntsville 3-2.

TEXAS LEAGUE   AA

EAST	**W**	**L**	**PCT**	**GB**	**Manager**
**Shreveport (Giants)	76	62	.551	—	Carlos Lezcano
Arkansas (Cardinals)	68	72	.486	9	Rick Mahler
Jackson (Astros)	66	73	.475	10½	Dave Engle
Tulsa (Rangers)	61	78	.439	15½	Bobby Jones
WEST	**W**	**L**	**PCT**	**GB**	**Manager**
**San Antonio (Dodgers)	84	55	.604	—	John Shelby
El Paso (Brewers)	74	66	.529	10½	Dave Machemer
Midland (Angels)	64	75	.460	20	Mitch Seoane
Wichita (Royals)	64	76	.457	20½	Ron Johnson

PLAYOFFS: Finals (best-of-7)—San Antonio defeated Shreveport 4-3.

CALIFORNIA LEAGUE   A

FREEWAY	**W**	**L**	**PCT**	**GB**	**Manager**
*Rancho Cuca. (Padres)	77	63	.550	—	Mike Basso
Visalia (Athletics)	71	69	.507	6	Tony DeFrancesco
*San Bern. (Dodgers)	68	72	.486	9	Del Crandall/Dino Ebel
Bakersfield (Giants)	62	78	.443	15	Glenn Tufts/Keith Bodie
Lake Elsinore (Angels)	61	79	.436	16	Don Long
VALLEY	**W**	**L**	**PCT**	**GB**	**Manager**
*High Desert (D'backs)	83	57	.593	—	Chris Speier
Lancaster (Mariners)	75	66	.532	8½	Rick Burleson
Modesto (Athletics)	74	67	.525	9½	Jeffrey Leonard
*Stockton (Brewers)	70	70	.500	13	Greg Mahlberg
San Jose (Giants)	60	80	.429	23	Frank Cacciatore

PLAYOFFS: First Round (best-of-3)—San Bernardino defeated Visalia 2-0; Lancaster defeated Stockton 2-1. **Semifinals** (best-of-5)—San Bernardino defeated Rancho Cucamonga 3-2; High Desert defeated Lancaster 3-0. **Finals** (best-of-5)—High Desert defeated San Bernardino 3-0.

CAROLINA LEAGUE   A

NORTH	**W**	**L**	**PCT**	**GB**	**Manager**
*Lynchburg (Pirates)	82	58	.586	—	Jeff Banister/Jeff Richardson
Prince William (Cardinals)	69	70	.496	12½	Roy Silver
*Frederick (Orioles)	69	71	.493	13	Dave Hilton
Wilmington (Royals)	62	78	.443	20	John Mizerock
SOUTH	**W**	**L**	**PCT**	**GB**	**Manager**
**Kinston (Indians)	87	53	.621	—	Joel Skinner
Salem (Rockies)	63	75	.457	23	Bill McGuire
Durham (Braves)	63	76	.453	23½	Paul Runge
Winston-Salem (White Sox)	63	77	.450	24	Mike Heath/Mark Haley

PLAYOFFS: Semifinals (best-of-3)—Lynchburg defeated Frederick 2-0. **Finals** (best-of-5)—Lynchburg defeated Kinston 3-1.

FLORIDA STATE LEAGUE   A

EAST	**W**	**L**	**PCT**	**GB**	**Manager**
*Kissimmee (Astros)	71	66	.518	—	John Tamargo
*Vero Beach (Dodgers)	70	67	.511	1	John Shoemaker
West Palm Beach (Expos)	69	66	.511	1	Doug Sisson
Daytona (Cubs)	65	73	.471	16½	Steve Roadcap
Brevard County (Marlins)	62	76	.449	19½	Lorenzo Bundy
St. Lucie (Mets)	54	81	.400	16	John Gibbons
WEST	**W**	**L**	**PCT**	**GB**	**Manager**
*St. Pete (Devil Rays)	81	56	.591	—	Bill Evers
*Lakeland (Tigers)	81	57	.587	½	Mark Meleski
Fort Myers (Twins)	81	58	.583	1	John Russell
Tampa (Yankees)	70	66	.515	10½	Lee Mazzilli
Clearwater (Phillies)	70	68	.507	11½	Roy Majtyka
Charlotte (Rangers)	68	71	.489	14	Butch Wynegar

| Sarasota (Red Sox) | 63 | 75 | .457 | 18½ | Rob Derksen |
| Dunedin (Blue Jays) | 57 | 82 | .410 | 25 | Dennis Holmberg |

PLAYOFFS: Semifinals (best-of-3)—Vero Beach defeated Kissimmee 2-1; St. Petersburg defeated Lakeland 2-0. **Finals** (best-of-5)—St. Petersburg defeated Vero Beach 3-2.

MIDWEST LEAGUE — A

EAST	W	L	PCT	GB	Manager
**West Michigan (Tigers)	92	39	.702	—	Bruce Fields
Michigan (Red Sox)	70	67	.511	25	Billy Gardner Jr.
Lansing (Royals)	69	68	.504	26	Bob Herold
Fort Wayne (Twins)	68	67	.504	26	Mike Boulanger
South Bend (D'backs)	54	83	.394	41	Dickie Scott
CENTRAL	W	L	PCT	GB	Manager
*Wisconsin (Mariners)	76	63	.547	—	Gary Varsho
*Kane County (Marlins)	70	68	.507	5½	Lynn Jones
Peoria (Cardinals)	70	69	.504	6	Joe Cunningham
Rockford (Cubs)	66	66	.500	8	Ruben Amaro
Beloit (Brewers)	60	73	.451	13	Luis Salazar
WEST	W	L	PCT	GB	Manager
*Burlington (Reds)	72	68	.514	—	Phillip Wellman
Clinton (Padres)	65	71	.478	5	Tom LeVasseur
*Cedar Rapids (Angels)	62	76	.449	9	Mario Mendoza
Quad City (Astros)	59	75	.440	10	Manny Acta

PLAYOFFS: First Round (best-of-3)—Cedar Rapids defeated Burlington 2-0; Kane County defeated Wisconsin 2-0; Fort Wayne defeated West Michigan 2-0; Lansing defeated Michigan 2-1. **Semifinals** (best-of-3)—Lansing defeated Fort Wayne 2-0; Kane County defeated Cedar Rapids 2-0. **Finals** (best-of-5)—Lansing defeated Kane County 3-2.

SOUTH ATLANTIC LEAGUE — A

NORTH	W	L	PCT	GB	Manager
**Charleston, W.Va. (Reds)	76	62	.551	—	Barry Lyons
Delmarva (Orioles)	77	65	.542	1	Tom Shields/Tom Trebelhorn
Cape Fear (Expos)	66	74	.471	11	Phil Stephenson
Hagerstown (Blue Jays)	65	73	.471	11	J.J. Cannon
CENTRAL	W	L	PCT	GB	Manager
*Capital City (Mets)	77	63	.550	—	D. Mansolino/J. Stephenson
Hickory (White Sox)	76	64	.543	1	Chris Cron
*Greensboro (Yankees)	75	65	.536	2	Tom Nieto
Piedmont (Phillies)	70	72	.493	8	Ken Oberkfell
Asheville (Rockies)	62	76	.449	14	Ron Gideon
Charleston, S.C. (Devil Rays)	60	82	.423	18	Scott Fletcher
SOUTH	W	L	PCT	GB	Manager
**Macon (Braves)	80	60	.571	—	Brian Snitker
Augusta (Pirates)	71	71	.500	10	Jeff Richardson/Scott Little
Savannah (Dodgers)	63	77	.450	17	John Shelby
Columbus (Indians)	62	76	.449	17	Jack Mull

PLAYOFFS: First Round (best-of-3)—Delmarva defeated Hickory 2-0; Greensboro defeated Capital City 2-0; Macon defeated Augusta 2-1; Charleston W.Va., defeated Cape Fear 2-0. **Semifinals** (best-of-3)—Greensboro defeated Macon 2-0; Delmarva defeated Charleston W.Va., 2-1. **Finals** (best-of-3)—Delmarva defeated Greensboro 2-0.

NEW YORK-PENN LEAGUE — SHORT-SEASON A

McNAMARA	W	L	PCT	GB	Manager
Pittsfield (Mets)	42	32	.568	—	Doug Davis
Lowell (Red Sox)	38	38	.500	5	Dick Berardino
New Jersey (Cardinals)	35	39	.473	7	Jeff Shireman
Hudson Valley (Devil Rays)	35	40	.467	7½	Julio Garcia
Vermont (Expos)	35	41	.461	8	Kevin Higgins
PINCKNEY	W	L	PCT	GB	Manager
Oneonta (Yankees)	49	25	.662	—	Joe Arnold
Watertown (Indians)	39	36	.520	10½	Ted Kubiak
Utica (Marlins)	36	38	.486	13	Juan Bustabad
Williamsport (Cubs)	29	46	.387	20½	Bobby Ralston
Auburn (Astros)	29	47	.382	21	Mike Rojas
STEDLER	W	L	PCT	GB	Manager
Erie (Pirates)	50	26	.658	—	Marty Brown
Batavia (Phillies)	47	27	.635	2	Greg Legg
St. Catharines (Blue Jays)	35	40	.467	14½	Rocket Wheeler
Jamestown (Tigers)	25	49	.338	24	Dwight Lowry/Matt Martin

PLAYOFFS: Semifinals (best-of-3)—Batavia defeated Oneonta 2-0; Pittsfield defeated Erie 2-0. **Finals** (best-of-3)—Pittsfield defeated Batavia 2-1.

NORTHWEST LEAGUE — SHORT-SEASON A

NORTH
NORTH	W	L	PCT	GB	Manager
Boise (Angels)	51	25	.671	—	Tom Kotchman
Spokane (Royals)	45	31	.592	6	Jeff Garber
Everett (Mariners)	29	47	.382	22	Orlando Gomez
Yakima (Dodgers)	23	53	.303	28	Joe Vavra

SOUTH	W	L	PCT	GB	Manager
Portland (Rockies)	44	32	.579	—	Jim Eppard
So. Oregon (Athletics)	41	35	.539	3	John Kuehl
Salem-Keizer (Giants)	40	36	.526	4	Shane Turner
Eugene (Braves)	31	45	.408	13	Jim Saul

PLAYOFFS: Finals (best-of-3)—Boise defeated Portland 2-0.

APPALACHIAN LEAGUE — ROOKIE

EAST	W	L	PCT	GB	Manager
Bluefield (Orioles)	40	29	.580	—	Bobby Dickerson
Princeton (Devil Rays)	39	30	.565	1	Charlie Montoyo
Burlington (Indians)	32	38	.471	7½	Harry Spilman/Joe Mikulik
Danville (Braves)	30	38	.441	9½	Rick Albert
Martinsville (Phillies)	29	39	.426	10½	Kelly Heath

WEST	W	L	PCT	GB	Manager
Pulaski (Rangers)	43	25	.632	—	Julio Cruz
Elizabethton (Twins)	38	30	.559	5	Jose Marzan
Kingsport (Mets)	37	31	.544	6	Ken Berry
Bristol (White Sox)	30	38	.441	13	Nick Capra
Johnson City (Cardinals)	23	45	.338	20	Steve Turco

PLAYOFFS: Semifinals (sudden death)—Bluefield defeated Princeton 1-0.
Finals (best-of-3)—Bluefield defeated Pulaski 2-0.

PIONEER LEAGUE — ROOKIE

NORTH	W	L	PCT	GB	Manager
*Great Falls (Dodgers)	40	32	.556	—	Mickey Hatcher
*Lethbridge (D'backs)	39	33	.542	1	Tommy Jones
Helena (Brewers)	37	34	.521	2½	Alex Morales
Medicine Hat (Blue Jays)	26	46	.361	14	Marty Pevey

SOUTH	W	L	PCT	GB	Manager
*Billings (Reds)	39	32	.549	—	Donnie Scott
*Idaho Falls (Padres)	39	33	.542	½	Don Werner
Ogden (Brewers)	37	35	.514	2½	Bernie Moncallo
Butte (Angels)	30	42	.417	9½	Bill Lachemann

PLAYOFFS: Semifinals (best-of-3)—Great Falls defeated Lethbridge 2-0; Billings defeated Idaho Falls 2-0. **Finals** (best-of-3)—Billings defeated Great Falls 2-0.

GULF COAST LEAGUE — ROOKIE

EAST	W	L	PCT	GB	Manager
St. Lucie Mets	42	18	.700	—	Mickey Brantley/Doug Flynn
Melbourne Marlins	31	28	.525	10½	Jon Deeble
West Palm Beach Expos	25	35	.417	17	Luis Dorante
West Palm Beach Braves	21	38	.356	20½	Frank Howard

NORTH	W	L	PCT	GB	Manager
Tampa Yankees	40	20	.667	—	Ken Dominguez
Lakeland Tigers	31	29	.517	9	Kevin Bradshaw
St. Petersburg Devil Rays	25	35	.417	15	Bobby Ramos
Kissimmee Astros	24	36	.400	16	Julio Linares

WEST	W	L	PCT	GB	Manager
Fort Myers Royals	36	24	.600	—	Al Pedrique
Port Charlotte Rangers	34	26	.567	2	James Byrd
Fort Myers Red Sox	31	28	.525	4½	Luis Aguayo
Fort Myers Twins	28	32	.467	8	Steve Liddle
Bradenton Pirates	27	32	.458	8½	Woody Huyke
Sarasota Orioles	27	33	.450	9	Butch Davis
Sarasota White Sox	26	34	.433	10	Roly de Armas

PLAYOFFS: Semifinals (sudden death)—Mets defeated Yankees 1-0; Rangers defeated Royals 1-0. **Finals** (best-of-3)—Mets defeated Rangers 2-0.

ARIZONA LEAGUE — ROOKIE

	W	L	PCT	GB	Manager
Mesa Cubs	34	21	.618	—	Terry Kennedy
Peoria Mariners	30	26	.536	5½	Darrin Garner
Phoenix Athletics	29	27	.518	6½	Juan Navarrete
Phoenix Diamondbacks	27	29	.482	7½	B.Butterfield/D. Wakamatsu
Peoria Padres	25	30	.455	9	Randy Whisler
Chandler Rockies	22	34	.393	12½	Tim Blackwell

PLAYOFFS: None.

INTERNATIONAL LEAGUE

Class AAA

Office Address: 55 S. High St., Suite 202, Dublin, OH 43017. **Telephone:** (614) 791-9300. **FAX:** (614) 791-9009. **E-Mail Address:** office@ilbaseball.com. **Website:** www.ilbaseball.com.

Years League Active: 1884-.

President/Treasurer: Randy Mobley.

Vice Presidents: Harold Cooper, Dave Rosenfield (Norfolk), Tex Simone (Syracuse), George Sisler Jr. **Corporate Secretary:** Richard Davis.

Randy Mobley

Directors: Peter Anlyan (Durham), Bruce Baldwin (Richmond), Don Beaver (Charlotte), Gene Cook (Toledo), Howard Darwin (Ottawa), Rick Muntean (Scranton/Wilkes-Barre), Bob Rich Jr. (Buffalo), Dave Rosenfield (Norfolk), Ken Schnacke (Columbus), Max Schumacher (Indianapolis), Naomi Silver (Rochester), John Simone (Syracuse), Mike Tamburro (Pawtucket), Dan Ulmer (Louisville).

Office Manager: Marcia Willison. **Administrative Assistant:** Nathan Blackmon.

1998 Opening Date: April 9. **Closing Date:** Sept. 7.

Regular Season: 144 games.

Division Structure: North—Buffalo, Ottawa, Pawtucket, Rochester, Scranton/Wilkes-Barre, Syracuse. **West**—Columbus, Indianapolis, Louisville, Toledo. **South**—Charlotte, Durham, Norfolk, Richmond.

Playoff Format: West winner plays South winner in best-of-5 series; wild-card club (non-division winner with best record) plays North winner in best-of-5 series. First-round winners meet in best-of-5 series for league championship.

All-Star Game: July 8 at Norfolk (IL vs. Pacific Coast League).

Roster Limit: 23 active, until midnight Aug. 10 when roster can expand to 25. **Player Eligibility Rule:** No restrictions.

Brand of Baseball: Rawlings ROM-INT.

Statistician: Howe Sportsdata International, Boston Fish Pier, West Bldg. #1, Suite 302, Boston MA 02210.

Umpires: Mark Barron (Lawrenceville, GA), Jorge Bauza (San Juan, PR), Mike Billings (Pembroke Pines, FL), C.B. Bucknor (Brooklyn, NY), Pat Connors (Berlin, WI), Field Culbreth (Inman, SC), Kerwin Danley (Chandler, AZ), Lazaro Diaz (Miami, FL), Paul Emmel (Sanford, MI), Mark Facto (Ellicott City, MD), Marty Foster (Beloit, WI), Brian Gibbons (South Bend, IN), Greg Gibson (Catlettsburg, KY), Ed Hickox (Daytona Beach, FL), Dan Iassogna (Smyrna, GA), Jerry Meals (Salem, OH), Paul Nauert (Lawrenceville, GA), Brian O'Nora (Youngstown, OH), Scott Potter (South Daytona, FL), Jim Reynolds (Wethersfield, CT), Willie Rodriguez (Bayamon, PR), Paul Schrieber (Louisville, KY), Jeff Schrupp (Birmingham, AL), Mitch Schwark (Battle Creek, MI), Tim Timmons (Columbus, OH), Mike VanVleet (Battle Creek, MI), Mark Wegner (Birchwood, MN), Bill Welke (Coldwater, MI), Hunter Wendelstedt (Ormond Beach, FL).

Stadium Information

Club	Stadium	Dimensions			Capacity	'97 Att.
		LF	CF	RF		
Buffalo#	North AmeriCare	325	404	325	21,050	696,193
Charlotte	Knights Castle	325	400	325	10,000	318,102
Columbus	Cooper	355	400	330	15,000	507,810
Durham†	Durham Bulls Athletic	305	400	327	10,000	381,589
Indianapolis#	Victory Field	320	402	320	15,500	618,095
Louisville#	Cardinal	360	405	312	33,600	408,550
Norfolk	Harbor Park	333	410	338	12,067	507,328
Ottawa	JetForm Park	325	404	325	10,332	266,568
Pawtucket	McCoy	325	380	325	7,002	474,557
Richmond	The Diamond	330	402	330	12,150	512,727
Rochester	Frontier Field	335	402	325	10,868	512,570
Scranton	Lackawanna County	330	408	330	10,982	441,413
Syracuse	P&C	328	404	328	11,602	400,804
Toledo	Ned Skeldon	325	410	325	10,025	325,532

#Member of disbanded American Association in 1997.
†Expansion team.

Buffalo BISONS

Office Address: 275 Washington St., Buffalo, NY 14203. **Mailing Address:** P.O. Box 450, Buffalo, NY 14205. **Telephone:** (716) 846-2000. **FAX:** (716) 852-6530. **E-Mail Address:** bisons@buffnet.net. **Website:** www.bisons.com.

Affiliation (first year): Cleveland Indians (1995). **Years in League:** 1886-90, 1912-70, 1998.

Ownership, Management

Operated by: Rich Products Corp.

Principal Owner/President: Robert E. Rich Jr. **Chairman:** Robert E. Rich Sr.

President, Rich Entertainment Group: Melinda Rich. **Executive Vice President, Rich Entertainment Group:** Jon Dandes. **Vice President /Treasurer:** David Rich. **Vice President/Secretary:** William Gisel Jr. **Vice President/Sales and Marketing:** Marta Hiczewski.

General Manager: Mike Buczkowski. **Controller:** John Dougherty. **Senior Account Representatives:** Jim Mack, Leigh Balcom, Ted Rich, Pete Sinagra, Kathleen Ascioti. **Stadium Operations Manager:** John Wiedeman. **Director, Public Relations/Marketing:** Tom Burns. **Assistant, Public Relations:** Matt Herring. **Game Day Director/CSP Assistant:** Alex Moser. **Coordinator, Community Relations:** Don Feldman. **Director, Ticket Sales:** Jim Mack. **Director, Merchandising:** Nancy Martin. **Director, Food Services:** Eric Nelson. **Office Manager:** Margaret Russo. **Head Groundskeeper:** Jim Hornung. **Director, Clubhouse Operations:** Ron Krauza.

Field Staff

Manager: Jeff Datz. **Coach:** Dave Keller. **Pitching Coach:** Bud Black. **Trainer:** Lee Kuntz.

Game Information

Radio Announcer: Jim Rosenhaus. **No. of Games Broadcast:** Home-72, Away-72. **Flagship Station:** WWKB 1520-AM.

PA Announcer: John Summers. **Official Scorers:** Duke McGuire, Mike Kelly.

Stadium Name (year opened): North AmeriCare Park (1988). **Location:** From north, take I-190 to Elm Street exit, left onto Swan Street. From east, take I-90 West to exit 51 (Route 33) to end, exit at Oak Street, right onto Swan Street. From west, take I-90 East, exit 53 to I-190 North, exit at Elm Street, left onto Swan Street.

Standard Game Times: 7:05 p.m.; Wed 1:05; Sat. 2:05, 7:05; Sun 2:05.

Visiting Club Hotel: Holiday Inn Downtown, 620 Delaware Ave., Buffalo, NY 14202. Telephone: (716) 886-2121.

Charlotte KNIGHTS

Office Address: 2280 Deerfield Dr., Fort Mill, SC 29715. **Mailing Address:** P.O. Box 1207, Fort Mill, SC 29716. **Telephone:** (704) 364-6637. **FAX:** (704) 329-2155, (803) 548-8055. **E-Mail Address:** knights1@mind-spring.com. **Website:** www.aaaknights.com.

Affiliation (first year): Florida Marlins (1995). **Years in League:** 1993-.

Ownership, Management

Operated by: Knights Baseball, LLC.

Principal Owners: Don Beaver, Derick Close, Bill Allen.

President/Chairman: Don Beaver.

Vice President/General Manager: Marty Steele. **Assistant General Manager:** Chris Carroll. **Director, Sales/Marketing:** Julie Sigmon. **Director, Promotions/Game Operations:** Derrick Grubbs. **Director, Broadcasting:** Matt Swierad. **Director, Community Relations:** Tommy John. **Director, Media/Public Relations:** Melissa Booker. **Director, Advertising/Event Operations:** Jon Percival. **Manager, Ticket Operations:** Jamie Hall. **Ticket Operations/Team Travel:** Erin Dunne. **Manager, Ticket Sales:** Randy Habluetzel. **Ticket Sales Representatives:** Anthony DeNino, Olivia Kaylor, Jack Murray. **Mascot Coordinator:** Billy Yandle. **Facility Manager:** Ed Hrynkow. **Head Groundskeeper:** Joey Simmons. **Assistant Groundskeeper:** Marty Kaufman. **Building Operations:** Dean Henry. **Office**

Manager: Marie Andersen. **Clubhouse Manager:** Jay Barnhouse.

Field Staff

Manager: Fredi Gonzalez. **Coach:** Adrian Garrett. **Pitching Coach:** Randy Hennis. **Trainer:** Mike Leon.

Game Information

Radio Announcers: Matt Swierad, Tommy John. **No. of Games Broadcast:** Home-72, Away-72. **Flagship Station:** Unavailable.

PA Announcer: Derrick Grubbs. **Official Scorer:** Sam Copeland.

Stadium Name (year opened): Knights Castle (1990). **Location:** Exit 88 off I-77, east on Gold Hill Road. **Standard Game Times:** 7 p.m., Sun. 2.

Visiting Club Hotel: Holiday Inn Express-Pineville, 9820 Leitner Dr., Pineville, NC 28134. Telephone: (704) 341-1190.

Columbus
CLIPPERS

Office Address: 1155 West Mound St., Columbus, OH 43223. **Telephone:** (614) 462-5250. **FAX:** (614) 462-3271. **E-Mail Address:** colsclippers@earthlink.net. **Website:** www.clippersbaseball.com.

Affiliation (first year): New York Yankees (1979). **Years in League:** 1955-70, 1977-.

Ownership, Management

Operated by: Columbus Baseball Team, Inc.

Principal Owner: Franklin County, Ohio.

Chairman: Donald Borror. **President:** Richard Smith.

General Manager: Ken Schnacke. **Assistant General Manager:** Mark Warren. **Assistant GM/Park Supervisor:** Dick Fitzpatrick. **Director, Stadium Operations:** Steve Dalin. **Director, Ticket Sales:** Scott Ziegler. **Director, Media Relations:** Keif Fetch. **Director, Sales:** Mark Galuska. **Director, Marketing:** Shawne Beck. **Director, Merchandising:** Danny Mummey. **Director, Advertising:** Todd Pfeil. **Director, Finance:** Chris Burleson. **Director, Publications:** Chris Daugherty. **Assistant to General Manager:** Judi Timmons. **Secretary:** Monica Schemrich. **Receptionist:** Kelly Ryther.

Field Staff

Manager: Stump Merrill. **Coaches:** Hop Cassady, Tony Perezchica. **Pitching Coach:** Oscar Acosta. **Trainer:** Darren London.

Game Information

Radio Announcers: Terry Smith, Brooks Melchior. **No. of Games Broadcast:** Home-72, Away-72. **Flagship Station:** WBNS 1460-AM.

PA Announcers: John Ross, Bob Lewis. **Official Scorers:** Chuck Emmerling, Kris Hutchins, Randy Parker, Jeff Rapp, Joe Santry.

Stadium Name (year opened): Cooper Stadium (1977). **Location:** From north/south, I-71 to I-70 West, exit at Mound Street. From west, I-70 East, exit at Broad Street, east to Glenwood, south to Mound Street. From east, I-70 West, exit at Mound Street. **Standard Game Times:** 7:15 p.m.; Sat. 6:15, 7:15; Sun. 2:15, 6:15.

Visiting Club Hotel: Best Western-Columbus North, 888 East Dublin-Granville Rd., Columbus, OH 43229. Telephone: (614) 888-8230.

Durham
BULLS

Office Address: 409 Blackwell St., Durham, NC 27701. **Mailing Address:** P.O. Box 507, Durham, NC 27702. **Telephone:** (919) 687-6500. **FAX:** (919) 687-6560.

Affiliation (first year): Tampa Bay Devil Rays (1998). **Years in League:** 1998.

Ownership, Management

Operated by: Capitol Broadcasting Co., Inc.

President/Chief Executive Officer: Jim Goodmon.

Division Vice President: George Habel. **Vice President/Legal Counsel:** Mike Hill.

Vice President/General Manager: Peter Anlyan. **Assistant General Manager:** Gillian Zucker. **Manager, Sales:** Matt West. **Manager, Ticket Sales:** Barry Gibson. **Manager, Accounting:** Raechel Chaney. **Manager,**

Office Systems: Andrea Harris. **Facility Superintendent:** Steve Banos. **Head Groundskeeper:** Mike Boekholder. **Assistant Head Grounds-keeper:** Ed Kovalesky. **Account Executives, Sponsorship:** Mike Davis, Chip Hutchinson, Melanie Weaver. **Coordinator, Promotions:** Brian Crichton. **Coordinator, Public Relations:** Missy Weening. **Assistant, Ticket Sales:** Tammy Weis. **Coordinators, Group Outings:** Ryan Fay, Jon Bishop. **Representative, Ticket Sales:** Mitch Mann. **Coordinator, Box Office:** Doug Augis. **Box Office:** Jerry Mach. **Supervisor, Operations:** Tim Neubauer. **Executive Secretary:** Valerie Bellamy. **Accouting Clerk:** Anna Maynard. **Assistant, Accouting/Ballpark:** Jewell White. **Mascot Coordinator:** Graham Hackett. **Receptionist/Secretary:** Barbara Goss.

Field Staff

Manager: Bill Evers. **Coach:** Dave Hilton. **Pitching Coach:** Pete Filson. **Trainer:** Paul Harker.

Game Information

Radio Announcer: Steve Barnes. **No. of Games Broadcast:** Home-72, Away-72. **Flagship Station:** WDNC 620-AM.

PA Announcer: Bill Law. **Official Scorer:** Brent Belvin.

Stadium Name (year opened): Durham Bulls Athletic Park (1995). **Location:** From Raleigh—I-40 West to Hwy. 147 North, exit 12B to Willard, two blocks on Willard to stadium. From I-85—Gregson Street exit to downtown, left on Chapel Hill Street, right on Mangum Street. **Standard Game Times:** 7 p.m.; Sun. 5.

Visiting Club Hotel: The Durham Omni, 201 Foster St., Durham, NC 27701. Telephone: (919) 683-6664.

Indianapolis INDIANS

Office Address: 501 West Maryland St., Indianapolis, IN 46225. **Telephone:** (317) 269-3542. **FAX:** (317) 269-3541. **E-Mail Address:** indians@indyindians.com. **Website:** www.indyindians.com.

Affiliation (first year): Cincinnati Reds (1993). **Years in League:** 1963, 1998.

Ownership, Management

Operated by: Indians, Inc.

Chairman/President: Max Schumacher.

General Manager: Cal Burleson. **Director, Business Operations:** Brad Morris. **Director, Stadium Operations:** Randy Lewandowski. **Head Groundskeeper:** Gary Shepherd. **Director, Media/Public Relations:** Mark Walpole. **Director, Sales/Marketing:** Daryle Keith. **Director, Community Relations:** Chris Herndon. **Director, Ticket Sales:** Mike Schneider. **Assistant Ticket Manager:** Tim Holms. **Director, Group Sales:** Suzy Pavone. **Director, Merchandising:** Mark Schumacher. **Director, Food Services:** Mike Moos. **Director, Special Projects:** Bruce Schumacher. **Clubhouse Operations:** John Rinaldi. **Manager, Personnel:** Belinda Shepherd. **Facility Director:** Bill Sampson. **Director, Maintenance:** Jack Kiplinger.

Field Staff

Manager: Dave Miley. **Coach:** Russ Nixon. **Pitching Coach:** Grant Jackson. **Trainer:** John Young.

Game Information

Radio Announcers: Howard Kellman, Brian Giffin. **No. of Games Broadcast:** Home-72, Away-72. **Flagship Stations:** WNDE 1260-AM, WSYW 107.1-FM.

PA Announcer: Bruce Schumacher. **Official Scorers:** Kim Rogers, Bill MacAfee.

Stadium Name (year opened): Victory Field (1996). **Location:** I-70 to West Street exit, north on West Street to ballpark; I-65 to Martin Luther King and West Street exit, south on West Street to ballpark. **Standard Game Times:** 7 p.m.; Sun. 2, 6.

Visiting Club Hotel: Ramada East, 7701 East 42nd St., Indianapolis, IN 46226. Telephone: (317) 897-4000.

Louisville REDBIRDS

Office Address: Cardinal Stadium, Phillips Lane at Freedom Way, Louisville, KY 40213. **Mailing Address:** P.O. Box 36407, Louisville, KY 40213. **Telephone:** (502) 367-9121. **FAX:** (502) 368-5120.

Affiliation (first year): Milwaukee Brewers (1998). **Years in League:** 1998-.

Ownership, Management
Operated by: Louisville Baseball Club, Inc.

Owners: Dan Ulmer, John A. Hillerich III, Dale Owens, C. Edward Glasscock, Kenny Huber, Jim Morrissey, Tom Musselman, Robert Stallings, Gary Ulmer.

Chairman: Dan Ulmer. **President:** Gary Ulmer.

Vice President/General Manager: Dale Owens. **Assistant General Manager:** Greg Galiette. **Director, Baseball Operations:** Mary Barney. **Director, Sales:** David Gardner. **Bookkeeper:** Michele Anderson. **Director, Broadcasting:** Jim Kelch. **Director, Stadium Operations:** Scott Shoemaker. **Account Executives:** Dave Allen, Dave Arnold. **Director, Public Relations:** Matt Gorsky. **Ticket Manager:** George Veith. **Sales:** Kevin Kelley, Wayne Willis. **Assistant, Operations:** Mark Shepherd.

Field Staff
Manager: Gary Allenson. **Coach:** Luis Salazar. **Pitching Coach:** Mike Caldwell. **Trainer:** Richard Stark.

Game Information
Radio Announcers: Mark Gorsky, Jim Kelch. **No. of Games Broadcast:** Home-72, Away-72. **Flagship Station:** WKJK 1080-AM.

PA Announcer: Charles Gazaway. **Official Scorer:** Unavailable.

Stadium Name (year opened): Cardinal Stadium (1956). **Location:** Intersection of I-65 and I-264 at Kentucky Fair and Expo Center. **Standard Game Times:** 7:05 p.m.; Tue. 12; Sun. 2.

Visiting Club Hotels: Executive Inn, 978 Phillips Lane, Louisville, KY 40209. Telephone: (502) 367-6161.

Norfolk TIDES

Office Address: 150 Park Ave., Norfolk, VA 23510. **Telephone:** (757) 622-2222. **FAX:** (757) 624-9090. **E-Mail Address:** info@norfolktides.com. **Website:** www.norfolktides.com.

Affiliation (first year): New York Mets (1969). **Years in League:** 1969-.

Ownership, Management
Operated by: Tides Baseball Club, LP.

President: Ken Young.

General Manager: Dave Rosenfield. **Assistant General Manager:** Joe Gorza. **Director, Sales/Promotions:** Jay Richardson. **Director, Media Relations:** Shon Sbarra. **Director, Broadcasting:** Jack Ankerson. **Director, Community Relations:** Susan Pinckney. **Director, Ticket Operations:** Glenn Riggs. **Ticket Manager:** Linda Waisanen. **Accounting Manager:** Lew Schwartz. **Director, Group Sales:** Dave Harrah. **Assistant, Group Sales:** Steve Podjasek. **Director, Merchandising:** Troy Waller. **Manager, Operations:** Chris Vtipl. **Receptionist:** Heather Harkins. **Manager, Equipment/Clubhouse:** Kevin Kierst. **Head Groundskeeper:** Ken Magner. **Assistant Groundskeeper:** Keith Collins.

Field Staff
Manager: Rick Dempsey. **Coach:** Tom Lawless. **Pitching Coach:** Ray Rippelmeyer. **Trainer:** Joe Hawkins.

Game Information
Radio Announcers: Rob Evans, Jack Ankerson. **No. of Games Broadcast:** Home-72, Away-72. **Flagship Station:** WTAR 850-AM.

PA Announcer: Frank Bennett. **Official Scorers:** Bob Moskowitz, Dave Lewis, Charlie Denn.

Stadium Name (year opened): Harbor Park (1993). **Location:** Exit 9, 11A or 11B off I-264, adjacent to the Elizabeth River in downtown Norfolk. **Standard Game Times:** 7:15 p.m.; Sun. (April-June) 1:15, (July-Sept.) 6:15.

Visiting Club Hotels: Omni Norfolk, 777 Waterside Dr., Norfolk, VA 23510. Telephone: (757) 622-6664; Doubletree Club Hotel, 880 North Military Highway, Norfolk, VA 23502. Telephone: (757) 461-9192.

Ottawa
LYNX

Office Address: 300 Coventry Rd., Ottawa, Ontario K1K 4P5. **Telephone:** (613) 747-5969. **FAX:** (613) 747-0003. **E-Mail Address:** lynx@ottawalynx.com. **Website:** www.ottawalynx.com.

Affiliation (first year): Montreal Expos (1993). **Years in League:** 1993-.

Ownership, Management
Operated By: Ottawa Triple-A Baseball Inc.
Principal Owner/President: Howard Darwin.
Director, Baseball Operations: Joe Bohringer. **Controller:** Richard Paulin. **Director, Stadium Operations:** Jack Darwin. **Head Groundskeepers:** Peter Webb, Brad Keith. **Director, Media/Public Relations:** Steve Keogh. **Director, Sales:** Mark Russet. **Senior Account Representative:** Peter Leyser. **Director, Promotions/Marketing:** Ron Lemaire. **Director, Ticket Sales:** Joe Fagan. **Administrative Manager:** Rupert Darwin. **Director, Merchandising:** Nancy Darwin. **Clubhouse Operations:** John Bryk. **Receptionist:** Lorraine Charrette. **Coordinator, Publications:** Annie Pare.

Field Staff
Manager: Pat Kelly. **Coach:** Billy Masse. **Pitching Coach:** Dean Treanor. **Trainer:** Alex Ochoa.

Game Information
Radio: None.
PA Announcer: Gord Breen. **Official Scorer:** Randy Fix.
Stadium Name (year opened): JetForm Park (1993). **Location:** Highway 417 to Riverside Drive/Vanier Parkway exit, Vanier Parkway north to Coventry Road, right on Coventry to stadium. **Standard Game Times:** 7:05 p.m.; Sat.-Sun. (April-May) 2:05, (June-Aug.) 7:05.
Visiting Club Hotel: The Chimo Hotel, 1199 Joseph Cyr St., Ottawa, Ontario K1J 7T4. Telephone: (613) 744-1060.

Pawtucket
RED SOX

Office Address: One Columbus Ave., Pawtucket, RI 02860. **Mailing Address:** P.O. Box 2365, Pawtucket, RI 02861. **Telephone:** (401) 724-7300. **FAX:** (401) 724-2140. **E-Mail Address:** pawsox@worldnet.att.net. **Website:** www.pawsox.com.

Affiliation (first year): Boston Red Sox (1973). **Years in League:** 1973-.

Ownership, Management
Operated by: Pawtucket Red Sox Baseball Club, Inc.
Chairman: Ben Mondor. **President:** Mike Tamburro.
Vice President/General Manager: Lou Schwechheimer. **Vice President, Treasurer:** Kathy Crowley. **Vice President, Sales and Marketing:** Michael Gwynn. **Vice President, Stadium Operations:** Mick Tedesco. **Vice President, Public Relations:** Bill Wanless. **Office Manager:** Kathy Davenport. **Ticket Manager:** Keith Kuceris. **Director, Community Relations:** Don Orsillo. **Director, Sales:** Daryl Jasper. **Account Executives:** Jeff Dooley, Larry Tocci. **Secretary;** Sandi Brown. **Clubhouse Manager:** Chris Parent. **Head Groundskeeper:** Larry DeVito. **Director, Stadium Services:** Derek Molhan. **Director, Concession Services:** Dave Johnson. **Director, Hospitality:** Kathy Walsh.

Field Staff
Manager: Ken Macha. **Coach:** Gerald Perry. **Pitching Coach:** John Cumberland. **Trainer:** Jim Young.

Game Information
Radio Announcers: Don Orsillo, Mike Logan. **No. of Games Broadcast:** Home-72, Away-72. **Flagship Station:** WLKW 790-AM
PA Announcer: Jim Martin. **Official Scorer:** Bruce Guindon.
Stadium Name (year opened): McCoy Stadium (1942). **Location:** I-95 North to exit 28 (School Street); I-95 South to exit 2A (Newport Avenue).

Standard Game Times: April-May 6 p.m.; June-Sept. 7; Sat. (April) 1, (May-Sept.) 7; Sun. 1.

Visiting Club Hotel: Comfort Inn, 2 George St., Pawtucket, RI 02860. Telephone: (401) 723-6700.

Richmond
BRAVES

Office Address: 3001 North Boulevard, Richmond, VA 23230. **Mailing Address:** P.O. Box 6667, Richmond, VA 23230. **Telephone:** (804) 359-4444. **FAX:** (804) 359-0731. **E-Mail Address:** rbraves@bznet.com. **Website:** www.rbraves.com.

Affiliation (first year): Atlanta Braves (1966). **Years in League:** 1884, 1915-17, 1954-64, 1966-.

Ownership, Management

Operated by: Atlanta National League Baseball, Inc.

Principal Owner: Ted Turner. **President:** Stan Kasten.

General Manager: Bruce Baldwin. **Assistant General Manager:** Ken Clary. **Office Manager:** Joanne Cornutt. **Manager, Stadium Operations:** Nate Doughty. **Manager, Public Relations:** Todd Feagans. **Manager, Group Sales:** Danny Saggese. **Assistant, Marketing/Group Sales:** Corey Bowdre. **Assistant Ticket Manager:** Kelly Harris. **Administrative Assistant:** Townley Goldsmith. **Manager, Field Maintenance:** Chad Mulholland. **Administrative Assistant:** Jin Wong. **Receptionist:** Janet Zimmerman.

Field Staff

Manager: Jeff Cox. **Coach:** Max Venable. **Pitching Coach:** Bill Fischer. **Trainer:** Jim Lovell.

Game Information

Radio Announcer: Robert Fish. **No. of Games Broadcast:** Home-72, Away-72. **Flagship Station:** WRNL 910-AM.

PA Announcer: Mike Blacker. **Official Scorer:** Leonard Alley.

Stadium Name (year opened): The Diamond (1985). **Location:** Exit 78 (Boulevard) at junction of I-64 and I-95, follow signs to park. **Standard Game Times:** 7 p.m., Sun. 2.

Visiting Club Hotel: Holiday Inn I-64 and West Broad, 6531 West Broad St., Richmond, VA 23230. Telephone: (804) 285-9951.

Rochester
RED WINGS

Office Address: One Morrie Silver Way, Rochester, NY 14608. **Telephone:** (716) 454-1001. **FAX:** (716) 454-1056. **E-Mail Address:** red wings@frontiernet.net. **Website:** www.redwingsbaseball.com.

Affiliation (first year): Baltimore Orioles (1961). **Years in League:** 1885-89, 1891-92, 1895-.

Ownership, Management

Operated by: Rochester Community Baseball, Inc.

Chairman: Fred Strauss. **President:** Elliot Curwin.

Chief Operating Officer: Naomi Silver. **General Manager:** Dan Mason. **Assistant General Manager:** Will Rumbold. **Controller:** Darlene Giardina. **Head Groundskeeper:** Gene Buonomo. **Director, Media/Public Relations:** Chuck Hinkel. **Director, Broadcasting:** Joe Castellano. **Director, Marketing:** Steve Salluzzo. **Assistant Director, Marketing:** Mike Lipani. **Accounting Assistant:** Dave Bills. **Director, Community Relations:** Wendy Rose. **Director, Ticket Sales:** Joe Ferrigno. **Director, Group Sales:** Russ Ruter. **Director, Merchandising:** Wendy Morrissette. **Assistant Director, Merchandising:** Josh Harris. **Manager, Payroll:** Paula LoVerde. **Account Executives:** John Caricati, Don Feldmann. **Director, Food Services:** Tom Sadtler. **Director, Administration:** Jennifer Waldow. **Clubhouse Operations:** Kenny Slough, Terry Costello.

Field Staff

Manager: Marv Foley. **Coach:** Dave Cash. **Pitching Coach:** Larry McCall. **Trainer:** Al Price.

Game Information

Radio Announcer: Joe Castellano. **No. of Games Broadcast:** Home-

72, Away-72. **Flagship Station:** WHTK 1280-AM.

PA Announcer: Kevin Spears. **Official Scorer:** Len Lustik.

Stadium Name (year opened): Frontier Field (1997). **Location:** New York State Thruway (I-90) connects with I-490 at exit 45 east of Rochester and exit 47 west of Rochester; exit 46 feeds into Routes 390 and 590, both of which connect with I-490 north of exit 46; from downtown area, use Plymouth Avenue exit. **Standard Game Times:** 7:15 p.m., Sun. 2:15.

Visiting Club Hotel: Crowne Plaza, 70 State St., Rochester, NY 14614. Telephone: (716) 546-3450.

Scranton/Wilkes-Barre
RED BARONS

Office Address: 235 Montage Mountain Rd., Moosic, PA 18507. **Mailing Address:** P.O. Box 3449, Scranton, PA 18505. **Telephone:** (717) 963-6556. **FAX:** (717) 963-6564. **E-Mail Address:** barons@epix.net. **Website:** www.redbarons.com.

Affiliation (first year): Philadelphia Phillies (1989). **Years in League:** 1989-.

Ownership, Management

Operated by: Lackawanna County Stadium Authority.

Chairman: Bill Jenkins.

General Manager: Rick Muntean. **Controller:** Tom Durkin. **Director, Media/Public Relations:** Mike Cummings. **Director, Stadium Operations:** Tom Staff. **Head Groundskeeper:** Bill Casterline. **Director, Sales/Marketing:** Rob Donovan. **Account Representatives:** Jim Petrie, Julie Martin. **Director, Ticket Sales:** Ron Prislupski. **Director, Group Sales:** Brian Bosley. **Director, Special Projects:** Karen Healy. **Clubhouse Operations:** Rick Renta. **Office Manager:** Donna McDonald. **Box Office:** Ann Marie Nocera.

Field Staff

Manager: Marc Bombard. **Coach:** Bill Robinson. **Pitching Coach:** Gary Ruby. **Trainer:** Craig Strobel.

Game Information

Radio Announcer: Kent Westling. **No. of Games Broadcast:** Home-72; Away-72. **Flagship Station:** WICK 1400-AM.

PA Announcer: John Davies. **Official Scorer:** Bob McGoff.

Stadium Name (year opened): Lackawanna County Stadium (1989). **Location:** I-81 to exit 51 (Davis Street). **Standard Game Times:** 7 p.m., 7:30; Sun. 1:30, 6.

Visiting Club Hotel: Radisson Lackawanna Station Hotel, 700 Lackawanna Ave., Scranton, PA 18503. Telephone: (717) 342-8300.

Syracuse
SKYCHIEFS

Office Address: P&C Stadium, One Tex Simone Dr., Syracuse, NY 13208. **Telephone:** (315) 474-7833. **FAX:** (315) 474-2658. **E-Mail Address:** baseball@skychiefs.com. **Website:** www.skychiefs.com.

Affiliation (first year): Toronto Blue Jays (1978). **Years in League:** 1885-89, 1891-92, 1894-1901, 1918, 1920-27, 1934-55, 1961-.

Ownership, Management

Operated by: Community Owned Baseball Club of Central New York, Inc.

Chairman: Richard Ryan. **President:** Donald Waful.

Executive Vice President/Chief Operating Officer: Anthony "Tex" Simone. **General Manager:** John Simone. **Assistant General Manager/Director, Media Relations, Sales:** Tom Van Schaack. **Director, Marketing/Promotions:** Stan Jakim. **Director, Group Sales:** Vic Gallucci. **Director, Ticket Sales:** H.J. Refici. **Business Manager:** Don Lehtonen. **Stadium Operations:** John Walters. **Clubhouse Operations:** Mike Maser, Ryan Abbott.

Field Staff

Manager: Terry Bevington. **Coach:** Lloyd Moseby. **Pitching Coach:** Scott Breeden. **Trainer:** Jon Woodworth.

Game Information

Radio Announcers: Ted DeLuca, Steve Hyder. **No. of Games**

Broadcast: Home-72, Away-72. **Flagship Station:** WHEN 620-AM.

PA Announcer: Dave Perkins. **Official Scorers:** Joel Marieniss, Tom Leo.

Stadium Name (year opened): P&C Stadium (1997). **Location:** New York State Thruway to exit 36 (I-81 South), to 7th North Street exit, left on 7th North, right on Hiawatha Boulevard. **Standard Game Times:** 7 p.m.; Sun. (April-May) 2, (June-Aug.) 6.

Visiting Club Hotel: Ramada Inn, 1305 Buckley Rd., Syracuse, NY 13212. Telephone: (315) 457-8670.

Toledo
MUD HENS

Office Address: 2901 Key St., Maumee, OH 43537. **Mailing Address:** P.O. Box 6212, Toledo, OH 43614. **Telephone:** (419) 893-9483. **FAX:** (419) 893-5847. **E-Mail Address:** mudhens@mudhens.com. **Website:** www.mudhens.com.

Affiliation (first year): Detroit Tigers (1987). **Years in League:** 1889, 1965-.

Ownership, Management

Operated by: Toledo Mud Hens Baseball Club, Inc.

President: Edwin Bergsmark. **Vice Presidents:** Michael Miller, David Huey. **Secretary-Treasurer:** Charles Bracken.

Vice President/Chief Executive Officer: Gene Cook. **Executive Director:** Joe Napoli. **Executive Director, Community Affairs:** Jeff Condon. **Director, Media Relations:** Greg Faist. **Director, Corporate Sales:** Scott Jeffer. **Director, Marketing and Promotions:** Neil Neukam. **Manager, Promotions:** Kerri White. **Director, Ticket Sales and Operations:** Bob Palmisano. **Manager, Group Sales:** Erik Ibsen. **Manager, Ticket Sales:** Glenn Sturtz. **Season Ticket and Group Sales Associates:** Joe Pfeiffer, Kelley Keast. **Director, Merchandising:** Kevin Marcy. **Associate, Merchandising:** Greg Setola. **Business Manager:** Dorothy Welniak. **Office Manager:** Carol Hamilton.

Field Staff

Manager: Gene Roof. **Coach:** Brad Komminsk. **Pitching Coach:** Jeff Jones. **Trainer:** Lon Pinhey.

Game Information

Radio Announcers: Jim Weber, Frank Gilhooley. **No. of Games Broadcast:** Home-72, Away-72. **Flagship Stations:** WMTR 96.1-FM, WFRO 900-AM/99.1-FM.

PA Announcer: John Keller. **Official Scorer:** John Wagner.

Stadium Name (year opened): Ned Skeldon Stadium (1965). **Location:** From Ohio Turnpike, exit 4, north to Toledo onto Reynolds, right onto Heatherdowns, right onto Key Street. From Detroit, I-75 South to exit 201A (Route 25), right onto Key Street. From Ann Arbor, Route 23 South to Route 475 South, exit 6, left at stoplight, follow Dussel Dr. to stadium. From Dayton, I-75 via Route 475 to Maumee exit (Route 24), left onto Key Street. **Standard Game Times:** 7 p.m., Sun. 2.

Visiting Club Hotel: Holiday Inn West, 2340 South Reynolds Rd., Toledo, OH 43614. Telephone: (419) 865-1361.

PACIFIC COAST LEAGUE

Class AAA

Mailing Address: 1631 Mesa Ave., Colorado Springs, CO 80906. **Telephone:** (719) 636-3399. **FAX:** (719) 636-1199. **E-Mail Address:** pclbaseball@earthlink.net.

Years League Active: 1903-.

President/Secretary-Treasurer: Branch B. Rickey.

Vice President: Russ Parker (Calgary).

Directors: Joe Adams (Omaha), Gary Arthur (Vancouver), Clay Bennett (Oklahoma), Joe Buzas (Salt Lake), John Carbray (Fresno), Rob Couhig (New Orleans), George Foster (Tacoma), Bob Goughan (Colorado Springs), Ken Grandquist (Iowa), Rick Holtzman (Tucson), Dean Jernigan (Memphis), Mel Kowalchuk (Edmonton), Pat McKernan (Albuquerque), Russ Parker (Calgary), Hank Stickney (Las Vegas), Mike Woleben (Nashville).

Branch Rickey

Director, Operations: George King. **Office Secretary:** Tammy Foe.

1998 Opening Date: April 7. **Closing Date:** Sept. 7.

Regular Season: 144 games (split schedule).

Division Structure: American Conference—Midwest: Albuquerque, Colorado Springs, Iowa, Omaha. **East:** Memphis, Nashville, New Orleans, Oklahoma. **Pacific Conference—South:** Fresno, Las Vegas, Salt Lake, Tucson. **West:** Calgary, Edmonton, Tacoma, Vancouver.

Playoff Format: West plays South and Midwest plays East in best-of-5 semifinal series. Winners meet in best-of-5 championship series.

All-Star Game: July 8 at Norfolk, VA (International League vs. PCL).

Roster Limit: 23 active, until midnight Aug. 10 when roster can be expanded to 25. **Player Eligibility Rule:** No restrictions.

Brand of Baseball: Rawlings ROM.

Umpires: Ron Barnes (Tucson, AZ), Lance Barksdale (Jackson, MS), Ted Barrett (Mesa, AZ), Fred Cannon (Brookhaven, MS), Eric Cooper (Des Moines, IA), Mark Carlson (Joliet, IL), John Dezelan (Imperial, PA), Mike DiMuro (Chandler, AZ), Ray DiMuro (Chandler, AZ), Bruce Dreckman (Marcus, IA), Robert Drake (Mesa, AZ), Doug Eddings (Las Cruces, NM), Mark Erramouspe (Rock Springs, WY), Mike Everitt (Chandler, AZ), Joel Fincher (Arlington, TX), Andy Fletcher (Memphis, TN), Dan Gnadt (Moorhead, MN), Morris Hodges (Helena, AL), Heath Jones (Glendale, AZ), Travis Katzenmeier (Liberal, KS), Jeff Kowalczyk (Bloomington, IL), Ron Kulpa (Florissant, MO), Ian Lamplugh (Victoria, BC), Alfonso Marquez (Anaheim, CA), Bill Miller (Aptos, CA), Scott Nance (Castle Rock, CO), Jeff Nelson (Cottage Grove, MN), Ken Page (Phoenix, AZ), Jeff Patterson (Imperial Beach, CA), Anthony Randazzo (Las Cruces, NM), Don Rea (Chandler, AZ), Kraig Sanders (Little Rock, AR), Chris Taylor (Kansas City, MO).

Stadium Information

Club	Stadium	Dimensions LF	CF	RF	Capacity	'97 Att.
Albuquerque	Albuquerque Sports	360	410	340	10,510	307,760
Calgary	Burns	345	400	345	8,000	291,918
Colo. Springs	Sky Sox	350	400	350	9,000	216,716
Edmonton	TELUS Field	340	420	320	9,200	432,504
Fresno†	Beiden Field	331	410	330	7,500	—
Iowa#	Sec Taylor	335	400	335	10,800	403,040
Las Vegas	Cashman Field	328	433	323	9,334	313,128
Memphis*	Tim McCarver	323	398	325	8,800	113,183
Nashville#	Herschel Greer	327	400	327	15,500	269,186
New Orleans	Zephyr Field	333	407	332	10,000	507,164
Oklahoma#	Southwestern Bell	325	400	325	15,000	325,582
Omaha#	Rosenblatt	332	408	332	22,000	—
Salt Lake	Franklin Quest Field	345	420	315	15,500	578,107
Tacoma	Cheney	325	425	325	9,600	305,281
Tucson	Tucson Electric	340	405	340	11,000	285,817
Vancouver	Nat Bailey	335	395	335	6,500	303,148

*Expansion team
#Member of disbanded American Association in 1997
†Franchise operated in Phoenix in 1997

Albuquerque
DUKES

Office Address: 1601 Avenida Cesar Chavez SE, Albuquerque, NM 87106. **Telephone:** (505) 243-1791. **FAX:** (505) 842-0561. **E-Mail Address:** coastdukes@aol.com. **Website:** www.dukes.fanlink.com.

Affiliation (first year): Los Angeles Dodgers (1972). **Years in League:** 1972-.

Ownership, Management
Operated by: Albuquerque Professional Baseball, Inc.
Principal Owner, Chairman: Bob Lozinak.
President/General Manager: P. Patrick McKernan. **Director, Media Relations:** David Sheriff. **Director, Accounting:** Dawnene Shoup. **Director, Sales:** Jim Guscott. **Director, Merchandising/Food Services:** Patrick J. McKernan. **Director, Stadium Operations:** Mick Byers. **Director, Ticket Operations:** Mark Spencer. **Director, Business Operations/Group Sales:** Pat Fachet.

Field Staff
Manager: Glenn Hoffman. **Coach:** Jon Debus. **Pitching Coach:** Claude Osteen. **Trainer:** Matt Wilson.

Game Information
Radio Announcers: Unavailable. **No. of Games Broadcast:** Home-72, Away-72. **Flagship Station:** Unavailable.
PA Announcer: David Sheriff. **Official Scorer:** Gary Herron.
Stadium Name (year opened): Albuquerque Sports Stadium (1969). **Location:** I-25 to Avenida Cesar Chavez exit, east to stadium. **Standard Game Times:** 7 p.m., Sun. 1.
Visiting Club Hotel: Plaza Inn Albuquerque, 900 Medical Arts NE, Albuquerque, NM 87106. Telephone: (505) 243-5693.

Calgary
CANNONS

Office Address: 2255 Crowchild Trail NW, Calgary, Alberta T2M 4S7. **Telephone:** (403) 284-1111. **FAX:** (403) 284-4343. **E-Mail Address:** cannons@telusplanet.net. **Website:** www.cannons.fanlink.com.

Affiliation (first year): Chicago White Sox (1998). **Years in League:** 1985-.

Ownership, Management
Operated by: Braken Holdings Ltd.
President: Russ Parker. **Secretary/Treasurer:** Diane Parker.
Vice President, Baseball Operations: John Traub. **Vice President, Marketing:** Bill Cragg. **Vice President, Finance:** Chris Poffenroth. **Director, Ticketing:** Greg Winthers. **Director, Events:** Darren Parker. **Coordinator, Public Relations:** Craig Burak. **Account Executive:** Jason MacAskill. **Marketing and Promotions:** Brent Andrew. **Administrative Assistant:** Dalyce Benette. **Clubhouse Managers:** Blair McAusland, Brian Miettinen.

Field Staff
Manager: Tom Spencer. **Coach:** Von Joshua. **Pitching Coach:** Kirk Champion. **Trainer:** Scott Johnson.

Game Information
Radio: Unavailable.
PA Announcer: Bill Clapham. **Official Scorer:** Fred Collins.
Stadium Name (year opened): Burns Stadium (1966). **Location:** Crowchild Trail NW to 24th Avenue, adjacent to McMahon Stadium. **Standard Game Times:** April 6:05 p.m.; May-August 7:05; Sat. (April-May) 1:35, (June-August) 7:05; Sun. 1:35.
Visiting Club Hotel: Calgary Marriott Hotel, 110 9th Ave. SE, Calgary, Alberta. Telephone: (403) 231-4527.

Colorado Springs
SKY SOX

Office Address: 4385 Tutt Blvd., Colorado Springs, CO 80922. **Telephone:** (719) 597-1449. **FAX:** (719) 597-2491. **E-Mail Address:** info@skysox.com. **Website:** www.skysox.com.

Affiliation (first year): Colorado Rockies (1993). **Years in League:** 1988-.

Ownership, Management

Operated by: Colorado Springs Sky Sox, Inc.

Principal Owner: David G. Elmore.

President/General Manager: Bob Goughan. **Senior Vice President, Administration:** Sam Polizzi. **Senior Vice President, Finance:** Carrol Payne. **Senior Vice President, Operations:** Dwight Hall. **Senior Vice President, Marketing:** Rai Henniger. **Senior Vice President, Stadium Operations:** Mark Leasure. **Vice President, Public Relations:** Chris Costello. **Vice President, Corporate Development:** Chad Starbuck. **Vice President, Advertising:** Nick Sciarratta. **Assistant General Manager, Group Sales:** Brien Smith. **Assistant General Manager, Merchandising:** Robert Stein. **Assistant, Merchandising:** Josh Beser. **Director, Finance:** Craig Levin. **Director, Community Relations:** Michael Hirsch. **Group Sales/Grounds Crew:** Chip Dreamer. **Home Clubhouse Manager/Marketing Representative:** Murlin Whitten. **Visiting Clubhouse Manager:** Brian Ochsie. **Marketing Representatives:** Andy Chidester, Eric Crook, Matt DeMargel, Ryan Ellis, Mike Humphreys, Eric Perez.

Field Staff

Manager: Paul Zuvella. **Coach:** Tony Torchia. **Pitching Coach:** Sonny Siebert. **Trainer:** Keith Dugger.

Game Information

Radio Announcers: Dick Chase, Dan Karcher, Norm Jones. **No. of Games Bradcast:** Home-72, Away-72. **Flagship Station:** KRDO 1240-AM.

PA Announcer: Nick Sciarratta. **Official Scorer:** Marty Grantz.

Stadium Name (year opened): Sky Sox Stadium (1988). **Location:** I-25 South to Woodmen Road exit, east on Woodmen to Powers Blvd., right on Powers to Barnes Road. **Standard Game Times:** 7:05 p.m.; Sat. (April-June 6) 1:35; Sun. 1:35.

Visiting Club Hotel: LeBaron Hotel, 314 West Bijou St., Colorado Springs, CO 80905. Telephone: (719) 471-8680.

Edmonton
TRAPPERS

Office Address: 10233 96th Ave., Edmonton, Alberta T5K 0A5. **Telephone:** (403) 414-4450. **FAX:** (403) 414-4475. **E-Mail Address:** trappers@planet.eon.net. **Website:** www.fanlink.com/edmonton~trappers.

Affiliation (first year): Oakland Athletics (1995). **Years in League:** 1981-.

Ownership, Management

Operated by: Trappers Baseball Corp.

Principal Owner/Chairman: Peter Pocklington.

President/General Manager: Mel Kowalchuk. **Assistant General Manager:** Dennis Henke. **Accountant:** Gabrielle Hampel. **Stadium Manager:** Don Benson. **Head Groundskeeper:** Jamie Rosnau. **Manager, Media/Public Relations:** Gary Tater. **Manager, Sales/Marketing:** Rob McGillis. **Senior Account Representatives:** Ken Charuk, Trent Houg, Ian Rose. **Manager, Community Relations/Special Events:** Lauri Holomis. **Office Manager/Tickets:** Debbie Zaychuk. **Manager, Group Sales:** Susan Jackson. **Clubhouse Operations:** Ian Rose.

Field Staff

Manager: Mike Quade. **Coach:** Orv Franchuk. **Pitching Coach:** Pete Richert. **Trainer:** Walt Horn.

Game Information

Radio Announcer: Al Coates. **No. of Games Broadcast:** Home-30, Away-30. **Flagship Station:** CHED 630-AM.

PA Announcer: Dean Parthenis. **Official Scorer:** Al Coates.

Stadium Name (year opened): TELUS Field (1995). **Location:** From north, 101st Street to 96th Ave., left on 96th, one block east; From south, Calgary Trail North to Queen Elizabeth hill, right across Walterdale Bridge, right on 96th Ave. **Standard Game Times:** 7:05; Sun. 2:05.

Visiting Club Hotel: Sheraton Grande, 10235 101 St., Edmonton, Alberta P5J 3E9. Telephone: (403) 428-7111.

Fresno
GRIZZLIES

Office Address: 1231 N St., Fresno, CA 93721. **Telephone:** (209) 442-1994. **FAX:** (209) 264-0795. **E-Mail Address:** info@fresnogrizzlies.com. **Website:** www.fresnogrizzlies.com.

Affiliation (first year): San Francisco Giants (1998). **Years in League:** 1998.

Ownership, Management

Operated by: Fresno Diamond Group.

Principal Owners: John Carbray, Diane Engelken, Rick Roush, Dave Cates. **Chairman:** William Connolly. **President:** John Carbray.

Vice President, Baseball Operations: Tim Cullen. **Vice President, Sales/Marketing:** Derek Leistra. **Director, Community Relations:** Gus Zernial. **Marketing Associates:** LeeAnne Hobbs, David Martin, Ron Thomas, Bob Wineger. **Director, Media Relations:** Michael Caires. **Director, Stadium Operations:** Glenn Wolff. **Director, Tickets:** Debbie Scott-Leistra. **Assistant, Tickets:** Angie Brondos. **Assistant, Operations:** Rick Finley. **Administrative Assistants:** Margaret Wilcox, Leticia Vazquez.

Field Staff

Manager: Jim Davenport. **Coach:** Joe Lefebvre. **Pitching Coach:** Joel Horlen. **Trainer:** Donna Papangellin.

Game Information

Radio Announcers: John Doskow, Paul Swearengin. **No. of Games Broadcast:** Home-72, Away-72. **Flagship Stations:** KYNO 1300-AM, KGST 1600-AM.

PA Announcer: Unavailable. **Official Scorer:** Unavailable.

Stadium Name (year opened): Beiden Field (1987). **Location:** Highway 41 to Shaw Ave., east to Cedar, left to stadium. **Standard Game Times:** 7:05 p.m., Sun. 2:05.

Visiting Club Hotel: Holiday Inn Centre Plaza, 2233 Ventura St., Fresno, CA 93721. Telephone: (209) 268-1000.

Iowa
CUBS

Office Address: 350 SW 1st St., Des Moines, IA 50309. **Telephone:** (515) 243-6111. **FAX:** (515) 243-5152. **Website:** www.iowacubs.com.

Affiliation (first year): Chicago Cubs (1981). **Years in League:** 1998.

Ownership, Management

Operated by: Greater Des Moines Baseball Co., Inc.

Principal Owner/President: Ken Grandquist.

General Manager: Sam Bernabe. **Assistant General Manager:** Jim Nahas. **Director, Media Relations:** Brett Dolan. **Controller:** Sue Tollefson. **Director, Stadium Operations:** Boyd Davis. **Director, Group Sales:** Nick Willey. **Director, Merchandising/Office Manager:** Karen Seitz. **Senior Account Executives:** Jeff Lantz, Steve Miller. **Head Groundskeeper:** Luke Yoder.

Field Staff

Manager: Terry Kennedy. **Coach:** Glenn Adams. **Pitching Coach:** Marty DeMerritt. **Trainer:** Bob Grimes.

Game Information

Radio Announcer: Deene Ehlis. **No. of Games Broadcast:** Home-72, Away-72. **Flagship Station:** KXTK 940-AM.

PA Announcer: Chuck Shockley, Mark Hendricks. **Official Scorer:** Dick McDonald, Dirk Brinkmeyer.

Stadium Name (year opened): Sec Taylor Stadium (1992). **Location:** I-235 to 3rd Street exit, south on 3rd Street to Tuttle Street, left on Tuttle. **Standard Game Times:** 7:15 p.m.; Sun. (April-May) 2:05, (June-Sept.) 6:05.

Visiting Club Hotel: Savery Hotel, 401 Locust St., Des Moines, IA 50309. Telephone: (515) 244-2151.

Las Vegas
STARS

Office Address: 850 Las Vegas Blvd. North, Las Vegas, NV 89101. **Telephone:** (702) 386-7200. **FAX:** (702) 386-7214. **Website:** lvstars.com. **Affiliation (first year):** San Diego Padres (1982). **Years in League:** 1982-.

Ownership, Management
Operated by: Mandalay Sports Enterprises.
Chief Executive Officer: Hank Stickney. **Managing Director:** Ken Stickney. **Chairman:** Peter Guber. **Vice Chairman:** Paul Schaeffer. **President:** Harley Frankel.
General Manager: Don Logan. **Assistant General Manager:** Mark Grenier. **Vice President, Business Operations:** Robert Murphy. **Senior Administrative Assistant:** Robert Blum. **Controller:** Allen Taylor. **Accounting:** Cindy Goodwyn, Christine Atherton. **Manager, Operations:** Nick Fitzenreider. **Director, Public Relations/Marketing:** Jon Sandler. **Manager, Marketing:** Lisa Talley. **Coordinator, Marketing/Community Relations:** Karin Tomcik. **Managers, Public Relations:** Brad Hickey, Steve Solomon. **Manager, Sales:** Steve Moser.
Corporate Account Executives: Eric Dornak, Chuck Johnson. **Director, Ticket Operations:** Eric Deutsch. **Coordinator, Ticketing:** Kim Kerschner. **Manager, Box Office:** Josh Levi. **Director, Special Projects:** Meredith Breen. **Director, Merchandising:** Laurie Wanser. **Manager, Ticket Sales:** Jeff Eiseman. **Manager, Administrative Services:** Mary McConnell. **Manager, Direct Sales:** Mike Levine. **Administrative Assistant, Direct Sales:** Summer Busbee.

Field Staff
Manager: Jerry Royster. **Coach:** Craig Colbert. **Pitching Coach:** Dave Smith. **Trainer:** Greg Poulis.

Game Information
Radio Announcers: Jon Sandler, Tim Neverett. **No. of Games Broadcast:** Home-72, Away-72. **Flagship Station:** KBAD 920-AM.
PA Announcer: Dan Bickmore. **Official Scorer:** Jim Gemma.
Stadium Name (year opened): Cashman Field (1983). **Location:** I-15 to U.S. 95 (exit downtown), east on 95 to Las Vegas Blvd. North exit, north on Las Vegas Boulevard. **Standard Game Times:** 7:05 p.m., Sun. 1:05.
Visiting Club Hotel: Las Vegas Club Hotel and Casino, 18 East Fremont St., Las Vegas, NV 89101. Telephone: (702) 385-1664.

Memphis
REDBIRDS

Office Address: 800 Home Run Lane, Memphis, TN 38104. **Telephone:** (901) 721-6000. **FAX:** (901) 721-6017. **Downtown Office Address:** 8 South Third St., Suite 101, Memphis, TN 38103. **Telephone:** (901) 523-7870. **FAX:** (901) 527-1642. **Website:** www.memphisredbirds.com.
Affiliation (first year): St. Louis Cardinals (1998). **Years in League:** 1998.

Ownership, Management
Operated By: Blues City Baseball, Inc..
Principal Owners: Dean Jernigan, Kristi Jernigan.
Chairman: Jim Thomas.
President, General Manager: Allie Prescott. **Assistant to President/General Manager:** Kipp Williams. **Assistant General Manager:** Dan Madden. **Controller:** Jonathan Martin. **Director, Development:** Gwen Driscoll. **Director, Project Development:** Ray Brown. **Coordinator, Special Projects:** Chris Jernigan. **Director, Stadium Operations:** Cecil Jernigan. **Game Day Manager:** Steele Ford. **Director, Field Operations:** Steve Horne. **Director, Marketing:** Kim Gaskill. **Graphic Designer:** Iris Horne. **Director, Promotions:** Richard Flight. **Director, Media Relations:** Tom Stocker. **Director, Sales:** Pete Rizzo. **Account Executive:** Angie Jernigan. **Director, Community Relations:** Reggie Williams. **Director, Ticket Operations/Ballpark Office Manager:** Julia Courtney.

Field Staff
Manager: Gaylen Pitts. **Coach:** Mitchell Page. **Pitching Coach:** Marty Mason. **Trainer:** Pete Fagan.

Game Information
Radio Announcers: Tom Stocker, David Wilson. **No. of Games Broadcast:** Home-72, Away-72. **Flagship Station:** WHBQ 560-AM.

PA Announcer: Unavailable. **Official Scorer:** John Guinozzo.

Stadium Name (year opened): Tim McCarver Stadium (1963). **Location:** I-40 West (Sam Cooper Blvd./Broad Street). **Location:** I-40 West (Sam Cooper Blvd./Broad Street), left onto East Parkway, left onto Central Ave., right onto Early Maxwell Blvd. **Standard Game Times:** 7:05 p.m., Sat. 6:05, Sun. 2:05.

Visiting Club Hotel: Sleep Inn at Court Square, 40 North Front St., Memphis, TN 38103. Telephone: (901) 522-9700.

Nashville
SOUNDS

Office Address: 534 Chestnut St., Nashville, TN 37203. **Mailing Address:** P.O. Box 23290, Nashville, TN 37202. **Telephone:** (615) 242-4371. **FAX:** (615) 256-5684.

Affiliation (first year): Pittsburgh Pirates (1998). **Years in League:** 1998.

Ownership, Management
Principal Owners: Al Gordon, Mike Murtaugh, Mike Woleben.

General Manager: Bill Larson. **Chief Financial Officer:** Glenn Yaeger. **Business Manager:** Judy Franke. **Director, Public Relations:** John Swandal. **Human Resources Director:** Rick Schlobach. **Director, Ticket Sales:** David Lorenz. **Director, Group Sales:** D. Smith. **Director, Merchandising:** Lisa Lorenz. **Group Sales Representatives:** Joe Hart, Keith Jenkins, Tim Sexton, Chuck Valenches. **Director, Systems Marketing:** Dave Stidham. **Director, Food Services:** Mark Lolli. **Office Manager:** Sharon Carson. **Head Groundskeeper:** Tom McAfee.

Field Staff
Manager: Trent Jewett. **Coach:** Richie Hebner. **Pitching Coach:** Bruce Tanner. **Trainer:** Sandy Krum.

Game Information
Radio Announcers: Steve Selby, Chuck Velenches. **No. of Games Broadcast:** Home-72, Away-72. **Flagship Station:** Unavailable.

PA Announcer: Unavailable. **Official Scorer:** Unavailable.

Stadium Name (year opened): Herschel Greer Stadium (1978). **Location:** I-65 to Wedgewood exit, west to 8th Ave., right on 8th to Chestnut Street, right on Chestnut. **Standard Game Times:** 7 p.m.; Sat. 4, 7; Sun. 2, 4.

Visiting Club Hotel: Days Inn-Opryland, #1 International Plaza, Nashville, TN 37217. Telephone: (615) 361-7666.

New Orleans
ZEPHYRS

Office Address: 6000 Airline Dr., Metairie, LA 70003. **Telephone:** (504) 734-5155. **FAX:** (504) 734-5118. **E-Mail Address:** zephyrs@zephyrsbaseball.com. **Website:** www.zephyrsbaseball.com.

Affiliation (first year): Houston Astros (1997). **Years in League:** 1998.

Ownership, Management
Operated by: New Orleans Zephyrs Baseball Club, LLC.

Principal Owners: Rob Couhig, Don Beaver. **President:** Rob Couhig.

Vice President/General Manager: Jay Miller. **Assistant General Manager:** Dan Hanrahan. **Director, Stadium Operations:** Rick Sneed. **Director, Media/Public Relations:** Les East. **Director, Sales/Marketing:** Dawn Mentel. **Account Executive:** Mike Schmittou. **Director, Community Relations:** Aaron Lombard. **Director, Ticket Sales:** Michelle Toussaint. **Director, Group Sales:** Scott Sidwell. **Director, Merchandising:** Heather Woods. **Director, Food Services:** Luis Martinez. **Head Groundskeeper:** Russell Brown. **Clubhouse Operations:** Richie Runnels. **Office Manager:** Jane Howard. **Accounting:** Shawn Kelly, Sherry Grimes.

Field Staff
Manager: John Tamargo. **Coach:** Al Pedrique. **Pitching Coach:** Jim Hickey. **Trainer:** Mike Freer.

Game Information
Radio Announcers: Ken Trahan, Ron Swoboda. **No. of Games Broadcast:** Home-72, Away-72. **Flagship Stations:** WWL 870-AM, WSMB 1350-AM.

PA Announcer: Unavailable. **Official Scorer:** J.L. Vangilder.

Stadium Name (year opened): Zephyr Field (1997). **Location:** I-10 to Clearview Parkway South exit, right on Airline Drive (Route 61). **Standard Game Times:** 7:05 p.m.; Sun. 6:05.

Visiting Club Hotel: Best Western Landmark, 2601 Severn Ave., Metairie, LA 70002. Telephone: (504) 888-9500.

Oklahoma
REDHAWKS

Mailing Address: Southwestern Bell Park, 2 South Mickey Mantle Dr., Oklahoma City, OK 73104. **Telephone:** (405) 218-1000. **FAX:** (405) 218-1001. **E-Mail Address:** redhawks@mail.icnet.net.

Affiliation (first year): Texas Rangers (1983). **Years in League:** 1963-1968, 1998.

Ownership, Management
Operated by: OKC Athletic Club, LP.

President: Clayton Bennett.

General Manager: Tim O'Toole. **Assistant General Manager:** Andy Thiem. **Director, Sales:** Brad Tammen. **Director, Media Relations:** John Allgood. **Manager, Tickets:** Amy Clelland. **Account Executives:** Jeb Cook, Bryan Bedford, Earle Haggard, Summer Williams. **Manager, Stadium Operations:** Tim Gorman. **Head Groundskeeper:** Monty McCoy. **Manager, Food Services:** Milton Neal. **Manager, Merchandise:** Mike Prange. **Manager, Maintenance:** Harlan Budde. **Administrative Assistant:** Amy Farnsworth.

Field Staff
Manager: Greg Biagini. **Pitching Coach:** Tom Brown. **Trainer:** Greg Harrel.

Game Information
Radio Announcer: Jack Damrill. **Flagship Station:** WKY 930-AM.

PA Announcers: Randy Kemp, David Patterson. **Official Scorers:** Pat Petree, Bob Colon, Max Nichols.

Stadium Name (year opened): Southwestern Bell Park (1998). **Location:** Intersection of I-35 and I-40, take Lincoln exit, west on Reno. **Standard Game Times:** 7:05; Sun. (April-May) 2:05, (June-August) 7:05.

Visiting Club Hotel: West Inn, One North Broadway, Oklahoma City, OK 73102. Telephone: (405) 235-2780.

Omaha
ROYALS

Office Address: Rosenblatt Stadium, 1202 Bert Murphy Dr., Omaha, NE 68107. **Mailing Address:** P.O. Box 3665, Omaha, NE 68103. **Telephone:** (402) 734-2550. **FAX:** (402) 734-7166. **E-Mail Address:** mmashanic@earthlink.net. **Website:** www.omaharoyals.com.

Affiliation (first year): Kansas City Royals (1969). **Years in League:** 1998.

Ownership, Management
Operated by: Omaha Royals, LP.

Principal Owners: Union Pacific Railroad, Warren Buffett, Walter Scott.

President: Joe Adams.

Vice President/General Manager: Bill Gorman. **Assistant General Manager/Director, Corporate Sales:** Terry Wendlandt. **Director, Media Relations:** Mike Mashanic. **Controller:** Jessica Graner. **Director, Marketing:** Mike Stephens. **Stadium Superintendent:** Jesse Cuevas. **Manager, Ticket Office:** Joe Volquartsen. **Assistant, Ticket Office:** Joe Pane. **Comptroller:** Sue Nicholson. **Corporate Sales Representatives:** Tony Duffek, Andy Lewis, Jeff Ryan. **Manager, Concessions:** Rick Bronwell. **Administrative**

Assistant: Kay Besta. **Controller:** Sue Nicholson. **Manager, Concessions:** Rick Bronwell.

Field Staff
Manager: Ron Johnson. **Coach:** U.L. Washington. **Pitching Coach:** Gary Lance. **Trainer:** Frank Kyte.

Game Information
Radio Announcer: Kevin McNabb. **No. of Games Broadcast:** Home-72, Away-72. **Flagship Station:** KOSR 1490-AM.

PA Announcer: Bill Jensen. **Official Scorers:** Steve Pivovar, Rob White.

Stadium Name (year opened): Rosenblatt Stadium (1948). **Location:** I-80 to 13th Street South exit, south one block. **Standard Game Times:** 7:05 p.m.; Wed. 12:05, Sun. 1:35.

Visiting Club Hotel: Ramada Hotel Central, 7007 Grover St., Omaha, NE 68106. Telephone: (402) 397-7030

Salt Lake BUZZ

Office Address: 77 West 1300 South, Salt Lake City, UT 84115. **Mailing Address:** P.O. Box 4108, Salt Lake City, UT 84110. **Telephone:** (801) 485-3800. **FAX:** (801) 485-6818. **E-Mail Address:** slbuzz@earthlink.net. **Website:** www.buzz.fanlink.com.

Affiliation (first year): Minnesota Twins (1994). **Years in League:** 1915-25, 1958-65, 1970-84, 1994-.

Ownership, Management
Operated by: Buzas Baseball, Inc.

Principal Owners: Joe Buzas, Penny Buzas.

President/General Manager: Joe Buzas. **Assistant General Managers:** Dorsena Picknell, Rob White. **Director, Business Operations:** Jackie Riley. **Director, Media/Public Relations:** Kent Haslam. **Director, Ticket Sales:** Michael O'Conor. **Assistant Manager, Sales:** Jim Hochstrasser. **Senior Account Executives:** Paul Hirst, Jennifer Church. **Director, Stadium Operations:** Mark Hildebrand. **Clubhouse Operations:** Eli Rice.

Field Staff
Manager: Phil Roof. **Coaches:** Bill Springman, Al Newman. **Pitching Coach:** Rick Anderson. **Trainer:** Rick McWane.

Game Information
Radio Announcer: Steve Klauke. **No. of Games Broadcast:** Home-72, Away-72. **Flagship Station:** KFNZ 1320-AM.

PA Announcers: Jeff Reeves. **Official Scorers:** Howard Nakagama, Bruce Hilton.

Stadium Name (year opened): Franklin Quest Field (1994). **Location:** From I-15/I-80, east at 1300 South exit to corner of 1300 South and West Temple. **Standard Game Times:** 7 p.m.; Sun. (April-May) 2, (June-Sept.) 5.

Visiting Club Hotel: Quality Inn City Center, 154 West 600 South, Salt Lake City, UT 84101. Telephone: (801) 521-2930.

Tacoma RAINIERS

Office Address: 2502 South Tyler, Tacoma, WA 98405. **Mailing Address:** P.O. Box 11087, Tacoma, WA 98411. **Telephone:** (253) 752-7707. **FAX:** (253) 752-7135. **E-Mail Address:** tacomapcl@aol.com. **Website:** www.rainiers.fanlink.com.

Affiliation (first year): Seattle Mariners (1995). **Years in League:** 1904-05, 1960-.

Ownership, Management
Operated by: George's Pastime, Inc.

Principal Owners: George Foster, Sue Foster.

President: George Foster.

Executive Vice President: Mel Taylor. **Director, Finance:** Laurie Yarbrough. **Director, Baseball Operations:** Kevin Kalal.

Director, Marketing Operations: Colleen Sullivan. **Director, Sales:** Dave Lewis. **Account Representatives:** Connie Littlejohn-Rivers, Carl

Edensword, Margaret McCormick. **Director, Media Sales:** Renee Waltz. **Director, Ticket Operations:** John Pesch. **Assistant, Ticket Operations:** Jenny Zalewski. **Director, Food Services:** Frank Maryott. **Director, Merchandise:** Jeanette Collett. **Director, Stadium Operations:** Twila Elrod. **Head Groundskeeper:** Bob Christofferson. **Clubhouse Managers:** Rob Reagle, Brian Kinney.

Field Staff

Manager: Dave Myers. **Coach:** Dave Brundage. **Pitching Coach:** Ron Romanick. **Trainer:** Randy Roetter.

Game Information

Radio Announcer: Bob Robertson. **No. of Games Broadcast:** Home-72, Away-72. **Flagship Station:** KHHO 850-AM.

PA Announcer: Jeff Randall. **Official Scorers:** Darin Padur, Mark Johnston.

Stadium Name (year opened): Cheney Stadium (1960). **Location:** From I-5, take exit 132 to Highway 16 West, take 19th Avenue East exit, right on Cheyenne Street. **Standard Game Times:** 7:05 p.m., Sun. 1:35.

Visiting Club Hotel: Howard Johnson Express Inn, 8702 South Hosmer, Tacoma, WA 98444. Telephone: (206) 535-3100.

Tucson
SIDEWINDERS

Office Address: 3400 East Ajo Way, Tucson, AZ 85713. **Mailing Address:** P.O. Box 27045, Tucson, AZ 85726. **Telephone:** (520) 325-2621. **FAX:** (520) 327-2371. **E-Mail Address:** tuffy@azstarnet.com. **Website:** tucsonsidewinders.com.

Affiliation (first year): Arizona Diamondbacks (1998). **Years in League:** 1969-.

Ownership, Management

Operated by: Professional Baseball, Inc.

Principal Owner/President: Martin Stone.

Vice President/General Manager: Mike Feder. **Assistant General Manager:** Todd Woodford. **Director, Community Relations/Group Sales:** Eric May. **Director, Marketing:** Becky Larsen. **Director, Media Relations:** Pete Tees. **Director, Merchandising:** Tom Newell. **Director, Operations:** Doug Leary. **Director, Sales/Ticketing:** Louis Butash. **Office Manager:** Pattie Feder. **Account Executives:** Kristin Taylor, Patrick Ware. **Clubhouse Operations:** Bill Gleason, Chris Rasnake.

Field Staff

Manager: Chris Speier. **Coach:** Mike Barnett. **Pitching Coach:** Chuck Kniffin. **Trainer:** Peter Kolb.

Game Information

Radio Announcer: Dave Brady. **No. of Games Broadcast:** Home-72, Away-72. **Flagship Station:** KTKT 990-AM.

PA Announcer: Anthony DeFazio. **Official Scorer:** George Doig.

Stadium Name (year opened): Tucson Electric Park (1998). **Location:** I-10, exit at Ajo Way, east ½ mile. **Standard Games Times:** 7 p.m., Fri.-Sat. 7:30.

Visiting Club Hotel: Ramada Inn-Foothills, 6944 Tanque Verde Rd., Tucson, AZ 85715. Telephone: (520) 886-9595.

Vancouver
CANADIANS

Office Address: 4601 Ontario St., Vancouver, B.C. V5V 3H4. **Telephone:** (604) 872-5232. **FAX:** (604) 872-1714. **E-Mail Address:** canadians@ultranet.com. **Website:** www.canadians.fanlink.com.

Affiliation (first year): Anaheim Angels (1993). **Years in League:** 1956-62, 1965-69, 1978-.

Ownership, Management

Operated by: Japan Sports Systems, Inc.

President: John McHale.

General Manager: Gary Arthur. **Director, Business Operations:** Harry Chan. **Manager, Marketing/Sales:** Ken Cooper. **Manager, Merchandising:** Torchy Pechet. **Manager, Ticket Sales:** Peter Daubaras. **Director,**

Media/Community Relations: Steve Hoem. **Director, Stadium Operations:** Bill Posthumus. **Clubhouse Operations:** Dick Phillips.

Field Staff

Manager: Mitch Seoane. **Coach:** Leon Durham. **Pitching Coach:** Greg Minton. **Trainer:** Don McGann.

Game Information

Radio: Unavailable.

PA Announcers: Jerry Landa, Brook Ward. **Official Scorer:** Pat Karl.

Stadium Name (year opened): Nat Bailey Stadium (1952). **Location:** From downtown, Cambie Street Bridge, left on East 33rd Street, left on Clancy Loringer Way, right to stadium. From south, Highway 99 to Oak Street, right on 41st Ave., left on Ontario. **Standard Game Times:** 7:05 p.m.; Wed. 12:15, Sun. 1:30.

Visiting Club Hotel: The Stay 'n' Save, 10551 St. Edwards Dr., Richmond, BC V6X 3L8. Telephone: (604) 273-1333.

EASTERN LEAGUE

Class AA

Office Address: 511 Congress St., 7th Floor, Portland, ME 04104. **Mailing Address:** P.O. Box 9711, Portland, ME 04104. **Telephone:** (207) 761-2700. **FAX:** (207) 761-7064. **E-Mail Address:** elpb@eastern-league.com. **Website:** www.easternleague.fanlink.com.

Years League Active: 1923-.
President/Treasurer: Bill Troubh.
Assistant to President: Joe McEacharn.
Executive Assistant: Mike Fiol.
Vice President: Greg Agganis (Akron).
Corporate Secretary: Gerry Berthiaume (New Britain).
Directors: Greg Agganis (Akron), Joe Buzas (New Britain), Charles Eshbach (Portland), Barry Gordon (Norwich), Peter Kirk (Bowie), Ed Massey (New Haven),

Bill Troubh

Steve Resnick (Harrisburg), Dick Stanley (Trenton), Craig Stein (Reading), Mike Urda (Binghamton).

1998 Opening Date: April 8. **Closing Date:** Sept. 7.
Regular Season: 142 games.
Division Structure: North—Binghamton, New Britain, New Haven, Norwich, Portland. **South**—Akron, Bowie, Harrisburg, Reading, Trenton.
Playoff Format: Top two teams in each division play best-of-5 series. Division playoff winners meet in best-of-5 series for league championship.
All-Star Game: July 8 at New Haven, CT (joint Double-A game).
Roster Limit: 23 active, until midnight Aug. 10 when roster can be expanded to 24. **Player Eligibility Rule:** No restrictions.
Brand of Baseball: Rawlings ROM-EL.
Statistician: Howe Sportsdata International, Boston Fish Pier, West Bldg. #1, Suite 302, Boston MA 02210.
Umpires: John Bennett (Shelbyville, KY), Troy Blades (Clark's Harbour, Nova Scotia), Robert Cook (Gahanna, OH), John Creek (Kalamazoo, MI), Philip Cuzzi (Nutley, NJ), Michael Fichter (Lansing, IL), Scott Hepinstall (Midland, MI), Matthew Hollowell (Whitehouse Station, NJ), Justin Klemm (Cataumet, MA), Patrick McGinnis (Joliet, IL), Timothy Pasch (Plant City, FL), Alexander Rea (Miami, FL), Brian Runge (El Cajon, CA), Patrick Spieler (Omaha, NE), Mark Winters (Pleasant Plains, IL).

Stadium Information

Club	Stadium	Dimensions			Capacity	'97 Att.
		LF	CF	RF		
Akron	Canal Park	331	400	337	9,097	473,232
Binghamton	Binghamton Municipal	330	400	330	6,012	200,513
Bowie	Prince George's	309	405	309	10,000	409,285
Harrisburg	RiverSide	335	400	335	6,200	242,431
New Britain	New Britain	330	400	330	6,146	151,718
New Haven	Yale Field	340	405	315	6,200	232,101
Norwich	Thomas J. Dodd	309	401	309	6,275	244,246
Portland	Hadlock Field	315	400	330	6,860	397,117
Reading	Municipal Memorial	330	400	330	8,500	398,182
Trenton	Waterfront Park	330	407	330	6,341	446,527

NOTE: Expansion franchises have been granted to Altoona, Pa., and Erie, Pa., for the 1999 season.

Akron
AEROS

Office Address: 300 South Main St., Akron, OH 44308. **Telephone:** (330) 253-5151. **FAX:** (330) 253-3300. **E-Mail Address:** aaeros@neo.lrun.com. **Website:** www.akronaeros.com.

Affiliation (first year): Cleveland Indians (1989). **Years in League:** 1989-.

Ownership, Management

Operated by: Akron Professional Baseball, Inc.
Principal Owners: Mike Agganis, Greg Agganis.
Chief Executive Officer: Mike Agganis. **President:** Greg Agganis.
Vice President/General Manager: Jeff Auman. **Assistant General Manager, Marketing and Communications:** Vinny Maculaitis. **Assistant General Manager, Ticket Operations:** Drew Cooke. **Assistant General Manager, Finance:** Bob Larkins. **Director, Community Relations:** Katie Dannemiller. **Manager, Media Relations:** James Carpenter. **Coordinator, Marketing:** Don Krizo. **Director, Ticket Sales:** Kurt Landes. **Director, Group Sales:** Jim Draper. **Assistant Director, Group Sales:** Ben Tolchinsky. **Manager, Season Ticket/Loge Services:** Matt Carr. **Account Representatives, Group Sales:** Thomas Craven, Matt Ippolito. **Director, Merchandising:** Kris Roukey. **Director, Field Maintenance:** Rick Izzo. **Receptionist:** Jean Dockus.

Field Staff

Manager: Joel Skinner. **Coach:** Billy Williams. **Pitching Coach:** Tony Arnold. **Trainer:** Dan DeVoe.

Game Information

Radio Announcers: Jim Clark, Todd Bell. **No. of Games Broadcast:** Home-71, Away-71. **Flagship Station:** WHLO 640-AM.
PA Announcer: Joe Dunn. **Official Scorer:** Dick Ziegler.
Stadium Name (year opened): Canal Park (1997). **Location:** From I-76 East or I-77 South, exit onto Route 59 East, exit at Exchange/Cedar and turn right onto Cedar, go left at Main Street. From I-76 West or I-77 North, exit at Main Street/Downtown, follow exit onto Broadway Street, left onto Exchange Street, right at Main Street. **Standard Game Times:** 7:05 p.m.; Sun. 2:05.
Visiting Club Hotel: Ramada Plaza, 20 West Mill St., Akron, OH 44308. Telephone: (330) 384-1500.

ALTOONA

(Eastern League expansion team, 1999)
Mailing Address: P.O. Box 1029, Altoona, PA 16603. **Telephone:** (814) 943-5400. **FAX:** (814) 949-9207.

Ownership, Management

Operated by: Altoona Baseball Properties.
Majority Owner: Bob Lozinak. **Minority Owners:** Mark Thomas, Tate DeWeese, Sal Baglieri.
General Manager: Sal Baglieri. **Assistant General Manager:** Steve Lozinak. **Director, Marketing/Community, Media Relations:** Jim Gregory.

Binghamton
METS

Office Address: 211 Henry St., Binghamton, NY 13901. **Mailing Address:** P.O. Box 598, Binghamton, NY 13902. **Telephone:** (607) 723-6387. **FAX:** (607) 723-7779. **E-Mail Address:** bmets@bmets.com. **Website:** www.bmets.com.

Affiliation (first year): New York Mets (1992). **Years in League:** 1923-37, 1940-63, 1966-68, 1992-.

Ownership, Management

Operated by: Binghamton Mets Baseball Club, Inc.
Principal Owners: David Maines, William Maines, R.C. Reuteman, George Scherer, Christopher Urda, Michael Urda.

President: Michael Urda.

General Manager: R.C. Reuteman. **Assistant General Manager:** Scott Brown. **Director, Stadium Operations:** Richard Tylicki. **Director, Food and Beverage:** Pete Brotherton. **Director, Corporate Sales/Community Affairs:** Melinda Mayne. **Director, Business Operations:** Jim Weed. **Director, Merchandising:** John Willi. **Manager, Group Sales:** Josh Passman. **Marketing Representative:** Mitch Gorton. **Administrative Assistant:** Sally Subik. **Bookkeeper:** Karen Micalizzi. **Head Grounds-keeper:** Craig Evans.

Field Staff

Manager: John Gibbons. **Coach:** Ken Berry. **Pitching Coach:** Rick Waits. **Trainer:** Jeff Weems.

Game Information

Radio Announcer: Dave Schultz. **No. of Games Broadcast:** Home-71, Away-71. **Flagship Station:** WNBF 1290-AM.

PA Announcer: Roger Neel. **Official Scorer:** Steve Kraly.

Stadium Name (year opened): Binghamton Municipal (1992). **Location:** I-81 to exit 4S (Binghamton), Route 11 exit to Henry Street. **Standard Game Times:** 7 p.m., Sat. (April-May 9) 1:30, Sun. 1:30.

Visiting Club Hotel: Holiday Inn Arena, 2-8 Hawley St., Binghamton, NY 13901. Telephone: (607) 722-1212.

Bowie
BAYSOX

Office Address: 4101 NE Crain Highway, Bowie, MD 20716. **Mailing Address:** P.O. Box 1661, Bowie, MD 20717. **Telephone:** (301) 805-6000. **FAX:** (301) 805-6008.

Affiliation (first year): Baltimore Orioles (1993). **Years In League:** 1993-.

Ownership

Operated by: Maryland Baseball, LP.

Principal Owners: Peter Kirk, Pete Simmons, Hugh Schindel, John Daskalakis, Frank Perdue.

Chairman/Chief Executive Officer: Peter Kirk. **President:** Pete Simmons.

General Manager: Jon Danos. **Assistant General Manager:** Mike Munter. **Director, Stadium Operations:** Will Gardner. **Head Groundskeeper:** Bob Butler. **Director, Media/Public Relations:** Dave Collins. **Senior Account Representatives:** Eric Landseadel, Jeff Baskin, Ray Hedrick. **Director, Community Relations:** Cheryl LeGohn-Tubbs. **Director, Ticket Operations:** Brenda Berger, Brian Sands. **Ticket Operations:** Chris Larrick, Doug George, Brad Sims, Anne Hinsberg, Stanley Cohen. **Clubhouse Operations:** Dave Dolney. **Office Manager:** Margo Carpenter. **Administrative Assistant:** Becci Velasco.

Field Staff

Manager: Joe Ferguson. **Coach:** Bien Figueroa. **Pitching Coach:** Bo McLaughlin. **Trainer:** Mitch Bibb.

Game Information

Radio Announcer: Dave Collins. **No. of Games Broadcast:** Unavailable. **Flagship Station:** Unavailable.

PA Announcer: Tom DeGroff. **Official Scorer:** Jeff Hertz.

Stadium Name (year opened): Prince George's Stadium (1994). **Location:** U.S. 50 to U.S. 301 South, left at second light. **Standard Game Times:** 7:05 p.m., Sun. 1:05.

Visiting Club Hotel: Days Inn-Historic Annapolis, 2520 Riva Rd., Annapolis, MD 21401. Telephone: (410) 224-2800.

ERIE

(Eastern League expansion team, 1999)

Office Address: 110 East 10th St., Erie, PA 16501. **Mailing Address:** P.O. Box 1776, Erie, PA 16507. **Telephone:** (814) 456-1300. **FAX:** (814) 456-7520.

Ownership, Management

Principal Owner: Alan Levin. **Vice President, Palisades Baseball:** Eric Haig.

General Manager: Andy Milovich.

Harrisburg
SENATORS

Office Address: RiverSide Stadium, City Island, Harrisburg, PA 17101. **Mailing Address:** P.O. Box 15757, Harrisburg, PA 17105. **Telephone:** (717) 231-4444. **FAX:** (717) 231-4445. **E-Mail Address:** hbgsenator @aol.com. **Website:** www.senatorsbaseball.com.

Affiliation (first year): Montreal Expos (1991). **Years in League:** 1924-35, 1987-.

Ownership, Management

Operated by: Harrisburg Civic Baseball Club, Inc.

Chairman of the Board: Greg Martini.

General Manager: Todd Vander Woude. **Business Manager:** Steve Resnick. **Assistant GM, Baseball Operations:** Mark Mattern. **Assistant GM, Business Operations:** Mark Clarke. **Director, Broadcasting/Media Relations:** Brad Sparesus. **Manager, Facilities:** Tim Foreman. **Manager, Concessions:** Steve Leininger. **Ticket Manager:** Paul Seeley. **Groundskeeper:** Joe Bialek. **Group Sales:** Brian Egli, Mickey Graham. **Picnic Operations:** Carol Baker. **Human Resources:** Sean Carroll. **Community Relations:** Jocelyn Johnson. **Ticket Sales:** Tom Wess.

Field Staff

Manager: Rick Sweet. **Coach:** Tim Leiper. **Pitching Coach:** Brent Strom. **Trainer:** Sean Bearer.

Game Information

Radio Announcers: Brad Sparesus, Mark Mattern. **No. of Games Broadcast:** Home-71, Away-71. **Flagship Station:** WKBO 1230-AM, WIOO 1000-AM.

PA Announcer: Chris Andre. **Official Scorer:** Gary Ritter.

Stadium Name (year opened): RiverSide Stadium (1987). **Location:** I-83, exit 23 (Second Street) to Market Street, bridge to City Island. **Standard Game Times:** 7:05 p.m.; Sun. 1:05.

Visiting Club Hotel: Hilton Hotel, One North 2nd St., Harrisburg, PA 17101. Telephone: (717) 233-6000.

New Britain
ROCK CATS

Office Address: South Main Street, New Britain, CT 06051. **Mailing Address:** P.O. Box 1718, New Britain, CT 06050. **Telephone:** (860) 224-8383. **FAX:** (860) 225-6267. **E-Mail Address:** buzas.assoc@snet.net. **Website:** gs1.com/rock/cats.html.

Affiliation (first year): Minnesota Twins (1995). **Years in League:** 1983-.

Ownership, Management

Operated by: Buzas Enterprises, Inc.

Principal Owner, Chairman: Joe Buzas. **President:** Hilary Buzas-Drammis.

General Manager: Gerry Berthiaume. **Assistant General Manager:** Mark Mogul. **Director, Stadium Operations:** Ryan Donahue. **Director, Media Relations/Community Relations:** Robin Wentz. **Director, Ticket Sales:** Sebastian Thomas. **Director, Group Sales:** Chris Faris. **Director, Food Services:** Donna Mogul.

Field Staff

Manager: John Russell. **Coach:** Rob Ellis. **Pitching Coach:** Eric Rasmussen. **Trainer:** Dave Pruemer.

Game Information

Radio: Unavailable.

PA Announcer: Roy Zurrell. **Official Scorer:** Unavailable.

Stadium Name (year opened): New Britain Stadium (1996). **Location:** From I-84, take U.S. 72 East (exit 35) or Route 9 South (exit 39A), left at Ellis Street (exit 25), left at South Main Street, stadium one mile on right. From Route 91 or Route 15, take Route 9 North to Route 71 (exit 24), first exit. **Standard Game Times:** April-May 6:35 p.m., June-Sept. 7; Sun. 2.

Visiting Club Hotel: Super 8, 1 Industrial Park Rd., Cromwell, CT 06416. Telephone: (860) 632-8888.

New Haven
RAVENS

Office Address: 252 Derby Ave., West Haven, CT 06516. Telephone: (203) 782-1666. FAX: (203) 782-3150. E-Mail Address: ravens@connix.com. Website: www.ravens.com.

Affiliation (first year): Colorado Rockies (1994). Years in League: 1916-32, 1994-.

Ownership, Management

Operated By: New Haven Ravens Baseball, LP.

Principal Owner: Edward Massey.

General Manager: Chris Canetti. Assistant General Manager: Joe Zajac. Controller: Tamara Nolin. Director, Stadium Operations: Roy Kirchner. Head Groundskeeper: Rick Capecelatro. Director, Media /Public Relations: Jessica Berry. Director, Ticket Sales: Mark Calabro. Director, Group Sales: Mike Thompson. Director, Food Services: Bill Brown. Office Manager: Lori McCarthy.

Field Staff

Manager: Tim Blackwell. Coach: Stu Cole. Pitching Coach: Jim Wright. Trainer: Bill Borowski.

Game Information

Radio Announcer: Matt Devlin. No. of Games Broadcast: Home-71, Away-71. Flagship Station: WAVZ 1300-AM.

PA Announcer: Unavailable. Official Scorer: Tim Bennett.

Stadium Name (year opened): Yale Field (1927). Location: From I-95, take eastbound exit 44 or westbound exit 45 to Route 10 and follow the Yale Bowl signs. From Merritt Parkway, take exit 57, follow to 34 East. Standard Game Times: 7:05 p.m., Sun. 2:05.

Visiting Club Hotel: Days Hotel, 490 Saw Mill Road, West Haven, CT 06516. Telephone: (203) 933-0344.

Norwich
NAVIGATORS

Office Address: 14 Stott Ave., Norwich, CT 06360. Mailing Address: P.O. Box 6003, Yantic, CT 06389. Telephone: (860) 887-7962. FAX: (860) 886-5996. E-Mail Address: gators@connix.com. Website: www.gators.com.

Affiliation (first year): New York Yankees (1995). Years in League: 1995-.

Ownership, Management

Operated by: Minor League Sports Enterprises, LP.

Principal Owners: Bob Friedman, Neil Goldman, Barry Gordon, Marc Klee, Hank Smith.

Chairman: Barry Gordon. President: Hank Smith.

General Manager: Brian Mahoney. Assistant General Manager, Stadium Operations: Geoff Brown. Assistant General Manager, Marketing: Tom Hinsch. Director, Finance: Richard Darling. Director, Media/Broadcasting: Shawn Holliday. Director, Ticket Sales: Chris Fritz. Ticket Manager: Adam Dolliver. Director, Group Sales: John Clark. Managers, Group Sales: Jackie Cirtello, Lou Ghetti. Director, Merchandising: Chris Augere. Director, Food Services: Richard Heimberg. Office Manager: Donna Arndt. Head Groundskeeper: Will Schnell.

Field Staff

Manager: Trey Hillman. Coach: Arnie Beyeler. Pitching Coach: Rick Tomlin. Trainer: Carl Randolph.

Game Information

Radio Announcers: Shawn Holliday, Mark Leinweaver. No. of Games Broadcast: Home-71, Away-71. Flagship Station: WSVB 980-AM.

PA Announcer: John Tuite. Official Scorer: Gene Gumbs.

Stadium Name (year opened): Senator Thomas J. Dodd Memorial Stadium (1995). Location: I-395 to exit 82, follow signs to Norwich Industrial Park, stadium is in back of industrial park. Standard Game Times: Mon.-Thur. (April-May) 6:35 p.m., (June-Sept.) 7:05; Fri. 7:05; Sat. (April-May)1:05, (June-Sept.) 7:05; Sun. (April-May) 1:05, (June-Sept.) 4:05.

Visiting Club Hotel: Days Inn-Niantic, 265 Flanders Road, Niantic, CT 06357. Telephone: (860) 739-6921.

Portland
SEA DOGS

Office Address: 271 Park Ave., Portland, ME 04102. **Mailing Address:** P.O. Box 636, Portland, ME 04104. **Telephone:** (207) 874-9300. **FAX:** (207) 780-0317. **Website:** portlandseadogs.com.

Affiliation (first year): Florida Marlins (1994). **Years in League:** 1994-.

Ownership, Management
Operated By: Portland, Maine, Baseball, Inc.
Principal Owner/Chairman: Daniel Burke.
President/General Manager: Charles Eshbach. **Assistant General Manager:** John Kameisha. **Director, Business Operations:** Jim Heffley. **Director, Business Development:** Elliott Barry. **Director, Stadium Operations:** Mike Fagerson. **Head Groundskeeper:** Rick Anderson. **Director, Sales/Marketing:** Mike Gillogly. **Director, Ticket Sales:** William Connolly. **Assistant Director, Tickets:** Jim Beaudoin. **Director, Group Sales:** Terryn Feeney. **Director, Merchandising:** Murray Roberts. **Director, Food Services:** Matthew Drivas. **Team Statistician:** Michael Beveridge. **Office Manager:** Judy Bray.

Field Staff
Manager: Lynn Jones. **Coach:** Sal Rende. **Pitching Coach:** Brian Peterson. **Trainer:** Tim Abraham.

Game Information
Radio Announcer: Andy Young. **No. of Games Broadcast:** Home-71, Away-71. **Flagship Station:** WZAN 970-AM.

PA Announcer: Dean Rogers. **Official Scorers:** Leroy Rand, Mike Beveridge.

Stadium Name (year opened): Hadlock Field (1994). **Location:** From south, I-295 to exit 5A, merge onto Congress Street, left at St. John Street, merge right onto Park Avenue; From north, I-295 to exit 6A, right on Park Avenue. **Standard Game Times:** April-May 6 p.m., June-Aug. 7; Sat. (April-May) 1, (June-Aug.) 7; Sun. (April-May) 1, (June-Aug.) 4.

Visiting Club Hotel: Radisson-Eastland, 157 High St., Portland, ME 04101. Telephone: (207) 775-5411.

Reading
PHILLIES

Office Address: Rt. 61 South/1900 Centre Ave., Reading, PA 19605. **Mailing Address:** P.O. Box 15050, Reading, PA 19612. **Telephone:** (610) 375-8469. **FAX:** (610) 373-5868. **E-Mail Address:** rphils@voicenet.com. **Website:** www.readingphillies.com.

Affiliation (first year): Philadelphia Phillies (1967). **Years in League:** 1933-35, 1952-61, 1963-65, 1967-.

Ownership, Management
Operated By: E&J Baseball Club, Inc.
Principal Owner/President: Craig Stein.
General Manager: Chuck Domino. **Assistant General Manager:** Scott Hunsicker. **Director, Operations:** Andy Bortz. **Assistant Director, Operations:** Jamie Keitsock. **Director, Communications/Community Development:** Mark Wallace. **Assistant Director, Communications/Community Development:** Rob Hackash. **Director, Tickets:** Zach Conen. **Director, Group Sales:** Jeff Tagliaferro. **Assistant Director, Group Sales:** Joe Pew. **Merchandise/Group Sales Associate:** Kevin Sklenarik. **Director, Business Development/Game Operations:** Troy Potthoff. **Director, Stadium Grounds:** Dan Douglas. **Director, Office Management:** Denise Haage.

Field Staff
Manager: Al LeBoeuf. **Coach:** Milt Thompson. **Pitching Coach:** Ross Grimsley. **Trainer:** Troy Hoffert.

Game Information
Radio Announcer: Steve Degler. **No. of Games Broadcast:** Home-71, Away-71. **Flagship Station:** WRAW 1340-AM.

PA Announcer: Dave Bauman. **Official Scorer:** John Lemcke.

Stadium Name (year opened): Reading Municipal Memorial Stadium (1950). **Location:** From east, take Pennsylvania Turnpike West to Morgantown exit, to 176 North, to 422 West, to 222 North, to Route 61 South exit. From west, take 422 East to Route 222 North, to Route 61 exit. From north, take 222 South to Sinking Spring exit, to Route 61 South exit and proceed four miles. From south, take 222 North to 422 West, at split remain on Route 222 North, exit at Route 61 South. **Standard Game Times:** 7:05; Sun. 1:05.

Visiting Club Hotel: Wellesley Inn, 910 Woodland Ave., Wyomissing, PA 19610. Telephone: (610) 374-1500.

Trenton
THUNDER

Office/Mailing Address: One Thunder Rd., Trenton, NJ 08611. **Telephone:** (609) 394-3300. **FAX:** (609) 394-9666. **E-Mail Address:** office@trentonthunder.com. **Website:** www.trentonthunder.com.

Affiliation (first year): Boston Red Sox (1995). **Years in League:** 1994-.

Ownership, Management

Operated by: Garden State Baseball, LP.

General Manager/Chief Operating Officer: Wayne Hodes. **Assistant General Manager:** Tom McCarthy. **Director, Stadium Operations:** John Fierko. **Controller:** John Coletta. **Assistant Controller:** Kelly Beach. **Director, Sales/Marketing:** Eric Lipsman. **Director, Production/Event Operation:** Rick Brenner. **Director, Public Relations:** Andrea Bunney. **Director, Ticket Sales:** Scott Gross. **Director, Group Sales:** Adam Palant. **Director, Broadcasting:** Andy Freed. **Director, Food Services:** Harry Smith. **Manager, Media Relations:** Kate McKenna. **Clubhouse Operations:** Donnie Phippen. **Office Manager:** Sue Chassen. **Head Groundskeeper:** Jeff Migliaccio.

Field Staff

Manager: DeMarlo Hale. **Coach:** Dave Gallagher. **Pitching Coach:** Ralph Treuel. **Trainer:** Bryan Jaquette.

Game Information

Radio Announcers: Tom McCarthy, Andy Freed. **No. of Games Broadcast:** Home-71, Away-71. **Flagship Station:** WHWH 1350-AM.

PA Announcer: Brandon Hardison. **Official Scorers:** Jay Dunn, Mike Maconi.

Stadium Name (year opened): Mercer County Waterfront Park (1994). **Location:** Route 129 North, left at Cass Street. **Standard Game Times:** 7:05 p.m.; Sat. (April-June) 1:05, (July-Aug.) 7:05; Sun. 1:05.

Visiting Club Hotel: McIntosh Inn, 3270 Brunswick Pike, Lawrenceville, NJ 08648. Telephone: (609) 896-3700.

SOUTHERNLEAGUE

Class AA

Mailing Address: One Depot St., Suite 300, Marietta, GA 30060. **Telephone:** (770) 428-4749. **FAX:** (770) 428-4849. **E-Mail Address:** soleague@bellsouth.net.

Years League Active: 1964-.

President/Secretary-Treasurer: Arnold Fielkow.

Vice President: Don Mincher (Huntsville).

Directors: Don Beaver (Knoxville), Peter Bragan Sr. (Jacksonville), Steve Bryant (Carolina), Frank Burke (Chattanooga), Steve DeSalvo (Greenville), Bill Hardekopf (Birmingham), David Hersh (West Tenn), John Higgins (Orlando), Eric Margenau (Mobile), Don Mincher (Huntsville).

Arnold Fielkow

Director, Business Development/ Marketing: Irvin Cohen. **Executive Assistant:** Monica Cooper.

1998 Opening Date: April 2. **Closing Date:** Sept. 7.

Regular Season: 140 games (split-schedule).

Division Structure: East—Carolina, Greenville, Jacksonville, Knoxville, Orlando. **West**—Birmingham, Chattanooga, Huntsville, Mobile, West Tenn.

Playoff Format: First-half division winners play second-half division winners in best-of-5 series. Division playoff winners meet in best-of-5 series.

All-Star Games: June 22 at Mobile, AL; July 8 at New Haven, CT (joint Double-A game).

Roster Limit: 23 active, until midnight Aug. 10 when roster can be expanded to 24. **Player Eligibility Rule:** No restrictions.

Brand of Baseball: Rawlings.

Statistician: Howe Sportsdata International, Boston Fish Pier, West Bldg. #1, Suite 302, Boston MA 02210.

Umpires: Mike Alvarado (Moses Lake, WA), Chris Boberg (Charlotte, NC), Cory Erickson (St. Petersburg, FL), Daryn Fredrickson (Louisville, KY), Chris Guccione (Salida, CO), William Haze (Gilbert, AZ), Jeff Head (Jasper, AL), Brian Knight (Helena, MT), Brian McCraw (Nashville, TN), Scott Nelson (Coshocton, OH), Ray Parrish (Lakeland, FL), Stu Robertson (Gretna, VA), Webb Turner (Hope Mills, NC), Roger Walling (Placentia, CA), Greg Williams (Fort Lauderdale, FL).

Stadium Information

Club	Stadium	Dimensions			Capacity	'97 Att.
		LF	CF	RF		
Birmingham	Hoover Metropolitan	340	405	340	10,800	302,144
Carolina	Five County	330	400	330	6,000	265,219
Chattanooga	Engel	325	471	318	7,500	228,391
Greenville	Greenville Municipal	345	400	345	7,048	254,049
Huntsville	Davis Municipal	345	405	330	10,200	285,580
Jacksonville	Wolfson Park	320	390	320	8,200	238,238
Knoxville	Bill Meyer	330	400	330	6,412	138,389
Mobile	Hank Aaron	325	400	310	6,000	332,639
Orlando	Tinker Field	340	425	320	5,104	147,241
*West Tenn	Pringles Park	310	395	320	6,000	113,183

*Franchise operated in Memphis in 1997

Birmingham
BARONS

Office Address: 100 Ben Chapman Dr., Birmingham, AL 35244. **Mailing Address:** P.O. Box 360007, Birmingham, AL 35236. **Telephone:** (205) 988-3200. **FAX:** (205) 988-9698. **E-Mail Address:** barons@quicklink.net

Affiliation (first year): Chicago White Sox (1986). **Years in League:** 1964-65, 1967-75, 1981-.

Ownership, Management

Operated by: Elmore Sports Group, Ltd.

Principal Owner: Dave Elmore. **President/Chief Executive Officer:** Bill Hardekopf.

Vice President/General Manager: Tony Ensor. **Assistant General Manager/Group Sales:** Jonathan Nelson. **Director, Stadium Operations:** Chris Jenkins. **Head Groundskeeper:** Mike Zullo. **Director, Media Relations:** David Lee. **Director, Community Relations:** Melanie McCullough. **Director, Ticket Sales:** Joe Drake. **Director, Food Services:** Thomas Deakle. **Office Manager:** Norma Rosebrough. **Accounting Clerk:** Kecia Arnold. **Catering Manager:** Joe Dorolek. **Manager, Clubhouse Operations:** Ken Dunlap. **Administrative Assistants:** Ed Crackle, Jennifer Sicola, Ashley Farrar, Melissa Copeland.

Field Staff

Manager: Dave Huppert. **Coach:** Steve Whitaker. **Pitching Coach:** Steve Renko. **Trainer:** Scott Takao.

Game Information

Radio Announcer: Curt Bloom. **No. of Games Broadcast:** Home-70, Away-70. **Flagship Station:** WAPI 1070-AM.

PA Announcer: Derek Scudder. **Official Scorer:** Bill Graham.

Stadium Name (year opened): Hoover Metropolitan Stadium (1988). **Location:** I-459 to Highway 150 (exit 10) in Hoover. **Standard Game Times:** 7 p.m.; Sun. (April-June) 2, (July-Sept.) 6.

Visiting Club Hotel: Riverchase Inn, 1800 Riverchase Dr., Birmingham, AL 35244. Telephone: (205) 985-7500.

Carolina
MUDCATS

Office Address: 1501 N.C. Highway 39, Zebulon, NC 27597. **Mailing Address:** P.O. Drawer 1218, Zebulon, NC 27597. **Telephone:** (919) 269-2287. **FAX:** (919) 269-4910. **E-Mail Address:** mudcats@bellsouth.net. **Website:** www.fanlink.com/carolinamudcats.

Affiliation (first year): Pittsburgh Pirates (1991). **Years in League:** 1991-.

Ownership, Management

Operated by: Carolina Mudcats Professional Baseball Club, Inc.

Principal Owner/President: Steve Bryant.

General Manager: Joe Kremer. **Assistant General Manager:** Joe Chatman. **Director, Stadium Operations:** Brian Becknell. **Head Groundskeeper:** Bill Riggan. **Director, Media Relations:** Jim Duzyk. **Director, Sales/Marketing:** Duke Sanders. **Director, Community Relations:** Holly Myers. **Director, Ticket Sales:** Steven Weydig. **Director, Group Sales:** Bob Lord. **Director, Merchandising:** Brian Tatum. **Director, Special Projects:** Jim Miller. **Office Manager:** Jackie DiPrimo. **Clubhouse Manager:** Kevin Bryant. **Director, Telemarketing:** Jeff Curtis.

Field Staff

Manager: Jeff Banister. **Coach:** Curtis Wilkerson. **Pitching Coach:** Dave Rajsich. **Trainer:** Mike Sandoval.

Game Information

Radio Announcer: Pete Schopen. **No. of Games Broadcast:** Home-70, Away-70. **Flagship Station:** WSAY 98.5-FM.

PA Announcer: Duke Sanders. **Official Scorer:** John Hobgood.

Stadium Name (year opened): Five County Stadium (1991). **Location:** From Raleigh, I-64 East to 264 East, exit at Highway 39 in Zebulon. **Standard Game Times:** 7:30 p.m.; Sun. (April-May) 2:05, (June-Sept.) 5:05.

Visiting Club Hotel: Plantation Inn-Raleigh, 6401 Capital Blvd., Raleigh, NC 27616. Telephone: (919) 876-1411.

Chattanooga
LOOKOUTS

Office Address: 1130 East Third St., Chattanooga, TN 37403. **Mailing Address:** P.O. Box 11002, Chattanooga, TN 37401. **Telephone:** (423) 267-2208. **FAX:** (423) 267-4258.

Affiliation (first year): Cincinnati Reds (1988). **Years in League:** 1964-65, 1976-.

Ownership, Management

Operated by: Engel Stadium Corporation.

Principal Owners: Frank Burke, Daniel Burke, Charles Eshbach.

President, General Manager: Frank Burke. **Assistant General Manager:** Rich Mozingo. **Director, Public Relations:** Brad Smith. **Head Groundskeeper:** Lee Batten. **Director, Merchandising:** Katie Harris. **Directors, Group Sales:** Matthew Louck, Jake Pierson. **Director, Concessions:** Tony DaSilveira. **Director, Ticket Operations:** Rob Hambor. **Office Manager:** Debra Berrigan.

Field Staff

Manager: Mark Berry. **Coach:** Mark Wagner. **Pitching Coach:** Mack Jenkins. **Trainer:** Billy Maxwell.

Game Information

Radio Announcers: Larry Ward, Todd Agne. **No. of Games Broadcast:** Home-70, Away-70. **Flagship Station:** WSGC 101.9-FM.

PA Announcer: Unavailable. **Official Scorer:** Wurt Gammon.

Stadium Name (year opened): Engel Stadium (1930). **Location:** I-24 to U.S. 27 North to 4th St. exit, 1¾ miles to O'Neal Street, right on O'Neal. **Standard Game Times:** 7 p.m.; Wed. 12:30, Sun. 2.

Visiting Club Hotel: Holiday Inn Southeast, 6700 Ringgold Rd., Chattanooga, TN 37412. Telephone: (423) 892-8100.

Greenville
BRAVES

Office Address: One Braves Ave., Greenville, SC 29607. **Mailing Address:** P.O. Box 16683, Greenville, SC 29606. **Telephone:** (864) 299-3456. **FAX:** (864) 277-7369.

Affiliation (first year): Atlanta Braves (1984). **Years in League:** 1984-.

Ownership, Management

Operated by: Atlanta National League Baseball Club, Inc.

Principal Owner: Ted Turner. **President:** Stan Kasten.

General Manager: Steve DeSalvo. **Assistant General Manager:** Jim Bishop. **Director, Ticket Sales:** Jimmy Moore. **Head Groundskeeper:** Matt Taylor. **Director, Stadium Operations:** Hollye Edwards. **Office Manager:** Brenda Yoder.

Field Staff

Manager: Randy Ingle. **Coach:** Mel Roberts. **Pitching Coach:** Mike Alvarez. **Trainer:** Jay Williams.

Game Information

Radio Announcer: Mark Hauser. **No. of Games Broadcast:** Home-70, Away-70. **Flagship Station:** WPCI 1490-AM.

PA Announcer: Tim Worley. **Official Scorer:** Jimmy Moore.

Stadium Name (year opened): Greenville Municipal Stadium (1984). **Location:** I-85 to exit 46 (Mauldin Road), east two miles. **Standard Game Times:** 7:15 p.m.; Sun. 2:15.

Visiting Club Hotel: Quality Inn, 50 Orchard Park Dr., Greenville, SC 29615. Telephone: (864) 297-9000.

Huntsville STARS

Office Address: 3125 Leeman Ferry Rd., Huntsville, AL 35801. **Mailing Address:** P.O. Box 2769, Huntsville, AL 35804. **Telephone:** (205) 882-2562. **FAX:** (205) 880-0801. **E-Mail Address:** stars@traveller.com. **Website:** www.huntsvillestars.com.

Affiliation (first year): Oakland Athletics (1985). **Years In League:** 1985-.

Ownership, Management

Operated by: Huntsville Stars Baseball, LLC.

President/General Manager: Don Mincher. **Vice President/Executive Director:** Patrick Nichol.

Assistant General Manager: Bryan Dingo. **Director, Business Operations:** Pat Mincher. **Director, Stadium Operations:** Mark Gorenc. **Head Groundskeeper:** Mike Dudash. **Director, Media/Public Relations:** Jim Riley. **Director, Ticket Sales:** Cynthia Giles. **Director, Merchandising:** Devin Rose. **Manager, Concessions:** Gregg Corbin.

Field Staff

Manager: Jeffrey Leonard. **Coach:** Dave Joppie. **Pitching Coach:** Bert Bradley. **Trainer:** Brian Thorson.

Game Information

Radio Announcer: Steve Kornya. **No. of Games Broadcast:** Home-70, Away-70. **Flagship Station:** WTKI 1450-AM.

PA Announcer: Tommy Hayes. **Official Scorer:** Larry Smith.

Stadium Name (year opened): Joe W. Davis Municipal Stadium (1985). **Location:** I-65 to I-565 East, south on Memorial Parkway to Drake Ave. exit. **Standard Game Times:** 7:05 p.m.; Sun. (April-June) 2:05, (July-Sept.) 7:05.

Visiting Club Hotel: La Quinta Inn, 3141 University Dr., Huntsville, AL 35805. Telephone: (205) 533-0756.

Jacksonville SUNS

Office Address: 1201 East Duval St., Jacksonville, FL 32202. **Mailing Address:** P.O. Box 4756, Jacksonville, FL 32201. **Telephone:** (904) 358-2846. **FAX:** (904) 358-2845. **E-Mail Address:** jaxsuns@bellsouth.net. **Website:** www.jaxsuns.com.

Affiliation (first year): Detroit Tigers (1995). **Years in League:** 1970-.

Ownership, Management

Operated by: Baseball Jax, Inc.

Principal Owner/President: Peter Bragan Sr. **Assistant to President:** Jerry LeMoine.

Vice President/General Manager: Peter Bragan Jr. **Assistant General Manager:** Todd Budnick. **Director, Stadium Operations:** Ryan Valerius. **Head Groundskeeper:** Mark Clay. **Director, Ticket Sales:** Christine Meyers. **Director, Marketing:** Kirk Goodman. **Director, Group Sales:** Jamie Smith. **Director, Concessions:** David Leathers. **Clubhouse Manager:** Ray Sterling. **Office Manager:** Cathy Wiggins. **Administrative Assistants:** Bryan Franker, Emily Mosier.

Field Staff

Manager: Dave Anderson. **Coach:** Matt Martin. **Pitching Coach:** Rich Bombard. **Trainer:** Matt Lewis.

Game Information

Radio Announcer: David Schultz. **No. of Games Broadcast:** Home-70, Away-70. **Flagship Station:** WBWL 600-AM.

PA Announcer: John Leard. **Official Scorer:** Paul Ivice.

Stadium Name (year opened): Wolfson Park (1955). **Location:** From I-95 North to 20th Street East exit, take to end, turn right before Jacksonville Municipal Stadium; From I-95 South to Emerson Street exit, take right to Hart Bridge, take Sports Complex exit, left at light to stop sign, take right and quick left; From Mathews Bridge, take A. Phillip Randolph exit, right off ramp, right at stop sign, left at second light to stadium. **Standard Game Times:** 7:35 p.m, 12:35.; Sun. 2:35, 5:35.

Visiting Club Hotels: La Quinta-Orange Park, 8555 Blanding Blvd., Jacksonville, FL 32244. Telephone: (904) 778-9539.

Knoxville
SMOKIES

Office Address: 633 Jessamine St., Knoxville, TN 37917. Telephone: (423) 637-9494. FAX: (423) 523-9913. E-Mail Address: smokies@1stresource.com. Website: www.1stresource.com/~ksmokies.

Affiliation (first year): Toronto Blue Jays (1980). Years in League: 1964-67, 1972-.

Ownership, Management

Operated by: Knoxville Smokies Baseball, Inc.
Principal Owner/President: Don Beaver.
General Manager: Dan Rajkowski. Assistant General Manager: Brian Cox. Executive Director, Sales/Marketing: Mark Seaman. Director, Group Sales/Marketing: Jeff Shoaf. Head Groundskeeper: Bob Shoemaker. Administrative Assistant: Heather Sharpe.

Field Staff

Manager: Omar Malave. Coach: J.J. Cannon. Pitching Coach: Bill Monbouquette. Trainer: Mike Wirsta.

Game Information

Radio: None.
PA Announcer: Unavailable. Official Scorer: Unavailable.
Stadium Name (year opened): Bill Meyer Stadium (1955). Location: I-40 to James White Parkway, right on Summit Hill Drive, right on Central Ave., right on Willow Ave to park. Standard Game Times: 7:15 p.m., Wed 12, Sun. 5.
Visiting Club Hotel: Best Western, 118 Merchants Dr., Knoxville, TN 37912. Telephone: (423) 688-3141.

Mobile
BAYBEARS

Office Address: 755 Bolling Bros. Blvd., Mobile, AL 36606. Mailing Address: P.O. Box 161663, Mobile, AL 36616. Telephone: (334) 479-2327. FAX: (334) 476-1147. E-Mail Address: mobilebaybears@mobilebaybears.com. Website: mobilebaybears.com.

Affiliation (first year): San Diego Padres (1997). Years in League: 1997-.

Ownership, Management

Operated by: United Sports Ventures.
Principal Owner: Eric Margenau.
General Manager: Tom Simmons. Assistant General Manager: Kevin Cummings. Director, Business Operations: Mark Ruckwardt. Director, Merchandising: Anthony Holman. Director, Group Sales: Dan Zusman. Director, Public Relations/Broadcasting: Tom Nichols. Director, Sales: Travis Toth. Coordinator, Ticket Sales: Doug Stephens. Manager, Special Events: Allen Jernigan. Director, Facility Operations: Pat White. Manager, Community Relations: Chris Morgan. Manager, Customer Relations: William Younce. Manager, Creative Services: Freddie Parce. Manager, Stadium Operations: Brian Hayes.

Field Staff

Manager: Mike Ramsey. Coach: Jim Bowie. Pitching Coach: Don Alexander. Trainer: Jason Haeussinger.

Game Information

Radio Announcer: Tom Nichols. No. of Games Broadcast: Home-70, Away-70. Flagship Station: WNSP 105.5-FM.
PA Announcer: Unavailable. Official Scorer: Unavailable.
Stadium Name (year opened): Hank Aaron Stadium (1997). Location: I-65 to Highway 90 East, right at McVay, right at Bolling Bros. Boulevard. Standard Game Times: 7:05 p.m.; Sun. (April-May) 2:05, (June-Sept.) 6:05.
Visiting Club Hotel: Holiday Inn-Historic District, 301 Government St., Mobile, AL 36602. Telephone (334) 694-0100.

Orlando
RAYS

Office Address: 287 Tampa Ave. South, Orlando, FL 32805. **Telephone:** (407) 649-7297. **FAX:** (407) 649-1637. **E-Mail Address:** orays@aol.com.
Affiliation (first year): Seattle Mariners (1998). **Years in League:** 1973-

Ownership, Management
Operated by: Orlando Rays Baseball, Inc.
Principal Owner: Tampa Bay Devil Rays, Ltd.
President: Vincent Naimoli.
General Manager: Thomas Ramsberger. **Assistant General Manager:** John Cody. **Director, Sales/Marketing:** Tom Albano. **Director, Public Relations:** Pat Hernan. **Director, Ticket Sales:** Lynn Barnette. **Director, Merchandising:** Mack Powell. **Head Groundskeeper:** Doug Lopas.

Field Staff
Manager: Dan Rohn. **Coach:** Henry Cotto. **Pitching Coach:** Pat Rice. **Trainer:** Rob Nodine.

Game Information
Radio: None.
PA Announcer: Tom Peters. **Official Scorer:** Tim Wilkening.
Stadium Name (year opened): Tinker Field (1964). **Location:** I-4 to Colonial Drive (State Road 50), west to Tampa Ave., left on Tampa Ave for 1½ miles. **Standard Game Times:** 7 p.m.; Sun. (April-June) 2, (July-August.) 6.
Visiting Club Hotel: Unavailable.

West Tenn
DIAMOND JAXX

Office Address: Pringles Park, 4 Fun Place, Jackson, TN 38305. **Telephone:** (901) 664-2020. **FAX:** (901) 988-5246. **E-Mail Address:** baseball@diamondjaxx.com. **Website:** www.diamondjaxx.com.
Affiliation (first year): Chicago Cubs (1998). **Years In League:** 1998-.

Ownership, Management
Operated by: Professional Sports and Entertainment Associates of Tennessee, LP.
President/General Manager: David Hersh.
Assistant General Manager: Jarrod Coates. **Director, Business Operations:** Debbie Swacker. **Regional Sales Managers:** Brian Cheever, Chad Hallett, Russ McBryde. **Controller:** Dianne Sherrod. **Director, Stadium Operations:** Matt Erwin. **Director, Media Relations/Broadcasting:** John Miller. **Media Assistant:** Amy Balthrop. **Director, Merchandising:** Terrie Hopper. **Customer Service Specialist:** Patty Haynes. **Executive Assistant:** Betsy Bailey. **Director, Food Services:** Robert Garcia. **Box Office Manager:** Steven Aldridge.

Field Staff
Manager: Dave Trembley. **Coach:** Tack Wilson. **Pitching Coach:** Alan Dunn. **Trainer:** Jim O'Reilly.

Game Information
Radio Announcer: John Miller. **No. of Games Broadcast:** Home-70, Away-70. **Flagship Station:** WNWS 101.5-FM.
PA Announcer: Brad McCoy. **Official Scorer:** Ron Barry.
Stadium Name (year opened): Pringles Park (1998). **Location:** From I-40, take exit 85 South to F.E. Wright Drive, left on Ridgecrest Extended, left to park. **Standard Game Times:** 7:05 p.m.; Sun. (April-June) 2:05, (July-Sept.) 5:05 p.m.
Visiting Club Hotel: Garden Plaza Hotel, 1770 Highway 45 Bypass, Jackson, TN 38305. Telephone: (901) 664-6900.

TEXAS LEAGUE

Class AA

Mailing Address: 2442 Facet Oak, San Antonio, TX 78232. **Telephone:** (210) 545-5297. **FAX:** (210) 545-5298. **E-Mail Address:** tkayser@texas-league.com.

Years League Active: 1888-1890, 1892, 1895-1899, 1902-1942, 1946-.

President/Treasurer: Tom Kayser.

Vice President: Bill Blackwell (Jackson). **Corporate Secretary:** Chuck Lamson (Tulsa).

Directors: Bill Blackwell (Jackson), Chuck Lamson (Tulsa), Taylor Moore (Shreveport), Rick Parr (El Paso), Miles Prentice (Midland), Steve Shaad (Wichita), Bill Valentine (Arkansas), Burl Yarbrough (San Antonio).

Administrative Assistant: Ronald Bartlett.

Tom Kayser

1998 Opening Date: April 2. **Closing Date:** Aug. 29.

Regular Season: 140 games (split-schedule).

Division Structure: East—Arkansas, Jackson, Shreveport, Tulsa. **West**—El Paso, Midland, San Antonio, Wichita.

Playoff Format: First-half division winners play second-half division winners in best-of-5 series. Division playoff winners meet in best-of-7 series for league championship.

1998 All-Star Game: July 28 at Little Rock, AR; July 8 at New Haven, CT (joint Double-A game).

Roster Limit: 23 active, until midnight Aug. 10 when roster can be expanded to 24. **Player Eligibility Rule:** No restrictions.

Brand of Baseball: Rawlings.

Statistician: Howe Sportsdata International, Boston Fish Pier, West Bldg. #1, Suite 302, Boston, MA 02210.

Umpires: David Aschwege (Lincoln, NE), Dave Baldwin (Reno, NV), Dave Brandt (Mission, KS), Wes Hamilton (Edmond, OK), Scott Higgins (Keizer, OR), John Lomayaya (Tempe, AZ), Steve Mattingly (Phoenix, AZ), Sean Randall (Olathe, KS), Pat Riley (Gilbert, AZ), Jack Samuels (Orange, CA), Jeff Spedoske (Lansing, MI), Jim Wolf (West Hills, CA).

Stadium Information

Club	Stadium	Dimensions			Capacity	'97 Att.
		LF	CF	RF		
Arkansas	Ray Winder Field	330	390	345	6,083	195,935
El Paso	Cohen	340	410	340	9,765	302,894
Jackson	Smith-Wills	330	400	330	5,200	160,587
Midland	Christensen	333	398	333	5,000	185,532
San Antonio	Wolff Municipal	310	402	340	6,200	336,542
Shreveport	Fair Grounds Field	330	400	330	6,200	164,922
Tulsa	Drillers	335	390	340	10,955	333,019
Wichita	Lawrence-Dumont	344	401	312	6,111	152,205

Arkansas
TRAVELERS

Office Address: Ray Winder Field at War Memorial Park, Little Rock, AR 72205. **Mailing Address:** P.O. Box 55066, Little Rock, AR 72215. **Telephone:** (501) 664-1555. **FAX:** (501) 664-1834. **E-Mail Address:** travs@aristotle.com. **Website:** www.travs.com

Affiliation (first year): St. Louis Cardinals (1966). **Years in League:** 1966-.

Ownership, Management

Operated by: Arkansas Travelers Baseball, Inc.
President: Bert Parke.
Executive Vice President/General Manager: Bill Valentine. **Assistant GM/Sales, Promotions:** Hap Seliga. **Assistant GM/Concessions, Merchandising:** John Evans. **Director, Stadium Operations:** Rob Kelly. **Park Superintendent:** Greg Johnston. **Assistant Park Superintendent:** Reggie Temple. **Bookkeeper:** Nena Valentine.

Field Staff

Manager: Chris Maloney. **Coach:** Luis Melendez. **Pitching Coach:** Rich Folkers. **Trainer:** B.J. Maack.

Game Information

Radio Announcer: Unavailable. **No. of Games Broadcast:** Home-70. **Flagship Station:** KARN 920-AM.

PA Announcer: Bill Downs. **Official Scorer:** George Avery.

Stadium Name (year opened): Ray Winder Field (1932). **Location:** I-630 at Fair Park Boulevard exit. **Standard Game Time:** 7:30 p.m., Sun 2.

Visiting Club Hotel: Little Rock Hilton, 925 South University, Little Rock, AR 72204. Telephone: (501) 664-6020.

El Paso
DIABLOS

Office Address: 9700 Gateway North Blvd., El Paso, TX 79924. **Mailing Address:** P.O. Drawer 4797, El Paso, TX 79914. **Telephone:** (915) 755-2000. **FAX:** (915) 757-0671. **E-Mail Address:** tickets@diablos.com.

Affiliation (first year): Milwaukee Brewers (1981). **Years in League:** 1962-70, 1972-.

Ownership, Management

Operated by: Diamond Sports, Inc.
Principal Owners: Peter Gray, Bill Pereira.
President/General Manager: Rick Parr. **Associate General Manager:** Andrew Wheeler. **Associate GM/Director, Stadium Operations:** Rob Sesich. **Controller:** Sue Peterson. **Head Groundskeeper:** Jody Skipworth. **Director, Public Relations:** Matt Hicks. **Director, Sales/Marketing:** Ken Schrom. **Account Representatives:** Bernie Ricono, Brett Pollock, Cori Vasquez. **Director, Ticket Sales:** Bret Beer. **Director, Group Sales:** Beverly Mowad. **Director, Food Services:** Jerry McClelland. **Office Manager:** Heather Smith. **Administrative Assistant:** Mary Hill.

Field Staff

Manager: Ed Romero. **Coach:** Jon Pont. **Pitching Coach:** Dwight Bernard. **Trainer:** Bryan Bute.

Game Information

Radio Announcers: Matt Hicks, Dave Popkin. **No. of Games Broadcast:** Home-70, Away-70. **Flagship Station:** KROD 600-AM.

PA Announcer: Tony Bravo. **Official Scorer:** Bernie Olivas.

Stadium Name (year opened): Cohen Stadium (1990). **Location:** I-10 to U.S. 54 (Patriot Freeway), east to Diana exit to Gateway North Boulevard. **Standard Game Times:** April-May 6:30 p.m., June-August 7; Sun. 6:30.

Visiting Club Hotel: Quality Inn, 6201 Gateway Blvd. West, El Paso, TX 79925. Telephone: (915) 778-6611.

Jackson
GENERALS

Office Address: 1200 Lakeland Dr., Jackson, MS 39216. Mailing Address: P.O. Box 4209, Jackson, MS 39296. Telephone: (601) 981-4664. FAX: (601) 981-4669. E-Mail Address: jagenerals@aol.com.

Affiliation (first year): Houston Astros (1991). Years in League: 1975-.

Ownership, Management
Operated by: Cowboy Maloney Supply Co., Inc.

Principal Owner/Chairman: J. Con Maloney. President: Eddie Maloney. Vice President/General Manager: Bill Blackwell. Assistant GM/Director, Food Services: Frank Buccieri. Head Groundskeeper: Joe Whipps. Director, Broadcasting/Sales: Bill Walberg. Director, Group Sales: Tim Attel. Director, Operations: Brian Heller. Clubhouse Operations: Hugh Staples, Pete Phillips. Office Manager: Judy Blackwell.

Field Staff
Manager: Jim Pankovits. Coach: Jorge Orta. Pitching Coach: Charley Taylor. Trainer: Mike Ra.

Game Information
Radio Announcer: Bill Walberg. No. of Games Broadcast: Home-70, Away-70. Flagship Station: WJDS 620-AM.

PA Announcer: Glen Waddle. Official Scorer: Blair Cash.

Stadium Name (year opened): Smith-Wills Stadium (1975). Location: I-55 to Lakeland Drive exit, ¼ mile on left at Cool Papa Bell Drive. Standard Game Times: 7 p.m.; Sun. 2:30 (April-May), 6 (June-August).

Visiting Club Hotel: Holiday Inn Southwest, 2649 Highway 80 West, Jackson, MS 39204. Telephone: (601) 355-3472.

Midland
ANGELS

Office Address: 4300 N. Lamesa Road, Midland, TX 79705. Mailing Address: P.O. Box 51187, Midland, TX 79710. Telephone: (915) 683-4251. FAX: (915) 683-0994. E-Mail Address: angels@iglobal.net. Website: www.midlandangels.org.

Affiliation (first year): Anaheim Angels (1985). Years in League: 1972-.

Ownership, Management
Operated by: Midland Sports, Inc.

Principal Owners: Miles Prentice, Bob Richmond.

President: Miles Prentice.

General Manager: Monty Hoppel. Assistant General Manager: Rick Carden. Director, Business Operations: Eloisa Robledo. Director, Stadium Operations/Concessions: Jeff Von Holle. Head Groundskeeper: Lee Velarde. Director, Media/Public Relations: Bob Hards. Director, Sales/Marketing: Harold Fuller. Sales and Marketing Representative: Bill Levy. Director, Community Relations: Jamie Richardson. Director, Group Sales: Bob Flannery. Director, Merchandising: Ray Fieldhouse. Office Manager: Noel Martinez (Midland), Claudia Jaquez (Odessa). Director, Youth Relations: Andy Alvarez. Manager, Facilities: Jeff Corbett. Director, Team Operations: Brad Haynes. Administrative Assistant: Pat Kerin.

Field Staff
Manager: Don Long. Coach: Todd Claus. Pitching Coach: Rick Wise.Trainer: Doug Baker.

Game Information
Radio Announcer: Bob Hards. No. of Games Broadcast: Home-70, Away-70. Flagship Station: KCRS 550-AM.

PA Announcer: Robert Hallmark. Official Scorer: Bobby Dunn.

Stadium Name (year opened): Christensen Stadium (1972). Location: Big Spring exit off Rankin Highway to Loop 250, exit right on Lamesa Road. Standard Game Times: 7 p.m.; Sun. 6.

Visiting Club Hotel: ClayDesta Inn, 4108 North Big Spring, Midland, TX 79705. Telephone: (915) 686-8733.

San Antonio
MISSIONS

Office Address: 5757 Highway 90 West, San Antonio, TX 78227. Telephone: (210) 675-7275. FAX: (210) 670-0001. E-Mail Address: sainfo@21stcenturyacess.com. Website: samissions.com.

Affiliation (first year): Los Angeles Dodgers (1977). Years In League: 1888, 1892, 1895-99, 1907-42, 1946-64, 1967-.

Ownership, Management

Operated by: Elmore Sports Group.

Principal Owner: Dave Elmore. President: Burl Yarbrough.

General Manager: David Oldham. Assistant General Manager: Jimi Olsen. Director, Business Operations: Marc Frey. Director, Stadium Operations: Jeff Long. Head Groundskeeper: Mike Pankey. Director, Media/Public Relations: Jim White. Director, Sales/Marketing: Tom Davis. Senior Account Representative: Trent Brown. Director, Community Relations: Shannon Walsh. Director, Ticket Sales: Ben Rivers. Director, Group Sales: Jeff Windle. Director, Merchandising: Bill Gerlt. Director, Food Services: Doug Campbell. Manager, Diamond Concessions: Candy Pena. Clubhouse Operations: Bill Cantrel. Office Manager: Delia Rodriguez.

Field Staff

Manager: Ron Roenicke. Coach: Lance Parrish. Pitching Coach: Edwin Correa. Trainer: Jim Cranmer.

Game Information

Radio Announcers: Roy Acuff, Brian Anderson. No. of Games Broadcast: Home-70, Away-70. Flagship Station: KKYX 680-AM.

PA Announcer: Stan Kelly. Official Scorer: David Humphrey.

Stadium Name (year opened): Nelson Wolff Municipal Stadium (1994). Location: From I-10, I-35 or I-37, take U.S. Hwy. 90 West to Callaghan Road exit. Standard Game Times: 7:05 p.m., Sun. 6:05.

Visiting Club Hotel: Thrifty Inn, 9806 I-10 West, San Antonio, TX 78230. Telephone: (210) 696-0810.

Shreveport
CAPTAINS

Office Address: 2901 Pershing Blvd., Shreveport, LA 71109. Mailing Address: P.O. Box 3448, Shreveport, LA 71133. Telephone: (318) 636-5555. FAX: (318) 636-5670. E-Mail Address: shvcaps@iamerica.net. Website: www.shreveportcaptains@iamerica.com.

Affiliation (first year): San Francisco Giants (1979). Years in League: 1895, 1908-10, 1915-32, 1938-42, 1946-57, 1968-.

Ownership, Management

Operated by: Shreveport Baseball, Inc.

Principal Owner/President: Taylor Moore.

General Manager: Daniel Robinson. Assistant GM/Director, Ticket Sales: Terri Sipes. Assistant GM/Director, Sales, Marketing and Promotions: Michael Beasley. Director, Stadium Operations: Gyla Whitlow. Head Groundskeeper: Steve Bange. Director, Media/Public Relations: Charles Cavell. Director, Food Services: Leroy Beasley. Administrative/Marketing Assistant: Sheila Martin.

Field Staff

Manager: Mike Hart. Coach: Frank Cacciatore. Pitching Coach: Todd Oakes. Trainer: Ben Potenziano.

Game Information

Radio Announcer: Dave Nitz. No. of Games Broadcast: Home-70, Away-70. Flagship Station: KWKH 1130-AM.

PA Announcer: Charles Cavell. Official Scorer: Jim Dawson.

Stadium Name (year opened): Fair Grounds Field (1986). Location: Hearne Ave. (U.S. 171) exit off I-20 at Louisiana State Fairgrounds. Standard Game Times: April-May 7:05 p.m., June-Aug. 7:35; Sat. 7:35; Sun. 6:05.

Visiting Club Hotel: Ramada Inn-Airport, 5116 Monkhouse Dr., Shreveport, LA 71109. Telephone (318) 635-7531.

Tulsa DRILLERS

Office Address: 4802 East 15th St., Tulsa, OK 74112. **Mailing Address:** P.O. Box 4448, Tulsa, OK 74159. **Telephone:** (918) 744-5998. **FAX:** (918) 747-3267.

Affiliation (first year): Texas Rangers (1977). **Years in League:** 1933-42, 1946-65, 1977-.

Ownership, Management

Operated by: Tulsa Baseball, Inc.
Principal Owner/President: Went Hubbard.
General Manager: Chuck Lamson. **Associate General Manager:** Chris Pound. **Bookkeeper:** Cheryll Moore. **Director, Media/Public Relations:** Brian Carroll. **Director, Stadium Operations:** Mark Hilliard. **Head Groundskeeper:** Sam Clay. **Director, Promotions:** Mike Melega. **Director, Ticket Sales:** Debbie Jones. **Manager, Group Sales:** Jeff Gladu. **Assistant, Ticket Sales:** Philip Cowan. **Manager, Merchandising:** Joe Benbow. **Manager, Food Services:** Clay Dixon.

Field Staff

Manager: Bobby Jones. **Pitching Coach:** Brad Arnsberg. **Trainer:** Mike Quinn.

Game Information

Radio Announcer: Mark Neely. **No. of Games Broadcast:** Home-70, Away-70. **Flagship Station:** KQLL 1430-AM.
PA Announcer: Kirk McAnany. **Official Scorer:** Unavailable.
Stadium Name (year opened): Drillers Stadium (1981). **Location:** Three miles north of I-44 and 1½ miles south of I-244 at 15th Street and Yale Avenue. **Standard Game Times:** Mon.-Thurs. (April-May 13) 7:05 p.m., (May 14-Aug.) 7:35; Sat. 7:35; Sun. (April-May) 2:05, (June-August) 6:05.
Visiting Club Hotel: Trade Winds Central, 3141 East Skelly Drive, Tulsa, OK 74105. Telephone: (918) 749-5561.

Wichita WRANGLERS

Office Address: 300 South Sycamore, Wichita, KS 67213. **Mailing Address:** P.O. Box 1420, Wichita, KS 67201. **Telephone:** (316) 267-3372. **FAX:** (316) 267-3382. **E-Mail Address:** wranglers@wichitawranglers.com. **Website:** www.wichitawranglers.com.

Affiliation (first year): Kansas City Royals (1995). **Years in League:** 1987-.

Ownership, Management

Operated by: Wichita Baseball, Inc.
Principal Owner: Rich Products Corp., Robert Rich Jr.
Vice President: Steve Shaad. **General Manager:** Lance Deckinger. **Assistant General Manager:** Chris Taylor. **Manager, Sales and Marketing:** Derrick Morgan. **Assistant, Marketing:** Natasha Frazier. **Stadium Manager:** Dave Wellenzohn. **Manager, Ticket Sales:** Erik Jordan. **Coordinator, Ticket Sales:** Pete Bell. **Account Executives:** Harry Centa, Angela Haar. **Assistant, Ticket Operations:** Shane Flater. **Assistant, Ticket Sales:** Tom Bergles. **Assistant GM/Events Unlimited:** Greg Kalkwarf. **Assistant Stadium Manager/Head Groundskeeper:** Matt Arneson. **Coordinator, Business:** Chris Kloepping.

Field Staff

Manager: John Mizerock. **Coach:** Phil Stephenson. **Pitching Coach:** Mike Mason. **Trainer:** John Finley.

Game Information

Radio Announcer: Dennis Higgins. **No. of Games Broadcast:** Home-70, Away-70. **Flagship Station:** KQAM 1480-AM.
PA Announcer: Brad Eldridge. **Official Scorer:** Ted Woodward.
Stadium Name (year opened): Lawrence-Dumont Stadium (1934). **Location:** I-135 to Kellogg Ave. West, north on Broadway, west on Lewis. **Standard Game Times:** 7:15 p.m.; Sun. (April-May) 2:15, (June-August) 6:15.
Visiting Club Hotel: Clarion Hotel Airport, 5805 West Kellogg, Wichita, KS 67209. Telephone: (316) 942-7911.

CALIFORNIA LEAGUE

Class A Advanced

Office Address: 2380 South Bascom Ave., Suite 200, Campbell, CA 95008. **Telephone:** (408) 369-8038. **FAX:** (408) 369-1409. **E-Mail Address:** cabaseball@aol.com. **Website:** www.californialeague.com.

Years League Active: 1941-1942, 1946-.

President/Treasurer: Joe Gagliardi.

Vice President: Harry Stavrenos (San Jose). **Corporate Secretary:** Bill Weiss.

Directors: Bobby Brett (High Desert), Chris Chen (Modesto), Mike Ellis (Lancaster), Acey Kohrogi (Visalia), Pat Patton (Bakersfield), Dick Phelps (Stockton), Harry Stavrenos (San Jose), Hank Stickney (Rancho Cucamonga), Ken Stickney (Lake Elsinore), Donna Tuttle (San Bernardino).

Joe Gagliardi

Administration Assistant: Kathleen Kelly. **Supervisor, Umpire Development:** John Oldham.

1998 Opening Date: April 2. **Closing Date:** Aug. 30.

Regular Season: 140 games (split schedule).

Division Structure: Freeway—Bakersfield, Lake Elsinore, Rancho Cucamonga, San Bernardino, Visalia. **Valley**—High Desert, Lancaster, Modesto, San Jose, Stockton.

Playoff Format: Six teams. Split-season winners in each division with best overall record earn first-round bye; other division split-season winners meet wild card with next-best overall record in best-of-3 quarterfinals. Winners meet teams which earned first-round byes in best-of-5 semifinals. Winners meet in best-of-5 series for league championship.

All-Star Game: June 16 at Lancaster.

Roster Limit: 25 active. **Player Eligibility Rule:** No more than two players and one player-coach on active list may have more than six years experience.

Brand of Baseball: Rawlings ROM.

Statistician: Howe Sportsdata International, Boston Fish Pier, West Bldg. #1, Suite 302, Boston MA 02210; P.O. Box 5061, San Mateo, CA 94402.

Stadium Information

Club	Stadium	LF	CF	RF	Capacity	'97 Att.
Bakersfield	Sam Lynn Ballpark	328	354	328	4,600	117,818
High Desert	Mavericks	340	401	340	3,808	157,605
Lake Elsinore	Diamond	330	400	310	7,866	341,393
Lancaster	Lancaster Municipal	350	410	350	4,500	298,465
Modesto	Thurman Field	312	400	319	4,000	140,861
R. Cucamonga	Epicenter	330	400	330	6,631	404,525
San Bernardino	The Ranch	330	410	330	5,000	273,739
San Jose	Municipal	320	400	320	4,200	146,151
Stockton	Billy Hebert Field	325	392	335	3,500	101,254
Visalia	Recreation Park	320	405	320	1,700	80,078

Bakersfield
BLAZE

Office Address: 4009 Chester Ave., Bakersfield, CA 93301. **Mailing Address:** P.O. Box 10031, Bakersfield, CA 93389. **Telephone:** (805) 322-1363. **FAX:** (805) 322-6199. **E-Mail Address:** blaze1@bakersfieldblaze.com. **Website:** www.bakersfieldblaze.com.

Affiliation: San Francisco Giants (1997). **Years In League:** 1941-42, 1946-75, 1978-79, 1982-.

Ownership, Management

Principal Owner/President: Pat Patton.

Vice President/General Manager: Jack Patton. **Assistant General Manager:** Susan Wells. **Administrative Assistant:** Dan Shanyfelt. **Director, Stadium Operations:** Craig Noren. **Head Groundskeeper:** Leon Williams. **Director, Community Relations:** Paul Sheldon. **Director, Ticket Sales:** Cricket Whitaker. **Account Executive:** Kent Bowersox. **Director, Broadcasting:** Mark Roberts.

Field Staff

Manager: Frank Reberger. **Pitching Coach:** Shawn Barton. **Trainer:** Rick Fuhriman.

Game Information

Radio Announcers: Mark Roberts, Dale Parsons. **No. of Games Broadcast:** Home-70, Away-70. **Flagship Station:** KGEO 1230-AM.

PA Announcer: Unavailable. **Official Scorer:** Tim Wheeler.

Stadium Name (year opened): Sam Lynn Ballpark (1941). **Location:** Highway 99 to California Avenue, east three miles to Chester Ave., north two miles to stadium. **Standard Game Times:** 7:30 p.m.

Visiting Club Hotel: Travelodge Hotel, 818 Real Rd., Bakersfield, CA 93309. Telephone: (805) 324-6666.

High Desert
MAVERICKS

Office Address: 12000 Stadium Way, Adelanto, CA 92301. **Telephone:** (760) 246-6287. **FAX:** (760) 246-3197.

Affiliation (first year): Arizona Diamondbacks (1997). **Years in League:** 1991-.

Ownership, Management

Operated by: High Desert Mavericks, Inc.

Principal Owner: Bobby Brett.

Vice President, Tickets and Administration: Mike Guarini. **Vice President, Business and Baseball Operations:** Pete Thuresson. **Assistant GM/Director, Marketing:** Kiyomi Endo. **Director, Stadium Operations and Concessions:** Mike Fleming. **Director, Ticket Sales:** Rick Janac. **Director, Group Sales:** Stacy Richner. **Group Sales Assistant:** Bryan Goldwater. **Director, Merchandising:** Scott Bolton. **Account Executive:** Charles Hackett. **Manager, Public Relations:** Jim Thornby. **Office Manager:** Kaye Allen. **Head Groundskeeper:** Tino Gonzalez. **Clubhouse Manager:** Mike Weil.

Field Staff

Manager: Don Wakamatsu. **Coach:** Ty Van Burkleo. **Pitching Coach:** Dennis Lewallyn. **Trainer:** Greg Barber.

Game Information

Radio Announcer: Unavailable. **No. of Games Broadcast:** Home-70, Away-70. **Flagship Station:** KROY 1590-AM.

PA Announcer: Art Hernandez. **Official Scorer:** Jim Erwin.

Stadium Name (year opened): Mavericks Stadium (1991). **Location:** I-15 North to Highway 395 to Adelanto Road. **Standard Game Times:** 7:05 p.m.; Sun. (April-May) 2:05, (June-Aug.) 5:05.

Visiting Club Hotel: Holiday Inn-Victorville, 15494 Palmdale Rd., Victorville, CA 92393 Telephone: (760) 241-1577.

Lake Elsinore
STORM

Office Address: 500 Diamond Drive, Lake Elsinore, CA 92530. **Mailing Address:** P.O. Box 535, Lake Elsinore, CA 92531. **Telephone:** (909) 245-4487. **FAX:** (909) 245-0305. **E-Mail Address:** lestorm@pe.net. **Website:** www.pe.net/storm.

Affiliation (first year): Anaheim Angels (1994). **Years in League:** 1994-.

Ownership, Management
Operated by: Mandalay Sports Entertainment.
Managing Director: Ken Stickney.
Chairman: Peter Guber. **Vice Chairman:** Paul Schaeffer.
General Manager: Kevin Haughian. **Assistant General Manager:** Chris Hill. **Director, Media/Public Relations:** Wayne Teats. **Director, Operations and Special Events:** Brent Boznanski. **Assistant Director, Sales and Marketing:** Darrin Gross. **Director, Merchandising:** Jennifer Bock. **Director, Business Administration:** Yvonne Hunneman. **Director, Broadcasting:** Sean McCall. **Director, Ticket Operations:** Kristie Schmitt. **Director, Ticketing:** Kyle Haden. **Managers, Corporate Marketing:** David Jojola, Larry Ryan. **Manager, Corporate Accounts:** Leann Rothrock. **Group Sales:** Mary Stanley. **Office Administrator:** Jo Equila.

Field Staff
Manager: Mario Mendoza. **Coach:** Joe Urso. **Pitching Coach:** Kernan Ronan. **Trainer:** Alan Russell.

Game Information
Radio Announcer: Sean McCall. **No. of Games Broadcast:** Home-70, Away-70. **Flagship Station:** Unavailable.
PA Announcer: Joe Martinez. **Official Scorer:** Dennis Bricker.
Stadium Name (year opened): Lake Elsinore Diamond (1994). **Location:** From I-15, exit at Diamond Drive, west for one mile to stadium. **Standard Game Times:** 7:05 p.m.; Sun. (April-May) 2:05, (June-Aug.) 5:05.
Visiting Club Hotel: Unavailable.

Lancaster
JETHAWKS

Office Address: 45116 Valley Central Way, Lancaster, CA 93536. **Telephone:** (805) 726-5400. **FAX:** (805) 726-5406. **E-Mail Address:** ljethawks@qnet.com. **Website:** www.jethawks.com.

Affiliation (first year): Seattle Mariners (1996). **Years in League:** 1996-.

Ownership, Management
Operated by: Clutch Play Baseball, LLC.
Chairman: Horn Chen. **President:** Mike Ellis.
General Manager: Matt Ellis. **Assistant General Manager:** Kevin Younkin. **Director, Sales:** Eileen Garcia. **Director, Ticket Sales:** Chris Hale. **Director, Merchandising:** Lori Mayle. **Manager, Stadium Operations:** John Laferney. **Manager, Media/Public Relations:** Bruce Battle. **Financial Analyst, FSM:** Michele Ellis. **General Manager, Food Services:** Wayne Berry. **Head Groundskeeper:** Dave Pfatenhauer.

Field Staff
Manager: Rick Burleson. **Coach:** Unavailable. **Pitching Coach:** Jim Slaton. **Trainer:** Troy McIntosh.

Game Information
Radio Announcers: Dan Hubbard, Rick DeReyes. **No. of Games Broadcast:** Home-70, Away-70. **Flagship Stations:** KUTY 1470-AM, KHJJ 1380-AM.
PA Announcer: Larry Thornhill. **Official Scorer:** David Guenther.
Stadium Name (year opened): Lancaster Municipal Stadium (1996). **Location:** Highway 14 in Lancaster to Avenue I exit, west on Avenue I to intersection of Avenue I, 25th Street West and Highway 14. **Standard Game Times:** 7:11 p.m.; Sun. (first half) 2, (second half) 5.
Visiting Club Hotel: Desert Inn, 44219 Sierra Highway, Lancaster, CA 93534. Telephone: (805) 942-9401.

Modesto
A's

Office Address: 601 Neece Dr., Modesto, CA 95351. Mailing Address: P.O. Box 883, Modesto, CA 95353. Telephone: (209) 572-4487. FAX: (209) 572-4490. E-Mail Address: fun@modestoathletics.com. Website: www.modestoathletics.com.

Affiliation (first year): Oakland Athletics (1975). Years in League: 1946-64, 1966-.

Ownership, Management
Operated by: Modesto A's Professional Baseball Club, Inc.
Principal Owner/President: Chris Chen.
Vice President, Business Development: Tim Marting.
General Manager: David Gottfried. Assistant GM/Stadium Operations: Jeff Colville. Assistant GM/Baseball Operations: John Katz. Director, Food Service: Alan Day. Director, Tickets/Group Sales: Jeff Titus. Director, Community Affairs: Tim Patnode. Administrative Assistant: Sara Scheffler. Head Groundskeeper: Walter Woodley. Clubhouse Manager: David Tomchuk.

Field Staff
Manager: Juan Navarrete. Coach: Brian McArn. Pitching Coach: Rick Rodriguez. Trainer: Blake Bowers.

Game Information
Radio Announcer: Rev Johnson. No. of Games Broadcast: Away-50. Flagship Station: KBUL 970-AM.
PA Announcer: Rev Johnson. Official Scorer: Sean Bohannon.
Stadium Name (year opened): John Thurman Field (1952). Location: Highway 99 in SW Modesto to Tuolomne Blvd. exit, west on Tuolomne Blvd. for one block to Neece Drive, left for ¼ mile to stadium. Standard Game Times: 7:05 p.m.; Sun. (April) 1:05, (May-Aug.) 6:05.
Visiting Club Hotel: Vagabond Inn, 1525 McHenry Ave., Modesto, CA 95350. Telephone: (209) 521-6340.

Rancho Cucamonga
QUAKES

Office Address: 8408 Rochester Ave., Rancho Cucamonga, CA 91730. Mailing Address: P.O. Box 4139, Rancho Cucamonga, CA 91729. Telephone: (909) 481-5000. FAX: (909) 481-5005. E-Mail Address: rcquakes@aol.com. Website: www.rcquakes.com.

Affiliation (first year): San Diego Padres (1993). Years In League: 1993-.

Ownership, Management
Operated by: Valley Baseball Inc.
President, General Manager: Hank Stickney.
Vice President, Assistant General Manager: Jay Middleton. Vice President, Sales and Marketing: Bob Teixeira. Director, Ticket Operations: Dennis O'Connor. Director, Broadcasting/Media Relations: Michael Curto. Senior Account Executive: Brant Ringler. Account Executives: Janet Beard, James Keyston. Ticket Office Manager: Kelli Pickwith. Office Manager: Frances Kolarz. Marketing Assistant: Marlene Merrill. Assistant to President: Marty Breen. Assistants, Corporate Sales: Mike Junga, Matt Gorman. Director, Group Sales: Maggie Cupp. Sales Assistant: Lynn Abele. Head Groundskeeper: Rex Whitney.

Field Staff
Manager: Mike Basso. Coach: Jason McLeod. Pitching Coach: Darrel Akerfelds. Trainer: Lance Cacanindin.

Game Information
Radio Announcer: Michael Curto. No. of Games Broadcast: Home-70, Away-70. Flagship Station: KNSE 1510-AM.
PA Announcer: David Achord. Official Scorer: Larry Kavanaugh.
Stadium Name (year opened): The Epicenter (1993). Location: I-10 to I-15 North, exit at Foothill Blvd., left on Foothill, left on Rochester. Standard Game Times: 7:15 p.m.; Sun. (April-June 7) 2:15, (June 21-Aug.) 6:15.
Visiting Club Hotel: Best Western Heritage Inn, 8179 Spruce Ave., Rancho Cucamonga, CA 91730. Telephone: (909) 466-1111.

San Bernardino
STAMPEDE

Office Address: 280 South E St., San Bernardino, CA 92401. **Telephone:** (909) 888-9922. **FAX:** (909) 888-5251. **E-Mail Address:** staff@stampedebaseball.com. **Website:** www.stampedebaseball.com.

Affiliation (first year): Los Angeles Dodgers (1995). **Years in League:** 1941, 1987-.

Ownership, Management
Operated by: Elmore Sports Group.
Principal Owners: David Elmore, Donna Tuttle.
President: Donna Tuttle.
General Manager: Jason Watson. **Assistant General Manager:** Blake Inman. **Controller:** Gayla Anhaeuser. **Director, Stadium Operations:** Greg Cozzo. **Head Groundskeeper:** Jerry Brown. **Director, Media/Public Relations:** Melissa Olds. **Manager, Corporate Sales:** Paul Stiritz. **Director, Community Relations:** Matt Kelly. **Director, Promotions:** Chris Harmon. **Director, Group Sales:** Lisa Mueller. **Director, Merchandising:** Stephanie Reed. **Director, Food Services:** Brian Morgan. **Clubhouse Operations:** Peter Thompson. **Office Manager:** Vanessa Ramos. **Account Executive:** Lorrie Payne. **Assistant Director, Food Services:** Debbie Hamlin-Kralun.

Field Staff
Manager: Mickey Hatcher. **Coach:** Monte Marshall. **Pitching Coach:** Charlie Hough. **Trainer:** Jason Mahnke.

Game Information
Radio Announcer: Mike Saeger. **No. of Games Broadcast:** Home-70, Away-70. **Flagship Station:** KCKC 1350-AM.
PA Announcer: J.J. Gould. **Official Scorer:** Ross French.
Stadium Name (year opened): The Ranch (1996). **Location:** I-215 to San Bernardino, exit at Mill Street, east on Mill Street, north on G Street.
Standard Game Times: 7:05 p.m.; Sun. (April-May) 2:05, (June-Aug.) 5:05.
Visiting Club Hotel: Radisson Hotel, 295 North E St., San Bernardino, CA 92401. Telephone: (909) 381-6181.

San Jose
GIANTS

Office Address: 588 East Alma Ave., San Jose, CA 95112. **Mailing Address:** P.O. Box 21727, San Jose, CA 95151. **Telephone:** (408) 297-1435. **FAX:** (408) 297-1453. **E-Mail Address:** sjgiants@ix.netcom.com. **Website:** www.sjgiants.com.

Affiliation (first year): San Francisco Giants (1988). **Years in League:** 1942, 1947-58, 1962-76, 1979-.

Ownership, Management
Operated by: Progress Sports Management.
Chairman: Richard Beahrs. **President:** Harry Stavrenos.
General Manager: Mark Wilson. **Assistant General Manager:** Steve Fields. **Director, Sales:** Linda Pereira. **Director, Public Relations:** Dave Moudry. **Manager, Group Sales/Tickets:** Rocky Koplik. **Stadium Operations:** Rick Tracy. **Groundskeeper:** Hector Gonzales.

Field Staff
Manager: Shane Turner. **Pitching Coach:** Bryan Hickerson. **Trainer:** Dave Groeschner.

Game Information
Radio: None.
PA Announcer: Jim Chapman. **Official Scorers:** John Pletsch, Brian Burkett.
Stadium Name (year opened): Municipal Stadium (1942). **Location:** From I-280, 10th Street exit to Alma, left on Alma, stadium on right. From US 101, Tully Road exit to Senter, right on Senter, left on Alma, stadium on left. **Standard Game Times:** 7:15 p.m.; Sat. 5; Sun. (April-June) 1, (July-Aug.) 5.
Visiting Club Hotel: Gateway Inn, 2585 Seaboard Ave., San Jose, CA 95131. Telephone: (408) 435-8800.

Stockton PORTS

Office Address: Billy Hebert Field, Alpine and Sutter Streets, Stockton, CA 95204. **Mailing Address:** P.O. Box 8550, Stockton, CA 95208. **Telephone:** (209) 944-5943. **FAX:** (209) 463-4937. **E-Mail Address:** fans@stocktonports.com. **Website:** www.stocktonports.com.

Affiliation (first year): Milwaukee Brewers (1979). **Years in League:** 1941, 1946-72, 1978-.

Ownership, Management
Operated by: Joy in Mudville.
Principal Owner: Richard Phelps.
General Manager: Dan Chapman. **Assistant General Manager:** Alfred Spear. **Director, Stadium Operations:** Chris Justen. **Director, Media/Merchandising:** John Schaars. **Office Manager:** Molly Rogers.

Field Staff
Manager: Bernie Moncallo. **Coach:** John Mallee. **Pitching Coach:** Saul Soltero. **Trainer:** Paul Anderson.

Game Information
Radio: None.
PA Announcer: Johnny Milford. **Official Scorer:** Tim Ankcorn.
Stadium Name (year opened): Billy Hebert Field (1927). **Location:** From I-5, March Lane exit east, south on Pacific Ave., east on Alpine Ave. From Hwy. 99 South, Wilson Way exit west to Alpine Ave., west on Alpine. **Standard Game Times:** 7:05 p.m.; Sun. 5.
Visiting Club Hotel: Best Western Stockton Inn, 4219 East Waterloo Road, Stockton, CA 95215. Telephone: (209) 931-3131.

Visalia OAKS

Office Address: 440 North Giddings Ave., Visalia, CA 93291. **Mailing Address:** P.O. Box 48, Visalia, CA 93279. **Telephone:** (209) 625-0480. **FAX:** (209) 739-7732. **E-Mail Address:** visoak@aol.com.

Affiliation: Oakland Athletics (1997). **Years in League:** 1946-62, 1968-75, 1977-.

Ownership, Management
Operated by: JSS/USA, Inc.
Chairman: Keiichi Tsukamoto.
General Manager: Andrew Bettencourt. **Director, Media/Public Relations:** Harry Kargenian. **Director, Ticket Sales:** Kathy Elick. **Head Groundskeeper:** Darren Holt.

Field Staff
Manager: Tony DeFrancesco. **Coach:** David Robb. **Pitching Coach:** Glenn Abbott. **Trainer:** Jeremy Loew.

Game Information
Radio: None.
PA Announcer/Official Scorer: Harry Kargenian.
Stadium Name (year opened): Recreation Park (1946). **Location:** From Highway 99, take 198 East to Mooney Blvd. exit, left on Giddings Ave. **Standard Game Times:** 7:05 p.m.; Sun. 6:05.
Visiting Club Hotel: Holiday Inn-Visalia, 9000 West Airport Drive, Visalia, CA 93277. Telephone: (209) 651-5000.

CAROLINA LEAGUE

Class A Advanced

Office Address: 1806 Pembroke Rd., Greensboro, NC 27408. **Mailing Address:** P.O. Box 9503, Greensboro, NC 27429. **Telephone:** (336) 691-9030. **FAX:** (336) 691-9070. **E-Mail Address:** office@carolinaleague.com. **Website:** www.carolina league.com.

Years League Active: 1945-.

President/Treasurer: John Hopkins.

Vice Presidents: Kelvin Bowles (Salem), Calvin Falwell (Lynchburg). **Corporate Secretary:** Art Silber (Prince William).

Directors: Don Beaver (Winston-Salem), Kelvin Bowles (Salem), Calvin Falwell (Lynchburg), George Habel (Danville), North Johnson (Kinston), Peter Kirk (Frederick), Matt Minker (Wilmington), Art Silber (Prince William).

John Hopkins

Administrative Assistants: Marnee Larkins, Michael Albrecht.

1998 Opening Date: April 10. **Closing Date:** Sept. 6.

Regular Season: 140 games (split schedule).

Division Structure: Northern—Frederick, Lynchburg, Prince William, Wilmington. **Southern**—Danville, Kinston, Salem, Winston-Salem.

Playoff Format: First-half division winners play second-half division winners in best-of-3 series. Division playoff winners meet in best-of-5 series for Mills Cup.

All-Star Game: June 23 at Wilmington, DE.

Roster Limit: 25 active. **Player Eligibility Rule:** No age limit. No more than two players and one player-coach on active list may have six or more years of prior minor league service.

Brand of Baseball: Rawlings.

Statistician: Howe Sportsdata International, Boston Fish Pier, West Bldg. #1, Suite 302, Boston MA 02210.

Stadium Information

Club	Stadium	LF	CF	RF	Capacity	'97 Att.
Danville#	Dan Daniel Memorial	330	400	330	2,588	—
Frederick	Harry Grove	325	400	325	5,500	274,894
Kinston	Grainger	335	390	335	4,100	151,953
Lynchburg	City	325	390	325	4,000	112,363
Prince William	Pfitzner	315	400	315	6,000	214,037
Salem	Salem Memorial	325	401	325	6,300	188,023
Wilmington	Frawley	325	400	325	5,911	326,201
Winston-Salem	Ernie Shore Field	325	400	325	6,280	156,285

#Franchise operated in Durham, N.C., in 1997

Danville 97s

Office Address: 302 River Park Dr., Danville, VA 24540. **Mailing Address:** P.O. Box 3637, Danville, VA 24543. **Telephone:** (804) 791-3346. **FAX:** (804) 791-3347. **E-Mail Address:** dbraves@gamewood.net. **Website:** www.danvillebraves.com.

Affiliation (first year): Atlanta Braves (1998). **Years in League:** 1945-58, 1998.

Ownership, Management

Operated by: Danville Braves, Inc.
Principal Owner: Capitol Broadcasting, Inc.
President: Jim Goodmon.
General Manager: Tim Cahill. **Assistant General Managers:** Brent Bartemeyer, Mike Drahush. **Director, Sales/Marketing:** Cole Spencer. **Director, Group Sales:** Dennis Mertha. **Office Manager:** Beth Hall.

Field Staff

Manager: Paul Runge. **Coach:** Bobby Moore. **Pitching Coach:** Bruce Dal Canton. **Trainer:** Willy Johnson.

Game Information

Radio: None.
PA Announcer: Unavailable. **Official Scorers:** Danny Miller, Stan Mitchell.
Stadium Name (year opened): Dan Daniel Memorial Park (1993). **Location:** U.S. 58 to Rivermont Road, follow signs to park; U.S. 29 bypass to Dan Daniel Park exit (U.S. 58 East), to Rivermont Road, follow signs. **Standard Game Times:** 7 p.m.; Sun. (April-May) 2, (June-Sept.) 7.
Visiting Club Hotel: Innkeeper West, 3020 Riverside Dr., Danville, VA 24541. Telephone: (804) 799-1202.

Frederick KEYS

Office Address: 6201 New Design Rd., Frederick, MD 21702. **Mailing Address:** P.O. Box 3169, Frederick, MD 21705. **Telephone:** (301) 662-0013. **FAX:** (301) 662-0018. **E-Mail Address:** frekeys@aol.com. **Website:** frederickkeys.com.

Affiliation (first year): Baltimore Orioles (1989). **Years In League:** 1989-.

Ownership, Management

Operated by: Maryland Baseball, LP.
Principal Owners: Peter Kirk, Hugh Schindel, Pete Simmons, Frank Perdue, John Daskalakis.
Chairman: Peter Kirk. **President:** Pete Simmons.
General Manager: Joe Preseren. **Assistant General Manager:** Joe Pinto. **Director, Stadium Operations:** Dave Wisner. **Head Groundskeeper:** Tommy Long. **Director, Media/Public Relations:** Ernie Stepoulos. **Director, Marketing:** Mark Zeigler. **Account Representative:** Debbie Beall. **Assistant Director, Public Relations** Shaun O'Neal. **Director, Food Services:** Mike Brulatour. **Clubhouse Operations:** George Bell, Danny Benn. **Director, Client Relations and Development:** Kent Hornbrook. **Director, Ticketing and Group Sales:** Gina Little. **Assistant Directors, Group Sales:** Heather Claybaugh, Laura Springer. **Assistant Ticket Directors:** DeeAnn Gonzalez, Nathan Kahl.

Field Staff

Manager: Tommy Shields. **Coach:** Todd Brown. **Pitching Coach:** Larry Jaster. **Trainer:** Dave Walker.

Game Information

Radio Announcer: Matt Noble. **No. of Games Broadcast:** Home-70, Away-70. **Flagship Station:** WXTR 820-AM.
PA Announcer: Rick McCauslin. **Official Scorers:** Bryan Hissey, George Richardson.
Stadium Name (year opened): Harry Grove Stadium (1990). **Location:** From I-70, take exit 54 (Market Street), left at light. From I-270, take exit 31A for two miles, stadium on left. **Standard Game Times:** 7:05 p.m.; Sun. 1:05.

Visiting Club Hotel: Comfort Inn, 420 Prospect Blvd., Frederick, MD 21701. Telephone: (301) 695-6200.

Kinston
INDIANS

Office Address: 400 East Grainger Ave., Kinston, NC 28501. **Mailing Address:** P.O. Box 3542, Kinston, NC 28502. **Telephone:** (919) 527-9111. **FAX:** (919) 527-2328. **E-Mail Address:** ktribe@kinstonindians.com. **Website:** www.kinstonindians.com.
Affiliation (first year): Cleveland Indians (1987). **Years in League:** 1956-57, 1962-74, 1978-.

Ownership, Management
Operated by: Slugger Partners, LP.
Principal Owners: Cam McRae, North Johnson.
Chairman: Cam McRae. **President/General Manager:** North Johnson.
Assistant General Manager: Dave Echols. **Director, Merchandising:** John Purvis. **Director, Group Sales:** Joe Welch. **Concessions Manager:** Rita Spence. **Head Groundskeeper:** Tommy Walston. **Clubhouse Operations:** Robert Smeraldo.

Field Staff
Manager: Mako Oliveras. **Coach:** Mike Sarbaugh. **Pitching Coach:** Dave Miller. **Trainer:** Teddy Blackwell.

Game Information
Radio Announcer: Josh Whetzel. **No. of Games Broadcast:** Home-70, Away-70. **Flagship Station:** Unavailable.
PA Announcer: Unavailable. **Official Scorers:** Karl Grant, Keith Spence.
Stadium Name (year opened): Grainger Stadium (1949). **Location:** U.S. Route 70 Business to Vernon Avenue, left on East Street. **Standard Game Times:** 7 p.m.; Sun. 2.
Visiting Club Hotel: Holiday Inn, Highway 70 Bypass, Kinston, NC 28501. Telephone: (919) 527-4155.

Lynchburg
HILLCATS

Office Address: City Stadium, 3180 Fort Ave., Lynchburg, VA 24501. **Mailing Address:** P.O. Box 10213, Lynchburg, VA 24506. **Telephone:** (804) 528-1144. **FAX:** (804) 846-0768. **E-Mail Address:** hillcats@inmind.com. **Website:** www.cl.org/baseball/lynchburg/.
Affiliation (first year): Pittsburgh Pirates (1995). **Years in League:** 1966-.

Ownership, Management
Operated by: Lynchburg Baseball Corp.
President: W. Calvin Falwell.
General Manager: Paul Sunwall. **Assistant General Manager:** Ronnie Roberts. **Head Groundskeeper/Sales:** Darren Johnson. **Clubhouse Operations:** Chuck Watson, Lou Watson. **Office Manager:** Karen East.

Field Staff
Manager: Jeff Richardson. **Coach:** Jeff Livesey. **Pitching Coach:** Jim Bibby. **Trainer:** Unavailable.

Game Information
Radio Announcer: Matt Provence. **No. of Games Broadcast:** Home-70, Away-70. **Flagship Station:** WBRG 1050-AM.
PA Announcers: Chuck Young, David Glass. **Official Scorers:** Malcolm Haley, Chuck Young.
Stadium Name (year opened): City Stadium (1940). **Location:** U.S. 29 South to City Stadium (exit 6); U.S. 29 North to Lynchburg College/City Stadium (exit 4). **Standard Game Times:** 7:05 p.m.; Sun. (April-June) 2:05, (July-Sept.) 6:05.
Visiting Club Hotel: Best Western, 2815 Candlers Mountain Rd., Lynchburg, VA 24502. Telephone: (804) 237-2986.

Prince William
CANNONS

Office Address: 7 County Complex Court, Woodbridge, VA 22192.
Mailing Address: P.O. Box 2148, Woodbridge, VA 22193. Telephone: (703)
590-2311. FAX: (703) 590-5716. E-Mail Address: pwcannons@aol.com.
Website: www.pwcannons.com.

Affiliation (first year): St. Louis Cardinals (1997). Years in League:
1978-.

Ownership, Management
Operated by: Prince William Professional Baseball Club, Inc.
Principal Owner/President: Art Silber.
Vice President/General Manager: Pat Filippone. Director, Media/
Public Relations: Mike Antonellis. Director, Sales: Tron Kohlhagen.
Director, Marketing: Rich Girardo. Manager, Stadium Operations/
Merchandising: Jason Van Liew. Director, Finance: Dean Sisco.
Director, Community Relations: Mark Gordon. Manager, Community
Relations/Marketing: Timothy Bickers. Director, Ticket Sales: Gerry
McKearney. Ticket Manager: Tim Phillips. Manager, Food Services: Rich
Arnold. Outside Sales Representative: Don Wallace.

Field Staff
Manager: Joe Cunningham. Coach: Boots Day. Pitching Coach: Mark
Grater. Trainer: Aaron Bruns.

Game Information
Radio Announcer: Mike Antonellis. No. of Games Broadcast: Home-
70; Away-70. Flagship Stations: WAGE 1200-AM, WPWC 1480-AM.
PA Announcer: Trip Morgan. Official Scorer: John Oravec.
Stadium Name (year opened): G. Richard Pfitzner Stadium (1984).
Location: From I-95, exit 158B and continue on Prince William Parkway for
five miles, right into County Complex Court. Standard Game Times: 7:30
p.m.; Sat. 7; Sun. (April-June) 1:30, (July-Sept.) 6.
Visiting Club Hotel: Inns of Virginia, 951 Annapolis Way, Woodbridge,
VA 22191. Telephone: (800) 248-2445.

Salem
AVALANCHE

Office Address: 1004 Texas St., Salem, VA 24153. Mailing Address:
P.O. Box 842, Salem, VA 24153. Telephone: (540) 389-3333. FAX: (540)
389-9710. E-Mail Address: info@salemavalanche.com. Website: www.
salemavalanche.com.

Affiliation (first year): Colorado Rockies (1995). Years In League:
1968-.

Ownership, Management
Operated by: Salem Professional Baseball Club, Inc.
Principal Owner/President: Kelvin Bowles.
General Manager: Dave Oster. Assistant GM, Sales and Marketing:
Christian Carlson. Assistant GM, Stadium Operations: Stan Macko. Head
Groundskeeper: Mark Bragunier. Director, Community Relations: Tracy
Beskid. Director, Ticket Sales: Mike Ranelli. Director, Group Sales:
Kathy Mair. Assistant Director, Ticket and Group Sales: Amy Young.
Assistant Director, Marketing: Eliza Folsom. Director, Merchandising
and Finance: Brian Bowles. Director, Food Services: Todd Lange.

Field Staff
Manager: Jay Loviglio. Coach: Elanis Westbrooks. Pitching Coach:
Jack Lamabe. Trainer: Paul Evans.

Game Information
Radio Announcer: Unavailable. No. of Games Broadcast: Home-70,
Away-70. Flagship Station: WROV 1240-AM.
PA Announcer: Bruce Reynolds. Official Scorer: Brian Hoffman.
Stadium Name (year opened): Salem Memorial Baseball Stadium
(1995). Location: I-81 exits to Salem Civic Center complex. Standard
Game Times: 7 p.m.; Sun. (April-June) 2, (July-Sept.) 6.
Visiting Club Hotel: Days Inn-Airport, 8118 Plantation Rd., Roanoke, VA
24019. Telephone: (540) 366-0341.

Wilmington
BLUE ROCKS

Office Address: 801 South Madison St., Wilmington, DE 19801. **Telephone:** (302) 888-2015. **FAX:** (302) 888-2032. **E-Mail Address:** info@bluerocks.com. **Website:** www.bluerocks.com.

Affiliation (first year): Kansas City Royals (1993). **Years in League:** 1993-.

Ownership, Management

Operated by: Wilmington Blue Rocks, LP.

Principal Owner/President: Matt Minker.

General Manager: Chris Kemple. **Director, Finance:** Craig Bailey. **Director, Stadium Operations:** Andrew Layman. **Head Groundskeeper:** Steve Gold. **Director, Media Relations and Broadcasting:** Mark Nasser. **Director, Sales and Marketing:** Doug Stewart. **Assistant Director, Marketing:** Jim Beck. **Director, Community Relations:** Chris Parise. **Director, Ticket Sales:** Marla Chalfie. **Assistant Director, Ticket Sales:** Jen Sabatine. **Director, Merchandising:** Paul Siegwarth. **Director, Food Services:** Tom Brady. **Equipment Manager:** Jeremy Vroman.

Field Staff

Manager: Darrell Evans. **Coach:** Kevin Long. **Pitching Coach:** Steve Crawford. **Trainer:** Chad Spaulding.

Game Information

Radio Announcers: Mark Nasser, Kevin Reiter. **No. of Games Broadcast:** Home-70, Away-70. **Flagship Station:** WJBR 1290-AM.

PA Announcer: John McAdams. **Official Scorers:** E.J. Casey, Dick Shute, Mike Brint.

Stadium Name (year opened): Judy Johnson Field at Daniel S. Frawley Stadium (1993). **Location:** I-95 North to Maryland Ave. (exit 6), right onto Maryland Ave., right on Read Street, right on South Madison Street to ballpark; I-95 South to Maryland Ave. (exit 6), left at Martin Luther King Blvd., right on South Madison Street. **Game Times:** 7:05 p.m.; Sat. (April-May) 2:05; Sun. 2:05.

Visiting Club Hotel: Quality Inn-Skyways, 147 North DuPont Highway, New Castle, DE 19720. Telephone: (302) 328-6666.

Winston-Salem
WARTHOGS

Office Address: 401 Deacon Blvd., Winston-Salem, NC 27105. **Mailing Address:** P.O. Box 4488, Winston-Salem, NC 27115. **Telephone:** (336) 759-2233. **FAX:** (336) 759-2042. **E-Mail Address:** warthogs@warthogs.com. **Website:** www.warthogs.com.

Affiliation (first year): Chicago White Sox (1997). **Years in League:** 1945-.

Ownership, Management

Operated by: Beaver Sports, Inc.

Principal Owner/President: Donald Beaver.

General Manager: Peter Fisch. **Assistant General Manager:** Mark Viniard. **Director, Broadcasting and Media Relations:** Tim Grubbs. **Director, Community Relations:** Donna Poyant. **Director, Sales:** Chris Semmens. **Director, Stadium Operations:** Jason Stacherski. **Director, Merchandise:** Mike Belton. **Ticket/Office Manager:** Liesa Ellis. **Head Groundskeeper:** Eddie Busque.

Field Staff

Manager: Chris Cron. **Coach:** Dallas Williams. **Pitching Coach:** Curt Hasler. **Trainer:** Matt Bekkadal.

Game Information

Radio Announcer: Tim Grubbs. **No. of Games Broadcast:** Home-70, Away-70. **Flagship Station:** WTOB 1380-AM.

PA Announcer: Unavailable. **Official Scorer:** Matt Roy.

Stadium Name (year opened): Ernie Shore Field (1956). **Location:** I-40 Business to Cherry Street exit, north through downtown to Deacon Blvd., right to park. **Standard Game Times:** 7:15 p.m.; Sun. 2:05.

Visiting Club Hotel: Hawthorne Inn, 420 High St., Winston-Salem, NC 27101. Telephone: (336) 777-3000.

FLORIDA STATE LEAGUE

Class A Advanced

Street Address: 103 East Orange Ave., Daytona Beach, FL 32114. **Mailing Address:** P.O. Box 349, Daytona Beach, FL 32115. **Telephone:** (904) 252-7479. **FAX:** (904) 252-7495. **E-Mail Address:** bball-league@mindspring.com.

Chuck Murphy

Years League Active: 1919-1927, 1936-1941, 1946-.

President/Treasurer: Chuck Murphy.

Vice Presidents: Ken Carson (Dunedin), Jordan Kobritz (Daytona). **Corporate Secretary:** David Hood.

Directors: Sammy Arena (Tampa), Ken Carson (Dunedin), Andy Dunn (Brevard County), Tony Flores (St. Petersburg), Marvin Goldklang (Fort Myers), Grant Griesser (Vero Beach), Jim Herlihy (Charlotte), Woody Hicks (Lakeland), Ed Kenney (Sarasota), Jordan Kobritz (Daytona), Jeff Maultsby (St. Lucie), Tim Purpura (Kissimmee), Rob Rabenecker (Jupiter), John Timberlake (Clearwater).

Office Secretary: Peggy Catigano.

1998 Opening Date: April 8. **Closing Date:** Sept. 6.

Regular Season: 140 games (split-schedule).

Division Structure: East—Brevard County, Daytona, Jupiter, Kissimmee, St. Lucie, Vero Beach. **West**—Charlotte, Clearwater, Dunedin, Fort Myers, Lakeland, St. Petersburg, Sarasota, Tampa.

Playoff Format: First-half division winners play second-half division winners in best-of-3 series. Division playoff winners meet in best-of-5 series for league championship.

All-Star Game: June 20 at Fort Myers.

Roster Limit: 25. **Player Eligibility Rule:** No age limit. No more than two players and one player-coach on active list may have six or more years of prior minor league service.

Brand of Baseball: Rawlings.

Statistician: Howe Sportsdata International, Boston Fish Pier, West Bldg. #1, Suite 302, Boston, MA 02210.

Stadium Information

Club	Stadium	Dimensions LF	CF	RF	Capacity	'97 Att.
Brevard Cty.	Space Coast	340	404	340	8,100	132,608
Charlotte	Charlotte County	340	410	340	5,626	69,072
Clearwater	Jack Russell Memorial	340	400	340	6,917	97,687
Daytona	Jackie Robinson Ballpark	317	400	325	4,200	86,704
Dunedin	Dunedin	335	400	315	6,106	54,544
Fort Myers	Hammond	330	405	330	7,500	88,266
Jupiter*	Roger Dean	335	400	325	6,871	—
Kissimmee	Osceola County	330	410	330	5,180	37,989
Lakeland	Joker Marchant	340	420	340	7,100	21,198
St. Lucie	Thomas J. White	338	410	338	7,347	60,210
St. Petersburg	Al Lang	330	410	330	7,004	154,610
Sarasota	Ed Smith	340	400	340	7,500	69,813
Tampa	Legends Field	318	408	314	10,386	149,191
Vero Beach	Holman	340	400	340	6,500	59,511

*Franchise operated in West Palm Beach in 1997

Brevard County
MANATEES

Office Address: 5800 Stadium Pkwy., Melbourne, FL 32940.
Telephone: (407) 633-9200. **FAX:** (407) 633-9210.

Affiliation (first year): Florida Marlins (1994). **Years in League:** 1994-.

Ownership, Management

Operated by: Florida Marlins of Brevard, Ltd.

Principal Owner: Wayne Huizenga. **President:** Don Smiley.

General Manager: Andy Dunn. **Director, Media Relations:** Kristin Vandeventer. **Coordinator, Corporate Sales:** Kim Hill. **Ticket Manager:** Trey Fraser. **Ground Superintendent:** Brian Cool. **Account Executives:** Creighton Rollins, Melonie Miller. **President, Brevard Concessions:** Roy Lake. **Facility Maintenance:** Jack Haberthier.

Field Staff

Manager: Rick Renteria. **Coach:** Jose Castro. **Pitching Coach:** Larry Pardo. **Trainer:** Mike McGowan.

Game Information

Radio: None.

PA Announcer: Gary Henderson. **Official Scorer:** Ron Jernick.

Stadium Name (year opened): Space Coast Stadium (1994). **Location:** I-95 North to Wickham Road (exit 73), left onto Wickham, right onto Lake Andrew Drive, left onto St. Johns, right onto Stadium Parkway; I-95 South to Fiske Blvd. (exit 74), left onto Fiske, follow Fiske/Stadium Parkway. **Standard Game Times:** 7:05 p.m., Sun. 1:35.

Visiting Club Hotel: Melbourne Airport Hilton, 200 Rialto Place, Melbourne, FL 32901. Telephone: (407) 768-0200.

Charlotte
RANGERS

Office Address: 2300 El Jobean Rd., Port Charlotte, FL 33948.
Telephone: (941) 625-9500. **FAX:** (941) 624-5168.

Affiliation (first year): Texas Rangers (1987). **Years in League:** 1987-.

Ownership, Management

Operated by: Texas Rangers Baseball Club, Ltd.

President: Tom Schieffer.

General Manager: Jim Herlihy. **Assistant General Manager:** Chris Snyder. **Director, Business Operations:** Pam Munz. **Director, Ticket Sales:** Matt LaBranch. **Head Groundskeeper:** Tom Vida. **Director, Media Relations:** Scott Borowick. **Director, Community Relations:** Tina Buonaiuto. **Director, Stadium Operations:** Matt Becker. **Clubhouse Operations:** Jason Hise.

Field Staff

Manager: James Byrd. **Pitching Coach:** Lee Tunnell. **Trainer:** Unavailable.

Game Information

Radio: None.

PA Announcer: Unavailable. **Official Scorer:** Unavailable.

Stadium Name (year opened): Charlotte County Stadium (1987). **Location:** I-75 South to exit 32, follow Toledo Blade Blvd. west for seven miles to stop sign at SR 776, right on 776 for one mile. **Standard Game Times:** 6 p.m., Fri.-Sat. 7, Sun. 2.

Visiting Club Hotel: Days Inn, 1941 Tamiami Trail, Murdock, FL 33948. Telephone: (941) 627-8900.

Clearwater
PHILLIES

Office Address: 800 Phillies Dr., Clearwater, FL 33755. Mailing Address: P.O. Box 10336, Clearwater, FL 33757. Telephone: (813) 441-8638. FAX: (813) 447-3924. E-Mail Address: leemcdaniel@worldnet.att.net.

Affiliation (first year): Philadelphia Phillies (1985). Years in League: 1985-.

Ownership, Management
Operated by: The Philadelphia Phillies.
President: David Montgomery.
Director, Florida Operations: John Timberlake. Business Manager, Florida Operations: Dianne Gonzalez. General Manager: Lee McDaniel. Director, Sales: Dan McDonough. Director, Public Relations/Marketing: Andy Shenk. Director, Tickets: Lauren Fortier. Director, Stadium Operations: Larry Hawkins. Head Groundskeeper: Opie Cheek. Clubhouse Operations: Cliff Armbruster.

Field Staff
Manager: Bill Dancy. Coach: Glenn Brummer. Pitching Coach: Darold Knowles. Trainer: Clete Sigwart.

Game Information
Radio: None.
PA Announcer: Don Guckian. Official Scorer: Unavailable.
Stadium Name (year opened): Jack Russell Memorial Stadium (1955). Location: U.S. 19 North to Drew Street, west to Greenwood Avenue, north to Seminole Street, right to park. Standard Game Times: 7 p.m., Sun. 2.
Visiting Club Hotel: Econo Lodge, 21252 U.S. 19 North, Clearwater, FL 33765. Telephone: (813) 796-3165.

Daytona
CUBS

Office Address: 105 East Orange Ave., Daytona Beach, FL 32114. Mailing Address: P.O. Box 15080, Daytona Beach, FL 32115. Telephone: (904) 257-3172. FAX: (904) 257-3382.

Affiliation (first year): Chicago Cubs (1993). Years in League: 1920-24, 1928, 1936-41, 1946-73, 1977-87, 1993-.

Ownership, Management
Operated by: Florida Professional Sports, Inc.
Principal Owner/President: Jordan Kobritz.
General Manager: Debbie Berg. Account Representatives: Jeff Hinton, Greg Coleman. Clubhouse Operations: Ryan Corner.

Field Staff
Manager: Steve Roadcap. Coach: Richie Zisk. Pitching Coach: Jose Santiago. Trainer: Alan Morales.

Game Information
Radio: None.
PA Announcer: Greg Coleman. Official Scorer: Lyle Fox.
Stadium Name (year opened): Jackie Robinson Ballpark (1930). Location: I-95 to International Speedway Blvd. exit (Route 92), east to Beach Street, south to Orange Ave., east to ballpark; A1A North/South to Orange Ave., west to ballpark. Standard Game Times: 7 p.m.; Sun.1.
Visiting Club Hotel: Clarion Inn Oceanfront, 905 South Atlantic Ave., Daytona Beach, FL 32118. Telephone: (904) 255-5432.

Dunedin
BLUE JAYS

Office Address: Dunedin Stadium, 373 Douglas Ave., Dunedin, FL 34698. Mailing Address: P.O. Box 957, Dunedin, FL 34697. Telephone: (813) 733-9302. FAX: (813) 734-7661.

Affiliation (first year): Toronto Blue Jays (1987). Years in League: 1978-79, 1987-.

Ownership, Management
Operated by: Toronto Blue Jays.
Director, Florida Operations/General Manager: Ken Carson.
Director, Sales/Marketing: Ed Vonnes. Director, Promotions: John Cook. Clubhouse Operations: Mickey McGee. Director, Food Services: Russ Williams. Head Groundskeeper: Steve Perry.

Field Staff
Manager: Rocket Wheeler. Coach: Dennis Holmberg. Pitching Coach: Rick Langford. Trainer: Unavailable.

Game Information
Radio: None.
PA Announcer: Ed Groth. Official Scorer: Larry Wiederecht.
Stadium Name (year opened): Dunedin Stadium at Grant Field (1990).
Location: From North, U.S. 19 to SR 580, west on 580 to Douglas Avenue, south on Douglas to stadium. From South, U.S. 19 to Sunset Point Road, west on Sunset Point, north on Douglas Avenue. Standard Game Times: 7 p.m.; Sun. 5.
Visiting Club Hotel: Comfort Inn, 27988 U.S. 19 North, Clearwater, FL 34621. Telephone: (813) 796-0135.

Fort Myers
MIRACLE

Office Address: 14400 Six Mile Cypress Pkwy., Fort Myers, FL 33912. Telephone: (941) 768-4210. FAX: (941) 768-4211. E-Mail Address: miracle@miraclebaseball.com. Website: www.miraclebaseball.com.
Affiliation (first year): Minnesota Twins (1993). Years in League: 1978-87, 1992-.

Ownership, Management
Operated by: Greater Miami Baseball Club, LP.
Principal Owner/Chairman: Marvin Goldklang. President: Mike Veeck.
General Manager: Derek Sharrer. Assistant General Manager: Dave Burke. Coordinator, Stadium Operations: Mark Rich. Director, Sales/Marketing: Linda McNabb. Director, Business Operations: Suzanne Reaves. Director, Media/Public Relations: Rob Malec. Coordinator, Ticket/Group Sales: Andrew Seymour. Director, Community Relations: Lou Slack. Senior Account Representatives: Tom Brock, Jody Clarke, Mark Hendrickson, Mike Combs. Groundskeepers: Scott Swenson, Terry Slausen.

Field Staff
Manager: Mike Boulanger. Coach: Jeff Carter. Pitching Coach: Stu Cliburn. Trainer: Lanning Tucker.

Game Information
Radio Announcer: Rob Malec. No. of Games Broadcast: Home-70, Away-70. Flagship Station: WGCQ 92.1-FM.
PA Announcer: Ted Fitzgeorge. Official Scorer: Unavailable.
Stadium Name (year opened): William Hammond Stadium (1991).
Location: Exit 21 off I-75, west on Daniels Parkway, left on Six Mile Cypress Parkway. Standard Game Times: 7:05 p.m.; Sun 5.
Visiting Club Hotel: Wellesley Inn Suites, 4400 Ford St. Extension, Fort Myers, FL 33909. Telephone: (941) 278-3949.

Jupiter
HAMMERHEADS

Office Address: 4751 Main St., Jupiter, FL 33458. **Mailing Address:** P.O. Box 8929, Jupiter, FL 33468. **Telephone:** (561) 775-1818. **FAX:** (561) 691-6886.

Affiliation (first year): Montreal Expos (1969). **Years in League:** 1998.

Ownership, Management
Operated by: Montreal Expos.
President: Claude Brochu.
General Manager: Rob Rabenecker. **Assistant General Manager:** Kevin Whalen. **Director, Stadium Operations:** Budgie Clark. **Director, Sales/Marketing:** Kelley Burke. **Account Representatives:** Bryan Monteleone, Jennifer Chalhub, Ian Olson, Brian Barnes, Todd Pund, Rick Tickner. **Director, Ticket Sales:** Mike Stubin. **Director, Merchandising:** Ashley Brown. **Office Manager:** Natalie Hargett. **Head Groundskeepers:** Joe Skrabak, Jorge Toro.

Field Staff
Manager: Doug Sisson. **Coach:** Steve Phillips. **Pitching Coach:** Wayne Rosenthal. **Trainer:** Brian Eggleston.

Game Information
Radio: None.
PA Announcer: Dick Sanford. **Official Scorer:** Ted Leshinski.
Stadium Name (year opened): Roger Dean Stadium (1998). **Location:** Exit I-95 at Donald Ross Road, east ¼ mile. **Standard Game Times:** 7:05 p.m., Sun. 2:05.
Visiting Club Hotel: Wellesley Inn, 34 Fishermans Wharf, Jupiter, FL 33477. Telephone: (561) 575-7201.

Kissimmee
COBRAS

Office Address: 1000 Bill Beck Blvd., Kissimmee, FL 34744. **Mailing Address:** P.O. Box 422229, Kissimmee, FL 34742. **Telephone:** (407) 933-5500. **FAX:** (407) 847-6237.

Affiliation (first year): Houston Astros (1985). **Years In League:** 1985-.

Ownership, Management
Operated by: Houston Astros.
Chairman: Drayton McLane. **President:** Tal Smith.
General Manager: Jeff Kuenzli. **Assistant General Manager:** David Barnes. **Head Groundskeeper:** Rick Raasch. **Office Manager:** Olga Torres.

Field Staff
Manager: Manny Acta. **Coach:** Mark Bailey. **Pitching Coach:** Jack Billingham. **Trainer:** Nate Lucero.

Game Information
Radio: None.
PA Announcer: Norm Allen. **Official Scorer:** Greg Kaye.
Stadium Name (year opened): Osceola County Stadium (1985). **Location:** Florida Turnpike exit 244, west on U.S. 192, right on Bill Beck Blvd.; I-4 exit onto 192 East for 12 miles, stadium on left; 17-92 South to U.S. 192, left for 3 miles. **Standard Game Times:** 7:05 p.m.; Sun. 1:05.
Visiting Club Hotel: Stadium Inn and Suites, 2039 East Irlo Bronson Hwy., Kissimmee, FL 34743. Telephone: (407) 846-7814.

Lakeland
TIGERS

Office Address: 2125 North Lake Ave., Lakeland, FL 33805. **Mailing Address:** P.O. Box 90187, Lakeland, FL 33804. **Telephone:** (941) 688-7911. **FAX:** (941) 688-9589. **Website:** www.lakeland-tigers.com.

Affiliation (first year): Detroit Tigers (1967). **Years in League:** 1919-26, 1953-55, 1960, 1962-64, 1967-.

Ownership, Management
Operated by: Detroit Tigers.
Principal Owner: Mike Ilitch. **President:** John McHale Jr.
General Manager: Woody Hicks. **Assistant General Manager:** Tripp Norton. **Director, Sales/Media Relations:** Zach Burek. **Director, Marketing/Community Relations:** Patti Sarano. **Director, Merchandising/Concessions:** Kay Lalonde. **Clubhouse Operations/Equipment Operations:** Dan Price.

Field Staff
Manager: Mark Meleski. **Coach:** Gary Green. **Pitching Coach:** Joe Georger. **Trainer:** Mark Gruesbeck.

Game Information
Radio: None.
PA Announcer: Wayne Koehler. **Official Scorer:** Sandy Shaw.
Stadium Name (year opened): Joker Marchant Stadium (1960). **Location:** Exit 19 on I-4 to Lakeland Hills Blvd., left 1½ miles. **Standard Game Times:** 7 p.m.; Sun. (April-June) 2, (July-Sept.) 6.
Visiting Club Hotel: Wellesley Inn, 3520 U.S. Hwy. 98, Lakeland, FL. Telephone: (941) 859-3399.

St. Lucie
METS

Office Address: 525 NW Peacock Blvd., Port St. Lucie, FL 34986. **Telephone:** (561) 871-2100. **FAX:** (561) 878-9802. **E-Mail Address:** slmets@gate.net.

Affiliation (first year): New York Mets (1988). **Years in League:** 1988-.

Ownership, Management
Operated by: Sterling Doubleday Entertainment, LP.
Chairman: Nelson Doubleday. **President:** Fred Wilpon.
General Manager: Jeff Maultsby. **Assistant General Manager:** Kevin Mahoney. **Director, Media/Public Relations:** George McClelland. **Director, Ticket Sales:** Grace Benway. **Office Manager:** Joanne Colenzo. **Administrative Assistants:** Derek Harnapp, Melvin Springs.

Field Staff
Manager: Howie Freiling. **Coach:** Gary Ward. **Pitching Coach:** Bob Stanley. **Trainer:** Brandon Sheppard.

Game Information
Radio Announcer: Paul Decastro. **No. Games Broadcast:** Unavailable. **Flagship Station:** WPSL 1590-AM.
PA Announcer: Unavailable. **Official Scorer:** George McClelland.
Stadium Name (year opened): Thomas J. White Stadium (1988). **Location:** Exit 63C (St. Lucie West Blvd.) off I-95, east ½ mile to NW Peacock, left on NW Peacock. **Standard Game Times:** 7 p.m., Sun. 1.
Visiting Club Hotel: Holiday Inn, 10120 South Federal Hwy., Port St. Lucie, FL 34952. Telephone: (561) 337-2200.

St. Petersburg
DEVIL RAYS

Office Address: 180 2nd Ave. SE, St. Petersburg, FL 33701. Mailing Address: P.O. Box 12557, St. Petersburg, FL 33733. Telephone: (813) 822-3384. FAX: (813) 895-1556.

Affiliation (first year): Tampa Bay Devil Rays (1997). Years In League: 1920-27, 1955-.

Ownership, Management
Operated by: Tampa Bay Devil Rays.
President: Vincent Naimoli.
General Manager: Tony Flores. Assistant General Manager: Steve Cohen. Director, Media/Public Relations: Raamen Bass. Director, Sales/Marketing: Pat O'Brien. Manager, Operations: Adrian Moore. Director, Community Relations: Abbie Garcia. Director, Group Sales: Dwayne Hairston. Director, Ticket Sales: Dineen Owen. Head Groundskeeper: Mike Williams.

Field Staff
Manager: Roy Silver. Coach: Steve Livesey. Pitching Coach: Greg Harris. Trainer: Mike Libby.

Game Information
Radio: None.
PA Announcer: Bill Couch. Official Scorer: Richard Martin.
Stadium Name (year opened): Al Lang Stadium (1977). Location: I-275 to exit 9, left on 1st Street South. Standard Game Times: 7:05 p.m., Sun. 5.
Visiting Club Hotel: Best Western Mirage, 5005 34th St. North, St. Petersburg, FL 33701. Telephone: (813) 525-1181.

Sarasota
RED SOX

Office Address: 2700 12th St., Sarasota, FL 34237. Mailing Address: P.O. Box 2816, Sarasota, FL 34230. Telephone: (941) 365-4460, ext. 230. FAX: (941) 365-4217.

Affiliation (first year): Boston Red Sox (1994). Years in League: 1927, 1961-65, 1989-.

Ownership, Management
Operated by: Red Sox of Florida, Inc.
Principal Owner: Boston Red Sox.
General Manager: Fred Seymour Jr.

Field Staff
Manager: Bob Geren. Coach: Victor Rodriguez. Pitching Coach: Jeff Gray. Trainer: Scott Haglund.

Game Information
Radio: None.
PA Announcer: Unavailable. Official Scorer: Walter Jacobus.
Stadium Name (year opened): Ed Smith Stadium (1989). Location: I-75 to exit 39, three miles west to Tuttle Ave., right on Tuttle ½ mile to 12th St., stadium on left. Standard Game Times: 7 p.m., Sun. 5.
Visiting Club Hotel: Wellesley Inn, 1803 North Tamiami Trail, Sarasota, FL 34234. Telephone: (941) 366-5128.

Tampa
YANKEES

Office Address: One Steinbrenner Dr., Tampa, FL 33614. **Telephone:** (813) 875-7753. **FAX:** (813) 673-3174. **E-Mail Address:** www.tyank1.com.

Affiliation (first year): New York Yankees (1994). **Years in League:** 1919-27, 1957-1988, 1994-.

Ownership, Management

Operated by: New York Yankees, LP.

Principal Owner: George Steinbrenner.

General Manager: Sam Arena. **Assistant General Manager:** Shaun Cully. **Director, Sales/Marketing:** Howard Grossworth. **Director, Ticket Sales:** Vance Smith. **Director, Community Relations:** John Spzonar. **Director, Stadium Operations:** Rick Onderko. **Assistant, Marketing:** Camille Garner. **Head Groundskeeper:** Mike Hurd.

Field Staff

Manager: Lee Mazzilli. **Coach:** Fred Langiotti, Ricky Ware. **Pitching Coach:** Mark Shiflett. **Trainer:** Russell Orr.

Game Information

Radio: None.

PA Announcer: Todd Wright. **Official Scorer:** J.J. Pizzio.

Stadium Name (year opened): Legends Field (1996). **Location:** From north, I-275 South to Martin Luther King, west on Martin Luther King to Dale Mabry; From south, I-275 North to Martin Luther King, west on Martin Luther King to Dale Mabry. **Standard Game Times:** 7 p.m., Sun. 1.

Visiting Club Hotel: Holiday Inn Express, 4732 North Dale Mabry, Tampa, FL 33614. Telephone: (813) 877-6061.

Vero Beach
DODGERS

Office Address: 4101 26th St., Vero Beach, FL 32960. **Mailing Address:** P.O. Box 2887, Vero Beach, FL 32961. **Telephone:** (561) 569-4900. **FAX:** (561) 567-0819. **E-Mail Address:** dodgers@vero.com. **Website:** www.vero.com/dodgers.

Affiliation (first year): Los Angeles Dodgers (1980). **Years in League:** 1980-.

Ownership, Management

Operated by: Los Angeles Dodgers, Inc.

President: Peter O'Malley.

General Manager: Grant Griesser. **Assistant General Manager:** Rob Croll. **Controller:** Link Stanton. **Head Groundskeeper:** John Yencho. **Director, Ticket Sales:** Louise Boissy. **Director, Food Services:** Bruce Callahan. **Clubhouse Operations:** Mike Parrish. **Administrative Assistants:** Kevin O'Malley, Nicole Turner, Brian Hines.

Field Staff

Manager: John Shoemaker. **Coach:** John Shelby. **Pitching Coach:** Gorman Heimueller. **Trainer:** Rob Giesecke.

Game Information

Radio Announcer: Bob DeCourcey. **No. of Games Broadcast:** Home-70, Away-70. **Flagship Station:** WAXE 1370-AM.

PA Announcer: Unavailable. **Official Scorer:** Randy Phillips.

Stadium Name (year opened): Holman Stadium (1953). **Location:** Exit I-95 at Route 60, east to 43rd Ave., north to Aviation Blvd., east on Aviation. **Standard Game Times:** 7 p.m.; Sun. (April-May) 1:30, (June-Sept.) 6.

Visiting Club Hotel: Vero Beach Inn, 4700 North A1A, Vero Beach, FL 32963. Telephone: (561) 231-1600.

MIDWEST LEAGUE

Class A

Office Address: 1118 Cranston Rd., Beloit, WI 53511. **Mailing Address:** P.O. Box 936, Beloit, WI 53512. **Telephone:** (608) 364-1188. **FAX:** (608) 364-1913. **E-Mail Address:** midwest@inwave.com. **Website:** www.minor-leaguebaseball.com/leagues/midwest.

Years League Active: 1947-.

President/Treasurer: George Spelius.

Vice President: Ed Larson. **Legal Counsel/Secretary:** Richard Nussbaum.

Directors: Lew Chamberlin (West Michigan), George Chaney (Clinton), William Collins III (Michigan), Dennis Conerton (Beloit), Tom Dickson (Lansing), Erik Haag (South Bend), Richard Holtzman (Quad City), Wally Krouse (Cedar Rapids), Eric Margenau (Fort Wayne), Mark McGuire (Rockford), Pete Vonachen (Peoria), Dave Walker (Burlington), Mike Woleben (Kane County), John Wollner (Wisconsin).

George Spelius

League Administrator: Stephanie Gray.

1998 Opening Date: April 9. **Closing Date:** Sept. 7.

Regular Season: 140 games (split-schedule).

Division Structure: Eastern—Fort Wayne, Lansing, Michigan, South Bend, West Michigan. **Central**—Beloit, Kane County, Peoria, Rockford, Wisconsin. **Western**—Burlington, Cedar Rapids, Clinton, Quad City.

Playoff Format: Eight teams qualify. First-half and second-half division champions, and two wild-card teams, meet in best-of-3 quarterfinal series. Winners advance to best-of-3 semifinals. Winners advance to best-of-5 final for league championship.

All-Star Game: June 23 at Clinton, IA.

Roster Limit: 25 active. **Player Eligibility Rule:** No age limit. No more than two players and one player-coach on active list may have more than five years experience.

Brand of Baseball: Rawlings ROM-MID.

Statistician: Howe Sportsdata International, Boston Fish Pier, West Bldg. #1, Suite 302, Boston MA 02210.

Stadium Information

Club	Stadium	Dimensions			Capacity	'97 Att.
		LF	CF	RF		
Beloit	Pohlman Field	325	380	325	3,501	81,564
Burlington	Community Field	338	403	315	3,502	52,152
Cedar Rapids	Veterans Memorial	325	385	325	6,000	124,629
Clinton	Riverview	335	390	325	3,000	50,597
Fort Wayne	Memorial	330	400	330	6,316	230,210
Kane County	Philip B. Elfstrom	335	400	335	5,900	436,505
Lansing	Oldsmobile Park	305	412	305	11,000	523,443
Michigan	C.O. Brown	323	401	336	6,600	126,947
Peoria	Pete Vonachen	335	383	335	5,200	148,585
Quad City	John O'Donnell	340	390	340	6,200	130,932
Rockford	Marinelli Field	335	405	335	4,500	86,716
South Bend	Coveleski Regional	336	410	336	5,000	197,864
West Michigan	Old Kent Park	327	402	327	10,900	536,029
Wisconsin	Fox Cities	325	405	325	5,500	227,104

Beloit
SNAPPERS

Office Address: 2301 Skyline Dr., Beloit, WI 53511. **Mailing Address:** P.O. Box 855, Beloit, WI 53512. **Telephone:** (608) 362-2272. **FAX:** (608) 362-0418. **E-Mail Address:** snappers@jv/net.com. **Website:** snappers-baseball.com.

Affiliation (first year): Milwaukee Brewers (1982). **Years in League:** 1982-.

Ownership, Management

Operated by: Beloit Professional Baseball Association, Inc.

Chairman: Dennis Conerton. **President:** Marcy Olsen.

General Manager: Matt Harris. **Assistant General Manager:** Dave Endress. **Director, Media/Public Relations:** Bryan Dolgin. **Director, Group Sales/Community Relations:** Jeff Brazzale. **Clubhouse Operations:** Tom Nibbio. **Head Groundskeeper:** Jim Haun. **Administrative Assistants:** Kyle Murphy, Tyler Burns, P.J. Connelly, Ben Lathrop, Tyler Nickel.

Field Staff

Manager: Don Money. **Coach:** Floyd Rayford. **Pitching Coach:** Randy Kramer. **Trainer:** Keith Sayers.

Game Information

Radio Announcer: Bryan Dolgin. **No. of Games Broadcast:** Home-70, Away-70. **Flagship Station:** WGEZ 1490-AM.

PA Announcer: Al Fagerli. **Official Scorer:** Dick Fitzwell.

Stadium Name (year opened): Pohlman Field (1982). **Location:** I-90 to exit 185-A, right at Cranston Road for 1½ miles. **Standard Game Times:** April-May 6:30 p.m.; June-September 7; Sat. (April-May) 2; Sun. 2.

Visiting Club Hotel: Comfort Inn, 2786 Milwaukee Rd., Beloit, WI 53511. Telephone: (608) 362-2666.

Burlington
BEES

Office Address: 2712 Mt. Pleasant St., Burlington, IA 52601. **Mailing Address:** P.O. Box 824, Burlington, IA 52601. **Telephone:** (319) 754-5705. **FAX:** (319) 754-5882.

Affiliation (first year): Cincinnati Reds (1997). **Years In League:** 1962-.

Ownership, Management

Operated by: Burlington Baseball Association, Inc.

President: David Walker.

General Manager: Kyle Fisher. **Assistant General Manager:** Kent Harman. **Director, Sales/Marketing:** Brenna Goetz. **Manager, Public Relations:** Jason Parry. **Head Groundskeeper:** Chuck Cannon.

Field Staff

Manager: Phillip Wellman. **Pitching Coach:** Derek Botelho. **Trainer:** Unavailable.

Game Information

Radio Announcer: Dan Vaughn. **No. of Games Broadcast:** Home-70, Away-70. **Flagship Station:** KBUR 1490-AM.

PA Announcer: Unavailable. **Official Scorer:** Scott Logas.

Stadium Name (year opened): Community Field (1973). **Location:** From U.S. 34, take U.S. 61 North to Mt. Pleasant Street, east ⅛ mile. **Standard Game Times:** 7 p.m.; Sat. (April-May 16) 2, (May 30-September) 7; Sun. (April-May 17) 2, (May 31-September) 6.

Visiting Club Hotel: Best Western-Pzazz, 3001 Winegard Dr., Burlington, IA 52601. Telephone: (319) 753-2223.

Cedar Rapids
KERNELS

Office Address: 950 Rockford Road SW, Cedar Rapids, IA 52404. **Mailing Address:** P.O. Box 2001, Cedar Rapids, IA 52406. **Telephone:** (319) 363-3887. **FAX:** (319) 363-5631. **E-Mail Address:** kernels@kernels.com. **Website:** www.kernels.com.

Affiliation (first year): Anaheim Angels (1993). **Years in League:** 1962-.

Ownership, Management

Operated by: Cedar Rapids Baseball Club, Inc.

President: Wally Krouse.

General Manager: Jack Roeder. **Assistant General Manager:** Blake Porter. **Head Groundskeeper:** Bud Curran. **Office Manager:** Nancy Cram. **Clubhouse Operations:** Ron Plein. **Director, Food Services:** John Bateman.

Field Staff

Manager: Garry Templeton. **Coach:** Tyrone Boykin. **Pitching Coach:** Jim Bennett. **Trainer:** Jeff Hostetler.

Game Information

Radio Announcer: John Rodgers. **No. of Games Broadcast:** Home-70, Away-70. **Flagship Station:** KCRG 1600-AM.

PA Announcer: Dale Brodt. **Official Scorer:** Andy Pantini.

Stadium Name (year opened): Veterans Memorial Stadium (1949). **Location:** I-380 to Wilson Ave., west to Rockford Road, right to corner of 8th Ave. and 15th Street SW. **Standard Game Times:** 7 p.m.; Sun., 2.

Visiting Club Hotels: Village Inn, 100 F Ave. NW, Cedar Rapids, IA 52405. Telephone (319) 366-5323.

Clinton
LUMBERKINGS

Office Address: Riverview Stadium, 6th Avenue North and 1st Street, Clinton, IA 52732. **Mailing Address:** P.O. Box 1295, Clinton, IA 52733. **Telephone:** (319) 242-0727. **FAX:** (319) 242-1433. **E-Mail Address:** lkings@clinton.net. **Website:** www.clinton.net/~lkings.

Affiliation (first year): San Diego Padres (1995). **Years in League:** 1956-.

Ownership, Management

Operated by: Clinton Baseball Club, Inc.

Chairman: Don Roode. **President:** George Chaney.

General Manager: Alfredo Portela. **Assistant General Manager:** Mike Lieberman. **Director, Ticket Sales:** Kelly Harvey. **Office Manager:** Terri Portela.

Field Staff

Manager: Tom LeVasseur. **Coach:** Dan Simonds. **Pitching Coach:** Tony Phillips. **Trainer:** Unavailable.

Game Information

Radio Announcer: Dylan Bry. **No. of Games Broadcast:** Home-70, Away-70. **Flagship Station:** KCLN 97.7-FM.

PA Announcer: Unavailable. **Official Scorer:** Unavailable.

Stadium Name (year opened): Riverview Stadium (1937). **Location:** Highway 30 East to 6th Avenue North, right on 6th, cross railroad tracks, stadium on right. **Standard Game Times:** 6:30 p.m.; Fri., 7; Sat. (April-May) 2, (June-Sept.) 7; Sun. 2.

Visiting Club Hotel: Ramada Inn, 1522 Lincolnway, Clinton, IA 52732. Telephone (319) 243-8841.

Fort Wayne
WIZARDS

Office Address: 4000 Parnell Ave., Fort Wayne, IN 46805. **Telephone:** (219) 482-6400. **FAX:** (219) 471-4678.

Affiliation (first year): Minnesota Twins (1993). **Years in League:** 1993-.

Ownership, Management
Operated by: United Sports Ventures, Inc.
Principal Owner: Eric Margenau. **Vice President:** Mike Tatoian.
General Manager: Bret Staehling. **Director, Business Operations:** Jeff Hyde. **Assistant General Manager:** Vince Saul. **Director, Merchandising:** Vince Slack. **Director, Broadcasting/Media Relations:** Alan Garrett. **Director, Marketing/Promotions:** Jason Hartlund. **Director, Ticket Sales:** Scott Brumfiel. **Director, Group Sales:** Jeremy Guest. **Assistant, Group Sales:** Christy Utes. **Assistant, Ticket Sales:** Seth Tipton. **Office Manager:** Nancy Murphy.

Field Staff
Manager: Jose Marzan. **Coach:** Riccardo Ingram. **Pitching Coach:** David Perez. **Trainer:** Chad Floyd.

Game Information
Radio Announcer: Alan Garrett. **No. of Games Broadcast:** Home-70, Away-70. **Flagship Station:** WHWD 1380-AM.
PA Announcer: Crash Davis. **Official Scorers:** Rich Tavierne, Mark Lazzer.
Stadium Name (year opened): Memorial Stadium (1993). **Location:** Exit 112A (Coldwater Road) off I-69 to Coliseum Blvd., left on Coliseum Blvd. to stadium. **Standard Game Times:** Mon.-Thur. (April-May) 6:30, (June-Aug.) 7; Fri.-Sat. 7 p.m.; Sun. (April-May) 2, (June-Aug.) 2, 6.
Visiting Club Hotel: Budgetel Inn, 1005 West Washington Center Rd., Fort Wayne, IN 46805. Telephone: (219) 489-2220.

Kane County
COUGARS

Office Address: 34W002 Cherry Lane, Geneva, IL 60134. **Telephone:** (630) 232-8811. **FAX:** (630) 232-8815. **Website:** www.kccougars.com.
Affiliation (first year): Florida Marlins (1993). **Years In League:** 1991-.

Ownership, Management
Operated by: Cougars Baseball Partners.
President: Al Gordon. **Vice President:** Mike Murtaugh. **Secretary-Treasurer:** Mike Woleben.
General Manager: Jeff Sedivy. **Assistant General Manager:** Curtis Haug. **Business Manager:** Mary Almlie. **Assistant Business Manager:** Doug Czurylo. **Manager, Personnel:** Patti Savage. **Director, Media Relations/Advertising:** Marty Cusack. **Coordinator, Season Tickets:** Jennifer Plesa. **Coordinator, Promotions:** Jeff Ney. **Office Manager:** Terry Berendt. **Creative Director/Computer Operations:** Kevin Gilsdorf. **Coordinators, Group Sales:** Sue Lesters, Amy Mason. **Account Executives:** John Knechtges, Brad Bober, Mike Moore, Kevin Sullivan, Bill Baker. **Facilities Management:** Mike Fik, Mike Kurns. **Manager, Concessions:** Rich Essegian. **Clubhouse:** Jose Torres.

Field Staff
Manager: Juan Bustabad. **Coach:** Matt Winters. **Pitching Coach:** Steve Luebber. **Trainer:** Harold Williams.

Game Information
Radio Announcer: Pat Kinas. **No. of Games Broadcast:** Home-70, Away-70. **Flagship Station:** WKKD 95.9-FM.
PA Announcer: Kirk Possehl. **Official Scorer:** Marty Cusack.
Stadium Name (year opened): Philip B. Elfstrom Stadium (1991). **Location:** I-88 (East-West Tollway) to Farnsworth Road North exit, 5 miles north to Cherry Lane, left to stadium. **Standard Game Times:** 7 p.m., Sat. 6, Sun. 2.
Visiting Club Hotel: Travelodge, 1617 Naperville Rd., Naperville, IL 60563. Telephone: (630) 505-0200.

Lansing
LUGNUTS

Office Address: 505 East Michigan Ave., Lansing MI 48912. **Telephone:** (517) 485-4500. **FAX:** (517) 485-4518. **E-Mail Address:** lugnuts@tcimet.net. **Website:** www.lansinglugnuts.com.

Affiliation (first year): Kansas City Royals (1996). **Years In League:** 1996-.

Ownership, Management

Operated by: Take Me Out To The Ball Game, LLC.

Principal Owner/President: Tom Dickson.

General Manager: Tom Glick. Director, Operations: Greg Rauch. Director, Marketing: Linda Frederickson. Director, Customer Service: Darla Bowen. Director, Finance/Human Resources: Kimberly Hengesbach. Director, Retail: Mary Kay Schultz. Ticket Manager: Jenny Frasco. Manager, Stadium Operations: Rich Zizek. Sponsorship Account Executive: Elizabeth Panich. Sponsorship Service Manager: Megan Frazer. Director, Corporate Sales: Tom Murphy. Director, Group Sales: Dorn McGaw. Head Groundskeeper: Tom Preslar.

Field Staff

Manager: Bob Herold. Coach: Rodney McCray. Pitching Coach: Larry Carter. Trainer: Jeff Stevenson.

Game Information

Radio Announcer: Jeff Walker. No. of Games Broadcast: Home-70, Away-70. Flagship Station: WJIM 1240-AM.

PA Announcer: Unavailable. Official Scorer: Michael Clark.

Stadium Name (year opened): Oldsmobile Park (1996). Location: I-96 East/West to U.S. 496, exit at Larch Street. Standard Game Times: 7:05 p.m.; April 6:05; Sun. (May-July) 2:05, (August-Sept.) 6:05.

Visiting Club Hotel: Holiday Inn South, 6820 South Cedar St., Lansing, MI 48911. Telephone: (517) 694-8123.

Michigan
BATTLE CATS

Office Address: 1392 Capital Ave. NE, Battle Creek, MI 49017. Telephone: (616) 660-2287. FAX: (616) 660-2288.

Affiliation (first year): Boston Red Sox (1995). Years in League: 1995-.

Ownership, Management

Operated by: American Baseball Capital, Inc.

Principal Owner/Chairman: William Collins III.

General Manager: Jerry Burkot. Controller: T.J. Egan. Director, Media Relations: Danielle Disch. Director, Corporate Sales: Anthony Errico. Director, Community Relations: Tonya Fenderbosch. Head Groundskeeper: Scott Dobbins.

Field Staff

Manager: Billy Gardner Jr. Coach: Bill Madlock. Pitching Coach: Larry Pierson. Trainer: Scott Hagland.

Game Information

Radio Announcers: Terry Newton, Ken Ervin. No. of Games Broadcast: Home-70; Away-70. Flagship Station: WBCK 930-AM.

PA Announcer: Unavailable. Official Scorer: Unavailable.

Stadium Name (year opened): C.O. Brown Stadium (1990). Location: I-94 to exit 98B (downtown), to Capital Ave. NE, east to stadium. Standard Game Times: 7 p.m.; Sat (April-May) 2, (June-August) 7; Sun. 2.

Visiting Club Hotel: Unavailable.

Peoria
CHIEFS

Office Address: 1524 West Nebraska Ave., Peoria, IL 61604. Telephone: (309) 688-1622. FAX: (309) 686-4516. E-Mail Address: peochfs@aol.com. Website: chiefsnet.com.

Affiliation (first year): St. Louis Cardinals (1995). Years in League: 1983-.

Ownership, Management

Operated by: Peoria Chiefs Community Baseball Club, LLC.

Principal Owner/President: Pete Vonachen.

General Manager: Rocky Vonachen. Assistant GM/Marketing, Promotions: Michael Baird. Assistant GM/Operations: Mark Vonachen. Senior Account Executive: Ralph Rashid. Director, Ticket Sales: John

Bientema. **Manager, Group Sales:** Jennifer Blackorby. **Head Grounds-keeper:** Dennis Rothlisberger. **Office Manager:** Barbara Linberg. **Game Day Ticket Operations:** Jay McCormick.

Field Staff
Manager: Jeff Shireman. **Coach:** Tony Diggs. **Pitching Coach:** Gary Buckels. **Trainer:** Drew McCarthy.

Game Information
Radio Announcer: Unavailable. **No. of Games Broadcast:** Home-70, Away-70. **Flagship Station:** WBGE 92.3-FM.

PA Announcer: Unavailable. **Official Scorer:** Unavailable.

Stadium Name (year opened): Pete Vonachen Stadium (1984). **Location:** I-74 exit 91B (University Street North), left on Nebraska Avenue, left to ballpark. **Standard Game Times:** 7:05 p.m.; Sun. (April-May) 2:05, (June-Sept.) 6:05.

Visiting Club Hotel: Holiday Inn City Centre, 500 Hamilton Blvd., Peoria, IL 61602. Telephone: (309) 674-2500.

Quad City
RIVER BANDITS

Office Address: 209 South Gaines St., Davenport, IA 52802. **Mailing Address:** P.O. Box 3496, Davenport, IA 52808. **Telephone:** (319) 324-2032. **FAX:** (319) 324-3109. **E-Mail Address:** rvrbandits@aol. **Website:** www.qconline.com/bandits.

Affiliation (first year): Houston Astros (1993). **Years in League:** 1960-.

Ownership, Management
Operated by: Quad City Professional Baseball Club, Inc.

Principal Owner/Chairman: Richard Holtzman.

General Manager: Tim Bawmann. **Assistant General Managers:** Holly Morgan, Heath Brown. **Director, Corporate Sales:** Chet Carey. **Director, Group Sales:** Erica Poag. **Office Manager:** Shelley Wheeler. **Director, Concessions:** Bryan Ellis. **Groundskeepers:** Matt Hildebrandt, Eric Mumma, Jason Veto.

Field Staff
Manager: Mike Rojas. **Coach:** Sid Holland. **Pitching Coach:** Bill Ballou. **Trainer:** Craig Yingling.

Game Information
Radio Announcers: Cory Dann, Tim Bawmann. **No. of Games Broadcast:** Home-70, Away-70. **Flagship Station:** WKBF 1270-AM.

PA Announcer: Pete Ivanic. **Official Scorer:** Jim Tappa.

Stadium Name (year opened): John O'Donnell Stadium (1931). **Location:** From I-74, south on SR 61 to corner of South Gaines Street and River Drive; From I-80, take Brady exit to River Drive, right on South Gaines. **Standard Game Times:** 7 p.m.; Sun. (April-May) 2, (June-Sept.) 5.

Visiting Club Hotel: Heartland Inn, 815 Golden Valley Dr., Bettendorf, IA 52807. Telephone: (319) 355-6336.

Rockford
CUBBIES

Office Address: 101 15th Ave., Rockford, IL 61104. **Mailing Address:** P.O. Box 6748, Rockford, IL 61125. **Telephone:** (815) 962-2827. **FAX:** (815) 961-2002.

Affiliation (first year): Chicago Cubs (1995). **Years in League:** 1988-.

Ownership, Management
Operated By: Chicago Cubs.

President: Mark McGuire. **Vice President:** Connie Kowal.

General Manager: Bruce Keiter. **Director, Community/Media Relations/Group Sales:** Sarah Couey. **Director, Ticket Operations:** Eric Robin. **Director, Stadium Operations:** Craig Girling. **Director, Concessions/Retail:** Sarah Skridla.

Field Staff
Manager: Ruben Amaro. **Coach:** Manny Trillo. **Pitching Coach:** Stan Kyles. **Trainer:** Chris Heitz.

Game Information

Radio Announcers: Andy Gannon, Jeff Cummings. **Games Broadcast:** Home games/Friday, Saturday. **Flagship Station:** WQFL 101 FM.

PA Announcer: Unavailable. **Official Scorer:** Dave Shultz.

Stadium Name (year opened): Marinelli Field (1988). **Location:** I-90 West to U.S. 20 West to Highway 2, north on Main Street to 15th Avenue. **Standard Game Times:** 6:30 p.m.; Sat (April-May) 2, (June-Sept.) 7; Sun. 2.

Visiting Club Hotel: Howard Johnson, 3909 11th St., Rockford, IL 61109. Telephone: (815) 397-9000.

South Bend
SILVER HAWKS

Office Address: 501 West South St., South Bend, IN 46601. **Mailing Address:** P.O. Box 4218, South Bend, IN 46634. **Telephone:** (219) 235-9988. **FAX:** (219) 235-9950. **Website:** www.silverhawks.com.

Affiliation (first year): Arizona Diamondbacks (1997). **Years in League:** 1988-.

Ownership, Management

Operated by: Palisades Baseball, Ltd.

Principal Owner: Alan Levin.

Vice President/General Manager: Erik Haag. **Assistant General Manager:** Jim Pool. **Director, Finance:** Andy Zmudzinski. **Assistant Director, Finance:** Renee Mitzenfelt. **Director, Marketing/Promotions:** Mike Foss. **Director, Stadium Operations:** Tom Reed. **Director, Ticket Operations:** Jon Zeitz. **Director, Group Sales:** Sharee Brandler. **Director, Concessions:** Troy Landrey. **Director, Media Relations/Broadcasting:** Mike Carver. **Assistant Director, Stadium Operations:** Matt Adamski. **Head Groundskeeper:** Joel Reinebold.

Field Staff

Manager: Roly de Armas. **Coaches:** Rick Schu, Jim Reinebold. **Pitching Coach:** Mike Parrott. **Trainer:** Dale Gilbert.

Game Information

Radio Announcer: Mike Carver. **No. of Games Broadcast:** Home-70, Away-70. **Flagship Station:** WSBT 960-AM.

PA Announcer: Unavailable. **Official Scorer:** Unavailable.

Stadium Name (year opened): Stanley Coveleski Regional Stadium (1987). **Location:** I-80/90 toll road to exit 77, take U.S. 31-33 south to South Bend, to downtown (Main Street), to Western Ave., right on Western, left on Taylor. **Standard Game Times:** 7 p.m.; Sat. 2 (April-May), 7 (June-August); Sun. 2.

Visiting Club Hotel: Ramada Inn, 52890 U.S. 31/33 North, South Bend, IN 46637. Telephone: (219) 272-5220.

West Michigan
WHITECAPS

Office Address: Old Kent Park, 4500 West River Dr., Comstock Park, MI 49321. **Mailing Address:** P.O. Box 428, Comstock Park, MI 49321. **Telephone:** (616) 784-4131. **FAX:** (616) 784-4911. **E-Mail Address:** whitecap@gr.cns.net. **Website:** www.whitecaps-baseball.com.

Affiliation (first year): Detroit Tigers (1997). **Years in League:** 1994-.

Ownership, Management

Operated by: Whitecaps Professional Baseball Corp.

Principal Owners: Dennis Baxter, Lew Chamberlin.

President: Dennis Baxter. **Vice President, Managing Partner:** Lew Chamberlin.

General Manager: Scott Lane. **Director, Sales:** John Guthrie. **Director, Baseball Operations:** Jim Jarecki. **Director, Group Sales:** Greg Hill. **Director, Media Relations/Merchandising:** Lori Clark. **Manager, Gameday Operations:** Matt O'Brien. **Ticket Manager:** Bruce Radley. **Manager, Concessions:** Eddie Sypniewski. **Manager, Community Relations:** Erin Kauth. **Account Executive:** Dan Morrison. **Manager, Facility Maintenance:** Joe Eimer. **Head Groundskeeper:** Heather Nabozny. **Coordinator, Human Resources:** Ellen Chamberlin. **Accountant:** Dean Haverdink.

Field Staff
Manager: Bruce Fields. **Coach:** Skeeter Barnes. **Pitching Coach:** Steve McCatty. **Trainer:** Bryan Goike.

Game Information
Radio Announcers: Rick Berkey, Rob Sanford. **No. of Games Broadcast:** Home-70, Away-70. **Flagship Station:** WOOD 1300-AM.

PA Announcers: Mike Dean, Don Thomas. **Official Scorers:** Bob Wells, Mike Newell.

Stadium Name (year opened): Old Kent Park (1994). **Location:** U.S. 131 North from Grand Rapids to exit 91 (West River Drive). **Standard Game Times:** April-May 6:35 p.m.; June-Sept. 7; Sat. (April-May) 2; Sun. 2.

Visiting Club Hotel: Days Inn-Downtown, 310 Pearl St. NW, Grand Rapids, MI 49504. Telephone: (616) 235-7611.

Wisconsin
TIMBER RATTLERS

Office Address: 2400 North Casaloma Dr., Appleton, WI 54915. **Mailing Address:** P.O. Box 464, Appleton, WI 54912. **Telephone:** (920) 733-4152. **FAX:** (920) 733-8032.

Affiliation (first year): Seattle Mariners (1993). **Years in League:** 1962-.

Ownership, Management
Operated by: Appleton Baseball Club, Inc.

Chairman: John Wollner. **President:** Kevin Doyle.

General Manager: Mike Birling. **Assistant General Manager:** Gary Mayse. **Controller:** Cathy Spanbauer. **Head Groundskeeper:** Chad Huss. **Director, Marketing:** Gary Radke. **Director, Corporate Sales:** Ryan Mangan. **Director, Ticket Sales:** Tim Okonek. **Director, Group Sales:** Kevin Hill. **Group Sales Representatives:** Drew Niehans, Rob Zerjav. **Office Manager:** Mary Robinson.

Field Staff
Manager: Gary Varsho. **Coach:** Omer Munoz. **Pitching Coach:** Steve Peck. **Trainer:** Jeff Carr.

Game Information
Radio Announcers: Tim McCord, Greg Hofer. **No. of Games Broadcast:** Home-70, Away-70. **Flagship Station:** WSGC 1050-AM.

PA Announcers: Bill Scott, Bill Schultz. **Official Scorers:** Doug Hahn, Dan Huber, Jim Youngwerth.

Stadium Name (year opened): Fox Cities Stadium (1995). **Location:** Highway 41 to Wisconsin Ave. exit, west to Casaloma Drive, right on Casaloma, stadium ½ mile on right. **Standard Game Times:** 7 p.m., Sun. 1.

Visiting Club Hotel: Fairfield Inn, 132 Mall Dr., Appleton, WI 54912. Telephone: (920) 954-0202.

SOUTH ATLANTIC LEAGUE

Class A

Office Address: 504 Crescent Hill, Kings Mountain, NC 28086. **Mailing Address:** P.O. Box 38, Kings Mountain, NC 28086. **Telephone:** (704) 739-3466. **FAX:** (704) 739-1974. **E-Mail Address:** sal@shelby.net.

Years League Active: 1948-1952, 1960-.
President/Secretary-Treasurer: John Moss.

Vice President: Winston Blenckstone (Hagerstown), Ron McKee (Asheville).

Directors: Don Beaver (Hickory), Winston Blenckstone (Hagerstown), Chuck Boggs (Charleston, W.Va.), William Collins III (Greensboro), Marv Goldklang (Charleston, S.C.), Larry Hedrick (Piedmont), Eric Margenau (Capital City), Ron McKee (Asheville), Chip Moore (Macon), Charles Morrow (Columbus), Charles Padgett (Cape Fear),

John Moss

Bill Scripps (Augusta), Ken Silver (Savannah), Pete Simmons (Delmarva).

Administrative Assistant: Elaine Moss.

1997 Opening Date: April 2. **Closing Date:** Aug. 30.

Regular Season: 142 games (split-schedule).

Division Structure: Central—Asheville, Capital City, Charleston SC, Greensboro, Hickory, Piedmont. **Northern**—Cape Fear, Charleston WV, Delmarva, Hagerstown. **Southern**—Augusta, Columbus, Macon, Savannah.

Playoff Format: Eight teams qualify. First-half and second-half division champions, and two wild-card teams, meet in best-of-3 quarterfinal series. Winners advance to best-of-3 semifinal series. Winners advance to best-of-3 final for league championship.

All-Star Game: June 16 at Charleston, SC.

Roster Limit: 25 active. **Player Eligibility Rule:** No age limit. No more than two players and one player-coach on active list may have more than five years of experience.

Brand of Baseball: Rawlings.

Statistician: Howe Sportsdata International, Boston Fish Pier, West Bldg. #1, Suite 302, Boston, MA 02210.

Stadium Information

Club	Stadium	LF	CF	RF	Capacity	'97 Att.
Asheville	McCormick Field	328	402	300	4,000	143,351
Augusta	Lake Olmstead	330	400	330	4,322	152,270
Cape Fear	J.P. Riddle	330	405	330	4,200	69,873
Capital City	Capital City	330	395	320	6,000	135,670
Charleston, SC	Riley Ballpark	306	386	336	5,800	231,006
Charleston, WV	Watt Powell Park	340	406	330	5,400	88,378
Columbus	Golden Park	330	415	330	5,000	119,646
Delmarva	Perdue	309	402	309	5,200	324,412
Greensboro	War Memorial	327	401	327	7,500	146,987
Hagerstown	Municipal	335	400	330	4,600	115,011
Hickory	L.P. Frans	330	401	330	5,062	196,394
Macon	Luther Williams	338	402	338	4,000	129,723
Piedmont	Fieldcrest Cannon	330	400	310	4,700	114,646
Savannah	Grayson	290	400	310	8,000	125,729

Asheville
TOURISTS

Office Address: McCormick Field, 30 Buchanan Place, Asheville, NC 28801. Mailing Address: P.O. Box 1556, Asheville, NC 28802. Telephone: (704) 258-0428. FAX: (704) 258-0320. E-Mail Address: touristsbb@mind-spring.com. Website: www.fanlink.com.

Affiliation (first year): Colorado Rockies (1994). Years in League: 1976-.

Ownership, Management
Operated by: Tourists Baseball, Inc.
Principal Owners: Peter Kern, Ron McKee.
President: Peter Kern.
General Manager: Ron McKee. Assistant General Managers: Chris Smith, Dave Meyer. Director, Business Operations: Carolyn McKee. Manager, Ticket Sales/Merchandising: Margarita Turner. Concessions Manager: Jane Lentz. Head Groundskeeper: Grady Gardner.

Field Staff
Manager: Ron Gideon. Coach: Billy White. Pitching Coach: Jerry Cram. Trainer: Travis Anderson.

Game Information
Radio: None.
PA Announcer: Sam Zurich. Official Scorers: Mike Gore, Bob Browning.
Stadium Name (year opened): McCormick Field (1992). Location: I-240 to Charlotte Street South exit, south one mile on Charlotte, left on McCormick Place. Standard Game Times: 7 p.m., Sun. 2.
Visiting Club Hotel: Days Inn, 199 Tunnel Rd., Asheville, NC 28805. Telephone: (704) 254-4311.

Augusta
GREENJACKETS

Office Address: 78 Milledge Rd., Augusta, GA 30904. Mailing Address: P.O. Box 3746, Hill Station, Augusta, GA 30904. Telephone: (706) 736-7889. FAX: (706) 736-1122.

Affiliation (first year): Pittsburgh Pirates (1988). Years in League: 1988-.

Ownership, Management
Operated by: Scripps Baseball Group, Inc.
Principal Owner/President: Bill Scripps.
General Manager: Chris Scheuer. Associate General Manager: Scott Skadan. Assistant General Manager: Marc Williamson. Business Manager: Nancy Crowe. Director, Media Relations/Group Sales: Jason Pellegrini Director, Promotions: Joe Distel. Head Groundskeeper: John Packer.

Field Staff
Manager: Marty Brown. Coach: Jeff Treadway. Pitching Coach: Scott Lovekamp. Trainer: Mark Shoen.

Game Information
Radio: None.
PA Announcer: Torye Hurst. Official Scorer: Frank Mercogliano.
Stadium Name (year opened): Lake Olmstead Stadium (1995). Location: I-20 to Washington Road exit, east to Broad Street exit, left on Milledge Road. Standard Game Times: 7:05 p.m; Sun. (April-May) 2:30, (June-August) 6:05.
Visiting Club Hotel: Holiday Inn West, 1075 Stevens Creek Rd., Augusta, GA 30907. Telephone: (706) 738-8811.

Cape Fear
CROCS

Office Address: 2823 Legion Road, Fayetteville, NC 28306. **Mailing Address:** P.O Box 64939, Fayetteville, NC 28306. **Telephone:** (910) 424-6500. **FAX:** (910) 424-4325. **E-Mail Address:** salcrocs@aol.com

Affiliation (first year): Montreal Expos (1997). **Years in League:** 1987-.

Ownership, Management

Operated by: Fayetteville Baseball Club, Inc.

Principal Owner/President: Charles G. Padgett.

President: Charles E. Padgett.

General Manager: Brad Taylor. **Director, Media/Public Relations:** Buck Rogers. **Director, Sales/Marketing:** Yvette Taylor. **Account Representative:** Rhonda Walker. **Office Manager:** Mary Mercer. **Director, Ticket Sales/Merchandising:** Tim Mueller. **Head Groundskeeper:** Houston Reece.

Field Staff

Manager: Luis Dorante. **Coach:** Bert Heffernan. **Pitching Coach:** Randy St. Claire. **Trainer:** Dave Cohen.

Game Information

Radio: None.

PA Announcer: Unavailable. **Official Scorer:** Unavailable.

Stadium Name (year opened): J.P. Riddle Stadium (1987). **Location:** From Route 301 (business 95), west on Owen Drive, left on Legion Road. **Standard Game Times:** 7:05 p.m.; Sun. (April-May) 2:05, (June-August) 5:05.

Visiting Club Hotel: Econo Lodge, 1952 Cedar Creek Road, Fayetteville, NC 28306. Telephone: (910) 433-2100.

Capital City
BOMBERS

Office Address: 301 South Assembly St., Columbia, SC 29201. **Mailing Address:** P.O. Box 7845, Columbia, SC 29202. **Telephone:** (803) 256-4110. **FAX:** (803) 256-4338. **E-Mail Address:** office@ccbombers.com. **Website:** www.ccbombers.com.

Affiliation (first year): New York Mets (1983). **Years in League:** 1960-61, 1983-.

Ownership, Management

Operated by: United Sports Ventures, Inc.

Principal Owner/President: Eric Margenau. **Vice President:** Bill Shanahan.

General Manager: Tim Swain. **Director, Sales:** Shirley Broughton. **Director, Marketing and Promotions:** Nancy Behenna. **Director, Stadium Operations:** Bob Hook. **Director, Media Relations:** Mark Bryant. **Account Executives:** Malcolm Dennis, Brian Spencer. **Director, Group Sales:** Eddie Dowling.

Field Staff

Manager: Doug Davis. **Coach:** Juan Lopez. **Pitching Coach:** Buzz Capra. **Trainer:** Bill Wagner.

Game Information

Radio Announcer: Mark Bryant. **No. of Games Broadcast:** Home-71, Away-71. **Flagship Station:** WISW 1320-AM.

PA Announcer: Unavailable. **Official Scorer:** Julian Gibbons.

Stadium Name (year opened): Capital City Stadium (1991). **Location:** I-26 East to Columbia, Elmwood Avenue to Assembly Street, right on Assembly for four miles; I-77 South to Columbia, exit at State Road 277 (Bull Street), right on Elmwood, left on Assembly. **Standard Game Times:** 7:05 p.m., Sun. 6:05.

Visiting Club Hotel: Travelodge, 2210 Bush River Road, Columbia, SC 29210. Telephone: (803) 798-9665.

Charleston, S.C.
RIVERDOGS

Office Address: 360 Fishburne St., Charleston, SC 29403. Mailing Address: P.O. Box 20849, Charleston, SC 29413. Telephone: (803) 723-7241. FAX: (803) 723-2641.

Affiliation (first year): Tampa Bay Devil Rays (1997). Years in League: 1973-78, 1980-.

Ownership, Management

Operated by: South Carolina Baseball Club, LP.

Principal Owner: Marv Goldklang. President: Mike Veeck.

Vice President/General Manager: Mark Schuster. Director, Corporate Sales: Marc Coplea. Director, Operations: Stan Hughes. Vice President, Marketing: Carol Killough. Senior Account Representative: Scott Hannion. Director, Public Relations: Rob Egan. Director, Community Relations: Melissa McCants. Director, Ticket Sales: David Sacchetti. Director, Special Projects: Meridith Anzulis. Group Sales Representatives: Kelly Davis, Michael Monahan, Wendy Nilsen, Nancy Bishop. Director, Stadium Operations: Albert Washington. Clubhouse Manager: Mary Jane McInnes.

Field Staff

Manager: Greg Mahlberg. Coach: Julio Garcia. Pitching Coach: Bryan Kelly. Trainer: Mike Klein.

Game Information

Radio Announcer: Rob Egan. No. of Games Broadcast: Home-70, Away-71. Flagship Station: WTMZ 910-AM.

PA Announcer: Ryan Walker. Official Scorer: Tony Ciuffo.

Stadium Name (year opened): Joseph P. Riley Jr. Ballpark (1997). Location: From U.S. 17, take Lockwood Drive North, right on Fishburne Street. Standard Game Times: 7:05 p.m.; Sun. (April-May) 2:05, (June-August) 5:05.

Visiting Club Hotel: Howard Johnson, 250 Spring St., Charleston, SC 29403. Telephone: (803) 722-4000.

Charleston, W.Va.
ALLEY CATS

Office Address: 3403 MacCorkle Ave. SE, Charleston, WV 25304. Mailing Address: P.O. Box 4669, Charleston, WV 25304. Telephone: (304) 344-2287. FAX: (304) 344-0083.

Affiliation (first year): Cincinnati Reds (1990). Years in League: 1987-.

Ownership, Management

Operated by: Wheelers Baseball, LP.

Managing Partner: Andy Paterno.

General Manager: Tim Bordner. Director, Media Relations/Broadcasting: Dan Loney. Assistant, Public Relations: Stephanie Renica. Director, Sales: Jay Brown. Director, Promotions: Shannon Sharp. Director, Group Sales: Joe Adkinson. Director, Concessions: Pat Twohig. Director, Stadium Operations: Mike Spencer. Assistant Director, Operations: Jordan Blizzard. Office Manager: Lisa Spoor. Head Groundskeeper: Bob Hartman.

Field Staff

Manager: Barry Lyons. Coach: Amador Arias. Pitching Coach: Andre Rabouin. Trainer: Dan Siegel.

Game Information

Radio Announcer: Dan Loney. No. of Games Broadcast: Home-71, Away-71. Flagship Station: Unavailable.

PA Announcer: Unavailable. Official Scorer: Kevin Pratt.

Stadium Name (year opened): Watt Powell Park (1949). Location: I-77 South/I-64 East to 35th Street Bridge exit. I-77 North/I-64 West to exit 95 (MacCorkle Avenue) to Route 61 North. Standard Game Times: 7:15 p.m.; Sun. 2:15.

Visiting Club Hotel: Travelodge of Dunbar, 1007 Dunbar Ave., Dunbar, WV 25064. Telephone: (304) 768-1000.

Columbus
REDSTIXX

Office Address: 100 Fourth St., Columbus, GA 31901. **Mailing Address:** P.O. Box 1886, Columbus, GA 31902. **Telephone:** (706) 571-8866. **FAX:** (706) 571-9107. **E-Mail Address:** redstixx@mindspring.com. **Website:** www.redstixx.com.

Affiliation (first year): Cleveland Indians (1991). **Years in League:** 1991-.

Ownership, Management

Operated by: Columbus RedStixx and Professional Baseball, Inc.
Principal Owner/President: Charles Morrow.
General Manager: Randy Schmidt. **Assistant General Manager:** Mark Littleton. **Director, Business Operations:** Jim White. **Director, Public/Community Relations:** Melea Hames. **Director, Promotions/Special Projects:** Jay Scarsi. **Account Executive:** Dave Turner. **Office Manager:** Rosemary Johnson. **Head Groundskeeper:** Brock Phipps.

Field Staff

Manager: Eric Wedge. **Coach:** Eric Fox. **Pitching Coach:** Ken Rowe. **Trainer:** Rick Jameyson.

Game Information

Radio: None.
PA Announcer: Steve Thiele. **Official Scorer:** Kathy Gierer.
Stadium Name (year opened): Golden Park (1951). **Location:** I-185 South to exit 1 (Victory Drive), west to 4th Street (Veterans Parkway). In South Commons Complex on left. **Standard Game Times:** 7:15 p.m.; Sun. 2:15.
Visiting Club Hotel: Holiday Inn-Airport North, 2800 Manchester Expressway, Columbus, GA 31904. Telephone: (706) 324-0231.

Delmarva
SHOREBIRDS

Office Address: 6400 Hobbs Rd., Salisbury, MD 21804. **Mailing Address:** P.O. Box 1557, Salisbury, MD 21802. **Telephone:** (410) 219-3112. **FAX:** (410) 219-9164.

Affiliation (first year): Baltimore Orioles (1997). **Years in League:** 1996-.

Ownership, Management

Operated by: Maryland Baseball, LP.
Principal Owners: John Daskalakis, Peter Kirk, Frank Perdue, Hugh Schindel, Pete Simmons.
Chairman: Peter Kirk. **President:** Pete Simmons.
General Manager: Jim Terrill. **Director, Group Sales:** Martin Ward. **Director, Client Services:** Kathy Clemmer. **Director, Marketing:** Chad Prior. **Director, Ticketing:** Renee Harris. **Director, Promotions:** Kevin Kulp. **Director, Media/Public Relations:** Mike James. **Director, Community Relations:** Ralph Murray. **Director, Stadium Operations:** Charlie Shahan. **Director, Clubhouse Operations:** Jerry Bass. **Assistant Director, Ticketing:** Jeff Tierney. **Account/Group Sales Representative:** Chris Ouellet. **Head Groundskeeper:** Ed Attala. **Office Manager:** Joyce Young. **Manager, Accounting:** Gail Potts. **Assistant, Marketing:** Mary Sparacino.

Field Staff

Manager: Dave Machemer. **Coach:** Bobby Rodriguez. **Pitching Coach:** Dave Schmidt. **Trainer:** Mike Myers.

Game Information

Radio Announcer: Bob Socci. **No. of Games Broadcast:** Home-71, Away-71. **Flagship Station:** WICO 1320-AM.
PA Announcer: Unavailable. **Official Scorers:** Barry Grimm, Doug Rupple.
Stadium Name (year opened): Arthur W. Perdue Stadium (1996). **Location:** From U.S. 50 East, right on Hobbs Road; From U.S. 50 West, left on Hobbs Road. **Standard Game Times:** 7:05 p.m., Sun. 2:05.
Visiting Club Hotel: Howard Johnson, 2625 North Salisbury Blvd., Salisbury, MD 21801. Telephone: (410) 742-7194.

Greensboro
BATS

Office Address: 510 Yanceyville St., Greensboro, NC 27405. **Telephone:** (336) 333-2287. **FAX:** (336) 273-7350. **Website:** www.greensborobats.com.

Affiliation (first year): New York Yankees (1990). **Years in League:** 1979-.

Ownership, Management

Operated by: Carolina Diamond Baseball Club, LP.

Principal Owners: William Collins Jr., William Collins III, John Horshok, Bill Lee, Tim Cullen, Harry Rhodes, George Nethercutt.

Chairman: William Collins III. **President:** William Collins Jr. **Chief Operating Officer:** John Horshok. **Chief Financial Officer:** T.J. Egan.

General Manager: John Frey. **Vice President, Sales:** David Mulholland. **Director, Stadium Operations/Head Groundskeeper:** Mel Lanford. **Director, Public Relations:** Chris Bates. **Director, Promotions:** Tim Clever. **Director, Group Sales:** Shelton Grant. **Directors, Merchandising:** Alan Ashkinazy, Will Dvoranchik. **Director, Business Operations:** Ellen Selby. **Director, Operations:** Jennifer Leung.

Field Staff

Manager: Tom Nieto. **Coach:** Jason Garcia. **Pitching Coach:** Tom Filer. **Trainer:** Chris DeLucia.

Game Information

Radio: Unavailable.

PA Announcer: Jim Scott. **Official Scorer:** Unavailable.

Stadium Name (year opened): War Memorial Stadium (1926). **Location:** I-40/I-85 to Highway 29, north to Lee Street, west to Bennett Avenue, right on Bennett. **Standard Game Times:** 7:15 p.m., Sun. 2:15.

Visiting Club Hotel: Travelodge, 2112 West Meadowview Rd., Greensboro, NC 27403. Telephone: (336) 292-2020.

Hagerstown
SUNS

Office Address: 274 East Memorial Blvd., Hagerstown, MD 21740. **Mailing Address:** P.O. Box 230, Hagerstown, MD 21741. **Telephone:** (301) 791-6266. **FAX:** (301) 791-6066. **E-Mail Address:** hagsuns@intrepid.net. **Website:** www.hagerstownsuns.com.

Affiliation (first year): Toronto Blue Jays (1993). **Years in League:** 1993-.

Ownership, Management

Operated by: Norwin Corporation.

Principal Owner/President: Winston Blenckstone.

General Manager: David Blenckstone. **Director, Business Operations:** Carol Gehr. **Director, Media Relations:** Michael Heckman. **Director, Public Relations:** Kimberly Bohle. **Director, Ticket Sales:** Les Seville. **Director, Food Services:** Morris Anderson. **Clubhouse Manager:** Mike White.

Field Staff

Manager: Marty Pevey. **Coach:** Paul Elliott. **Pitching Coach:** Hector Berrios. **Trainer:** Unavailable.

Game Information

Radio Announcer: Karl Schalk. **No. of Games Broadcast:** Home-71, Away-71. **Flagship Station:** WHAG 1410-AM.

PA Announcer: Rich Daniels. **Official Scorer:** Jan Marcus.

Stadium Name (year opened): Municipal Stadium (1931). **Location:** Exit 32B (U.S. 40 West) on I-70 West, left at Eastern Blvd.; Exit 6A (U.S. 40 East) on I-81 South, right at Cleveland Ave. **Standard Game Times:** 7:05 p.m.; Mon. 6:05; Sun. (April-June 15) 2:05, (June 15-August) 5:05.

Visiting Club Hotel: Best Western Venice Inn, 431 Dual Highway, Hagerstown, MD 21740. Telephone: (301) 733-0830.

Hickory
CRAWDADS

Office Address: 2500 Clement Blvd. NW, Hickory, NC 28601. **Mailing Address:** P.O. Box 1268, Hickory, NC 28603. **Telephone:** (704) 322-3000. **FAX:** (704) 322-6137. **E-Mail Address:** crawdad@abts.net. **Website:** www.hickorycrawdads.com.

Affiliation (first year): Chicago White Sox (1993). **Years in League:** 1952, 1960, 1993-.

Ownership, Management
Operated by: Hickory Baseball, Inc.
Principal Owners: Don Beaver, Luther Beaver, Charles Young.
President: Don Beaver. **Vice President:** Tim Newman.
General Manager: David Haas. **Director, Stadium Operations:** Nick Reese. **Director, Media/Broadcasting:** Evan Malter. **Director, Ticket Sales:** Mike Congro. **Director, Group Sales/Ticket Services:** Adam Deschenes. **Director, Merchandising:** Melanie Zimmermann. **Director, Ticket Administration/Game Operations:** Heidi Komery. **Office Manager:** Jan Hutchison. **Account Representatives:** Shane Flater, Vance Spinks, David Heath.

Field Staff
Manager: Mark Haley. **Coach:** Gregg Ritchie. **Pitching Coach:** Sean Snedeker. **Trainer:** Joe Geck.

Game Information
Radio Announcer: Evan Malter. **No. of Games Broadcast:** Home-71, Away-71. **Flagship Station:** WMNC 92.1-FM.
PA Announcer: JuJu Phillips. **Official Scorer:** Gary Olinger.
Stadium Name (year opened): L.P. Frans Stadium (1993). **Location:** I-40 to Exit 123 (Lenoir North), 321 North to Clement Blvd., left for ¼ mile. **Standard Game Times:** 7 p.m.; Sun. (April-June) 2, (July-August) 6.
Visiting Club Hotel: Red Roof Inn, 1184 Lenoir Rhyne Blvd., Hickory, NC 28602. Telephone: (704) 323-1500.

Macon
BRAVES

Office Address: Central City Park, 7th Street, Macon, GA 31201. **Mailing Address:** P.O. Box 4525, Macon, GA 31208. **Telephone:** (912) 745-8943. **FAX:** (912) 743-5559.

Affiliation (first year): Atlanta Braves (1991). **Years in League:** 1962-63, 1980-87, 1991-.

Ownership, Management
Operated by: Atlanta National League Baseball Club, Inc.
Principal Owner: Ted Turner. **President:** Stan Kasten.
General Manager: Michael Dunn. **Director, Stadium Operations:** Terry Morgan. **Head Groundskeeper:** George Stephens. **Director, Sales/Marketing:** Jim Tessmer. **Director, Special Projects:** Mike Miskavech. **Office Manager:** Kimberly Lykins.

Field Staff
Manager: Brian Snitker. **Coach:** Glenn Hubbard. **Pitching Coach:** Mark Ross. **Trainer:** Mike Graus.

Game Information
Radio: None.
PA Announcer: Jimmy Jones. **Official Scorer:** Kevin Coulombe.
Stadium Name (year opened): Luther Williams Field (1929). **Location:** Exit 4 off I-16, across Otis Redding Bridge to Riverside Drive, follow signs to Central City Park. **Standard Game Times:** 7 p.m., Sun. 2.
Visiting Club Hotel: Comfort Inn, 2690 Riverside Dr., Macon, GA 31204. Telephone: (912) 746-8855.

Piedmont
BOLL WEEVILS

Office Address: 2888 Moose Rd., Kannapolis, NC 28083. Mailing Address: P.O. Box 64, Kannapolis, NC 28082. Telephone: (704) 932-3267. FAX: (704) 938-7040.

Affiliation (first year): Philadelphia Phillies (1995). Years in League: 1995-.

Ownership, Management
Operated by: Iredell Trading Co.
Principal Owners: Larry Hedrick, Sue Hedrick.
President: Larry Hedrick.
Vice President, General Manager: Todd Parnell. Director, Stadium/Baseball Operations: Eric Allman. Director, Business Development: Patrick Coakley. Director, Public Relations/Promotions: Randy Long. Director, Tickets/Publications: Melissa Dudek. Director, Group Sales/Merchandise: Jennifer Violand. Bookkeeper: Deb Hall. Director, Sales: Pete Laven. Head Groundskeeper: Eric Allman.

Field Staff
Manager: Ken Oberkfell. Pitching Coach: Ken Westray. Trainer: Paul Gabrielson.

Game Information
Radio Announcer: Matt Park. No. of Games Broadcast: Home-71, Away-71. Flagship Stations: WRNA 1140-AM, WRKB 1460-AM.
PA Announcer: Unavailable. Official Scorer: Unavailable.
Stadium Name (year opened): Fieldcrest Cannon Stadium (1995). Location: Exit 63 on I-85. Standard Game Times: 7:05 p.m.; Sun. 2:05.
Visiting Club Hotel: Sleep Inn, 321 Bendix Dr., Salisbury, NC 28146. Telephone: (704) 633-5961.

Savannah
SAND GNATS

Office Address: 1401 East Victory Dr., Savannah, GA 31404. Mailing Address: P.O. Box 3783, Savannah, GA 31414. Telephone: (912) 351-9150. FAX: (912) 352-9722. E-Mail Address: savgnats@aol.

Affiliation (first year): Texas Rangers (1998). Years in League: 1962, 1984-.

Ownership, Management
Operated by: Savannah Professional Baseball Club, Inc.
Principal Owners: Ken Silver, Ken Savin.
General Manager: Ric Sisler. Assistant General Manager: David Ellington. Director, Media/Public Relations: David Maloney. Director, Food Services: Nick Brown. Director, Group Sales: Chris Gulley. Office Manager: Deleah Garcia. Head Groundskeeper: Bob Neikirk.

Field Staff
Manager: Paul Carey. Pitching Coach: Dan Gakeler. Trainer: Gene Basham.

Game Information
Radio: None.
PA Announcer: Unavailable. Official Scorer: Unavailable.
Stadium Name (year opened): Grayson Stadium (1941). Location: I-16 to 37th Street exit, left on 37th, right on Abercorn Street, left on Victory Drive. Standard Game Times: 7:15 p.m; Sun. (April-June 15) 2, (June 16-August) 4.
Visiting Club Hotel: Econo Lodge Midtown, 7500 Abercorn St., Savannah, GA 31406. Telephone: (912) 352-1657.

NEW YORK-PENN LEAGUE

Short-Season Class A

Mailing Address: 1629 Oneida St., Utica, NY 13501. **Telephone:** (315) 733-8036. **FAX:** (315) 797-7403.

Years League Active: 1939-.

President: Bob Julian.

Vice President: Sam Nader (Oneonta).

Treasurer: Bill Gladstone (Pittsfield). **Corporate Secretary:** Tony Torre (New Jersey).

Directors: Mike Ferguson (Jamestown), Rob Fowler (Utica), Stan Getzler (Watertown), Bill Gladstone (Pittsfield), Barry Gordon (New Jersey), Alan Levin (Erie), Sam Nader (Oneonta), Ray Pecor (Vermont), Leo Pinckney (Auburn), Brad Rogers (Batavia), Clyde Smoll (Lowell), Greg Sorbara (St. Catharines), Paul Velte (Williamsport), Skip Weisman (Hudson Valley).

Bob Julian

Executive Assistant: Pamela Stagliano.

1998 Opening Date: June 16. **Closing Date:** Sept. 3.

Regular Season: 76 games (split-schedule).

Division Structure: McNamara—Hudson Valley, Lowell, New Jersey, Pittsfield, Vermont. **Pinckney**—Auburn, Oneonta, Utica, Watertown, Williamsport. **Stedler**—Batavia, Erie, Jamestown, St. Catharines.

Playoff Format: Three division winners and wild-card team meet in best-of-3 semifinals. Winners meet in best-of-3 series for league championship.

All-Star Game: None.

Roster Limit: 25 active. **Player Eligibility Rule:** No more than two players who are 23 or older. No more than three players on active list may have four or more years of prior service.

Brand of Baseball: Rawlings.

Statistician: Howe Sportsdata International, Boston Fish Pier, West Bldg. #1, Suite 302, Boston MA 02210.

Stadium Information

		Dimensions				
Club	Stadium	LF	CF	RF	Capacity	'97 Att.
Auburn	Falcon Park	330	400	330	2,800	51,260
Batavia	Dwyer	325	400	325	2,600	41,192
Erie	Jerry Uht Park	312	400	328	6,000	196,212
Hudson Valley	Dutchess	325	400	325	4,320	161,771
Jamestown	Diethrick Park	335	410	353	4,200	51,775
Lowell	Alumni Field	337	400	302	4,863	106,862
New Jersey	Skylands Park	330	392	330	4,336	171,244
Oneonta	Damaschke Field	352	406	350	4,200	53,447
Pittsfield	Wahconah Park	334	374	333	4,500	82,935
St. Catharines	Community Park	320	400	320	2,500	53,520
Utica	Donovan	324	400	324	4,000	52,185
Vermont	Centennial Field	330	405	323	4,000	91,694
Watertown	Duffy Fairgrounds	330	405	325	3,250	36,359
Williamsport	Bowman Field	345	405	350	4,200	58,795

Auburn
DOUBLEDAYS

Office Address: 108 North Division St., Auburn, NY 13021. **Telephone:** (315) 255-2489. **FAX:** (315) 255-2675. **E-Mail Address:** auburndd @relex.com.

Affiliation (first year): Houston Astros (1982). **Years in League:** 1958-80, 1982-.

Ownership, Management

Operated by: Auburn Community Baseball, Inc.

Chairman, Chief Executive Officer: Ann Bunker. **President:** Leo Pinckney.

General Manager: Paul Taglieri. **Assistant General Manager:** Paul Marriott. **Head Groundskeeper:** Rich Wild.

Field Staff

Manager: Lyle Yates. **Coach:** Brad Wellman. **Pitching Coach:** Darwin Pennye. **Trainer:** Shawn Moffitt.

Game Information

Radio Announcer: Unavailable. **No of Games Broadcast:** Home-38, Away-38. **Flagship Station:** WMBO 1340-AM

PA Announcer: Unavailable. **Official Scorer:** Jason Kuffs.

Stadium Name (year opened): Falcon Park (1995). **Location:** I-90 to exit 40, right on Route 34 for 8 miles to York Street, right on York, left on North Division Street. **Standard Game Times:** 7:05 p.m., Sun. 6.

Visiting Club Hotel: Auburn Super 8, 9 McMaster St., Auburn, NY 13021. Telephone: (315) 253-8886.

Batavia
MUCKDOGS

Office Address: Dwyer Stadium, 299 Bank St., Batavia, NY 14020. **Telephone:** (716) 343-5454. **FAX:** (716) 343-5620.

Affiliation (first year): Philadelphia Phillies (1988). **Years in League:** 1939-53, 1957-59, 1961-.

Ownership, Management

Operated by: Genesee County Professional Baseball, Inc.

President: Larry Roth.

General Manager: Jason Smorol. **Assistant General Manager:** Steve Lenox. **Administrative Assistant:** Linda Crook.

Field Staff

Manager: Unavailable. **Coach:** Alberto Fana. **Pitching Coach:** John Martin. **Trainer:** Unavailable.

Game Information

Radio Announcer: Steve Lenox. **No. of Games Broadcast:** Away-38. **Flagship Station:** WBSU 89.1-FM.

PA Announcer/Official Scorer: Wayne Fuller.

Stadium Name (year opened): Dwyer Stadium (1996). **Location:** I-90 to exit 48, left on Route 98 South, left on Richmond Ave., left on Bank Street. **Standard Game Times:** 7:05 p.m.

Visiting Club Hotel: Unavailable.

Erie
SEAWOLVES

Office Address: 110 East 10th St., Erie, PA 16501. **Mailing Address:** P.O. Box 1776, Erie, PA 16507. **Telephone:** (814) 456-1300. **FAX:** (814) 456-7520. **E-Mail Address:** seawolve@erie.net. **Website:** www.sea-wolves.com.

Affiliation (first year): Pittsburgh Pirates (1995). **Years in League:** 1944-45, 1954-63, 1967, 1981-93, 1995-.

Ownership, Management

Operated by: Seawolves Partners.

Principal Owner: Alan Levin.

General Manager: Andy Milovich. Assistant General Manager: Keith Hallal. Director, Operations: Ken Fogel. Director, Group Sales: Dave Smith. Assistant Director, Group Sales: Andrew Minister. Assistant Director, Ticket Operations: Kim Usselman. Accountant: Bernadette Mulvihill.

Field Staff

Manager: Tracy Woodson. Coach: Joe Lonnett. Pitching Coach: Chris Lein. Trainer: Unavailable.

Game Information

Radio Announcer: Unavailable. No. of Games Broadcast: Unavailable. Flagship Station: WFLP 1330-AM.

PA Announcer: Rick Shigo. Official Scorer: Les Caldwell.

Stadium Name (year opened): Jerry Uht Park (1995). Location: U.S. 79 North to East 12th Street exit, left on State Street, right on 10th Street. Standard Game Times: 7 p.m., Sun. 2.

Visiting Club Hotel: Avalon Hotel, 16 West 10th St., Erie, PA 16501. Telephone: (814) 459-2220.

Hudson Valley RENEGADES

Office Address: Dutchess Stadium, Route 9D, Wappingers Falls, NY 12590. Mailing Address: P.O. Box 661, Fishkill, NY 12524. Telephone: (914) 838-0094. FAX: (914) 838-0014. E-Mail Address: info@hvrenegades.com.

Affiliation (first year): Tampa Bay Devil Rays (1996). Years in League: 1994-.

Ownership, Management

Operated by: Keystone Professional Baseball Club, Inc.

Principal Owner/Chairman: Marv Goldklang.

President/General Manager: Skip Weisman. Assistant General Manager/Merchandising: Kathy Butsko. Assistant General Manager /Sales: Steve Gliner. Director, Operations: Elmer LeSuer. Director, Business Operations: Sharon Evans-Weisman. Coordinator, Customer Service: Dottie Paponetti. Head Groundskeeper: Tom Hubmaster. Director, Ticket Operations: Sally Berry. Administrative Assistants: Aaron Grubel, L.A. Ross, Melissa Tuck. Director, Food Services: Mike Beadles. Manager, Clubhouse: Mike Valovich.

Field Staff

Manager: Charlie Montoyo. Coach: Brad Rippelmeyer. Pitching Coach: Ray Searage. Trainer: Jeff Stay.

Game Information

Radio Announcers: Bill Rogan, Rick Schultz. No. of Games Broadcast: Home-38, Away-38. Flagship Station: WBNR 1260-AM, WLNA 1420-AM, WALL 1340-AM.

PA Announcer: Lisa Morris. Official Scorer: Bob Beretta.

Stadium Name (year opened): Dutchess Stadium (1994). Location: From east, I-84 West to exit 11 (Route 9D North), north 1 mile to stadium; From north, south and west, New York State Thruway to exit 17 in Newburgh, to I-84 East over Newburgh-Beacon Bridge exit 11 (Route 9D North), north 1 mile to stadium. Standard Game Times: 7:15 p.m., Sun. 5:15.

Visiting Club Hotel: Ramada Inn, 1055 Union Ave., Newburgh, NY 12550. Telephone: (914) 564-4500.

Jamestown JAMMERS

Office Address: 485 Falconer St., Jamestown, NY 14702. Mailing Address: P.O. Box 638, Jamestown, NY 14702. Telephone: (716) 664-0915. FAX: (716) 664-4175. E-Mail Address: jammergm@juno.com. Website: jamestownjammers.com.

Affiliation (first year): Detroit Tigers (1994). Years in League: 1939-57, 1961-73, 1977-.

Ownership, Management

Operated by: Rich Entertainment Group.

Chairman: Robert Rich Sr. **President:** Robert Rich Jr.

General Manager: Mike Ferguson. **Controller:** John Dougherty. **Director, Group Sales/Ticket Sales:** Jeffery Buser. **Director, Merchandising:** Mike Ferguson. **Director, Food Services:** Rich Ruggerio. **Clubhouse Operations:** Cal Chiffon. **Head Groundskeeper:** Tom Casler. **Office Manager:** Norma Marvell.

Field Staff

Manager: Tim Torricelli. **Pitching Coach:** Unavailable. **Trainer:** Matt Rankin.

Game Information

Radio Announcers: Greg Mayer, Bernie Walsh. **No. of Games Broadcast:** Home-38, Away-38. **Flagship Station:** WKSN 1340-AM.

PA Announcer: Unavailable. **Official Scorer:** Jim Riggs.

Stadium Name (year opened): Russell Diethrick Park (1941). **Location:** From I-90, south on Route 60, left on Buffalo Street, left on Falconer Street. **Standard Game Times:** 7:05 p.m.

Visiting Club Hotel: Holiday Inn, 150 West Fourth St., Jamestown, NY 14701. Telephone: (716) 664-3400.

Lowell
SPINNERS

Office Address: 450 Aiken St., Lowell, MA 01854. **Telephone:** (978) 459-2255. **FAX:** (978) 459-1674. **E-Mail Address:** generalinfo@lowellspinners.com. **Website:** www.lowellspinners.com.

Affiliation (first year): Boston Red Sox (1996). **Years in League:** 1996-.

Ownership, Management

Operated by: Diamond Action, Inc.

Principal Owner/President: Drew Weber.

General Manager: Shawn Smith. **Assistant General Manager**: Brian Lindsay. **Director, Media/Community Relations:** Dan Hoffman. **Corporate Controller:** Layla Hey. **Director, Ticket Operations:** Melissa Spury. **Assistant Director, Ticket Operations:** Tami Reynolds. **Director, Merchandising:** Joann Weber. **Manager, Merchandising/Group Sales Associate:** Darren Garrity. **Account Executive:** Brent Olyowski.

Field Staff

Manager: Dick Berardino. **Coach:** Unavailable. **Pitching Coach:** Dennis Rasmussen. **Trainer:** Stan Skolfield.

Game Information

Radio Announcer: Bob Ellis, Chaz Scoggins. **No. of Games Broadcast:** Home-22, Away-38. **Flagship Station:** WLLH 1400-AM.

PA Announcer: Unavailable. **Official Scorer:** Unavailable.

Stadium Name (year opened): Edward LeLacheur Park (1998). **Location:** From Routes 495 and 3, take exit 35C (Lowell Connector), follow connector to exit 5B, Thorndike Street onto Dutton Street, past city hall, left onto Father Morrissette Blvd., right on Aiken Street. **Standard Game Times:** 7 p.m., Sun. 5.

Visiting Club Hotel: DoubleTree Inn, 50 Warren St., Lowe. Telephone: (978) 452-1200.

New Jersey
CARDINALS

Office Address: 94 Championship Place, Suite 2, Augusta, NJ 07822. **Telephone:** (973) 579-7500. **FAX:** (973) 579-7502. **E-Mail Address:** office@njcards.com. **Website:** www.njcards.com.

Affiliation (first year): St. Louis Cardinals (1994). **Years in League:** 1994-.

Ownership, Management

Operated by: Minor League Heroes, LP.

Chairman: Barry Gordon. **President:** Marc Klee.

Vice President/General Manager: Tony Torre. **Director, Finance:** Warren Brown. **Head Groundskeeper:** Ralph Naiffe. **Director, Media Relations:** Herm Sorcher. **Office Manager:** Christine Sutton. **Director, Promotions:** Bob Commentucci. **Director, Group Sales:** John Martin. **Director, Sales:** Bart Springur. **Director, Merchandising:** Don Wilson.

Director, Ticketing: Brian Eggers.

Field Staff
Manager: Jose Oquendo. **Pitching Coach:** Joe Rigoli. **Trainer:** Unavailable.

Game Information
Radio Announcer: Phil Pepe. **No. of Games Broadcast:** Home-38. **Flagship Station:** WNNJ 1360-AM, WHCY 106.3-FM.

PA Announcer: Unavailable. **Official Scorer:** Ken Hand.

Stadium Name (year opened): Skylands Park (1994). **Location:** I-80 exit 34B (Rt. 15 North) to Rt. 565 East; I-84 to Rt. 6 (Matamoras) to Rt. 209 to Rt. 206, south to Rt. 565; Route 206 North to junction of 565 and 15, then 565 east. **Standard Game Times:** 7:15 p.m.; Sat. 5; Sun. 1.

Visiting Club Hotel: Best Western at Hunt's Landing, 900 Rts. 6 and 209, Matamoras, PA 18336. Telephone: (800) 308-2378.

Oneonta
YANKEES

Office Address: 95 River St., Oneonta, NY 13820. **Telephone:** (607) 432-6326. **FAX:** (607) 432-1965. **E-Mail:** naderas@telenet.net.

Affiliation (first year): New York Yankees (1967). **Years in League:** 1966-.

Ownership, Management
Operated by: Oneonta Athletic Corp., Inc.

President/General Manager: Sam Nader. **Assistant General Manager:** John Nader. **Controller:** Sidney Levine. **Head Groundskeeper:** Ted Christman. **Director, Media/Public Relations:** Suzanne Longo. **Director, Special Projects:** Mark Nader. **Director, Food Services:** Bob Zeh. **Director, Sales/Marketing:** Alice O'Conner.

Field Staff
Manager: Joe Arnold. **Coach:** Bobby DeJardin. **Pitching Coach:** Steve Webber. **Trainer:** Unavailable.

Game Information
Radio: None.

PA Announcer: Doug Decker. **Official Scorer:** David Bishop.

Stadium Name (year opened): Damaschke Field (1940). **Location:** Exit 15 off I-88. **Standard Game Times:** 7 p.m., Sun. 6.

Visiting Club Hotel: Town House Motor Inn, 318 Main St., Oneonta, NY 13820. Telephone: (607) 432-1313.

Pittsfield
METS

Office Address: 136 South St., Pittsfield, MA 01201. **Mailing Address:** P.O. Box 328, Pittsfield, MA 01201. **Telephone:** (413) 499-6387. **FAX:** (413) 443-7144. **E-Mail Address:** pittmets@berkshire.net

Affiliation (first year): New York Mets (1989). **Years in League:** 1989-.

Ownership, Management
Operated by: National Pastime Corporation.

Principal Owners: William Gladstone, Martin Barr, John Burton, Alfred Roberts, Stephen Siegel.

President: William Gladstone.

General Manager: Richard Murphy. **Assistant General Manager:** Richard Lenfest. **Director, Media/Public Relations:** Ethan Wilson. **Head Groundskeeper:** Jason Mancivalano.

Field Staff
Manager: Roger LaFrancois. **Coach:** Tony Tijerina. **Pitching Coach:** Doug SImons. **Trainer:** Mike Stoopes.

Game Information
Radio Announcer: George Miller. **No. of Games Broadcast:** Home-38, Away-38. **Flagship Station:** WBRK 101.7-FM.

PA Announcer: Unavailable. **Official Scorer:** Ethan Wilson.

Stadium Name (year opened): Wahconah Park (1950). **Location:** From east, Mass Pike exit 2 to Route 7 North to Pittsfield, right on North Street, left on Wahconah Street; From west, Route 295E to 41 North to 20E into

Pittsfield, left on Route 7, right on North Street, left on Wahconah. **Standard Game Times:** 7 p.m.; Sun. 6.

Visiting Club Hotels: Berkshire Crown Plaza, Berkshire Common, Pittsfield, MA 01201. Telephone: (413) 499-2000. Holiday Inn of the Berkshires, 40 Main St., North Adams, MA 01247. Telephone: (413) 663-6500.

St. Catharines
STOMPERS

Office Address: 174 St. Paul St., St. Catharines, Ontario L2R 3M2. **Telephone:** (905) 641-5297. **FAX:** (905) 641-3007. **E-Mail Address:** stompers@vaxxine.com. **Website:** http://vaxxine.com/stompers.

Affiliation (first year): Toronto Blue Jays (1986). **Years in League:** 1986-.

Ownership, Management
Operated by: St. Catharines Baseball Club, Ltd.
Principal Owners: Home Innings, Inc.; Leadoff Investments, Ltd.; Ernie Whitt.
President: Greg Sorbara.
General Manager: John Belford. **Director, Ticket Sales/Special Projects:** David Shaw. **Office Manager:** Eleanor Bowman.

Field Staff
Manager: Duane Larson. **Coach:** Hector Torres. **Pitching Coach:** Neil Allen. **Trainer:** Trevor Carter.

Game Information
Radio: Unavailable.
PA Announcer: Rod Mawhood. **Official Scorers:** Ann Rudge, Marcel Landry.
Stadium Name (year opened): Community Park (1987). **Location:** From east, Queen Elizabeth Expressway to Glendale exit, turn left then right on Merritt Street, right on Seymour Ave.; From west, Queen Elizabeth Expressway to 406 South, left at Glendale Ave. exit, left on Merritt Street, right on Seymour Ave. **Standard Game Times:** 7:05 p.m., Sun: 6:05.
Visiting Club Hotel: Ramada Inn, 327 Ontario St., St. Catharines, Ontario L2R 5L3. Telephone: (905) 688-2324.

Utica
BLUE SOX

Office Address: 1700 Sunset Ave., Utica, NY 13502. **Mailing Address:** P.O. Box 751, Utica, NY 13503. **Telephone:** (315) 738-0999. **FAX:** (315) 738-0992.

Affiliation (first year): Florida Marlins (1996). **Years in League:** 1977-.

Ownership, Management
Operated by: Utica Baseball Club, Ltd.
Principal Owner/President: Bob Fowler.
General Manager: Rob Fowler. **Director, Stadium Operations:** Jim Griffiths. **Head Groundskeeper:** Carmen Russo. **Clubhouse Operations:** Bob Perry.

Field Staff
Manager: Ken Joyce. **Coach:** Steve McFarland. **Pitching Coach:** Bill Sizemore. **Trainer:** John Gianini.

Game Information
Radio: None.
PA Announcer: Unavailable. **Official Scorer:** Unavailable.
Stadium Name (year opened): Donovan Stadium (1976). **Location:** New York State Thruway to exit 31 (Genesee Street), south to Burrstone Rd., right to stadium. **Standard Game Times:** 7 p.m.
Visiting Club Hotel: Horizon Hotel, Oneida County Airport, 5920 Airport Rd., Oriskany, NY 13424. Telephone: (315) 736-3377.

Vermont
EXPOS

Office Address: 1 Main Street, Box 4, Winooski, VT 05404. **Telephone:** (802) 655-4200. **FAX:** (802) 655-5660. **E-Mail Address:** vtexpos@together.net. **Website:** www.vermontexpos.com.

Affiliation (first year): Montreal Expos (1994). **Years in League:** 1994-.

Ownership, Management
Operated by: Vermont Expos, Inc.
Principal Owner/President: Ray Pecor.
General Manager: Kyle Bostwick. **Assistant General Manager:** C.J Knudsen. **Director, Business Operations:** Monica LaLime. **Controller:** Mia Ouellette. **Head Groundskeeper:** Lee Keller. **Director, Media Relations:** Paul Stanfield. **Director, Community Relations/Public Relations:** Marie Heikkinen. **Director, Sales/Marketing:** Chris Corley. **Director, Ticket Sales:** Mike Simpson. **Director, Food Services:** Steve Bernard. **Clubhouse Operations:** Phil Schelzo.

Field Staff
Manager: Unavailable. **Pitching Coach:** Unavailable. **Trainer:** Liam Frawley.

Game Information
Radio Announcer: George Commo. **No. of Games Broadcast:** Home-25, Away-25. **Flagship Station:** WXPS 96.7-FM.
PA Announcer: Rich Haskell. **Official Scorer:** Ev Smith.
Stadium Name (year opened): Centennial Field (1922). **Location:** I-89 to exit 14W, right on East Ave for one mile, right at light onto Colchester Avenue. **Standard Game Times:** 7:05 p.m., Sun. 2:05.
Visiting Club Hotel: Econo Lodge, 1076 Williston Rd., South Burlington, VT 05403. Telephone: (802) 863-1125.

Watertown
INDIANS

Watertown Indians

Office Address: Duffy Fairgrounds, 900 Coffeen St., Watertown, NY 13601. **Mailing Address:** P.O. Box 802, Watertown, NY 13601. **Telephone:** (315) 788-8747. **FAX:** (315) 788-8841.

Affiliation (first year): Cleveland Indians (1989). **Years in League:** 1983-.

Ownership, Management
Operated by: Sandlot Sports, Inc.
President: Stanley Getzler. **Vice President:** Joshua Getzler.
General Manager: Jeff Dumas. **Director, Stadium Operations:** Ed Montani. **Director, Food Services:** Tim Mosher. **Clubhouse Operations:** Mark Baker.

Field Staff
Manager: Ted Kubiak. **Coach:** Willis Aviles. **Pitching Coach:** Steve Lyons. **Trainer:** Nick Paparesta.

Game Information
Radio: None.
PA Announcer: Brian Hunsicker. **Official Scorer:** Unavailable.
Stadium Name (year opened): Alex T. Duffy Fairgrounds (1983). **Location:** I-81 to exit 46, east on Coffeen Street, left on Duffy Drive. **Standard Game Times:** 7 p.m., Sun. 6.
Visiting Club Hotel: Days Inn, 1142 Arsenal St., Watertown, NY 13601. Telephone: (315) 782-2700.

Williamsport
CUBS

Office Address: Bowman Field, 1700 West 4th St., Williamsport, PA 17701. **Mailing Address:** P.O. Box 3173, Williamsport, PA 17701. **Telephone:** (717) 326-3389. **FAX:** (717) 326-3494. **E-Mail Address:** wcubs@aol.com. **Website:** www.wcubs.fanlink.com.

Affiliation (first year): Chicago Cubs (1994). **Years in League:** 1923-37, 1968-72, 1994-.

Ownership, Management

Operated by: Geneva Cubs Baseball, Inc.

Principal Owner/President: Paul Velte.

General Manager: Doug Estes. **Director, Marketing/Public Relations:** Gabe Sinicropi. **Director, Stadium Operations:** Scott Stevenson. **Head Groundskeeper:** Matt Duncan.

Field Staff

Manager: Bob Ralston. **Coach:** Damon Farmar. **Pitching Coach:** Charlie Greene. **Trainer:** Unavailable.

Game Information

Radio: None.

PA Announcer: Tom Scott. **Official Scorer:** Ken Myers.

Stadium Name (year opened): Bowman Field (1926). **Location:** From south, Route 15 to Maynard Street, right on Maynard, left on 4th Street for one mile; From north, Route 15 to 4th Street, left on 4th. **Standard Game Times:** 7:05 p.m.

Visiting Club Hotel: Holiday Inn, 1840 East 3rd St., Williamsport, PA 17701. Telephone: (717) 326-1981.

NORTHWEST LEAGUE

Short-Season Class A

Office Address: 5900 North Granite Reef Rd., Suite 105, Scottsdale, AZ 85250. **Mailing Address:** P.O. Box 4941, Scottsdale, AZ 85261. **Telephone:** (602) 483-8224. **FAX:** (602) 443-3450. **E-Mail Address:** bobrichmond@worldnet.att.net. **Website:** www.fanlink.com.

Years League Active: 1901-1922, 1937-1942, 1946-.

President/Treasurer: Bob Richmond.

Vice President: Bill Pereira (Boise). **Corporate Secretary:** John Cunningham.

Directors: Bob Bavasi (Everett), Bob Beban (Eugene), Bobby Brett (Spokane), Jack Cain (Portland), Dave Connell (Yakima), Fred Herrmann (Southern Oregon), Bill Pereira (Boise), Jerry Walker (Salem-Keizer).

Administrative Assistant: Rob Richmond.

Bob Richmond

1998 Opening Date: June 16. **Closing Date:** Sept. 2.

Regular Season: 76 games.

Division Structure: North—Boise, Everett, Spokane, Yakima. **South**—Eugene, Portland, Salem-Keizer, Southern Oregon.

Playoff Format: Division winners play best-of-5 series for league championship.

All-Star Game: None.

Roster Limit: 25 active, 35 under control. **Player Eligibility Rule:** No more than four players who are 23 or older. No more than three players on active list may have four or more years of prior service.

Brand of Baseball: Rawlings.

Statistician: Howe Sportsdata International, Boston Fish Pier, West Bldg. #1, Suite 302, Boston MA 02210.

Stadium Information

Club	Stadium	Dimensions			Capacity	'97 Att.
		LF	CF	RF		
Boise	Memorial	335	400	335	4,500	154,819
Eugene	Civic	335	400	328	6,800	135,926
Everett	Everett Memorial	330	395	330	3,682	79,918
Portland	Civic	308	407	348	23,150	213,242
Salem-Keizer	Volcanoes	325	400	325	4,100	136,836
Southern Oregon	Miles Field	332	384	344	2,900	68,757
Spokane	Seafirst	335	398	335	7,100	185,304
Yakima	Yakima County	295	406	295	3,000	80,003

Boise
HAWKS

Office Address: 5600 Glenwood St., Boise, ID 83714. Telephone: (208) 322-5000. FAX: (208) 322-7432. E-Mail Address: carnefx@primenet.com.

Affiliation (first year): Anaheim Angels (1989). Years in League: 1975-76, 1978, 1985-.

Ownership, Management

Operated by: Diamond Sports, Inc.

Principal Owner: Bill Pereira.

Chairman: Peter Gray. President: Cord Pereira. Executive Vice President: Eric Trapp.

General Manager: John Cunningham. Controller: Lee Ryan. Head Groundskeeper: Joe Kelly. Director, Public Relations: Jack Carnefix. Director, Sales/Marketing: Dennis Burbank. Director, Ticket Sales: Denise Jones. Director, Promotions: Matt Gentil. Director, Group Sales: Jake Hines. Ticket Account Executive: Ryan Brach. Creative Director: Craig Sarton. Accountant: Tiffany Stevenson. Director, Advertising: Gerry Eickhoff.

Field Staff

Manager: Tom Kotchman. Coach: Charlie Romero. Pitching Coach: Howie Gershberg. Trainer: Todd Hine.

Game Information

Radio Announcer: Rob Simpson. No. of Games Broadcast: Home-38, Away-38. Flagship Stations: KTIK 1340-AM.

PA Announcer: Greg Culver. Official Scorer: Dan Ward.

Stadium Name (year opened): Memorial Stadium (1989). Location: I-84 to Cole Road, north to Western Idaho Fairgrounds. Standard Game Times: 7:05 p.m.; Sun. 6:05.

Visiting Club Hotel: Unavailable.

Eugene
EMERALDS

Office Address: 2077 Willamette St., Eugene, OR 97405. Mailing Address: P.O. Box 5566, Eugene, OR 97405. Telephone: (541) 342-5367. FAX: (541) 342-6089. E-Mail Address: ems@go-ems.com. Website: www.go-ems.com.

Affiliation (first year): Atlanta Braves (1995). Years in League: 1955-68, 1974-.

Ownership, Management

Operated by: Eugene Baseball, Inc.

Principal Owner: David Elmore.

President/General Manager: Bob Beban. Business Manager: Eileen Beban. Assistant General Managers: Todd Rahr, Jere Hanks. Director, Media Relations/Ticket Sales: Chris Metz. Director, Group Sales: Brian Rogers. Director, Promotions/Client Services: Jeff Benjamin. Facilities Director: David Puente. Grounds Superintendent: Tom Nielsen.

Field Staff

Manager: Jim Saul. Coach: Dan Norman. Pitching Coach: Jerry Nyman. Trainer: Justin Sharpe.

Game Information

Radio Announcer: Dave Hahn. No. of Games Broadcast: Home-38, Away-38. Flagship Station: KUGN 590-AM.

PA Announcer: Ray Martin. Official Scorer: Unavailable.

Stadium Name (year opened): Civic Stadium (1938). Location: From I-5, take Hwy. 126 to downtown, west to Pearl Street, south to 20th Ave. Standard Game Times: 7:05 p.m; Sun. 2:05, 6:05.

Visiting Club Hotel: Crossland Economy Studios, 520 Harlow Rd., Springfield, OR 97477. Telephone: (541) 741-3908.

Everett
AQUASOX

Office Address: 3802 Broadway, Everett, WA 98201. Mailing Address: P.O. Box 7893, Everett, WA 98201. Telephone: (425) 258-3673. FAX: (425) 258-3675. E-Mail Address: aquasox@aquasox.com. Website: www.aqua-sox.com.

Affiliation (first year): Seattle Mariners (1995). Years in League: 1984-.

Ownership, Management

Operated by: Farm Club Sports, Inc.

President: Bob Bavasi. Vice President: Margaret Bavasi.

Controller: Don Anderson. Director, Corporate Sales: Aimee Bavasi. Director, Client Services: Brian Sloan. Director, Media Relations /Operations: Robb Stanton. Director, Ticket Services: Kim Echols. Director, Ballpark Operations: Gary Farwell. Director, Broadcasting: Pat Dillon. Manager, Ticket Operations: Nick Griffith.

Field Staff

Manager: Terry Pollreisz. Coaches: Andy Bottin, Tommy Cruz. Pitching Coach: Gary Wheelock. Trainer: Spyder Webb.

Game Information

Radio Announcer: Pat Dillon. No. of Games Broadcast: Home-38, Away-38. Flagship Station: KSER 90.7/90.5 FM.

PA Announcer: Tom Lafferty. Official Scorer: John VanSandt.

Stadium Name (year opened): Everett Memorial Stadium (1984). Location: I-5, exit 192. Standard Game Times: 7:05 p.m.; Sat., Sun. 6:05.

Visiting Club Hotel: Holiday Inn Hotel, 101 128th St. SE, Everett, WA 98208. Telephone: (425) 337-2900.

Portland
ROCKIES

Office Address: 1844 SW Morrison, Portland, OR 97205. Mailing Address: P.O. Box 998, Portland, OR 97207. Telephone: (503) 223-2837. FAX: (503) 223-2948. E-Mail Address: rockies@telport.com. Website: www.portlandrockies.com.

Affiliation (first year): Colorado Rockies (1995). Years in League: 1973-77, 1995-.

Ownership, Management

Operated by: Portland Baseball, Inc.

Principal Owners: Jack Cain, Mary Cain. President: Jack Cain.

General Manager: Mark Helminiak. Director, Merchandise: Bob Cain. Director, Ticket Sales: Corey Kearsley. Office Manager: Katie Reeder. Administrative Assistant: Sarah Keaney. Clubhouse Operations: Travis McQuire. Account Executives: Bard Arnsmeier, Dick Johnson, Jeff Robbins, Berinda Post, Tom Shepherd, Bryan Beban, Hank Sadorus, Akinobu Yokoyama.

Field Staff

Manager: Jim Eppard. Coach: Al Bleser. Pitching Coach: Tom Edens. Trainer: Scott Gehret.

Game Information

Radio Announcers: Bryan Beban, Mike O'Brien. No. of Games Broadcast: Home-38, Away-38. Flagship Station: KKSN 910-AM.

PA Announcer: Dan Folwick. Official Scorers: Chuck Charnquist, John Hilsenteger.

Stadium Name (year opened): Civic Stadium (1926). Location: I-405 to West Burnside exit, SW 20th Street to stadium. Standard Game Times: 7:05 p.m.; Sun. 2:05.

Visiting Club Hotel: Ramada Plaza, 1441 NE Second Ave., Portland, OR 97232. Telephone: (503) 233-2401.

Salem-Keizer
VOLCANOES

Street Address: 6700 Field of Dreams Way NE, Keizer, OR 97307.
Mailing Address: P.O. Box 20936, Keizer, OR 97307. **Telephone:** (503) 390-2225. **FAX:** (503) 390-2227. **E-Mail Address:** probasebal@aol.com
Affiliation (first year): San Francisco Giants (1997). **Years in League:** 1997-.

Ownership, Management

Operated By: Sports Enterprises, Inc.
Principal Owners: Jerry Walker, Bill Tucker.
President/General Manager: Jerry Walker.
Manager, Corporate Sales/Director, Promotions: Lisa Walker. **Director, Business Operations:** Rick Nelson. **Director, Tickets/Group Sales:** Tony Brown. **Director, Sales/Media Relations:** Pat Lafferty. **Director, Stadium Operations/Community Relations:** Katrinka Rau. **Director, Merchandising:** Kimberly Spicer. **Director, Food Services:** Carol Unruh. **Facility Management:** Nate Holeman, Lois Holeman. **Head Groundskeeper:** Brian Radke.

Field Staff

Manager: Carlos Lezcano. **Coach:** Bert Hunter. **Pitching Coach:** Keith Comstock. **Trainer:** Eric Reisinger.

Game Information

Radio Announcer: Pat Lafferty. **No. of Games Broadcast:** Home-38, Away-38. **Flagship Station:** KYKN 1430-AM.
PA Announcer: Dave Jarvis. **Official Scorer:** Scott Bigham.
Stadium Name (year opened): Volcanoes Stadium (1997). **Location:** I-5 exit 260, west one block to Radiant Drive, north six blocks to stadium. **Standard Game Times:** 7:05 p.m.; Sun. 2:05, 6:05.
Visiting Club Hotel: Quality Inn, 3301 Market St. NE, Salem, OR 97301. Telephone: (503) 370-7888.

Southern Oregon
TIMBERJACKS

Office Address: 1801 South Pacific Highway, Medford, OR 97501.
Mailing Address: P.O. Box 1457, Medford, OR 97501. **Telephone:** (541) 770-5364. **FAX:** (541) 772-4466. **E-Mail Address:** athletic@mind.net.
Website: www.mind.net/tjacks.
Affiliation (first year): Oakland Athletics (1979). **Years in League:** 1967-71, 1979-.

Ownership, Management

Operated by: National Sports Organization, Inc.
Chairman/President: Fred Herrmann.
General Manager: Dan Kilgras. **Director, Stadium Operations:** Jamie Brown. **Director, Ticket Sales:** Jordell Hasha. **Head Groundskeeper:** Richard Steinmuller. **Account Executives:** Seth Distler, Dan Smith, Jamie Brown, John White. **Office Manager:** Carol Miner.

Field Staff

Manager: Greg Sparks. **Coach:** Jim Pransky. **Pitching Coach:** Gil Lopez. **Trainer:** Unavailable.

Game Information

Radio Announcer: Bob Hamilton. **No. of Games Broadcast:** Home-38, Away-38. **Flagship Station:** Unavailable.
PA Announcer: Unavailable. **Official Scorer:** B.G. Gould.
Stadium Name (year opened): Jackson and Perkins Garden at Miles Field (1951). **Location:** I-5 to exit 27, west on Barnett Road for ½ mile, left on South Pacific Highway for one mile. **Standard Game Times:** 7:05 p.m.; Sun. 6:05.
Visiting Club Hotel: Economy Inn, 954 Alba Dr., Medford, OR 97504. Telephone: (541) 773-1579.

Spokane
INDIANS

Office Address: 602 North Havana, Spokane, WA 99202. Mailing Address: P.O. Box 4758, Spokane, WA 99202. Telephone: (509) 535-2922. FAX: (509) 534-5368.

Affiliation (first year): Kansas City Royals (1995). Years in League: 1972, 1983-.

Ownership, Management
Operated by: Longball, Inc.
Principal Owners: Bobby Brett, George Brett, Ken Brett, J.B. Brett.
President: Andrew Billig. Chairman: Bobby Brett.
General Manager: Paul Barbeau. Executive Director/Sponsorships: Otto Klein. Controller: Carol Dell. Director, Stadium Operations: Chad Smith. Head Groundskeeper: Anthony Lee. Director, Public Relations: Rob Leslie. Director, Corporate Ticket Sales: Eric Marglous. Account Executives: Brett Binkley, Matt Clay. Executive Administrative Assistant: Barbara Klante. Director, Promotions: Kyle McFarlane. Director, Group Sales: Brent Miles. Manager, Ticket Office: Grant Riddle. Coordinator, Group Sales: Paul Zilm. Director, Special Projects: Dave Pier.

Field Staff
Manager: Jeff Garber. Coach: Steve Balboni. Pitching Coach: Rick Mahler. Trainer: Unavailable.

Game Information
Radio Announcer: Craig West. No. of Games Broadcast: Home-38, Away-38. Flagship Station: KTRW 970-AM.
PA Announcer: Mike Lindskog. Official Scorer: Dave Edwards.
Stadium Name (year opened): Seafirst Stadium at Interstate Fairgrounds (1958). Location: I-90 to Havana exit, follow directions to Interstate Fairgrounds.
Standard Game Times: 7:05 p.m.; Sun. 6:05.
Visiting Club Hotel: Cavanaugh's 4th Avenue, 110 East 4th Ave., Spokane, WA 99202. Telephone: (509) 838-6101.

Yakima
BEARS

Office Address: 810 West Nob Hill Blvd., Yakima, WA 98902. Mailing Address: P.O. Box 483, Yakima, WA 98907. Telephone: (509) 457-5151. FAX: (509) 457-9909.

Affiliation (first year): Los Angeles Dodgers (1990). Years in League: 1955-66, 1990-.

Ownership, Management
Operated by: Tradition Sports, Inc.
Principal Owners: Dave Connell, Ed Kershaw, Nick Temple, Mike Smith, Steve Zwight.
President: Dave Connell.
General Manager: Bob Romero. Assistant General Manager: Benjy Mogensen. Director, Ticket Sales: Joel Lehocky. Clubhouse Operations: Craig Hyatt. Office Manager: DeAnne Munson. Head Groundskeeper: Kory Leadon.

Field Staff
Manager: Tony Harris. Coach: Mitch Webster. Pitching Coach: Mark Brewer. Trainer: Beau Clay.

Game Information
Radio Announcer: Craig Dunkin. No. of Games Broadcast: Home-38, Away-38. Flagship Station: KMWX 1460-AM.
PA Announcer: Todd Lyons. Official Scorer: Gene Evans.
Stadium Name (year opened): Yakima County Stadium (1993). Location: I-82 to exit 34 (Nob Hill Blvd.), west to Fair Avenue, right on Fair, right on Pacific. Standard Game Times: 7:05 p.m.; Sun. 6:05.
Visiting Club Hotel: Days Inn, 2408 Rudkin Rd., Union Gap, WA 98903. Telephone: (509) 248-9700.

APPALACHIANLEAGUE

Rookie Advanced Classification

Mailing Address: 283 Deerchase Circle, Statesville, NC 28625. **Telephone:** (704) 873-5300. **FAX:** (704) 873-4333. **E-Mail Address:** appylg@i-america.net.

Years League Active: 1921-25, 1937-55, 1957-.

President/Treasurer: Lee Landers. **Corporate Secretary:** Dan Moushon (Burlington).

Directors: Tom Foley (Princeton), Mike Jorgensen (Johnson City), Deric Ladnier (Danville), Reid Nichols (Pulaski), Steve Noworyta (Bristol), Jim Rantz (Elizabethton), Mark Shapiro (Burlington), Syd Thrift (Bluefield), Del Unser (Martinsville), Jim Duquette (Kingsport).

Lee Landers

Administrative Assistant: Bobbi Landers.

1998 Opening Date: June 17. **Closing Date:** Aug. 26.

Regular Season: 68 games.

Division Structure: East—Bluefield, Burlington, Danville, Martinsville, Princeton. **West**—Bristol, Elizabethton, Johnson City, Kingsport, Pulaski.

Playoff Format: Division winners meet in best-of-3 series for league championship.

All-Star Game: None.

Roster Limit: 30 active. **Player Eligibility Rule:** No more than 12 players who are 21 or older; no more than two of the 12 may be 23 or older.

Brand of Baseball: Rawlings.

Statistician: Howe Sportsdata International, Boston Fish Pier, West Bldg. #1, Suite 302, Boston, MA 02210.

Stadium Information

Club	Stadium	Dimensions			Capacity	'97 Att.
		LF	CF	RF		
Bluefield	Bowen Field	335	365	335	2,500	43,300
Bristol	DeVault Memorial	325	400	310	2,500	25,105
Burlington	Burlington Athletic	335	410	335	3,000	46,915
Danville	Dan Daniel Memorial	330	400	330	2,588	75,745
Elizabethton	Joe O'Brien Field	335	414	326	1,500	17,397
Johnson City	Howard Johnson	320	410	320	2,500	43,300
Kingsport	Hunter Wright	330	410	330	2,500	48,396
Martinsville	Hooker Field	330	402	330	3,200	39,947
Princeton	Hunnicutt Field	330	396	330	1,537	36,481
Pulaski	Calfee Park	335	405	310	2,000	23,898

Bluefield
ORIOLES

Mailing Address: P.O. Box 356, Bluefield, WV 24701. **Telephone:** (540) 326-1326. **FAX:** (540) 326-1318.

Affiliation (first year): Baltimore Orioles (1957). **Years in League:** 1946-55, 1957-.

Ownership, Management
Operated by: Bluefield Baseball Club, Inc.
Director: Syd Thrift (Baltimore Orioles).
President/General Manager: George McGonagle. **Assistant General Manager/Director, Group Sales:** Kim Long. **Controller:** Charles Peters. **Directors, Special Projects:** John Duffy, Tuillio Ramella.

Field Staff
Manager: Andy Etchebarren. **Coach:** Jerry Greeley. **Pitching Coach:** Charlie Puleo. **Trainer:** P.J. Mainville.

Game Information
Radio: Unavailable.
PA Announcer: Unavailable. **Official Scorer:** Kristi Maupin.
Stadium Name (year opened): Bowen Field (1939). **Location:** I-77 Bluefield exit, Route 290 to Route 460 West, right onto Leatherwood Lane, left at first light, past Chevron station and turn right, stadium ¼ mile on left. **Standard Game Times:** 7 p.m.
Visiting Club Hotel: Ramada Inn-East River, 3175 East Cumberland Rd., Bluefield, WV 24701. Telephone: (304) 325-5421.

Bristol
SOX

Office Address: 1501 Euclid Ave., Bristol, VA 24201. **Mailing Address:** P.O. Box 1434, Bristol, VA 24203. **Telephone:** (540) 645-7275. **FAX:** (540) 645-7377.

Affiliation (first year): Chicago White Sox (1995). **Years in League:** 1921-25, 1940-55, 1969-.

Ownership, Management
Operated by: Bristol Baseball, Inc.
Director: Steve Noworyta (Chicago White Sox).
President: Boyce Cox. **General Manager:** Robert Childress.

Field Staff
Manager: Nick Capra. **Coach:** Darryl Boston. **Pitching Coach:** J.R. Perdew. **Trainer:** Unavailable.

Game Information
Radio: None.
PA Announcer: Boyce Cox. **Official Scorer:** Allen Shepherd.
Stadium Name (year opened): DeVault Memorial Stadium (1969). **Location:** I-81 to exit 3 onto Commonwealth Ave., right on Euclid Ave. for ½ mile. **Standard Game Times:** 7 p.m.
Visiting Club Hotel: Ramada Inn, 2121 Euclid Ave., Bristol, VA 24201. Telephone: (540) 669-7171.

Burlington
INDIANS

Office Address: 1450 Graham St., Burlington, NC 27217. **Mailing Address:** P.O. Box 1143, Burlington, NC 27216. **Telephone:** (336) 222-0223. **FAX:** (336) 226-2498. **E-Mail Address:** bindians@aol.com.

Affiliation (first year): Cleveland Indians (1986). **Years in League:** 1986-.

Ownership, Management
Operated by: Burlington Baseball Club, Inc.
Director: Mark Shapiro (Cleveland Indians).
Principal Owner/President: Miles Wolff. **Vice President:** Dan Moushon.

General Manager: Mike Edwards. **Assistant General Manager:** Bryan Garruto. **Director, Group Sales:** Lisa LaRosa.

Field Staff

Manager: Joe Mikulik. **Coach:** Jack Mull. **Pitching Coach:** Carl Willis. **Trainer:** Dave Lassiter.

Game Information

Radio Announcer: Mike Blucher. **No. of Games Broadcast:** Home-36, Away-32. **Flagship Station:** WBAG 1150-AM.

PA Announcer: Unavailable. **Official Scorer:** Unavailable.

Stadium Name (year opened): Burlington Athletic Stadium (1960). **Location:** I-40/85 to exit 145, north on Route 100 (Maple Avenue) for 1½ miles, right on Mebane Street for 1½ miles, right on Beaumont, left on Graham. **Standard Game Times:** 7 p.m.

Visiting Club Hotel: Holiday Inn, 2444 Maple Ave., Burlington, NC 27215. Telephone: (336) 229-5203.

Danville
BRAVES

Office Address: Dan Daniel Memorial Park, 302 River Park Dr., Danville, VA 24540. **Mailing Address:** P.O. Box 3637, Danville, VA 24543. **Telephone:** (804) 791-3346. **FAX:** (804) 791-3347. **E-Mail Address:** dbraves@gamewood.net. **Website:** www.danvillebraves.com.

Affiliation (first year): Atlanta Braves (1993). **Years in League:** 1993-.

Ownership, Management

Operated by: Danville Braves, Inc.

Director: Deric Ladnier (Atlanta Braves).

President/General Manager: Tim Cahill. **Assistant General Manager:** Brent Bartemeyer. **Vice President, Business Operations:** Mike Drahush. **Director, Marketing:** Cole Spencer. **Director, Group Sales:** Dennis Mertha. **Office Manager:** Beth Hall.

Field Staff

Manager: Franklin Stubbs. **Coach:** Ralph Henriquez. **Pitching Coach:** Bill Slack. **Trainer:** Chris Shaff.

Game Information

Radio: None.

PA Announcer: Unavailable. **Official Scorers:** Danny Miller, Stan Mitchell.

Stadium Name (first year): Dan Daniel Memorial Park (1993). **Location:** U.S. 58 to Rivermont Road, follow signs to park; U.S. 29 bypass to Dan Daniel Park exit (U.S. 58 East), to Rivermont Road, follow signs. **Standard Game Times:** 7 p.m.

Visiting Club Hotel: Innkeeper-West, 3020 Riverside Dr., Danville, VA 24541. Telephone: (804) 799-1202.

Elizabethton
TWINS

Office Address: 136 South Sycamore St., Elizabethton, TN 37643. **Telephone:** (423) 543-4395. **FAX:** (423) 542-1510.

Affiliation (first year): Minnesota Twins (1974). **Years in League:** 1937-42, 1945-51, 1974-.

Ownership, Management

Operated by: City of Elizabethton.

Director: Jim Rantz (Minnesota Twins).

President: Harold Mains.

General Manager: Ray Smith. **Assistant General Manager:** Lisa Story. **Director, Business Operations:** Harold Ray. **Director, Stadium Operations:** Willie Church. **Head Groundskeeper:** Jim Barker. **Director, Media/Public Relations:** Lou Getman. **Director, Sales/Marketing:** Shelley Cornett. **Director, Community Relations:** David Ornduff. **Director, Promotions:** Jim Barker. **Director, Ticket Sales:** Jane Crow. **Director, Food Services:** Jane Hardin. **Clubhouse Operations:** David McQueen. **Office Manager:** Paula Bishop.

Field Staff

Manager: Jon Mathews. **Coach:** Ray Smith. **Pitching Coach:** Jim Shellenback. **Trainer:** Tony Leo.

Game Information

Radio Announcers: Frank Santore, Doug Jennett. **No. of Games Broadcast:** Home-34, Away-16. **Flagship Station:** WBEJ 1240-AM.

PA Announcer: Tom Banks. **Official Scorer:** Joe Dodd.

Stadium Name (year opened): Joe O'Brien Field (1974). **Location:** I-81 to I-181, exit at Highway 321/67, left at Holly Lane. **Standard Game Times:** 7 p.m.

Visiting Club Hotel: Days Inn, 505 West Elk Ave., Elizabethton, TN 37643. Telephone: (423) 543-3344.

Johnson City CARDINALS

Office Address: 401 Cranberry St., Johnson City, TN 37601. **Mailing Address:** P.O. Box 568, Johnson City, TN 37605. **Telephone:** (423) 461-4850. **FAX:** (423) 461-4864.

Affiliation (first year): St. Louis Cardinals (1975). **Years in League:** 1921-24, 1937-55, 1957-61, 1964-.

Ownership, Management

Operated By: Johnson City Cardinals Baseball Club.

Director: Mike Jorgensen (St. Louis Cardinals).

Chairman: Jack Chinouth. **President:** Lonnie Lowe.

General Manager: Rebecca Hilbert. **Assistant General Manager/Controller:** Mary Ann Marsh. **Clubhouse Operations:** Carl Black. **Head Groundskeeper:** Eddie Teague.

Field Staff

Manager: Steve Turco. **Coaches:** Jose Oquendo, Dave Ricketts. **Pitching Coach:** Mike Snyder. **Trainer:** Brad Bluestone.

Game Information

Radio Announcer: Marky Billson. **No. of Games Broadcast:** Home-34. **Flagship Station:** WKPT 1590-AM.

PA Announcer/Official Scorer: Joe Dodd.

Stadium Name (year opened): Howard Johnson Field (1956). **Location:** I-181 to exit 32, left on Commonwealth, left on State of Franklin, left on Legion Street. **Standard Game Times:** 7 p.m., Sun. 3.

Visiting Club Hotel: Ramada Inn, 2406 North Roan St., Johnson City, TN 37601. Telephone: (423) 282-2161.

Kingsport METS

Office Address: 433 East Center St., Kingsport, TN 37662. **Mailing Address:** P.O. Box 1128, Kingsport, TN 37662. **Telephone:** (423) 378-3744. **FAX:** (423) 392-8538. **E-Mail Address:** info@kmets.com. **Website:** www.kmets.com.

Affiliation (first year): New York Mets (1980). **Years in League:** 1921-25, 1938-52, 1957, 1960-63, 1969-82, 1984-.

Ownership, Management

Operated by: S/H Baseball.

Director: Jim Duquette (New York Mets).

Principal Owners: Rick Spivey, Steve Harville.

President: Rick Spivey. **Vice President:** Steve Harville.

General Manager: Jim Arnold.

Field Staff

Manager: Unavailable. **Coach:** Lee May Jr. **Pitching Coach:** Bill Champion. **Trainer:** Patrick Huber.

Game Information

Radio Announcer: Scott Gray. **No. of Games Broadcast:** Home-34, Away-12. **Flagship Station:** WKPT 1400-AM.

PA Announcer: Don Spivey. **Official Scorer:** Eddie Durham.

Stadium Name (year opened): Hunter Wright Stadium (1995). **Location:** I-81 to I-181 North, exit 11E (Stone Drive), left on West Stone

Drive (U.S. 11W), right on Granby Road. **Standard Game Times:** 7 p.m.
Visiting Club Hotel: Comfort Inn, 100 Indian Center Court, Kingsport, TN 37660. Telephone: (423) 378-4418.

Martinsville
PHILLIES

Office Address: Hooker Field, Commonwealth Blvd. and Chatham Heights Road, Martinsville, VA 24112. **Mailing Address:** P.O. Box 3614, Martinsville, VA 24115. **Telephone:** (540) 666-2000. **FAX:** (540) 666-2139. **E-Mail Address:** mphillies@kimbanet.com.
Affiliation (first year): Philadelphia Phillies (1988). **Years in League:** 1988-.

Ownership, Management
Operated by: Martinsville Phillies Professional Baseball, Inc.
Director: Del Unser (Philadelphia Phillies).
General Manager: Carper Cole. **Assistant General Manager:** Rachel Byrd. **Head Groundskeeper:** Sam Pickeral.

Field Staff
Manager: Greg Legg. **Coach:** Unavailable. **Pitching Coach:** Carlos Arroyo. **Trainer:** Unavailable.

Game Information
Radio: None.
PA Announcer: Unavailable. **Official Scorer:** Unavailable.
Stadium Name (year opened): Hooker Field (1988). **Location:** U.S. 220 Business to Commonwealth Blvd., east for three miles; U.S. 58 to Chatham Heights Road, north two blocks. **Standard Game Times:** 7 p.m.
Visiting Club Hotel: Dutch Inn, 633 Virginia Ave., Collinsville, VA 24078. Telephone: (540) 647-3721.

Princeton
DEVIL RAYS

Office Address: Hunnicutt Field, Old Bluefield-Princeton Road, Princeton, WV 24740. **Mailing Address:** P.O. Box 5646, Princeton, WV 24740. **Telephone:** (304) 487-2000. **FAX:** (304) 487-8762.
Affiliation (first year): Tampa Bay Devil Rays (1997). **Years in League:** 1988-.

Ownership, Management
Operated by: Princeton Baseball Association, Inc.
Director: Tom Foley (Tampa Bay).
President: Dewey Russell.
General Manager: Jim Holland. **Account Representative:** Paul Lambert. **Director, Stadium Operations:** Mick Bayle. **Head Groundskeeper:** Frankie Bailey.

Field Staff
Manager: Dave Howard. **Coach:** Mike Tosar. **Pitching Coach:** Milt Hill. **Trainer:** Craig Payment.

Game Information
Radio: None.
PA Announcer: Jason Choate. **Official Scorer:** Dick Daisey.
Stadium Name (year opened): Hunnicutt Field (1988). **Location:** Exit 9 off I-77, U.S. 460 West to downtown exit, left on Stafford Drive, stadium located behind Mercer County Technical Education Center. **Standard Game Times:** 7 p.m.
Visiting Club Hotel: Days Inn, I-77 and Route 460, Princeton, WV 24740. Telephone: (304) 425-8100.

Pulaski
RANGERS

Office Address: 5th and Pierce SE, Pulaski, VA 24301. **Telephone:** (540) 994-8696. **FAX:** (540) 980-3055.

Affiliation (first year): Texas Rangers (1997). **Years in League:** 1946-50, 1952-55, 1957-58, 1969-77, 1982-92, 1997-.

Ownership, Management
Operated by: Pulaski Baseball.
Director: Reid Nichols (Texas Rangers).
President: Hi Nicely.
General Manager: Tom Compton. **Controller:** Wayne Carpenter. **Director, Stadium Operations:** Dave Hart. **Head Groundskeeper:** Don Newman. **Director, Ticket Sales:** Rick Mansell. **Director, Special Projects:** Dave Edmonds.

Field Staff
Manager: Unavailable. **Pitching Coach:** Aris Tirado. **Trainer:** Unavailable.

Game Information
Radio: None.
PA Announcer: Unavailable. **Official Scorer:** Unavailable.
Stadium Name (year opened): Calfee Park (1935). **Location:** I-81 to exit 89 (Route 11), north to Pulaski, right on Pierce Avenue. **Standard Game Times:** 7 p.m.
Visiting Club Hotel: Unavailable.

PIONEER LEAGUE

Rookie Advanced Classification

Office Address: 812 West 30th St., Spokane, WA 99203. **Mailing Address:** P.O. Box 2546, Spokane, WA 99220. **Telephone:** (509) 456-7615. **FAX:** (509) 456-0136. **E-Mail Address:** baseball@lor.com.

Jim McCurdy

Years League Active: 1939-1942, 1946-.

President/Secretary-Treasurer: Jim McCurdy.

Vice President: Mike Ellis (Lethbridge).

Directors: Dave Baggott (Ogden), Mike Ellis (Lethbridge), Bill Fanning (Butte), Larry Geske (Great Falls), Kevin Greene (Idaho Falls), Dennis O'Meara (Medicine Hat), Rob Owens (Helena), Bob Wilson (Billings).

Administrative Assistant: Teryl McDonald.

1998 Opening Date: June 16. **Closing Date:** Sept. 3.

Regular Season: 76 games (split-schedule).

Division Structure: North—Great Falls, Helena, Lethbridge, Medicine Hat. **South**—Butte, Billings, Idaho Falls, Ogden.

Playoff Format: First-half division winners play second-half division winners in best-of-3 series. Division playoff winners meet in best-of-3 series.

All-Star Game: None.

Roster Limit: 30 active. **Player Eligibility Rule:** No more than 17 players 21 and older, provided that no more than three of the 17 are 23 or older. No player on active list may have more than three years of prior service.

Brand of Baseball: Rawlings.

Statistician: Howe Sportsdata International, Boston Fish Pier, West Bldg. #1, Suite 302, Boston, MA 02210.

Stadium Information

Club	Stadium	Dimensions			Capacity	'97 Att.
		LF	CF	RF		
Billings	Cobb Field	335	405	325	4,200	97,708
Butte	Alumni Coliseum	335	450	355	1,500	32,854
Great Falls	Legion Park	335	414	335	3,800	58,595
Helena	Kindrick Field	335	400	325	2,010	35,161
Idaho Falls	McDermott Field	340	400	350	2,800	56,039
Lethbridge	Henderson	330	410	330	2,750	46,909
Medicine Hat	Athletic Park	350	400	350	3,000	46,770
Ogden	Lindquist Field	335	399	335	4,800	101,256

Billings
MUSTANGS

Office Address: Cobb Field, 901 North 27th St., Billings, MT 59103.
Mailing Address: P.O. Box 1553, Billings, MT 59103. Telephone: (406)
252-1241. FAX: (406) 252-2968. E-Mail Address: mustangs@wtp.net.
Website: www.wtp.net/mustangs.

Affiliation (first year): Cincinnati Reds (1974). Years in League: 1948-
63, 1969-.

Ownership, Management

Operated by: Billings Pioneer Baseball Club, Inc.
Chairman: Ron May.
President/General Manager: Bob Wilson. Assistant General
Manager: Gary Roller. Head Groundskeeper: Francis Rose.

Field Staff

Manager: Russ Nixon. Coach: Amador Arias. Pitching Coach: Terry
Abbott. Trainer: Tom Spencer.

Game Information

Radio Announcer: Unavailable. No. of Games Broadcast: Home-38,
Away-38. Flagship Station: KCTR 970-AM.
PA Announcer: Hank Cox. Official Scorer: Jack Skinner.
Stadium Name (year opened): Cobb Field (1948). Location: I-90 to
27th Street exit, north to 9th Ave. North. Standard Game Times: 7 p.m.,
Sun. 6.
Visiting Club Hotel: Rimrock Inn, 1203 North 27th St., Billings, MT
59101. Telephone: (406) 252-7107.

Butte
COPPER KINGS

Office Address: West Park Street, Butte, MT 59701. Mailing Address:
P.O. Box 888, Butte, MT 59703. Telephone: (406) 723-8206. FAX: (406)
723-3376. E-Mail Address: copkings@montana.com. Website: www.cop-
perkings.com.
Affiliation: Anaheim Angels (1997). Years in League: 1978-85, 1987-.

Ownership, Management

Operated by: Silverbow Baseball Corp.
Principal Owners: Mike Veeck, Bill Murray, Bill Fanning, Annie
Huidekoper, Rich Taylor, Cynthia Gitt, Miles Wolff.
Chairman: Mike Veeck. President: Bill Fanning.
Vice President/General Manager: Ted Tornow.

Field Staff

Manager: Bill Lachemann. Coach: Orlando Mercado. Pitching Coach:
Zeke Zimmerman. Trainer: Jaime Macias.

Game Information

Radio Announcer: Unavailable. No. of Games Broadcast: Home-38,
Away-38. Flagship Station: KXTL 1370-AM.
PA Announcer: Unavailable. Official Scorer: Unavailable.
Stadium Name (year opened): Alumni Coliseum (1962). Location: I-90
to Montana Street exit, north to Park Street, west to stadium (on Montana
Tech campus). Standard Game Times: 7 p.m., Sun. 2.
Visiting Club Hotel: War Bonnet Inn, 2100 Cornell, Butte, MT 59701.
Telephone: (406) 494-7800.

Great Falls
DODGERS

Office Address: 11 5th St. North, Great Falls, MT 59401. Mailing
Address: P.O. Box 1621, Great Falls, MT 59403. Telephone: (406) 452-
5311. FAX: (406) 454-0811.
Affiliation (first year): Los Angeles Dodgers (1984). Years in League:
1948-63, 1969-.

Ownership, Management

Operated by: Great Falls Baseball Club, Inc.
President: Larry Geske.
General Manager: Jim Keough. **Director, Stadium Operations:** Billy Chaffin. **Director, Media/Public Relations:** Gene Black. **Director, Merchandising:** Sandy Geske. **Director, Food Services:** Larry Lucero. **Office Manager:** Angela Lanning.

Field Staff

Manager: Dino Ebel. **Coach:** Tom Thomas. **Pitching Coach:** Max Leon. **Trainer:** Homer Zulucia.

Game Information

Radio Announcer: Gene Black. **No. of Games Broadcast:** Home-38, Away-38. **Flagship Station:** KEIN 92.9-FM.
PA Announcer: Unavailable. **Official Scorer:** Unavailable.
Stadium Name (year opened): Legion Park (1956). **Location:** From I-15, take 10th Ave. South (exit 281) for four miles to 26th Street, left to 8th Ave. North, left to 25th Street North, right to ballpark. **Standard Game Times:** 7 p.m., Sun. 5.
Visiting Club Hotel: Midtowne Hotel, 526 2nd Ave. North, Great Falls, MT 59401. Telephone: (406) 453-2411.

Helena
BREWERS

Office Address: 1103 North Main, Helena, MT 59601. **Mailing Address:** P.O. Box 4606, Helena, MT 59604. **Telephone:** (406) 449-7616. **FAX:** (406) 449-6979. **E-mail Address:** helbrewers@aol.com.
Affiliation (first year): Milwaukee Brewers (1985). **Years in League:** 1978-.

Ownership, Management

Operated by: Never Say Never, Inc.
Principal Owners: Rob Owens, Stanley Owens, Linda Gach Ray.
General Manager: Stephanie Taylor. **Assistant General Manager:** Pam Bailey. **Head Groundskeeper:** Tim Estesen. **Director, Media/Public Relations:** Phil Elson. **Account Representative:** Dan Peterson. **Director, Ticket Sales:** Jill Erickson. **Director, Group Sales:** Julie Cummings.

Field Staff

Manager: Tom Houk. **Coach:** Quinn Mack. **Pitching Coach:** R.C. Lichtenstein. **Trainer:** Greg Barajas.

Game Information

Radio Announcer: Dan Peterson. **No. of Games Broadcast:** Home-38, Away-38. **Flagship Station:** KBLL 1240-AM.
PA Announcer: Unavailable. **Official Scorer:** Dan Peterson.
Stadium Name (year opened): Kindrick Legion Field (1939). **Location:** Cedar Street exit off I-15, west to Main Street, left at Memorial Park. **Standard Game Times:** 7:05 p.m.
Visiting Club Hotel: Super 8, 2201 11th Ave., Helena, MT 59601. Telephone: (406) 443-2450.

Idaho Falls
BRAVES

Office Address: 568 West Elva, Idaho Falls, ID 83402. **Mailing Address:** P.O. Box 2183, Idaho Falls, ID 83403. **Telephone:** (208) 522-8363. **FAX:** (208) 522-9858. **E-Mail Address:** ifbraves@cyberhighway.net.
Affiliation (first year): San Diego Padres (1995). **Years in League:** 1940-42, 1946-.

Ownership, Management

Operated by: The Elmore Group.
Principal Owner: David Elmore.
President/General Manager: Kevin Greene. **Vice President/Director of Administration:** Paul Fetz. **Assistant General Managers:** Marcus Loyola, David Plante. **Head Groundskeeper:** Craig Evans.

Field Staff
Manager: Don Werner. **Coach:** Gary Kendall. **Pitching Coach:** Darryl Milne. **Trainer:** Unavailable.

Game Information
Radio Announcers: Jim Garshow, Geoff Flynn, John Balginy. **No. of Games Broadcast:** Home-38, Away-38. **Flagship Station:** KUPI 980-AM.

PA Announcer: Kelly Beckstead. **Official Scorer:** John Balginy.

Stadium Name (year opened): McDermott Field (1976). **Location:** I-15 to West Broadway exit, left onto Memorial Drive to Mound Ave., right ¼ mile to stadium. **Standard Game Times:** 7:15 p.m., Sun. 5.

Visiting Club Hotel: Unavailable.

Lethbridge
BLACK DIAMONDS

Office Address: 2425 North Parkside Drive South, Lethbridge, Alberta T1J 3Y2. **Mailing Address:** P.O. Box 1986, Lethbridge, Alberta T1J 4K5. **Telephone:** (403) 327-7975. **FAX:** (403) 327-8085. **E-Mail Address:** lethb-dbb@telustlanet.net **Website:** www.dtmn.com/LBD_BB/

Affiliation (first year): Arizona Diamondbacks (1996). **Years in League:** 1975-83, 1992-.

Ownership, Management
Operated by: Home Plate, Ltd.

Principal Owner/President: Mike Ellis.

Vice Presidents: Mike McMurray, Judy Ellis, Laura McMurray, Matt Ellis.

Acting General Manager: Shelly Poitras. **Sales Manager:** Matt Medina.

Financial Analyst: Michele Ellis.

Field Staff
Manager: Joe Almaraz. **Coach:** Jeff Davenport. **Pitching Coach:** Dave Jorn. **Trainer:** Gord Watt.

Game Information
Radio: None.

PA Announcer: Merv Caven. **Official Scorer:** Mary Oikawa.

Stadium Name (year opened): Henderson Stadium (1975). **Location:** Highway 314 to Mayor Magrath Drive, to North Parkside Drive South. **Standard Game Times:** 7:05 p.m., Sun. 5:05.

Visiting Club Hotel: Sandman Inn, 421 Mayor Magrath Drive South, Lethbridge, Alberta T1J 3Y2. Telephone: (403) 328-1111.

Medicine Hat
BLUE JAYS

Office Address: 361 First St. SE, Medicine Hat, Alberta T1A 0A5. **Mailing Address:** P.O. Box 465, Medicine Hat, Alberta T1A 7G2. **Telephone:** (403) 526-0404. **FAX:** (403) 526-4000.

Affiliation (first year): Toronto Blue Jays (1978). **Years in League:** 1977-.

Ownership, Management
Operated By: Whycon Holdings Ltd.

Principal Owner/President: Bill Yuill.

General Manager: Larry Plante. **Director, Business Operations:** Candace Hansen. **Controller:** Katherine Kirkup. **Head Groundskeeper:** Ryan Schlosser. **Director, Ticket Sales:** Peggy Plante.

Field Staff
Manager: Rolando Pino. **Coach:** Randy Phillips. **Pitching Coach:** Les Stryker. **Trainer:** Mike Frostad.

Game Information
Radio: None.

PA Announcer: Unavailable. **Official Scorers:** John Doucett, Hubie Schlenker.

Stadium Name: Athletic Park (1977). **Location:** First Street SW exit off Trans Canada Highway, left on River Road. **Standard Game Times:** 7:05 p.m.

Visiting Club Hotel: Medicine Hat Inn, 530 4th St. SE, Medicine Hat, Alberta T1B 3T8. Telephone: (403) 526-1313.

Ogden RAPTORS

Office Address: 2330 Lincoln Ave., Ogden, UT 84401. Telephone: (801) 393-2400. FAX: (801) 393-2473. E-Mail Address: homerun@Ogden-Raptors.com. Website: www.ogden-raptors.com.

Affiliation: Milwaukee Brewers (1996). Years in League: 1939-42, 1946-55, 1966-74, 1994-.

Ownership, Management

Operated by: Ogden Professional Baseball, Inc.

Principal Owners: Dave Baggott, John Lindquist.

Chairman/President: Dave Baggott.

General Manager: John Stein. Assistant General Manager: Paige Jackson. Head Groundskeeper: Ken Kopinski. Director, Media/Community Relations: Pete Diamond. Director, Merchandising: Geri Kapinski. Director, Food Services: Jason Athay.

Field Staff

Manager: Ed Sedar. Pitching Coach: Steve Cline. Trainer: Jeff Paxson.

Game Information

Radio Announcers: Kurt Wilson, Willy Ambos. No. of Games Broadcast: Home-38, Away-38. Flagship Station: KSOS 800-AM.

PA Announcer: Dave Baggott. Official Scorer: Unavailable.

Stadium Name: Lindquist Field (1997). Location: I-15 North to 24th Street, east to Lincoln; from south, I-15 South to 21st Street, east to Lincoln, south to park. Standard Game Times: 7:11 p.m., Sun. 1:30.

Visiting Club Hotel: Days Inn of Ogden, 3306 Washington Blvd., Odgen, UT 84403. Telephone: (801) 399-5671.

ARIZONA LEAGUE

Rookie Classification

Street Address: 5900 North Granite Reef Road, Suite 105, Scottsdale, AZ 85250. **Mailing Address:** P.O. Box 4941, Scottsdale, AZ 85261. **Telephone:** (602) 483-8224. **FAX:** (602) 443-3450. **E-Mail Address:** bobrichmond@worldnet.att.net.

Years League Active: 1988-.
President/Treasurer: Bob Richmond.
Vice President: Tommy Jones (Diamondbacks). **Corporate Secretary:** Ted Polakowski (Athletics).
Administrative Assistant: Rob Richmond.
1998 Opening Date: June 24. **Closing Date:** August 31.
Division Structure: None.
Regular Season: 56 games.
Playoff Format: None.
All-Star Game: None.
Roster Limit: 30 active, 35 under control. **Player Eligibility Rule:** No more than eight players 20 or older, and no more than two players 21 or older. At least 10 pitchers. No more than two years of prior service, excluding Rookie leagues outside the United States and Canada.
Brand of Baseball: Rawlings.
Statistician: Howe Sportsdata International, Boston Fish Pier, West Bldg. #2, Suite 306, Boston, MA 02210.

Clubs	Playing Site	Manager
Athletics	Papago Park Sports Complex, Phoenix.	John Kuehl
Cubs	Fitch Park, Mesa	Nate Oliver
Diamondbacks	Kino Baseball Complex, Tucson	Mike Brumley
Mariners	Peoria Sports Complex, Peoria	Darrin Garner
Padres	Peoria Sports Complex, Peoria	Randy Whisler
Rockies	Hi Corbett Field, Tucson	P.J. Carey
White Sox	Tucson Electric Park, Tucson	Tony Pena

GULF COAST LEAGUE

Rookie Classification

Mailing Address: 1503 Clower Creek Dr., Suite H-262, Sarasota, FL 34231. **Telephone:** (941) 966-6407. **FAX:** (941) 966-6872.

Years League Active: 1964-.
President/Treasurer: Tom Saffell.
First Vice President: John Boles (Marlins). **Second Vice President:** Bob Schaefer (Red Sox).
Executive Secretary: Anne Doyle.
1998 Opening Date: June 19. **Closing Date:** Aug. 27.
Regular Season: 60 games.
Division Structure: Eastern—Braves, Expos, Marlins, Mets. **Northern**—Astros, Devil Rays, Tigers, Yankees. **Western**—Orioles, Pirates, Rangers, Red Sox, Royals, Twins.
Playoff Format: Northern and Eastern Division winners play one game. Top two teams in Western Division play one game. Winners advance to best-of-3 series for league championship.
All-Star Game: None.
Roster Limit: 30 active. **Player Eligibility Rule:** No more than eight players 20 or older, and no more than two players 21 or older. No more than two years of prior service, excluding Rookie leagues outside the United States and Canada.
Brand of Baseball: Rawlings.
Statistician: Howe Sportsdata International, Boston Fish Pier, West Bldg. #2, Suite 306, Boston, MA 02210.

Clubs	Playing Site	Manager
Astros	Osceola County Stadium, Kissimmee	Julio Linares
Braves	Disney World, Orlando	Rick Albert
Devil Rays	Devil Rays Complex, St. Petersburg	Bobby Ramos
Expos	Roger Dean Stadium, Jupiter	Frank Kremblas
Marlins	Carl Barger Baseball Complex, Melbourne	Jon Deeble

Mets	St. Lucie County Sports Complex	John Stephenson
Orioles	Twin Lakes Park, Sarasota	Butch Davis
Pirates	Pirate City Complex, Bradenton	Woody Huyke
Rangers	Charlotte County Stadium, Port Charlotte	Darryl Kennedy
Red Sox	Minor league complex, Fort Myers	Luis Aguayo
Royals	Lee County Stadium, Fort Myers	Andre David
Tigers	Tigertown, Lakeland	Kevin Bradshaw
Twins	Lee County Stadium, Fort Myers	Steve Liddle
Yankees	Yankee Complex, Tampa	Ken Dominguez

Minor League Schedules

CLASS AAA

International League

Buffalo
APRIL
9-10 .... Rochester
16-17-18-19 .. Pawtucket
20-21-22 .... Ottawa
MAY
3.................... Rochester
4-5 .... Scranton
7-8-9-10 .... Syracuse
19-20-21-22 .... Toledo
23-24-25-26 .. Columbus
JUNE
4-5-6-7 .... Norfolk
9-10-11 .... Ottawa
20-21-22-23.... Louisville
25-26-27-28...... Durham
JULY
2-3 .... Scranton
4-5-6 .... Rochester
13-14-15-16 .. Indianapolis
25-26-27-28 ... Charlotte
AUGUST
3-4-5-6 .... Richmond
7-8-9-10 .... Pawtucket
15-16-17-18 .... Scranton
25-26 .... Ottawa
27-28 .... Syracuse
SEPTEMBER
2-3................. Syracuse
4-5 .... Rochester

Charlotte
APRIL
16-17-18-19............ Indy
20-21-22 ...... Louisville
29-30 .... Toledo
MAY
1 .... Toledo
2-3.................. Richmond
11-12-13-14... Buffalo
15-16-17.......... Durham
19-20-21-22 ...... Norfolk
JUNE
1-2-3-4.......... Pawtucket
8-9-10-11 .... Scranton
12-13-14-15 .. Columbus
25-26-27-28 .. Richmond
JULY
4-5-6 .... Durham
14-15-16 .... Toledo
17-18-19-20 ... Syracuse
30-31 .... Columbus
AUGUST
1-2................. Indianapolis
3-4-5-6 .... Ottawa
11-12-13-14 .. Rochester
22-23.............. Richmond
24-25-26........ Louisville
27-28-29-30 ...... Norfolk
SEPTEMBER
3-4 .... Durham

Columbus
APRIL
16-17-18-19 ...... Norfolk
20-21-22-23 ... Richmond
24-25 .... Toledo
MAY
2-3.............. Indianapolis
5-6-7 .... Charlotte
8-9-10 ....Durham

Durham
APRIL
16-17-18-19... Louisville
20-21-22 .... Indianapolis
29-30............. Richmond
MAY
1 .... Richmond
2-3 .... Toledo
4-5-6 .... Norfolk
18 .... Charlotte
19-20-21-22 .. Rochester
23-24-25-26 ... Syracuse
JUNE
5-6-7 .... Charlotte
12-13-14-15 .... Buffalo
16-17-18-19 .. Columbus
29-30 .... Richmond
JULY
3 .... Charlotte
9-10-11-12 .... Pawtucket
13-14-15-16 ...... Ottawa
25-26-27-28 .... Scranton
30-31 .... Toledo
AUGUST
1-2................. Columbus
5-6 .... Norfolk
14-15-16 ... Indianapolis
17-18 .... Louisville
24-25-26 .... Richmond
27-28 .... Toledo
31....................... Norfolk
SEPTEMBER
1-2................... Norkolk
5-6-7 .... Charlotte

Indianapolis
APRIL
9-10-11-12 .... Toledo
13-14............. Columbus
23-24 .... Durham
25-26-27-28..... Charlotte
30 .... Louisville
MAY
1 .... Louisville
11-12-13-14 ... Pawtucket
15-15-16-17 .... Scranton
27-28-29-30 ...... Buffalo
31 .... Richmond

19-20-21-22 .... Ottawa
JUNE
1-2-3-4 .... Scranton
5-6-7 .... Louisville
8-9-10-11 ...... Pawtucket
22-23 .... Rochester
25-26-27-28 . Indianapolis
JULY
4-5-6 .... Toledo
9-10 .... Rochester
11-12 .... Richmond
21-22-23-24 ...... Buffalo
25-26 .... Norfolk
27-28-29 .... Toledo
AUGUST
3-4-5-6 .... Syracuse
7-8-9................ Louisville
17-18-19 .... Charlotte
21-22-23........... Durham
27-28 .... Louisville
29-30 .... Indianapolis

Louisville
APRIL
9-10-11-12 .... Columbus
13-14-15 .... Toledo
23-24 .... Charlotte
25-26-27-28..... Durham
MAY
8-9-10 .... Indianapolis
11-12-13-14 .... Scranton
15-16-17-18.. Pawtucket
27-28-29-30 .. Richmond
31 .... Buffalo
JUNE
1-2-3 .... Buffalo
12-13-14-15 ... Syracuse
16-17-18-19 .... Ottawa
29-30 .... Indianapolis
JULY
1-2-3 .... Toledo
6................. Indianapolis
9-10 .... Charlotte
11-12................. Norfolk
13-14-15-16 .. Rochester
23-24 .... Norfolk
25-26 .... Toledo
27-28.............. Richmond
AUGUST
11-12 .... Durham
13-14 .... Norfolk
15-16 .... Charlotte
31 .... Columbus
SEPTEMBER
1-2-3 .... Columbus
6-7 .... Indianapolis

Norfolk
APRIL
9-10-11-12........ Durham
13-14-15 .... Charlotte
26-27............. Richmond
28-29-30 ...... Columbus
MAY
1 .... Columbus
2-3................. Louisville
15-16-17-18 .. Rochester
23-24 .... Richmond

JUNE
1-2-3 .... Richmond
12-13-14-15 .... Ottawa
16-17-18-19 ... Syracuse
20-21 .... Rochester
JULY
1-2-3 .... Columbus
4-5 .... Louisville
9-10 .... Norfolk
11-12 .... Rochester
21-22 .... Norfolk
23-24 .... Toledo
25-26............. Richmond
AUGUST
7-8-9-10........... Durham
11-12 .... Norfolk
20-21 .... Charlotte
22-23 .... Louisville
24-25-26 .... Columbus
SEPTEMBER
2-3 .... Toledo
4-5 .... Louisville

27-29-30-31 ...... Pawtucket

JUNE
1-2-3 .... Toledo
12-13-14-15 ..... Scranton
16-17-18-19 ...... Buffalo
29-30 .... Charlotte

JULY
1-2 .... Durham
3 .... Richmond
13-14-15-16 ..... Syracuse
17-18-19-20 .... Louisville
27-28-29 .... Indianapolis
30-31 .... Ottawa

AUGUST
1-2 .... Ottawa
3-4 .... Durham
7-8-9 .... Charlotte
15-16 .... Columbus
17-18-19 ..... Indianapolis
24-25-26 .... Toledo

SEPTEMBER
3-4-5 .... Richmond

Ottawa

APRIL
9-10-11-12 ...... Scranton
13-14-15 .... Buffalo
24-25-26 .... Syracuse
27-28-29-30 .. Pawtucket

MAY
11-12-13-14 .... Norfolk
15-16-17-18 .... Toledo
28-29-30-31 .... Columbus

JUNE
1-2-3 .... Rochester
4-5-6-7 ...... Indianapolis
20-21-22-23 ...... Durham
25-26-27-28 .... Louisville
29-30 .... Buffalo

JULY
1 .... Buffalo
9-10-11-12 .... Scranton
21-22-23-24 .... Charlotte
25-26 .... Rochester
28-29 .... Syracuse

AUGUST
7-8-9-10 .... Richmond
16-17-18 .... Syracuse
19-20 .... Buffalo
21-22-23-24 .. Pawtucket

SEMPTEMBER
1-2-3 .... Rochester

Pawtucket

APRIL
9-10-11 .... Syracuse
20-21-22 .... Rochester
24-25-26 .... Buffalo

MAY
4-5-6 .... Ottawa
7-8-9-10 .... Richmond
19-20-21-22 . Indianapolis
23-24-25-26.... Louisville

JUNE
5-6-7 .... Rochester
16-17-18 .... Charlotte
20-21-22-23 ...... Norfolk
25-26 .... Scranton

JULY
2-3 .... Ottawa
4-5-6 .... Syracuse
17-18-19-20 .... Columbus
21-22-23-24 ...... Durham
30-31 .... Buffalo

AUGUST
1-2 .... Rochester
3-4-5-6 .... Scranton
12-13-14 .... Ottawa

15-16-17-18 .... Toledo
19-20 .... Syracuse
27-28 .... Scranton
29-30-31 .... Buffalo

Richmond

APRIL
9-10-11-12 ...... Charlotte
13-14-15 .... Durham
24-25 .... Norfolk

MAY
4-5-6 .... Louisville
15-16-17-18 ...... Buffalo
20-20-21-22 ... Syracuse
25-26 .... Norfolk

JUNE
4-5-6-7 .... Toledo
9-10-11 .... Durham
20-21 .... Columbus
22-23 .... Indianapolis

JULY
1-2 .... Charlotte
4-5 .... Norfolk
13-14-15-16 .. Pawtucket
17-18-19-20 ...... Ottawa
21-22-23-24 .... Scranton
30-31 .... Indianapolis

AUGUST
1-2 .... Toledo
11-12-13-14 .. Columbus
15-16-17-18 .. Rochester
19-20-21 .... Louisville
27-28 .... Indianapolis
29-30 .... Durham

SEPTEMBER
1-2 .... Charlotte
6-7 .... Norfolk

Rochester

APRIL
11-12 .... Buffalo
14-15 .... Pawtucket
23-24-25-26 .... Scranton
27-28-29-30 ... Syracuse

MAY
1-2 .... Buffalo
7-8-9-10 .... Ottawa
11-12-13-14 .. Columbus
23-24-25-26 .... Charlotte
28-29-30-31 ...... Durham

JUNE
8-9-10-11 .... Norfolk
12-13-14-15 .. Richmond
25-26-27-28 ...... Toledo
30 .... Pawtucket

JULY
1 .... Pawtucket
2-3 .... Syracuse
17-18-19-20 . Indianapolis
23-24 .... Syracuse
28-29 .... Pawtucket

AUGUST
3-4-5-6 .... Louisville
7-8-9-10 .... Scranton
21-22-23-24 .... Buffalo
25-26 .... Pawtucket
27-28 .... Ottawa

SEPTEMBER
6-7 .... Ottawa

Scranton/W-B

APRIL
13-14 .... Syracuse
16-17-18-19 .. Rochester
27-28-29-30 .... Buffalo

MAY
1-2-3 .... Ottawa
7-8-9-10 .... Norfolk

19-20-21-22.... Louisville
23-24-25-26 . Indianapolis

JUNE
5-6-6-7 .... Syracuse
16-17-18-19 .. Richmond
20-21-22-23 .... Charlotte
27-28-29 .... Pawtucket

JULY
4-5 .... Ottawa
13-14-15-16 .. Columbus
17-18-19-20 ...... Durham
30-31 .... Rochester

AUGUST
1-2 .... Buffalo
11-12-13-14 .... Toledo
19-20 .... Rochester
25-26 .... Syracuse
29-30-31 .... Ottawa

SEPTEMBER
1-2-3-4-5 .... Pawtucket
6-7 .... Buffalo

Syracuse

APRIL
16-17-18-19-19 .. Ottawa
20-21-22 .... Scranton

MAY
1-2-3 .... Pawtucket
4-5 .... Rochester
11-12-13-14 .. Richmond
15-16-17-18 .. Columbus
28-29-30-31 .... Charlotte

JUNE
1-2-3-4 .... Durham
8-9-10-11 .. Indianapolis
20-21-22-23 .... Toledo
25-26-27-28 ...... Norfolk
29 .... Rochester
30 .... Scranton

JULY
1 .... Scranton
9-10-11-12 .... Buffalo
21-22 .... Rochester
25-26-27 ...... Pawtucket
30-31 .... Louisville

AUGUST
1-2 .... Louisville
11-12-13-14 .... Buffalo
15 .... Ottawa
21-22-23 .... Scranton
29-30-31 .... Rochester

SEPTEMBER
4-5 .... Ottawa
6-7 .... Pawtucket

Toledo

APRIL
16-17-18-19 .. Richmond
20-21-22 .... Norfolk
26-27 .... Columbus

MAY
4-5-6 .... Indianapolis
8-9-10 .... Charlotte
11-12-13-14 ...... Durham
23-24-25-26 ...... Ottawa
28-29-30-31 .... Scranton

JUNE
8-9-10-11 .... Louisville
12-13-14-15 .. Pawtucket
16-17-18-19 .. Rochester
29-30 .... Columbus

JULY
9-10 .... Richmond
11-12-13 .... Charlotte
17-18-19-20 ...... Buffalo
21-22 .... Louisville

AUGUST
4-5-6 .... Indianapolis
7-8-9-10 .... Syracuse

19-20 .... Durham	29-30 .... Louisville	**SEPTEMBER**
21-22-23 .... Norfolk	31 .... Indianapolis	1 .... Indianapolis
		4-5-6-7 .... Columbus

Pacific Coast League

Albuquerque

APRIL
7-8-9-10 ... New Orleans
11-12-13-14 .. Oklahoma
25-26-27-28 ...... Fresno
30 .... Omaha

MAY
1-2-3 ....Omaha
13-14-15-16 .... Memphis
17-18-19-20 .. Edmonton
26-27-28-29 ...... Tucson
30-31 .... Colo. Spr.

JUNE
1-2 .... Colo. Spr.
4-5-6-7 .... Vancouver
22-23-24-25 .... Iowa

JULY
4-4-5-5 .... Tacoma
13-14-15-16 .. Colo. Spr.
17-18-19-20 .. Nashville
29-30-31 .... Calgary

AUGUST
1........................ Calgary
2-3-4-5 .... Las Vegas
19-20-21-22 .... Iowa
31 .... Salt Lake

SEPTEMBER
1-2-3 .... Salt Lake
4-5-6-7 .... Omaha

Calgary

APRIL
16-17-18-19 ...... Tucson
21-22-23-24 . Las Vegas

MAY
9-10-11-12 .... Tacoma
13-14-15-16 ...... Omaha
26-27-28-29 .... Nashville
30-31 .... Fresno

JUNE
1-2 .... Fresno
13-14-15-16 .. Colo. Spr.
18-19-20-21 .. Albuquerque
26-27-28-29 .. New Orleans
30 .... Salt Lake

JULY
1-2-3 .... Salt Lake
13-14-15-16 . Vancouver
17-18-19-20 ...... Tacoma
21-22-23-24 .... Memphis

AUGUST
2-3-4-5 .... Edmonton
6-7-8-9 .... Iowa
11-12-13-14 .. Oklahoma
19-20-21-22 ...Edmonton
31 .... Vancouver

SEPTEMBER
1-2-3 .... Vancouver

Colo. Springs

APRIL
7-8-9-10 .... Oklahoma
21-22-23-24 .... Fresno
25-26-27-28 New Orleans

MAY
9-10-11-12 .... Iowa
13-14-15-16 . Vancouver
22-23-24-25 .. Edmonton
26-27-28-29 . Las Vegas

JUNE
4-5-6-7 .... Memphis
9-10-11-12 Albuquerque

22-23-24-25 ...... Calgary
26-27-28-29 .... Iowa

JULY
4-5-5-6 .... Tucson
9-10-11-12 .... Omaha
21-22-23-24 ...... Nashville
25-26-27-28 .. Salt Lake

AUGUST
11-12-13-14... Albuquerque
23-24-25-26 ...... Tacoma
31 .... Omaha

SEPTEMBER
1-2-3 .... Omaha

Edmonton

APRIL
21-22-23-24 ...... Tucson
25-26-27-28 ...... Calgary

MAY
9-10-11-12 .... Omaha
13-14-15-16 ...... Tacoma
26-27-28-29 ...... Fresno
30-31 .... Nashville

JUNE
1-2 .... Nashville
13-14-15-16... Albuquerque
18-19-20-21 .. Colo. Spr.
26-27-28-29 .. Salt Lake
30 .... New Orleans

JULY
1-2-3 .... New Orleans
9-10-11-12 .... Calgary
17-18-19-20 .... Memphis
21-22-23-24 ...... Tacoma

AUGUST
4-5-6-7 .... Vancouver
15-16-17-18 .. Oklahoma
23-24-25-26 . Las Vegas
31 .... Iowa

SEPTEMBER
1-2-3 .... Iowa
4-5-6-7 .... Vancouver

Fresno

APRIL
7-8-9-10 .... Calgary
16-17-18-19 .... Omaha
29-30 .... Memphis

MAY
1-3 .... Memphis
13-14-15-16 .. Oklahoma
17-18-19-20 ...... Tucson
22-23-24-25 Albuquerque

JUNE
9-10-11-12 .... Vancouver
13-14-15-16 .. Salt Lake
18-19-20-21 ...... Tacoma

JULY
4-5-5-6 .... Las Vegas
9-10-11-12 ...... Salt Lake
25-26-27-28 .... Iowa
29-30-31 ...... Las Vegas

AUGUST
1 .... Las Vegas
2-3-4-5 .... Tucson
11-12-13-14 .. New Orleans
15-16-17-18 .. Colo. Spr.
19-20-21-22 .... Nashville
27-28-29-30 .. Edmonton

Iowa

APRIL
7-8-9-10 .... Nashville
11-12-13-14 .... Memphis

25-26-27-28 ...... Tacoma
30 .... Vancouver

MAY
1-2-3 .... Vancouver
13-14-15-16 .. New Orleans
17-18-19-20 .. Colo. Spr.
30-31 .... Omaha

JUNE
1-2 .... Omaha
4-5-6-7 .... Calgary
18-19-20-21 ...... Tucson

JULY
4-5-5-6 .... Oklahoma
9-10-11-12 Albuquerque
17-18-19-20 ...... Fresno
29-30-31 .... Omaha

AUGUST
1 .... Omaha
2-3-4-5 .... Colo. Spr.
11-12-12-14 .. Edmonton
15-16-17-18 . Las Vegas
23-24-25-26 .. Salt Lake
27-28-29-30... Albuquerque

Las Vegas

APRIL
7-8-9-10 .... Edmonton
11-12-13-14 ...... Calgary
25-26-27-28 .... Memphis
30 .... Oklahoma

MAY
1-2-3 .... Oklahoma
13-14-15-16 .... Tucson
17-18-19-20 . Vancouver
30-31 .... Salt Lake

JUNE
1-2 .... Salt Lake
4-5-6-7 .... Fresno
22-23-24-25 ...... Omaha
30 .... Nashville

JULY
1-2-3 .... Nashville
13-14-15-16 ...... Fresno
21-22-23-24 .... Iowa
25-26-27-28... Albuquerque

AUGUST
6-7-8-9 .... New Orleans
11-12-13-14.... Salt Lake
27-28-29-30 ...... Tacoma
31 ....Tucson

SEPTEMBER
1-2-3 .... Tucson
4-5-6-7 .... Colo. Spr.

Memphis

APRIL
16-17-18-19 .. Colo. Spr.
21-22-23-24.. Albuquerque

MAY
5-6-7-8 .... Calgary
9-10-11-12.... Las Vegas
17-18-19-20 .... Nashville
22-23-24-25 .. New Orleans
26-27-28-29 .. Salt Lake

JUNE
13-14-15-16 .... Iowa
18-19-20-21 .. Oklahoma
26-27-28-29 ...... Fresno
30 .... Omaha

JULY
1-2-3 ....Omaha
13-14-15-16 .. New Orleans

25-26-27-28 .. Edmonton

AUGUST
6-7-8-9............... Tucson
11-12-13-14 ...... Tacoma
19-20-21-22 . Vancouver
23-24-25-26 .... Nashville

SEPTEMBER
4-5-6-7 .... Oklahoma

Nashville

APRIL
11-12-13-14 ... Colo. Spr.
16-17-18-19 . Albuquerque
30...................... Calgary

MAY
1-2-3 .... Calgary
5-6-7-8 .... Las Vegas
22-23-24-25 ... Salt Lake

JUNE
4-5-6-7 .... Oklahoma
9-10-11-12 .... Iowa
22-23-24-25 .... Fresno

JULY
4-5-5-6 .... Memphis
9-10-11-12 New Orleans
13-14-15-16 .. Oklahoma
25-26-27-28....... Omaha
29-30-31 .... Edmonton

AUGUST
1...................... Edmonton
6-7-8-9.............. Tacoma
11-12-13-14 ...... Tucson
15-16-17-18 . Vancouver
27-28-29-30 .. New Orleans
31 .... Memphis

SEPTEMBER
1-2-3 .... Memphis

New Orleans

APRIL
11-12-13-14 .. Edmonton
16-17-18-19........... Iowa
23-24-25-26 .... Alb.

MAY
5-6-7-8 .... Salt Lake
9-10-11-12 .... Fresno
26-27-28-29 ...... Tacoma
30-31 .... Memphis

JUNE
1-2 .... Memphis
4-5-6-7............... Omaha
18-19-20-21 . Las Vegas
22-23-24-25 .. Oklahoma

JULY
4-5-5-6 .... Calgary
17-18-19-20 .... Tucson
21-22-23-24 . Vancouver
29-30-31........ Colo. Spr.

AUGUST
1...................... Colo. Spr.
15-16-17-18.... Memphis
31.................... Oklahoma

SEPTEMBER
1-2-3 .... Oklahoma
4-5-6-7 .... Nashville

Oklahoma

APRIL
16-17-18-19 .. Edmonton
21-22-23-24........... Iowa
25-26-27-28..... Nashville

MAY
5-6-7-8 .... Fresno
9-10-11-12...... Salt Lake
26-27-28-29 ...... Omaha
30-31 .... Tacoma

JUNE
1-2 .... Tacoma

9-10-11-12 ...... Memphis
13-14-15-16 . Las Vegas
26-27-28-29 .... Nashville
30.............. Albuquerque

JULY
1-2-3 .... Albuquerque
9-10-11-12 ...... Memphis
17-18-19-20 . Vancouver
21-22-23-24 .... Tucson
25-26-27-28 . New Orleans

AUGUST
7-7-8-9 .... Colo. Spr.
20-21-22-23 . New Orleans
27-28-29-30 ... Calgary

Omaha

APRIL
7-8-9-10 .... Memphis
21-22-23-24 ...... Tacoma
25-26-27-28 . Vancouver
30.............. Albuquerque

MAY
5-6-7-8................... Iowa
17-18-19-20.. New Orleans
21-22-23-24 . Las Vegas

JUNE
9-10-11-12 ...... Calgary
13-14-15-16 ...... Tucson
26-27-28-29.. Albuquerque

JULY
4-5-5-6 .... Edmonton
13-14-15-16......... Iowa
17-18-19-20 .. Colo. Spr.
21-22-23-24 .... Fresno

AUGUST
2-3-4-5............ Nashville
6-7-8-9 ...... Albuquerque
19-20-21-22 .. Colo. Spr.
23-24-25-26 .. Oklahoma
27-28-29-30 ... Salt Lake

Salt Lake

APRIL
7-8-9-10 .... Tacoma
11-12-13-14 ...... Fresno
25-26-27-28 ...... Tucson
30 .... Colo. Spr.

MAY
1-2-3 .... Colo. Spr.
13-14-15-16 .... Nashville
17-18-19-20 .. Oklahoma

JUNE
4-5-6-7 .... Edmonton
9-10-11-12 .... Las Vegas
18-19-20-21....... Omaha
22-23-24-25 .... Memphis

JULY
4-5-5-6 .... Vancouver
17-18-19-20 . Las Vegas
21-22-23-24.. Albuquerque

AUGUST
2-3-4-5 ..... New Orleans
6-7-8-9 .... Fresno
15-16-17-18 ...... Calgary
19-20-21-22 ...... Tucson

SEPTEMBER
4-5-6-7..................... Iowa

Tacoma

APRIL
11-12-13-14.. Vancouver
16-17-18-19 ... Salt Lake
30.................. Edmonton

MAY
1-2-3 .... Edmonton
5-6-7-8 ...... Albuquerque
17-18-19-20 ...... Calgary
22-23-24-25........... Iowa

27-28-28-30 . Las Vegas

JUNE
4-5-6-7............... Tucson
9-10-11-12 New Orleans
13-14-15-16 ... Nashville
26-27-28-29 . Vancouver
30 .... Colo. Spr.

JULY
1-2-3 .... Colo. Spr.
13-14-15-16 .. Edmonton
29-30-31 .... Oklahoma

AUGUST
1...................... Oklahoma
2-3-4-5 .... Memphis
15-16-17-18....... Omaha
31 .... Fresno

SEPTEMBER
1-2-3 .... Fresno
4-5-6-7 .... Calgary

Tucson

APRIL
7-8-9-10 .... Vancouver
11-12-13-14 .... Omaha
30 .... New Orleans

MAY
1-2-3 ...... New Orleans
5-6-7-8 .... Colo. Spr.
9-10-11-12 ...... Nashville
22-23-24-25 .. Oklahoma

JUNE
9-10-11-12 .... Edmonton
22-23-24-25 ...... Tacoma
26-27-28-29 . Las Vegas
30 .... Iowa

JULY
1-2-3 .... Iowa
9-10-11-12 ... Las Vegas
13-14-15-16 .. Salt Lake
25-26-27-28 ...... Calgary
29-30-31 ...... Salt Lake

AUGUST
1...................... Salt Lake
15-16-17-18... Albuquerque
23-24-25-26 ...... Fresno
27-28-29-30.... Memphis

SEPTEMBER
4-5-6-7 .... Fresno

Vancouver

APRIL
16-17-18-19 . Las Vegas
21-22-23-24 .. Salt Lake

MAY
5-6-7-8 .... Edmonton
9-10-11-12 Albuquerque
22-23-24-25 ...... Calgary
26-27-28-29 .... Iowa
30-31 .... Tucson

JUNE
1-2 .... Tucson
13-14-15-16 New Orleans
18-19-20-21 .. Nashville
22-23-24-25 .. Edmonton
30...................... Fresno

JULY
1-2-3 .... Fresno
9-10-11-12 ...... Tacoma
25-26-27-28 ... Tacoma
29-30-31 .... Memphis

AUGUST
1...................... Memphis
2-3-4-5 .... Oklahoma
11-12-13-14....... Omaha
23-24-25-26 ...... Calgary
27-28-29-30 . Colo. Spr.

CLASSAA

Eastern League

Akron
APRIL
10-11-12 .... Bowie
13-14-15 .... Portland
24-25-26 ..... New Britain
27-28-29 .... Trenton
MAY
8-9-10 .... Reading
18-19-20-21 New Haven
22-23-24 ...... Harrisburg
29-30-31 .... Reading
JUNE
1-2-3-4 .... Norwich
15-16-17-18.... Binghamton
19-20-21 ...... Harrisburg
23-24 .... Trenton
29-30 .... Reading
JULY
10 ....Reading
10-11-12 ...... Harrisburg
16-17-18-19 New Britain
21-22-23 .... Reading
31 .... Binghamton
AUGUST
1-2 .... Binghamton
10-11-12-13 ..... Portland
14-15-16 ..... New Haven
17-18-19 .... Norwich
31 .... Bowie
SEPTEMBER
1-2 .... Bowie
4-5-6-7 .... Trenton

Binghamton
APRIL
9-10-11 .... New Britain
14-15 .... New Haven
16-17 .... Akron
24-25-26 .... Norwich
MAY
4-5 .... Bowie
6-7 .... Akron
8-9-10 .... Trenton
18-19-20 .... Portland
22-23-24 .... Reading
JUNE
1-2-3-4 .... Harrisburg
5-6-7 .... Akron
12-13-14 ..... New Haven
23-24-25 .... Norwich
JULY
2-3-4-5-6 .... Bowie
9-10 .... Portland
14-15 .... Akron
16-17-18-19 ..... Reading
27-28-29-30 New Britain
AUGUST
6-7-8-9 .... Trenton
10-11-12 .... Norwich
21-22-23 ...... Harrisburg
25-26 .... New Britain
29-30 .... New Haven
31 .... Portland
SEPTEMBER
1-2-3 .... Portland

Bowie
APRIL
13-14-15-16-17 . Trenton
18-19 .... Akron

28-29 .... New Britain
30 .... Harrisburg
MAY
1-2-3 .... Harrisburg
8-9-10 .... Norwich
11-12-13-14 ..... Reading
25-26-27 .... Akron
JUNE
2-3-4 .... Portland
5-6-7 .... Reading
19-20-21-22.... Binghamton
25-26-27-28 ...... Trenton
JULY
11-12-13-14-15 ...... N.B.
16-17-18-19 New Haven
27-28-29-30 ...... Akron
AUGUST
3-4-5 .... Binghamton
6-7-8-9 .... Portland
10-11-12 ..... New Haven
20-21-22-23 ..... Norwich
24-25-26-27-28. Harrisburg
SEPTEMBER
6-7 .... Reading

Harrisburg
APRIL
9-10-11-12 ...... Portland
13-15 .... Reading
20 ....Reading
24-25-26 .... Trenton
27-28-29 ..... New Haven
MAY
4-5 .... Akron
6-7 .... Bowie
11-12-13-14 .... Norwich
15-16-17 ..... Binghamton
18-19-20 ..... New Britain
29-30-31 .... Bowie
JUNE
5-6-7 .... Norwich
15-16-17 .... Trenton
23-24 .... Bowie
25-26-27-28 .... Akron
JULY
2-3-4 .... Reading
13-14-15 .... Trenton
20-21-22-23.... Binghamton
24-25-26 .... Akron
AUGUST
3-4-5-6 .... New Haven
7-8-9 .... Reading
14-15-16 .... Portland
17-18-19-20 New Britain
29-30 .... Bowie

New Britain
APRIL
16-17 .... Harrisburg
18-19 .... Binghamton
20-21-22 .... Bowie
MAY
1-2-3 .... Portland
4-5-6 .... Trenton
11-12-13-14 ...... Akron
21-22-23-24 .... Norwich
25-26-27 ..... New Haven
28-29-30-31.... Binghamton
JUNE
5-6-7 .... Portland

12-13-14...... Harrisburg
15-16-17 .... Reading
26-27-28 .... Binghamton
29-30 .... Bowie
JULY
5-6 .... Harrisburg
9-10 .... Bowie
20-21 .... New Haven
24-25-26 .... Portland
31 .... Norwich
AUGUST
1-2 .... Norwich
7-8-9 .... Akron
10-11-12-13 ..... Reading
21-22-23-24 ...... Trenton
31 .... New Haven
SEPTEMBER
1-2-3 .... New Haven
6-7 .... Norwich

New Haven
APRIL
10-11-12 .... Norwich
20-21-22 .... Binghamton
23-24-25-26 ...... Bowie
MAY
4-5-6 .... Portland
7-8-9-10 ..... New Britain
15-16-17 .... Akron
22-23-24 .... Bowie
JUNE
1-2-3 .... New Britain
4-5-6-7 .... Trenton
8-9-10-11 ..... Harrisburg
15-16-17 .... Portland
18-19-20-21 ..... Reading
29-30 .... Harrisburg
JULY
1 .... Harrisburg
2-3-4 .... Norwich
22-23 .... New Britain
24-25-26 .... Trenton
27-28-29 .... Portland
AUGUST
7-8-9 .... Norwich
20-21-22-23 .... Akron
24-25-26 .... Reading
27-28 .... Binghamton
SEPTEMBER
4-5-6-7 .... Binghamton

Norwich
APRIL
13-14-15 ..... New Britain
17-18-19 ..... New Haven
27-28-29 .... Reading
MAY
1-2-3 .... Binghamton
25-26-28 .... Trenton
29-30-31 ..... New Haven
JUNE
8-9-10-11 ..... New Britain
12-13-14 .... Akron
15-16-17 .... Bowie
19-20-21 .... Portland
26-27-28 ..... New Haven
29-30 .... Binghamton
JULY
1 .... Binghamton
5 .... Trenton

9-10-11-12 .... Reading	3-4 .... New Britain
17-18-19 .... Portland	17-18-19............. Bowie
24-25-26 .... Binghamton	20-21-22-23 ..... Reading
27-28-29-30.. Harrisburg	24-25-26-27 .... Akron

AUGUST

	SEPTEMBER
3-4-5-6 .... Akron	4-5-6-7 .... Harrisburg
13-14-15-16......... Bowie	
25-26-27 .... Trenton	
28-29-30 .... Portland	

Reading

APRIL

SEPTEMBER

1-2-3 .... Harrisburg	10-11-12............ Trenton
4-5 .... New Britain	21-22 .... Harrisburg

Portland

APRIL

	23-24-25-26 ..... Portland
17-18-19 .... Reading	30........................ Akron
20-21-22........... Norwich	**MAY**
28-29-30 .... Binghamton	1-2-3 .... Akron

MAY

8-9-10 .... Harrisburg	5-6-7 .... Norwich
11-12-13 ..... New Haven	15-16-17 ..... New Britain
15-16-17........... Norwich	19-20-21 .... Bowie
25-26-27 .... Binghamton	25-26-27-28.. Harrisburg
29-30-31 .... Trenton	**JUNE**

JUNE

8-9-10 .... Akron	8-9-10-11 .... Binghamton
11-12-13-14........ Bowie	12-13-14 .... Trenton
22-23-24-25 New Britain	22-23-24-25 New Haven
	26-27-28 .... Portland

JULY

2-3-4 .... New Britain	5-6...................... Akron
5-6 .... New Haven	13-14-15.............Akron
11-12-13..... Binghamton	20-21-22-23 ..... Norwich
14-15-16........... Norwich	24-25-26.............. Bowie
20-21-22-23 .... Trenton	31 .... Harrisburg
30-31 .... New Haven	**AUGUST**

AUGUST

1-2 .... New Haven	1-2 .... Harrisburg
	3-4-5 .... Trenton
	14-15-16 ... Binghamton
	17-18-19..... New Haven
	27-28-29-30 New Britain

Trenton

APRIL

8-9 .... Norwich
18-19 .... Harrisburg
20-21-22 .... Akron

MAY

1-2-3 .... New Haven
12-13-14 .... Binghamton
15-16-17 .... Bowie
18-19-19-20 ..... Norwich
21-22-23-24 ..... Portland

JUNE

1-2-3 .... Reading
8-9-10 .... Bowie
18-19-20-21 .New Britain
29-30 .... Portland

JULY

1.......................... Portland
2-3-4 .... Akron
6 .... Norwich
9-10-11-12 .. New Haven
16-17-18-19.. Harrisburg
28-29-30 .... Reading
31 .... Bowie

AUGUST

1-2 .... Bowie
11-12-13 .... Harrisburg
14-15-16 ..... New Britain
17-18-19-20... Binghamton
28-29-30 .... Akron
31 .... Reading

SEPTEMBER

1-2 .... Reading

SEPTEMBER

3-4-5 .... Bowie

Southern League

Birmingham

APRIL

	JUNE	JULY
7-8-9-10 .... Carolina	4-5-6-7 ...... Chattanooga	4-5-6 .... Orlando
11-12-13-14 .... Knoxville	9-10-11-12........ Orlando	18-19-20-21... Huntsville
25-26-27-28........ Mobile	18-19-20-21 .. Greenville	22-23-24-25 ... Jacksonville
30.............. Jacksonville	27-28-29-30 .... Knoxville	30-31 .... West Tenn

MAY

	JULY	AUGUST
1-2-3 .... Jacksonville	1-2-3 .... Chattanooga	1-2 .... West Tenn
8-9-10........... West Tenn	14-15-16-17.... Huntsville	4-5-6-7 .... Knoxville
21-22-23-24...... Orlando	26-27-28-29 ... West Tenn	22-23-24-25........ Mobile
	30-31.......... Birmingham	27-28-29-30 ...... Carolina

JUNE

	AUGUST	
4-5-6-7 .... Greenville	1-2 ....Birmingham	**Greenville**
13-14-15-16.... Huntsville	18-19-20-21 .... Mobile	**APRIL**
18-19-20-21 .. Chattanooga	22-23-24-25 .. Jacksonville	2-3-4-5...... Chattanooga
	31 .... Greenville	16-17-18-19.... Birmingham

JULY

	SEPTEMBER	
4-5-6 .... West Tenn	1-2-3 .... Greenville	21-22-23-24 ... Jacksonville
9-10-11-12 .... Carolina	4-5-6-7 .... Orlando	**MAY**
14-15-16-17 .... Knoxville		8-9-10 .... Huntsville
26-27-28-29 .. Jacksonville	**Chattanooga**	16-17-18-19 . West Tenn
	APRIL	26-27-28-29...... Orlando

AUGUST

4-5-6-7.............. Orlando	11-12-13-14.... Jacksonville	30-31 .... Carolina
8-9-10-11 .... Huntsville	16-17-18-19........ Orlando	**JUNE**
18-19-20-21 .. Greenville	25-26-27-28 . West Tenn	1-2 .... Carolina
26-27-28-29...... Mobile	30 .... Huntsville	9-10-11-12 ...... Knoxville
31 .... Chattanooga	**MAY**	13-14-15-16........ Mobile
	1-2-3 .... Huntsville	23-24-25-26...... Carolina

SEPTEMBER

		JULY
1-2-3 .... Chattanooga	4-5-6 .... Greenville	4-5-6 .... Jacksonville
	16-17-18-19 .... Carolina	18-19-20-21 ... Knoxville
Carolina	21-22-23-24 .... Knoxville	22-23-24-25........ Mobile
APRIL	30-31.......... Birmingham	**AUGUST**
16-17-18-19 .... Knoxville	**JUNE**	4-5-6-7........... Huntsville
21-22-23-24 .... Mobile	1-2 .... Birmingham	13-14-15-16 .. Chattanooga
MAY	9-10-11-12 .... Mobile	22-23-24-25 . West Tenn
8-9-10 .... Jacksonville	23-24-25-26... Birmingham	27-28-29-30...... Orlando
12-13-14-15... Huntsville	27-28-29-30 .. Greenville	**SEPTEMBER**
21-22-23-24 . West Tenn		4-5-6-7 .... Birmingham
26-27-28-29.... Birmingham		

Huntsville
APRIL
7-8-9-10.............. Mobile
11-12-13-14 ..... Carolina
21-22-23-24 .. Chattanooga
25-26-27-28...... Orlando
MAY
4-5-6 .... Birmingham
16-17-18-19 .... Knoxville
21-22-23-24 .. Greenville
30-31 .... Jacksonville
JUNE
1-2 .... Jacksonville
18-19-20-21 . West Tenn
23-24-25-26..... Orlando
JULY
1-2-3 .... Knoxville
9-10-11-12 .... Greenville
22-23-24-25 .. Birmingham
30-31 .... Mobile
AUGUST
1-2 .... Mobile
13-14-15-16 ..... Carolina
18-19-20-21 .. Chattanooga
27-28-29-30 .. Jacksonville
31 .... West Tenn
SEPTEMBER
1-2-2..............West Tenn

Jacksonville
APRIL
2-3-4-5 .... West Tenn
7-8-9-10 .... Greenville
25-26-27-28 ..... Carolina
MAY
4-5-6 .... Knoxville
12-13-14-15 .. Chattanooga
16-17-18-19.... Birmingham
21-22-23-24 .... Mobile
JUNE
9-10-11-12 ..... Huntsville
13-14-15-16..... Orlando
27-28-29-30..... Mobile
JULY
1-2-3 .... Birmingham
14-15-16-17 .. Chattanooga
18-19-20-21 ..... Carolina
30-31............ Greenville
AUGUST
1-2................ Greenville
8-9-10-11 .... Orlando
13-14-15-16 ..... Knoxville
18-19-20-21 . West Tenn
SEPTEMBER
4-5-6-7 .... Huntsville

Knoxville
APRIL
2-3-4-5 .... Huntsville
7-8-9-10.... Chattanooga
21-22-23-24.... Birmingham
25-26-27-28 .. Greenville
MAY
8-9-10 .... Mobile
26-27-28-29 . Jacksonville
30-31 .... Orlando
JUNE
1-2 .... Orlando
4-5-6-7 ..... West Tenn
13-14-15-16..... Carolina
23-24-25-26 . Jacksonville
JULY
4-5-6 .... Carolina
9-10-11-12 .... Mobile
22-23-24-25 . West Tenn
26-27-28-29 ....Huntsville
31 .... Orlando
AUGUST
1-2-3.................. Orlando
8-9-10-11 ...... Greenville
22-23-24-25... Birmingham
SEPTEMBER
4-5-6-7..... Chattanooga

Mobile
APRIL
2-3-4-5 .... Birmingham
11-12-13-14 .. West Tenn
16-17-18-19 ... Huntsville
30.................... Carolina
MAY
1-2-3 .... Carolina
4-5-6................. Orlando
12-13-14-15 .. Greenville
26-27-28-29 .. Chattanooga
JUNE
4-5-6-7 ...... Jacksonville
18-19-20-21 ... Knoxville
JULY
4-5-6 .... Huntsville
14-15-16-17 .. Greenville
18-19-20-21..... Orlando
26-27-28-29 Chattanooga
AUGUST
4-5-6-7 ...... Jacksonville
8-9-10-11 .... Carolina
13-14-15-16 . Birmingham
31..................... Knoxville
SEPTEMBER
1-2-3 .... Knoxville
4-5-6-7 .... West Tenn

Orlando
APRIL
2-3-4-5 .... Carolina
7-8-9-10 .... West Tenn
11-12-13-14 .. Greenville
30.................... Knoxville
MAY
1-2-3 .... Knoxville
8-9-10 .... Chattanooga
12-13-14-15.... Birmingham
16-17-18-19..... Mobile
JUNE
4-5-6-7 .... Huntsville
18-19-20-21 .. Jacksonville
27-28-29-30... Birmingham
JULY
1-2-3 .... Mobile
9-10-11-12 Chattanooga
22-23-24-25..... Carolina
26-27-28-29 .. Greenville
AUGUST
13-14-15-16 . West Tenn
17-18-19-20..... Knoxville
22-23-24-25... Huntsville
31................ Jacksonville
SEPTEMBER
1-2-3 .... Jacksonville

West Tenn
APRIL
16-17-18-19 .. Jacksonville
21-22-23-24...... Orlando
30.................. Greenville
MAY
1-2-3 .... Greenville
4-5-6 .... Carolina
12-13-14-15 .... Knoxville
26-27-28-29 .. Huntsville
30-31 .... Mobile
JUNE
1-2 .... Mobile
9-10-11-12 . Birmingham
13-14-15-16 .. Chattanooga
23-24-25-26..... Mobile
27-28-29-30... Huntsville
JULY
1-2-3 .... Greenville
9-10-11-12 . Jacksonville
14-15-16-17...... Orlando
18-19-20-21... Birmingham
AUGUST
4-5-6-7 .... Carolina
8-9-10-11 .. Chattanooga
27-28-29-30 ... Knoxville

Texas League

Arkansas
APRIL
13-14-15-16-17..... Jack.
18-18-19-20-21..... Tulsa
28-30-30...... Shreveport
MAY
1-2 .... Shreveport
15-16-16-18-19 ...... El P
20-21-22-23-23. Midland
JUNE
1-2-3-4-5-6 .... Tulsa
13-13-15-16-17-18 Jack.
19-20-20-21-22-23.. Shr.
JULY
9-10-11-11-13-14.... S.A.
15-16-17-18-18-20 ... Wich.
30-31 .... Shreveport
AUGUST
1-1-3 .... Shreveport

10-11-12-13-14 Jackson
15-15-17-18-19..... Tulsa

El Paso
APRIL
2-3-4-5-6.... San Antonio
18-19-20-21-22 . Wichita
23-24-25-26-27. Midland
MAY
4-5-6-7-8 .... Arkansas
9-10-11-12-13 .. Jackson
26-27-28-29-30-31 . Wich.
JUNE
13-14-15-16-17-18 . Mid.
19-20-21-22-23-24...... S.A.
JULY
2-3-4-5-6-7 .. Shreveport
9-10-11-12-13-14.. Tulsa
30-31 .... San Antonio

AUGUST
1-2-3 .... San Antonio
10-11-12-13-14.. Wichita
15-16-17-18-19. Midland

Jackson
APRIL
7-8-9-10-11... Shreveport
23-24-25-26-27 ... Arkansas
28-29-30 .... Tulsa
MAY
1-2 .... Tulsa
15-16-17-18-19 ...... Mid.
20-21-22-23-24. El Paso
JUNE
1-2-3-4-5-6 .. Shreveport
7-8-9-10-11-12.... Arkansas
19-20-21-22-23-24.... Tulsa

JULY
2-3-4-5-6-7 .... S.A.
9-10-11-12-13-14... Wichita
30-31 .... Tulsa
AUGUST
1-2-3 .... Tulsa
4-5-6-7-8...... Shreveport
20-21-22-23-24... Arkansas

Midland
APRIL
2-3-4-5-6 .... Wichita
7-8-9-10-11 ... El Paso
18-19-20-21-22 ...... S.A.
MAY
4-5-6-7-8 .... Jackson
9-10-11-12-13. Arkansas
26-27-28-29-30-31 . S.A.
JUNE
1-2-3-4-5-6 .... El Paso
19-20-21-22-23-24 ... Wich.
JULY
2-3-4-5-6-7 .... Tulsa
9-10-11-12-13-14.... Shr.
30-31 .... Wichita
AUGUST
1-2-3................... Wichita
4-5-6-7-8........... El Paso
20-21-22-23-24 ...... S.A.

San Antonio
APRIL
7-8-9-10-11 .... Wichita
13-14-15-16-17. El Paso
28-29-30 .... Midland
MAY
1-2 .... Midland
15-16-17-18-19... Shreveport
20-21-22-23-24..... Tulsa

JUNE
1-2-3-4-5-6 .... Wichita
7-8-9-10-11-12.. El Paso
26-27-28-29-30 ..... Mid.
JULY
1 .... Midland
15-16-17-18-19-20 Jack.
22-23-24-25-26-27 .. Ark.
AUGUST
4-5-6-7-8 .... Wichita
10-11-12-13-14....... Mid.
25-26-27-28-29. El Paso

Shreveport
APRIL
2-3-4-5-6 .... Arkansas
13-14-15-16-17..... Tulsa
18-19-20-21-22..... Jack.
MAY
4-5-6-7-8.... San Antonio
9-9-10-11-12....... Wichita
25-26-27-28-29-30.. Ark.
JUNE
13-14-15-16-17-18..... Tulsa
26-27-28-29-30 ..... Jack.
JULY
1 .... Jackson
15-16-17-18-19-20 El Paso
21-22-23-24-25-26 . Mid.
AUGUST
10-11-12-13-14 ..... Tulsa
15-16-17-18-19..... Jack.
25-26-27-28-29 .... Ark.

Tulsa
APRIL
2-3-4-5-6 .... Jackson
7-8-9-10-11..... Arkansas
23-24-25-26-27 .... Shr.

MAY
4-5-6-7-8 .... Wichita
9-10-11-12-13... San Antonio
26-27-28-29-30-31 Jack.
JUNE
7-8-9-10-11-12 . Shreveport
26-27-28-29-30... Arkansas
JULY
1 .... Arkansas
15-16-17-18-19-20 . Mid.
22-23-24-25-26-27..... El P
AUGUST
4-5-6-7-8 .... Arkansas
20-21-22-23-24 .... Shr.
25-26-27-28-29 Jackson

Wichita
APRIL
13-14-15-16-17 ...... Mid.
23-24-25-26-27.... San Antonio
28-29-30 .... El Paso
MAY
1-2 .... El Paso
15-16-17-18-19..... Tulsa
20-21-22-23-24....... Shr.
JUNE
7-8-9-10-11-12.. Midland
13-14-15-16-17-18 . S.A.
26-27-28-29-30 ...... El P
JULY
1 .... El Paso
2-3-4-5-6-7 ..... Arkansas
22-23-24-25-26 Jack.
AUGUST
15-16-17-18-19 ...... S.A.
20-21-22-23-24 ...... El P
25-26-27-28-29 ...... Mid.

CLASS A

California League

Bakersfield
APRIL
12-13-14 .... Visalia
15-16-17 .... San Bern.
18-19-20......... Modesto
28-29-30.. Lake Elsinore
MAY
1-2-3 .... San Jose
12-13-14 .... Visalia
18-19-20-21 . R. Cucamonga
26-27-28......... Modesto
29-30-31 .... High Desert
JUNE
4-5-6-7 .... Stockton
9-10-11 .... Lancaster
24-25-26.... R. Cucamonga
JULY
1-2-3.......... Lake Elsinore
7-8-9 ...... R. Cucamonga
10-11-12..... High Desert
16-17-18-19........ Visalia
28-29-30......... Stockton
AUGUST
6-7-8-9............. Modesto
11-12-13....... Lancaster
14-15-16 ...... San Bern.
25-26-27 .... San Jose
28-29-30........ Stockton

High Desert
APRIL
9-10-11 ...... Bakersvfield
12-13-14 .... San Bern.
15-16-17.. R. Cucamonga
25-26-27......... Stockton
28-29-30 .... San Jose
MAY
4-5-6................ Modesto
7-8-9-10....... Lancaster
19-20-25 .... San Bern.
26-27-28 .... San Jose
JUNE
4-5-6-7 .... Lake Elsinore
9-10-11 .... Visalia
18-19-20.. R. Cucamonga
21-22-23.......... Stockton
JULY
4-5-6 .... Lancaster
13-14-15 .... Modesto
24-25-26-27 .. San Bern.
28-29-30.. Lake Elsinore
31 .... Bakersfield
AUGUST
1-2 .... Bakersfield
6-7-8-9 .... San Jose
14-15-16 .... Visalia
17-18-19.. R. Cucamonga
28-29-30 .... Lancaster

Lake Elsinore
APRIL
2-3-4-5 .... San Bern.
6-7-8 ..... R. Cucamonga
18-19-20 .... San Jose
22-23-24 .... High Desert
25-26-27...... Bakersfield
MAY
8-9-10....R. Cucamonga
15-16-17........... Modesto
18-19-20-21... Lancaster

Stockton
29-30-31.......... Stockton
JUNE
1-2-3 .... Visalia
12-13-14 .... High Desert
21-22-23.......... Lancaster
24-25-26 .... San Bern.
JULY
4-5-6 .... San Bern.
7-8-9 .... San Jose
13-14-15.......... Lancaster
16-17-18-19 .. High Des.
July 31............. Modesto
AUGUST
1-2 .... Modesto
3-4-5............. Bakersfield
11-12-13.......... Stockton
20-21-22-23 .. R. Cuca.
25-26-27 .... Visalia

Lancaster
APRIL
2-3-4-5 .. R. Cucamonga
6-7-8 .... High Desert
15-16-17 .... San Jose
18-19-20.......... Stockton
MAY
1-2-3.........Lake Elsinore
12-13-14.. Lake Elsinore
15-16-17 ... High Desert
22-23-24 ...... Bakersfield
26-27-28 .... San Bern.
29-30-31 .... Visalia
JUNE
4-5-6-7 .... Modesto
18-19-20.. R. Cucamonga
24-25-26.......... Modesto
27-28-29..... Bakersfield
JULY
1-2-3 ..... R. Cucamonga
7-8-9 .... Visalia
24-25-26-27 .... L.E.
28-29-30 .... San Jose
AUGUST
3-4-5................. Modesto
14-15-16....... Stockton
17-18-19 .... San Bern.
20-21-22-23 .. High Des.

Modesto
APRIL
9-10-11 .... Stockton
12-13-14 .... Lancaster
15-16-17.. Lake Elsinore
25-26-27 .... Visalia
28-29-30.. R. Cucamonga
MAY
1-2-3 .... San Bern.
7-8-9-10....... Bakersfield
18-19-20-21 ... San Jose
22-23-24.......... Stockton
JUNE
1-2-3 .... High Desert
12-13-14........ Lancaster
18-19-20........ Lancaster
21-22-23 .... San Jose
JULY
4-5-6.......... Bakersfield
10-11-12........ San Bern.
16-17-18-19.... Lancaster
24-25-26-27 .... Stockton

R. Cucamonga
APRIL
9-10-11 .... Lancaster
12-13-14 .... San Jose
22-23-24 ...... Bakersfield
25-26-27 .... Lancaster
MAY
1-2-3 .... Visalia
4-5-6-7 ... Lake Elsinore
12-13-14 .... High Desert
15-16-17.... Bakersfield
26-27-28 .... Stockton
29-30-31.......... Modesto
JUNE
4-5-6-7 ....San. Bern.
21-22-23.........San Bern.
JULY
4-5-6 .... Visalia
10-11-12.. Lake Elsinore
13-14-15 .... San Bern.
21-22-23.......... Modesto
24-25-26-27. Bakersfield
AUGUST
6-7-8-9.......... Lancaster
11-12-13..... High Desert
14-15-16 .... San Jose
25-26-27....... Stockton
28-29-30.. Lake Elsinore

San Bernardino
APRIL
6-7-8 .... Bakersfield
9-10-11 .... Lake Elsinore
18-19-20.. R. Cucamonga
22-23-24 .... Stockton
MAY
4-5-6 .... Lancaster
7-8-9-10............. Visalia
12-13-14.......... Modesto
21-22-23-24 .. High Des.
29-30-31 .... San Jose
JUNE
1-2-3 ...... R. Cucamonga
9-10-11 .... Lake Elsinore
18-19-20........ Stockton
27-28-29...... Modesto
JULY
1-2-3............High Desert
7-8-9 ...... High Desert
16-17-18-19 . R. Cucamonga
21-22-23....... Bakersfield
28-29-30 .... Visalia
AUGUST
6-7-8-9 .... Lake Elsinore
11-12-13...... San Jose
25-26-27....... Lancaster
28-29-30 .... Visalia

San Jose
APRIL
2-3-4-5 .... High Desert
9-10-11 .... Visalia
22-23-24.......... Modesto

25-26-27 .... San Bern.
MAY
4-5-6........... Bakersfield
8-9-10............. Stockton
15-16-17........... Visalia
22-23-24.. Lake Elsinore
25 .... Stockton
JUNE
1-2-3............. Lancaster
9-10-11 .... Modesto
12-13-14.. R. Cucamonga
24-25-26 .... High Desert
27-28-29.. Lake Elsinore
JULY
4-5-6............... Stockton
10-11-12 .... Lancaster
13-14-15........ Stockton
21-22-23 .... High Desert
24-25-26-27 ...... Visalia
31 .... R. Cucamonga
AUGUST
1-2......... R. Cucamonga
3-4-5 .... San Bern.
17-18-19 ..... Bakersfield
20-21-22-23..... Modesto

Stockton
APRIL
2-3-4-5............. Modesto

6-7-8 .... San Jose
12-13-14.. Lake Elsinore
28-29-30........ Lancaster
MAY
1-2-3 .... High Desert
12-13-14 .... San Jose
15-16-17 ...... San Bern.
18-19-20-21 ...... Visalia
JUNE
1-2-3............. Bakersfield
9-10-11 .. R. Cucamonga
12-13-14..... Bakersfield
24-25-26 .... Modesto
27-28-29 .... High Desert
JULY
1-2-3 .... Modesto
7-8-9 .... Modesto
10-11-12 .... Visalia
16-17-18-19 .. San Bern.
21-22-23 ...... Lancaster
31 .... San Bern.
AUGUST
1-2 .... San Bern.
3-4-5 ..... R. Cucamonga
17-18-19.. Lake Elsinore
20-21-22-23. Bakersfield

Visalia
APRIL
2-3-4-5........ Bakersfield
6-7-8................. Modesto
15-16-17........... Stockton
18-19-20 .... High Desert
22-23-24........ Lancaster
28-29-30 ...... San Bern.
MAY
4-5-6............... Stockton
22-23-24 .... R. Cuca.
25-26-27.. Lake Elsinore
JUNE
4-5-6-7 .... San Jose
12-13-14 ...... San Bern.
18-19-20 .... San Jose
21-22-23...... Bakersfield
27-28-29.. R. Cucamonga
JULY
1-2-3 .... San Jose
13-14-15...... Bakersfield
21-22-23.. Lake Elsinore
31 .... Lancaster
AUGUST
1-2 .... Lancaster
3-4-5 .... High Desert
6-7-8-9 .... Stockton
17-18-19.......... Modesto
20-21-22-23 .. San Bern.

Carolina League

Danville
APRIL
10-11-12. Prince William
20-21-22-23 ..... Kinston
24-25-26................. W-S
MAY
1-2-3 .... Lynchburg
4-5-6-7 .... Salem
8-9 .... Lynchburg
15-16-17...... Wilmington
19-20-21........ Frederick
30-31 .... Lynchburg
JUNE
8-9-10............... Kinston
11-12-13-14........... W-S
16-17-18 .... Salem
28-29-30. Prince William
JULY
8-9-10 .... Frederick
18-19-20 .... Lynchburg
28-29-30........... Kinston
31.......... Winston-Salem
AUGUST
11-12-13............. Salem
14-15-16-17 Prince William
18-19 .... Winston-Salem
22-23-24-25. Wilmington
26-27-28-29 ... Frederick
31 .... Wilmington
SEPTEMBER
1-2 .... Wilmington

Frederick
APRIL
17-18-19 .... Salem
20-21-22-23.. Lynchburg
MAY
1-2-3............ Wilmington
4-5-6-7 .... W-S
11-12-13-14...... Danville
22-23-24. Prince William
25-26-27............ Kinston
JUNE
5-6-7 .... Salem

8-9-10 .... Lynchburg
19-20-21 ...... Wilmington
25-26-27 .... W-S
JULY
1-2-3................... Kinston
11-12-13. Prince William
15-16-17....... Danville
24-25-26-27 .... Salem
28-29-30 ...... Lynchburg
AUGUST
7-8-9-10....... Wilmington
11-12-13 .... W-S
18-19-20-21 ...... Kinston
30-31....... Prince William
SEPTEMBER
1-2 .... Prince William
3-4-5 .... Danville

Kinston
APRIL
10-11-12 .... Lynchburg
14-15-16........... Danville
24-25-26........... Frederick
28-29-30...... Wilmington
MAY
8-9-10...... Prince William
19-20-21............... W-S
22-23-24 .... Salem
28-29-30-31 Prince William
JUNE
1-2-3-4............... Danville
11-12-13-14...... Frederick
15-16-17-18. Wilmington
28-29-30 .... Lynchburg
JULY
8-9-10 .... Salem
11-12-13 .... W-S
18-19-20. Prince William
21-22-23 .... Danville
31 .... Frederick
AUGUST
1-2 .... Frederick
4-5-6............. Wilmington
14-15-16-17.. Lynchburg
26-27-28-29 .... W-S

30-31................... Salem
SEPTEMBER
1-2 .... Salem

Lynchburg
APRIL
14-15-16......... Frederick
17-18-19............ Kinston
28-29-30. Prince William
MAY
10 .... Danville
11-12-13-14. Wilmington
15-16-17................ W-S
25-26-27 .... Salem
28-29 .... Danville
JUNE
1-2-3-4 .... Frederick
5-6-7 .... Kinston
15-16-17-18 Prince William
19-20-21 .... Danville
JULY
1-2-3............. Wilmington
4-5-6 .... Salem
8-9-10 .... W-S
11-12 .... Salem
21-22-23.......... Frederick
24-25-26-27 ...... Kinston
AUGUST
4-5-6....... Prince-William
7-8-9-10........... Danville
19-20-21 ...... Wilmington
30-31 .... Winston-Salem
SEPTEMBER
1-2 .... Winston-Salem
5-6......................... Salem

Prince William
APRIL
17-18-19.......... Danville
20-21-22-23 .... W-S
MAY
1-2-3................. Kinston
4-5-6-7.......... Lynchburg
11-12-13-14 .... Salem
15-16-17........ Frederick

25-26-27...... Wilmington

JUNE

5-6-7................. Danville
8-9-10...................... W-S
19-20-21............. Kinston
25-26-27....... Lynchburg

JULY

1-2-3 .... Salem
4-5-6.............. Frederick
15-16-17....... Wilmington
24-25-26-27...... Danville
28-29-30................ W-S

AUGUST

7-8-9-10 .... Kinston
11-12-13 .... Lynchburg
19-20-21 .... Salem
22-23-24-25 ... Frederick

SEPTEMBER

3-4-5-6......... Wilmington

Salem

APRIL

10-11-12-13............ W-S
14-15-16...... Wilmington
24-25-26. Prince William
27-28-29-30...... Danville

MAY

8-9-10............. Frederick
15-16-17............ Kinston
19-20-21...... Lynchburg
29-30-31................ W-S

JUNE

1-2-3-4........... Wilmington
11-12-13-14. Prince William
25-26-27........... Danville
28-29-30......... Frederick

JULY

13 .... Lynchburg
15-16-17............ Kinston
18-19-20................ W-S
21-22-23...... Wilmington
31 .... Prince William

AUGUST

1-2 .... Prince William
4-5-6................. Danville
14-15-16-17 .... Frederick
22-23-24-25 .... Kinston
26-27-28-29.. Lynchburg

SEPTEMBER

3-4 .... Lynchburg

Wilmington

APRIL

10-11-12......... Frederick
20-21-22-23 .... Salem
24-25-26 .... Lynchburg

MAY

4-5-6-7 .... Kinston
8-9-10.................... W-S
19-20-21. Prince William
22-23-24............ Danville
28-29-30-31 .... Frederick

JUNE

8-9-10 .... Salem
11-12-13-14 ..Lynchburg
25-26-27............. Kinston
28-29-30................ W-S

JULY

4-5-6 .... Danville
8-9-10..... Prince William
11-12-13-14...... Danville
18-19-20......... Frederick

28-29-30 .... Salem
31 .... Lynchburg

AUGUST

1-2 .... Lynchburg
11-12-13............ Kinston
14-15-16-17 .... W-S
26-27-28-29 Prince William

Winston-Salem

APRIL

14-15-16. Prince William
17-18-19...... Wilmington
28-29-30....... Frederick

MAY

1-2-3 .... Salem
11-12-13-14....... Kinston
22-23-24 .... Lynchburg
25-26-27 ....Danville

JUNE

1-2-3-4... Prince William
5-6-7........... Wilmington
15-16-17-18 .... Frederick
19-20-21 .... Salem

JULY

1-2-3............... Danville
4-5-6................. Kinston
15-16-17...... Lynchburg
21-22-23. Prince William
24-25-26-27. Wilmington

AUGUST

1-2 .... Danville
4-5-6.............. Frederick
7-8-9-10 .... Salem
20-21 .... Danville
22-23-24-25.. Lynchburg

SEPTEMBER

3-4-5................. Kinston

Florida State League

Brevard County

APRIL

8 .... Vero Beach
10...................... Daytona
12-13 .... St. Lucie
23-24 .... Vero Beach
26...................... Daytona
29-30 .... Jupiter

MAY

1-2 .... Jupiter
3-4-5-6 .... Fort Myers
9-10-11-12 ... Kissimmee
21-22-23-24.... Charlotte
29-30-31 .... Lakeland

JUNE

1 .... Lakeland
5-6 .... Daytona
7-8.................... St. Lucie
15-16-17-18 ... Sarasota
24-25 .... Jupiter
30 ....Vero Beach

JULY

1 .... Vero Beach
2....................... Daytona
4 .... St. Lucie
8 ....St. Lucie
9-10-11-12 .... Tampa
17-18.................. Jupiter
20-21 .... Kissimmee
22-23-24-25 . Clearwater

AUGUST

3-4-5-6 .... Dunedin
7-8-9-10 . St. Petersburg
13...................... Daytona
16 .... Vero Beach
24 .... Vero Beach

---

31 .... Kissimmee

SEPTEMBER

2-3 .... Daytona
5 .... Vero Beach
6 .... Kissimmee

Charlotte

APRIL

11 .... Fort Myers
14-15 .... Tampa
16-17-18-19........ Jupiter
22-23 .... Dunedin
26-27 .... Lakeland

MAY

1-2 .... Clearwater
3-4-5-6 .... St. Lucie
8.................. Fort Myers
13-14 .... Fort Myers
15-16..... St. Petersburg
17-18 .... Lakeland
27-28.... St. Petersburg
30................ Clearwater

JUNE

2.................... Fort Myers
7-8 .... Sarasota
14................ Clearwater
15-16-17-18.. Vero Beach
22 .... St. Petersburg
26-27-28-29..... Brevard
30..................... Dunedin

JULY

1..................... Dunedin
2-3 .... Clearwater
4.................... Fort Myers
6-8 .... Lakeland
17-18-19-20 ..... Daytona

27-28-29-30. Kissimmee
31 .... Tampa

AUGUST

1 .... Tampa
7-8 .... Sarasota
12-13 .... Lakeland
17....................... Sarasota
18-19 .... Dunedin
21-22 .... Fort Myers
26-27 .... Tampa
31..................... Sarasota

SEPTEMBER

2 .... St. Petersburg

Clearwater

APRIL

9............. St. Petersburg
10...................... Dunedin
12 .... Lakeland
13............. St. Petersburg
15....................... Sarasota
16-17-18-19 ..... Daytona
30..................... Sarasota

MAY

3............. St. Petersburg
8 .... Tampa
15-16 .... Fort Myers
17-18-19-20...... Brevard
22...................... Dunedin
24...................... Dunedin
26-27 .... Lakeland
29 .... St. Petersburg

JUNE

1 .... Tampa
3-4.................. Fort Myers
7 .... Tampa

9-10 .... Charlotte
11 .... Dunedin
12 .... Lakeland
15-16-17-18. Kissimmee
22 .... Dunedin
23 .... Charlotte
26-27-28-29 ...... Jupiter

JULY
4 .... Tampa
6 .... Tampa
13-14-15-16 Vero Beach
17 .... Dunedin
19-20 .... Sarasota
27-28-29-30 .... St. Lucie
31 .... Dunedin

AUGUST
1 .... Sarasota
12 .... Sarasota
13 .... Tampa
14 .... Lakeland
15 .... Charlotte
18-19 ...... St. Petersburg
24 .... Lakeland
25 .... Charlotte
28 ....Charlotte
29 .... Dunedin
31 .... St. Petersburg

SEPTEMBER
4-5 .... Fort Myers
6 .... St. Petersburg

Daytona
APRIL
8 .... Kissimmee
11 .... Brevard County
13-13-14-15 ... Vero Beach
24 .... Kissimmee
27 .... Brevard County

MAY
7-8 .... Brevard County
9-10-11-12 ..... Charlotte
13-14 .... Kissimmee
15-16 .... St. Lucie
21-22-22-23 ..... Fort Myers

JUNE
3-4 .... St. Lucie
7-8 .... Jupiter
9 .... Kissimmee
11-12-13-14 .... Sarasota
15-16-17-18 ..... Lakeland
29-29 .... Kissimmee
30 .... Jupiter

JULY
1 .... Jupiter
3-6 .... Brevard County
9-10-10-11 ... St. Pete
13-14 ..... Brevard County
22-23-24-25 ..... Dunedin
31 .... St. Lucie

AUGUST
1 .... St. Lucie
3-4-5-6 .... Tampa
7-8-9-10 .... Clearwater
11-12-14-15 Vero Beach
16 .... Kissimmee
26-27 .... Jupiter
31 .... St. Lucie

SEPTEMBER
1 .... St. Lucie

Dunedin
APRIL
11 .... Clearwater
12 .... St. Petersburg
13 .... Sarasota
15 .... Lakeland
17 .... Sarasota
18-19-20-21 ...... Brevard

MAY

3-4-5-6 .... Daytona
15-16 .... Kissimmee
17 .... St. Petersburg
21-23 .... Clearwater
25-26 .... Charlotte
27 .... Tampa
29-30 .... Kissimmee

JUNE
2 .... Clearwater
3-4 .... Sarasota
5-6 .... Tampa
10 .... Lakeland
12-13 .... Charlotte
14 .... Tampa
15-16 .... Fort Myers
18 .... St. Petersburg
23 .... Lakeland
24-25 .... Charlotte
27 .... Tampa
28-29 .... Sarasota

JULY
6 .... St. Petersburg
15 .... Tampa
18 .... Clearwater
19-20 .... Lakeland
27-28-29-30 Vero Beach

AUGUST
1 .... Lakeland
12 .... Fort Myers
13-14-15-16 ... St. Lucie
17 .... Clearwater
20 .... Tampa
21-25 ...... St. Petersburg
26-27 .... Clearwater
28 .... Tampa
31 .... Fort Myers

SEPTEMBER
1 .... Fort Myers
2-3-4-5 .... Jupiter
6 .... Fort Myers

Fort Myers
APRIL
8-9 .... Lakeland
10 .... Charlotte
12-13-14-15 .... Jupiter
18-19 ...... St. Petersburg
24-25-26-27 ..... Dunedin

MAY
7 .... Charlotte
9-10 .... Clearwater
11-12 .... Sarasota
17-18-19-20 .... Tampa
25-26-27-28 .... St. Lucie
29-30 .... Sarasota
31 .... Charlotte

JUNE
5-6 .... Lakeland
11-12-13-14 Vero Beach
22-23-24-25 ..... Daytona
26-27 .... Sarasota
30 .... Clearwater

JULY
1 .... Clearwater
2-3 .... Dunedin
5 .... Charlotte
8 .... Sarasota
18 .... Lakeland
24-25 ...... St. Petersburg
27-28-29-30 ...... Brevard
31 .... St. Petersburg

AUGUST
1 .... St. Petersburg
3-4 .... Charlotte
5 .... Lakeland
10-11 .... Charlotte
13 .... Sarasota
24-25 .... Tampa
26-27-28-29. Kissimmee

SEPTEMBER
2-3 .... Clearwater

Jupiter
APRIL
9-11 .... St. Lucie
20-21-22-23 . Clearwater
24-25-26-27 .... Tampa

MAY
5-6 .... Kissimmee
7-8-9-10 .... Dunedin
11-12-13-14 .... St. Pete
16-18-19-20 ... Vero Beach
29-30-31 .... Daytona

JUNE
1 .... Daytona
3-4-9-10 .... Brevard
11-12 .... Kissimmee
15 .... St. Lucie
22-23 .... Brevard County

JULY
2-3-4-5 .... Sarasota
9-10-11-12 ... Fort Myers
13-14-15-16 .... Charlotte
21 .... St. Lucie
22-23-24-25 .... Lakeland

AUGUST
3-4 .... Vero Beach
7-8-11 .... St. Lucie
17-18-19-20. Kissimmee
21-22-23-24 ... Daytona
28-29 .... Vero Beach

SEPTEMBER
6 .... St. Lucie

Kissimmee
APRIL
9..................... Daytona
11 .... Vero Beach
12-13 .... Charlotte
14-15 .... St. Lucie
20-21 .... Vero Beach
22-23 .... Lakeland
25...................... Daytona
29-30 .... Fort Myers

MAY
1-2.................. Fort Myers
3-4 .... Jupiter
17-18-19-20 .... Sarasota
25-26-27-28 .... Brevard

JUNE
1-2.................... St. Lucie
3-4 .... Lakeland
5-6 .... Charlotte
8 .... Vero Beach
10............................ Daytona
13-14 .... Jupiter
26-27 .... Daytona
30........... St. Petersburg

JULY
1 .... St. Petersburg
2-6 .... Vero Beach
8.......................... Daytona
13-14 ...... St. Petersburg
15-16.... Brevard County
17-18 .... St. Lucie
22-23-24-25 .... Tampa
31 .... Jupiter

AUGUST
1 .... Jupiter
3-4-5-6 .... Clearwater
7-8-9-10 .... Dunedin
12 .... Jupiter
14-15.... Brevard County
24-25 .... St. Lucie

SEPTEMBER
1 .... Jupiter
4-5 .... Daytona

Lakeland

APRIL
10.................... Sarasota
13 .... Tampa
14...................... Dunedin
16-17 .... Fort Myers
19...................... Sarasota
20-21 .... Charlotte
24.......... St. Petersburg
29-30 .... St. Lucie

MAY
1-2.................... St. Lucie
3-4-5-6........ Vero Beach
8............. St. Petersburg
10-11-12 .... Tampa
13-14-16 .... Sarasota
19-20 .... Charlotte
21-22-23-24...... Jupiter
28................. Clearwater

JUNE
7-8-9 .... Dunedin
13-24-25 .... Clearwater

JULY
4-5 .... Kissimmee
9-10 .... Dunedin
11-12 .... Clearwater
13-14 .... Tampa
15-16 .... Daytona
17 .... Fort Myers
27-29... St. Petersburg

AUGUST
3-4............. St. Petersburg
6-7-8 .... Fort Myers
16 .... Charlotte
17-18.... Brevard County
20 .... Charlotte
21-22 .... Kissimmee
25.................... Sarasota
26-27.... Brevard County
28-29 .... Daytona

SEPTEMBER
1 .... Charlotte
3...................... Sarasota
4 .... Charlotte
6...................... Sarasota

St. Lucie

APRIL
8-10 .... Jupiter
16-17 .... Vero Beach
20-21-22-23........ Tampa
24-25-26-27. Clearwater

MAY
7-8 .... Kissimmee
9-10........St. Petersburg
11-12-13-14 .....Dunedin
17-18-19-20 ...... Daytona
29-30 .... Vero Beach

JUNE
5-6............ St. Petersburg
11-12-13-14 ...... Brevard
16-17-18............ Jupiter
24-25 .... Vero Beach
30 .... Lakeland

JULY
1-2-3 .... Lakeland
5........... Brevard County
6........................ Jupiter
9-10-11-12 ... Kissimmee
13-14-15-16 ....Ft. Myers
20 .... Jupiter
22-23-24-25 .... Charlotte

AUGUST
3-4-5-6............ Sarasota
10 .... Jupiter
12......... Brevard County
17-18-19-20 ..... Daytona
21-22 .... Vero Beach

St. Petersburg

APRIL
8.................... Clearwater
10 .... Tampa
14-15-16-17...... Brevard
20-21-22-23 ...... Daytona
25................... Lakeland
29-30 .... Charlotte

MAY
1-2 .... Sarasota
4.................... Clearwater
7 .... Lakeland
18-19-20 .... Dunedin
21-22-23-24. Kissimmee
25................... Clearwater
30 .... Tampa

JUNE
7-8-9-10 .... Fort Myers
11 .... Lakeland
13 .... Tampa
14 .... Lakeland
15 .... Tampa
17 .... Dunedin
23-24 .... Tampa
26-27-28-29 .... St. Lucie

JULY
3 .... Tampa
4-5 .... Dunedin
8.................... Clearwater
15-16 .... Sarasota
17-18-19-20 .. Vero Beach
22-23 .... Fort Myers
28-30 .... Lakeland

AUGUST
2-6 .... Charlotte
13-14-15-16...... Jupiter
17 .... Tampa
20 .... Clearwater
22-24 .... Dunedin
28................... Sarasota

SEPTEMBER
1 .... Clearwater
3 .... Charlotte
4 .... Sarasota
5 ....Charlotte

Sarasota

APRIL
8-9 .... Charlotte
11...................... Lakeland
14................... Clearwater
16...................... Dunedin
18 .... Lakeland
20-21-22-23 ...... Ft.Myers
24-25 .... Charlotte
26-27.... St. Petersburg
29.................. Clearwater

MAY
3 .... Tampa
5-6........... St. Petersburg
7-8-9-10...... Vero Beach
15 .... Lakeland
21-22-23-24 .... St. Lucie
25-26-27-28...... Jupiter

JUNE
1....................... Dunedin
2 .... Tampa
5-6 .... Clearwater
22-23-24-25. Kissimmee
30 .... Tampa

JULY
1 .... Tampa
6................... Fort Myers
9-10 .... Clearwater
11-12-13-14 ..... Dunedin
17 .... Tampa
27-28-29-30 ..... Daytona

Tampa

APRIL
8-9 .... Dunedin
11 .... St. Petersburg
12................... Sarasota
16-17-18-19.. Kissimmee
29-30 .... Daytona

MAY
1-2 .... Daytona
4 .... Sarasota
5-6-7 .... Clearwater
9 .... Lakeland
13-14-15-16 ...... Brevard
25 .... Lakeland
26............. St. Petersburg
28................... Dunedin
29 .... Charlotte

JUNE
3-4 .... Charlotte
8................... Clearwater
9-10 .... Sarasota
11 .... Charlotte
12-16.... St. Petersburg
17-18 .... Fort Myers
22 .... Lakeland
25............. St. Petersburg
26.................... Dunedin
28-29 .... Fort Myers

JULY
2 .... St. Petersburg
5.................... Clearwater
8-16 .... Dunedin
18................... Sarasota
19-20 .... Fort Myers
27-28-29-30...... Jupiter

AUGUST
7-8-9-10...... Vero Beach
12............. St. Petersburg
14 .... Charlotte
15 .... Lakeland
16................... Clearwater
18................... Sarasota
19 .... Lakeland
21-22 .... Clearwater
29............. St. Petersburg
31 .... Lakeland

SEPTEMBER
2-3-4-5 .... St. Lucie
6 .... Charlotte

Vero Beach

APRIL
9........... Brevard County
10 .... Kissimmee
18-19............... St. Lucie
25-25.... Brevard County
26-27 .... Kissimmee
29-30 .... Dunedin

MAY
1-2 .... Dunedin
11-12-13-14 . Clearwater
15-17 .... Jupiter
21-22-23-24........ Jupiter
25-26-27-28 ..... Daytona

JUNE
1-2-3-4 ... St. Petersburg
5-6 .... Jupiter

7 .... Kissimmee	22-23-24-25 .... Sarasota	26-27 .... St. Lucie
9-10-22-23 ...... St. Lucie	31 .... Brevard County	31 .... Jupiter
26-27-28-29.... Lakeland	**AUGUST**	**SEPTEMBER**
JULY	1 .... Brevard	1 .... Brevard County
3 .... Kissimmee	5-6 .... Jupiter	2-3 .... Kissimmee
4-5 .... Daytona	13 .... Kissimmee	4 .... Brevard
8 .... Jupiter	17-18-19-20 .. Ft.Meyers	
9-10-11-12 ...... Charlotte	25 .... Brevard County	

Midwest League

Beloit

APRIL
13-14-15-16... Kane Cty.
22-23 .... Peoria
26-27-28-29 .... Rockford
30 .... Lansing

MAY
1-2-3 .... Lansing
12-13-14-15 ... Michigan
16-17-18-19 ...... Clinton
29-30-31 ..... Fort Wayne

JUNE
1 .... Fort Wayne
6-7 .... Peoria
10-11-12-13 .. Wisconsin
18-19-20-21 .. Burlington
25-26-27-28.. South Bend

JULY
3-4-5-6 .... Peoria
16-17-18-19 .... C.R.
24-25-26 .... Wisconsin

AUGUST
5-6-7 .... Rockford
10-11 .... Kane County
18-19 .... Rockford
20-21 .... Quad City
25-26-27-28. West Mich.
31 .... Kane County

SEPTEMBER
1 .... Kane County
2-3 .... Quad City
6-7 .... Wisconsin

Burlington

APRIL
14-15 .... Peoria
18-19 ...... Cedar Rapids
28-29 .... Peoria
30 .... Clinton

MAY
1-2-3 .... Clinton
6-7 .... Quad City
8-9 .... Cedar Rapids
14-15 .... Quad City
16-17-18-19 ..... Lansing
25-26-27-28 .... Beloit
29-30-31 .... Michigan

JUNE
1 .... Michigan
10-11-12-13 .... Rockford
14-15-16-17 Fort Wayne
25-26-27-28. West Mich.

JULY
1-2 .... Clinton
4-5 .... Quad City
14-15 .... Wisconsin
16-17-18-19... Kane Cty.
22-23 ...... Cedar Rapids
28-29 .... South Bend
31 .... Quad City

AUGUST
6-7 .... Clinton
8-9-10 .... Quad City
14-15 .... Cedar Rapids
18-19 .... Wisconsin
29-30 .... Clinton

Cedar Rapids

APRIL
11 .... Quad City
14-15 .... Clinton
20-21 .... Burlington
22-23-24-25 ... Kane Cty.
28-29 .... Wisconsin
30 .... Wisconsin

MAY
1-2-3 .... Wisconsin
10-11 .... Burlington
16-17-18-19 .... Michigan
21-22-23-24 ...... Beloit

JUNE
2 .... Quad City
4-5 .... Quad City
6-7-8-9 .... Lansing
18-19-20-21 Fort Wayne
29-30 .... Quad City

JULY
4-5 .... Clinton
8-9-10-11 .... Rockford
20-21 .... Burlington
24-25-26-27.. South Bend

AUGUST
4-5 .... Quad City
8-9-10-11 ..... West Mich.
12-13 .... Burlington
16-17-18-19 .... Peoria
23-26-27-28 .... Clinton
31 .... Burlington

SEPTEMBER
1 .... Burlington
6-7 .... Quad City

Clinton

APRIL
9-10-11-12 .... Burlington
16-17 .... Cedar Rapids
18-19-20-21 .. Wisconsin
24-25 .... Quad City
26-27 .... Cedar Rapids

MAY
8-9 .... Quad City
12-13-14-15 ..... Lansing
25-26-27-28 Fort Wayne

JUNE
2-3-4-5 .... South Bend
6-7-8-9 .... Rockford
14-15-16-17 ...... W.Mich.
25-26-27-28.. Kane Cty.
29-30 .... Burlington

JULY
3 .... Cedar Rapids
12-13-14-15 .... Beloit
16-17-18-19 .... Peoria
24-25-26-27 .. Cedar Rapids

AUGUST
4-5 .... Burlington
12-13-14-15 .... Michigan
20-21-22 . Cedar Rapids
31 .... Quad City

Fort Wayne

APRIL
15-16 ..... West Michigan
20-21 .... Michigan
22-23-24-25.. South Bend
26-27 .... Lansing
30 .... West Michigan

MAY
1 .... West Michigan
4-5-6-7 .... Peoria
8-9-10-11 .... Rockford
16-17-18-19..... Kane Cty.
21-22-23-24 .. Quad City

JUNE
2-3-4-5 .... Burlington
6-7 .... Michigan
10-11 .... Lansing
25-26-27-28 .. Wisconsin
30 .... West Michigan

JULY
1-2 .... West Michigan
12-13-14-15 .... C.R.
16-17-18-19 ..... Lansing
24-25-26-27 ..... Clinton
30-31 .... Clinton

AUGUST
1-2 .... Clinton
8-9 .... South Bend
12-13-14-15 .... Beloit
19 .... South Bend
29-30 ....South Bend

SEPTEMBER
2-3 .... West Michigan

Kane County

APRIL
9-10-11-12 .... Peoria
26-27-28-29 .. Wisconsin
30 .... Rockford

MAY
1 .... Rockford
8-9-10-11 .... Beloit
12-13-14-15 .... C.R.
25-26-27-28 .. Quad City
29-30-31 .... Clinton

JUNE
1 .... Clinton
6-7-8-9 .... Burlington
18-19-20-21.. South Bend
30 .... Beloit

JULY
1-2 .... Beloit
3-4 .... Rockford
8-9-10-11 .... Lansing
22-23 .... Rockford
24-25-26-27 .... Peoria

AUGUST
4-5-6-7 .... Fort Wayne
8-9 .... Beloit
12-13-14-15. West Mich.
16-17-18-19 .... Michigan
26-27-28 .... Wisconsin

29-30 .... Rockford
SEPTEMBER
4-5 .... Wisconsin

Lansing
APRIL
14-15-16-17 .... Michigan
22-23-24-25 .. Burlington
28-29 .... Fort Wayne
MAY
4-5-6-7 .... Clinton
8-9-10-11 .... Peoria
21-22-23-24 .. Kane Cty.
29-30-31..... South Bend
JUNE
1 .... South Bend
2-3-4-5... West Michigan
12-13 .... Fort Wayne
14-15-16-17 .. Quad City
25-26-27-28 .... C.R.
29-30 .... Rockford
JULY
1-2 .... Rockford
5-6 .... West Michigan
12-13 .... Michigan
20-21-22-23 .... Beloit
24-25-26 .... West Mich.
28-29 .... Wisconsin
AUGUST
6-7 .... South Bend
16-17-18 ..... Fort Wayne
22-23 .... Michigan
29-30 .... Wisconsin
SEPTEMBER
4-5 .... Fort Wayne
6-7 .... South Bend

Michigan
APRIL
9-10-11-12............ Beloit
18-19 .... Fort Wayne
26-27-28-29 .. Quad City
30 .... South Bend
MAY
1 .... South Bend
4-5 .... West Michigan
8-9 .... South Bend
21-22-23-24 ...... Clinton
25-26-27-28 ...... Lansing
JUNE
2-3-4-5........... Kane Cty.
8-9 .... Fort Wayne
14-15-16-17 .... Rockford
25-26-27-28 .... Peoria
30 .... South Bend
JULY
1 .... South Bend
8-9-10-11 ...... Burlington
14-15 .... Lansing
18-19 .... South Bend
20-21 ..... West Michigan
30-31 .... Cedar Rapids
AUGUST
1-2........... Cedar Rapids
6-7 .... West Michigan
8-9-10-11 ....Wisconsin
21 .... Lansing
26-27-28 ...... Fort Wayne
29-30 .... West Michigan
SEPTEMBER
2-3 .... Lansing
6-7 .... Fort Wayne

Peoria
APRIL
16-17............ Burlington
18-19............. Quad City
24-25.....................Beloit
26-27............ Burlington
30 .... Quad City
MAY
1 .... Quad City
12-13-14-15.. South Bend
16-17-18-19. West Mich.
25-26-27-28 .... Rockford
29-30-31 .... Wisconsin
JUNE
1 .... Wisconsin
8-9 .... Beloit
10-11-12-13 .... C.R.
14-15-16-17... Kane Cty.
29-30 .... Wisconsin
JULY
1-2 .... Wisconsin
9-10-11 .... Beloit
12-13-14 ...... Kane Cty.
20-21-22-23 Fort Wayne
28-29 .... Michigan
30-31 .... Lansing
AUGUST
1-2 .... Lansing
8-9-10-11 .... Clinton
22-23 .... Rockford
29-30 .... Beloit
SEPTEMBER
2-3 .... Kane County
4-5 .... Michigan
6-7 .... Rockford

Quad City
APRIL
9-10........ Cedar Rapids
12 ....Cedar Rapids
14-15 .... Wisconsin
20-21 .... Peoria
22-23.................. Clinton
MAY
2-3 .... Peoria
4-5................ Burlington
10-11 ....Clinton
12-13.................Burlington
16-17-18-19.. South Bend
29-30-31 ...... West Mich.
JUNE
1 .... West Michigan
3.............. Cedar Rapids
8-9 .... Wisconsin
10-11-12-13 ... Kane Cty.
18-19-20-21 .... Michigan
JULY
1-2 .... Cedar Rapids
3..................... Burlington
8-9-10-11 .... Fort Wayne
12-13-14-15 ... Rockford
28-29 .... Beloit
AUGUST
1-2.............. Burlington
6-7......... Cedar Rapids
12-13-14-15...... Lansing
16-17-18-19 ... Clinton
22-23 .... Beloit
26-27-28 ...... Burlington
29-30...... Cedar Rapids
SEPTEMBER
4-5 .... Clinton

Rockford
APRIL
14-15-16-17.. South Bend
18-19-20-21 .. Kane Cty.
22-23-24-25 .... Michigan
MAY
2-3 .... Kane County
4-5-6-7 .... Beloit
12-13-14-15. West Mich.
16-17-18-19 .. Wisconsin

29-30-31 . Cedar Rapids
JUNE
1 .... Cedar Rapids
2-3-4-5 .... Peoria
18-19-20-21 .... Clinton
25-26-27-28 .. Quad City
JULY
5 .... Kane County
16-17-18-19 .. Wisconsin
20-21 ...... Kane County
24-25-26-27 .. Burlington
28-29 .... Fort Wayne
AUGUST
4 .... Beloit
8-9-10-11 .... Lansing
16-17 .... Beloit
20-21 .... Peoria
26-27-28 .... Peoria
31 .... Fort Wayne
SEPTEMBER
1 .... Fort Wayne
5 .... Beloit

South Bend
APRIL
9-10-11-12 .. Fort Wayne
18-19-20-21 ..... Lansing
28-29 ..... West Michigan
MAY
2-3 .... Michigan
4-5-6-7 .... Cedar Rapids
10-11 .... Michigan
21-22-23-24 .... Rockford
25-26-27-28 .. Wisconsin
JUNE
6-7 .... West Michigan
10-11-12-13 .... Clinton
14-15-16-17 .... Beloit
JULY
2...................... Michigan
3-4-5-6........ Fort Wayne
12-13-14-15. West Mich.
16-17 .... Michigan
20-21-22-23 .. Quad City
30-31 ...... Kane County
AUGUST
1-2............ Kane County
4-5 .... Lansing
12-13-14-15 .... Peoria
20-21-22-23 .. Burlington
26-27-28 .... Lansing
31 .... Michigan
SEPTEMBER
1.................... Michigan

West Michigan
APRIL
9-10-11-12 .... Lansing
13-14 .... Fort Wayne
17-18-19-20 .... Beloit
26-27 .... South Bend
MAY
2-3 .... Fort Wayne
6-7 .... Michigan
8-9-10-11 .... Wisconsin
21-22-23-24 .. Burlington
25-26-27-28 .... C.R.
JUNE
8-9 .... South Bend
10-11-12-13 .... Michigan
18-19-20-21 .... Peoria
JULY
3-4 .... Lansing
8-9-10-11 .... Clinton
16-17-18-19 .. Quad City
22-23 .... Michigan
28-29 .... Kane County
30-31 .... Rockford

AUGUST
1-2 .... Rockford
5 .... Michigan
16-17-18..... South Bend
20-21-22-23 Fort Wayne
31 .... Lansing
SEPTEMBER
1 .... Lansing
4-5 .... South Bend
6-7 .... Kane County

Wisconsin
APRIL
9-10-11-12 ...... Rockford

16-17............. Quad City
22-23-24-25. West Mich.
MAY
4-5-6-7............. Kane Cty.
12-13-14-15 Fort Wayne
21-22-23-24 .... Peoria
JUNE
2-3-4-5 .... Beloit
6-7 .... Quad City
14-15-16-17 ...... C.R.
18-19-20-21 ...... Lansing
JULY
3-4-5-6 .... Michigan
8-9-10-11 ..... South Bend

12-13............. Burlington
20-21-22-23 .... Clinton
30-31 .... Beloit
AUGUST
1-2 .... Beloit
5-6-7 .... Peoria
13-14-15 ...... Rockford
16-17............. Burlington
20-21-22-23... Kane Cty.
31............. Peoria
SEPTEMBER
1........................ Peoria
2-3 .... Rockford

South Atlantic League

Asheville
APRIL
6-7-8-9 .... Cape Fear
10-11-12-13 .. Columbus
14-15................. Hickory
27-28-29-30 .. Char., SC
MAY
1-2-3 .... Piedmont
4-5-6-7............... Macon
14-15-16............ Hickory
18-19-20-21 Capital City
22-23-24-25.... Delmarva
30-31 ....Greensboro
JUNE
1-2 .... Greensboro
4-5 .... Hickory
18-19-20-21.. Char., WV
JULY
8-9 .... Piedmont
10-11-12-13...... Augusta
16-17-18-19....... Hagerstown
27-28-29-30... Char., SC
AUGUST
4-5-6-7 .... Greensboro
13-14................. Hickory
17-18-19-20 .. Savannah
21-22 .... Piedmont
28-29-30 ..... Capital City

Augusta
APRIL
2-3-4-5 .... Char., WV
14-15................. Savannah
16-17-18-19 .... Asheville
27-28-29-30 .. Columbus
MAY
1-2-3................. Macon
8-9-10-11 ...... Char., SC
18-19-20-21 ...... Savannah
22-23-24-25........ Macon
30-31 .... Piedmont
JUNE
11-12-13-14....... Hickory
18-19-20-21 .. Savannah
26-27-28 .... Columbus
29-30 .... Macon
JULY
1-2 .... Macon
8-9 .... Columbus
16-17-18-19....... G'boro
20-21 .... Macon
27-28............... Piedmont
AUGUST
4-5-6-7 .... Hagerstown
8-9-10-11 ...... Columbus
12-13-14-15 ....Columbia
28-29-30 .... Savannah

Cape Fear
APRIL
10-11-12-13.. Char., SC

14-15 ....Char., WV
27-28-29-30.. Char., WV
MAY
1-2-3 .... Hagerstown
4-5-6-7............. G'boro
18-19-20-21 ... Delmarva
22-23-24-25 Hagerstown
26-27-28-29..... Macon
JUNE
3-4-5-6 .... Capital City
8-9-10.............. Delmarva
18-19-20-21 .... Delmarva
22-23-24-25 ..... Augusta
JULY
8-9 .... Delmarva
10-11-12-13 .. Char., WV
14-15.............. Hagerstown
23-24-25-26 .... Asheville
AUGUST
8-9-10-11 .... Hagerstown
17-18-19-20 ... Piedmont
21-22-23-24 ...... Hickory
28-29-30 ..... Char., WV

Capital City
APRIL
2-3-4-5................. G'boro
6-7-8-9 .... Char., WV
14-15 .... Char., SC
16-17-18-19 . Hagerstown
27-28-29-30 .. Piedmont
MAY
1-2-3................. Hickory
4-5-6-7 .... Augusta
14-15-16........ Char., SC
26-27-28-29 .... Asheville
30-31 .... Savannah
JUNE
1-2 .... Savannah
18-19-20-21 .. Piedmont
22-23-24-25 .. Columbus
JULY
3-4-5-6 .... Asheville
16-17-18-19 . Cape Fear
27-28-29-30 .. Delmarva
31 .... Hickory
AUGUST
1-2-3................. Hickory
17-18-19-20... Char., SC
21-22-23-24 ...... Macon
25-26-27 .... G'boro

Charleston, SC
APRIL
2-3-4-5 .... Asheville
16-17-18-19 .. Savannah
20-21 .... Greensboro
22-23-24-25 Capital City
MAY
12-13.......... Greensboro
18-19-20-21 . Hagerstown

22-23-24-25.. Char., WV
26-27-28-29 ... Piedmont
JUNE
8-9-10................. Hickory
18-19-20-21....... G'boro
22-23-24-25 ... Piedmont
26-27-28 ..... Capital City
JULY
3-4-5-6 .... Augusta
8-9 .... Hickory
10-11-12-13........ Macon
14-15 .... Capital City
20-21 .... Hickory
31 .... Columbus
AUGUST
1-2-3 .... Columbus
4-5-6-7 .... Cape Fear
12-13-14-15 ... Delmarva
25-26-27 .... Asheville

Charleston, WV
APRIL
10-11-12-13...... Hickory
20-21.......... Hagerstown
22-23-24-25 ... Asheville
MAY
1-2-3 .... Delmarva
4-5-6-7 .... Piedmont
14-15-16 ...... Cape Fear
18-19-20-21 .. Columbus
26-27-28-29 ... Delmarva
30-31 .... Hagerstown
JUNE
1-2 .... Hagerstown
11-12-13-14 .. Cape Fear
22-23-24-25 .. Savannah
JULY
3-4-5-6 .... Cape Fear
14-15 .... Delmarva
16-17-18-19... Char., SC
20-21 .... Cape Fear
31 .... Hagerstown
AUGUST
1-2-3 .... Hagerstown
4-5-6-7 .... Capital City
8-9-10-11 ...... Delmarva
17-18-19-20........ G'boro
25-26-27 .... Hagerstown

Columbus
APRIL
2-3-4-5 .... Hagerstown
6-7-8-9 .... Augusta
16-17-18-19........ G'boro
20-21 .... Augusta
22-23-24-25........ Macon
MAY
4-5-6-7.......... Char., SC
8-9-10-11 .. Capital City
12-13............. Savannah
14-15-16........... Augusta

26-27-28-29 .. Savannah

JUNE

3-4-5-6 .... Piedmont
8-9-10 .... Macon
18-19-20-21........ Macon
29-30............... Asheville

JULY

1-2.................... Asheville
14-15.................. Macon
16-17-18-19 ...... Hickory
23-24-25-26 ..... Augusta
27-28-29-30 .. Savannah

AUGUST

12-13-14-15 . Cape Fear
25-26-27 .... Savannah

Delmarva

APRIL

10-11-12-13 Capital City
16-17-18-19.. Char., WV
20-21........... Cape Fear
27-28-29-30 . Hagerstown

MAY

8-9-10-11...... Cape Fear
12-13 .... Char., WV
14-15-16 .... Hagerstown
30-31 .... Char., SC

JUNE

1-2 .... Char., SC
4-5-6-7 .... Augusta
11-12-13-14........ G'boro
22-23-24-25 . Hagerstown
26-27-28 .... Char., WV
29-30............ Cape Fear

JULY

1-2................ Cape Fear
16-17-18-19 ... Piedmont
20-21.......... Hagerstown
31.................... Asheville

AUGUST

1-2-3 .... Asheville
4-5-6-7 .... Hickory
17-18-19-20 .. Columbus
21-22-23-24.. Char., WV
25-26-27 ...... Cape Fear

Greensboro

APRIL

6-7-8-9 .... Hagerstown
22-23.............. Piedmont
27-28-29-30 ...... Hickory

MAY

1-2-3.............. Char., SC
10-11 .... Hickory
14-15-16 .... Piedmont
22-23-24-25 Capital City
26-27-28-29 ..... Augusta

JUNE

3-4-5-6.......... Char., WV
8-9-10 .... Asheville
22-23-24-25 ...... Asheville

JULY

3-4-5-6........... Delmarva
8-9 .... Capital City
10-11 .... Hickory
20-21 .... Capital City
23-24-25-26... Char., SC
27-28-29-30........ Macon
31 .... Cape Fear

AUGUST

1-2-3 .... Cape Fear
8-9-10-11 ...... Savannah
12-13-14-15 ... Piedmont
21-22-23-24 .. Columbus

Hagerstown

APRIL

10-11-12-13 ... Piedmont
14-15 .... Delmarva
23-24-25-26 . Cape Fear

MAY

4-5-6-7 .... Delmarva
8-9-10 ....Char., WV
12-13............ Cape Fear
26-27-28-29 ...... Hickory

JUNE

3-4-5-6.......... Savannah
8-9-10-11 ...... Char., WV
11-12-13-14 .... Asheville
26-27-28 ...... Cape Fear
29-30.......... Greensboro

JULY

1-2.............. Greensboro
8-9 .... Char., WV
10-11-12-13 ... Delmarva
23-24-25-26 Capital City
27-28-29-30 . Cape Fear

AUGUST

13-14-15-16 ...Char., WV
17-18-19-20........ Macon
21-22-23-24... Char., SC
28-29-30 .... Delmarva

Hickory

APRIL

6-7-8-9........... Char., SC
16-17-18-19........ Macon
20-21 .... Capital City
23-24-25-26 ... Delmarva

MAY

8-9.............. Greensboro
12-13 .... Capital City
20-21.............. Piedmont
22-23-24-25 .. Columbus
30-31 .... Cape Fear

JUNE

1-2................ Cape Fear
6-7.................... Asheville
18-19-20-21 . Hagerstown
26-27-28 ....Asheville
29-30 .... Capital City

JULY

1-2 .... Capital City
3-4-5-6 .... Savannah
12-13.......... Greensboro
14-15............... Asheville
23-24.............. Piedmont
27-28-29-30.. Char., WV

AUGUST

8-9-10-11 .... Char., SC
15-16............... Asheville
17-18-19-20 ..... Augusta
25-26-27 .... Piedmont
28-29-30......Greensboro

Macon

APRIL

2-3-4-5........... Delmarva
10-11-12-13...... Augusta
14-15............ Columbus
20-21............ Savannah
29-30............ Savannah

MAY

12-13............... Augusta
14-15-16 .... Savannah
18-19-20-21........ G'boro
30-31............ Columbus

JUNE

1-2................ Columbus
4-5-6-7........... Char., SC

11-12-13-14 Capital City
22-23-24-25 ...... Hickory

JULY

3-4-5-6 .... Columbus
8-9................. Savannah
16-17-18-19 .. Savannah
23-24-25-26.. Char., WV
31 .... Augusta

AUGUST

1-2-3................. Augusta
4-5-6-7 .... Piedmont
8-9-10-11 .... Asheville
25-26-27........... Augusta
28-29-30 .... Columbus

Piedmont

APRIL

2-3-4-5 .... Hickory
6-7-8-9 .... Delmarva
14-15.......... Greensboro
16-17-18-19 . Cape Fear
20-21............... Asheville
24-25.......... Greensboro

MAY

8-9-10-11 .... Macon
12-13............... Asheville
18-19.................. Hickory

JUNE

1-2..................... Augusta
8-9-10 .... Capital City
11-12-13-14... Char., SC
26-27-28............. G'boro
29-30 .... Char., WV

JULY

1-2 .... Char., WV
3-4-5-6 .... Hagerstown
10-11-12-13 .. Columbus
14-15.......... Greensboro
20-21............... Asheville
25-26.................. Hickory
29-30................ Augusta
31 .... Savannah

AUGUST

1-2-3 .... Savannah
8-9-10-11 .... Capital City
23-24............... Asheville
28-29-30........ Char., SC

Savannah

APRIL

2-3-4-5 .... Cape Fear
6-7-8-9................ Macon
10-11-12-13 Greensboro
22-23-24-25 ..... Augusta
27-28 .... Macon

MAY

1-2-3 .... Columbus
4-5-6-7 .... Hickory
8-9-10-11 .... Asheville
22-23-24-25 ... Piedmont

JUNE

8-9-10............... Augusta
11-12-13-14 .. Columbus
26-27-28............. Macon
29-30 .... Char., SC

JULY

1-2 .... Char., SC
10-11-12-13 Capital City
14-15................ Augusta
20-21............. Columbus
23-24-25-26 ... Delmarva

AUGUST

4-5-6-7 .... Columbus
12-13-14-15........ Macon
21-22-23-24 ..... Augusta

SHORTSEASON

CLASS A

New York-Penn League

Auburn

JUNE
17 .... Utica
18 .... Watertown
22-23-24-25 .... Williams.
26-27 .... Oneonta

JULY
2 .... Batavia
7-8 .... Pittsfield
9-11 .... Utica
15-16 .... Jamestown
19-20 .... Erie
23-25 .... Utica
30-31 .... Watertown

AUGUST
3-4 .... St. Catharines
5-6 .... Oneonta
8-10 .... Watertown
12 .... Batavia
13-14 .... Lowell
22 .... Utica
24-25 .... Williamsport
26-27 .... Oneonta
30-31 .... New Jersey

SEPTEMBER
2 .... Watertown

Batavia

JUNE
16-17 .... Erie
19-21 .... Jamestown
28-29-30 .... Vermont

JULY
1 .... Vermont
3 .... Auburn
4-5 .... Utica
9-10 .... New Jersey
13 .... St. Catharines
21-22 .... Oneonta
25-26 .... Watertown
28-29 .... Williamsport
30 .... St. Catharines

AUGUST
1-2 .... Erie
3-4 .... Pittsfield
6 .... St. Catharines
11 .... Auburn
14 .... Jamestown
15-16 .... Erie
18-19 ...... Hudson Valley
24-26-28. St. Catharines
31 .... Jamestown

SEPTEMBER
1-2 .... Jamestown

Erie

JUNE
18-19-20-21 .... St. Cath.
28-29 .... Auburn
30 .... Oneonta

JULY
1-2-3 .... Oneonta
11-12 .... Batavia
14 .... Utica
15-16 ...... Hudson Valley
17-18 .... New Jersey
23-24 ...... St. Catharines

28-29-30-31 .... Lowell

AUGUST
3-4 .... Utica
6 .... Jamestown
7-8-9-10 .... Batavia
17-18 .... Pittsfield
21 .... Jamestown
22-23 .... Williamsport
25-27-29 ..... Jamestown

Hudson Valley

JUNE
17 .... New Jersey
22-23-24-25 .... Erie
26-27 .... Utica

JULY
4-5 .... Auburn
8 .... New Jersey
13-14 .... Lowell
19-20 .... Batavia
21-22 .... Lowell
23-24 .... Vermont
25-26 .... Pittsfield

AUGUST
1 .... New Jersey
5-6 .... Williamsport
7-8 .... Vermont
9-10 .... Oneonta
13-14-15-16 .... Pittsfield
22-23 .... Lowell
26-28 .... New Jersey
30-31 .... Vermont

SEPTEMBER
2 .... New Jersey

Jamestown

JUNE
18-20 .... Batavia
22-23 .... New Jersey
26-27 .... Pittsfield
28-29 .... Utica
30 .... Lowell

JULY
1 .... Lowell
6-7 .... Utica
9-10 .... Williamsport
11-12 .... Watertown
13 .... Erie
17-18 ...... Hudson Valley
21-22 .... Auburn
23-24 .... Batavia
25-26-27-28 .... St. Cath.

AUGUST
5 .... Erie
7-8 .... New Jersey
13 .... Batavia
20 .... Erie
22-23 ...... St. Catharines
24-26-28 .... Erie
30 .... Batavia

Lowell

JUNE
22-23 .... Vermont
24-25-26-27 ...... Batavia
28-29 .... New Jersey

JULY
2-3 .... Hudson Valley

9-10-11-12 .. St. Catharines
15-16 .... Pittsfield
19-20 .... Watertown
23-24-25-26.. New Jersey

AUGUST
1-2 .... Jamestown
7-8 .... Pittsfield
11-12 ...... Hudson Valley
18-19-20-21 ..... Vermont
24-25 ...... Hudson Valley
28-29 .... Auburn
30-31 .... Pittsfield

New Jersey

JUNE
16 .... Hudson Valley
18-19-20-21 .... Lowell
24-25 .... Jamestown
30 .... Pittsfield

JULY
1 .... Pittsfield
2-3 .... Utica
4-5 .... Williamsport
7 .... Hudson Valley
13-14-15-16 ..... Vermont
19-20-21-22 .... Pittsfield
28-29 .... Vermont

AUGUST
2 .... Hudson Valley
3-4 .... Lowell
9-10 .... Jamestown
11-12-13-14.... St. Cath.
24-25 .... Watertown
27-29 ...... Hudson Valley

SEPTEMBER
1 .... Hudson Valley

Oneonta

JUNE
16-17 .... Williamsport
22-23 .... Batavia
28-29 ..... St. Catharines

JULY
4-5 .... Lowell
7-8 .... St. Catharines
9-10 .... Watertown
13-14 .... Auburn
18-20 .... Utica
25-26 .... Erie
28-29 .... Auburn
30-31 .... Williamsport

AUGUST
1-2 .... Auburn
3-4 .... Jamestown
11-12-13-14...Watertown
15-16 .... Auburn
18-19 .... New Jersey
21-24-29-31 .... Utica

Pittsfield

JUNE
16-17 .... Lowell
20-21-28-29 .. Hud. Valley

JULY
2-3 .... Williamsport
4-5 .... Jamestown
9-10 .... Erie
11-12 .... Oneonta

17-18.................. Batavia
23-24............ Watertown
27-28...... Hudson Valley
30-31........ New Jersey

AUGUST

5-6....................... Lowell
9-10........ St. Catharines
11-12................. Vermont
20-21-22-23 .... N.J.
26-27-28-29 .... Vermont

SEPTEMBER

1-2....................... Lowell

St. Catharines

JUNE

16-17............ Jamestown
22-23-24-25... Pittsfield
26-27............ Watertown
30...................... Auburn

JULY

1...................... Auburn
2-3-4-5 .... Vermont
14...................... Batavia
15-16 .... Williamsport
21-22 .... Erie
25-26 .... Jamestown
31 .... Batavia

AUGUST

1-2...................... Utica
5 .... Batavia
7-8 .... Oneonta
17-18........... Jamestown
20-21...... Hudson Valley
25-27-29 .... Batavia
30-31 .... Erie

SEPTEMBER

1-2 .... Erie

Utica

JUNE

16...................... Auburn
18-19...... Hudson Valley
20-22............ Watertown
24-25 .... Vermont
30 .... Williamsport

JULY

1 .... Williamsport

10-12 ....Auburn
13-14 .... Pittsfield
15-16 ....Batavia
17-19 .... Oneonta
21-22 .... Williamsport
24-26 .... Auburn
29 .... Watertown
30-31...... Hudson Valley

AUGUST

5 .... Watertown
11-12 .... Jamestown
13-14 .... Williamsport
16-18 .... Watertown
20 .... Oneonta
23 .... Auburn
25 .... Oneonta
26-27 .... Lowell
28-30 .... Oneonta

Vermont

JUNE

18-19 .... Pittsfield
20-21 .... Auburn
26-27 .... New Jersey

JULY

7-8 .... Lowell
9-10-11-12 .. Hud. Valley
17-18 .... Lowell
19-20... St. Catharines
21-22............ Watertown
30-31.......... Jamestown

AUGUST

1-2 .... Pittsfield
3-4 .... Hudson Valley
5-6 .... New Jersey
9-10 .... Lowell
13-14 .... Erie
15-16 .... New Jersey
22-23 .... Batavia
24-25 .... Pittsfield

SEPTEMBER

1-2 .... Oneonta

Watertown

JUNE

16-17 .... Vermont
19...................... Auburn

21-23.................... Utica
24-25 .... Oneonta
30 .... Hudson Valley

JULY

1 .... Hudson Valley
2-3............... Jamestown
4-5-6-7 .... Erie
13-14 .... Williamsport
15-16 .... Oneonta
17-18.... St. Catharines
28 .... Utica

AUGUST

1-2 .... Williamsport
6................ .... Utica
7-9 .... Auburn
15-17................ .. Utica
20-21 .... Batavia
22-23 .... Oneonta
26-27-28-29 .... Williams.

SEPTEMBER

1......................... Auburn

Williamsport

JUNE

18-19-20-21..... Oneonta
26-27 .... Erie
28-29 .... Watertown

JULY

7-8 .... Batavia
11-12 .... New Jersey
17-18 .... Auburn
19-20............ Jamestown
23-24 .... Oneonta
25-26 .... Vermont

AUGUST

3-4 .... Watertown
7-8-9-10 .... Utica
11-12.................... Erie
15-16.................. Lowell
18-19-20-21 ...... Lowell
30-31 .... Watertown

SEPTEMBER

1-2................... .... Utica

Northwest League

Boise

JUNE

16-17-18 .... Spokane
22-23-24-25-26. Eugene

JULY

2-3-4 .... Yakima
8-9-10-11-12 .. S. Oregon
19-20-21 .... Yakima
28-29-30-31 .... Salem

AUGUST

1..................... Salem
5-6-7-8-9-10....... Everett
14-15-16-17-18 Portland
31 .... Spokane

SEPTEMBER

1-2................... Spokane

Eugene

JUNE

18........................ Salem
19-20-21 .... Portland
27-28-29-30 ...... Everett

JULY

1....................... Everett
4-5-6 .... Portland
14-15-16-17-18 .... Boise
19-20-21 .... S. Oregon
28-29-30-31 .... Spokane

AUGUST

1...................... Spokane
8-9-10 .... Salem
11-12-13 .... S. Oregon
20-21-22-23-24.. Yakima
27-28.................. Salem

Everett

JUNE

16-17-18 .... Yakima
22-23-24-25-26. S. Oregon

JULY

2-3-4 .... Spokane
8-9-10-11-12 ..... Eugene
19-20-21 .... Spokane
28-29-30-31 .... Portland

AUGUST

1....................... Portland
11-12-13 .... Yakima
14-15-16-17-18 .... Salem
25-26-27-28-29-30 ... Boise

Portland

JUNE

16-17-18 .... S. Oregon
22-23-24-25-26 . Spokane

JULY

2-3 .... Eugene

7...................... Eugene
8-9-10-11-12...... Yakima
22-23-24-25-26 .... Boise

AUGUST

2-3-4 .... Eugene
11-12-13.............. Salem
20-21-22-23-24 .. Everett
28-29-30 .... S. Oregon
31 .... Salem

SEPTEMBER

1-2...................... Salem

Salem

JUNE

16-17 .... Eugene
22-23-24-25-26.. Yakima

JULY

2-3-4 .... S. Oregon
8-9-10-11-12 ... Spokane
19-20-21 .... Portland
22-23-24-25-26.. Everett

AUGUST

2-3-4 .... S. Oregon
5-6-7 .... Portland
20-21-22-23-24 .... Boise
25-26 .... Eugene
29-30 .... Eugene

So. Oregon

JUNE
19-20-21 .... Salem
27-28-29-30 .... Boise

JULY
1 .... Boise
5-6-7 .... Salem
14-15-16-17-18.. Everett
28-29-30-31 .... Yakima

AUGUST
1 .... Yakima
5-6-7 .... Eugene
8-9-10 .... Portland
20-21-22-23-24 . Spokane
25-26-27 .... Portland
31 .... Eugene

SEPTEMBER
1-2 .... Eugene

Spokane

JUNE
19-20-21 .... Everett
27-28-29-30 .... Salem

JULY
1 .... Salem
5-6-7 .... Boise
14-15-16-17-18 Portland
22-23-24-25-26 . S. Oregon

AUGUST
2-3-4 .... Everett
5-6-7 .... Yakima
11-12-13 .... Boise
14-15-16-17-18. Eugene
28-29-30 .... Yakima

Yakima

JUNE
19-20-21 .... Boise
27-28-29-30 ..... Portland

JULY
1 .... Portland
5-6-7 .... Everett
14-15-16-17-18 ... Salem
22-23-24-25-26. Eugene

AUGUST
2-3-4 .... Boise
8-9-10 .... Spokane
14-15-16-17-18. S. Oregon
25-26-27 .... Spokane
31 .... Everett

SEPTEMBER
1-2 .... Everett

ROOKIE LEAGUES

Appalachian League

Bluefield

JUNE
17 .... Princeton
19-20-21... Johnson City
22-23-24 .... Pulaski
28-29-30.... Elizabethton

JULY
5-6 .... Burlington
8-9-10-11 .... Danville
20-21-22 .... Bristol
28 .... Burlington
29-30-31 ...... Martinsville

AUGUST
5-6 .... Pulaski
7-8-9 .... Danville
17-18-19 .... Princeton
20-21-22 .... Kingsport
25-26 .... Princeton

Bristol

JUNE
17 .... Kingsport
22-23-24 ...... Martinsville
25-26-27 .... Burlington

JULY
3 .... Johnson City
6 .... Elizabethton
9 .... Kingsport
12-13 .... Johnson City
14-15-16 .... Bluefield
17-18-19 .... Danville
24-25 .... Elizabethton
30-31 .... Johnson City

AUGUST
2-3 .... Kingsport
7-8 .... Kingsport
10-11-12 .... Princeton
13-14-15 .... Pulaski
25-26 .... Elizabethton

Burlington

JUNE
17-18 .... Danville
19-20-21 .... Princeton
28-29-30.......... Danville

JULY
1-2-3 .... Elizabethton
4 .... Bluefield
10-11 .... Martinsville
12-13 .... Princeton
20-21-22 .... Pulaski
24-25 .... Bluefield

AUGUST
4-5-6 .... Kingsport

7-8-9 .... Johnson City
11-12 .... Danville
17-18-19 .... Bristol
20-21-22...... Martinsville
25 .... Danville

Danville

JUNE
19-20-21...... Martinsville
25-26-27 .... Elizabethton

JULY
1-2-3 .... Pulaski
4-5-6 .... Princeton
12-13 .... Martinsville
14-15-16 .... Kingsport
26-27 .... Burlington

AUGUST
1-2-3 .... Bluefield
4-5-6 .... Johnson City
10 .... Burlington
20-21-22 .... Bluefield
26 .... Burlington

Elizabethton

JUNE
18 .... Johnson City
19-20-21 ...... Kingsport
22-23-24 .... Princeton

JULY
4-5 .... Bristol
8-9 .... Johnson City
10-11 .... Bristol
17-18-19 .... Pulaski
20-21-22... Johnson City
23 .... Bristol
29-30-31 ...... Burlington

AUGUST
7-8-9 .... Martinsville
10-11-12 .... Bluefield
17-18-19 .... Danville
23-24 .... Kingsport

Johnson City

JUNE
17 .... Elizabethton
22-23-24 .... Danville
25-26-27 ... Martinsville

JULY
1-2 .... Bristol
10-11 .... Kingsport
14-15-16.... Elizabethton
17-18-19 .... Princeton
23-24-25 .... Kingsport
27-28 .... Elizabethton
29 .... Bristol

7-8-9 .... Johnson City
11-12 .... Danville
17-18-19 .... Bristol
20-21-22...... Martinsville
25 .... Danville

AUGUST
1-2-3 .... Burlington
10-11-12 .... Pulaski
13-14-15 .... Bluefield
23-24 .... Bristol

Kingsport

JUNE
18 ....Bristol
22-23-24 ...... Burlington
25-26-27 .... Pulaski

JULY
4-5-6 .... Johnson City
8 .... Bristol
12-13 .... Elizabethton
17-18-19 .... Bluefield
20-21-22 .... Danville
27-28 .... Bristol
29-30-31 .... Princeton

AUGUST
1 .... Bristol
9 .... Bristol
10-11-12 ...... Martinsville
13-14-15 .... Elizabethton
25-26 .... Johnson City

Martinsville

JUNE
17-18 .... Pulaski
28-29-30 ...... Kingsport

JULY
1-2-3 .... Bluefield
8-9 .... Burlington
14-15-16 .... Princeton
17-18-19 .... Burlington
23-24-25 .... Pulaski

AUGUST
1-2-3 .... Elizabethton
4-5-6 .... Bristol
13-14-15 .... Danville
17-18-19... Johnson City
23-24 .... Danville
25 .... Pulaski

Princeton

JUNE
18 .... Bluefield
25-26-27 .... Bluefield
28-29-30............. Bristol

JULY
1-2-3 .... Kingsport
10-11 .... Pulaski
20-21-22...... Martinsville
23-24-25 .... Danville
26-27 .... Bluefield

AUGUST
1-2-3 .... Pulaski
4-5-6 .... Elizabethton
13-14-15 .... Burlington
20-21-22 .. Johnson City
23-24 .... Burlington

Pulaski
JUNE
19-20-21 .... Bristol
28-29-30 ... Johnson City
JULY
4-5-6 .... Martinsville
8-9 .... Princeton
12-13 .... Bluefield
14-15-16 ...... Burlington

27-28 .... Martinsville
29-30-31 .... Danville
AUGUST
4 .... Bluefield
7-8-9 .... Princeton
17-18-19 .... Kingsport
20-21-22 .. Elizabethton
23-24 .... Bluefield
26 .... Martinsville

Pioneer League

Billings
JUNE
16-17-18 .... Butte
22-23 .... Butte
JULY
1-2-3 .... Idaho Falls
4-5-6 .... Ogden
12-13-14-15. Great Falls
21-22-23-24 .... Helena
25-26-27-28 .... Butte
31 .... Medicine Hat
AUGUST
1-2-3 .... Med. Hat
8-9-10-11 ...... Lethbridge
17-18-19 ...... Idaho Falls
23-24-25-26 .... Ogden

Butte
JUNE
19-20-21 .... Ogden
24-25 .... Billings
26-27-28 ...... Idaho Falls
JULY
1-2-3 .... Ogden
8-9-10-11 ..... Great Falls
16-17-18-19 .... Helena
29-30 .... Billings
AUGUST
4-5-6-7 .... Lethbridge
13-14-15-16 .... Med. Hat
23-24-25-26. Idaho Falls
27-28-29 .... Billings
SEPTEMBER
2-3 .... Billings

Great Falls
JUNE
16-17-18-19 .... Med. Hat
24-25-26 .... Lethbridge
27-28 .... Helena
JULY
4-5-6 .... Helena
16-17-18-19 .... Ogden
21-22-23-24 . Idaho Falls
25-26 .... Helena
AUGUST
4-5-6-7 .... Billings
8-9-10-11 .... Butte
17-18-19 ...... Lethbridge
21-22 .... Medicine Hat

30-31 .... Medicine Hat
SEPTEMBER
1 .... Medicine Hat

Helena
JUNE
16-17-18-19 . Lethbridge
20-21-22-23. Great Falls
29-30 .... Medicine Hat
JULY
8-9-10-11 .... Idaho Falls
12-13-14-15 .... Ogden
28-29-30 ...... Great Falls
31 .... Butte
AUGUST
1-2-3 .... Butte
13-14-15-16 ...... Billings
21-22 .... Lethbridge
28-29 .... Medicine Hat
30-31 .... Lethbridge
SEPTEMBER
1 .... Lethbridge
2-3 .... Medicine Hat

Idaho Falls
JUNE
19-20-21 .... Billings
22-23 .... Ogden
29-30 .... Billings
JULY
4-5-6 .... Butte
12-13-14-15 ... Med. Hat
17-18-19-20 . Lethbridge
29-30 .... Ogden
AUGUST
9-10-11-12 .... Helena
13-14-15-16. Great Falls
21-22 .... Billings
27-28-29 .... Ogden
30-31 .... Butte
SEPTEMBER
1 .... Butte
2-3 .... Ogden

Lethbridge
JUNE
20-21-22-23... Med. Hat
29-30 .... Great Falls
JULY
1-2-3 .... Helena

8-9-10-11 .... Billings
12-13-14-15 .... Butte
28-29-30 ...... Med. Hat
31 .... Idaho Falls
AUGUST
1-2-3 .... Idaho Falls
13-14-15-16........ Ogden
20 .... Great Falls
23-24-25 .... Helena
26-27-28-29. Great Falls
SEPTEMBER
2-3 .... Great Falls

Medicine Hat
JUNE
24-25-26 .... Helena
27-28 .... Lethbridge
JULY
1-2-3 .... Great Falls
4-5-6 .... Lethbridge
17-18-19-20 ...... Billings
21-22-23-24 .... Butte
26-27 .... Lethbridge
AUGUST
4-5-6-7 .... Idaho Falls
9-10-11-12 .... Ogden
17-18-19-20 ...... Helena
23-24-25 ...... Great Falls
26-27 .... Helena

Ogden
JUNE
16-17-18 ...... Idaho Falls
24-25 .... Idaho Falls
26-27-28 .... Billings
29-30 .... Butte
JULY
8-9-10-11 .... Med. Hat
21-22-23-24 . Lethbridge
25-26-27-28. Idaho Falls
31 .... Great Falls
AUGUST
1-2-3 .... Great Falls
4-5-6-7 .... Helena
18-19-20-21-22 .....Butte
30-31 .... Billings
SEPTEMBER
1 .... Billings

Independent Leagues

1997 STANDINGS

*Split-season champion

Big South League

	W	L	PCT	GB		W	L	PCT	GB
Tupelo	43	19	.678	—	*Meridian	33	29	.532	10
*Greenville	39	21	.650	3	Tullahoma	9	55	.148	35

PLAYOFFS: Finals (best-of-5)—Greenville defeated Meridian 3-0.

Frontier League

EAST	W	L	PCT	GB	WEST	W	L	PCT	GB
*Johnstown	47	33	.588	—	*Evansville	46	33	.582	—
*Canton	45	35	.563	2	*Richmond	43	37	.538	3½
Chillicothe	41	38	.519	5	Springfield	42	37	.532	4
Ohio Valley	21	59	.263	26	Kalamazoo	33	46	.418	13

PLAYOFFS: Semifinals (best-of-3)—Canton defeated Johnstown 2-0; Evansville defeated Richmond 2-1. **Finals** (best-of-3)—Canton defeated Evansville 2-0.

Heartland League

NORTH	W	L	PCT	GB	SOUTH	W	L	PCT	GB
*Altoona	36	36	.500	—	**Tennessee	55	15	.786	—
*Anderson	33	36	.478	1½	Columbia	39	31	.557	16
Will County	31	39	.443	4	Clarksville	32	40	.444	24
Lafayette	30	41	.423	5½	Dubois County	27	45	.375	29

PLAYOFFS: Semifinals (best-of-3)—Anderson defeated Altoona 2-0; Columbia defeated Tennessee 2-1. **Finals** (best-of-5)—Columbia defeated Anderson 3-1.

Northeast League

NORTH	W	L	PCT	GB	SOUTH	W	L	PCT	GB
*Albany	51	33	.607	—	*Waterbury	46	37	.554	—
*Massachusetts	45	37	.549	5	*Elmira	44	38	.537	1½
Adirondack	45	38	.542	5½	Allentown	39	43	.476	6½
Bangor	40	43	.482	10½	Catskill	21	62	.253	25

PLAYOFFS: Semifinals (best-of-3)—Albany defeated Massachusetts 2-0; Elmira defeated Waterbury 2-0. **Finals** (best-of-3)—Elmira defeated Albany 2-0.

Northern League

EAST	W	L	PCT	GB	WEST	W	L	PCT	GB
*St. Paul	45	39	.536	—	*Winnipeg	53	30	.639	—
*Duluth-Superior	39	44	.470	5	Sioux City	50	34	.595	3½
Thunder Bay	36	48	.429	9	*Fargo-Moorhead	47	37	.560	6½
Madison	34	50	.405	11	Sioux Falls	31	53	.369	22½

PLAYOFFS: Semifinals (best-of-5)—Duluth-Superior defeated St. Paul 3-2; Winnipeg defeated Fargo-Moorhead 3-2. **Finals** (best-of-5)—Duluth-Superior defeated Winnipeg 3-2.

Prairie League

NORTH	W	L	PCT	GB	SOUTH	W	L	PCT	GB
*Regina	39	27	.591	—	*Southern Minny	42	24	.636	—
*Saskatoon	38	28	.576	1	*Minot	43	28	.606	1½
Moose Jaw	16	25	.390	10½	Grand Forks	33	34	.493	9½
West Man	16	45	.262	25½	Aberdeen	27	43	.386	17

PLAYOFFS: Semifinals (best-of-3)—Regina defeated Saskatoon 2-1; Minot defeated Southern Minny 2-0. **Finals** (best-of-5)—Minot defeated Regina 3-0.

Texas-Louisiana League

	W	L	PCT	GB		W	L	PCT	GB
*Amarillo	55	33	.625	—	Rio Grande Valley	39	49	.443	16
Tyler	48	40	.545	7	Lubbock	38	50	.432	17
*Alexandria	48	40	.545	7	Abilene	36	52	.409	19

PLAYOFFS: Finals (best-of-5)—Alexandria defeated Amarillo 3-1.

Western League

NORTH	W	L	PCT	GB	SOUTH	W	L	PCT	GB
**Reno	55	35	.611	—	**Sonoma County	56	34	.622	—
Grays Harbor	49	41	.544	6	Chico	45	45	.500	11
Bend	39	51	.433	16	Salinas	43	47	.478	13
Tri-Cities	34	56	.378	21	Mission Viejo	39	51	.433	17

PLAYOFFS: Semifinals (best-of-3)—Reno defeated Grays Harbor 2-1; Chico defeated Sonoma County 2-1. **Finals** (best-of-5)—Chico defeated Reno 3-1.

INDEPENDENT LEAGUES

ATLANTIC LEAGUE

Mailing Address: 31 Turner Lane, West Chester, PA 19380. **Telephone:** (610) 696-8662. **FAX:** (610) 696-8667. **E-Mail Address:** atllg@aol.com.
Year Founded: 1998.
Chairman: Frank Boulton. **President:** Bud Harrelson. **Corporate Secretary/General Counsel:** Tony Rosenthal.
Executive Director/Director, Player Development: Joe Klein. **Assistant Director, Player Development:** Ben Fonseca.
1998 Opening Date: May 20. **Closing Date:** Sept. 6.
Regular Season: 100 games.
Playoff Format: Unavailable.
All-Star Game: July 15 at Atlantic City.
Roster Limit: 27 (23 active). **Eligibility Rule:** No restrictions.

ATLANTIC CITY SURF

Office Address: 545 North Albany Ave., Atlantic City, NJ 08401. **Telephone:** (609) 344-7873. **FAX:** (609) 344-7010.
Operated by: Atlantic City Surf Professional Baseball Club, Inc.
President/General Manager: Ken Shepherd. **Assistant General Manager:** Dave Gardner. **Director, Ticket Sales:** Mark Porch. **Representative, Ticket Sales:** Joe Harrington. **Director, Media Relations/Broadcasting:** Ryan Patrick.
Manager: Doc Edwards. **Pitching Coach:** Unavailable.

BRIDGEPORT BLUEFISH

Office Address: 500 Main St., Bridgeport, CT 06604. **Telephone:** (203) 333-1608. **FAX:** (203) 333-1610.
Operated by: Bridgeport Bluefish Professional Baseball Club, LLC.
Principal Owners: Mary-Jane Foster, Mickey Herbert, Jack McGregor, Ken Paul, Bridgeport Waterfront Investors.
Senior Vice President: Ken Paul.
General Manager: Charlie Dowd. **Assistant General Manager:** John Brandt. **Director, Sales/Marketing:** Mike Burke. **Director, Public/Media Relations:** Steve Schoenfeld. **Director, Community Relations/Promotions:** Rachael DiLauro. **Director, Merchandising:** Dave Fowler.
Manager: Willie Upshaw. **Pitching Coach:** Unavailable.

NASHUA PRIDE

Office Address: 100 Main St. #1, Nashua, NH 03060. **Telephone:** (603) 883-2255. **FAX:** (603) 883-0880.
Operated by: Nashua Pride Professional Baseball, LLC.
Principal Owner/President: Chris English.
General Manager: Billy Johnson. **Manager, Promotions:** Andy Taylor. **Manager, Group Events:** Chris Ames. **Manager, Business Development:** David Ryan. **Manager, Baseball Operations:** Jim Cardello.
Manager: Mike Easler. **Coach:** Jim Cardello.

NEWARK BEARS

Office Address: P.O. Box 6, Creskill, NJ 07626. **Telephone:** (203) 333-1608. **FAX:** (203) 333-1610.
Owned/Operated by: Newark Bears Professional Baseball Club, Inc.
President: Rick Cerone.
Manager: Tom O'Malley.

NEWBURGH BLACK DIAMONDS

Office Address: 375 Washington St., Newburgh, NY 12550. **Telephone:** (914) 565-2288. **FAX:** (914) 565-1379.
Operated by: Lehigh Valley Professional Sports Clubs, Inc.
President: Tom Flaherty.
General Manager: Ross Vecchio. **Assistant General Manager:** Gary Rigley. **Director, Newburgh Operations:** Jack Tracz.
Manager: Wayne Krenchicki. **Pitching Coach:** Steve Foucault.

SOMERSET PATRIOTS

Office Address: 20 West Main St., Somerville, NJ 08876. **Mailing Address:** P.O. Box 543, Somerville NJ 08876. **Telephone:** (908) 252-0700. **FAX:** (908) 252-0776.
Operated by: Somerset Patriots Professional Baseball Club, LLC.
Principal Owners: Steven Kalafer, Michael Kalafer, Jack Cust, Byron Brisby.
Chairman: Steven Kalafer. **President:** Michael Kalafer.
General Manager: David Gasaway. **Director, Player Procurement:** Jim Frey.
Manager: Sparky Lyle. **Player-Coach:** Dane Lyle.

Mailing Address: P.O. Box 2662, Zanesville, OH 43702. **Telephone:** (740) 452-7400. **FAX:** (740) 452-2999.

Year Founded: 1993.

Commissioner: Bill Lee. **President:** Chris Hanners (Chillicothe). **Vice President:** Doug James (Kalamazoo). **Treasurer:** Bob Wolfe.

Administrative Assistant: Kathy Lee. **Supervisor of Umpires:** Jim Schaly.

1998 Opening Date: June 4. **Closing Date:** Aug. 31.

Regular Season: 80 games (split-schedule).

Division Structure: East—Canton, Chillicothe, Johnstown, Ohio Valley. **West**—Evansville, Kalamazoo, Richmond, Springfield.

Playoff Format: First-half division winners play second-half division winners in best-of-3 playoff. Winners meet in best-of-3 series for league championship.

All-Star Game: July 20, site unavailable.

Roster Limit: 22 minimum, 24 maximum. **Eligibility Rule:** Minimum of 11 first-year players; maximum of eight players with one year of professional experience; maximum of three with unlimited experience. No player may be 27 before June 1, 1998.

CANTON CROCODILES

Office Address: 2501 Allen Ave. SE, Canton, OH 44707. **Telephone:** (330) 455-2255. **FAX:** (330) 454-4835.

Operated by: Canton Frontier League Baseball, LLC.

Managing Partners: Richard Ehrenreich, Pete Heitman, Matt Perry.

General Manager: Joe Scrivner. **Assistant General Manager/ Marketing, Communications:** Tom Delamater. **Assistant General Manager, Sales:** Bob Jones. **Director, Operations:** Chip Meiers. **Assistant, Operations:** Neil Swanson. **Director, Ticket Sales:** Matt Miloch. **Manager:** Unavailable. **Pitching Coach:** Mike Arner.

Stadium Name: Thurman Munson Memorial Stadium. **Standard Game Times:** 7:05 p.m.; Sun. 6:05.

CHILLICOTHE PAINTS

Office Address: 59 North Paint St., Chillicothe, OH 45601. **Telephone:** (740) 773-8326. **FAX:** (740) 773-8338.

Operated by: Chillicothe Paints Professional Baseball Association, Inc.

Principal Owner: Chris Hanners. **President:** Shirley Bandy.

General Manager: Bryan Wickline. **Director, Stadium Operations:** Valerie Cook. **Head Groundskeeper:** Ralph Moore. **Director, Community Relations:** Harry Chenault. **Director, Ticket Sales:** Brandi Munn.

Manager/Director, Baseball Operations: Roger Hanners. **Coaches:** Steve Dawes, Marty Dunn. **Pitching Coach:** Eric Welch. **Trainer:** Scott Kaser.

Stadium Name: V.A. Memorial Stadium. **Standard Game Times:** 7:05 p.m.; Sun. 6:05.

EVANSVILLE OTTERS

Office Address: 1701 North Main St., Evansville, IN 47711. **Telephone:** (812) 435-8686. **FAX:** (812) 435-8688.

Operated by: Old Time Sports I, LLC.

President: Charles Jacey Jr.

Executive Vice President/Chief Operating Officer: Curtis Jacey.

General Manager: Jim Miller. **Assistant General Manager:** Pam Miller. **Director, Media Relations/Operations:** Steve Tahsler. **Director, Public Relations:** Taryn Nance. **Director, Special Projects:** Ryan Forim.

Manager: Greg Tagert. **Pitching Coach:** J.R. Seymour. **Trainer:** Wes Keller.

Stadium Name: Bosse Field. **Standard Game Time:** 7:05 p.m.; Sun. 6:05.

JOHNSTOWN JOHNNIES

Office Address: 430 Main St., 2nd Floor, Johnstown, PA 15901. **Telephone:** (814) 536-8326. **FAX:** (814) 539-0056.

Operated by: Johnstown Professional Baseball, Inc.

Principal Owners: Thomas Sullivan, Tom Begel, Tom Lindemuth. **Chairman:** Thomas Sullivan.

President/General Manager: Tom Lindemuth.

Assistant GM/Sales: Brent Martin. **Assistant GM/Promotions:** Patty Sladki. **Head Groundskeeper:** Greg Avramis. **Office Manager:** Dotty Clark.

Manager: Stephan Rapaglia. **Coaches:** John Couture, Dee Dee Osborne. **Director, Player Procurement:** Charlie Sullivan.

Stadium Name: Point Stadium. **Standard Game Times:** 7:05 p.m.; Sun. 6:05.

KALAMAZOO KODIAKS

Office Address: 251 Mills St., Kalamazoo, MI 49003. **Telephone:** (616)

383-4487. **FAX:** (616) 383-4492.

Operated by: Kalamazoo Professional Baseball, LLC.

Principal Owner: James Kuhn. **Chairman:** Doug James.

President/General Manager: John Kuhn. **Assistant General Manager:** John Spolyar. **Director, Media/Community Relations:** Stephanie John. **Director, Ticket Sales:** Michelle Vandenboss.

Manager: Alan Riffle. **Coach:** Don Leppert.

Stadium Name: Sutherland Field. **Standard Game Times:** 7:05 p.m.; Sun. 2:05.

OHIO VALLEY REDCOATS

Mailing Address: P.O. Box 1583, Parkersburg, WV 26102. **Telephone:** (304) 422-0426. **FAX:** (304) 422-2791.

Operated by: Ohio Valley Redcoats Professional Baseball Inc.

President: Jim Nelson.

General Manager: Steve Swisher. **Head Groundskeeper:** J.C. McGee. **Director, Ticket Sales:** Dave Satow.

Manager: Greg LeMaster. **Trainer:** Troy Nelson.

Stadium Name: Bennett Stump Field. **Standard Game Times:** 7:05 p.m.; Sun. 6:05.

RICHMOND ROOSTERS

Mailing Address: 201 NW 13th St., Richmond, IN 47374. **Telephone:** (765) 935-7529. **FAX:** (765) 962-7047.

Ownership, Management

Operated by: Richmond Baseball, LLC.

Managing Partner/Director, Baseball Operations: John Cate.

Director, Business Operations: Duke Ward. **Account Executive:** Gary Kitchel. **Food Service:** Deanna Beaman. **Ticket Sales:** Sam Hodges.

Manager: John Cate. **Coach:** Morgan Burkhart. **Pitching Coach:** Bill Richardson. **Trainer:** Scott Lambert.

Stadium Name: Don McBride Stadium. **Standard Game Times:** 7:05 p.m.; Sun. 5:05.

SPRINGFIELD CAPITALS

Office Address: 1351 North Grand Ave. East, Springfield, IL 62702. **Telephone:** (217) 525-5500. **FAX:** (217) 525-5508.

Operated by: Hathaway Corporation. **Chairman:** Gary Jones.

General Manager: John Wallenstein. **Director, Business Operations:** Marc Sanson. **Head Groundskeeper:** Larry Rockford. **Director, Sales/Marketing:** Todd Fulk.

Manager: Mal Fichman. **Coach:** Tom Tornicasa. **Director, Baseball Operations/Pitching Coach:** Paul Fletcher.

Stadium Name: Robin Roberts Stadium. **Standard Game Times:** 7:05 p.m.; Sun. 4:05.

HEARTLAND LEAGUE

Mailing Address: 3582 Canterbury Dr., Lafayette, IN 47905. **Telephone:** (765) 474-5341. **FAX:** (765) 474-6462. **E-Mail Address:** swolf8@aol.com.

Year Founded: 1995.

President: David Arch (Cook County). **Vice President:** Ray Rytel (DuBois County). **Treasurer/Corporate Secretary:** Jeff Gamble (Tennessee).

Commissioner: Allen Wolf. **Director of Umpires:** Eric Harmon.

1998 Opening Date: May 29. **Closing Date:** August 22.

Regular Season: 78 games (split-schedule).

Member Clubs: Cook County Cheetahs (Crestwood, Ill.), Dubois County Dragons (Huntingburg, Ind.), Huntington (W.Va.) RailKings, Lafayette (Ind.) Leopards, Tennessee Tomahawks (Winchester, Tenn.), Tupelo (Miss.) Tornado.

Playoff Format: First-half winner plays second-half winner in best-of-3 series for league championship.

Roster Limit: 23. **Eligibility Rule:** No college-eligible players without waiver.

NORTHEAST LEAGUE

Mailing Address: 1306 Davos Pointe, Woodbridge, NY 12789. **Telephone:** (914) 436-0411. **FAX:** (914) 436-6864. **E-Mail Address:** info @ northeastleague.com. **Website:** northeastleague.com.

Year Founded: 1995.

President: Tom Sullivan. **Vice President:** Dean Gyorgy. **Treasurer:** Charles Jacey. **Executive Director:** Michael McGuire.

1998 Opening Date: May 29. **Closing Date:** Sept. 1.

Regular Season: 84 games (split-schedule).

Division Structure: North—Adirondack, Albany, Massachusetts, Waterbury. **South**—Allentown, Catskill, Elmira, New Jersey.

Playoff Format: First-and second- half winners meet in best-of-3 division

series. Winners meet in best-of-3 series for league championship.
Roster Limit: 24. **Player Eligibility Rule:** No restrictions.

ADIRONDACK LUMBERJACKS

Office Address: 15 Dix Ave., Glens Falls, NY 12801. **Telephone:** (518) 743-9618. **FAX:** (518) 743-9721.

Operated by: Old Time Sports II, LLC.

Principal Owner/President: Charles Jacey.

General Manager: Curt Jacey. **Assistant General Manager:** Jim Davidson. **Head Groundskeeper:** Sean Marshall. **Director, Media/Special Projects:** Heather LaVine. **Director, Sales/Community Relations:** Kevin Graber.

Manager/Director, Player Procuremnt: Kevin Graber.

Stadium Name: East Field Stadium. **Standard Game Time:** 7 p.m.

ALBANY-COLONIE DIAMOND DOGS

Office Address: 780 Watervliet-Shaker Rd., Albany, NY 12211. **Telephone:** (513) 869-9234. **FAX:** (518) 869-5291.

Operated by: Diamond Dogs Sports, Inc.

Principal Owner/President: Tom Sullivan.

General Manager: Charlie Voelker. **Vice President, Sales:** Rip Rowan. **Director, Promotions:** Kevin Forrester. **Director, Merchandising:** Erinn McNeil.

Manager/Director, Player Procurement: Charlie Sullivan. **Trainer:** Chris Andriski.

Stadium Name: Heritage Park. **Standard Game Times:** 7 p.m.; Sun. 2.

ALLENTOWN AMBASSADORS

Office Address: 1511-25 Hamilton St., Allentown, PA 18102. **Telephone:** (610) 437-6800. **FAX:** (610) 437-6804.

Operated by: Allentown Ambassadors Professional Baseball Team, Inc.

Principal Owner/President: Peter Karoly.

General Manager: David Hieter. **Controller:** Tom Arnold. **Director, Media/Public Relations:** Karin Crossley. **Director, Promotions:** Barbara Zahn.

Manager: Ed Ott. **Coach:** Denton Lakatosh. **Pitching Coach:** Dean Lakatosh. **Director, Player Procurement:** Joe Calfapietra.

Stadium Name: Bicentennial Park. **Standard Game Times:** 7:05 p.m.; Sun. 2:05.

CATSKILL COUGARS

Office Address: 67 Main St., Mountaindale, NY 12763. **Mailing Address:** P.O. Box 113, Mountaindale, NY 12763. **Telephone:** (914) 436-4263. **FAX:** (914) 436-4722.

Operated by: Sullivan County Baseball.

Principal Owners: Bill Resnick, Patsy Resnick.

General Manager: Mike Babcock. **Assistant General Manager:** Stephanie Findling. **Director, Sales/Marketing:** Steve Pinto. **Director, Ticket Sales:** Richard Feigenbaum. **Director, Stadium Operations:** Benjamin Budd. **Director, Special Projects:** John Lamendella.

Manager: Gates Brown. **Trainer:** Donnie Woods.

Stadium Name: Baxter Stadium. **Standard Game Time:** 7:05 p.m.

ELMIRA PIONEERS

Office Address: 546 Luce St., Elmira, NY 14904. **Telephone:** (607) 734-1270. **FAX:** (607) 734-0891.

Operated by: Elmira Baseball, LLC.

President: John Ervin. **Director, Business Operations:** Steve Ervin.

General Manager: Randy Youmans. **Assistant General Manager:** Rye Pothakos. **Director, Ticket/Group Sales:** Matt Hufnagel. **Director, Marketing:** Joe Kosmicki.

Manager: Dan Shwam. **Assistant Coach:** John Booher. **Batting Coach:** Rick Sellers. **Pitching Coach:** Frank Gonzales. **First Base Coach:** Bill Limoncelli. **Trainer:** Chad Mathieu.

Stadium Name: Dunn Field. **Standard Game Times:** 7:05 p.m.; Sun. 5:05.

MASSACHUSETTS MAD DOGS

Office Address: 359 Western Ave., Lynn, MA 01904. **Mailing Address:** P.O. Box 8292, Lynn, MA 01904. **Telephone:** (781) 592-2255. **FAX:** (781) 592-8814.

Operated by: Flyball, Inc.

Principal Owner/Chairman: Jonathan Fleisig. **President/General Manager:** Michael Kardamis.

Director, Business Operations: Peter Oldytowski. **Director, Stadium Operations:** Robert Ruggiero. **Director, Group Sales:** Travis Ellingson.

Manager/Director, Player Procurement: George Scott. **Coach:** Tom Donahue. **Trainer:** William Coffee.

Stadium Name: Fraser Field. **Standard Game Times:** 7:05 p.m.; Sun.

6:05.

NEW JERSEY JACKALS

Office Address: One Hall Dr., Little Falls, NJ 07424. **Telephone:** (973) 746-3131.

Operated by: Floyd Hall Enterprises, LLC.

Principal Owner/Chairman: Floyd Hall. **President:** Greg Lockard.

General Manager: Leo Kirk. **Director, Business Operations:** Jennifer Fertig. **Head Groundskeeper:** Larry Castoro. **Director, Food Services:** Jim Aldworth. **Office Manager:** Anita Wall.

Manager/Director, Player Procurement: Kash Beauchamp.

Stadium Name: Yogi Berra Stadium. **Standard Game Times:** 7:35 p.m.; Sun. 6:35.

WATERBURY SPIRIT

Office Address: 1200 Watertown Ave., Waterbury, CT 06722. **Mailing Address:** P.O. Box 1876, Waterbury, CT 06722. **Telephone:** (203) 419-0393. **FAX:** (203) 419-0396.

Operated by: WC Sports, LLC.

Principal Owner/Chairman: David Carpenter. **President:** Bob Wirz.

General Manager: Russ Ardolina. **Assistant General Manager:** Jay Baldacci. **Director, Marketing:** Mike Weisbart. **Director, Media/Public Relations:** Ryan Piurek. **Director, Food Services:** Joe Caiazzo.

Manager: Stan Hough.

Stadium Name: Municipal Stadium. **Standard Game Times:** 7:05 p.m.; Sun 2:05, (July-Aug) 5:05.

NORTHERN LEAGUE

Office Address: 524 South Duke St., Durham, NC 27701. **Mailing Address:** P.O. Box 1282, Durham, NC 27702. **Telephone:** (919) 956-8150. **FAX:** (919) 683-2693. **E-Mail Address:** northernlg@earthlink.net.

Year Founded: 1993.

President/Commissioner: Miles Wolff. **Executive Director:** Dan Moushon. **Supervisor, Umpires:** Butch Fisher.

Director, Baseball Operations: Nick Belmonte, 16395 Malibu Drive, Fort Lauderdale, FL 33326. Telephone: (954) 389-5286. FAX: (954) 389-5128.

1998 Opening Date: May 28. **Closing Date:** Sept. 2.

Regular Season: 86 games (split-schedule).

Division Structure: East—Duluth-Superior, Madison, St. Paul, Thunder Bay. **West**—Fargo-Moorhead, Sioux City, Sioux Falls, Winnipeg.

All-Star Game: Aug. 3 at Sioux City.

Playoff Format: First-half division winners play second-half division winners in best-of-5 playoff series. Winners meet in best-of-5 league championship series.

Roster Limit: 22. **Eligibility Rule:** Minimum of five first-year players; maximum of four veterans (at least four years of professional service).

DULUTH-SUPERIOR DUKES

Office Address: 207 West Superior St., Suite 206, Duluth, MN 55802. **Mailing Address:** P.O. Box 205, Duluth, MN 55801. **Telephone:** (218) 727-4525. **FAX:** (218) 727-4533. **E-Mail Address:** hitnrun@dsdukes.com. **Website:** www.dsdukes.com.

Years in League: 1993-

Ownership, Management

Operated By: Dukes Baseball Corp.

President/Chief Executive Officer: Jim Wadley.

Vice President/General Manager: Bob Gustafson. **Director, Stadium Operations:** Rob Hargraves. **Director, Media Relations:** Dave McMillan. **Head Groundskeeper:** Ray Adameak.

Manager: George Mitterwald. **Coach:** Jackie Hernandez. **Pitching Coach:** Mike Cuellar. **Trainer:** Chris Gebeck.

Game Information

Radio Announcer: Unavailable. **No. of Games Broadcast:** Home—43, Away—43. **Flagship Station:** 104.3/106.3-FM.

Stadium Name: Wade Stadium. **Location:** I-35 to 40th Ave. West exit, three blocks west to Grand Avenue, right six blocks to 34th Avenue, right two blocks to park. **Standard Game Times:** 7:05 p.m.; Sun. 2:05.

Visiting Club Hotel: Black Bear Hotel, 1789 Highway 210, Carlton, MN 55718. Telephone: (218) 878-7400.

FARGO-MOORHEAD REDHAWKS

Office Address: 1515 15th Ave. North, Fargo, ND 58102. **Mailing Address:** P.O. Box 5258, Fargo, ND 58105. **Telephone:** (701) 235-6161. **FAX:** (701) 297-9247. **E-Mail Address:** redhawks@fmredhawks.com. **Website:** www.fmredhawks.com.

Years in League: 1996-

Ownership, Management
Operated by: Fargo Baseball, LLC.
Principal Owners: Mid-States Development Corp., Gene Allen.
President: Bruce Thom.
Vice President/General Manager: John Dittrich. **Assistant General Manager:** Tim Flakoll. **Ticket/Office Manager:** Lois Dittrich. **Manager, Accounting:** Trish Wiste. **Assistant Manager, Accounting:** Jeremy Lewis. **Director, Advertising:** Jan Plaude. **Director, Promotions:** Kris Breuer. **Assistant Director, Promotions:** Josh Krueger. **Director, Media Relations:** Josh Buchholz. **Director, Community Relations:** Nate Hancock. **Director, Merchandising:** Chris Coste.
Manager/Director, Player Procurement: Doug Simunic. **Pitching Coach:** Jeff Bittiger. **Trainer:** Leo Dougherty.

Game Information
Radio Announcer: Jack Michaels. **No. of Games Broadcast:** Home—43, Away—43. **Flagship Station:** KVOX 1280-AM.
Stadium Name: Newman Outdoor Field. **Location:** I-29 North to 19th Avenue North (exit 67), right (east) on 19th to FargoDome, right on Albrecht Avenue, four blocks to stadium. **Standard Game Times:** 7:05 p.m.; Sun. 2:05.
Visiting Club Hotel: Comfort Inn-West, 3825 9th Ave. SW, Fargo, ND 58103. Telephone: (701) 282-9596.

MADISON BLACK WOLF
Office Address: 2920 North Sherman Ave., Madison, WI 53704. **Telephone:** (608) 244-5666. **FAX:** (608) 244-6996. **E-Mail Address:** madwolf@madwolf.com. **Website:** www.madwolf.com.
Years in League: 1996-

Ownership, Management
Operated by: Madison Baseball, LLC.
Chairman: Patrick Sweeney.
President/General Manager: Bill Terlecky. **Director, Baseball Operations:** Ryan Richeal. **Director, Media/Public Relations:** Jennifer Watkins. **Director, Sales/Marketing:** Jason McCaffrey. **Director, Community Relations:** Stephane Dionne.
Manager: Al Gallagher. **Pitching Coach:** Dennis Burtt. **Trainer:** Justin Byers.

Game Information
Stadium Name: Warner Park. **Location:** From south, I-90 north to Highway 30, exit onto Northport Drive, left on Sherman Avenue. From north, I-90 south to Highway 151 south, exit onto Aberg Avenue to Northport Drive, left on Sherman Avenue. **Standard Game Times:** 7 p.m.; Sun. 1:30.
Visiting Club Hotel: Econo Lodge, 4726 East Washington Ave., Madison, WI 53704. Telephone: (608) 241-4171.

ST. PAUL SAINTS
Office Address: 1771 Energy Park Dr., St. Paul, MN 55108. **Telephone:** (612) 644-3517. **FAX:** (612) 644-1627. **E-Mail Address:** funsgood@spsaints.com. **Website:** www.spsaints.com.
Years in League: 1993-

Ownership, Management
Operated by: St. Paul Saints Baseball Club, Inc.
Principal Owners: Marvin Goldklang, Mike Veeck, Bill Murray, Van Schley.
Chairman: Marvin Goldklang. **President:** Mike Veeck.
General Manager: Bill Fanning. **Director, Operations:** Tom Whaley. **Bookkeeper:** Pat Cunningham. **Director, Stadium Operations:** Bob Klepperich. **Head Groundskeeper:** Connie Rudolph. **Director, Media/Public Relations:** Eric Webster. **Director, Sales/Marketing:** Bob St. Pierre. **Director, Community Relations:** Jody Beaulieu. **Director, Promotions:** Elizabeth Adams. **Director, Merchandising:** Bill Fisher. **Director, Food Services:** John Marso, Steven Marso.
Manager/Director, Player Procurement: Marty Scott. **Batting Coach:** Barry Moss. **Coach:** Wayne Terwilliger.

Game Information
Radio Announcers: Jim Lucas, Don Wardlow. **No. of Games Broadcast:** Home—43, Away—43. **Flagship Station:** KKMS-980 AM.
Stadium Name: Midway Stadium. **Location:** From I-94, north on Snelling Avenue, west on Energy Park Drive to stadium. **Standard Game Times:** 7:05 p.m.; Sun. 2:05.
Visiting Club Hotel: Ramada Hotel, 2540 North Cleveland Ave., Roseville, MN 55113. Telephone: (612) 636-4567.

SIOUX CITY EXPLORERS
Office Address: 3400 Line Dr., Sioux City, IA 51106. **Telephone:** (712)

277-9467. **FAX:** (712) 277-9406.
    Year in League: 1993-

Ownership, Management
    Operated by: Sioux City Explorers Baseball Club LLC.
    Principal Owner/President: Ed Nottle.
    Vice President/General Manager: Tim Utrup. **Controller:** Joe Hecht.
Head Groundskeeper: Eugene Carlson. **Director, Sales/Marketing:** Kevin
Farlow. **Director, Ticket Sales:** Paxton Bennett. **Director, Group Sales:**
Kerry White. **Ticket Account Executive:** Shane Caldwell.
    Manager: Ed Nottle. **Pitching Coach:** Lee Stange. **Trainer:** Mike Wright.
Director, Player Procurement: Harry Stavrenos.

Game Information
    Radio Announcers: Brian Dolgin, Joe Hecht. **No. of Games
Broadcast:** Home—43, Away—43. **Flagship Station:** KSCJ 1360-AM.
    Stadium Name: Lewis and Clark Park. **Location:** I-29 to Industrial Road
North, right at Line Drive. **Standard Game Times:** 7:05 p.m.; Sun. 6:05.
    Visiting Club Hotel: Best Western, 130 Nebraska St., Sioux City, IA
51101. **Telephone:** (712) 277-1550.

SIOUX FALLS CANARIES
    Office Address: 1001 North West Ave., Sioux Falls, SD 57104. **Mailing
Address:** P.O. Box 84412, Sioux Falls, SD 57118. **Telephone:** (605) 333-
0179. **FAX:** (605) 333-0139. **E-Mail Address:** canaries@iw.net. **Website:**
www.iw.net/canaries.
    Years in League: 1993-

Ownership, Management
    Operated By: Sioux Falls Canaries Professional Baseball.
    Principal Owners: Marvin Goldklang, Mike Veeck.
    Chairman: Marvin Goldklang. **President:** Mike Veeck.
    General Manager: Ripper Hatch. **Assistant General Managers:** Larry
McKenney, George Stavrenos. **Director, Ticket Sales:** Brad Seymour.
Director, Group Sales: Joel Elesland.
    Manager: Unavailable. **Coaches:** Unavailable.

Game Information
    Radio Announcer: Unavailable. **No. of Games Broadcast:** Home—43,
Away—43. **Flagship Station:** KWSN 1230-AM.
    Stadium Name: Sioux Falls Stadium. **Location:** I-29 to Russell Street
exit, 1¼ miles to West Avenue, right on West. **Standard Game Times:** 7:05
p.m.; Sun. 1:35.
    Visiting Club Hotel: Comfort Inn, 3216 South Carolyn Ave., Sioux Falls,
SD 57106. **Telephone:** (605) 361-2822.

THUNDER BAY WHISKEY JACKS
    Office Address: 425 Winnipeg Ave., Thunder Bay, Ontario P7B 6B7.
Mailing Address: P.O. Box 864, Station F, Thunder Bay, Ontario P7C 4X7.
Telephone: (807) 344-5225. **FAX:** (807) 343-4611.
    Years in League: 1993-

Ownership, Management
    Principal Owner: Whiskey Jack Partners LP.
    Operated By: Sports Capital Management Inc.
    President: Bill Terlecky.
    Vice President/General Manager: Rob Trippe. **Director, Promotions:**
Thomas Ruttan. **Director, Ticket Sales:** Jennifer Bilous. **Director, Baseball
Administration:** Pat Tilmon.
    Manager: Jay Ward.

Game Information
    Radio Announcer: Unavailable. **No. of Games Broadcast:** Home—12,
Away—16. **Flagship Station:** CKPR 580-AM.
    Stadium Name: Port Arthur Stadium. **Location:** Highway 61 North, right
onto Harbour Expressway, left on Memorial Ave., ballpark one mile north on
left. **Standard Game Times:** 7:05 p.m.; Sun. 6:05.
    Visiting Club Hotel: Prince Arthur Hotel, 17 North Cumberland St.,
Thunder Bay, Ontario P7A 4K8. **Telephone:** (807) 345-5411.

WINNIPEG GOLDEYES
    Office Address: 1430 Maroons Rd., Winnipeg, Manitoba R3G 0L5.
Telephone: (204) 982-2273. **FAX:** (204) 982-2274. **E-Mail Address:** gold-
eyes@mts.net. **Website:** www.goldeyes.aroundmanitoba.com.
    Years in League: 1994-

Ownership, Management
    President/Principal Owner: Sam Katz.
    General Manager: John Hindle. **Vice President, Finance:** Andrew
Collier. **Director, Communications:** Jonathan Green. **Director, Sales/
Marketing:** Kevin Moore. **Director, Promotions:** Barb McTavish. **Director,**

Ticket Sales: Dennis McLean.

Manager: Hal Lanier. **Coach:** Scott Neiles. **Pitching Coach:** Bob Kipper.

Game Information

Radio Announcer: Paul Edmonds. **No. of Games Broadcast:** Home—26, Away—26. **Flagship Station:** CJOB 680-AM.

Stadium Name: Winnipeg Stadium. **Location:** North on Pembina Highway (Highway 75), west on McGillivray Boulevard, north on Kenaston Boulevard, east on Ness Ave, north on St. James Street, east on Maroons Road to stadium. **Standard Game Times:** 7:05 p.m.; Sun. 1:35.

Visiting Club Hotel: Ramada Marlborough, 331 Smith St., Winnipeg, Manitoba R3B 2G9. Telephone: (204) 942-6411.

TEXAS-LOUISIANA LEAGUE

Mailing Address: 401 Cypress St., Suite 300, Abilene, TX 79601. **Telephone:** (915) 673-7364. **FAX:** (915) 673-5074. **E-Mail Address:** baseball@txproball.com.

Year Founded: 1994.

President: Byron Pierce. **Vice President/Chief Executive Officer:** Rick Ivey. **Administrative Assistants:** Jay Hansen, Chad Holt.

1998 Opening Date: May 21. **Closing Date:** Aug. 31.

Regular Season: 84 games.

All-Star Game: July 13 at Fort Worth.

Playoff Format: Top two teams meet in best-of-5 league championship series.

Roster Limit: 22.

ABILENE PRAIRIE DOGS

Office Address: 401 Cypress St., Suite 300, Abilene, TX 79601. **Telephone:** (915) 673-7364. **FAX:** (915) 673-5051.

Operated by: Abilene Baseball, LLC.

Chairman: Horn Chen.

President/General Manager: Byron Pierce. **Assistant GM/Sales and Marketing:** Bruce Unrue. **Assistant GM/Stadium Operations:** Mindy Cheek. **Director, Baseball Operations:** Travis Hartgraves.

Manager: Barry Jones. **Trainer:** Richard Vandever.

Stadium Name: Crutcher-Scott Field. **Standard Game Time:** 7:05 p.m.

ALEXANDRIA ACES

Office Address: 1 Babe Ruth Dr., Alexandria, LA 71301. **Mailing Address:** P.O. Box 6005, Alexandria, LA 71307. **Telephone:** (318) 473-2237. **FAX:** (318) 473-2229.

Operated by: Alexandria Baseball Club, LC.

General Manager: Craig Brasfield. **Assistant General Manager:** Reldon Owens. **Director, Stadium Operations:** Jodie White. **Head Groundskeeper:** John Hickman. **Director, Sales/Media Relations:** Todd Carter. **Director, Group Sales/Promotions:** Carroll DeMas.

Manager: Stan Cliburn. **Coach:** Walter Guillory. **Trainer:** Mike Palumbo.

Stadium Name: Bringhurst Field. **Standard Game Time:** 6:35 p.m.

AMARILLO DILLAS

Street Address: 501 West 9th St., Amarillo, TX 79101. **Mailing Address:** P.O. Box 31241, Amarillo, TX 79120. **Telephone:** (806) 342-3455. **FAX:** (806) 374-2269.

Operated by: Amarillo Baseball Club, LC.

Executive General Manager: Bob Miller. **Assistant General Manager:** Dena Lambert. **Director, Media/Public Relations:** Richard Durrett. **Account Representative:** Daren Brown. **Director, Community Relations:** Stephanie Ollinger. **Director, Group Sales:** Elisa Franco.

Manager: Glenn Wilson. **Pitching Coach:** Al Kermode.

Stadium Name: Potter County Memorial Stadium. **Standard Game Times:** 7:05 p.m.; Sun. 5:05.

BAYOU BULLFROGS

Mailing Address: 601 West Congress St., Lafayette, LA 70501. **Telephone:** (318) 233-0998. **FAX:** (318) 237-3539.

General Manager: Ryan Gribble. **Director, Group Sales:** Lydia Bergeron. **Director, Media/Broadcasting:** Doug Greenwald. **Director, Ticket Operations:** Jim Tennison.

Manager: Unavailable. **Trainer:** Unavailable.

Stadium Name: Moore Field. **Standard Game Time:** Unavailable.

GREENVILLE BLUESMEN

Mailing Address: 119 North Broadway, Greenville, MS 38701. **Telephone:** (601) 335-2583. **FAX:** (601) 335-7742.

Operated by: Greenville Professional Club, LLC.

President: George Hood.

General Manager: Arthur O'Bright. **Assistant General Manager/Sales:**

Jeff Brown. **Director, Sales/Marketing:** Todd Merton.
  Manager: Unavailable. **Trainer:** Unavailable.
  Stadium Name: Legion Field. **Standard Game Times:** Unavailable.

LUBBOCK CRICKETS

  Office Address: 1605 Broadway, Lubbock, TX 79401. **Mailing Address:** P.O. Box 2608, Lubbock, TX 79408. **Telephone:** (806) 749-2255. **FAX:** (806) 749-6625.
  General Manager: Bob Flanagan. **Assistant GM/Sales/Marketing:** Anthony DeVincenzo. **Assistant GM/Ticket Sales:** Ryan Ferguson. **Director, Baseball Operations:** Alex Geche.
  Manager/Director, Player Procurement: Glenn Sullivan.
  Stadium Name: Dan Law Field. **Standard Game Times:** 7:05 p.m.; Sun. 6:05.

RIO GRANDE VALLEY WHITEWINGS

  Mailing Address: 1216 Fair Park Blvd., Harlingen, TX 78550. **Telephone:** (956) 412-9464. **FAX:** (956) 412-9479.
  General Manager: Andy Berg. **Director, Business Operations:** Marilyn Farley. **Director, Stadium Operations:** Russ Tefertiller. **Director, Public Relations:** Erin Cassity.
  Manager: Unavailable. **Trainer:** Unavailable.
  Stadium Name: Harlingen Field. **Standard Game Times:** 7:05 p.m.

WESTERN LEAGUE

  Mailing Address: P.O. Box 19555, Portland, OR 97280. **Telephone:** (503) 203-8557. **FAX:** (503) 203-8438. **E-Mail Address:** office@western-baseball.com.
  Year Founded: 1995.
  President: Bruce Engel. **Treasurer/Corporate Secretary:** Bob Linscheid. **Executive Director:** Tom Kowitz.
  1998 Opening Date: May 22. **Closing Date:** Sept. 2.
  Regular Season: 90 games (split-schedule).
  Division Structure: North—Bend, Grays Harbor, Reno, Tri-City. **South**—Chico, Mission Viejo, Pacific, Sonoma County.
  Playoff Format: First-half division winners meet second-half winners in best-of-3 division series. Winners meet in best-of-5 league championship series.
  All-Star Game: July 13 at Chico.
  Roster Limit: 22. **Player Eligibility Rule:** Minimum of five first-year players; maximum of six veterans (five or more years of professional service).

BEND BANDITS

  Office Address: 1012 NW Wall St., Suite 250, Bend, OR 97701. **Mailing Address:** P.O. Box 1027, Bend, OR 97709. **Telephone:** (541) 383-1983. **FAX:** (541) 383-2004.
  Operated by: Central Oregon Professional Baseball, Inc. **President:** Dave Alden.
  General Manager: Mike Smith. **Co-General Manager:** Dean Stiles. **Director, Business Operations:** Larry Hix. **Director, Stadium Operations:** Jude Quilter. **Director, Media/Public Relations:** Tom Hamilton. **Office Manager:** Linda Longwell.
  Manager: Wally Backman. **Pitching Coach:** Chuck Clair.
  Stadium Name: Vince Genna Stadium. **Standard Game Times:** 6:35 p.m.; Sun. 5:35.

CHICO HEAT

  Street Address: 250 Vallombrosa Ave., Suite 200, Chico, CA 95926. **Mailing Address:** P.O. Box 5362, Chico, CA 95927. **Telephone:** (530) 343-4328. **FAX:** (530) 894-1799.
  Operated by: Chico Heat Baseball Club, LLC.
  President: Steve Nettleton.
  Vice President/General Manager: Bob Linscheid. **Vice President, Sales and Marketing:** Jeff Kragel. **Controller:** Allan Guidi. **Director, Media Relations/Group Sales:** Rory Miller. **Director, Ticket Sales:** Brian Ceccon.
  Manager: Bill Plummer. **Pitching Coach:** Jeff Pico. **Trainer:** Jason Bennett.
  Stadium Name: Nettleton Stadium. **Standard Game Times:** 7:05 p.m.

GRAYS HARBOR GULLS

  Office Address: 101 28th St., Hoquiam WA 98550. **Telephone:** (360) 532-4488. **FAX:** (360) 533-8762.
  Operated by: Hometown Baseball, LLC.
  President: Dale Giles.
  Vice President/General Manager: Pat Brown. **Head Groundskeeper:** Al Dick. **Director, Media/Public Relations:** Mike Warchol.
  Manager: Charley Kerfeld. **Coach:** Dan Madsen. **Pitching Coach:** Mike Voelkel.

Stadium Name: Olympic Stadium. **Standard Game Times:** 7:05 p.m.; Sun. 1:05.

MISSION VIEJO VIGILANTES

Office Address: 27301 La Paz Rd., Mission Viejo, CA 92692. **Telephone:** (714) 699-1616. **FAX:** (714) 699-1620.

Operated by: P&P Sports Enterprises.

President: Patrick Elster.

General Manager: Paula Pyers. **Assistant General Manager:** Bobby Grich. **Director, Media/Public Relations:** Randy Miller.

Manager/Director, Player Procurement: Buck Rodgers. **Trainer:** Brad McReynolds.

Stadium Name: Mission Viejo Stadium. **Standard Game Times:** 6:55 p.m.; Sun. 5:35.

PACIFIC SUNS

Office Address: 210 West Seventh St., Suite C, Oxnard, CA 93030. **Telephone:** (805) 247-9192. **FAX:** (805) 247-1931.

Operated by: Channel Island Sports Management.

President: Don DiCarlo.

General Manager: Michael Begley. **Director, Business Operations:** Mary Pat Trainor. **Director, Stadium Operations:** Tony DiCarlo. **Director, Media/Public Relations:** Paul Regina. **Director, Sales/Marketing:** Peter Erdos. **Director, Community Relations:** Karen DiCarlo. **Director, Promotions:** Leanna Bowman.

Manager: Jim Derrington. **Coach:** Pat Woods. **Pitching Coach:** John Wood. **Director, Player Procurement:** Frank Valdez.

Stadium Name: College Park. **Standard Game Times:** 7:05 p.m.; Sat. 6:05; Sun. 1:20.

RENO CHUKARS

Office Address: 240 West Moana Lane, Reno, NV 89509. **Telephone:** (702) 829-7890. **FAX:** (702) 829-7895.

Operated By: Reno Chukars, LLC.

President: Bruce Engel.

Vice President, Sales/Marketing: Larry Linde. **Director, Promotions/Ticket Sales:** Joe Henderson.

Manager/Director, Player Procurement: Butch Hughes. **Coaches:** John Noce, Tony Muser Jr. **Pitching Coach:** Al Endress. **Trainer:** Jeff Collins.

Stadium Name: Moana Stadium. **Standard Game Times:** 6:35 p.m.; Sun. 5:05.

SONOMA COUNTY CRUSHERS

Office Address: 5900 Labath Ave., Rohnert Park, CA 94928. **Telephone:** (707) 588-8300. **FAX:** (707) 588-8721.

Operated by: Sonoma County Professional Baseball, Inc.

President/General Manager: Robert Fletcher. **Director, Business Operations:** Susan Fletcher. **Director, Media/Public Relations:** David Raymond. **Director, Ticket Sales/Promotions:** Kevin Wolski.

Manager: Dick Dietz. **Coach:** Kevin Higgins. **Pitching Coach:** Dolf Hes.

Stadium Name: Rohnert Park Stadium. **Standard Game Times:** 7:05 p.m.; Wed. 1:30; Sat. 5:05; Sun. 1:30.

TRI-CITY POSSE

Office Address: 6200 Burden Rd., Pasco, WA 99301. **Telephone:** (509) 547-6773. **FAX:** (509) 547-4008.

Operated By: Tri-City Posse Baseball Inc.

President: John Montero. **General Manager:** Sean Kelly. **Director, Media/Community Relations:** Rich Buel. **Director, Promotions:** David Vogel. **Director, Ticket Sales:** Rick Marple.

Manager: Jamie Nelson. **Trainer:** Tressa Perkins.

Stadium Name: Posse Stadium. **Standard Game Times:** 7:05 p.m.; Sun. 5:05.

INDEPENDENT SCHEDULES

Frontier League

Canton
JUNE
9-10-11-12 ... Johnstown
13-14 .... Chillicothe
20-21-22-23 .. Richmond
28-29-30 ...... Springfield
JULY
1 .... Springfield
4-5 .... Chillicothe
13-14-15-16 Ohio Valley
17-18 .... Johnstown
31 .... Evansville
AUGUST
1-2-3 .... Evansville
8-9 .... Johnstown
11-12-13-14. Kalamazoo
22-23-24-25.. Chillicothe
28-29-30-31 Ohio Valley

Chillicothe
JUNE
9-10-11-12 .. Ohio Valley
20-21-22-23 .. Evansville
28-29-30 ...... Kalamazoo
JULY
1 .... Kalamazoo
2-3 .... Canton
11-12 .... Canton
13-14-15-16 . Johnstown
17-18 .... Ohio Valley
22-23-24-25 .... Canton
AUGUST
4-5-6-7 .... Richmond
15-16-17-18 . Springfield
20-21 .... Ohio Valley
28-29-30-31 . Johnstown

Evansville
JUNE
4-5-6-7 .... Kalamazoo
13-14 .... Richmond
24-25-26-27 ..... Canton
28-29-30 ...... Johnstown
JULY
1 .... Johnstown
4-5 .... Richmond
7-8-9-10 .... Springfield
22-23-24-25 Kalamazoo

AUGUST
4-5-6-7 .... Ohio Valley
11-12-13-14 .. Chillicothe
20-21-22-23 . Springfield
24-25-26-27 .. Richmond

Johnstown
JUNE
4-5-6-7 .... Chillicothe
13-14 .... Ohio Valley
16-17-18-19 . Springfield
24-25-26-27 .. Richmond
JULY
4-5 .... Ohio Valley
7-8-9-10 .... Canton
22-23-24-25 Ohio Valley
27-28-29-30 .. Chillicothe
AUGUST
4-5-6-7 .... Kalamazoo
16-17-18-19 .. Evansville
20-21 .... Canton
26-27 .... Canton

Kalamazoo
JUNE
9-10-11-12 .... Richmond
16-17-18-19 ...... Canton
20-21-22-23 . Johnstown
JULY
4-5 .... Springfield
11-12 .... Springfield
13-14-15-16 .. Evansville
27-28-29-30 . Springfield
31 .... Chillicothe
AUGUST
1-2-3 .... Chillicothe
8-9 .... Richmond
15-16-17-18 Ohio Valley
20-21 .... Richmond
28-29-30-31 .. Evansville

Ohio Valley
JUNE
4-5-6-7 .... Canton
16-17-18-19 .. Evansville
24-25-26-27 Kalamazoo
JULY
2-3 .... Johnstown

7-8-9-10 .... Chillicothe
11-12 .... Johnstown
27-28-29-30 .... Canton
31 .... Richmond
AUGUST
1-2-3 .... Richmond
8-9 .... Chillicothe
11-12-13-14 .. Springfield
22-23-24-25 . Johnstown
26-27 .... Chillicothe

Richmond
JUNE
4-5 .... Springfield
7-8 .... Springfield
16-17-18-19 .. Chillicothe
28-29-30 .... Ohio Valley
JULY
1 .... Ohio Valley
2-3 .... Evansville
7-8-9-10 .... Kalamazoo
11-12 .... Evansville
17-18 .... Kalamazoo
27-28-29-30 .. Evansville
AUGUST
11-12-13-14 . Johnstown
15-16-17-18 ...... Canton
22-23 .... Kalamazoo
28-29-30-31 . Springfield

Springfield
JUNE
9-10-11-12 .... Evansville
13-14 .... Kalamazoo
20-21-22-23 Ohio Valley
24-25-26-27 .. Chillicothe
JULY
2-3 .... Kalamazoo
13-14-15-16 .. Richmond
17-18 .... Evansville
22-23-24-25 . Richmond
31 .... Johnstown
AUGUST
1-2-3 .... Johnstown
4-5-6-7 .... Canton
8-9 .... Evansville
24-25-26-27 .Kalamazoo

Northeast League

Adirondack
JUNE
2-3-4 .... New Jersey
5-6-7 .... Catskill
12-13-14 .... Waterbury
23-24-25 .... Mass.
30 .... Albany
JULY
1-2 .... Albany
3-4-5 .... Allentown
7-8-9 .... Elmira
17-18-19 ..... New Jersey
28-29-30 .... Allentown
31 .... Massachusetts
AUGUST
1-2 .... Massachusetts
14-15-16 .... Elmira

18-19-20 .... Waterbury
27-28-29 .... Catskill
30-31 .... Albany
SEPTEMBER
1 .... Albany

Albany
MAY
29-30-31 .... Catskill
JUNE
2-3-4 .... Allentown
9-10-11 .... Adirondack
12-13-14 .... Mass.
23-24-25 ...... Waterbury
JULY
3-4-5 .... Elmira
13-14-15 ..... New Jersey
24-25-26 ...... Adirondack

28-29-30 .... Elmira
AUGUST
7-8-9 .... Waterbury
11-12-13 .... Allentown
18-19-20 .... Mass.
21-22-23 .... Catskill
27-28-29 ..... New Jersey

Allentown
MAY
29-30-31 .... Mass.
JUNE
9-10-11 .... Catskill
16-17-18 .... Elmira
19-20-21 ...... Adirondack
26-27-28 .... Albany
30 .... New Jersey

Northern League

14-15-16...... Sioux Falls
17-18-19.............. Fargo
28-29-30............. Duluth

Sioux Falls
JUNE
1-2-3............ Winnipeg
5-6-7.................. Duluth
15-16-17.......... St. Paul
19-20-21.......... Madison
27.................. Sioux City
30.................... Fargo
JULY
1-2 .... Fargo
3-4-5.......Thunder Bay
13-15............ Sioux City
17-18-19.......... St. Paul
27-28-29... Thunder Bay
31 .... Winnipeg
AUGUST
1-2.................. Winnipeg
10-11-12.......... Madison
24-25-26............. Duluth

27-28-29-30......... Fargo
31...................... Sioux City
SEPTEMBER
1-2 .... Sioux City

Thunder Bay
JUNE
1-2-3................ St. Paul
5-6-7 .... Fargo
15-16-17........ Winnipeg
19-20-21........ Sioux City
26-27-28 .... Duluth
30 .... Madison
JULY
1-2 .... Madison
10-11-12 ...... Sioux Falls
17-18-19........ Winnipeg
20-21-22...... Sioux Falls
30-31 .... St. Paul
AUGUST
1 .... St. Paul
4-5-6 .... Fargo
14-15-16 .... Duluth

20-21-22-23..... Madison
24-25-26 .... Sioux City

Winnipeg
JUNE
5-6-7 .... Madison
9-10-11 .... Thunder Bay
19-20-21 .... Duluth
22-23-24 ..... Sioux Falls
28-28-29 ...... Sioux City
JULY
10-11-12 ...... St. Paul
13-14-15 .... Fargo
25-25-26 .... Madison
27-28-29 .... Duluth
AUGUST
7-8-9 .... Thunder Bay
10-11-12-13 .. Sioux City
17-18-19 ..... Sioux Falls
28-29-30........... St. Paul
31........................ Fargo
SEPTEMBER
1-2 .... Fargo

Texas-Louisiana League

Abilene
MAY
28-29-30-31 Rio Grande
JUNE
4-5-6-7......... Alexandria
8-9-10............. Lafayette
11-12 .... Lubbock
26-27-28-29 .. Greenville
JULY
3-4 .... Lubbock
6-7-8................. Amarillo
18-19-20 .... Greenville
30-31 .... Lafayette
AUGUST
1-2 .... Lafayette
3-4-5-6............. Amarillo
18-19-20...... Alexandria
21-22-23 ..... Rio Grande
29-30-31 .... Lubbock

Alexandria
MAY
23 .... Lafayette
28-29-30-31...... Amarillo
JUNE
1-2-3.................. Abilene
8-9-10 .... Lubbock
19-20-21-22..... Lubbock
23-24-25 ..... Greenville
30 .... Rio Grande
JULY
1-2 .... Rio Grande
14-15-16-17.... Lafayette
25-26-27-28....... Abilene
AUGUST
10-11-12-13 .. Greenville
14-15-16-17 Rio Grande
21-22 .... Lafayette
28-29-30........... Amarillo

Amarillo
MAY
21-22-23 .... Lubbock
24-25-26-27 .... Abilene

JUNE
4-5-6-7 .... Rio Grande
8-9-10 .... Greenville
19-20-21-22.... Lafayette
JULY
3-4-5 .... Alexandria
9-10-11 .... Lafayette
14-15-16-17 .. Greenville
30-31 .... Alexandria
AUGUST
1-2 .... Alexandria
7-8-9................... Abilene
17 .... Lubbock
18-19-20 .... Rio Grande
25-26-27 .... Lubbock

Greenville
MAY
28-29-30-31.... Lafayette
JUNE
1-2-3................. Amarillo
11-12-13-14 .. Alexandria
15-16-17 .... Lubbock
19-20-21-22 Rio Grande
30 .... Abilene
JULY
1-2 .... Abilene
9-10-11 .... Rio Grande
21-22-23-24...... Amarillo
25-26-27-28..... Lubbock
AUGUST
14-15-16-17....... Abilene
18-19-20......... Lafayette
25-26-27......... Alexandria

Lafayette
MAY
21-22 .... Alexandria
24-25-26-27 .. Greenville
JUNE
15-16-17.......... Abilene
18 .... Alexandria
23-24-25......... Amarillo
30 .... Lubbock
JULY
1-2 .... Lubbock

3-4-5 .... Rio Grande
6-7 .... Alexandria
21-22-23-24 Rio Grande
25-26-27-28...... Amarillo
AUGUST
7-8-9 .... Greenville
10-11-12-13 ..... Lubbock
23-24 .... Alexandria
25-26-27-28...... Abilene

Lubbock
JUNE
1-2-3 .... Rio Grande
4-5-6-7........... Lafayette
13-14 .... Abilene
26-27-28-29...... Amarillo
JULY
5 .... Abilene
6-7-8 .... Greenville
9-10-11 .... Alexandria
18-19-20......... Lafayette
21-22-23-24...... Abilene
30-31 .... Rio Grande
AUGUST
1-2 .... Rio Grande
3-4-5-6............. Alexandria
14-15-16.......... Amarillo
21-22-23-24 ...Greenville

Rio Grande Valley
MAY
21-22-23 .... Greenville
24-25-26-27..... Lubbock
JUNE
11-12-13-14 .... Lafayette
15-16-17.......... Amarillo
23-24-25............ Abilene
26-27-28-29.. Alexandria
JULY
14-15-16-17....... Abilene
18-19-20....... Alexandria
AUGUST
3-4-5-6 .... Greenville
7-8-9 .... Lubbock
10-11-12-13...... Amarillo
29-30-31 .... Lafayette

Western League

Bend

MAY
29-30-31 .... Tri-City
JUNE
1 .... Tri-City
2-3-4 .... Chico
5-6-7 .... Mission Viejo
16-17-18 .... Pacific
19-20-21 ..... Sonoma Co.
30 .... Reno
JULY
1-2-3 .... Reno
8-9-10-11 . Grays Harbor
24-25-26 .... Tri-City
28-29-30 .... Pacific
31 .... Mission Viejo
AUGUST
1-2 .... Mission Viejo
18-19-20 .... Chico
21-22-23 .. Sonoma Co.
28-29-30 .... Reno
31 .... Grays Harbor
SEPTEMBER
1-2 .... Grays Harbor

Chico

MAY
29-30-31 .. Mission Viejo
JUNE
1 .... Mission Viejo
9-10-11 .... Bend
12-13-14 .... Reno
23-24-25 .... Tri-City
26-27-28 .. Grays Harbor
JULY
2-3 .... Sonoma County
4-5-6-7 .... Pacific
24-25-26 .. Mission Viejo
AUGUST
4-5-6 .... Bend
11-12-13 .. Grays Harbor
14-15-16 .... Tri-City
21-22-23 .... Reno
24-25-26-27-28 . Sonoma
31 .... Pacific
SEPTEMBER
1-2 .... Pacific

Grays Harbor

MAY
22-23-24 .... Reno
25-26-27 .... Bend
JUNE
2-3-4 .... Sonoma County
5-6-7 .... Pacific
16-17-18 .. Mission Viejo
19-20-21 .... Chico
JULY
4-5-6 .... Tri-City
16-17-18-19 .... Reno

20-21-22-23 .... Bend
28-29-30 .... Chico
31 .... Sonoma County
AUGUST
1-2 .... Sonoma County
18-19-20 .... Pacific
21-22-23 .. Mission Viejo
24-25-26-27 .... Tri-City

Mission Viejo

MAY
23-24-25 .... Chico
26-27-28 ... Sonoma Co.
JUNE
9-10-11 .... Grays Harbor
12-13-14 .... Tri-City
23-24-25 .... Reno
26-27-28 .... Bend
30 .... Pacific
JULY
1 .... Pacific
9-10-11 .... Pacific
15-16-17-18 .... Chico
19-20-21-22 ..... Sonoma
AUGUST
4-5-6 .... Tri-City
7-8-9 .... Grays Harbor
11-12-13 .... Reno
14-15-16 .... Bend
29-30 .... Pacific

Pacific

MAY
23-24-25 .... Sonoma
26-27-28 .... Chico
JUNE
9-10-11 .... Tri-City
12-13-14 .. Grays Harbor
23-24-25 .... Bend
26-27-28 .... Reno
JULY
2-3 .... Mission Viejo
15-16-17-18 ... Sonoma Co.
19-20-21-22 .... Chico
AUGUST
4-5-6 .... Grays Harbor
7-8-9 .... Tri-City
11-12-13 .... Bend
14-15-16 .... Reno
24-25-26-27-28 M. Viejo

Reno

MAY
29-30-31 .. Grays Harbor
JUNE
1 .... Grays Harbor
2-3-4 .... Mission Viejo
5-6-7 .... Chico
16-17-18 ... Sonoma Co.
19-20-21 .... Pacific

JULY
4-5-6 .... Bend
8-9-10-11 .... Tri-City
24-25-26 .. Grays Harbor
28-29-30 .. Mission Viejo
31 .... Pacific
AUGUST
1-2 .... Pacific
7-8-9 .... Chico
18-19-20 ... Sonoma Co.
24-25-26-27 .... Bend
31 .... Tri-City
SEPTEMBER
1-2 .... Tri-City

Sonoma County

MAY
29-30-31 .... Pacific
JUNE
9-10-11 .... Reno
12-13-14 .... Bend
23-24-25 .. Grays Harbor
26-27-28 .... Tri-City
30 .... Chico
JULY
1 .... Chico
4-5-6-7 .. Mission Viejo
9-10-11 .... Reno
23-24-25-26 .... Pacific
AUGUST
4-5-6 .... Reno
7-8-9 .... Bend
11-12-13 .... Tri-City
14-15-16 .. Grays Harbor
29-30 .... Chico
31 .... Mission Viejo
SEPTEMBER
1-2 .... Mission Viejo

Tri-City

MAY
22-23-24 .... Bend
25-26-27 .... Reno
JUNE
2-3-4 .... Pacific
5-6-7 .... Sonoma County
16-17-18 .... Chico
19-20-21 .. Mission Viejo
30 .... Grays Harbor
JULY
1-2-3 .... Grays Harbor
15-16-17-18 .... Bend
20-21-22-23 .... Reno
28-29-30 ... Sonoma Co.
31 .... Chico
AUGUST
1-2 .... Chico
18-19-20 .. Mission Viejo
21-22-23 .... Pacific
28-29-30 .. Grays Harbor

Foreign Leagues

1997 STANDINGS

*Split-season champion

Mexican League

Triple-A

CENTRAL	W	L	PCT	GB	SOUTH	W	L	PCT	GB
*Mexico City Reds	83	38	.686	—	*Tabasco	67	52	.563	—
*Mexico City Tigers	77	40	.658	4	*Quintana Roo	61	56	.521	5
Poza Rica	67	52	.563	15	Yucatan	54	64	.458	12½
Oaxaca	53	69	.434	30½	Campeche	46	64	.418	16½
Aguascalientes	46	73	.387	36	Minatitlan	42	76	.356	24½

NORTH	W	L	PCT	GB		W	L	PCT	GB
*Monterrey	68	52	.567	—	Saltillo	55	64	.462	12½
Monclova	65	56	.537	3½	Laredo	55	64	.462	12½
*Reynosa	60	57	.513	6½	Union Laguna	48	70	.407	19

PLAYOFFS: Quarterfinals (best-of-7)—Quintana Roo defeated Monterrey 4-2; Mexico City Reds defeated Reynosa 4-0; Mexico City Tigers defeated Poza Rica 4-0; Tabasco defeated Monclova 4-0. **Semifinals** (best-of-7)—Mexico City Tigers defeated Tabasco 4-1; Mexico City Reds defeated Quintana Roo 4-2. **Finals** (best-of-7)—Mexico City Tigers defeated Mexico City Reds 4-1

Japan Leagues

CENTRAL	W	L	T	PCT	GB	PACIFIC	W	L	T	PCT	GB
Yakult	83	52	2	.615	—	Seibu	76	56	3	.576	—
Yokohama	72	63	0	.533	11	Orix	71	61	3	.538	5
Hiroshima	66	69	0	.489	17	Kintetsu	68	63	4	.519	7½
Yomiuri	63	72	0	.467	20	Nippon Ham	63	71	1	.470	14
Hanshin	62	73	0	.459	21	Fukuoka	63	71	1	.470	14
Chunichi	59	76	1	.437	24	Chiba Lotte	56	76	2	.429	19½

PLAYOFFS: Finals (best-of-7)—Yakult defeated Seibu 4-1.

Taiwan Leagues

CPBL	W	L	PCT	GB	*Weichuan	46	46	.500	13½
President	58	31	.652	—	Sinon	45	48	.484	15
Mercury	46	44	.511	12½	*China Times	41	51	.446	18½
Brother	45	44	.506	13	China Trust	39	56	.411	22

PLAYOFFS: Finals (best-of-7)—Weichuan defeated China Times, 4-2.

TAIWAN MAJOR	W	L	PCT	GB		W	L	PCT	GB
Chia-nan	53	42	.558	—	Kao-ping	42	51	.452	10
Taipei	53	43	.552	½	Taichung	41	53	.436	11½

PLAYOFFS: Finals (best-of-7)—Chia-nan defeated Taipei, 4-3.

Dominican Summer League

Rookie Classification

S.D. EAST	W	L	PCT	GB		W	L	PCT	GB
Dodgers I	50	18	.735	—	Pirates	29	40	.420	18
Tigers	47	24	.662	4½	Devil Rays	27	41	.397	19½
Marlins	41	30	.577	10½	Padres	14	56	.200	33½
Brewers	40	32	.556	12					
Mariners	39	32	.549	12½	SAN PEDRO	W	L	PCT	GB
Athletics East	38	32	.543	13	Dodgers II	58	12	.828	—
Diamondbacks	32	39	.451	19½	Blue Jays	40	32	.556	19
Cardinals	28	43	.394	23½	Astros	36	35	.507	22½
Expos	19	50	.275	31½	Braves	35	37	.486	24
Rockies	18	52	.257	33	Giants	30	40	.428	28
					Red Sox	25	46	.352	33½
S.D. WEST	W	L	PCT	GB	Orioles	24	46	.342	34
Rangers I	47	22	.681	—					
Mets	41	27	.603	5½	CIBAO	W	L	PCT	GB
Yankees	40	30	.571	7½	Rangers II	49	23	.681	—
Athletics West	39	30	.565	8	Indians	37	34	.521	11½
Cubs	39	30	.565	8	Royals	35	36	.493	13½
					Phillies	22	50	.306	27

PLAYOFFS: Semifinals (best-of-3)—Dodgers I defeated Rangers I 2-1; Dodgers II defeated Rangers II 2-0. **Finals** (best-of-5)—Dodgers II defeated Dodgers I 3-2.

Venezuelan Summer League

Rookie Classification

	W	L	T	PCT	GB		W	L	T	PCT	GB
Guacara 2	32	24	4	.567	—	Maracay 1	28	27	5	.508	3½
San Joaquin 2	30	27	3	.525	2½	San Joaquin 1	25	32	3	.442	7½
Maracay 2	30	28	2	.517	3	Guacara 1	24	31	5	.442	7½

MEXICAN LEAGUE

Class AAA

NOTE: The Mexican League is a member of the National Association of Professional Baseball Leagues and has a Triple-A classification. However, its member clubs operate largely independent of the 30 major league teams, and for that reason the league is listed in the international and winter league section.

Mailing Address: Angel Pola #16, Col. Periodista, Mexico, D.F. CP 11220. **Telephone:** 011-525-557-10-07, 011-525-557-14-08. **FAX:** 011-525-395-24-54.

Years League Active: 1955-.

President: Pedro Treto Cisneros. **Vice President:** Roberto Mansur Galan.

Assistant to President/Public Relations: Nestor Alva Brito. **Treasurer:** Salvador Velazquez Andrade. **Secretary:** Socorro Becerra Campos.

1998 Opening Date: March 18. **Closing Date:** August 6.

No. of Games, Regular Season: 122.

Division Structure: Central—Aguascalientes, Mexico City Red Devils, Mexico City Tigers, Oaxaca, Minatitlan. **North**—Laredo, Monclova, Monterrey, Reynosa, Saltillo, Union Laguna. **South**—Campeche, Cancun, Chetumal, Tabasco, Yucatan.

Playoff Format: Three-tier playoffs involving top two teams in each zone, plus two wild-card teams. Two finalists meet in best-of-7 series for league championship.

All-Star Game: June 1 at Merida, Yucatan.

Roster Limit: 25. **Roster Limit, Imports:** 5.

Brand of Baseball: Rawlings.

Statistician: Ana Luisa Perea Talarico, Angel Pola #16, Col. Periodista, CP 11220 Mexico, D.F.

AGUASCALIENTES RAILROADMEN

Office Address: General Manuel Madrigal 110, Col. Heroes, CP 20190, Aguascalientes, Aguascalientes. **Telephone:** (49) 15-84-22. **FAX:** (49) 18-77-78.

President: Oscar Lomelin Ibarra. **General Manager:** Unavailable.

Manager: Juan Rodriguez.

CAMPECHE PIRATES

Office Address: Unidad Deportiva 20 de Noviembre, Local 4, CP 24000, Col. Centro, Campeche, Campeche. **Telephone:** (981) 6-60-71. **FAX:** (981) 6-38-07.

President: Gustavo Ortiz Avila. **General Manager:** Socorro Morales Martinez.

Manager: Carlos Paz.

CANCUN LOBSTERMEN

Office Address: Av. Kabah Super Manzana 31, Lote 25 Manzana 6, Altos. Cancun, Quintana Roo. **Telephone:** (98) 87-40-11.

President: Ariel Magana Carrillo. **General Manager:** Luis Bolio Mendez.

Manager: Francisco Estrada.

CHETUMAL MAYAS

Office Address: Av. Heroes de Chapultepec No. 9, Col. Centro C.P. 77000, Chetumal, Quintana Roo. **Telephone:** (983) 2-31-42. **FAX:** (983) 2-30-28.

President: Carlos Paredes Verastegui. **General Manager:** Raul Cano.

Manager: Jesus Sommers.

OWLS OF THE TWO LAREDOS

Office Address: Paseo Colon, No. 2421, Col. Madero C.P. 88270, Nuevo Laredo, Tamaulipas. **Telephone:** (87) 19-12-35. **FAX:** (87) 14-90-04.

President: Manuel Canales Escamilla. **General Manager:** Niria Judith Salinas.

Manager: Andres Mora.

MEXICO CITY RED DEVILS

Office Address: Av. Cuauhtemoc No. 451-101, Col. Piedad Narvarte, CP 03020, Mexico, D.F. **Telephone:** (905) 639-87-22.

Co-Presidents: Roberto Mansur Galan, Alfredo Harp Helu. **General Manager:** Pedro Mayorquin Aguilar.

Manager: Marco Vazquez.

MEXICO CITY TIGERS

Office Address: Tuxpan No. 45-A, Sto. Piso Col. Roma Sur, CP 06760, Mexico, D.F. **Telephone:** (905) 584-02-16. **FAX:** (590) 564-02-49.
President: Carlos Peralta. **General Manager:** Alfonso Lopez.
Manager: Dan Firova.

MINATITLAN COLTS

Office Adress: Avila Camacho Esq. Ninos Heroes S/N, Col. Los Maestros, CP 96850, Minatitlan, Veracruz. **Telephone:** (922) 3-50-03.
President: Javier Rios Lopez.
Manager: Alfredo Lopez.

MONCLOVA STEELERS

Office Address: Cuauhtemoc #1002, Col. Ciudad Deportiva, CP 25750, Monclova, Coahuila. **Telephone:** (86) 34-21-72. **FAX:** (86) 34-21-76.
President: Alonso Ancira Gonzalez. **General Manager:** Carlos de la Garza Barajas.
Manager: Unavailable.

MONTERREY SULTANS

Office Address: Ave. Manuel L. Barragan S/N, Estadio Monterrey, CP 64460, Monterrey, Nuevo Leon. **Telephone:** (08) 351-86-34, 351-02-09. **FAX:** (08) 351-91-86.
President: Jose Maiz Garcia. **General Manager:** Roberto Magdaleno Ramirez.
Manager: Derek Bryant.

OAXACA WARRIORS

Office Address: Privada del Chopo No. 105, Fraccionamiento El Chopo, CP 68050, Oaxaca, Oaxaca. **Telephone:** (951) 5-55-22. **FAX:** (951) 5-49-66.
President: Vicente Perez Avella. **General Manager:** Roberto Castellon Yuen.
Manager: Unavailable.

REYNOSA BRONCOS

Office Address: Blvd. Hidalgo 102, Col. Adolfo Lopez Mateos, CP 88650, Reynosa, Tamaulipas. **Telephone:** (89) 24-17-50. **FAX:** (89) 24-26-95.
President: Eduardo Trevino. **General Manager:** Jose Manuel Ortiz.
Manager: Unavailable.

SALTILLO SARAPE MAKERS

Office Address: Blvd. Nazario S. Ortiz esq. Blvd. Jesus Valdez Sanchez, CP 25280, Saltillo, Coahuila. **Telephone:** (84) 16-94-55.
President: Javier Cabello Siller. **General Manager:** David Wong.
Manager: Marcelo Juarez Moreno.

TABASCO CATTLEMEN

Office Address: Explanada de la Ciudad Deportiva, Estadio de Beisbol Centenario del 27 de Fabrero, Col. Atasta de Serra, CP 86100, Villahermosa, Tabasco. **Telephone:** (93) 15-32-37.
President: Diego Rosique Palavicini. **General Manager:** Juan Alberto Nava Comsilie.
Manager: Unavailable.

UNION LAGUNA COTTON PICKERS

Office Address: Calle Juan Gutemberg, S/N, Estadio de la Revolucion, CP 27000, Torreon, Coahuila. **Telephone:** (17) 17-43-35. **FAX:** (17) 18-55-15.
President: Francisco Gomez.
Manager: Jose Cano.

YUCATAN LIONS

Office Address: Calle 50 #406-B, Col. Jesus Carranza, CP 97109, Merida, Yucatan. **Telephone:** (99) 26-30-22. **FAX:** (99) 26-36-31.
President: Gustavo Ricalde Duran. **General Manager:** Jose Rivero Ancona.
Manager: Unavailable.

MEXICAN ACADEMY

Rookie Classification

Mailing Address: Angel Pola #16 Col. Periodista CP, Mexico, DF 11220. **Telephone:** 011-525-577-1007. **FAX:** 011-525-395-2454.
Years League Active: 1997-.
Commissioner: Unavailable.
Member Clubs: Unavailable.

JAPANESE LEAGUES

Mailing Address: Imperial Tower, 10F, 1-1-1 Uchisaiwai-cho, Chiyoda-ku, Tokyo 100-0011 Japan. **Telephone:** 011-81-03-3502-0022. **FAX:** 011-81-03-3502-0140.

Commissioner: TBA

Executive Secretary: Yoshiaki Kanai. **Assistant Director, International Affairs:** Nobuhisa "Nobby" Ito.

Japan Series: Best-of-7 series between Central and Pacific League champions, begins Oct. 17 at home of Central League club.

All-Star Series: July 22 at Nagoya Dome, July 23 at Chiba Marine Stadium.

Roster Limit: 70 per organization (one major league club, one minor league club). Major league club is permitted to register 28 players at a time, though only 25 may be available for each game. **Roster Limit, Imports:** 4 (2 position players, 2 pitchers) in majors; unlimited in minors.

CENTRAL LEAGUE

Mailing Address: Asahi Bldg. 3F, 6-6-7 Ginza, Chuo-ku, Tokyo 104-0061. **Telephone:** 03-3572-1673. **FAX:** 03-3571-4545.

Years League Active: 1950-.

President: Hiromori Kawashima.

Secretary General: Ryoichi Shibusawa. **Planning Department:** Masaaki Nagino.

1998 Opening Date: April 3. **Closing Date:** Sept. 28.

Regular Season: 135 games.

Playoff Format: None.

CHUNICHI DRAGONS

Mailing Address: Chunichi Bldg. 6F, 4-1-1 Sakae, Naka-ku, Nagoya 460-0008. **Telephone:** 052-252-5226. **FAX:** 052-263-7696.

Chairman: Hirohiko Oshima. **President:** Tsuyoshi Sato. **General Manager:** Osamu Ito.

Field Manager: Senichi Hoshino.

1997 Attendance: 2,607,500.

1998 Foreign Players: Leo Gomez, Kevin Jarvis, Jeong Bum Lee (Korea), Sun Dong Yol (Korea).

HANSHIN TIGERS

Mailing Address: 1-47 Koshien-cho, Nishinomiya-shi, Hyogo-ken 663-8152. **Telephone:** 0798-46-1515. **FAX:** 0798-40-0934.

Chairman: Shunjiro Kuma. **President:** Kazuhiko Miyoshi. **General Manager:** Katsuyoshi Nozaki.

Field Manager: Yoshio Yoshida.

1997 Attendance: 2,268,000.

1998 Foreign Players: Doug Creek, Dave Hansen, Tateo Kaku-ri (Taiwan), Alonzo Powell, Ben Rivera, Desi Wilson.

HIROSHIMA TOYO CARP

Mailing Address: 5-25 Motomachi, Naka-ku, Hiroshima 730-0011. **Telephone:** 082-221-2040. **FAX:** 082-228-5013.

Chairman: Kohei Matsuda. **General Manager:** Chitomi Takahashi.

Field Manager: Toshiyuki Mimura.

1997 Attendance: 1,163,000.

1998 Foreign Players: Nate Minchey, Felix Perdomo, Timoniel Perez, Alfonso Soriano.

YAKULT SWALLOWS

Mailing Address: Shimbashi MDV Bldg. 5F, 5-13-5 Shimbashi, Minato-ku, Tokyo 105-0021. **Telephone:** 03-5470-8415. **FAX:** 03-5470-8416.

Chairman: Jun Kuwahara. **President/General Manager:** Itaru Taguchi.

Field Manager: Katsuya Nomura.

1997 Attendance: 2,117,000.

1998 Foreign Players: Mark Acre, Travis Driskill, Dwayne Hosey, Lyle Mouton.

YOKOHAMA BAYSTARS

Mailing Address: Nihon Seimei Yokohama Hon-machi Bldg. 6F, 2-22 Hon-machi, Naka-ku, Yokohama 231-0005. **Telephone:** 045-681-0811. **FAX:** 045-661-2500.

Chairman: Keijiro Nakabe. **President:** Takashi Ohori. **General Manager:** Takeo Minatoya.

Field Manager: Hiroshi Gondo.

1997 Attendance: 1,683,000.

1998 Foreign Players: Pat Mahomes, Jose Malave, Bobby Rose.

YOMIURI GIANTS

Mailing Address: Takebashi 3-3 Bldg., 3-3 Kanda Nishiki-cho, Chiyoda-ku, Tokyo 101-0054. **Telephone:** 03-3295-7711. **FAX:** 03-3295-7708.

Chairman: Tsuneo Watanabe. **General Manager:** Yoshinori Fukaya.
Field Manager: Shigeo Nagashima.
1997 Attendance: 3,645,000.
1998 Foreign Players: Mariano Duncan, Balvino Galvez, Eric Hillman, Cho Sung Min (Korea).

PACIFIC LEAGUE

Mailing Address: Asahi Bldg. 9F, 6-6-7 Ginza, Chuo-ku, Tokyo 104-0061. **Telephone:** 03-3573-1551. **FAX:** 03-3572-5843.
Years League Active: 1950-.
President: Kazuo Harano.
Secretary General: Shigeru Murata. **Public Relations:** Hiroshi Yoshimura.
1998 Opening Date: April 4. **Closing Date:** Sept. 29.
Regular Season: 135 games.
Playoff Format: None.

CHIBA LOTTE MARINES

Mailing Address: WBG Marive West 25F, 2-6 Nakase, Mihama-ku, Chiba-shi, Chiba-ken 261-7125. **Telephone:** 043-297-2101. **FAX:** 043-297-2181.
Chairman: Takeo Shigemitsu. **General Manager:** Mitsumasa Mitsuno.
Field Manager: Akihito Kondo. **Foreign Coach:** Lenn Sakata.
1997 Attendance: 1,002,000.
1998 Foreign Players: Mark Carreon, Joe Crawford, Shane Dennis, Julio Franco, Mark Holzemer.

FUKUOKA DAIEI HAWKS

Mailing Address: Fukuoka Dome 6F, 2-2-2 Jigyohama, Chuo-ku, Fukuoka 810-0065. **Telephone:** 092-844-1189. **FAX:** 092-844-4600.
Chairman: Isao Nakauchi. **President:** Hiroshi Murakami. **General Manager:** Seiji Kishitani.
Field Manager: Sadaharu Oh.
1997 Attendance: 2,307,000.
1998 Foreign Players: Luis Lopez, Ryan Thompson, Brian Williams.

KINTETSU BUFFALOES

Mailing Address: Midosuji Grand Bldg. 5F, 2-2-3 Namba, Chuo-ku, Osaka 542-0076. **Telephone:** 06-212-9744. **FAX:** 06-212-6834.
Chairman: Yoshinori Ueyama. **President:** Hironobu Chikuma. **General Manager:** Yoshio Ikoma.
Field Manager: Kyosuke Sasaki.
1997 Attendance: 1,866,000.
1998 Foreign Players: Phil Clark, Phil Leftwich, Rob Mattson, Tuffy Rhodes.

NIPPON HAM FIGHTERS

Mailing Address: Roppongi Denki Bldg. 6F, 6-1-20 Roppongi, Minato-ku, Tokyo 106-0032. **Telephone:** 03-3403-9131. **FAX:** 03-3403-9143.
Chairman: Yoshinori Okoso. **President/General Manager:** Takeshi Kojima.
Field Manager: Toshiharu Ueda.
1997 Attendance: 1,678,000.
1998 Foreign Players: Jerry Brooks, Kip Gross, Rafael Orellano, Erik Schullstrom, Nigel Wilson.

ORIX BLUEWAVE

Mailing Address: Kanri Center 2F, Midoridai, Suma-ku, Kobe 654-0163. **Telephone:** 078-795-1001. **FAX:** 078-795-1005.
Chairman: Yoshihiko Miyauchi. **President:** Yasushi Iwai. **General Manager:** Steve Ino.
Field Manager: Akira Ogi.
1997 Attendance: 1,712,000.
1998 Foreign Players: James Bonnici, Chris Donnels, Willie Fraser, Edwin Hurtado, Harvey Pulliam.

SEIBU LIONS

Mailing Address: Seibu Lions Stadium, 2135 Kami-Yamaguchi, Tokorozawa-shi, Saitama-ken 359-1153. **Telephone:** 0429-24-1155. **FAX:** 0429-28-1919.
Chairman: Yoshiaki Tsutsumi. **President:** Iwao Nisugi. **General Manager:** Kenji Ono.
Field Manager: Osamu Higashio.
1997 Attendance: 1,447,500.
1998 Foreign Players: Terry Bross, Giovanni Carrara, Domingo Martinez, Rudy Pemberton, Brian Raabe.

OTHER LEAGUES

DOMINICAN REPUBLIC

DOMINICAN SUMMER LEAGUE
Rookie Classification

Mailing Address: c/o Banco del Progreso, Av. John F. Kennedy, No. 3, Santo Domingo, Dominican Republic. **Telephone/FAX:** (809) 565-0714.

Years League Active: 1985-.

President: Freddy Jana. **Administrative Assistant:** Orlando Diaz.

Member Clubs, 1998: Unavailable.

1998 Opening Date: June 1. **Closing Date:** Aug. 22.

Regular Season: 72 games.

Playoff Format: Four division winners meet in best-of-3 series. Winners meet in best-of-5 series for league championship.

Roster Limit: 30 active. **Player Eligibility Rule:** No more than eight players 20 or older and no more than two players 21 or older. At least 10 players must be pitchers. No more than two years of prior service, excluding Rookie leagues outside the U.S. and Canada.

VENEZUELA

VENEZUELAN SUMMER LEAGUE
Rookie Classification

Address: Estadio Jose Perez Colmenares, Maracay, Aragua, Venezuela. **Telephone:** 011-58-43-54-4632. **FAX:** 011-58-43-54-4134.

Years League Active: 1997-.

Administrator: Saul Gonzalez. **Coordinator:** Ramon Fereira.

Member Clubs, 1998: Unavailable.

1998 Opening Date: June 1. **Closing Date:** Aug. 22.

Regular Season: 60 games.

Playoffs: None.

Roster Limit: 30 active. **Player Eligibility Rule:** No player on active list may have more than three years of minor league service. Open to players from all Latin American Spanish-speaking countries except Mexico, the Dominican Republic and Puerto Rico.

TAIWAN

CHINESE PROFESSIONAL BASEBALL LEAGUE

Mailing Address: 14F, No. 126, Sec. 4, Nanking East Road, Taipei, Taiwan. **Telephone:** 886-2-577-6992. **FAX:** 886-2-577-2606.

Years League Active: 1990-.

Commissioner: C.K. Chen. **Secretary General:** Wayne Lee.

Member Clubs: Brother Elephants (Taipei), China Trust Wales (Taipei), Mercury Tigers (Taipei), President Lions (Tainan), Sinon Bulls (Taichung), Weichuan Dragons (Taipei).

Regular Season: 96 games (split schedule).

1998 Opening Date: Feb. 19. **Closing Date:** Oct. 25.

Import Rule: Twelve import players may be registered during a season, eight active (only three import players on field at one time).

TAIWAN MAJOR LEAGUE

Mailing Address: 8F, No. 214, Tunhua North Rd., Taipei, Taiwan. **Telephone:** 886-2-2545-9566. **FAX:** 886-2-2514-7607. **Website:** nalu 036@naluwan.com.tw.

Years League Active: 1997-.

President: Felix S.T. Chen. **General Manager:** Joey Chen. **Secretary General:** Huang Po-ying.

Member Clubs: Chia-nan Luka, Kao-ping Fala, Taichung Agan, Taipei Gida.

Regular Season: 108 games.

1998 Opening Date: Feb. 28. **Closing Date:** Oct. 18.

Import Rule: Seven (three on field at one time, four if one is the pitcher).

SOUTH KOREA

KOREA BASEBALL ORGANIZATION

Mailing Address: The Hall of Baseball, 946-16 Dogok-Dong, Kangnam-gu, Seoul, South Korea. **Telephone:** 011-82-2-3461-7887. **FAX:** 011-82-2-3472-7800.

Years League Active: 1982-.

Commissioner: Ki-Choon Kim. **Secretary General:** Deok Seon Chang.

Member Clubs: Haitai Tigers (Kwangju), Hanhwa Eagles (Daejeon), Hyundai Unicorns (Inchon), LG Twins (Seoul), Lotte Giants (Pusan), OB Bears (Seoul), Samsung Lions (Daegu), Sangbangwool Raiders (Jeonju).

Winter Baseball

1997-98 STANDINGS

CARIBBEAN WORLD SERIES

	W	L	PCT	GB		W	L	PCT	GB
Dominican Republic	6	0	1.000	—	Mexico	1	5	.167	5
Puerto Rico	4	2	.667	2	Venezuela	1	5	.167	5

Dominican League

Regular Season	W	L	Pct.	GB	Round-Robin	W	L	Pct.	GB
Licey	30	20	.600	—	Licey	13	4	.765	—
Escogido	28	22	.560	2	Aguilas	12	6	.667	1½
Aguilas	26	24	.520	4	Estrellas	5	12	.294	8
Estrellas	24	27	.471	6½	Escogido	5	13	.278	8½
Northeast	23	28	.451	7½					
Azucareros	20	30	.400	10					

PLAYOFFS: Finals (best-of-7)—Aguilas defeated Licey 4-1.

Mexican Pacific League

	W	L	Pct.	GB		W	L	Pct.	GB
*Los Mochis	38	23	.623	—	Mexicali	28	32	.467	9½
Culiacan	34	25	.576	3	Guasave	28	32	.467	9½
Navojoa	31	31	.500	7½	Hermosillo	27	34	.443	11
*Mazatlan	30	32	.484	8½	Obregon	27	34	.443	11

*Split-season champions

PLAYOFFS: Quarterfinals (best-of-7)—Culiacan defeated Guasave 4-0; Los Mochis defeated Mexicali 4-0; Mazatlan defeated Navojoa 4-2. **Semifinals** (best-of-7)—Mazatlan defeated Culiacan 4-2; Navojoa defeated Los Mochis 4-3. **Finals** (best-of-7)—Mazatlan defeated Navojoa 4-3.

Puerto Rican League

	W	L	Pct.	GB		W	L	Pct.	GB
San Juan	40	22	.645	—	Ponce	30	32	.484	10
Mayaguez	34	27	.557	5½	Arecibo	26	35	.426	13½
Caguas	30	32	.484	10	Santurce	25	37	.403	15

PLAYOFFS: Semifinals (best-of-7)—San Juan defeated Ponce 4-3; Mayaguez defeated Caguas 4-3. **Finals** (best-of-9)—Mayaguez defeated San Juan 5-4.

Venezuelan League

EAST	W	L	Pct.	GB	WEST	W	L	Pct.	GB
Magallanes	37	27	.578	—	Lara	43	21	.672	—
Caracas	35	29	.547	2	Occidente	34	30	.531	9
Oriente	30	34	.469	7	Aragua	26	38	.406	17
La Guaira	25	39	.391	12	Zulia	26	38	.406	17
Round-Robin	W	L	Pct.	GB	Magallanes	8	8	.500	4
Caracas	12	4	.750	—	Oriente	7	9	.438	5
Lara	10	6	.625	2	Occidente	3	13	.188	9

PLAYOFFS: Finals (best-of-7)—Lara defeated Caracas 4-3.

Arizona Fall League

NORTH	W	L	Pct.	GB	SOUTH	W	L	Pct.	GB
Peoria	28	17	.622	—	Grand Canyon	29	16	.644	—
Sun Cites	22	23	.489	6	Phoenix	21	24	.467	8
Scottsdale	20	25	.444	8	Mesa	15	30	.333	14

PLAYOFFS: Finals (best-of-3)—Peoria defeated Grand Canyon 2-1.

Australian Baseball League

	W	L	Pct.	GB		W	L	Pct.	GB
Mel. Monarchs	32	20	.615	—	Perth	30	23	.566	2½
Sydney	32	22	.592	1	Adelaide	26	27	.490	6½
Mel. Reds	30	21	.588	1½	Brisbane	20	33	.377	12½
Gold Coast	31	22	.584	1½	Hunter	10	43	.188	22½

PLAYOFFS: Semifinals (round-robin)—Unavailable. **Finals** (best-of-3)—Unavailable.

Hawaii Winter Baseball

OUTRIGGER	W	L	Pct.	GB	VOLCANO	W	L	Pct.	GB
Honolulu	27	27	.500	—	Hilo	29	24	.547	—
West Oahu	26	27	.491	½	Maui	25	29	.463	4½

PLAYOFFS: Finals (sudden death)—Honolulu defeated Hilo 1-0.

WINTER BASEBALL

CARIBBEAN BASEBALL CONFERATION

Mailing Address: Frank Feliz Miranda No. 1 Naco, Santo Domingo, Dominican Republic. **Telephone:** (809) 562-4737, 562-4715. **FAX:** (809) 565-4654.

Commissioner: Juan Fco. Puello Herrera.

Member Leagues: Dominican Republic, Mexican Pacific, Puerto Rican, Venezuelan.

1999 Caribbean World Series: Feb. 4-9 at San Juan, Puerto Rico.

DOMINICAN LEAGUE

Mailing Address: Estadio Quisqueya, Santo Domingo, Dominican Republic. **Telephone:** (809) 567-6371. **FAX:** (809) 567-5720.

Years League Active: 1951-.

President: Leonardo Matos. **Vice President/Treasurer:** Marcos Rodriguez. **Secretary:** Dr. Francisco Pellerano. **Public Relations Director:** Enrique Mota.

1997 Opening Date: Oct. 24. **Closing Date:** Dec. 30.

Regular Season: 50 games.

Playoff Format: Top four teams meet in an 18-game round-robin tournament. Top two finishers meet in a best-of-7 series for league championship. Winner advances to Caribbean World Series.

Roster Limit: 30. **Roster Limit, Imports:** 7.

AGUILAS

Street Address: Estadio Cibao, Ave. Imbert, Santiago, Dom. Rep. **Mailing Address:** EPS B-225, P.O. Box 02-5360, Miami, FL 33102. **Telephone:** (809) 575-4310, 575-1810. **FAX:** (809) 575-0865.

Primary Working Agreement: None.

President: Ricardo Hernandez. **General Manager:** Quilvio Hernandez.

1997-98 Manager: Tony Pena.

AZUCAREROS

Mailing Address: Estadio Francisco Micheli, La Romana, Dom. Rep. **Telephone:** (809) 556-6188. **FAX:** (809) 550-1550.

Primary Working Agreement: Los Angeles Dodgers.

President: Arturo Gil. **General Manager:** Pablo Peguero.

1997-98 Managers: Mickey Hatcher, Teddy Martinez.

ESCOGIDO LIONS

Street Address: Estadio Quisqueya, Ens. la Fe, Santo Domingo, Dom. Rep. **Mailing Address:** P.O. Box 1287, Santo Domingo, Dom. Rep. **Telephone:** (809) 565-1910. **FAX:** (809) 567-7643.

Primary Working Agreement: None.

President: Daniel Aquino-Mendez.

1997-98 Manager: Miguel Dilone.

ESTRELLAS

Street Address: Av. Lope de Vega No. 46, Altos, Ens. Piantini, San Pedro de Macoris, Dom. Rep. **Mailing Address:** P.O. Box 025577, Miami, FL 33102. **Telephone:** (809) 476-0080. **FAX:** (809) 476-0084.

Primary Working Agreement: None.

President: Federico Antun. **General Manager:** Manuel Antun.

1997-98 Manager: Alfredo Griffin.

LICEY TIGERS

Mailing Address: Estadio Quisqueya, Santo Domingo, Dom. Rep. **Telephone:** (809) 567-3090. **FAX:** (809) 542-7714.

Primary Working Agreement: None.

President: Miguel Heded. **General Manager:** Rafael Landestoy.

1997-98 Manager: Dave Jauss.

NORTHEAST GIANTS

Street Address: Estadio Julian Javier, San Francisco de Macoris, Dom. Rep. **Mailing Address:** EPS No. F-1447, P.O. Box 02-5301, Miami, FL 33103. **Telephone:** (809) 588-8882. **FAX:** (809) 588-8733.

Primary Working Agreement: None.

President: Jose Vargas. **General Manager:** Julian Javier.

1997-98 Manager: Alex Taveras.

MEXICAN PACIFIC LEAGUE

Mailing Address: Pesqueria No. 401-R Sur Altos, Navojoa, Sonora, Mexico. **Telephone:** (52-642) 2-3100. **FAX:** (52-642) 2-7250.

Years League Active: 1958-.
President: Dr. Arturo Leon Lerma. **Vice President:** Victor Cuevas.
General Manager: Oviel Denis Gonzalez.
1997 Opening Date: Oct. 18. **Closing Date:** Dec. 29.
Regular Season: 62 games.
Playoff Format: Six teams advance to best-of-7 quarterfinals. Three winners and losing team with best record advance to best-of-7 semifinals. Winners meet in best-of-7 series for league championship. Winner advances to Caribbean World Series.
Roster Limit: 27. **Roster Limit, Imports:** 5.

CULIACAN TOMATO GROWERS
Street Address: Ave. Alvaro Obregon 348 Sur, Col. Almada, CP 80200 Culiacan, Sinaloa, Mexico. **Telephone:** (67) 12-24-46 or 13-33-69. **FAX:** (67) 15-68-28.
President: Juan Manuel Ley Lopez. **General Manager:** Jaime Blancarte.
1997-98 Manager: Paquin Estrada.

GUASAVE COTTONEERS
Mailing Address: Ave. Obregon #43, Guasave, Sinaloa, Mexico. **Telephone:** (68) 72-14-31. **FAX:** (68) 72-29-98.
President: Reynaldo Valencia Amador. **General Manager:** Narciso Orona de los Palos.
1997-98 Managers: Fernando Villaescusa, Aurelio Rodriguez.

HERMOSILLO ORANGE GROWERS
Mailing Address: Nayarit 130, Local 4, Hermosillo, Sonora, Mexico. **Telephone:** (62) 14-07-80, (62) 14-21-23. **FAX:** (62) 15-57-31.
President: Enrique Mazon. **General Manager:** Marco Antonio Manzo.
1997-98 Manager: Derek Bryant.

LOS MOCHIS SUGARCANE GROWERS
Mailing Address: Angel Flores #532 Sur, Los Mochis, Sinaloa, Mexico CP 81200. **Telephone:** (68) 15-00-82. **FAX:** (68) 15-00-45.
President: Mario Lopez Valdez. **General Manager:** Antonio Castro.
1997-98 Manager: Juan Navarrete.

MAZATLAN DEER
Mailing Address: Av. Gutierrez Navera No. 821 Centro, CP 82000, Mazatlan, Sinaloa, Mexico. **Telephone:** (69) 81-17-10. **FAX:** (69) 81-17-11.
President: Hermilo Diaz Bringas. **General Manager:** Alejandro Vega Reyna.
1997-98 Manager: Raul Cano.

MEXICALI EAGLES
Street Address: Calzada Aviacion S/N Ciudad Deportiva, Mexicali, Baja California. **Mailing Address:** P.O. Box 7844, Calexico, CA 92231. **Telephone:** (65) 67-00-40. **FAX:** (65) 67-00-95.
President: Dio Alberto Murillo Rogers. **General Manager:** Leonardo Ovies Olea.
1997-98 Managers: Jesus Sommers, Dan Firova.

NAVOJOA MAYOS
Mailing Address: Allende #208, Dpto. 2, Novojoa, Sonora, Mexico, CP 85800. **Telephone:** (64) 22-14-33, (64) 22-37-64. **FAX:** (64) 22-89-97.
President: Victor Cuevas Garibay. **General Manager:** Lauro Villalobos.
1997-98 Manager: Lorenzo Bundy.

OBREGON YAQUIS
Mailing Address: Yucatan y Nainari #294 North, Ciudad Obregon, Sonora, Mexico, CP 85000. **Telephone:** (64) 14-11-56. **FAX:** (64) 14-11-56.
President: Luis Felipe Garcia DeLeon. **General Manager:** Miguel Sitten.
1997-98 Manager: Antonio Villaescusa.

PUERTO RICAN LEAGUE

Mailing Address: P.O. Box 1852, Hato Rey, PR 00919. **Telephone:** (787) 765-6285, 765-7285. **FAX:** (787) 767-3028.
Years League Active: 1938-.
President: Elpidio Batista. **Executive Director/Administrator:** Benny Agosto.
1997-98 Opening Date: Oct. 31, 1997. **Closing Date:** Jan. 12, 1998.
Regular Season: 62 games.
Playoff Format: Top four teams meet in best-of-7 semifinal series. Winners meet in best-of-9 series for league championship. Winner advances to Caribbean World Series.
Roster Limit: 26. **Roster Limit, Imports:** 4. Up to six more may be used to replace native players who are injured or are major leaguers who

elect not to play.

ARECIBO WOLVES

Street Address: Road #10, Rodriguez Olmo Stadium, Arecibo, PR 00613. **Mailing Address:** P.O. Box 141425, Arecibo, PR 00613. **Telephone:** (787) 879-0309. **FAX:** (787) 817-2323.
  Primary Working Agreement: None.
  President: Josue Vega. **Assistant to President:** Pachy Rodriguez.
  1997-98 Manager: Felix Millan.

CAGUAS CRIOLLOS

Mailing Address: P.O. Box 1415, Caguas, PR 00726. **Telephone:** (787) 258-2222. **FAX:** (787) 743-0545.
  Primary Working Agreement: None.
  General Manager: Jose Antonio Conde.
  1997-98 Manager: Ed Romero.

MAYAGUEZ INDIANS

Street Address: Estadio Isidoro Garcia, Mayaguez, PR. **Mailing Address:** P.O. Box 3089, Marina Station, Mayaguez, PR 00681. **Telephone:** (787) 834-5211. **FAX:** (787) 834-7480.
  Primary Working Agreement: None.
  President/General Manager: Ivan Mendez.
  1997-98 Manager: Tom Gamboa.

PONCE LIONS

Mailing Address: P.O. Box 7444, Pampanos Station, Ponce, PR 00732. **Telephone:** (787) 848-0050. **FAX:** (787) 848-8884.
  Primary Working Agreement: Florida Marlins.
  General Manager: Wito Conde.
  1997-98 Manager: Carlos Lezcano.

SAN JUAN SENATORS

Street Address: Estadio Hiram Bithorn, Ave. Roosevelt, Hato Rey, PR 00959. **Mailing Address:** P.O. Box 366246, San Juan, PR 00936. **Telephone:** (787) 754-1300. **FAX:** (787) 763-2217.
  Primary Working Agreement: Kansas City Royals.
  General Manager: Jackie Nieves.
  1997-98 Manager: Mako Oliveras.

SANTURCE CRABBERS

Mailing Address: P.O. Box 1077, Hato Rey, PR 00919. **Telephone:** (787) 274-0240, 274-0241. **FAX:** (787) 765-0410.
  Primary Working Agreement: Houston Astros.
  General Manager/1997-98 Manager: Frankie Thon.

VENEZUELAN LEAGUE

Mailing Address: Avenida Sorbona, Edificio Marta No. 25, Colinas de Bello Monte, Caracas, Venezuela. **Telephone:** (011-58-2) 751-2079, 753-6897, 751-1891. **FAX:** (011-58-2) 751-0891.
  Years League Active: 1946-.
  President: Carlos Cordido. **First Vice President:** Jaime Benitez. **Second Vice President:** Jesus Efrain Munoz. **General Manager:** Domingo Alvarez.
  Division Structure: Eastern—Caracas, La Guaira, Magallanes, Oriente. **Western**—Aragua, Lara, Pastora, Zulia.
  1997 Opening Date: Oct. 15. **Closing Date:** Dec. 30.
  Regular Season: 64 games.
  Playoff Format: Top two teams in each division, plus a wild-card team, meet in 16-game round-robin series. Top two finishers meet in a best-of-7 series for league championship. Winner advances to Caribbean World Series.
  Roster Limit: 26. **Roster Limit, Imports:** 7.

ARAGUA TIGERS

Address: Estadio Jose Perez Colmenares, Avenida Campo Elias, Barrio Democratico, Maracay, Aragua, Venezuela. **Telephone:** (58-043) 54-4134 or 4332. **FAX:** (58-043) 54-4134.
  Primary Working Agreement: None.
  President: Jose Maria Pages. **General Manager:** Carlos Isava.
  1997-98 Manager: Trey Hillman.

CARACAS LIONS

Street Address: Av. Francisco de Miranda, Centro Seguros La Paz, piso 4, Caracas, Venezuela 1070. **Telephone:** (58-2) 238-7733 or 8919. **FAX:** (58-2) 238-0691.
  Primary Working Agreement: Los Angeles Dodgers.
  President: Pablo Morales. **Vice President/General Manger:** Oscar Prieto.
  1997-98 Manager: Phil Regan.

LA GUAIRA SHARKS
Mailing Address: Primera Avenida, Urbanizacion Miramar, Detras del Periferico de Pariata, Maiquetia, Venezuela. **Telephone:** (58-31) 25-579. **FAX:** (58-31) 23-116.
Primary Working Agreement: None.
President/General Manager: Pedro Padron Panza.
1997-98 Manager: John McLaren.

LARA CARDINALS
Mailing Address: Avenida Rotaria, cruce con Avenida Corpahuaico, Estadio Barquisimeto, Barquisimeto, Venezuela 3001. **Telephone:** (58-051) 42-8321 or 3132 or 4543. **FAX:** (58-051) 42-1921.
Primary Working Agreement: Toronto Blue Jays.
President: Adolfo Alvarez. **General Manager:** Humberto Oropeza.
1997-98 Manager: Omar Malave.

MAGALLANES NAVIGATORS
Address: Avenida Centro Comercial Caribbean Plaza, Modulo 8, Local 173, Valencia, Venezuela. **Telephone:** (58-041) 24-0321 or 0980. **FAX:** (58-041) 24-0705.
Primary Working Agreement: Houston Astros.
President/General Manager: Alfredo Guadarrama.
1997-98 Managers: John Tamargo, Al Pedrique.

OCCIDENTE PASTORA
Mailing Address: Estadio Bachiller Julio Hernandez Molina, Avenida Romulo Gallegos, Aruare, Venezuela. **Telephone:** (055) 22-2945. **FAX:** (055) 21-8595.
Primary Working Agreement: None.
President: Enrique Finol. **General Manager:** Andres Finol.
1997-98 Manager: Domingo Carrasquel.

ORIENTE CARIBBEANS
Mailing Address: Avenida Estadio Alfonso Carrasquel, Oficina del Equipo de Caribes de Oriente, Centro Comercial Novocentro, Piso 2, Local 2-4, Puerto la Cruz, Sucre, Venezuela. **Telephone:** (081) 66-2536 or 66-7054. **FAX:** (081) 66-7054.
Primary Working Agreement: Cleveland Indians.
President: Gioconda de Marquez. **Vice President:** Pablo Ruggeri.
1997-98 Manager: Pompeyo Davalillo.

ZULIA EAGLES
Mailing Address: Avenida 8, Edificio Santa Rita, Las Carolinas, Mezanina Local M-10, Maracaibo, Zulia, Venezuela. **Telephone:** (58-061) 97-9835. **FAX:** (58-061) 98-0210.
Primary Working Agreement: None.
President: Lucas Rincon. **Vice President/General Manager:** Luis Rodolfo Machado Silva.
1997-98 Manager: Greg Biagini.

OTHER WINTER LEAGUES

ARIZONA FALL LEAGUE
Mailing Address: 10201 South 51st St., Suite 230, Phoenix, AZ 85044. **Telephone:** (602) 496-6700. **FAX:** (602) 496-6384. **E-Mail Address:** afl@goodnet.com. **Website:** www.majorleaguebaseball.com/special/arizona2.sml
Years League Active: 1992-.
Operated by: Major League Baseball.
Executive Vice President: Steve Cobb. **Administrative Assistant:** Joan McGrath.
Division Structure: North—Peoria, Scottsdale, Sun Cities. **South**—Grand Canyon, Mesa, Phoenix.
1998 Opening Date: Sept. 30. **Closing Date:** Nov. 19.
Regular Season: 45 games.
Playoff Format: Division champions meet in best-of-3 series for league championship.
Roster Limit: 29. No players from Puerto Rico, Dominican Republic or Venezuela. Players with less than one year of major league service are eligible.

GRAND CANYON RAFTERS
Mailing Address: See league address.
Working Agreements: Arizona Diamondbacks, Atlanta Braves, Detroit Tigers, Kansas City Royals, New York Mets, Philadelphia Phillies, Pittsburgh Pirates.
1997 Manager: Paul Runge (Braves).

MESA SAGUAROS
Mailing Address: See league address.
Working Agreements: Chicago Cubs, Chicago White Sox, Cleveland Indians, Philadelphia Phillies, Pittsburgh Pirates, St. Louis Cardinals.
1997 Manager: Jeff Datz (Indians).

PEORIA JAVELINAS
Mailing Address: See league address.
Working Agreements: Baltimore Orioles, Florida Marlins, Los Angeles Dodgers, Montreal Expos, Seattle Mariners, Tampa Bay Devil Rays.
1997 Manager: Mike Scioscia (Dodgers).

PHOENIX DESERT DOGS
Mailing Address: See league address.
Working Agreements: Anaheim Angels, Baltimore Orioles, Boston Red Sox, New York Yankees, Oakland Athletics, Tampa Bay Devil Rays, Toronto Blue Jays.
1997 Manager: Garth Iorg (Blue Jays).

SCOTTSDALE SCORPIONS
Mailing Address: See league address.
Working Agreements: Anaheim Angels, Arizona Diamondbacks, Cincinnati Reds, Colorado Rockies, San Francisco Giants, Texas Rangers.
1997 Manager: Ron Wotus (Giants).

SUN CITIES SOLAR SOX
Mailing Address: See league address.
Working Agreements: Houston Astros, Kansas City Royals, Milwaukee Brewers, Minnesota Twins, San Diego Padres, Tampa Bay Devil Rays.
1997 Manager: Al Newman (Twins).

AUSTRALIAN BASEBALL LEAGUE

Mailing Address: Level 2, 48 Atchison St., St. Leonards, New South Wales 2065 Australia. **Telephone:** (011-61-2) 9437-4622. **FAX:** (011-61-2) 9437-4155.
Chairman: Rod Byrne. **Manager, Baseball Operations:** Don Knapp. **Administration Manager:** Jane Taylor. **Director, Umpiring:** Geoff Robertson. **Manager, Game Operations:** Neil Barrowcliff.
1997-98 Opening Date: Oct. 29, 1997. **Closing Date:** Feb. 7, 1998.
Regular Season: 54 games.
Playoff Format: Top four teams meet in best-of-3 series. Winners meet in best-of-3 final for league championship.

ADELAIDE GIANTS
Mailing Address: P.O. Box 301, Kensington Park, SA 5068, Australia. **Telephone:** (08) 8364-3231. **FAX:** (08) 8364-3237.
Primary Working Agreement: Los Angeles Dodgers.
General Manager: Colin Alexander.
1997-98 Manager: Tony Harris.

BRISBANE BANDITS
Address: 127 Charlotte St., Brisbane, Queensland 4000, Australia. **Telephone:** (07) 3211-0080. **FAX:** (07) 3211-0082.
Primary Working Agreements: Detroit Tigers, San Diego Padres.
Chairman: Brian Richards. **Operations Manager:** Murdoch Campbell.
1997-98 Manager: Greg Wade.

GOLD COAST COUGARS
Address: Carrara Sports Stadium, Broadbeach Road, Nerang, Queensland 4211 Australia. **Telephone:** (075) 57-99972. **FAX:** (075) 57-99983.
Primary Working Agreement: Boston Red Sox.
General Manager: Glen Partridge.
1997-98 Manager: Bob Geren.

HUNTER EAGLES
Address: 44 Yeo St., Narara, New South Wales 2250, Australia. **Telephone:** (024) 328-3507. **FAX:** (024) 329-5037.
Primary Working Agreement: New York Mets.
General Manager: Paul Birch.
1996-97 Manager: Shane Barclay.

MELBOURNE MONARCHS
Address: P.O. Box 447, Berwick, Victoria 3806, Australia. **Telephone:** (03) 9705-1533. **FAX:** (03) 9705-1577.
Primary Working Agreement: Atlanta Braves.
Chief Operating Executive: Don Fenwick. **General Manager:** Phil Dale.
1997-98 Manager: Jon Deeble.

MELBOURNE REDS

Street Address: Moorabbin Reserve, Linton Street, Moorabbin, Victoria 3189, Australia. **Telephone:** (03) 9553-3202. **FAX:** (03) 9553-3257.

Primary Working Agreement: New York Yankees.

General Manager: Bruce Utting.

1997-98 Manager: Tom Nieto.

PERTH HEAT

Street Address: 159 Adelaide Terrace, Suite 12, Perth, Western Australia 6000. **Telephone:** (08) 9221-9799. **FAX:** (089) 9221-9798.

Primary Working Agreement: Baltimore Orioles.

General Manager: Douglas Mateljan.

1997-98 Manager: Bobby Dickerson.

SYDNEY STORM

Mailing Address: 48 Atchison St., Level 1, St. Leonards, New South Wales 2065, Australia. **Telephone:** (02) 9437-5546. **FAX:** (02) 9437-5834.

Primary Working Agreement: Toronto Blue Jays.

President: Trevor Jarrett. **General Manager:** David Balfour.

1997-98 Manager: Paul Elliott.

HAWAII WINTER BASEBALL

Mailing Address: 905 Makahiki Way, Unit C, Honolulu, HI 96826. **Telephone:** (808) 973-7247. **FAX:** (808) 973-7117.

Years League Active: 1993-.

Owner/Chairman: Duane Kurisu. **President:** Frank Kudo.

1997 Member Clubs: Hilo Stars, Honolulu Sharks, Maui Stingrays, West Oahu Canefires.

NOTE: League has suspended operations for 1998 season.

College Baseball

COLLEGE BASEBALL

NATIONAL COLLEGIATE
ATHLETIC ASSOCIATION

Mailing Address: 6201 College Blvd., Overland Park, KS 66211. **Telephone:** (913) 339-1906. **FAX:** (913) 339-0043.

Executive Director: Cedric Dempsey. **Director, Championships:** Dennis Poppe. **Contact, College World Series:** Jim Wright. **Contact, Statistics:** John Painter.

Chairman, Baseball Committee: Ron Wellman (athletic director, Wake Forest). **Baseball Committee:** Rich Alday (baseball coach, New Mexico), Jay Bergman (baseball coach, Central Florida), Joe Castiglione (athletic director, Missouri), John Easterbrook (athletic director, Cal State Fullerton), Paul Fernandes (associate athletic director, Columbia), Mike Knight (athletic director, Nicholls State), Dick Rockwell (athletic director, LeMoyne), Tim Weiser (athletic director, Eastern Michigan).

1999 National Convention: Jan. 9-12 at San Antonio.

1998 Championship Tournaments
NCAA Division I

College World Series .... Omaha, NE, May 29-June 6
Regionals .... Campus sites, May 21-24
Play-ins.. Campus sites, May 14-16

NCAA Division II

World Series .... Montgomery, AL, May 23-30

NCAA Division III

World Series .... Salem, VA, May 23-27

NATIONAL ASSOCIATION
OF INTERCOLLEGIATE ATHLETICS

Mailing Address: 6120 South Yale Ave., Suite 1450, Tulsa, OK 74136. **Telephone:** (918) 494-8828. **FAX:** (918) 494-8841.

Chief Executive Officer: Steve Baker. **Director, Championship Events:** Tim Kramer. **Baseball Event Coordinator:** John Mark Adkison.

1998 Championship Tournament

NAIA World Series... Tulsa, OK, May 18-23

NATIONAL JUNIOR COLLEGE
ATHLETIC ASSOCIATION

Mailing Address: P.O. Box 7305, Colorado Springs, CO 80933. **Telephone:** (719) 590-9788. **FAX:** (719) 590-7324.

Executive Director: George Killian. **Director, Division I Baseball Tournament:** Sam Suplizio. **Director, Division II Tournament:** John Daigle. **Director, Division III Tournament:** Barry Bower.

1998 Championship Tournaments
Division I

Junior College World Series .... Grand Junction, CO, May 23-30

Division II

World Series .... Millington, TN, May 23-29

Division III

World Series .... Batavia, NY, May 16-22

COMMUNITY COLLEGE LEAGUE
OF CALIFORNIA

Mailing Address: 2017 O St., Sacramento, CA 95814. **Telephone:** (916) 444-1600. **FAX:** (916) 444-2616.

Commissioner of Athletics: Joanne Fortunato. **Interim Associate Commissioner of Athletics:** Stuart Van Horn.

1998 Championship Tournament

State Championships .... Fresno City College, May 23-25

AMERICAN BASEBALL
COACHES ASSOCIATION

Office Address: 108 South University Ave., Suite 3, Mt. Pleasant, MI 48858. **Telephone:** (517) 775-3300. **FAX:** (517) 775-3600.

Executive Director: Dave Keilitz. **Assistant to Executive Director:** Betty Rulong. **Administrative Assistant:** Nick Williams.

President: Gary Pullins (Brigham Young University).

1999 National Convention: Jan. 7-10 at Atlanta.

NCAA DIVISION I CONFERENCES

AMERICA EAST CONFERENCE

Mailing Address: 10 High St., Suite 860, Boston, MA 02110. **Telephone:** (617) 695-6369. **FAX:** (617) 695-6385. **E-Mail Address:** bourque@americaeast.com. **Website:** www.americaeast.org.

Baseball Members (First Year): Delaware (1992), Drexel (1992), Hartford (1990), Hofstra (1995), Maine (1990), Northeastern (1990), Towson (1996), Vermont (1990).

Assistant Commissioner/Communications: Matt Bourque.

1998 Tournament: Four teams, double-elimination. May 14-16 at Frawley Stadium, Wilmington, DE.

ATLANTIC COAST CONFERENCE

Office Address: 4512 Weybridge Lane, Greensboro, NC 27407. **Mailing Address:** P.O. Drawer ACC, Greensboro, NC 27417. **Telephone:** (336) 851-6062. **FAX:** (336) 854-8797.

Baseball Members (First Year): Clemson (1953), Duke (1953), Florida State (1992), Georgia Tech (1980), Maryland (1953), North Carolina (1953), North Carolina State (1953), Virginia (1955), Wake Forest (1953).

Director, Media Relations: Brian Morrison. **Baseball Contact:** Emily Watkins.

1998 Tournament: Nine teams, double-elimination. May 12-17 at Durham Bulls Athletic Park, Durham, NC.

ATLANTIC-10 CONFERENCE

Mailing Address: 2 Penn Center Plaza, Suite 1410, Philadelphia, PA 19102. **Telephone:** (215) 751-0500. **FAX:** (215) 751-0770. **E-Mail Address:** rcella@atlantic10.org. **Website:** www.atlantic10.org.

Baseball Members (First Year): East—Fordham (1996), Massachusetts (1977), Rhode Island (1981), St. Bonaventure (1980), St. Joseph's (1983), Temple (1983). **West**—Dayton (1996), Duquesne (1977), George Washington (1977), LaSalle (1996), Virginia Tech (1996), Xavier (1996).

Assistant Commissioner/Communications: Ray Cella.

1998 Tournament: Four teams, double-elimination. May 8-10 at Boyertown, PA.

BIG EAST CONFERENCE

Mailing Address: 56 Exchange Terrace, Providence, RI 02903. **Telephone:** (401) 272-9108. **FAX:** (401) 751-8540. **E-Mail Address:** rcarolla@bigeast.org. **Website:** www.bigeast.org.

Baseball Members (First Year): Boston College (1985), Connecticut (1985), Georgetown (1985), Notre Dame (1996), Pittsburgh (1985), Providence (1985), Rutgers (1996), St. John's (1985), Seton Hall (1985), Villanova (1985), West Virginia (1996).

Assistant Director, Public Relations: Rob Carolla.

1998 Tournament: Six teams, double-elimination. May 13-16 at Thomas J. Dodd Stadium, Norwich, CT.

BIG SOUTH CONFERENCE

Mailing Address: 6428 Bannington Dr., Suite A, Charlotte, NC 28226. **Telephone:** (704) 341-7990. **FAX:** (704) 341-7991.

Baseball Members (First Year): Charleston Southern (1983), Coastal Carolina (1983), Liberty (1991), Maryland-Baltimore County (1992), UNC Asheville (1985), Radford (1983), Winthrop (1983).

Director, Public Relations: Shannon Fritts.

1998 Tournament: Four teams, double-elimination. May 8-10 at Knights Castle, Fort Mill, SC.

BIG TEN CONFERENCE

Mailing Address: 1500 West Higgins Rd., Park Ridge, IL 60068. **Telephone:** (847) 696-1010. **FAX:** (847) 696-1110. **E-Mail Address:** jchristman@big10.org. **Website:** www.bigten.org.

Baseball Members (First Year): Illinois (1896), Indiana (1899), Iowa (1899), Michigan (1896), Michigan State (1950), Minnesota (1896), Northwestern (1896), Ohio State (1912), Penn State (1990), Purdue (1896).

Communications Intern: Jim Christman.

1998 Tournament: Four teams, double-elimination. May 14-17 at regular-season champion.

BIG 12 CONFERENCE

Mailing Address: 2201 Stemmons Freeway, 28th Floor, Dallas, TX 75207. **Telephone:** (214) 742-1212, ext. 202. **FAX:** (214) 742-2046. **E-Mail Address:** bcarter@email.big12.com. **Website:** www.big12conf.com.

Baseball Members (First Year): Baylor (1997), Iowa State (1997), Kansas (1997), Kansas State (1997), Missouri (1997), Nebraska (1997), Oklahoma (1997), Oklahoma State (1997), Texas (1997), Texas A&M (1997), Texas Tech (1997).

Director, Service Bureau: Bo Carter.

1998 Tournament: Six teams, double-elimination. May 14-17 at The Ballpark in Bricktown, Oklahoma City, OK.

BIG WEST CONFERENCE

Mailing Address: 2 Corporate Park, Suite 206, Irvine, CA 92606. **Telephone:**

(714) 261-2525. **FAX:** (714) 261-2528. **E-Mail Address:** gathca@apollo. adcom.uci.edu. **Website:** www.uidaho.edu/admin/ncaa/bigwest.

Baseball Members (First Year): Cal Poly San Luis Obispo (1997), UC Santa Barbara (1970), Cal State Fullerton (1975), Long Beach State (1970), Nevada (1993), New Mexico State (1992), Pacific (1972), Sacramento State (1997).

Assistant Information Director: Mike Villamor.

1998 Tournament: Six teams, double-elimination. May 14-17 at Cal State Fullerton.

COLONIAL ATHLETIC ASSOCIATION

Mailing Address: 8625 Patterson Ave., Richmond, VA 23229. **Telephone:** (804) 754-1616. **FAX:** (804) 754-1830. **E-Mail Address:** svehorn@richmond.edu. **Website:** www.caasports.com.

Baseball Members (First Year): East Carolina (1986), George Mason (1986), James Madison (1986), UNC Wilmington (1986), Old Dominion (1992), Richmond (1986), Virginia Commonwealth (1996), William & Mary (1985).

Sports Information Director: Steve Vehorn.

1998 Tournament: Eight teams, double-elimination. May 12-16 at Grainger Stadium, Kinston, NC.

CONFERENCE USA

Mailing Address: 35 East Wacker Dr., Suite 650, Chicago, IL 60601. **Telephone:** (312) 553-0483. **FAX:** (312) 553-0495. **E-Mail Address:** rdanderson.@c-usa.org. **Website:** www.c-usa.org.

Baseball Members (First Year): Alabama-Birmingham (1996), Cincinnati (1996), Houston (1997), Louisville (1996), Memphis (1996), UNC Charlotte (1996), Saint Louis (1996), South Florida (1996), Southern Mississippi (1996), Tulane (1996).

Assistant Director, Communications: Russ Anderson.

1998 Tournament: Ten teams, double-elimination. May 12-17 at Zephyr Field, New Orleans, LA.

IVY LEAGUE

Mailing Address: 330 Alexander St., Princeton, NJ 08544. **Telephone:** (609) 258-6426. **FAX:** (609) 258-1690.

E-Mail Address: yrigoyen@princeton.edu. **Website:** www.ivyleague.princeton.edu.

Baseball Members (First Year): Rolfe—Brown (1993), Dartmouth (1993), Harvard (1993), Yale (1993). **Gehrig**—Columbia (1993), Cornell (1993), Pennsylvania (1993), Princeton (1993).

Associate Director/Communications: Chuck Yrigoyen.

1998 Tournament: Best-of-3 series between division champions. May 9-10 at Gehrig champion.

METRO ATLANTIC ATHLETIC CONFERENCE

Mailing Address: 1090 Amboy Ave., Edison, NJ 08837. **Telephone:** (732) 225-0202, ext. 5. **FAX:** (732) 225-5440. **E-Mail Address:** mike.scala@maac.org. **Website:** www.maac.org.

Baseball Members (First Year): North—Canisius (1990), LeMoyne (1990), Marist (1998), Niagara (1990), Siena (1990). **South**—Fairfield (1982), Iona (1982), Manhattan (1982), Rider (1998), St. Peter's (1982).

Director, Media Relations: Mike Scala.

1998 Tournament: Four teams, double-elimination. May 8-10 at Dutchess Stadium, Fishkill, NY.

MID-AMERICAN CONFERENCE

Mailing Address: Four Sea Gate, Suite 102, Toledo, OH 43604. **Telephone:** (419) 249-7177, ext. 305. **FAX:** (419) 242-4022. **E-Mail Address:** srobinson@midamconf.com. **Website:** www.midamconf.com.

Baseball Members (First Year): East—Akron (1992), Bowling Green State (1952), Kent (1951), Marshall (1996), Miami (1947), Ohio (1946). **West**—Ball State (1973), Central Michigan (1971), Eastern Michigan (1971), Northern Illinois (1996), Toledo (1950), Western Michigan (1947).

Assistant Director, Communications: Shawn Robinson.

1998 Tournament: Six teams, double-elimination. May 13-16 at regular-season champion.

MID-CONTINENT CONFERENCE

Mailing Address: 340 West Butterfield Rd., Suite 3-D, Elmhurst, IL 60126. **Telephone:** (630) 516-0661. **FAX:** (630) 516-0673.

Baseball Members (First Year): East—Central Connecticut State (1994), C.W. Post (1995), New York Tech (1995), Pace (1995), Youngstown State (1992). **West**—Chicago State (1994), Northeastern Illinois (1994), Oral Roberts (1998), Valparaiso (1982), Western Illinois (1982).

Assistant Commissioner: Mark Simpson.

1998 Tournament: Six teams, double-elimination. May 7-10 at Oral Roberts University.

MID-EASTERN ATHLETIC CONFERENCE

Mailing Address: 102 North Elm St., Suite 401, P.O. Box 21205, Greensboro, NC 27420. **Telephone:** (336) 275-9961. **FAX:** (336) 275-9964. **E-Mail Address:** meac@nr.infi.net. **Website:** www.greensboro.com/meac/.

Baseball Members (First Year): North—Coppin State (1985), Delaware State (1970), Howard (1970), Maryland-Eastern Shore (1970). **South**—Bethune-Cookman (1979), Florida A&M (1979), Norfolk State (1998), North Carolina A&T

(1970).

Director, Media Relations: Larry Barber.

1998 Tournament: Eight teams, double-elimination. May 1-3 at Daytona Beach, FL.

MIDWESTERN COLLEGIATE CONFERENCE

Mailing Address: 201 South Capitol Ave., Suite 500, Indianapolis, IN 46214. **Telephone:** (317) 237-5622. **FAX:** (317) 237-5620.

E-Mail Address: mbonifas@mccnet.org. **Website:** www.mccnet.org.

Baseball Members (First Year): Butler (1979), Cleveland State (1994), Detroit (1980), Illinois-Chicago (1994), Wisconsin-Milwaukee (1994), Wright State (1994).

Assistant Director, Communications: Megan Bonifas.

1998 Tournament: Six teams, double-elimination. May 8-10 at Chicago, IL.

MISSOURI VALLEY CONFERENCE

Mailing Address: 1016 I Century Oaks Dr., Suite 105, St. Louis, MO 63103. **Telephone:** (314) 421-0339. **FAX:** (314) 421-3505. **E-Mail Address:** watkins@ mvc.org. **Website:** www.mvc.org.

Baseball Members (First Year): Bradley (1955), Creighton (1976), Evansville (1994), Illinois State (1980), Indiana State (1976), Northern Iowa (1991), Southern Illinois (1974), Southwest Missouri State (1990), Wichita State (1945).

Assistant Commissioner: Jack Watkins. **Assistant, Communications:** Melody Yount.

1998 Tournament: Six teams, double-elimination. May 13-16 at Bosse Field, Evansville, IN.

NORTHEAST CONFERENCE

Mailing Address: 220 Old New Brunswick Rd., Piscataway, NJ 08854. **Telephone:** (732) 562-0877. **FAX:** (732) 562-8838. **E-Mail Address:** omgormley@aol.com. **Website:** www.northeastconference.org.

Baseball Members (First Year): Fairleigh Dickinson (1981), Long Island (1981), Monmouth (1985), Mount St. Mary's (1989), St. Francis, N.Y. (1981), Wagner (1981).

Assistant Commissioner: Denise Gormley.

1998 Tournament: Four teams, double-elimination. May 8-10 at Waterfront Park, Trenton, NJ.

OHIO VALLEY CONFERENCE

Mailing Address: 278 Franklin Rd., Suite 103, Brentwood, TN 37027. **Telephone:** (615) 371-1698. **FAX:** (615) 371-1788. **E-Mail Address:** rwashburn@ovc.org. **Website:** www.ovc.org.

Baseball Members (First Year): Austin Peay State (1963), Eastern Illinois (1996), Eastern Kentucky (1948), Middle Tennessee State (1952), Morehead State (1948), Murray State (1948), Southeast Missouri State (1991), Tennessee-Martin (1992), Tennessee Tech (1949).

Assistant Commissioner: Rob Washburn.

1998 Tournament: Six teams, double-elimination. May 7-9, site unavailable.

PACIFIC-10 CONFERENCE

Mailing Address: 800 South Broadway, Suite 400, Walnut Creek, CA 94596. **Telephone:** (510) 932-4411. **FAX:** (510) 932-4601. **E-Mail Address:** btom@pac-10.org. **Website:** www.pac-10.org.

Baseball Members (First Year): North—Oregon State (1916), Portland State (1982), Washington (1916), Washington State (1917). **South**—Arizona (1979), Arizona State (1979), California (1916), UCLA (1928), Southern California (1922), Stanford (1917).

Baseball Intern: Brian Tom.

1998 Tournament: Best-of-3 series between division champions. May 14-16 at Northern Division champion.

PATRIOT LEAGUE

Mailing Address: 3897 Adler Place, Bldg. C, Suite 310, Bethlehem, PA 18017. **Telephone:** (610) 691-2414. **FAX:** (610) 691-8414. **E-Mail Address:** tan0@lehigh.edu. **Website:** www.lehigh.edu\~inPat.

Baseball Members (First Year): Army (1993), Bucknell (1991), Holy Cross (1991), Lafayette (1991), Lehigh (1991), Navy (1993).

Associate Executive Director: Todd Newcomb.

1998 Tournament: Best-of-3 series. May 2-3 at No. 1 seed.

SOUTHEASTERN CONFERENCE

Mailing Address: 2201 Civic Center Blvd., Birmingham, AL 35203. **Telephone:** (205) 458-3010. **FAX:** (205) 458-3030. **E-Mail Address:** cbloom@ sec.org. **Website:** secsports.com.

Baseball Members (First Year): East—Florida (1933), Georgia (1933), Kentucky (1933), South Carolina (1991), Tennessee (1933), Vanderbilt (1933). **West**—Alabama (1933), Arkansas (1991), Auburn (1933), Louisiana State (1933), Mississippi (1933), Mississippi State (1933).

Assistant Commissioner: Charles Bloom.

1998 Tournament: Eight teams, modified double-elimination. May 13-17 at Hoover Metropolitan Stadium, Birmingham, AL.

SOUTHERN CONFERENCE

Mailing Address: One West Pack Square, Suite 1508, Asheville, NC 28801. **Telephone:** (704) 255-7872. **FAX:** (704) 251-5006. **E-Mail Address:** socon@

socon.org. **Website:** www.socon.org.

Baseball Members (First Year): Appalachian State (1971), The Citadel (1936), Davidson (1991), East Tennessee State (1978), Furman (1936), Georgia Southern (1991), UNC Greensboro (1998), Virginia Military Institute (1924), Western Carolina (1976), Wofford (1998).

Assistant Commisioner: Heather Czeczok.

1998 Tournament: Eight teams, double-elimination. April 30-May 3 at The Citadel, Charleston, SC.

SOUTHLAND CONFERENCE

Mailing Address: 8150 North Central Expressway, Dallas, TX 75206. **Telephone:** (214) 750-7522. **FAX:** (214) 750-8077. **E-Mail Address:** bludlow@southland.org.

Baseball Members (First Year): McNeese State (1971), Nicholls State (1991), Northeast Louisiana (1982), Northwestern State (1987), Sam Houston State (1987), Southeastern Louisiana (1998), Southwest Texas State (1987), Texas-Arlington (1987), Texas-San Antonio (1991).

Director, Media Relations: Bruce Ludlow.

1998 Tournament: Six teams, double-elimination. May 13-16 at Fair Grounds Field, Shreveport, LA.

SOUTHWESTERN ATHLETIC CONFERENCE

Mailing Address: Louisiana Superdome, 1500 Sugar Bowl Dr., New Orleans, LA 70112. **Telephone:** (504) 523-7574. **FAX:** (504) 523-7513. **E-Mail Address:** lhardy@swac.org. **Website:** www.swac.org.

Baseball Members (First Year): East—Alabama State (1982), Alcorn State (1962), Jackson State (1958), Mississippi Valley State (1968). **West**—Grambling State (1958), Prairie View A&M (1920), Southern (1934), Texas Southern (1954).

Assistant Commissioner, Media Relations: Lonza Hardy.

1998 Tournament: Four teams, double-elimination. April 17-19 at New Orleans, LA.

SUN BELT CONFERENCE

Mailing Address: One Galleria Blvd., Suite 2115, Metairie, LA 70001. **Telephone:** (504) 834-6600. **FAX:** (504) 834-6806. **E-Mail Address:** reynolds@sunbeltsports.org. **Website:** www.sunbeltsports.org.

Baseball Members (First Year): Arkansas-Little Rock (1991), Arkansas State (1991), Jacksonville (1976), Lamar (1991), Louisiana Tech (1991), New Orleans (1976), South Alabama (1976), Southwestern Louisiana (1991), Texas-Pan American (1991), Western Kentucky (1982).

Assistant Director, Media Services: Jeff Reynolds.

1998 Tournament: Six teams, double-elimination. May 13-16 at Hank Aaron Stadium, Mobile, AL.

TRANSAMERICA ATHLETIC CONFERENCE

Mailing Address: The Commons, 3370 Vineville Ave., Suite 108-B, Macon, GA 31204. **Telephone:** (912) 474-3394. **FAX:** (912) 474-4272.

Baseball Members (First Year): East—Campbell (1994), Charleston (1991), Georgia State (1983), Mercer (1978). **South**—Central Florida (1992), Florida Atlantic (1993), Florida International (1990), Stetson (1985). **West**—Centenary (1978), Jacksonville State (1996), Samford (1978), Troy State (1998).

Director, Information: Tom Snyder.

1998 Tournament: Twelve teams, best-of-3, May 8-9 at No. 1 and 2 seeds of each division; championship, double elimination, May 13-15 at Kissimmee, FL.

WEST COAST CONFERENCE

Mailing Address: 400 Oyster Point Blvd., Suite 221, South San Francisco, CA 94080. **Telephone:** (650) 873-8622. **FAX:** (650) 873-7846. **E-Mail Address:** wcc@westcoast.org. **Website:** www.westcoast.org.

Baseball Members (First Year): Gonzaga (1996), Loyola Marymount (1968), Pepperdine (1968), Portland (1996), St. Mary's (1968), San Diego (1979), San Francisco (1968), Santa Clara (1968).

Assistant, Public Relations: Mark Papadopoulos.

1998 Tournament: None.

WESTERN ATHLETIC CONFERENCE

Mailing Address: 9250 East Costilla Ave., Suite 300, Englewood, CO 80112. **Telephone:** (303) 799-9221. **FAX:** (303) 799-3888. **E-Mail Address:** wac@wac.org. **Website:** www.wac.org.

Baseball Members (First Year): North—Air Force (1980), Brigham Young (1962), Grand Canyon (1995), Utah (1962). **South**—Nevada-Las Vegas (1996), New Mexico (1962), Rice (1996), Texas Christian (1996). **West**—Fresno State (1992), Hawaii (1979), San Diego State (1978), San Jose State (1996).

Associate Director, Communications: Vicki Boillot.

1998 Tournament: Six teams, double-elimination. May 13-16, site unavailable.

*Recruiting coordinator

AIR FORCE ACADEMY Falcons
Conference: Western Athletic (North).
Mailing Address: 2169 Field House, USAF Academy, CO 80840.
Head Coach: Eric Campbell. **Assistant Coaches:** *Mike Barbato, Manny Robinson. **Telephone:** (719) 333-2057. ■ **Baseball SID:** Dave Toller. **Telephone:** (719) 333-2313. **FAX:** (719) 333-3798.
Home Field: Falcon Field. **Seating Capacity:** 1,000. **Outfield Dimensions:** LF—349, CF—400, RF—316. **Press Box Telephone:** (719) 333-3472.

AKRON Zips
Conference: Mid-American (East).
Mailing Address: JAR Arena, Carroll Street, Akron, OH 44325.
Head Coach: Dave Fross. **Assistant Coaches:** Tim Berenyi, Marc Thomas. **Telephone:** (330) 972-7277. ■ **Baseball SID:** Tom Liggett. **Telephone:** (330) 972-7468. **FAX:** (330) 374-8844.
Home Field: Lee R. Jackson Field. **Seating Capacity:** 2,500. **Outfield Dimensions:** LF—330, CF—405, RF—330. **Press Box Telephone:** (330) 972-8896.

ALABAMA Crimson Tide
Conference: Southeastern (West).
Mailing Address: P.O. Box 870391, Tuscaloosa, AL 35487.
Head Coach: Jim Wells. **Assistant Coaches:** Kirk Blount, Todd Butler, *Mitch Gaspard. **Telephone:** (205) 348-6171. ■ **Baseball SID:** Barry Allen. **Telephone:** (205) 348-6084. **FAX:** (205) 348-8840/8841.
Home Field: Sewell-Thomas Stadium. **Seating Capacity:** 4,007. **Outfield Dimensions:** LF—325, CF—405, RF—325. **Press Box Telephone:** (205) 348-4927.

ALABAMA-BIRMINGHAM Blazers
Conference: Conference USA.
Mailing Address: 617 13th St. South, Room 115, Birmingham, AL 35294.
Head Coach: Pete Rancont. **Assistant Coaches:** Brian Pompili, Frank Walton. **Telephone:** (205) 934-5181. ■ **Baseball SID:** Chris Pika. **Telephone:** (205) 934-0722. **FAX:** (205) 934-7505.
Home Field: Jerry D. Young Memorial Field. **Seating Capacity:** 1,000. **Outfield Dimensions:** LF—337, CF—390, RF—330. **Press Box Telephone:** (205) 975-0200.

ALABAMA STATE Hornets
Conference: Southwestern Athletic (East).
Mailing Address: P.O. Box 271, Montgomery, AL 36101.
Head Coach: Larry Watkins. **Assistant Coaches:** John Broom, James Graham. **Telephone:** (334) 293-4507, ext. 4228. ■ **Baseball SID:** Peter Forest. **Telephone:** (334) 229-4511. **FAX:** (334) 262-2971.

ALCORN STATE Braves
Conference: Southwestern Athletic (East).
Mailing Address: 1000 ASU Drive, No. 510, Lorman, MS 39096.
Head Coach: Willie McGowan. **Assistant Coach:** David Robinson. **Telephone:** (601) 877-6279. ■ **Baseball SID:** Derick Hackett. **Telephone:** (601) 877-6466. **FAX:** (601) 877-3821.

APPALACHIAN STATE Mountaineers
Conference: Southern.
Mailing Address: Broome-Kirk Gymnasium, Boone, NC 28608.
Head Coach: Jim Morris. **Assistant Coaches:** John Barrow, *Troy Heustess, Daryl Walls. **Telephone:** (704) 262-6097. ■ **Baseball SID:** Will Prewitt. **Telephone:** (704) 262-2268. **FAX:** (704) 262-6106.

ARIZONA Wildcats
Conference: Pacific-10 (South).
Mailing Address: P.O. Box 210096, Tucson, AZ 85721.
Head Coach: Jerry Stitt. **Assistant Coaches:** *Bill Kinneberg, Victor Solis. **Telephone:** (520) 621-4102. ■ **Baseball SID:** David Hardee. **Telephone:** (520) 621-4163. **FAX:** (520) 621-2681.
Home Field: Frank Sancet Field. **Seating Capacity:** 6,700. **Outfield Dimensions:** LF—360, CF—400, RF—360. **Press Box Telephone:** (520) 621-4440.

ARIZONA STATE Sun Devils
Conference: Pacific-10 (South).
Mailing Address: P.O. Box 872505, Tempe, AZ 85287.
Head Coach: Pat Murphy. **Assistant Coaches:** Nino Giarratano, *Doug Schreiber, Chris Sinacori. **Telephone:** (602) 965-6085. ■ **Baseball SID:** Aimee Dombroski. **Telephone:** (602) 965-6592. **FAX:** (602) 965-5408.
Home Field: Packard Stadium. **Seating Capacity:** 7,875. **Outfield Dimensions:** LF—340, CF—395, RF—340. **Press Box Telephone:** (602) 965-1509.

ARKANSAS Razorbacks
Conference: Southeastern (West).
Mailing Address: P.O. Box 7777, Fayetteville, AR 72702.
Head Coach: Norm DeBriyn. **Assistant Coaches:** Doug Clark, Chip Durham,

*Tim Montez. **Telephone:** (501) 575-6739. ■ **Baseball SID:** Kevin Trainor. **Telephone:** (501) 575-2751. **FAX:** (501) 575-7481.

Home Field: Baum Stadium. **Seating Capacity:** 3,300. **Outfield Dimensions:** LF—320, CF—400, RF—320. **Press Box Telephone:** (501) 444-0031.

ARKANSAS-LITTLE ROCK Trojans

Conference: Sun Belt.

Mailing Address: 2801 South University, Little Rock, AR 72204.

Head Coach: Brian Rhees. **Assistant Coaches:** Mark Coca, *Karl Kuhn. **Telephone:** (501) 663-8095. ■ **Baseball SID:** Jason Whaley. **Telephone:** (501) 569-3449. **FAX:** (501) 569-3030.

ARKANSAS STATE Indians

Conference: Sun Belt.

Mailing Address: P.O. Box 1000, State University, AR 72467.

Head Coach: Bill Bethea. **Assistant Coaches:** Skip Blythe, David Grimes, David Kenley. **Telephone:** (870) 972-2700. ■ **Baseball SID:** Scott Costello. **Telephone:** (870) 972-2541. **FAX:** (870) 972-3367.

Home Field: Tomlinson Stadium—Kell Field. **Seating Capacity:** 1,000. **Outfield Dimensions:** LF—335, CF—400, RF—335. **Press Box Telephone:** (870) 972-3383.

ARMY Cadets

Conference: Patriot.

Mailing Address: Howard Road, Building 639, West Point, NY 10996.

Head Coach: Dan Roberts. **Assistant Coach:** Joe Sottolano. **Telephone:** (914) 938-3712. ■ **Baseball SID:** Bob Beretta. **Telephone:** (914) 938-3512. **FAX:** (914) 446-2556.

AUBURN Tigers

Conference: Southeastern (West).

Mailing Address: P.O. Box 351, Auburn, AL 36831.

Head Coach: Hal Baird. **Assistant Coaches:** *Steve Renfroe, Tom Slater. **Telephone:** (334) 844-9767. ■ **Baseball SID:** Scott Stricklin. **Telephone:** (334) 844-9800. **FAX:** (334) 844-9807.

Home Field: Hitchcock Field at Plainsman Park. **Seating Capacity:** 3,186. **Outfield Dimensions:** LF—315, CF—385, RF—331. **Press Box Telephone:** (334) 844-4138.

AUSTIN PEAY STATE Governors

Conference: Ohio Valley.

Mailing Address: P.O. Box 4515, Clarksville, TN 37044.

Head Coach: Gary McClure. **Assistant Coaches:** Steve Cornelison, *Brian Hetland, Kris Runk. **Telephone:** (931) 648-7903. ■ **Baseball SID:** Peter Sullivan. **Telephone:** (931) 648-7561. **FAX:** (931) 648-7562.

BALL STATE Cardinals

Conference: Mid-American (West).

Mailing Address: 2000 University Ave., Muncie, IN 47306.

Head Coach: Rich Maloney. **Assistant Coaches:** Rob Gamble, Ken Jones, John Lowery. **Telephone:** (765) 285-8226. ■ **Baseball SID:** Bob Moore. **Telephone:** (765) 285-8242. **FAX:** (765) 285-8929.

Home Field: Ball Diamond. **Seating Capacity:** 1,700. **Outfield Dimensions:** LF—330, CF—400, RF—330. **Press Box Telephone:** (765) 285-8932.

BAYLOR Bears

Conference: Big 12.

Mailing Address: 150 Bear Run, Waco, TX 76711.

Head Coach: Steve Smith. **Assistant Coaches:** Steve Johnigan, *Mitch Thompson. **Telephone:** (254) 710-3029. ■ **Baseball SID:** Jason Archinal. **Telephone:** (254) 710-3066. **FAX:** (254) 710-1369.

Home Field: Ferrell Field. **Seating Capacity:** 1,700. **Outfield Dimensions:** LF—330, CF—400, RF—330. **Press Box Telephone:** (254) 754-5546.

BETHUNE-COOKMAN Wildcats

Conference: Mid-Eastern Athletic (South).

Mailing Address: 640 Mary McLeod Bethune Blvd., Daytona Beach, FL 32114.

Head Coach: Richard Skeel. **Assistant Coaches:** Arthur McConnehead, Mervyl Melendez. **Telephone:** (904) 255-1401, ext. 308. ■ **Baseball SID:** Julius Benford. **Telephone:** (904) 258-7621. **FAX:** (904) 253-4231.

BOSTON COLLEGE Eagles

Conference: Big East.

Mailing Address: 321 Conte Forum, Chestnut Hill, MA 02167.

Head Coach: Moe Maloney. **Assistant Coach:** Mike Martin. **Telephone:** (617) 552-3092. ■ **Baseball SID:** Dick Kelley. **Telephone:** (617) 552-3039. **FAX:** (617) 552-4903.

Home Field: Commander Shea Field. **Seating Capacity:** 1,000. **Outfield Dimensions:** LF—315, CF—390, RF—310. **Press Box Telephone:** None.

BOWLING GREEN STATE Falcons

Conference: Mid-American (East).

Mailing Address: Perry Stadium, Bowling Green, OH 43403.

Head Coach: Danny Schmitz. **Assistant Coaches:** L.J. Archambeau, Mark Nell. **Telephone:** (419) 372-7065. ■ **Baseball SID:** Mark Kunstmann. **Telephone:** (419) 372-7076. **FAX:** (419) 372-6015.

BRADLEY Braves

Conference: Missouri Valley.
Mailing Address: 1501 West Bradley Ave., Peoria, IL 61625.
Head Coach: Dewey Kalmer. **Assistant Coaches:** John Dyke, John Young. **Telephone:** (309) 677-2684. ■ **Baseball SID:** Bo Ryan. **Telephone:** (309) 677-2627. **FAX:** (309) 677-2626.
Home Field: Vonachen Stadium. **Seating Capacity:** 6,200. **Outfield Dimensions:** LF—335, CF—383, RF—335. **Press Box Telephone:** (309) 688-2653.

BRIGHAM YOUNG Cougars

Conference: Western Athletic (North).
Mailing Address: 30 SFH, Provo, UT 84602.
Head Coach: Gary Pullins. **Assistant Coaches:** Todd Armstrong, *Bob Noel. **Telephone:** (801) 378-5049. ■ **Baseball SID:** Ralph Zobell. **Telephone:** (801) 378-4909. **FAX:** (801) 378-3520.
Home Field: Cougar Field. **Seating Capacity:** 4,000. **Outfield Dimensions:** LF—345, CF—390, RF—345. **Press Box Telephone:** (801) 378-4041.

BROWN Bears

Conference: Ivy League (Rolfe).
Mailing Address: Box 1932, Providence, RI 02912.
Head Coach: Marek Drabinski. **Assistant Coach:** Dennis Dwyer. **Telephone:** (401) 863-3090. ■ **Baseball SID:** Gordon Morton. **Telephone:** (401) 863-2219. **FAX:** (401) 863-1436.

BUCKNELL Bison

Conference: Patriot.
Mailing Address: Davis Gym, Lewisburg, PA 17837.
Head Coach: Gene Depew. **Assistant Coaches:** Brian Hoyt, Brian McRoberts. **Telephone:** (717) 523-3593. ■ **Baseball SID:** Bob Behler. **Telephone:** (717) 524-1227. **FAX:** (717) 524-1660.

BUTLER Bulldogs

Conference: Midwestern Collegiate.
Mailing Address: 4600 Sunset Ave., Indianapolis, IN 46208.
Head Coach: Steve Farley. **Assistant Coaches:** Tony Baldwin, Matt Buczkowski. **Telephone:** (317) 940-9721. ■ **Baseball SID:** Tony Hamilton. **Telephone:** (317) 940-9671. **FAX:** (317) 940-9808.

C.W. POST Pioneers

Conference: Mid-Continent (East).
Mailing Address: 720 Northern Blvd., Brookville, NY 11548.
Head Coach: Dick Vining. **Assistant Coaches:** Dan Mascia, Pete Timmes. **Telephone:** (516) 299-2288. ■ **Baseball SID:** Jeremy Kniffin. **Telephone:** (516) 299-4156. **FAX:** (516) 299-3155.

CALIFORNIA Golden Bears

Conference: Pacific-10 (South).
Mailing Address: 210 Memorial Stadium, Berkeley, CA 94720.
Head Coach: Bob Milano. **Assistant Coaches:** *David Lawn, Scott Murray, Pat Shine. **Telephone:** (510) 643-6006. ■ **Baseball SID:** Scott Ball. **Telephone:** (510) 643-1741. **FAX:** (510) 643-7778.
Home Field: Evans Diamond. **Seating Capacity:** 4,000. **Outfield Dimensions:** LF—320, CF—395, RF—320. **Press Box Telephone:** (510) 642-3098.

UCLA Bruins

Conference: Pacific-10 (South).
Mailing Address: P.O. Box 24044, Los Angeles, CA 90024.
Head Coach: Gary Adams. **Assistant Coaches:** *Vince Beringhele, Brian Criss, Tim Leary. **Telephone:** (310) 794-8210. ■ **Baseball SID:** Jeff Blank. **Telephone:** (310) 206-7870. **FAX:** (310) 825-8664.
Home Field: Jackie Robinson Stadium. **Seating Capacity:** 1,250. **Outfield Dimensions:** LF—365, CF—395, RF—365. **Press Box Telephone:** (310) 794-8213.

UC SANTA BARBARA Gauchos

Conference: Big West (South).
Mailing Address: 1000 Robertson Gym, Santa Barbara, CA 93106.
Head Coach: Bob Brontsema. **Assistant Coaches:** John Kirkgard, Shad Knighton, Tom Myers. **Telephone:** (805) 893-3690. ■ **Baseball SID:** Tim Cummins. **Telephone:** (805) 893-8603. **FAX:** (805) 893-4537.
Home Field: Caesar Uyesaka Stadium. **Seating Capacity:** 1,000. **Outfield Dimensions:** LF—335, CF—400, RF—335. **Press Box Telephone:** (805) 893-4671.

CAL POLY SAN LUIS OBISPO Mustangs

Conference: Big West (South).
Mailing Address: One Grand Ave., San Luis Obispo, CA 93407.
Head Coach: Ritch Price. **Assistant Coaches:** Tom Kunis, Rob Neal, Mike Oakland. **Telephone:** (805) 756-6367. ■ **Baseball SID:** Mickey Seward. **Telephone:** (805) 756-6531. **FAX:** (805) 756-2650.
Home Field: San Luis Obispo Stadium. **Seating Capacity:** 3,500. **Outfield Dimensions:** LF—333, CF—410, RF—333. **Press Box Telephone:** (805) 756-2410.

CAL STATE FULLERTON Titans

Conference: Big West (South).
Mailing Address: 800 North State College Blvd., PE 133C, Fullerton, CA 92634.
Head Coach: George Horton. **Assistant Coaches:** Mike Kirby, *Dave Ser-

rano, Rick Vanderhook. **Telephone:** (714) 278-3789. ■ **Baseball SID:** Michael Greenlee. **Telephone:** (714) 278-3970. **FAX:** Unavailable.

    Home Field: Titan Field. **Seating Capacity:** 1,750. **Outfield Dimensions:** LF—330, CF—400, RF—330. **Press Box Telephone:** (714) 278-5327.

CAL STATE NORTHRIDGE Matadors

    Conference: Independent.

    Mailing Address: 18111 Nordhoff St., Northridge, CA 91330.

    Head Coach: Mike Batesole. **Assistant Coaches:** Randy Cooper, Grant Hohman. **Telephone:** (818) 677-7055. ■ **Baseball SID:** Daniel Lathey. **Telephone:** (818) 677-3243. **FAX:** (818) 677-4762.

    Home Field: Matador Field. **Seating Capacity:** 1,200. **Outfield Dimensions:** LF—325, CF—400, RF—330. **Press Box Telephone:** (818) 677-4293.

CAMPBELL Fighting Camels

    Conference: TransAmerica Athletic (East).

    Mailing Address: P.O. Box 10, Buies Creek, NC 27506.

    Head Coach: Chip Smith. **Assistant Coaches:** Jeff Bock, *Randy Hood. **Telephone:** (910) 893-1354. ■ **Baseball SID:** Stan Cole. **Telephone:** (910) 893-1331. **FAX:** (910) 893-1330.

CANISIUS Golden Griffins

    Conference: Metro Atlantic (North).

    Mailing Address: 2001 Main St., Buffalo, NY 14208.

    Head Coach: Don Colpoys. **Assistant Coach:** Ray Hennessy, David Penafeather. **Telephone:** (716) 858-7030. ■ **Baseball SID:** John Maddock. **Telephone:** (716) 888-2977. **FAX:** (716) 888-2980.

CENTENARY Gents

    Conference: Trans America Athletic (West).

    Mailing Address: Box 41188, Shreveport, LA 71134.

    Head Coach: Mark Linden. **Assistant Coaches:** Scott Leach, Ed McCann. **Telephone:** (318) 869-5095. ■ **Baseball SID:** Craig Lawson. **Telephone:** (318) 869-5092. **FAX:** (318) 869-5145.

CENTRAL CONNECTICUT STATE Blue Devils

    Conference: Mid-Continent (East).

    Mailing Address: Kaiser Hall, 1615 Stanley St., New Britain, CT 06050.

    Head Coach: George Redman. **Assistant Coaches:** Mike Church, Craig Schmitt. **Telephone:** (860) 832-3074. ■ **Baseball SID:** Bill Peterson. **Telephone:** (860) 832-3059. **FAX:** (860) 832-3084.

CENTRAL FLORIDA Golden Knights

    Conference: Trans America Athletic (South).

    Mailing Address: P.O. Box 163555, Orlando, FL 32816.

    Head Coach: Jay Bergman. **Assistant Coaches:** Craig Cozart, *Greg Frady, Rookie Gage. **Telephone:** (407) 823-0140. ■ **Baseball SID:** Stephanie Burchill. **Telephone:** (407) 823-2464. **FAX:** (407) 823-5266.

    Home Field: UCF Baseball Complex. **Seating Capacity:** 2,500. **Outfield Dimensions:** LF—330, CF—400, RF—330. **Press Box Telephone:** (407) 823-5002.

CENTRAL MICHIGAN Chippewas

    Conference: Mid-American (West).

    Mailing Address: 108 West Hall, Mt. Pleasant, MI 48859.

    Head Coach: Dean Kreiner. **Assistant Coaches:** *Jim Fuller, Jud Folske, Tom Tresh. **Telephone:** (517) 774-6670. ■ **Baseball SID:** Fred Stabley Jr. **Telephone:** (517) 774-3277. **FAX:** (517) 774-7324.

    Home Field: Theunissen Stadium. **Seating Capacity:** 4,100. **Outfield Dimensions:** LF—330, CF—390, RF—330. **Press Box Telephone:** (517) 774-3579/3594.

CHARLESTON Cougars

    Conference: Trans America Athletic (East).

    Mailing Address: 26 George St., Charleston, SC 29424.

    Head Coach: Ralph Ciabattari. **Assistant Coaches:** Scott Foxhall, R.J. Kackley, Greg Mucerino. **Telephone:** (803) 953-5916. ■ **Baseball SID:** Tony Ciuffo. **Telephone:** (803) 953-5465. **FAX:** (803) 953-6534.

CHARLESTON SOUTHERN Buccaneers

    Conference: Big South.

    Mailing Address: P.O. Box 118087, Charleston, SC 29411.

    Head Coach: Gary Murphy. **Assistant Coaches:** Jeff Kinne, Rex Graves. **Telephone:** (803) 863-7591. ■ **Baseball SID:** Ken Gerlinger. **Telephone:** (803) 863-7122. **FAX:** (803) 863-7695.

CHICAGO STATE Cougars

    Conference: Mid-Continent (West).

    Mailing Address: 9500 South King Dr., Chicago, IL 60628.

    Head Coach: Kevin McCray. **Assistant Coaches:** Terrence Jackson, Steve Spielman. **Telephone:** (773) 995-3659. ■ **Baseball SID:** Terrence Jackson. **Telephone:** (773) 995-2217. **FAX:** (773) 995-3656.

CINCINNATI Bearcats

    Conference: Conference USA.

    Mailing Address: Mail Location 21, Cincinnati, OH 45221.

Head Coach: Brian Cleary. **Assistant Coach:** David Sinnes. **Telephone:** (513) 556-0566. ■ **Baseball SID:** Thomas Samuel. **Telephone:** (513) 556-5191. **FAX:** (513) 556-0619.

Home Field: Johnny Bench Field. **Seating Capacity:** 500. **Outfield Dimensions:** LF—327, CF—385, RF—330. **Press Box Telephone:** (513) 556-0818.

THE CITADEL Bulldogs

Conference: Southern.

Mailing Address: P.O. Box 7, Citadel Station, Charleston, SC 29409.

Head Coach: Fred Jordan. **Assistant Coaches:** Bo Betchman, Chris Lemonis, *Dan McDonnell. **Telephone:** (803) 953-5901. ■ **Baseball SID:** Art Chase. **Telephone:** (803) 953-5120. **FAX:** (803) 953-5058.

Home Field: Riley Park (6,000). **Outfield Dimensions:** LF—315, CF—436, RF—290. **Press Box Telephone:** Unavailable.

CLEMSON Tigers

Conference: Atlantic Coast.

Mailing Address: P.O. Box 31, Clemson, SC 29633.

Head Coach: Jack Leggett. **Assistant Coaches:** Tim Corbin, Kevin Erminio, John Pawlowski. **Telephone:** (864) 656-1947. ■ **Baseball SIDs:** Bob Bradley, Brian Hennessy. **Telephone:** (864) 656-2114. **FAX:** (864) 656-0299.

Home Field: Tiger Field. **Seating Capacity:** 5,000. **Outfield Dimensions:** LF—328, CF—400, RF—338. **Press Box Telephone:** (864) 654-3326.

CLEVELAND STATE Vikings

Conference: Midwestern Collegiate.

Mailing Address: CSU Convocation Center, 2000 Prospect, Cleveland, OH 44115.

Head Coach: Jay Murphy. **Assistant Coaches:** Dennis Healy, Dave Sprochi. **Telephone:** (216) 687-4822. ■ **Baseball SID:** Dale Horba. **Telephone:** (216) 687-4818. **FAX:** (216) 523-7257.

COASTAL CAROLINA Chanticleers

Conference: Big South.

Mailing Address: P.O. Box 261954, Conway, SC 29528.

Head Coach: Gary Gilmore. **Assistant Coaches:** Bill Jarmen, Matt Schilling, Mac Smith. **Telephone:** (803) 349-2816. ■ **Baseball SID:** Matt Hogue. **Telephone:** (803) 349-2822. **FAX:** (803) 349-2819.

COLUMBIA Lions

Conference: Ivy League (Gehrig).

Mailing Address: Dodge Physical Fitness Center, 3030 Broadway, New York, NY 10027.

Head Coach: Paul Fernandes. **Assistant Coaches:** Derek England, Chris Hayes. **Telephone:** (212) 854-2543. ■ **Baseball SID:** Heather Croze. **Telephone:** (212) 854-2534. **FAX:** (212) 854-8168.

CONNECTICUT Huskies

Conference: Big East.

Mailing Address: U-78, 2095 Hillside Road, Storrs, CT 06269.

Head Coach: Andy Baylock. **Assistant Coaches:** Jerry LaPenta, Jim Penders. **Telephone:** (860) 486-2458. ■ **Baseball SID:** Kyle Muncy. **Telephone:** (860) 486-3531. **FAX:** (860) 486-5085.

Home Field: J.O. Christian Field. **Seating Capacity:** 2,500. **Outfield Dimensions:** LF—340, CF—405, RF—340. **Press Box Telephone:** Unavailable.

COPPIN STATE Eagles

Conference: Mid-Eastern Athletic (North).

Mailing Address: 2500 West North Ave., Baltimore, MD 21216.

Head Coach: Paul Blair. **Assistant Coaches:** Jamal Davis, Andy Srebroski. **Telephone:** (410) 383-5686. ■ **Baseball SID:** Matt Burton. **Telephone:** (410) 383-5981. **FAX:** (410) 383-2511.

CORNELL Big Red

Conference: Ivy League (Rolfe).

Mailing Address: Schoellkopf House, Campus Road, Ithaca, NY 14851.

Head Coach: Tom Ford. **Assistant Coaches:** Carmen Carcone, Tim Fisher. **Telephone:** (607) 255-6604. ■ **Baseball SID:** Laura Spang. **Telephone:** (607) 255-3753. **FAX:** (607) 255-9791.

CREIGHTON Blue Jays

Conference: Missouri Valley.

Mailing Address: 2500 California Plaza, Omaha, NE 68178.

Head Coach: Jack Dahm. **Assistant Coaches:** Mike Filipowicz, Bill Olson, Ed Servais. **Telephone:** (402) 280-5545. ■ **Baseball SID:** Bobby Parker. **Telephone:** (402) 280-2488. **FAX:** (402) 280-2495.

Home Field: Creighton Sports Complex. **Seating Capacity:** 2,000. **Outfield Dimensions:** LF—330, CF—405, RF—330. **Press Box Telephone:** (402) 490-4454.

DARTMOUTH Big Green

Conference: Ivy League (Rolfe).

Mailing Address: 6083 Alumni Gym, Hanover, NH 03755.

Head Coach: Bob Whalen. **Assistant Coaches:** Mik Aoki, Chris Dotolo. **Telephone:** (603) 646-2477. ■ **Baseball SID:** Ken Golner. **Telephone:** (603) 646-2468. **FAX:** (603) 646-1286.

DAVIDSON Wildcats
Conference: Southern.
Mailing Address: P.O. Box 1750, Davidson, NC 28036.
Head Coach: Dick Cooke. **Assistant Coaches:** *Brett Boretti, Chris Pollard.
Telephone: (704) 892-2368. ■ **Baseball SID:** Rick Bender. **Telephone:** (704) 892-2123. **FAX:** (704) 892-2636.

DAYTON Flyers
Conference: Atlantic-10 (West).
Mailing Address: Box 1238, 300 College Park, Dayton, OH 45469.
Head Coach: Chris Sorrell. **Assistant Coaches:** Clint Albert, Terry Bell, Brian Schwade. **Telephone:** (937) 229-4456. ■ **Baseball SID:** Mike DeGeorge. **Telephone:** (937) 229-4460. **FAX:** (937) 229-4461.

DELAWARE Fightin' Blue Hens
Conference: America East.
Mailing Address: 631 South College Ave., Newark, DE 19716.
Head Coach: Bob Hannah. **Assistant Coaches:** Dan Hammer, Paul Gillerlain, Jim Sherman. **Telephone:** (302) 831-8596. ■ **Baseball SID:** Adam Wolff. **Telephone:** (302) 831-2186. **FAX:** (302) 831-8653.

DELAWARE STATE Hornets
Conference: Mid-Eastern Athletic (North).
Mailing Address: 1200 North DuPont Highway, Dover, DE 19901.
Head Coach: Harry Van Sant. **Assistant Coach:** Robert Probst. **Telephone:** (302) 739-3529. ■ **Baseball SID:** Dennis Jones. **Telephone:** (302) 739-4926. **FAX:** (302) 739-5241.

DETROIT Titans
Conference: Midwestern Collegiate.
Mailing Address: 4001 West McNichols Rd., Detroit, MI 48219.
Head Coach: Bob Miller. **Assistant Coaches:** Lee Bjerke, Dean Rovinelli. **Telephone:** (313) 993-1725. ■ **Baseball SID:** John Martin. **Telephone:** (313) 993-1745. **FAX:** (313) 993-1765.

DREXEL Dragons
Conference: America East.
Mailing Address: 32nd and Chestnut Streets, Building 14-312, Philadelphia, PA 19104.
Head Coach: Don Maines. **Assistant Coaches:** Chris Calciano, Darren Munns. **Telephone:** (215) 895-1782. ■ **Baseball SID:** Chris Beckett. **Telephone:** (215) 590-8951. **FAX:** (215) 590-8668.

DUKE Blue Devils
Conference: Atlantic Coast.
Mailing Address: 115 Cameron Indoor Stadium, Durham, NC 27706.
Head Coach: Steve Traylor. **Assistant Coaches:** *Dave Koblentz, Chris McMullan. **Telephone:** (919) 684-2358. ■ **Baseball SID:** Rich Pefley. **Telephone:** (919) 684-2633. **FAX:** (919) 684-2489.
Home Field: Jack Coombs Field. **Seating Capacity:** 2,000. **Outfield Dimensions:** LF—330, CF—400, RF—330. **Press Box Telephone:** None.

DUQUESNE Dukes
Conference: Atlantic-10 (West).
Mailing Address: A.J. Palumbo Center, Pittsburgh, PA 15282.
Head Coach: Mike Wilson. **Assistant Coaches:** Norm Frey, Jay Stoner. **Telephone:** (412) 396-5245. ■ **Baseball SID:** George Nieman. **Telephone:** (412) 396-6560. **FAX:** (412) 396-6210.

EAST CAROLINA Pirates
Conference: Colonial Athletic.
Mailing Address: Ward Sports Medicine Building, Greenville, NC 27858.
Head Coach: Keith LeClair. **Assistant Coaches:** Tommy Eason, Randy Mazey. **Telephone:** (919) 328-1981. ■ **Baseball SID:** Jerry Trickie. **Telephone:** (919) 328-4522. **FAX:** (919) 328-4528.

EAST TENNESSEE STATE Buccaneers
Conference: Southern.
Mailing Address: P.O. Box 70641, Johnson City, TN 37614.
Head Coach: Ken Campbell. **Assistant Coach:** Johnny Cloud. **Telephone:** (423) 439-4496. ■ **Baseball SID:** Sanford Rogers. **Telephone:** (423) 439-5612. **FAX:** (423) 439-6138.

EASTERN ILLINOIS Panthers
Conference: Ohio Valley.
Mailing Address: Lantz Gym, Charleston, IL 61920.
Head Coach: Jim Schmitz. **Assistant Coaches:** Melesio Salazar, Chris Hall, Steve Dunlop. **Telephone:** (217) 581-2522. ■ **Baseball SID:** Pat Osterman. **Telephone:** (217) 581-6408. **FAX:** (217) 581-6434.

EASTERN KENTUCKY Colonels
Conference: Ohio Valley.
Mailing Address: 118 Alumni Coliseum, Richmond, KY 40475.
Head Coach: Jim Ward. **Assistant Coaches:** Joey Golinski, Steve Roof, Jason Stein. **Telephone:** (606) 622-2128. ■ **Baseball SID:** Karl Park. **Telephone:** (606) 622-1253. **FAX:** (606) 622-1230.

EASTERN MICHIGAN Eagles

Conference: Mid-American (West).
Mailing Address: 200 Bowen Fieldhouse, Ypsilanti, MI 48197.
Head Coach: Roger Coryell. **Assistant Coach:** Jake Boss. **Telephone:** (313) 487-0315. ■ **Baseball SID:** Jim Streeter. **Telephone:** (313) 487-0317. **FAX:** (313) 485-3840.
Home Field: Oestrike Stadium. **Seating Capacity:** 2,500. **Outfield Dimensions:** LF—330, CF—390, RF—330. **Press Box Telephone:** (313) 484-1396.

EVANSVILLE Purple Aces

Conference: Missouri Valley.
Mailing Address: 1800 Lincoln Ave., Evansville, IN 47722.
Head Coach: Jim Brownlee. **Assistant Coaches:** Ryan Brownlee, Tim Brownlee, Jeff Lystra. **Telephone:** (812) 479-2059. ■ **Baseball SID:** Kris Holzmeyer. **Telephone:** (812) 488-1024. **FAX:** (812) 479-2090.

FAIRFIELD Stags

Conference: Metro Atlantic (South).
Mailing Address: North Benson Road, Fairfield, CT 06430.
Head Coach: John Slosar. **Assistant Coaches:** Drew Brown, Vince DiGrande, Sean Martin, Dennis Whalen. **Telephone:** (203) 254-4000, ext. 2605. ■ **Baseball SID:** Drew Brown. **Telephone:** (203) 254-4000, ext. 2878. **FAX:** (203) 254-4117.

FAIRLEIGH DICKINSON Knights

Conference: Northeast.
Mailing Address: Temple Avenue, Rothman Center, Hackensack, NJ 07601.
Head Coach: Dennis Sasso. **Assistant Coaches:** Jerry DeFabbia, Ed Ward. **Telephone:** (201) 692-2245. ■ **Baseball SID:** Bob Rothwell. **Telephone:** (201) 692-2204. **FAX:** (201) 692-9361.

FLORIDA Gators

Conference: Southeastern (East).
Mailing Address: P.O. Box 14485, Gainesville, FL 32607.
Head Coach: Andy Lopez. **Assistant Coaches:** Rick Eckstein, *Gary Henderson, Steve Kling. **Telephone:** (352) 375-4683, ext. 4457. ■ **Baseball SID:** Steve Shaff. **Telephone:** (352) 375-4683, ext. 6130. **FAX:** (352) 375-4809.
Home Field: McKethan Stadium at Perry Field. **Seating Capacity:** 4,500. **Outfield Dimensions:** LF—329, CF—400, RF—325. **Press Box Telephone:** (352) 375-4683, ext. 4451.

FLORIDA A&M Rattlers

Conference: Mid-Eastern Athletic (South).
Mailing Address: Room 205, Gaither Athletic Center, Tallahassee, FL 32307.
Head Coach: Joe Durant. **Assistant Coaches:** Rozzeto Gordon, Harry Sapp. **Telephone:** (850) 599-3202. ■ **Baseball SID:** Alvin Hollins. **Telephone:** (850) 599-3200. **FAX:** (850) 599-3206.

FLORIDA ATLANTIC Owls

Conference: Trans America Athletic (South).
Mailing Address: 777 Glades Rd., Boca Raton, FL 33431.
Head Coach: Kevin Cooney. **Assistant Coaches:** Kerwin Belle, John McCormack, Steve Whitaker. **Telephone:** (561) 297-3956. ■ **Baseball SID:** Katrina McCormack. **Telephone:** (561) 297-3163. **FAX:** (561) 297-2996.

FLORIDA INTERNATIONAL Golden Panthers

Conference: TransAmerica Athletic (South).
Mailing Address: University Park Campus, Miami, FL 33199.
Head Coach: Danny Price. **Assistant Coaches:** Marc Calvi, *Rolando Casanova, Ken Foster. **Telephone:** (305) 348-3166. ■ **Baseball SID:** Rich Kelch. **Telephone:** (305) 348-3164. **FAX:** (305) 348-2963.
Home Field: University Park. **Seating Capacity:** 1,000. **Outfield Dimensions:** LF—325, CF—400, RF—325. **Press Box Telephone:** (305) 554-8694.

FLORIDA STATE Seminoles

Conference: Atlantic Coast.
Mailing Address: P.O. Box 2195, Tallahassee, FL 32316.
Head Coach: Mike Martin. **Assistant Coaches:** Chip Baker, Mike Martin Jr., *Jamey Shouppe. **Telephone:** (850) 644-1073. ■ **Baseball SID:** Amy Farnum. **Telephone:** (850) 644-0615. **FAX:** (850) 644-3820.
Home Field: Dick Howser Stadium. **Seating Capacity:** 5,000. **Outfield Dimensions:** LF—340, CF—400, RF—320. **Press Box Telephone:** (850) 644-1553.

FORDHAM Rams

Conference: Atlantic-10 (East).
Mailing Address: 441 East Fordham Road, Bronx, NY 10458.
Head Coach: Dan Gallagher. **Assistant Coaches:** John Ceprini, Tony Mellaci. **Telephone:** (718) 817-4292. ■ **Baseball SID:** Joe DiBari. **Telephone:** (718) 817-4240. **FAX:** (718) 817-4244.

FRESNO STATE Bulldogs

Conference: Western Athletic (West).
Mailing Address: 5305 North Campus Drive, Room 153, Fresno, CA 93740.
Head Coach: Bob Bennett. **Assistant Coaches:** Jim Fisher, Todd Johnson,

Steve Pearse, *Mike Rupcich. **Telephone:** (209) 278-2178. ■ **Baseball SID:** Josh Lehman. **Telephone:** (209) 278-2509. **FAX:** (209) 278-4689.

Home Field: Beiden Field. **Seating Capacity:** 4,575. **Outfield Dimensions:** LF—330, CF—400, RF—330. **Press Box Telephone:** (209) 278-7678.

FURMAN Paladins

Conference: Southern.
Mailing Address: 3300 Poinsett Highway, Greenville, SC 29613.
Head Coach: Ron Smith. **Assistant Coaches:** *Jeff Massey, Greg McVey. **Telephone:** (864) 294-2146. ■ **Baseball SID:** Kylie Inman. **Telephone:** (864) 294-3062. **FAX:** (864) 294-3061.

GEORGE MASON Patriots

Conference: Colonial Athletic.
Mailing Address: 4400 University Dr., Fairfax, VA 22030.
Head Coach: Bill Brown. **Assistant Coaches:** Ken Munoz, Chris Murphy, *J.J. Picollo. **Telephone:** (703) 993-3288. ■ **Baseball SID:** Ben Trittipoe. **Telephone:** (703) 993-3263. **FAX:** (703) 993-3259.

GEORGE WASHINGTON Colonials

Conference: Atlantic-10 (West).
Mailing Address: 600 22nd St. NW, Washington, DC 20052.
Head Coach: Tom Walter. **Assistant Coaches:** *Joe Raccuia, Terry Rooney. **Telephone:** (202) 994-7399. ■ **Baseball SID:** Jason Guy. **Telephone:** (202) 994-0339. **FAX:** (202) 994-2713.

GEORGETOWN Hoyas

Conference: Big East.
Mailing Address: McDonough Gym, 37th & O Streets NW, Washington, DC 20057.
Head Coach: Kirk Mason. **Assistant Coaches:** Don Fontana, Pat Hart, Josh Levey, Pete Wilk. **Telephone:** (202) 687-2462. ■ **Baseball SID:** Pat McBride. **Telephone:** (202) 687-2492. **FAX:** (202) 687-2491.

Home Field: Georgetown Baseball Field. **Seating Capacity:** 2,000. **Outfield Dimensions:** LF—301, CF—410, RF—310. **Press Box Telephone:** None.

GEORGIA Bulldogs

Conference: Southeastern (East).
Mailing Address: P.O. Box 1472, Athens, GA 30603.
Head Coach: Robert Sapp. **Assistant Coaches:** Matt Donahue, *David Perno. **Telephone:** (706) 542-7971. ■ **Baseball SID:** Christopher Lakos. **Telephone:** (706) 542-1621. **FAX:** (706) 542-7993.

Home Field: Foley Field. **Seating Capacity:** 3,200. **Outfield Dimensions:** LF—350, CF—410, RF—320. **Press Box Telephone:** (706) 542-6162/6161.

GEORGIA SOUTHERN Eagles

Conference: Southern.
Mailing Address: P.O. Box 8095, Statesboro, GA 30460.
Head Coach: Jack Stallings. **Assistant Coaches:** *Scott Baker, Buddy Holder, Darin Van Tassell. **Telephone:** (912) 681-5187. ■ **Baseball SID:** Tom McClellan. **Telephone:** (912) 681-5239. **FAX:** (912) 681-0046.

Home Field: J.I. Clements Stadium. **Seating Capacity:** 2,000. **Outfield Dimensions:** LF—330, CF—380, RF—330. **Press Box Telephone:** (912) 681-2508.

GEORGIA STATE Panthers

Conference: TransAmerica Athletic (East).
Mailing Address: University Plaza, Atlanta, GA 30303.
Head Coach: Mike Hurst. **Assistant Coaches:** *David Hartley, Bob Keller. **Telephone:** (404) 651-1198. ■ **Baseball SID:** Ramsey Baker. **Telephone:** (404) 651-3168. **FAX:** (404) 651-3204.

GEORGIA TECH Yellow Jackets

Conference: Atlantic Coast.
Mailing Address: 150 Bobby Dodd Way NW, Atlanta, GA 30332.
Head Coach: Danny Hall. **Assistant Coaches:** Jeff Guy, *Mike Trapasso. **Telephone:** (404) 894-5443. ■ **Baseball SID:** Mike Stamus. **Telephone:** (404) 894-5445. **FAX:** (404) 894-1248.

Home Field: Russ Chandler Stadium. **Seating Capacity:** 2,500. **Outfield Dimensions:** LF—320, CF—400, RF—330. **Press Box Telephone:** (404) 894-3167.

GONZAGA Bulldogs

Conference: West Coast.
Mailing Address: East 502 Boone Ave, Spokane, WA 99258.
Head Coach: Steve Hertz. **Assistant Coaches:** Greg Gores, Mark Machtolf. **Telephone:** (509) 328-4220, ext. 4226. ■ **Baseball SID:** Oliver Pierce. **Telephone:** (509) 328-4220, ext. 6373. **FAX:** (509) 324-5730.

GRAMBLING STATE Tigers

Conference: Southwestern Athletic/West.
Mailing Address: P.O. Box N, Grambling, LA 71245.
Head Coach: Wilbert Ellis. **Assistant Coach:** James Randall. **Telephone:** (318) 274-6121. ■ **Baseball SID:** Scott Boatright. **Telephone:** (318) 274-6199 /6281. **FAX:** (318) 274-2761.

GRAND CANYON Antelopes

Conference: Western Athletic (North).
Mailing Address: P.O Box 11097, Phoenix, AZ 85061.
Head Coach: Gil Stafford. **Assistant Coaches:** Dave Stapleton, Ed Wolfe.
Telephone: (602) 589-2810. ■ **Baseball SID:** Deron Filip. **Telephone:** (602)
589-2795. **FAX:** (602) 589-2529.
Home Field: Brazell Stadium. **Seating Capacity:** 2,000. **Outfield Dimensions:** LF—325, CF—390, RF—325. **Press Box Telephone:** (602) 589-2719.

HARTFORD Hawks

Conference: America East.
Mailing Address: 200 Bloomfield Ave., West Hartford, CT 06117.
Head Coach: Bob Nenna. **Assistant Coaches:** Unavailable. **Telephone:**
(860) 768-4656. ■ **Baseball SID:** Jim Keener. **Telephone:** (860) 768-4620. **FAX:**
(860) 768-4068.

HARVARD Crimson

Conference: Ivy League (Rolfe).
Mailing Address: Department of Athletics, 60 John F. Kennedy St.,
Cambridge, MA 02138.
Head Coach: Joe Walsh. **Assistant Coaches:** Gary Donovan, Marty
Nastasia. **Telephone:** (617) 495-2629. ■ **Baseball SID:** Paul McNeely. **Telephone:** (617) 495-2206. **FAX:** (617) 495-2130.

HAWAII Rainbows

Conference: Western Athletic (West).
Mailing Address: Sports Events Arena, Room 205, 1355 Lower Campus
Road, Honolulu, HI 96822.
Head Coach: Les Murakami. **Assistant Coaches:** Carl Furutani, Dave
Murakami, Les Nakama. **Telephone:** (808) 956-6247. ■ **Baseball SID:** Markus
Owens. **Telephone:** (808) 956-7523. **FAX:** (808) 956-4470.
Home Field: Rainbow Stadium. **Seating Capacity:** 4,312. **Outfield Dimensions:** LF—340, CF—400, RF—340. **Press Box Telephone:** (808) 956-6253.

HAWAII-HILO Vulcans

Conference: Independent.
Mailing Address: 200 West Kawili St., Hilo, HI 96720.
Head Coach: Joey Estrella. **Assistant Coaches:** Richard DeSa, Kallen
Miyataki. **Telephone:** (808) 974-7700. ■ **Baseball SID:** Kelly Leong. **Telephone:**
(808) 974-7606/7520. **FAX:** (808) 974-7711.

HOFSTRA Flying Dutchmen

Conference: America East.
Mailing Address: 1000 Hempstead Turnpike, PFC 240, Hempstead, NY
11549.
Head Coach: Reggie Jackson. **Assistant Coaches:** *Kevin Delaney, Larry
Minor. **Telephone:** (516) 463-5065. ■ **Baseball SID:** Jim Sheehan. **Telephone:**
(516) 463-6764. **FAX:** (516) 463-5033.

HOLY CROSS Crusaders

Conference: Patriot.
Mailing Address: One College St., Worcester, MA 01610.
Head Coach: Jack Whalen. **Assistant Coaches:** Paul Pearl, Tim Whalen.
Telephone: (508) 793-3628. ■ **Baseball SID:** John Butman. **Telephone:** (508)
793-2583. **FAX:** (508) 793-2309.

HOUSTON Cougars

Conference: Conference USA.
Mailing Address: 3100 Cullen Rd., Houston, TX 77204.
Head Coach: Rayner Noble. **Assistant Coaches:** *Trip Couch, Todd
Whitting. **Telephone:** (713) 743-9396. ■ **Baseball SID:** John Sullivan.
Telephone: (713) 743-9404. **FAX:** (713) 743-9411.
Home Field: Cougar Field. **Seating Capacity:** 4,500. **Outfield Dimensions:**
LF—330, CF—390, RF—330. **Press Box Telephone:** (713) 743-0840.

HOWARD Bison

Conference: Mid-Eastern Athletic (North).
Mailing Address: Sixth and Girard Street NW, Drew Hall, Washington, DC
20059.
Head Coach: Chuck Hinton. **Assistant Coaches:** Chico Hinton, Eric
Johnson. **Telephone:** (202) 806-5162. ■ **Baseball SIDs:** Anthony Estelle, Kevin
Page. **Telephone:** (202) 806-7188. **FAX:** (202) 806-9090.

ILLINOIS Fighting Illini

Conference: Big Ten.
Mailing Address: 1700 South Fourth St,, Champaign, IL 61820.
Head Coach: Itch Jones. **Assistant Coaches:** *Dan Hartleb, Todd Murphy.
Telephone: (217) 333-8605. ■ **Baseball SID:** Michelle Warner. **Telephone:**
(217) 333-1391. **FAX:** (217) 333-5540.
Home Field: Illinois Field. **Seating Capacity:** 1,500. **Outfield Dimensions:**
LF—330, CF—400, RF—330. **Press Box Telephone:** (217) 333-1227.

ILLINOIS-CHICAGO Flames

Conference: Midwestern Collegiate.
Mailing Address: 1101 West Taylor St., Suite 310, Chicago, IL 60680.
Head Coach: Dean Refakes. **Assistant Coaches:** Wally Berhns, Dan

Kusinski. **Telephone:** (312) 355-8645. ■ **Baseball SID:** Anne Schoenherr. **Telephone:** (312) 996-5880. **FAX:** (312) 996-5882.

ILLINOIS STATE Redbirds

Conference: Missouri Valley.

Mailing Address: Campus Box 7130, Normal, IL 61790.

Head Coach: Jeff Stewart. **Assistant Coach:** Tim Johnson. **Telephone:** (309) 438-5151. ■ **Baseball SID:** Todd Kober. **Telephone:** (309) 438-3249. **FAX:** (309) 438-5634.

INDIANA Hoosiers

Conference: Big Ten.

Mailing Address: 17th & Fee Lane, Assembly Hall, Bloomington, IN 47405.

Head Coach: Bob Morgan. **Assistant Coaches:** Jeff Calcaterra, Scott Googins. **Telephone:** (812) 855-1680. ■ **Baseball SID:** Josh Rawitch. **Telephone:** (812) 855-9399. **FAX:** (812) 855-9401.

Home Field: Sembower Field. **Seating Capacity:** 3,000. **Outfield Dimensions:** LF—333, CF—380, RF—333. **Press Box Telephone:** (812) 855-2754.

INDIANA STATE Sycamores

Conference: Missouri Valley.

Mailing Address: Student Services Building, Room A-15, Terre Haute, IN 47809.

Head Coach: Bob Warn. **Assistant Coaches:** Shohn Doty, *Mitch Hannahs. **Telephone:** (812) 237-4051. ■ **Baseball SID:** Doug Hoffman. **Telephone:** (812) 237-4073. **FAX:** (812) 237-4157.

Home Field: Sycamore Field. **Seating Capacity:** 2,500. **Outfield Dimensions:** LF—340, CF—402, RF—340. **Press Box Telephone:** (812) 237-4187.

IONA Gaels

Conference: Metro Atlantic (South).

Mailing Address: Mulcahy Center, 715 North Ave., New Rochelle, NY 10801.

Head Coach: Al Zoccolillo. **Assistant Coaches:** J.B. Buono, Marcel Galligani, Stephan Rapaglia. **Telephone:** (914) 633-2319. ■ **Baseball SID:** Dave Cagianello. **Telephone:** (914) 633-2334. **FAX:** (914) 633-2072.

IOWA Hawkeyes

Conference: Big Ten.

Mailing Address: 340 Carver-Hawkeye Arena, Iowa City, IA 52242.

Head Coach: Scott Broghamer. **Assistant Coaches:** Ken Charipar, *Elvis Dominguez. **Telephone:** (319) 335-9390. ■ **Baseball SID:** Kristy Fick. **Telephone:** (319) 335-9411. **FAX:** (319) 335-9417.

Home Field: Iowa Field. **Seating Capacity:** 3,000. **Outfield Dimensions:** LF—330, CF—400, RF—330. **Press Box Telephone:** (319) 335-9520.

IOWA STATE Cyclones

Conference: Big 12.

Mailing Address: Jacobson Athletic Building, 1800 South Fourth St., Ames, IA 50011.

Head Coach: Lyle Smith. **Assistant Coaches:** Jim Murphy, Tony Trumm. **Telephone:** (515) 294-4201. ■ **Baseball SID:** Mike Green. **Telephone:** (515) 294-1393. **FAX:** (515) 294-0558.

Home Field: Cap Timm Field. **Seating Capacity:** 3,000. **Outfield Dimensions:** LF—330, CF—400, RF—330. **Press Box Telephone:** (515) 294-1640.

JACKSON STATE Tigers

Conference: Southwestern Athletic (East).

Mailing Address: 1325 J.R. Lynch St., Jackson, MS 39217.

Head Coach: Robert Braddy. **Assistant Coaches:** Lewis Braddy, Mark Salter, Stanley Stubbs. **Telephone:** (601) 968-2450. ■ **Baseball SID:** Sam Jefferson. **Telephone:** (601) 968-2273. **FAX:** (601) 968-2000.

JACKSONVILLE Dolphins

Conference: Sun Belt.

Mailing Address: 2800 University Blvd. North, Jacksonville, FL 32211.

Head Coach: Terry Alexander. **Assistant Coaches:** *Rusty Green, Johnny Wiggs. **Telephone:** (904) 745-7476. ■ **Baseball SID:** George Sorensen. **Telephone:** (904) 745-7402. **FAX:** (904) 743-0067.

Home Field: Brest Field. **Seating Capacity:** 2,300. **Outfield Dimensions:** LF—340, CF—405, RF—340. **Press Box Telephone:** Unavailable.

JACKSONVILLE STATE Gamecocks

Conference: Trans America Athletic (West).

Mailing Address: Gamecock Fieldhouse, 700 Pelham Road N., Jacksonville, AL 36265.

Head Coach: Rudy Abbott. **Assistant Coach:** *Skipper Jones. **Telephone:** (205) 782-5367. ■ **Baseball SID:** Greg Seitz. **Telephone:** (205) 782-5279. **FAX:** (205) 782-5958.

JAMES MADISON Dukes

Conference: Colonial Athletic.

Mailing Address: South Main, Harrisonburg, VA 22807.

Head Coach: Spanky McFarland. **Assistant Coaches:** Barry Given, *Todd Raleigh. **Telephone:** (540) 568-6467. ■ **Baseball SID:** Curt Dudley. **Telephone:** (540) 568-6154. **FAX:** (540) 568-3703.

Home Field: Long Field/Mauck Stadium. **Seating Capacity:** 1,200. **Outfield**

Dimensions: LF—340, CF—400, RF—320. **Press Box Telephone:** (540) 568-6545.

KANSAS Jayhawks

Conference: Big 12.

Mailing Address: 202 Allen Fieldhouse, Lawrence, KS 66045.

Head Coach: Bobby Randall. **Assistant Coaches:** Mike Bard, Wilson Kilmer. **Telephone:** (785) 864-7907. ■ **Baseball SID:** Craig Pinkerton. **Telephone:** (785) 864-3417. **FAX:** (785) 864-7944.

Home Field: Hoglund-Maupin Stadium. **Seating Capacity:** 1,320. **Outfield Dimensions:** LF—350, CF—380, RF—350. **Press Box Telephone:** (785) 864-4037.

KANSAS STATE Wildcats

Conference: Big 12.

Mailing Address: Suite 144, Bramlage Coliseum, 1800 College Ave., Manhattan, KS 66502.

Head Coach: Mike Clark. **Assistant Coaches:** Mike Hensley, Robbie Moen. **Telephone:** (785) 532-5723. ■ **Baseball SID:** Andy Bartlett. **Telephone:** (785) 532-6735. **FAX:** (785) 532-6093.

Home Field: Frank Myers Field. **Seating Capacity:** 5,000. **Outfield Dimensions:** LF—340, CF—400, RF—325. **Press Box Telephone:** (785) 532-6926.

KENT Golden Flashes

Conference: Mid-American (East).

Mailing Address: P.O. Box 5190, 154 Memorial Gym, Kent, OH 44242.

Head Coach: Rick Rembielak. **Assistant Coaches:** Greg Beals, Mike Birkbeck. **Telephone:** (330) 672-3696. ■ **Baseball SID:** Heather Brocious. **Telephone:** (330) 672-2110. **FAX:** (330) 672-2112.

Home Field: Gene Michael Field. **Seating Capacity:** 2,000. **Outfield Dimensions:** LF—330, CF—400, RF—330. **Press Box Telephone:** (330) 672-2036.

KENTUCKY Wildcats

Conference: Southeastern (East).

Mailing Address: Room 23, Memorial Coliseum, Lexington, KY 40506.

Head Coach: Keith Madison. **Assistant Coaches:** Daron Schoenrock, Jan Weisberg, Jeff Young. **Telephone:** (606) 257-6900. ■ **Baseball SID:** Andre Foushee. **Telephone:** (606) 257-3838. **FAX:** (606) 323-4310.

Home Field: Cliff Hagan Stadium. **Seating Capacity:** 2,500. **Outfield Dimensions:** LF—340, CF—390, RF—310. **Press Box Telephone:** (606) 257-8027.

LAFAYETTE Leopards

Conference: Patriot.

Mailing Address: Room 17, Watson Hall, High Street, Easton, PA 18042.

Head Coach: Greg Vogel. **Assistant Coaches:** Lloyd Brewer, Clayton Gum. **Telephone:** (610) 250-5476. ■ **Baseball SID:** Brian Laubscher. **Telephone:** (610) 250-5518. **FAX:** (610) 250-5519.

LAMAR Cardinals

Conference: Sun Belt.

Mailing Address: Box 10066, LU Station, Beaumont, TX 77710.

Head Coach: Jim Gilligan. **Assistant Coaches:** Brian Biggers, Jim Ricklefson. **Telephone:** (409) 880-8315. ■ **Baseball SID:** Davey Crizer. **Telephone:** (409) 880-8329. **FAX:** (409) 880-2338.

Home Field: Vincent-Beck Stadium. **Seating Capacity:** 3,500. **Outfield Dimensions:** LF—325, CF—380, RF—325. **Press Box Telephone:** (409) 880-8327.

LA SALLE Explorers

Conference: Atlantic-10 (West).

Mailing Address: 1900 West Olney Ave., Philadelphia, PA 19141.

Head Coach: Larry Conti. **Assistant Coaches:** Steve Bongard, John Polillo. **Telephone:** (215) 951-1995. ■ **Baseball SID:** Kevin Currie. **Telephone:** (215) 951-1605. **FAX:** (215) 951-1694.

LEHIGH Mountain Hawks

Conference: Patriot.

Mailing Address: Taylor Gym, 641 Taylor St., Bethlehem, PA 18015.

Head Coach: Sean Leary. **Assistant Coaches:** Craig Anderson, Jerry Mack. **Telephone:** (610) 758-4315. ■ **Baseball SID:** Glenn Hofmann. **Telephone:** (610) 758-3174. **FAX:** (610) 758-4407.

LE MOYNE Dolphins

Conference: Metro Atlantic (North).

Mailing Address: Springfield Road, Syracuse, NY 13214.

Head Coach: John King. **Assistant Coaches:** Pete Hoy, Bobby Nandin. **Telephone:** (315) 445-4415. ■ **Baseball SID:** Mike Tuberosa. **Telephone:** (315) 445-4412. **FAX:** (315) 445-4678.

LIBERTY Flames

Conference: Big South.

Mailing Address: 1971 University Blvd., Lynchburg, VA 24506.

Head Coach: Dave Pastors. **Assistant Coaches:** Jeff Edwards, Randy Tomlin. **Telephone:** (804) 582-2100. ■ **Baseball SID:** Mike Montoro. **Telephone:** (804) 582-2292. **FAX:** (804) 582-2076.

LONG BEACH STATE 49ers

Conference: Big West (South).

Mailing Address: 1250 Bellflower Blvd., Long Beach, CA 90840.

Head Coach: Dave Snow. **Assistant Coaches:** Don Barbara, Mike Stembridge, John Strauss, *Mike Weathers, Jim Yogi. **Telephone:** (562) 987-0457. ■ **Baseball SID:** Steve Janisch. **Telephone:** (562) 985-7797. **FAX:** (562) 985-8197.

Home Field: Blair Field. **Seating Capacity:** 3,000. **Outfield Dimensions:** LF—348, CF—400, RF—348. **Press Box Telephone:** (562) 930-0714.

LONG ISLAND Blackbirds

Conference: Northeast.

Mailing Address: One University Plaza, Brooklyn, NY 11201.

Head Coach: Frank Giannone. **Assistant Coaches:** Chris Bagley, Mike Ryan. **Telephone:** (718) 488-1538. ■ **Baseball SID:** Greg Fox. **Telephone:** (718) 488-1420. **FAX:** (718) 488-3302.

LOUISIANA STATE Tigers

Conference: Southeastern (West).

Mailing Address: P.O. Box 25095, Baton Rouge, LA 70894.

Head Coach: Skip Bertman. **Assistant Coaches:** Dan Canevari, Tim Lanier, *Jim Schwanke. **Telephone:** (504) 388-4148. ■ **Baseball SID:** Bill Franques. **Telephone:** (504) 388-4148. **FAX:** (504) 388-1861.

Home Field: Alex Box Stadium. **Seating Capacity:** 7,006. **Outfield Dimensions:** LF—330, CF—405, RF—330. **Press Box Telephone:** (504) 388-4149.

LOUISIANA TECH Bulldogs

Conference: Sun Belt.

Mailing Address: P.O. Box 3166, Ruston, LA 71272.

Head Coach: Randy Davis. **Assistant Coaches:** Brian Rountree, Sean Teague, Jared Baker. **Telephone:** (318) 257-4111. ■ **Baseball SID:** Larry Little. **Telephone:** (318) 257-3144. **FAX:** (318) 257-3757.

LOUISVILLE Cardinals

Conference: Conference USA.

Mailing Address: Student Activities Center, Louisville, KY 40292.

Head Coach: Lelo Prado. **Assistant Coaches:** Keith Chester, *Brian Mundorf, Larry Owens. **Telephone:** (502) 852-0103. ■ **Baseball SID:** Nancy Smith. **Telephone:** (502) 852-6581. **FAX:** (502) 852-0815.

Home Field: Cardinal Stadium. **Seating Capacity:** 20,000. **Outfield Dimensions:** LF—360, CF—405, RF—320. **Press Box Telephone:** (502) 367-5000.

LOYOLA MARYMOUNT Lions

Conference: West Coast.

Mailing Address: 7900 Loyola Blvd., Los Angeles, CA 90045.

Head Coach: Frank Cruz. **Assistant Coaches:** David Eldredge, Ron Hauczinger, Kelly Nicholson. **Telephone:** (310) 338-2765. ■ **Baseball SID:** Dan Smith. **Telephone:** (310) 338-7643. **FAX:** (310) 338-2703.

MAINE Black Bears

Conference: America East.

Mailing Address: 186 Memorial Gym, Orono, ME 04469.

Head Coach: Paul Kostacopoulos. **Assistant Coaches:** Mike Coutts, Ted Novio. **Telephone:** (207) 581-1096. ■ **Baseball SID:** David Lang. **Telephone:** (207) 581-3646. **FAX:** (207) 581-3297.

Home Field: Mahaney Diamond. **Seating Capacity:** 4,000. **Outfield Dimensions:** LF—330, CF—400, RF—330. **Press Box Telephone:** (207) 581-1049/4734.

MANHATTAN Jaspers

Conference: Metro Atlantic (South).

Mailing Address: Manhattan College Parkway, Riverdale, NY 10471.

Head Coach: Gary Puccio. **Assistant Coach:** Mike Francese. **Telephone:** (718) 862-7486. ■ **Baseball SID:** Jeff Bernstein. **Telephone:** (718) 862-7228. **FAX:** (718) 862-8020.

MARIST Red Foxes

Conference: Metro Atlantic (North).

Mailing Address: McCann Center, 290 North Rd., Poughkeepsie, NY 12601.

Head Coach: John Szefc. **Assistant Coaches:** Mark Barron, Al Hammell, Chris Webb. **Telephone:** (914) 575-3000, ext. 2570. ■ **Baseball SID:** Dawn Derosa. **Telephone:** (914) 575-3000 ext. 2322. **FAX:** (914) 471-0466.

MARSHALL Thundering Herd

Conference: Mid-America (East).

Mailing Address: P.O. Box 1360, Huntington, WV 25715.

Head Coach: Craig Antush. **Assistant Coaches:** Matt Spade, *Dave Piepenbrink. **Telephone:** (304) 696-5277. ■ **Baseball SID:** Jake Keys. **Telephone:** (304) 696-5275. **FAX:** (304) 696-2325.

MARYLAND Terrapins

Conference: Atlantic Coast.

Mailing Address: P.O. Box 295, College Park, MD 20741.

Head Coach: Tom Bradley. **Assistant Coaches:** Jim Flack, *Kelly Kulina. **Telephone:** (301) 314-7122. ■ **Baseball SID:** Mark Ragonese. **Telephone:** (301) 314-7062. **FAX:** (301) 314-9094.

Home Field: Shipley Field. **Seating Capacity:** 2,200. **Outfield Dimensions:** LF—320, CF—360, RF—370. **Press Box Telephone:** None.

MARYLAND-BALTIMORE COUNTY Retrievers
Conference: Big South.
Mailing Address: 1000 Hilltop Circle, Baltimore, MD 21250.
Head Coach: John Jancuska. **Assistant Coach:** Bob Mumma. **Telephone:** (410) 455-2239. ■ **Baseball SID:** David Gansell. **Telephone:** (410) 455-2639. **FAX:** (410) 455-3994.

MARYLAND-EASTERN SHORE Hawks
Conference: Mid-Eastern Athletic (North).
Mailing Address: Tawes Gymnasium, Backbone Road, Princess Anne, MD 21853.
Head Coach: Kaye Pinhey. **Assistant Coach:** Brian Hollamon. **Telephone:** (410) 651-6539. ■ **Baseball SID:** Romanda Noble. **Telephone:** (410) 651-6499. **FAX:** (410) 651-7600.

MASSACHUSETTS Minutemen
Conference: Atlantic-10 (East).
Mailing Address: 255A Boyden Building, Commonwealth Avenue, Amherst, MA 01003.
Head Coach: Mike Stone. **Assistant Coaches:** Raphael Cerrato, Scott Meaney. **Telephone:** (413) 545-3120. ■ **Baseball SID:** Ken Dewey. **Telephone:** (413) 545-2439. **FAX:** (413) 545-1556.

McNEESE STATE Cowboys
Conference: Southland.
Mailing Address: P.O. Box 92735, Lake Charles, LA 70609.
Head Coach: Mike Bianco. **Assistant Coaches:** Jeremy Moore, Daniel Tomlin. **Telephone:** (318) 475-5482. ■ **Baseball SID:** Louis Bonnette. **Telephone:** (318) 475-5207. **FAX:** (318) 475-5202.

MEMPHIS Tigers
Conference: Conference USA.
Mailing Address: 205 Athletic Office Building, 570 Normal, Memphis, TN 38152.
Head Coach: Jeff Hopkins. **Assistant Coaches:** *Rob McDonald, Eric Page. **Telephone:** (901) 678-2452. ■ **Baseball SID:** Brian Zimmer. **Telephone:** (901) 678-2337. **FAX:** (901) 678-4134.
Home Field: Nat Buring Stadium. **Seating Capacity:** 2,000. **Outfield Dimensions:** LF—320, CF—380, RF—320. **Press Box Telephone:** (901) 678-2862.

MERCER Bears
Conference: Trans America Athletic (East).
Mailing Address: 1400 Coleman Ave., Macon, GA 31207.
Head Coach: Barry Myers. **Assistant Coaches:** Craig Gibson, Jim Cole, Buck Phillips. **Telephone:** (912) 752-2738. ■ **Baseball SID:** Kevin Coulombe. **Telephone:** (912) 752-2735. **FAX:** (912) 752-5350.

MIAMI Hurricanes
Conference: Independent.
Mailing Address: Box 248167, Coral Gables, FL 33146.
Head Coach: Jim Morris. **Assistant Coaches:** Gino DiMare, *Turtle Thomas. **Telephone:** (305) 284-4171. ■ **Baseball SID:** Phil de Montmollin. **Telephone:** (305) 284-3244. **FAX:** (305) 284-2807.
Home Field: Mark Light Stadium. **Seating Capacity:** 5,000. **Outfield Dimensions:** LF—330, CF—400, RF—330. **Press Box Telephone:** Unavailable.

MIAMI Redskins
Conference: Mid-American (East).
Mailing Address: 230 Millett Hall, Oxford, OH 45056.
Head Coach: Tracy Smith. **Assistant Coaches:** Bill Doran, *Tom Kinkelaar, Micah Nori. **Telephone:** (513) 529-6631. ■ **Baseball SID:** Kelby Siler. **Telephone:** (513) 529-4327. **FAX:** (513) 529-6729.
Home Field: Stanley G. McKie Field. **Seating Capacity:** 1,500. **Outfield Dimensions:** LF—330, CF—390, RF—330. **Press Box Telephone:** (513) 529-4327.

MICHIGAN Wolverines
Conference: Big Ten.
Mailing Address: 1000 South State St., Ann Arbor, MI 48109.
Head Coach: Geoff Zahn. **Assistant Coaches:** *Chris Harrison, Matt Hyde. **Telephone:** (313) 647-4550. ■ **Baseball SID:** Jim Schneider. **Telephone:** (313) 763-4423. **FAX:** (313) 647-1188.
Home Field: Ray Fisher Stadium. **Seating Capacity:** 4,000. **Outfield Dimensions:** LF—330, CF—400, RF—330. **Press Box Telephone:** (313) 647-1283.

MICHIGAN STATE Spartans
Conference: Big Ten.
Mailing Address: 401 Olds Hall, East Lansing, MI 48824.
Head Coach: Ted Mahan. **Assistant Coaches:** Greg Gunderson, Eddie Turek. **Telephone:** (517) 355-4486. ■ **Baseball SID:** Jay Davey. **Telephone:** (517) 355-2271. **FAX:** (517) 353-9636.
Home Fields (Seating Capacity): Kobs Field (4,000), Oldsmobile Park (6,000). **Outfield Dimensions:** Kobs Field/LF—340, CF—400, RF—301;

Oldsmobile Park/LF—330, CF—412 , LF—337. **Press Box Telephone:** Kobs Field/(517) 353-3009; Oldsmobile Park/(517) 485-2616.

MIDDLE TENNESSEE STATE Blue Raiders

Conference: Ohio Valley.
Mailing Address: 1500 Greenland Dr., Murfreesboro, TN 37132.
Head Coach: Steve Peterson. **Assistant Coaches:** Buddy Custer, *Jim McGuire. **Telephone:** (615) 898-2120. ■ **Baseball SIDs:** Jim Horten, Matt Gillespie. **Telephone:** (615) 898-2968. **FAX:** (615) 898-5626.

MINNESOTA Golden Gophers

Conference: Big Ten.
Mailing Address: Bierman Building, Room 208, 516 15th Ave. SE, Minneapolis, MN 55455.
Head Coach: John Anderson. **Assistant Coaches:** Mike Dee, *Rob Fornasiere. **Telephone:** (612) 625-1060. ■ **Baseball SID:** Rhonda Lundin. **Telephone:** (612) 625-4090. **FAX:** (612) 625-0359.
Home Fields (Seating Capacity): Siebert Field (2,500), Metrodome (55,000).
Outfield Dimensions: Siebert Field/LF—330, CF—380, RF—330; Metrodome/LF—343, CF—408, RF—327. **Press Box Telephone:** Siebert Field/(612) 625-4031; Metrodome/(612) 625-4000.

MISSISSIPPI Rebels

Conference: Southeastern (West).
Mailing Address: P.O. Box 217, University, MS 38677.
Head Coach: Pat Harrison. **Assistant Coaches:** Darby Carmichael, Tom Fleenor, *Keith Kessinger. **Telephone:** (601) 232-7538. ■ **Baseball SID:** Rick Stunak. **Telephone:** (601) 232-7522. **FAX:** (601) 232-7006.
Home Field: Oxford University Stadium. **Seating Capacity:** 3,000. **Outfield Dimensions:** LF—330, CF—400, RF—330. **Press Box Telephone:** (601) 236-1931.

MISSISSIPPI STATE Bulldogs

Conference: Southeastern (West).
Mailing Address: P.O. Box 5327, Starkville, MS 39762.
Head Coach: Pat McMahon. **Assistant Coaches:** Jim Case, Tommy Raffo. **Telephone:** (601) 325-3597. ■ **Baseball SID:** Joe Dier. **Telephone:** (601) 325-8040. **FAX:** (601) 325-3654.
Home Field: Dudy Noble Field/Polk-DeMent Stadium. **Seating Capacity:** 15,000. **Outfield Dimensions:** LF—325, CF—390, RF—325. **Press Box Telephone:** (601) 325-3776.

MISSISSIPPI VALLEY STATE Delta Devils

Conference: Southwestern Athletic (East).
Mailing Address: 14000 Highway 82 West, Itta Bena, MS 38941.
Head Coach: Cleotha Wilson. **Telephone:** (601) 254-3398. ■ **Baseball SID:** Chuck Prophet. **Telephone:** (601) 254-3550. **FAX:** (601) 254-3639.

MISSOURI Tigers

Conference: Big 12.
Mailing Address: 330 Hearnes Center, Columbia, MO 65211.
Head Coach: Tim Jamieson. **Assistant Coach:** Chal Fanning. **Telephone:** (573) 882-0731. ■ **Baseball SID:** Jeremy McNeive. **Telephone:** (573) 884-2437. **FAX:** (573) 882-4720.
Home Field: Simmons Field. **Seating Capacity:** 2,000. **Outfield Dimensions:** LF—340, CF—400, RF—340. **Press Box Telephone:** (573) 882-2112.

MONMOUTH Hawks

Conference: Northeast.
Mailing Address: Cedar Avenue, West Long Branch, NJ 07764.
Head Coach: Dean Ehehalt. **Assistant Coaches:** Jeff Barbalinardo, Joe Litterio. **Telephone:** (732) 263-5186. ■ **Baseball SID:** Chris Risden. **Telephone:** (732) 263-5180. **FAX:** (732) 571-3535.

MOREHEAD STATE Eagles

Conference: Ohio Valley.
Mailing Address: UPO 1023, Morehead, KY 40351.
Head Coach: John Jarnagin. **Assistant Coaches:** Mitch Dunn, Larry Lipker. **Telephone:** (606) 783-2882. ■ **Baseball SID:** Randy Stacy. **Telephone:** (606) 783-2500. **FAX:** (606) 783-2550.

MOUNT ST. MARY'S Mountaineers

Conference: Northeast.
Mailing Address: Route 15, Emmitsburg, MD 21727.
Head Coach: Scott Thomson. **Assistant Coach:** Trevor Buckley. **Telephone:** (301) 447-5296. ■ **Baseball SID:** Eric Kloiber. **Telephone:** (301) 447-5384. **FAX:** (301) 447-5300.

MURRAY STATE Thoroughbreds

Conference: Ohio Valley.
Mailing Address: P.O. Box 9, Stewart Stadium, Murray, KY 42071.
Head Coach: Mike Thieke. **Assistant Coaches:** Dave Jarvis, Chris Moddelmog. **Telephone:** (502) 762-4892. ■ **Baseball SID:** Steve Parker. **Telephone:** (502) 762-4270. **FAX:** (502) 762-6814.

NAVY Midshipmen

Conference: Patriot.
Mailing Address: Ricketts Hall, 566 Brownson Road, Annapolis, MD 21402.
Head Coach: Bob MacDonald. **Assistant Coaches:** Jim Bell, Glenn Davis, Joe Kinney. **Telephone:** (410) 293-5571. ■ **Baseball SIDs:** Jim Mateiko, Scott Strasemeier. **Telephone:** (410) 293-4517. **FAX:** (410) 269-6779.

NEBRASKA Cornhuskers

Conference: Big 12.
Mailing Address: 1141 Avery Ave., Lincoln, NE 68588.
Head Coach: Dave Van Horn. **Assistant Coach:** Mike Anderson. **Telephone:** (402) 472-2269. ■ **Baseball SID:** Trevor Parks. **Telephone:** (402) 472-2263/3290. **FAX:** (402) 472-2005.
Home Field: Buck Beltzer Stadium. **Seating Capacity:** 1,500. **Outfield Dimensions:** LF—330, CF—400, RF—330. **Press Box Telephone:** (402) 472-2279.

NEVADA Wolf Pack

Conference: Big West (North).
Mailing Address: Mail Stop 232, Reno, NV 89557.
Head Coach: Gary Powers. **Assistant Coaches:** Jason Gill, Gary McNamara, *Stan Stolte. **Telephone:** (702) 784-4180. ■ **Baseball SID:** Ken Mocarski. **Telephone:** (702) 784-4215. **FAX:** (702) 784-4386.
Home Field: Peccole Park. **Seating Capacity:** 1,500. **Outfield Dimensions:** LF—340, CF—401, RF—340. **Press Box Telephone:** (702) 784-1585.

NEVADA-LAS VEGAS Rebels

Conference: Western Athletic (South).
Mailing Address: 4505 Maryland Parkway, Las Vegas, NV 89154.
Head Coach: Rod Soesbe. **Assistant Coaches:** Jim Pace, Mel Stottlemyre Jr. **Telephone:** (702) 895-3499. ■ **Baseball SID:** Jim Gemma. **Telephone:** (702) 895-3995. **FAX:** (702) 895-0989.
Home Field: Earl E. Wilson Stadium. **Seating Capacity:** 3,000. **Outfield Dimensions:** LF—335, CF—400, RF—335. **Press Box Telephone:** (702) 895-1595.

NEW MEXICO Lobos

Conference: Western Athletic (South).
Mailing Address: South Campus, Albuquerque, NM 87131.
Head Coach: Rich Alday. **Assistant Coaches:** Paul Huitt, *Mark Martinez, Luke Oglesby, Kevin Takahashi. **Telephone:** (505) 925-5720. ■ **Baseball SID:** Bryan Satter. **Telephone:** (505) 925-5528. **FAX:** (505) 925-5529.
Home Field: Lobo Field. **Seating Capacity:** 500. **Outfield Dimensions:** LF—340, CF—405, RF—340. **Press Box Telephone:** Unavailable.

NEW MEXICO STATE Aggies

Conference: Big West (North).
Mailing Address: Athletics Department MSC 3145, P.O. Box 30001, Las Cruces, NM 88003.
Head Coach: Rocky Ward. **Assistant Coaches:** Tim Tuma, Brad Meador. **Telephone:** (505) 646-5813. ■ **Baseball SID:** Andy Wengerd. **Telephone:** (505) 646-3929. **FAX:** (505) 646-2425.
Home Field: Presley Askew Field. **Seating Capacity:** 1,000. **Outfield Dimensions:** LF—340, CF—400, RF—340. **Press Box Telephone:** (505) 646-5700.

NEW ORLEANS Privateers

Conference: Sun Belt.
Mailing Address: Lakefront Arena, New Orleans, LA 70148.
Head Coach: Tom Schwaner. **Assistant Coaches:** Kenny Bonura, *Jeff Twitty. **Telephone:** (504) 280-7021. ■ **Baseball SID:** Ed Cassiere. **Telephone:** (504) 280-6284. **FAX:** (504) 280-7240.
Home Field: Privateer Park. **Seating Capacity:** 5,225. **Outfield Dimensions:** LF—330, CF—405, RF—330. **Press Box Telephone:** (504) 280-7027.

NEW YORK TECH Bears

Conference: Mid-Continent (East).
Mailing Address: Northern Boulevard, Old Westbury, NY 11568.
Head Coach: Bob Hirschfield. **Assistant Coach:** *Scott Hatten, Bill Timmes. **Telephone:** (516) 686-7513. ■ **Baseball SID:** Tom Riordan. **Telephone:** (516) 686-7626. **FAX:** (516) 626-0750.

NIAGARA Purple Eagles

Conference: Metro Atlantic (North).
Mailing Address: O'Shea Hall, Niagara University, NY 14109.
Head Coach: Jim Mauro. **Assistant Coach:** Bob Kowalski. **Telephone:** (716) 286-8602. ■ **Baseball SID:** Mark Vandergrift. **Telephone:** (716) 286-8602. **FAX:** (716) 286-8609.

NICHOLLS STATE Colonels

Conference: Southland.
Mailing Address: P.O. Box 2032, Thibodaux, LA 70310.
Head Coach: Jim Pizzolatto. **Assistant Coaches:** Gerald Cassard, Rocke Musgraves, *Everett Russell. **Telephone:** (504) 448-4808. ■ **Baseball SID:** Jack Duggan. **Telephone:** (504) 448-4281. **FAX:** (504) 448-4924.

NORFOLK STATE Spartans

Conference: Mid-Eastern Athletic (South).

Mailing Adress: 2401 Corprew Ave., Norfolk, VA 23504.

Head Coach: Marty Miller. **Assistant Coach:** Anthony Jones. **Telephone:** (757) 683-9539. ■ **Baseball SID:** Traci Allen. **Telephone:** (757) 683-2934. **FAX:** (757) 683-8199.

NORTH CAROLINA Tar Heels

Conference: Atlantic Coast.

Mailing Address: P.O. Box 2126, Chapel Hill, NC 27515.

Head Coach: Mike Roberts. **Assistant Coaches:** Chad Holbrook, Roger Williams. **Telephone:** (919) 962-2351. ■ **Baseball SID:** Matt Bowers. **Telephone:** (919) 962-2123. **FAX:** (919) 962-0612.

Home Field: Boshamer Stadium. **Seating Capacity:** 3,500. **Outfield Dimensions:** LF—335, CF—400, RF—335. **Press Box Telephone:** Unavailable.

UNC ASHEVILLE Bulldogs

Conference: Big South.

Mailing Address: One University Heights, Asheville, NC 28804.

Head Coach: Bill Hillier. **Assistant Coach:** Eric Filipek. **Telephone:** (704) 251-6920. ■ **Baseball SID:** Mike Gore. **Telephone:** (704) 251-6923. **FAX:** (704) 251-6386.

UNC CHARLOTTE 49ers

Conference: Conference USA.

Mailing Address: 9201 University City Blvd., Charlotte, NC 28223.

Head Coach: Loren Hibbs. **Assistant Coaches:** Matt Criss, Jay Matthews, Mike Shildt. **Telephone:** (704) 547-3935. ■ **Baseball SID:** James McCoy. **Telephone:** (704) 510-6313. **FAX:** (704) 547-4918.

Home Field: Tom and Lib Phillips Field. **Seating Capacity:** 2,000. **Outfield Dimensions:** LF—335, CF—390, RF—335. **Press Box Telephone:** (704) 547-3148.

UNC GREENSBORO Spartans

Conference: Southern.

Mailing Address: 1000 Spring Garden St., Greensboro, NC 27412.

Head Coach: Mike Gaski. **Assistant Coaches:** *Neil Avent, Matt Faulkner, Tonka Maynor. **Telephone:** (910) 334-3247. ■ **Baseball SID:** Jeremy Agor. **Telephone:** (910) 334-5615. **FAX:** (910) 334-3182.

UNC WILMINGTON Seahawks

Conference: Colonial Athletic.

Mailing Address: 601 South College Road, Wilmington, NC 28403.

Head Coach: Mark Scalf. **Assistant Coach:** *Todd Wilkinson. **Telephone:** (910) 962-3570. ■ **Baseball SID:** Joe Browning. **Telephone:** (910) 962-3236. **FAX:** (910) 962-3686.

NORTH CAROLINA A&T Aggies

Conference: Mid-Eastern Athletic (South).

Mailing Address: 1601 East Market St., Moores Gym, Greensboro, NC 27411.

Head Coach: Keith Shumate. **Assistant Coaches:** Ric Chandgie, Larry Farrer. **Telephone:** (910) 334-7371. ■ **Baseball SID:** B.J. Evans. **Telephone:** (910) 334-7371. **FAX:** (910) 334-7272.

NORTH CAROLINA STATE Wolfpack

Conference: Atlantic Coast.

Mailing Address: P.O. Box 8501, Raleigh, NC 27695.

Head Coach: Elliott Avent. **Assistant Coaches:** *Billy Best, Mark Fuller, Scott Lawler. **Telephone:** (919) 515-3613. ■ **Baseball SID:** Bruce Winkworth. **Telephone:** (919) 515-1182. **FAX:** (919) 515-2898.

Home Field: Doak Field. **Seating Capacity:** 3,000. **Outfield Dimensions:** LF—340, CF—400, RF—340. **Press Box Telephone:** (919) 515-7643/7645.

NORTHEAST LOUISIANA Indians

Conference: Southland.

Mailing Address: 308 Stadium Dr., Monroe, LA 71209.

Head Coach: Smoke Laval. **Assistant Coaches:** Allen Chance, *Brad Holland. **Telephone:** (318) 342-3589. ■ **Baseball SID:** Troy Mitchell. **Telephone:** (318) 342-3589. **FAX:** (318) 342-5464.

NORTHEASTERN Huskies

Conference: America East.

Mailing Address: 360 Huntington Ave., Boston, MA 02115.

Head Coach: Neil McPhee. **Assistant Coach:** Matt Noone. **Telephone:** (617) 373-3657. ■ **Baseball SID:** Jack Grinold. **Telephone:** (617) 373-2691. **FAX:** (617) 373-3152.

NORTHEASTERN ILLINOIS Golden Eagles

Conference: Mid-Continent (West).

Mailing Address: 5500 North St. Louis Ave., Chicago, IL 60625.

Head Coach: Jim Hawrysko. **Assistant Coaches:** Unavailable. **Telephone:** (773) 794-2884. ■ **Baseball SID:** Damion Jones. **Telephone:** (773) 794-6241. **FAX:** (773) 794-6244.

NORTHERN ILLINOIS Huskies

Conference: Mid-American (West).

Mailing Address: 112 Evans Fieldhouse, DeKalb, IL 60115.
Head Coach: Frank Del Medico. Assistant Coaches: Unavailable.
Telephone: (815) 753-0147. ■ Baseball SID: Robert Hester. Telephone: (815) 753-1706. FAX: (815) 753-9540.

NORTHERN IOWA Panthers

Conference: Missouri Valley.
Mailing Address: 23rd and College, Upper NW UNI-Dome, Cedar Falls, IA 50614.
Head Coach: Dave Schrage. Assistant Coaches: Wade Brinkof, Scott Douglas, Jack Sole. Telephone: (319) 273-6323. ■ Baseball SID: Lis Erickson. Telephone: (319) 273-2932. FAX: (319) 273-3602.

NORTHWESTERN Wildcats

Conference: Big Ten.
Mailing Address: 1501 Central St., Evanston, IL 60208.
Head Coach: Paul Stevens. Assistant Coaches: Joe Keenan, Ron Klein, Tim Stoddard. Telephone: (847) 491-7503. ■ Baseball SID: Chris Hughes. Telephone: (847) 491-7503. FAX: (847) 491-8818.
Home Field: Rocky Miller Park. Seating Capacity: 1,000. Outfield Dimensions: LF—330, CF—400, RF—330. Press Box Telephone: (847) 491-4200.

NORTHWESTERN STATE Demons

Conference: Southland.
Mailing Address: 112 Prather Coliseum, Natchitoches, LA 71459.
Head Coach: John Cohen. Assistant Coach: Sean McCann. Telephone: (318) 357-4134. ■ Baseball SID: Doug Ireland. Telephone: (318) 357-6467. FAX: (318) 357-4515.

NOTRE DAME Fighting Irish

Conference: Big East.
Mailing Address: Joyce Center, 2nd Floor, Notre Dame, IN 46556.
Head Coach: Paul Mainieri. Assistant Coaches: Cory Mee, *Brian O'Connor. Telephone: (219) 631-8466. ■ Baseball SID: Pete LaFleur. Telephone: (219) 631-7516/4780. FAX: Unavailable.
Home Field: Frank Eck Stadium. Seating Capacity: 2,500. Outfield Dimensions: LF—331, CF—401, RF—331. Press Box Telephone: (219) 631-9018/9476.

OHIO Bobcats

Conference: Mid-American (East).
Mailing Address: 105 Convocation Center, Athens, OH 45701.
Head Coach: Joe Carbone. Assistant Coaches: Dusty Lepper, John Lombardo, Bill Toadvine. Telephone: (614) 593-1180. ■ Baseball SID: George Mauzy. Telephone: (614) 593-1298. FAX: (614) 593-2420.
Home Field: Bob Wren Stadium. Seating Capacity: 3,000. Outfield Dimensions: LF—330, CF—390, RF—330. Press Box Telephone: Unavailable.

OHIO STATE Buckeyes

Conference: Big Ten.
Mailing Address: 124 St. John Arena, 410 Woody Hayes Drive, Columbus, OH 43210.
Head Coach: Bob Todd. Assistant Coaches: Pat Bangston, *Greg Cypret. Telephone: (614) 292-1075. ■ Baseball SID: Greg Aylsworth. Telephone: (614) 292-6861. FAX: (614) 292-8547.
Home Field: Bill Davis Stadium. Seating Capacity: 3,000. Outfield Dimensions: LF—330, CF—400, RF—330. Press Box Telephone: (614) 292-0021/0024.

OKLAHOMA Sooners

Conference: Big 12.
Mailing Address: 180 West Brooks, Room 235, Norman, OK 73019.
Head Coach: Larry Cochell. Assistant Coaches: Bill Mosiello, Aric Thomas, Jackson Todd. Telephone: (405) 325-8354. ■ Baseball SID: Chris Williams. Telephone: (405) 325-8349. FAX: (405) 325-7623.
Home Field: L. Dale Mitchell Park. Seating Capacity: 2,700. Outfield Dimensions: LF—335, CF—411, RF—335. Press Box Telephone: (405) 325-8363.

OKLAHOMA STATE Cowboys

Conference: Big 12.
Mailing Address: 100 Allie P. Reynolds Stadium, Stillwater, OK 74078.
Head Coach: Tom Holliday. Assistant Coaches: John Farrell, Robbie Wine. Telephone: (405) 744-5849. ■ Baseball SID: Neal Freeman. Telephone: (405) 744-5749. FAX: (405) 744-7754.
Home Field: Allie P. Reynolds Stadium. Seating Capacity: 5,200. Outfield Dimensions: LF—330, CF—400, RF—330. Press Box Telephone: (405) 744-5757.

OLD DOMINION Monarchs

Conference: Colonial Athletic.
Mailing Address: Building 136, Athletic Administration, Norfolk, VA 23529.
Head Coach: Tony Guzzo. Assistant Coaches: Jayson Nave, Danny Nellum, *Rick Robinson. Telephone: (757) 683-4230. ■ Baseball SID: Carol Hudson. Telephone: (757) 683-3372. FAX: (757) 683-3119.
Home Field: Bud Metheny Stadium. Seating Capacity: 3,000. Outfield

Dimensions: LF—320, CF—395, RF—320. **Press Box Telephone:** (757) 683-5036.

ORAL ROBERTS Golden Eagles
Conference: Mid-Continent (West).
Mailing Address: 7777 South Lewis Ave., Tulsa, OK 74171.
Head Coach: Sunny Golloway. **Assistant Coaches:** Jim Freeman, Scott Marr, *Bob Miller. **Telephone:** (918) 495-7130. ■ **Baseball SID:** Todd Addington. **Telephone:** (918) 495-7102. **FAX:** (918) 495-7142.

OREGON STATE Beavers
Conference: Pacific-10 (North).
Mailing Address: Gill Coliseum, Room 127, Corvallis, OR 97331.
Head Coach: Pat Casey. **Assistant Coaches:** Tony Murillo, Ron Northcutt, Dan Spencer. **Telephone:** (541) 737-2825. ■ **Baseball SID:** Kip Carlson. **Telephone:** (541) 737-3720. **FAX:** (541) 737-3072.
Home Field: Coleman Field. **Seating Capacity:** 2,310. **Outfield Dimensions:** LF—330, CF—400, RF—330. **Press Box Telephone:** (541) 737-7475.

PACE Setters
Conference: Mid-Continent (East).
Mailing Address: 861 Bedford Road, Pleasantville, NY 10570.
Head Coach: Fred Calaicone. **Assistant Coaches:** Tim Kelly, Cris Crispino, Hank Milano. **Telephone:** (914) 773-3411. ■ **Baseball SID:** Nick Renda. **Telephone:** (914) 773-3888. **FAX:** (914) 773-3491.

PACIFIC Tigers
Conference: Big West (North).
Mailing Address: 3601 Pacific Ave., Stockton, CA 95211.
Head Coach: Quincey Noble. **Assistant Coaches:** Joe Moreno, Jim Yanko. **Telephone:** (209) 946-2512. ■ **Baseball SID:** Mike Millerick. **Telephone:** (209) 946-2479. **FAX:** (209) 946-2757.
Home Field: Billy Hebert Field. **Seating Capacity:** 3,500. **Outfield Dimensions:** LF—325, CF—392, RF—330. **Press Box Telephone:** (209) 944-5951.

PENNSYLVANIA Quakers
Conference: Ivy League (Gehrig).
Mailing Address: Weightman Hall South, 235 South 33rd St., Philadelphia, PA 19104.
Head Coach: Bob Seddon. **Assistant Coaches:** Bill Wagner, Dan Young. **Telephone:** (215) 898-6282. ■ **Baseball SID:** Carla Shultzberg. **Telephone:** (215) 898-1748. **FAX:** (215) 898-1747.

PENN STATE Nittany Lions
Conference: Big Ten.
Mailing Address: 112 Bryce Jordan Center, University Park, PA 16802.
Head Coach: Joe Hindelang. **Assistant Coaches:** *Jeff Ditch, Randy Ford, John Ramsey. **Telephone:** (814) 763-0239. ■ **Baseball SID:** Alan Ashby. **Telephone:** (814) 865-1757. **FAX:** (814) 863-3165.
Home Field: Beaver Field. **Seating Capacity:** 1,500. **Outfield Dimensions:** LF—350, CF—405, RF—350. **Press Box Telephone:** None.

PEPPERDINE Waves
Conference: West Coast.
Mailing Address: 24255 Pacific Coast Highway, Malibu, CA 90263.
Head Coach: Frank Sanchez. **Assistant Coaches:** Dave Esquer, David Rhoades. **Telephone:** (310) 456-4199. ■ **Baseball SID:** Michael Zapolski. **Telephone:** (310) 456-4333. **FAX:** (310) 456-4322.
Home Field: Eddy D. Field Stadium. **Seating Capacity:** 2,200. **Outfield Dimensions:** LF—330, CF—400, RF—330. **Press Box Telephone:** (310) 456-4598.

PITTSBURGH Panthers
Conference: Big East.
Mailing Address: P.O. Box 7436, Pittsburgh, PA 15213.
Head Coach: Joe Jordano. **Assistant Coaches:** Joel Dombkowski, Lou Schaper. **Telephone:** (412) 648-8208. ■ **Baseball SID:** Johanna Sarnowski. **Telephone:** (412) 648-8240. **FAX:** (412) 648-8248.
Home Field: Trees Field. **Seating Capacity:** 500. **Outfield Dimensions:** LF—328, CF—380, RF—335. **Press Box Telephone:** None.

PORTLAND Pilots
Conference: West Coast.
Mailing Address: 5000 North Willamette Blvd., Portland, OR 97203.
Head Coach: Chris Sperry. **Assistant Coach:** Ed Gustafson. **Telephone:** (503) 283-7707. ■ **Baseball SID:** Steve Walker. **Telephone:** (503) 283-7439. **FAX:** (503) 283-7242.

PORTLAND STATE Vikings
Conference: Pacific-10 (North).
Mailing Address: P.O. Box 751, Portland, OR 97207.
Head Coach: Dave Dangler. **Assistant Coach:** Hal DeBarry. **Telephone:** (503) 725-3852. ■ **Baseball SID:** Larry Sellers. **Telephone:** (503) 725-2525. **FAX:** (503) 725-5610.
Home Field: Civic Stadium. **Seating Capacity:** 23,000. **Outfield Dimensions:** LF—309, CF—399, RF—339. **Press Box Telephone:** (503) 294-2942.

PRAIRIE VIEW A&M Panthers

Conference: Southwestern Athletic (West).
Mailing Address: P.O. Box 97, Prairie View, TX 77446.
Head Coach: John Tankersley. **Assistant Coaches:** Matt Berly, Raymond Burgess, Scipio Johnson. **Telephone:** (409) 857-4290. ■ **Baseball SID:** Harlan Robinson. **Telephone:** (409) 857-2114. **FAX:** (409) 857-2408.

PRINCETON Tigers

Conference: Ivy League (Gehrig).
Mailing Address: Jadwin Gym, Princeton, NJ 08544.
Head Coach: Scott Bradley. **Assistant Coach:** Tom Crowley. **Telephone:** (609) 258-5059. ■ **Baseball SID:** Melissa Lempke. **Telephone:** (609) 258-3568. **FAX:** (609) 258-2399.

PROVIDENCE Friars

Conference: Big East.
Mailing Address: River Avenue, Providence, RI 02918.
Head Coach: Charlie Hickey. **Assistant Coaches:** John Navilliat, Sean O'Connor. **Telephone:** (401) 865-2273. ■ **Baseball SID:** Tim Connor. **Telephone:** (401) 865-2208. **FAX:** (401) 865-2583.
Home Field: Hendricken Field. **Seating Capacity:** 1,000. **Outfield Dimensions:** LF—330, CF—401, RF—301. **Press Box Telephone:** None.

PURDUE Boilermakers

Conference: Big Ten.
Mailing Address: 1790 Mackey Arena, West Lafayette, IN 47907.
Head Coach: Steve Green. **Assistant Coaches:** Mark Kingston, Bob Shepherd. **Telephone:** (765) 494-3217. ■ **Baseball SID:** Brett Swick. **Telephone:** (765) 494-3202. **FAX:** (765) 494-5447.
Home Field: Lambert Field. **Seating Capacity:** 1,100. **Outfield Dimensions:** LF—343, CF—400, RF—342. **Press Box Telephone:** (765) 494-1522.

RADFORD Highlanders

Conference: Big South.
Mailing Address: P.O. Box 6916, Radford, VA 24142.
Head Coach: Lew Kent. **Assistant Coach:** Wayne Smith. **Telephone:** (540) 831-5881. ■ **Baseball SID:** Chris King. **Telephone:** (540) 831-5211. **FAX:** (540) 831-5036.

RHODE ISLAND Rams

Conference: Atlantic-10 (East).
Mailing Address: 3 Keaney Rd., Suite 1, Kingston, RI 02881.
Head Coach: Frank Leoni. **Assistant Coaches:** John LaRose, Scott Norris, Pat Sullivan. **Telephone:** (401) 874-4550. ■ **Baseball SID:** Jamie Zeitz. **Telephone:** (401) 874-2409. **FAX:** (401) 874-5354.

RICE Owls

Conference: Western Athletic (South).
Mailing Address: P.O. Box 1892, MS 548, Houston, TX 77251.
Head Coach: Wayne Graham. **Assistant Coaches:** Chris Feris, *Jon Prather. **Telephone:** (713) 527-6022. ■ **Baseball SID:** Bill Cousins. **Telephone:** (713) 527-4034. **FAX:** (713) 527-6019.
Home Field: Cameron Field. **Seating Capacity:** 2,000. **Outfield Dimensions:** LF—330, CF—400, RF—330. **Press Box Telephone:** (713) 527-4931.

RICHMOND Spiders

Conference: Colonial Athletic.
Mailing Address: Robins Center, Richmond, VA 23173.
Head Coach: Ron Atkins. **Assistant Coaches:** Braxton Bell, Mark McQueen, Bobby Goode. **Telephone:** (804) 289-8391. ■ **Baseball SID:** Phil Stanton. **Telephone:** (804) 289-8320. **FAX:** (804) 289-8820.

RIDER Broncs

Conference: Metro Atlantic (South).
Mailing Address: 2083 Lawrenceville Road, Lawrenceville, NJ 08648.
Head Coach: Sonny Pittaro. **Assistant Coaches:** Tom Petroff, Jeff Plunkett. **Telephone:** (609) 896-5055. ■ **Baseball SID:** Bud Focht. **Telephone:** (609) 896-5138. **FAX:** (609) 896-0341.

RUTGERS Scarlet Knights

Conference: Big East.
Mailing Address: P.O. Box 1149, Piscataway, NJ 08855.
Head Coach: Fred Hill. **Assistant Coaches:** Tom Baxter, Jay Blackwell, Glen Gardner. **Telephone:** (732) 445-3553. ■ **Baseball SID:** Scott Novak. **Telephone:** (732) 445-6545. **FAX:** (732) 445-6546.
Home Field: Class of '53 Stadium. **Seating Capacity:** 1,500. **Outfield Dimensions:** LF—330, CF—410, RF—320. **Press Box Telephone:** None.

SACRAMENTO STATE Hornets

Conference: Big West (North).
Mailing Address: 6000 J St., Sacramento, CA 95819.
Head Coach: John Smith. **Assistant Coaches:** Jim Barr, Brian Hewitt, Buck Martinez. **Telephone:** (916) 278-7225. ■ **Baseball SID:** Holly Caldwell. **Telephone:** (916) 278-6896. **FAX:** (916) 278-5429.
Home Field: Hornet Field. **Seating Capacity:** 1,500. **Outfield Dimensions:** LF—333, CF—400, RF—333. **Press Box Telephone:** None.

ST. BONAVENTURE Bonnies

Conference: Atlantic-10 (East).
Mailing Address: Department of Athletics, St. Bonaventure, NY 14778.
Head Coach: Larry Sudbrook. **Assistant Coach:** Chris Goyette. **Telephone:** (716) 375-2641. ■ **Baseball SID:** Mike Hardisky. **Telephone:** (716) 375-2319. **FAX:** (716) 375-2383.

ST. FRANCIS Terriers

Conference: Northeast.
Mailing Address: 180 Remsen St., Brooklyn, NY 11201.
Head Coach: Frank Del George. **Assistant Coach:** Tony Barone, Mike Lopiparo, Frank Salzone. **Telephone:** (718) 489-5490. ■ **Baseball SID:** Jim Hoffman. **Telephone:** (718) 489-5490. **FAX:** (718) 797-2140.

ST. JOHN'S Red Storm

Conference: Big East.
Mailing Address: 8000 Utopia Parkway, Jamaica, NY 11439.
Head Coach: Ed Blankmeyer. **Assistant Coaches:** Anthony Fallacaro, Mike Maertan, *Kevin McMullan. **Telephone:** (718) 990-6148. ■ **Baseball SID:** Chris DeLorenzo. **Telephone:** (718) 990-6367. **FAX:** (718) 969-8468.
Home Field: McCallen Field. **Seating Capacity:** 1,000. **Outfield Dimensions:** LF—340, CF—400, RF—340. **Press Box Telephone:** (718) 990-6057.

ST. JOSEPH'S Hawks

Conference: Atlantic-10 (East).
Mailing Address: 5600 City Ave., Philadelphia, PA 19131.
Head Coach: Jim Ertel. **Assistant Coaches:** Jack Stanczak, Bill Black. **Telephone:** (610) 660-1718. ■ **Baseball SID:** Ken Krsolovic. **Telephone:** (610) 660-1704. **FAX:** (610) 660-1660.

SAINT LOUIS Billikens

Conference: Conference USA.
Mailing Address: 3672 West Pine Rd., St. Louis, MO 63108.
Head Coach: Bob Hughes. **Assistant Coaches:** Frank Mormino, Dan Nicholson, Mark Valle. **Telephone:** (314) 977-3172. ■ **Baseball SID:** Chris Cook. **Telephone:** (314) 977-3463. **FAX:** (314) 977-7193.
Home Field: Billiken Sports Center. **Seating Capacity:** 1,000. **Outfield Dimensions:** LF—330, CF—395, RF—330. **Press Box Telephone:** (314) 977-3560.

ST. MARY'S Gaels

Conference: West Coast.
Mailing Address: 1928 St. Mary's Rd., Moraga, CA 94575.
Head Coach: Rod Ingram. **Assistant Coaches:** John Baptista, Glen McCormick. **Telephone:** (510) 631-4400/4637. ■ **Baseball SID:** Andy McDowell. **Telephone:** (510) 631-4402. **FAX:** (510) 631-4405.

ST. PETER'S Peacocks

Conference: Metro Atlantic (South).
Mailing Address: 2641 Kennedy Blvd., Jersey City, NJ 07306.
Head Coach: Bruce Sabatini. **Assistant Coaches:** Brian Callahan, John Way. **Telephone:** (201) 915-9459. ■ **Baseball SID:** Brian Callahan. **Telephone:** (201) 915-9101. **FAX:** (201) 915-9102.

SAM HOUSTON STATE Bearkats

Conference: Southland.
Mailing Address: 500 Bowers Blvd., Huntsville, TX 77341.
Head Coach: John Skeeters. **Assistant Coach:** Carlo Gott. **Telephone:** (409) 294-1731. ■ **Baseball SID:** Paul Ridings. **Telephone:** (409) 294-1764. **FAX:** (409) 294-3538.

SAMFORD Bulldogs

Conference: Trans America Athletic (West).
Mailing Address: 800 Lakeshore Dr., Birmingham, AL 35229.
Head Coach: Tim Parenton. **Assistant Coach:** Todd Buczek. **Telephone:** (205) 870-2134. ■ **Baseball SID:** Riley Adair. **Telephone:** (205) 870-2966. **FAX:** (205) 870-2132.

SAN DIEGO Toreros

Conference: West Coast.
Mailing Address: 5998 Alcala Park, San Diego, CA 92110.
Head Coach: John Cunningham. **Assistant Coaches:** Glenn Godwin, Jake Molina. **Telephone:** (619) 260-8894. ■ **Baseball SID:** Mike Daniels. **Telephone:** (619) 260-4745. **FAX:** (619) 292-0388.

SAN DIEGO STATE Aztecs

Conference: Western Athletic (West).
Mailing Address: Department of Athletics, San Diego, CA 92182.
Head Coach: Jim Dietz. **Assistant Coaches:** Rusty Filter, Pat Oliverio, Stacy Parker. **Telephone:** (619) 594-6889. ■ **Baseball SID:** Dave Kuhn. **Telephone:** (619) 594-5547. **FAX:** (619) 582-6541.
Home Field: Tony Gwynn Stadium. **Seating Capacity:** 3,000. **Outfield Dimensions:** LF—340, CF—412, RF—340. **Press Box Telephone:** (619) 594-4103.

SAN FRANCISCO Dons

Conference: West Coast.
Mailing Address: 2130 Fulton St., San Francisco, CA 94117.
Head Coach: Rich Hill. **Assistant Coaches:** Chad Konishi, Nate Rodriguez.
Telephone: (415) 422-2934/2393. ■ **Baseball SID:** Kyle McRae. **Telephone:** (415) 422-6161/6162. **FAX:** (415) 422-2929.

SAN JOSE STATE Spartans

Conference: Western Athletic (West).
Mailing Address: One Washington Square, San Jose, CA 95192.
Head Coach: Sam Piraro. **Assistant Coaches:** Scott Hertler, Dean Madsen, Doug Thurman. **Telephone:** (408) 924-1255. ■ **Baseball SID:** Hung Tsai. **Telephone:** (408) 924-1217. **FAX:** (408) 924-1291.
Home Field: Municipal Stadium. **Seating Capacity:** 5,200. **Outfield Dimensions:** LF—340, CF—400, RF—340. **Press Box Telephone:** (408) 924-7276.

SANTA CLARA Broncos

Conference: West Coast.
Mailing Address: Toso Pavilion, Santa Clara, CA 95053.
Head Coach: Mike Cummins. **Assistant Coaches:** Troy Buckley, Greg Gohr. **Telephone:** (408) 554-4882. ■ **Baseball SID:** Jim Young. **Telephone:** (408) 554-4661. **FAX:** (408) 554-6942.
Home Field: Buck Shaw Stadium. **Seating Capacity:** 6,800. **Outfield Dimensions:** LF—350, CF—400, RF—330. **Press Box Telephone:** None.

SETON HALL Pirates

Conference: Big East.
Mailing Address: 400 South Orange Ave., South Orange, NJ 07079.
Head Coach: Mike Sheppard. **Assistant Coaches:** Ed Lyons, *Rob Sheppard. **Telephone:** (973) 761-9557. ■ **Baseball SID:** Dwayne Harrison. **Telephone:** (973) 761-9493. **FAX:** (973) 761-9061.
Home Field: Owen T. Carroll Field. **Seating Capacity:** 1,500. **Outfield Dimensions:** LF—330, CF—410, RF—312. **Press Box Telephone:** None.

SIENA Saints

Conference: Metro Atlantic (North).
Mailing Address: 515 Loudon Road, Loudonville, NY 12211.
Head Coach: Tony Rossi. **Assistant Coaches:** Tony Curro, Dave Perry, Paul Thompson. **Telephone:** (518) 786-5044. ■ **Baseball SID:** Chris Wallace. **Telephone:** (518) 783-2411. **FAX:** (518) 783-2992.

SOUTH ALABAMA Jaguars

Conference: Sun Belt.
Mailing Address: 1151 HPELS Building, Mobile, AL 36688.
Head Coach: Steve Kittrell. **Assistant Coaches:** Robert Flippo, Ron Pelletier, Ronnie Powell. **Telephone:** (334) 460-6876. ■ **Baseball SID:** Matt Smith. **Telephone:** (334) 460-7035. **FAX:** (334) 460-7297.
Home Field: Eddie Stanky Field. **Seating Capacity:** 3,500. **Outfield Dimensions:** LF—330, CF—400, RF—330. **Press Box Telephone:** (334) 460-7126.

SOUTH CAROLINA Gamecocks

Conference: Southeastern (East).
Mailing Address: 1300 Rosewood Drive, Columbia, SC 29208.
Head Coach: Ray Tanner. **Assistant Coaches:** Tripp Keister, Jerry Meyers, *Jim Toman. **Telephone:** (803) 777-5834. ■ **Baseball SIDs:** John Butts, Tom Price. **Telephone:** (803) 777-5204. **FAX:** (803) 777-2967.
Home Field: Sarge Frye Field. **Seating Capacity:** 4,000. **Outfield Dimensions:** LF—330, CF—390, RF—320. **Press Box Telephone:** (803) 777-6648/6691.

SOUTH FLORIDA Bulls

Conference: Conference USA.
Mailing Address: 4202 East Fowler Ave., Tampa, FL 33620.
Head Coach: Eddie Cardieri. **Assistant Coaches:** Bryan Peters, *Mark Rose. **Telephone:** (813) 974-3105. ■ **Baseball SID:** Fred Huff. **Telephone:** (813) 974-4087. **FAX:** (813) 974-5328.
Home Field: Red McEwen Field. **Seating Capacity:** 1,500. **Outfield Dimensions:** LF—340, CF—400, RF—340. **Press Box Telephone:** (813) 974-3604.

SOUTHEAST MISSOURI STATE Indians

Conference: Ohio Valley.
Mailing Address: One University Plaza, Cape Girardeau, MO 63701.
Head Coach: Mark Hogan. **Assistant Coaches:** *Greg Goff, Brian Schaefer, Mark Wasikowski. **Telephone:** (573) 651-2645. ■ **Baseball SID:** Ron Hines. **Telephone:** (573) 651-2937. **FAX:** (573) 651-2810.

SOUTHEASTERN LOUISIANA Lions

Conference: Southland.
Mailing Address: SLU Station 390, Hammond, LA 70402.
Head Coach: Greg Marten. **Assistant Coaches:** Johnny Brechtel, Mark Gosnell. **Telephone:** (504) 549-2253. ■ **Baseball SID:** Barry Niemeyer. **Telephone:** (504) 549-3774/2142. **FAX:** (504) 549-3495.

SOUTHERN Jaguars

Conference: Southwestern Athletic (West).
Mailing Address: P.O. Box 1085D, Baton Rouge, LA 70813.
Head Coach: Roger Cador. **Assistant Coaches:** Richard Gaines, Don

Thomas. **Telephone:** (504) 771-2513. ■ **Baseball SID:** Roderic Moseley. **Telephone:** (504) 771-2601. **FAX:** (504) 771-4400.

SOUTHERN CALIFORNIA Trojans

Conference: Pacific-10 (South).

Mailing Address: HER-103, University Park, Los Angeles, CA 90089.

Head Coach: Mike Gillespie. **Assistant Coaches:** Rob Klein, Andy Nieto, *John Savage. **Telephone:** (213) 740-5762. ■ **Baseball SID:** Roger Horne. **Telephone:** (213) 740-8480. **FAX:** (213) 740-7584.

Home Field: Dedeaux Field. **Seating Capacity:** 1,800. **Outfield Dimensions:** LF—335, CF—395, RF—335. **Press Box Telephone:** (213) 748-3449.

SOUTHERN ILLINOIS Salukis

Conference: Missouri Valley.

Mailing Address: SIU Arena, Lingle Hall, Room 130D, Carbondale, IL 62901.

Head Coach: Dan Callahan. **Assistant Coaches:** Dan Davis, *Ken Henderson. **Telephone:** (618) 453-2802. ■ **Baseball SID:** Gene Green. **Telephone:** (618) 453-5470. **FAX:** (618) 536-2152.

Home Field: Abe Martin Field. **Seating Capacity:** 1,800. **Outfield Dimensions:** LF—340, CF—410, RF—340. **Press Box Telephone:** (618) 453-3794.

SOUTHERN MISSISSIPPI Golden Eagles

Conference: Conference USA.

Mailing Address: Southern Station, Box 5161, Hattiesburg, MS 39406.

Head Coach: Corky Palmer. **Assistant Coaches:** *Scott Dwyer, Michael Federico, Dan Wagner. **Telephone:** (601) 266-5017. ■ **Baseball SID:** Ricky Hazel. **Telephone:** (601) 266-4503. **FAX:** (601) 266-4507.

Home Field: Pete Taylor Park. **Seating Capacity:** 3,678. **Outfield Dimensions:** LF—365, CF—400, RF—365. **Press Box Telephone:** (601) 266-5684.

SOUTHERN UTAH Thunderbirds

Conference: Independent.

Mailing Address: 351 West Center St., Cedar City, UT 84720.

Head Coach: DeLynn Corry. **Assistant Coaches:** Marty Haynie, Kevin Howard. **Telephone:** (435) 586-7932. ■ **Baseball SID:** Neil Gardner. **Telephone:** (435) 586-7753. **FAX:** (435) 865-8037.

SOUTHWEST MISSOURI STATE Bears

Conference: Missouri Valley.

Mailing Address: 901 South National Ave., Springfield, MO 65804.

Head Coach: Keith Guttin. **Assistant Coaches:** *Paul Evans, Brent Thomas. **Telephone:** (417) 836-5242. ■ **Baseball SID:** Mark Stillwell. **Telephone:** (417) 836-5402. **FAX:** (417) 836-4868.

SOUTHWEST TEXAS STATE Bobcats

Conference: Southland.

Mailing Address: Jowers Center, Room 118, San Marcos, TX 78666.

Head Coach: Howard Bushong. **Assistant Coaches:** *Monte Cain, Marcus Hendry. **Telephone:** (512) 245-3586. ■ **Baseball SID:** Corey Bobo. **Telephone:** (512) 245-2966. **FAX:** (512) 245-2967.

SOUTHWESTERN LOUISIANA Ragin' Cajuns

Conference: Sun Belt.

Mailing Address: 201 Reinhardt Dr., Lafayette, LA 70506.

Head Coach: Tony Robichaux. **Assistant Coaches:** Anthony Babineaux, Jason Gonzales, *Wade Simoneaux. **Telephone:** (318) 482-6189. ■ **Baseball SID:** Chad Schexnaydre. **Telephone:** (318) 482-6330. **FAX:** (318) 482-6649.

Home Field: Moore Field. **Seating Capacity:** 5,000. **Outfield Dimensions:** LF—330, CF—400, RF—330. **Press Box Telephone:** (318) 482-6331.

STANFORD Cardinal

Conference: Pacific-10 (South).

Mailing Address: Department of Athletics, Stanford, CA 94305.

Head Coach: Mark Marquess. **Assistant Coaches:** Tom Dunton, Dave Nakama, *Dean Stotz. **Telephone:** (650) 723-4528. ■ **Baseball SID:** Scott Leykam. **Telephone:** (650) 723-4418. **FAX:** (650) 725-2957.

Home Field: Sunken Diamond. **Seating Capacity:** 4,000. **Outfield Dimensions:** LF—335, CF—400, RF—335. **Press Box Telephone:** (650) 723-4629.

STETSON Hatters

Conference: Trans America Athletic (South).

Mailing Address: Woodland Blvd., Campus Box 8317, DeLand, FL 32720.

Head Coach: Pete Dunn. **Assistant Coaches:** Derek Johnson, Larry Jones, *Tom Riginos. **Telephone:** (904) 822-8106. ■ **Baseball SID:** Cris Belvin. **Telephone:** (904) 822-8131. **FAX:** (904) 822-8132.

Home Field: Conrad Park. **Seating Capacity:** 1,200. **Outfield Dimensions:** LF—352, CF—418, RF—352. **Press Box Telephone:** (904) 736-7360.

TEMPLE Owls

Conference: Atlantic-10 (East).

Mailing Address: Vivacqua Hall, 4th Floor, Philadelphia, PA 19122.

Head Coach: Skip Wilson. **Assistant Coaches:** Shawn Dawds, Dan Kusters, Joseph McNally. **Telephone:** (215) 204-7447. ■ **Baseball SID:** Vince Bigregrio. **Telephone:** (215) 204-4824. **FAX:** (215) 204-7499.

TENNESSEE Volunteers

Conference: Southeastern (East).
Mailing Address: P.O. Box 15016, Knoxville, TN 37901.
Head Coach: Rod Delmonico. **Assistant Coaches:** Mike Maack, *Larry Simcox. **Telephone:** (423) 974-2057. ■ **Baseball SID:** Jeff Muir. **Telephone:** (423) 974-1212. **FAX:** (423) 974-1269.
Home Field: Lindsey Nelson Stadium. **Seating Capacity:** 5,500. **Outfield Dimensions:** LF—335, CF—404, RF—330. **Press Box Telephone:** (423) 974-3376.

TENNESSEE-MARTIN Skyhawks

Conference: Ohio Valley.
Mailing Address: 40 Skyhawk Fieldhouse, Martin, TN 38238.
Head Coach: Vernon Prather. **Assistant Coach:** Michael Spaulding. **Telephone:** (901) 587-7667. ■ **Baseball SID:** Lee Wilmot. **Telephone:** (901) 587-7632. **FAX:** (901) 587-7624.

TENNESSEE TECH Golden Eagles

Conference: Ohio Valley.
Mailing Address: P.O. Box 5057, Cookeville, TN 38505.
Head Coach: David Mays. **Assistant Coaches:** *Donley Canary, Brent Chaffin. **Telephone:** (931) 372-3925. ■ **Baseball SID:** Rob Schabert. **Telephone:** (931) 372-3088. **FAX:** (931) 372-6139.

TEXAS Longhorns

Conference: Big 12.
Mailing Address: P.O. Box 7399, Austin, TX 78713.
Head Coach: Augie Garrido. **Assistant Coaches:** *Tommy Harmon, Burt Hooton, Jason Moler. **Telephone:** (512) 471-5732. ■ **Baseball SID:** Mike Forcucci. **Telephone:** (512) 471-6039. **FAX:** (512) 471-6040.
Home Field: Disch-Falk Field. **Seating Capacity:** 6,649. **Outfield Dimensions:** LF—340, CF—400, RF—325. **Press Box Telephone:** (512) 471-1146.

TEXAS-ARLINGTON Mavericks

Conference: Southland.
Mailing Address: P.O. Box 19079, Arlington, TX 76019.
Head Coach: Butch McBroom. **Assistant Coaches:** Clay Gould, Ron Liggett. **Telephone:** (817) 272-2032. ■ **Baseball SID:** Steve Weller. **Telephone:** (817) 273-2239. **FAX:** (817) 272-2254
Home Field: Allan Saxe Field. **Seating Capacity:** 1,200. **Outfield Dimensions:** LF—330, CF—400, RF—330. **Press Box Telephone:** (817) 460-3522.

TEXAS-PAN AMERICAN Broncs

Conference: Sun Belt.
Mailing Address: 1201 West University Dr., Edinburg, TX 78539.
Head Coach: Reggie Tredaway. **Assistant Coaches:** Mike Brown, Scott Wright. **Telephone:** (956) 381-2235. ■ **Baseball SID:** Jim McKone. **Telephone:** (956) 381-2240. **FAX:** (956) 381-2398.

TEXAS-SAN ANTONIO Roadrunners

Conference: Southland.
Mailing Address: 6900 NW Loop 1604, San Antonio, TX 78249.
Head Coach: Mickey Lashley. **Assistant Coach:** David Coleman. **Telephone:** (210) 458-4805. ■ **Baseball SID:** Rick Nixon. **Telephone:** (210) 458-4551. **FAX:** (210) 458-4569.

TEXAS A&M Aggies

Conference: Big 12.
Mailing Address: Joe Routt Boulevard, College Station, TX 77843.
Head Coach: Mark Johnson. **Assistant Coaches:** Bill Hickey, *Jim Lawler. **Telephone:** (409) 845-9534. ■ **Baseball SID:** Alan Cannon. **Telephone:** (409) 845-5725. **FAX:** (409) 845-0564.
Home Field: Olsen Field. **Seating Capacity:** 7,053. **Outfield Dimensions:** LF—330, CF—400, RF—330. **Press Box Telephone:** (409) 845-4810.

TEXAS CHRISTIAN Horned Frogs

Conference: Western Athletic (South).
Mailing Address: P.O. Box 297600, Fort Worth, TX 76129.
Head Coach: Lance Brown. **Assistant Coaches:** Craig Farmer, Nolan Ryan, *Donnie Watson. **Telephone:** (817) 921-7985. ■ **Baseball SID:** Trey Carmichael. **Telephone:** (817) 921-7969. **FAX:** (817) 921-7964.
Home Field: TCU Diamond. **Seating Capacity:** 1,500. **Outfield Dimensions:** LF—330, CF—390, RF—320. **Press Box Telephone:** (817) 921-7966.

TEXAS SOUTHERN Tigers

Conference: Southwestern Athletic (West).
Mailing Address: 3100 Cleburne St., Houston, TX 77004.
Head Coach: Candy Robinson. **Assistant Coaches:** Arthur Jenkins, Brian White. **Telephone:** (713) 313-7993. ■ **Baseball SID:** Gary Abernathy. **Telephone:** (713) 313-7270/7271. **FAX:** (713) 313-1945.

TEXAS TECH Red Raiders

Conference: Big 12.
Mailing Address: 6th and Red Raider Ave., Lubbock, TX 79409.
Head Coach: Larry Hays. **Assistant Coaches:** *Frank Anderson, Greg Evans, Marty Lamb. **Telephone:** (806) 742-3355. ■ **Baseball SID:** Greg Hotch-

kiss. **Telephone:** (806) 742-2770. **FAX:** (806) 742-1970.

Home Field: Dan Law Field. **Seating Capacity:** 5,614. **Outfield Dimensions:** LF—330, CF—405, RF—330. **Press Box Telephone:** (806) 742-3688.

TOLEDO Rockets

Conference: Mid-American (West).

Mailing Address: 2801 West Bancroft St., Toledo, OH 43606.

Head Coach: Joe Kruzel. **Assistant Coaches:** Mike Kendall, Steve Parrill. **Telephone:** (419) 530-2526. ■ **Baseball SID:** Kevin Gabinski. **Telephone:** (419) 530-3790. **FAX:** (419) 530-3795.

TOWSON STATE Tigers

Conference: America East.

Mailing Address: 8000 York Rd., Towson, MD 21252.

Head Coach: Mike Gottlieb. **Assistant Coaches:** John Matheis, Mike Vota. **Telephone:** (410) 830-3775. ■ **Baseball SID:** Dan O'Connell. **Telephone:** (410) 830-2232. **FAX:** (410) 830-3861.

TROY STATE Trojans

Conference: Trans America Athletic (West).

Mailing Address: Davis Field House, Troy State University, Troy, AL 36082.

Head Coach: John Mayotte. **Assistant Coaches:** Jerry Martinez, *Rod McWhorter. **Telephone:** (334) 670-3489. ■ **Baseball SID:** Brad Grice. **Telephone:** (334) 670-3229. **FAX:** (334) 670-3278.

TULANE Green Wave

Conference: Conference USA.

Mailing Address: Wilson Center, Ben Weiner Drive, New Orleans, LA 70118.

Head Coach: Rick Jones. **Assistant Coaches:** Rob Cooper, Jim Schlossnagle. **Telephone:** (504) 862-8239. ■ **Baseball SID:** Joel Quevillon. **Telephone:** (504) 865-5506. **FAX:** (504) 865-5512.

Home Field: Turchin Stadium. **Seating Capacity:** 5,000. **Outfield Dimensions:** LF—325, CF—400, RF—325. **Press Box Telephone:** (504) 862-8224.

UTAH Utes

Conference: Western Athletic (North).

Mailing Address: John Huntsman Center, Salt Lake City, UT 84112.

Head Coach: Tim Esmay. **Assistant Coaches:** Todd Delnoce, John Flores. **Telephone:** (801) 581-3526. ■ **Baseball SID:** Mickelle Marston. **Telephone:** (801) 581-3511. **FAX:** (801) 581-4358.

Home Field: Franklin Quest Field. **Seating Capacity:** 15,500. **Outfield Dimensions:** LF—345, CF—420, RF—315. **Press Box Telephone:** (801) 464-6938.

VALPARAISO Crusaders

Conference: Mid-Continent (West).

Mailing Address: 651 South College Ave., Valparaiso, IN 46383.

Head Coach: Paul Twenge. **Assistant Coaches:** Tim Holmes, *John Olson. **Telephone:** (219) 464-5239. ■ **Baseball SID:** Bill Rogers. **Telephone:** (219) 464-5232. **FAX:** (219) 464-5762.

VANDERBILT Commodores

Conference: Southeastern (East).

Mailing Address: Box 120158, 2601 Jess Neely Drive, Nashville, TN 37212.

Head Coach: Roy Mewbourne. **Assistant Coaches:** John Barlowe, *Ross Jones, Matt Elliott. **Telephone:** (615) 322-4122. ■ **Baseball SID:** Tom Weber. **Telephone:** (615) 322-4121. **FAX:** (615) 343-7064.

Home Field: McGugin Field. **Seating Capacity:** 1,000. **Outfield Dimensions:** LF—328, CF—362, RF—316. **Press Box Telephone:** (615) 320-0436.

VERMONT Catamounts

Conference: America East.

Mailing Address: 226 Patrick Gym, Burlington, VT 05405.

Head Coach: Bill Currier. **Assistant Coaches:** Steve Trimper, Len Whitehouse. **Telephone:** (802) 656-7701. ■ **Baseball SID:** Paul Stanfield. **Telephone:** (802) 656-1109. **FAX:** (802) 656-8328.

VILLANOVA Wildcats

Conference: Big East.

Mailing Address: 800 Lancaster Ave., Jake Nevin Field House, Villanova, PA 19085.

Head Coach: George Bennett. **Assistant Coach:** Lou Soscia. **Telephone:** (610) 519-4529. ■ **Baseball SID:** Dean Kenefick. **Telephone:** (610) 519-4120. **FAX:** (610) 519-7323.

Home Field: McGeehan Field. **Seating Capacity:** 2,000. **Outfield Dimensions:** LF—332, CF—402, RF—332. **Press Box Telephone:** None.

VIRGINIA Cavaliers

Conference: Atlantic Coast.

Mailing Address: P.O. Box 3785, Charlottesville, VA 22903.

Head Coach: Dennis Womack. **Assistant Coaches:** *Steve Heon, Steve Whitmyer. **Telephone:** (804) 982-5775. ■ **Baseball SID:** Charlie Bare. **Telephone:** (804) 982-5500. **FAX:** (804) 982-5525.

Home Field: Virginia Baseball Field. **Seating Capacity:** 2,300. **Outfield Dimensions:** LF—347, CF—400, RF—347. **Press Box Telephone:** (804) 295-9262.

VIRGINIA COMMONWEALTH Rams
Conference: Colonial Athletic.
Mailing Address: 819 West Franklin St., Richmond, VA 23284.
Head Coach: Paul Keyes. **Assistant Coaches:** Jay Ashcraft, Chris Finwood, Hank Kraft. **Telephone:** (804) 828-4820. ■ **Baseball SID:** Mark Halstead. **Telephone:** (804) 828-7000. **FAX:** (804) 828-9428.

VIRGINIA MILITARY INSTITUTE Keydets
Conference: Southern.
Mailing Address: Cameron Hall, Lexington, VA 24450.
Head Coach: Scott Gines. **Assistant Coaches:** *Chris Chernisky, Mike Parker. **Telephone:** (540) 464-7609. ■ **Baseball SID:** Pete Lefresne. **Telephone:** (540) 464-7253. **FAX:** (540) 464-7583.

VIRGINIA TECH Hokies
Conference: Atlantic-10 (West).
Mailing Address: 364 Jamerson Center, Blacksburg, VA 24061.
Head Coach: Chuck Hartman. **Assistant Coaches:** Jon Hartness, Josh Herman, *Jay Phillips. **Telephone:** (540) 231-3671. ■ **Baseball SID:** Dave Smith. **Telephone:** (540) 231-6726. **FAX:** (540) 231-6984.

WAGNER Seahawks
Conference: Northeast.
Mailing Address: 631 Howard Ave., Staten Island, NY 10301.
Head Coach: Rich Vitaliano. **Assistant Coaches:** Mike Arsenuk, Jason Tuthill. **Telephone:** (718) 390-3154. ■ **Baseball SID:** Bob Balut. **Telephone:** (718) 390-3215. **FAX:** (718) 390-3347.

WAKE FOREST Demon Deacons
Conference: Atlantic Coast.
Mailing Address: P.O. Box 7426, Winston-Salem, NC 27109.
Head Coach: George Greer. **Assistant Coaches:** *Bobby Moranda, Kyle Wagner. **Telephone:** (910) 758-5570. ■ **Baseball SID:** Chris Capo. **Telephone:** (910) 758-5640. **FAX:** (910) 758-5140.
Home Field: Hooks Stadium. **Seating Capacity:** 2,500. **Outfield Dimensions:** LF—340, CF—400, RF—315. **Press Box Telephone:** (910) 758-9711.

WASHINGTON Huskies
Conference: Pacific-10 (North).
Mailing Address: Box 354070, Seattle, WA 98195.
Head Coach: Ken Knutson. **Assistant Coaches:** Kevin Johnston, *Joe Ross, Joe Weis. **Telephone:** (206) 616-4335. ■ **Baseball SID:** Jeff Bechthold. **Telephone:** (206) 543-2230. **FAX:** (206) 543-5000.
Home Field: Husky Ballpark. **Seating Capacity:** 2,500. **Outfield Dimensions:** LF—327, CF—395, RF—317. **Press Box Telephone:** Unavailable.

WASHINGTON STATE Cougars
Conference: Pacific-10 (North).
Mailing Address: P.O. Box 641602, Pullman, WA 99164.
Head Coach: Steve Farrington. **Assistant Coaches:** *Russ Swan, Buzz Verduzco. **Telephone:** (509) 335-0211. ■ **Baseball SID:** Jeff Evans. **Telephone:** (509) 335-2684. **FAX:** (509) 335-0267.
Home Field: Buck Bailey Field. **Seating Capacity:** 3,500. **Outfield Dimensions:** LF—330, CF—400, RF—335. **Press Box Telephone:** (509) 335-2684.

WEST VIRGINIA Mountaineers
Conference: Big East.
Mailing Address: P.O. Box 0877, Morgantown, WV 26507.
Head Coach: Greg Van Zant. **Assistant Coaches:** Bruce Cameron, *Doug Little, Ron Moore. **Telephone:** (304) 293-2308. ■ **Baseball SID:** John Antonik. **Telephone:** (304) 293-2821. **FAX:** (304) 293-4105.
Home Field: Hawley Field. **Seating Capacity:** 1,500. **Outfield Dimensions:** LF—325, CF—390, RF—325. **Press Box Telephone:** (304) 293-5988.

WESTERN CAROLINA Catamounts
Conference: Southern.
Mailing Address: 2517 Ramsey Center, Cullowhee, NC 28723.
Head Coach: Rodney Hennon. **Assistant Coaches:** Dan Kyslinger, *Mike Tidick. **Telephone:** (704) 227-7373. ■ **Baseball SID:** Steve White. **Telephone:** (704) 227-7171. **FAX:** (704) 227-7688.
Home Field: Childress Field/Hennon Stadium. **Seating Capacity:** 1,500. **Outfield Dimensions:** LF—325, CF—390, RF—325. **Press Box Telephone:** (704) 293-9315.

WESTERN ILLINOIS Leathernecks
Conference: Mid-Continent (West).
Mailing Address: Western Hall 213, Macomb, IL 61455.
Head Coach: Dick Pawlow. **Assistant Coaches:** Chris Lachapell, Jim Morsovillo. **Telephone:** (309) 298-1521. ■ **Baseball SID:** Debbie Pilant. **Telephone:** (309) 298-1133. **FAX:** (309) 298-3366.

WESTERN KENTUCKY Hilltoppers
Conference: Sun Belt.
Mailing Address: One Big Red Way, Bowling Green, KY 42101.
Head Coach: Joel Murrie. **Assistant Coaches:** Clyde Keller, Dan Mosier.

Telephone: (502) 745-6023. ■ **Baseball SID:** Jeff Patrick. **Telephone:** (502) 745-4298. **FAX:** (502) 745-3444.

WESTERN MICHIGAN Broncos
Conference: Mid-American (West).
Mailing Address: B-205 Ellsworth Hall, Kalamazoo, MI 49008.
Head Coach: Fred Decker. **Assistant Coaches:** Rich Morales, Scott Demetral. **Telephone:** (616) 387-8149. ■ **Baseball SID:** John Beatty. **Telephone:** (616) 387-4138. **FAX:** (616) 387-4139.
Home Field: Hyames Field. **Seating Capacity:** 4,000. **Outfield Dimensions:** LF—325, CF—390, RF—340. **Press Box Telephone:** (616) 387-8630.

WICHITA STATE Shockers
Conference: Missouri Valley.
Mailing Address: 1845 Fairmount St., Campus Box 18, Wichita, KS 67260.
Head Coach: Gene Stephenson. **Assistant Coaches:** *Brent Kemnitz, Steve Miller, Jim Thomas. **Telephone:** (316) 978-5301. ■ **Baseball SID:** Joe Mc-Donald. **Telephone:** (316) 978-3265. **FAX:** (316) 978-3336.
Home Field: Tyler Field-Eck Stadium. **Seating Capacity:** 5,665. **Outfield Dimensions:** LF—330, CF—390, RF—330. **Press Box Telephone:** (316) 978-3390.

WILLIAM & MARY Tribe
Conference: Colonial Athletic.
Mailing Address: P.O. Box 399, Williamsburg, VA 23187.
Head Coach: Jim Farr. **Assistant Coaches:** *John Cole, Marlin Ikenberry. **Telephone:** (757) 221-3399. ■ **Baseball SID:** John Barker. **Telephone:** (757) 221-3368. **FAX:** (757) 221-3412.

WINTHROP Eagles
Conference: Big South.
Mailing Address: Winthrop Coliseum, Rock Hill, SC 29733.
Head Coach: Joe Hudak. **Assistant Coaches:** Mike McRea, Mike McGuire. **Telephone:** (803) 323-2129, ext. 235. ■ **Baseball SID:** Everett Hutto. **Telephone:** (803) 323-2129, ext. 246. **FAX:** (803) 323-2433.

WISCONSIN-MILWAUKEE Panthers
Conference: Midwestern Collegiate.
Mailing Address: P.O. Box 413, Milwaukee, WI 53201.
Head Coach: Jerry Augustine. **Assistant Coaches:** Scott Doffek, Todd Frohwirth. **Telephone:** (414) 229-5670. ■ **Baseball SID:** Chad Krueger. **Telephone:** (414) 229-4593. **FAX:** (414) 229-6759.

WOFFORD Terriers
Conference: Southern.
Mailing Address: 429 North Church St., Spartanburg, SC 29303.
Head Coach: Ernie May. **Assistant Coach:** *Andy Kiah. **Telephone:** (864) 597-4100. ■ **Baseball SID:** Bill English. **Telephone:** (864) 597-4092. **FAX:** (864) 597-4129.

WRIGHT STATE Raiders
Conference: Midwestern Collegiate.
Mailing Address: 3640 Colonel Glenn Highway, Dayton, OH 45435.
Head Coach: Ron Nischwitz. **Assistant Coaches:** Bo Bilinski, Dan Bassler. **Telephone:** (937) 775-2771. ■ **Baseball SID:** Robert Noss. **Telephone:** (937) 775-2816. **FAX:** (937) 775-2818.

XAVIER Musketeers
Conference: Atlantic 10 (West).
Mailing Address: 3800 Victory Parkway, Cincinnati, OH 45207.
Head Coach: John Morrey. **Assistant Coaches:** Ryan McGinnis, *Joe Regruth. **Telephone:** (513) 745-2890. ■ **Baseball SID:** Leslie Murry. **Telephone:** (513) 745-3416. **FAX:** (513) 745-2825.

YALE Bulldogs
Conference: Ivy League (Rolfe).
Mailing Address: P.O. Box 208216, New Haven, CT 06520.
Head Coach: John Stuper. **Assistant Coaches:** Dick Jeynes, Dan Scarpa. **Telephone:** (203) 432-7422. ■ **Baseball SID:** Steve Conn. **Telephone:** (203) 432-1455. **FAX:** (203) 432-1454.

YOUNGSTOWN STATE Penguins
Conference: Mid-Continent (East).
Mailing Address: One University Dr., Youngstown, OH 44555.
Head Coach: Dan Kubacki. **Assistant Coach:** Brad Ziegler. **Telephone:** (330) 742-3685. ■ **Baseball SID:** Rocco Gasparro. **Telephone:** (330) 742-3192. **FAX:** (330) 742-3191.

Amateur Baseball

High School Baseball • Youth Baseball

HIGHSCHOOLBASEBALL

NATIONAL FEDERATION
OF STATE HIGH SCHOOL ASSOCIATIONS
Office Address: 11724 NW Plaza Circle, Kansas City, MO 64153. **Mailing Address:** P.O. Box 20626, Kansas City, MO 64195. **Telephone:** (816) 464-5400. **FAX:** (816) 464-5571. **Website:** www.nfhsa.org.

Executive Director: Robert Kanaby. **Associate Director:** Fritz McGinness. **Assistant Director/Baseball Rules Editor:** Brad Rumble. **Director, Public Relations:** Bruce Howard.

NATIONAL HIGH SCHOOL
BASEBALL COACHES ASSOCIATION
Mailing Address: P.O. Box 12354, Omaha, NE 68112. **Telephone/FAX:** (402) 457-1962.

Executive Director: Jerry Miles. **Administrative Assistant:** Elaine Miles. **President:** Dom Cecere (Eastchester, NY).

1998 National Convention: Dec. 4-6 at Tulsa, OK.

NATIONAL CLASSIC
HIGH SCHOOL TOURNAMENT
Mailing Address: El Dorado High School, 1651 North Valencia Ave., Placentia, CA 92870. **Telephone:** (714) 993-5350. **FAX:** (714) 524-2458.

Tournament Director: Iran Novick.

1998 Tournament: April 13-16 in Orange County, CA (16 teams).

SUNBELT BASEBALL CLASSIC SERIES
Mailing Address: 505 North Boulevard, Edmond, OK 73034. **Telephone:** (405) 348-3839.

Chairman: Gordon Morgan. **Director:** John Schwartz.

1998 Series: Seminole, Shawnee and Tecumseh, OK, June 23-27 (8 states: Arizona, California, Florida, Georgia, Maryland, Ohio, Oklahoma, Texas).

NATIONAL SHOWCASE EVENTS

(For High School Players)

AREA CODE GAMES
Mailing Address: P.O. Box 213, Santa Rosa, CA 95402. **Telephone:** (707) 525-0498. **FAX:** (707) 525-0214.

President, Goodwill Series, Inc.: Bob Williams.

1998 Area Code Games: Aug. 10-15, Blair Field, Long Beach, CA.

Friendship X Series: Aug. 8-18, Beijing, China. **Goodwill Series V:** Dec. 18-31, Adelaide, Australia.

TEAM ONE NATIONAL SHOWCASE
Mailing Address: P.O. Box 8943, Cincinnati, OH 45208. **Telephone/FAX:** (606) 291-4463.

President, Team One Sports: Jeff Spelman.

Assistant Director: Stan Brzezicki. **Telephone:** (814) 899-8407.

1998 Team One National Showcase: July 10-12, Tropicana Field/Al Lang Stadium, St. Petersburg, FL. **Regional Showcases:** June 12-14, Tempe, AZ (Arizona State University); July 17-19, Clemson, SC (Clemson University); Aug. 7-9, Lexington, KY (University of Kentucky).

EASTERN PROFESSIONAL BASEBALL SHOWCASE
Mailing Address: 601 South College Rd., Wilmington, NC 28403. **Telephone:** (910) 962-3570.

Facility Director: Mark Scalf.

1998 Showcase: Aug. 5-8, Wilmington, NC (UNC Wilmington).

NATIONAL AMATEUR ALL-STAR
BASEBALL TOURNAMENT
Mailing Address: 400 North Michigan Ave., Suite 1016, Chicago, IL 60611. **Telephone:** (800) 622-2877. **FAX:** (312) 245-8088.

Operated by: Amateur Baseball, Inc.

Chairman: Allan Cox. **President:** Ron Berryman.

League Members: American Amateur Baseball Congress, Dixie Baseball, National Amateur Baseball Federation, National Association of Police Athletic Leagues, Reviving Baseball In Inner Cities, PONY Baseball.

1998 Tournament: Chicago, IL, dates unavailable.

BASEBALL FACTORY
Office Address: 3920 Pine Orchard Lane, Suite D, Ellicott City, MD 21042. **Telephone:** (800) 641-4487. **FAX:** (410) 418-5434.

President: Steve Sclafani. **Vice President:** Rob Naddelman.

TOP GUNS SHOWCASE
Mailing Address: P.O. Box 71680, Las Vegas, NV 89170. **Telephone:** (208) 762-1100. **FAX:** (208) 762-1100.

President: Larry Rook.

AMATEURBASEBALL

INTERNATIONAL OLYMPIC COMMITTEE
Mailing Address: Chateau de Vidy, 1007 Lausanne, Switzerland.
Telephone: 41-21-621-61-11. **FAX:** 41-21-621-62-16. **Website:** www.
olympic.org.
President: Juan Antonio Samaranch. **Administrative Assistant,
Department of International Cooperation/Public Information:** Betty
Guignard.

SYDNEY OLYMPIC ORGANIZING COMMITTEE
Street Address: Level 14, The Maritime Centre, 207 Kent St., Sydney,
New South Wales 2000 Australia. **Mailing Address:** GPO Box 2000,
Sydney, New South Wales 2000 Australia. **Telephone:** (61-29) 297-2000.
FAX: (61-29) 297-2020. **Website:** www.sydney.olympic.org.
President: Michael Knight. **Chief Executive Officer:** Sandy Hollway.
General Manager, Sport: Bob Elphinston.
Games of the XXVIIth Olympiad: Sept. 15-Oct. 1, 2000.

U.S. OLYMPIC COMMITTEE
Mailing Address: One Olympic Plaza, Colorado Springs, CO 80909.
Telephone: (719) 632-5551. **FAX:** (719) 578-4654.
President: William Hybl. **Executive Director:** Dick Schultz. **Assistant
Executive Director, Media/Public Affairs:** Mike Moran.
Olympics, 2000: Sept. 15-Oct. 1, 2000 at Sydney, Australia.

GOODWILL GAMES, INC.
Mailing Address: One CNN Center, P.O. Box 105366, Atlanta, GA
30348. **Telephone:** (404) 827-3400. **FAX:** (404) 827-1394.
President: Mike Plant. **Vice President, Sports:** David Raith. **Director,
Publicity:** Michael Lewellen.
Goodwill Games, 1998: July 19-Aug. 2, 1998 at New York.

PAN AMERICAN GAMES SOCIETY, INC.
Mailing Address: 500 Shaftesbury Blvd., Winnipeg, Manitoba, R3P
0M1. **Telephone:** (204) 985-1999. **FAX:** (204) 985-1993.
President/Chief Executive Officer: Don MacKenzie. **Manager,
Communications:** Diane Ulrich. **Manager, Public Relations:** Ernie Nairn.
Manager, Media Services: George Einarson.
Pan American Games, 1999: July 24-Aug. 8, 1999 at Winnipeg.

INTERNATIONAL BASEBALL ASSOCIATION
Mailing Address: Avenue de Mon-Repos 24, Case Postale 131, 1000
Lausanne 5, Switzerland. **Telephone:** 41-21-311-18-63. **FAX:** (41-21) 311-
18-64. **E-Mail Address:** iba@dial.eunet.ch. **Website:** alpcom.it/digesu/
index/html.
President: Aldo Notari (Italy). **Secretary General:** John Ostermeyer
(Australia). **Executive Director:** Miquel Ortin.

1998 Events
Americas Qualifying Tournament* .... Managua, Nicaragua, June
AA World Youth Championship .... Fairview Heights, IL, July 8-19
World Senior Baseball Cup .... Italy, July 21-Aug. 2
AAA European Championship** .. Ostrava, Czech Rep., July 25-Aug. 1
World Children's Baseball Fair .... Shizuoka City, Japan, Aug. 2-8
European B Pool Senior Championship*** .. Vienna, Austria, Aug. 8-16
AAA Asian Championship** .... Osaka, Japan, Sept. 4-13
AAA Americas Junior Championship** ...... Cartagena, Colombia, Sept.
President's Cup .... Buenos Aires, Argentina, Oct. 10-18

*Qualifying tournament for 1998 World Senior Cup
**Qualifying tournament for 1999 AAA World Youth Championship
***Qualifying tournament for 2000 Olympics

USA BASEBALL
Mailing Address, Corporate Headquarters: Hi Corbett Field, 3400
East Camino Campestre, Tucson, AZ 85716. **Telephone:** (520) 327-9700.
FAX: (520) 327-9221. **E-Mail Address:** usabasebal@aol.com. **Website:**
www.usabaseball.com.
Chairman: Cliff Lothery. **President:** Mark Marquess. **Executive Vice
President:** Neil Lantz. **Secretary:** Tom Hicks. **Treasurer:** Gale Mont-

gomery.

Executive Director/Chief Executive Officer: Dan O'Brien Sr. **Director, Marketing/Business Affairs:** Jeff Odenwald. **Director, National Team Baseball Operations:** Paul Seiler. **Director, Media Relations:** George Doig. **Assistant, Marketing/Youth Baseball Coordinator:** Ray Darwin. **Senior Advisor to National Teams/Alumni Affairs:** Jerry Kindall.

National Members: Amateur Athletic Union, American Amateur Baseball Congress, American Baseball Coaches Association, American Legion Baseball, Dixie Baseball, Little League Baseball, National Amateur Baseball Federation, National Association of Intercollegiate Athletics, National Baseball Congress, National Collegiate Athletic Association, National Federation of State High School Athletic Associations, National High School Baseball Coaches Association, National Junior College Athletic Association, Police Athletic League, PONY Baseball, YMCAs of the USA.

1998 Events

Senior World Cup Qualifier	Nicaragua, June
Junior Olympic Championships (16)	Tucson, AZ, June 19-28
AA World Youth Championship (16)	Fairview Heights, IL, July 11-19
Senior World Cup	Italy, July 21-Aug. 2
World Junior Champ. Qualifier (18)	Cartagena, Colombia, Sept.

BASEBALL CANADA

Mailing Address: 1600 James Naismith Dr., Suite 208, Ottawa, Ontario K1B 5N4. **Telephone:** (613) 748-5606. **FAX:** (613) 748-5767. **E-Mail Address:** info@baseball.ca. **Website:** www.baseball.ca.

Director General: Duncan Grant.

NATIONAL BASEBALL CONGRESS

Mailing Address: P.O. Box 1420, Wichita, KS 67201. **Telephone:** (316) 267-3372. **FAX:** (316) 267-3382.

Year Founded: 1931.

President: Robert Rich Jr. **Executive Vice President:** Melinda Rich. **Vice President:** Steve Shaad. **National Commissioner/Tournament Director:** Larry Davis. **General Manager:** Lance Deckinger. **Director, Administration:** Dian Overaker. **National Coordinator:** Mark Chiarucci. **Stadium Manager:** Dave Wellenzohn. **Coordinator, Marketing/Public Relations:** Justin Givens.

1998 NBC World Series (non-professional, ex-professional): July 31-Aug. 14, Lawrence-Dumont Stadium, Wichita, KS.

INTERNATIONAL BASEBALL FOUNDATION

Mailing Address: 1313 13th St. South, Birmingham, AL 35205. **Telephone:** (205) 558-4235. **FAX:** (205) 918-0800.

Executive Director: David Osinski.

Summer College Leagues

National Alliance of Collegiate Summer Baseball

Office Address: 6201 College Blvd., Overland Park, KS 66211. **Telephone:** (913) 339-1906. **FAX:** (913) 339-0026.

NCAA Compliance Representative: Dave Brunk.

NCAA Certified Leagues: Atlantic Collegiate League, Cape Cod League, Central Illinois Collegiate League, Great Lakes League, New England Collegiate League, Northeastern League, Northwest Collegiate League, San Diego Collegiate League, Shenandoah Valley League.

ALASKA BASEBALL LEAGUE

Mailing Address: P.O. Box 318, Kenai, AK 99611. **Telephone:** (907) 283-7133. **FAX:** (907) 283-3390.

Year Founded: 1974 (reunited, 1998).

Executive Director: Jack Slama (Gig Harbor, WA). **Director, Publicity:** Dick Lobdell.

1998 Opening Date: June 7. **Closing Date:** July 31.

Regular Season: 29 league games.

Playoff Format: None. Top two teams advance to National Baseball Congress World Series.

Roster Limit: 21, plus exemption for Alaska residents.

ALASKA GOLDPANNERS

Mailing Address: P.O. Box 71154, Fairbanks, AK 99707. **Telephone:** (907) 451-0095. **FAX:** (907) 451-0095.

President: Bill Stroecker. **General Manager:** Don Dennis. **Head Coach:** Dan Cowgill (Los Angeles, Calif., CC).

ANCHORAGE BUCS

Mailing Address: P.O. Box 24-0061, Anchorage, AK 99524. **Telephone:** (907) 561-2827. **FAX:** (907) 561-2920.

Executive Director: Brian Crawford. **General Manager:** Dennis

Mattingly. **Head Coach:** Mike Oakland (Cal Poly San Luis Obispo).

ANCHORAGE GLACIER PILOTS

Mailing Address: P.O. Box 100895, Anchorage, AK 99510. **Telephone:** (907) 274-3627. **FAX:** (907) 274-3628.

President: Chuck Shelton. **General Manager:** Ron Okerlund. **Head Coach:** Kevin Smallcomb (Mendocino, Calif., CC).

HAWAII ISLAND MOVERS

Mailing Address: P.O. Box 17865, Honolulu, HI 96817. **Telephone:** (808) 832-4805. **FAX:** (808) 841-2321.

President: Donald Takaki. **Manager, Operations:** Thomas Gushiken. **Head Coach:** Kalen Miyatake (U. of Hawaii-Hilo).

KENAI PENINSULA OILERS

Mailing Address: P.O. Box 318, Kenai, AK 99611. **Telephone:** (907) 283-7133. **FAX:** (907) 283-3390.

President: John Lohrke. **Manager, Baseball Operations:** Mike Baxter. **Head Coach:** Scott Marr (Oral Roberts U.).

MAT-SU MINERS

Mailing Address: P.O. Box 1633, Palmer, AK 99645. **Telephone:** (907) 745-4901. **FAX:** (907) 745-7275.

President: Bill Bartholomew. **General Manager:** Stan Zaborac. **Head Coach:** Pete Wilk (Georgetown U.).

ARIZONA COLLEGIATE LEAGUE

Mailing Address: P.O. Box 872505, Tempe, AZ 85287. **Telephone:** (602) 965-6085. **FAX:** (602) 965-9309.

Year Founded: 1989.

Commissioner/President: Chris Sinacori.

Member Clubs: Athletics, Braves, Giants, Marlins, Royals, Yankees.

1998 Opening Date: July 1. **Closing Date:** Aug. 10.

Regular Season: 35 games.

Playoff Format: Top two teams meet in best-of-3 championship series.

Roster Limit: 22 (limited to Arizona natives or Arizona college players).

ATLANTIC COLLEGIATE LEAGUE

Mailing Address: 26 Eric Trail, Sussex, NJ 07461. **Telephone:** (973) 702-1755. **FAX:** (973) 702-1898.

Year Founded: 1967.

Acting President: Tom Bonekemper. **Commissioner:** Robert Pertsas. **Director, Publicity:** Ben Smookler.

Member Clubs: Delaware Gulls, Jersey City (N.J.) Colonels, Jersey Pilots, Metro New York Cadets, New York Generals, Nassau (N.Y.) Collegians, Quakertown (Pa.) Blazers, Scranton/Wilkes-Barre (Pa.) Twins, West Deptford (N.J.) Storm.

1998 Opening Date: June 3. **Closing Date:** July 29.

Regular Season: 36 games.

Playoff Format: Top four teams meet in best-of-3 semifinals. Winners meet in one-game championship.

Roster Limit: 21 (college-eligible players only).

CALIFORNIA COASTAL LEAGUE

Mailing Address: 1398-B Washington Blvd., Concord, CA 94521. **Telephone:** (805) 566-1476, (510) 604-8058.

Year Founded: 1993.

President/Commissioner: Tony Dress.

Member Clubs: Fresno Barons, Oxnard Destroyers, San Francisco Seals, San Luis Obispo Blues, Santa Barbara Foresters, Santa Maria Stars.

Playoff Format: League champion advances to NBC World Series.

1998 Opening Date: May 9. **Closing Date:** July 31.

Regular Season: 24 games.

CAPE COD LEAGUE

Mailing Address: Tabor Academy, Marion, MA 02738. **Telephone/FAX:** (508) 996-5004. **E-Mail Address:** capecod@gbwebworks.com. **Website:** www.capecodbaseball.com.

Year Founded: 1885.

Commissioner: Richard Marr. **President:** Judy Scarafile.

Senior Vice President: Don Tullie. **Vice Presidents:** Jim Higgins, Bonnie Jacobs.

Director, Public Relations: Missy Ilg-Alaimo. **Assistant Director, Public Relations:** Cathie Nichols.

Division Structure: East—Brewster, Chatham, Harwich, Orleans, Yarmouth-Dennis. **West**—Bourne, Cotuit, Falmouth, Hyannis, Wareham.

1998 Opening Date: June 11. **Closing Date:** Aug. 15.

Regular Season: 44 games.

All-Star Game: Aug. 1 at Chatham.

Playoff Format: Top two teams in each division meet in best-of-3 semi-finals. Winners meet in best-of-5 series for league championship.

Roster Limit: 23 (college-eligible players only).

BOURNE BRAVES

Mailing Address: P.O. Box 895, Monument Beach, MA 02553. Telephone/FAX: (508) 999-4306.

President: Ed Ladetto. General Manager: Cathie Nichols. Head Coach: Jason King (U. of Massachusetts-Boston).

BREWSTER WHITECAPS

Mailing Address: P.O. Box 2349, Brewster, MA 02631. Telephone: (617) 720-7870. FAX: (617) 720-7877.

Executive Director: Sol Yas. General Manager: Howard Wayne. Head Coach: Bill Mosiello (U. of Oklahoma).

CHATHAM ATHLETICS

Mailing Address: P.O. Box 428, Chatham, MA 02633. Telephone: (508) 945-3841. FAX: (508) 945-9616.

President: Paul Galop. General Manager: Charles Thoms. Head Coach: John Schiffner (Plainville, Conn., HS).

COTUIT KETTLEERS

Mailing Address: P.O. Box 411, Cotuit, MA 02635. Telephone/FAX: (508) 428-9075.

President: Bruce Murphy. General Manager: George Streeter. Head Coach: Tom Walter (George Washington U.).

FALMOUTH COMMODORES

Mailing Address: 33 Wintergreen Rd., Mashpee, MA 02649. Telephone: (508) 477-5724. FAX: (508) 540-3835.

President: Steve Spitz. General Manager: Chuck Sturtevant. Head Coach: Harvey Shapiro (Bowdoin, Maine, College).

HARWICH MARINERS

Mailing Address: P.O. Box 201, Harwich Port, MA 02646. Telephone/FAX: (508) 432-8515.

President: Mary Henderson. General Manager: Ken Keenan. Head Coach: Chad Holbrook (U. of North Carolina).

HYANNIS METS

Mailing Address: P.O. Box 852, Hyannis, MA 02601. Telephone: (508) 778-0275. FAX: (508) 790-1803.

President: Everett Martin. General Manager: Steve Norton. Head Coach: Steve Mrowka (Georgia College).

ORLEANS CARDINALS

Mailing Address: P.O. Box 516, East Orleans, MA 02643. Telephone: (508) 240-5867. FAX: (508) 240-5871.

General Manager: Dave Reed. Head Coach: Don Norris (Georgia College).

WAREHAM GATEMEN

Mailing Address: 71 Towhee Rd., Wareham, MA 02571. Telephone: (508) 295-3956. FAX: (508) 295-8821.

President: Donna Joseph. General Manager: John Wylde. Head Coach: Don Reed.

YARMOUTH-DENNIS RED SOX

Mailing Address: P.O. Box 814, South Yarmouth, MA 02664. Telephone: (508) 394-9387. FAX: (508) 398-2239.

President: Stuart Schulman. General Managers: Gary Ellis, Jim Hagemeister. Head Coach: Unavailable.

CENTRAL ILLINOIS COLLEGIATE LEAGUE

Mailing Address: RR 13, Box 369, Bloomington, IL 61704. Telephone: (309) 828-4429. FAX: (309) 827-4652.

Year Founded: 1963.

President: Duffy Bass. Commissioner: Mike Woods.

Member Clubs, Division Structure: East—Danville Dans, Decatur Blues, Twin City Stars. West—Springfield Rifles, Bluff City Bombers, Quincy Gems.

1998 Opening Date: June 4. Closing Date: July 31.

Regular Season: 48 games.

All-Star Game: July 5 at Quincy.

Playoff Format: Single-elimination tournament.

Roster Limit: 23 (college-eligible players only).

CLARK GRIFFITH COLLEGIATE LEAGUE

Mailing Address: 4917 North 30th St., Arlington, VA 22207. **Telephone:** (703) 536-1729. **FAX:** (703) 536-1729.

Year Founded: 1945.

President/Commissioner: John Depenbrock. **Director, Publicity:** Dennis Dwyer.

Member Clubs: Arlington (Va.) Senators, Herndon (Va.) Optimists, Prince William (Va.) Gators, Reston (Va.) Hawks, Southern Maryland Battlecats.

1998 Opening Date: May 30. **Closing Date:** Aug. 1.

Regular Season: 40 games (split-schedule).

Playoff Format: Top four teams meet in best-of-three semifinal. Winners meet in best-of-3 series for league championship.

Roster Limit: 24 (players 20 and under).

COASTAL PLAIN LEAGUE

Mailing Address: 4900 Waters Edge Dr., Suite 201, Raleigh, NC 27606. **Telephone:** (919) 852-1960. **FAX:** (919) 852-1973. **Website:** www.coastalplain.com.

Year Founded: 1997.

Chairman/Chief Executive Officer: Jerry Petitt. **President:** Pete Bock. **Director, Operations:** Mark Cryan. **Director, Media Relations:** Steve Mac-Donald.

1998 Opening Date: May 29. **Closing Date:** Aug. 8.

Regular Season: 50 games (split-schedule).

Playoff Format: First-half winner meets second-half winner in best-of-3 series for league championship.

Roster Limit: 20 (college-eligible players only).

DURHAM BRAVES

Mailing Address: P.O. Box 125, Durham, NC 27701. **Telephone:** (919) 956-9555. **FAX:** (919) 956-9557.

General Manager: Unavailable. **Head Coach:** Chris Pollard (Davidson College).

EDENTON

Mailing Address: P.O. Box 86, Edenton, NC 27932. **Telephone:** (252) 482-4080. **FAX:** Unavailable.

General Manager: Greg Grall. **Head Coach:** Kevin Erminio (Clemson U.).

FLORENCE REDWOLVES

Mailing Address: P.O. Box 809, Florence, SC 29503. **Telephone:** (843) 629-0700. **FAX:** (843) 629-0703.

General Manager: David Sandler. **Head Coach:** Chris McMullan (Duke U.).

ROCKY MOUNT ROCKFISH

Mailing Address: P.O. Box 153, Rocky Mount, NC 27802. **Telephone:** (252) 446-1907. **FAX:** (252) 446-2997.

General Manager: Unavailable. **Head Coach:** Roger Williams (U. of North Carolina).

WILMINGTON SHARKS

Mailing Address: P.O. Box 15233, Wilmington, NC 28412. **Telephone:** (910) 343-5621. **FAX:** (910) 343-8932.

General Manager: Curt Van Derzee. **Head Coach:** Tripp Keister (U. of South Carolina).

WILSON TOBS

Mailing Address: P.O. Box 633, Wilson, NC 27894. **Telephone:** (252) 291-8627. **FAX:** (252) 291-1224.

General Manager: Jason Matlock. **Head Coach:** Mike Rikard (Elon, N.C., College).

GREAT LAKES LEAGUE

Office Address: 24700 Center Ridge Rd., Suite 10, Westlake, OH 44116. **Mailing Address:** P.O. Box 16679, Cleveland, OH 44116. **Telephone:** (440) 871-5724. **FAX:** (440) 871-4221.

Year Founded: 1986.

Commissioner: Brian Sullivan. **President:** Barry Ruben.

Member Clubs (all teams located in Ohio): Central Ohio Cows, Columbus All-Americans, Grand Lake Mariners, Lake County Admirals, Lima Locos, Sandusky Bay Stars.

1998 Opening Date: June 10. **Closing Date:** Aug. 2.

Regular Season: 40 games.

All-Star Game: July 26 at Lima.

Playoff Format: Top four teams meet in best-of-3 series. Winners meet in best-of-3 final for championship.

Roster Limit: 25 (college-eligible players only).

JAYHAWK LEAGUE

Mailing Address: 5 Adams Place, Halstead, KS 67056. **Telephone:** (316) 755-2361. **FAX:** (316) 755-1285.

Year Founded: 1976.

Commissioner: Bob Considine. **President:** Don Carlile. **Director, Public Relations:** Pat Chambers. **Statistician:** Gary Karr.

Member Clubs: El Dorado (Kan.) Broncos, Elkhart (Kan.) Dusters, Hays (Kan.) Larks, Liberal (Kan.) Bee Jays, Nevada (Mo.) Griffons, Topeka (Kan.) Capitols.

1998 Opening Date: May 29. **Closing Date:** July 18.

Regular Season: 48 games.

Playoff Format: League champion advances to NBC World Series.

Roster Limit: 25.

NEW ENGLAND COLLEGIATE LEAGUE

Mailing Address: 8 Southpond Rd., South Glastonbury, CT 06073. **Telephone/FAX:** (860) 633-3222.

Year Founded: 1993.

Commissioner: Joel Cooney. **Chairman/President:** Fay Vincent.

Member Clubs: Central Mass Collegians (Sterling, Mass.), Danbury (Conn.) Westerners, Eastern Tides (Willimantic, Conn.), Keene (N.H.) Swamp Bats, Middletown (Conn.) Giants, Rhode Island Reds (West Warwick, R.I.), Torrington (Conn.) Twisters.

1998 Opening Date: June 4. **Closing Date:** July 31.

Regular Season: 42 games.

All-Star Game: July 18 at Torrington.

Playoff Format: Top four teams meet in best-of-3 series. Winners meet in beat-of-3 series for league championship.

Roster Limit: 23 (college-eligible players only).

NORTHEASTERN COLLEGIATE LEAGUE

Mailing Address: 3148 Riverside Dr., Wellsville, NY 14895. **Telephone/FAX:** (716) 593-3923.

Year Founded: 1986.

Commissioner: Dave Chamberlain. **Chairman:** Bob Bellizzi. **Publicity Director:** Dick Cuydendall.

Member Clubs (all teams located in New York)**:** Cortland Apples, Geneva Knights, Hornell Dodgers, Ithaca Lakers, Little Falls Knickerbockers, Newark Raptors, Rome Indians, Schenectady Mohawks, Wellsville Nitros.

1998 Opening Date: June 6. **Closing Date:** July 31.

Regular Season: 40 games.

Playoff Format: Top four teams meet in best-of-3 series. Winners meet in one-game final for league championship.

Roster Limit: 24 (college-eligible players only).

NORTHWEST COLLEGIATE BASEBALL

Mailing Address: 16077 Bailer Way, Sherwood, OR 97140. **Telephone:** (503) 725-5634. **FAX:** (503) 725-5610.

Year Founded: 1992.

Commissioner: Reed Rainey. **Vice President:** Hal DeBerry.

Member Clubs (all teams located in Oregon)**:** Bucks, Dukes, Lobos, Ports, Stars, Toros.

1998 Opening Date: June 5. **Closing Date:** Aug. 8.

Regular Season: 36 games (split-schedule).

Playoff Format: First-half winner meets second-half winner in best-of-3 series for league championship.

Roster Limit: 19 (college-eligible players only).

NORTHWOODS LEAGUE

Mailing Address: P.O. Box 1234, Highland City, FL 33846. **Telephone:** (941) 644-4022. **FAX:** (941) 644-1238.

Year Founded: 1994.

President: George MacDonald Jr. **Vice Presidents:** Dick Radatz Jr., Bill McKee, John Wendel.

Member Clubs: North—Brainerd (Minn.) Mighty Gulls, Grand Forks (N.D.) Channel Cats, St. Cloud (Minn.) River Bats, Wausau (Wis.) Woodchucks. **South**—Kenosha (Wis.) Kroakers, Rochester (Minn.) Honkers, Southern Minny Starts (Austin, Minn.), Waterloo (Iowa) Bucks.

1998 Opening Date: June 5. **Closing Date:** Aug. 9.

Regular Season: 64 games.

All-Star Game: July 25 at Brainerd.

Playoff Format: North winner meets South winner in best-of-3 series for league championship.

Roster Limit: 22 (college-eligible players only).

PACIFIC INTERNATIONAL LEAGUE

Mailing Address: 504 Yale Ave. North, Seattle, WA 98109. **Telephone:** (206) 623-8844. **FAX:** (602) 623-8361.

Year Founded: 1988.

President: Mickie Schmith. **Commissioner:** Seth Dawson.

Member Clubs: Coquitlam (B.C.) Athletics, Everett (Wash.) Merchants, Kelowna (B.C.) Grizzlies, Ontario Orchard (Ore.) Meadowlarks, Performance Radiator Studs (Seattle), Richmond (B.C.) Budgies, Tacoma (Wash.) Timbers, Seattle Cruisers, Seattle Hackers, Yakima (Wash.) Chiefs.

1998 Opening Date: June 1. **Closing Date:** Aug. 1.

Regular Season: 32 games.

Playoff Format: League champion advances to NBC World Series.

Roster Limit: 25.

SAN DIEGO COLLEGIATE LEAGUE

Mailing Address: 948 Jasmine Ct., Carlsbad, CA 92009. **Telephone:** (760) 438-0347.

Year Founded: 1984.

Commissioner: Gerald Clements. **Vice Commissioner:** John Gunther. **Publicity Director:** Dave Kuhn.

Member Clubs, Division Structure: National—Beach City Cubs, El Cajon Padres, North County Mets. **American**—East County Orioles, San Diego Royals, South Bay Indians.

1998 Opening Date: June 1. **Closing Date:** Aug. 3.

Regular Season: 30 games (split-schedule).

Playoff Format: First-half division winners meet second-half division winners in one-game playoff. Winners meet in best-of-3 series for league championship.

Roster Limit: 21 (college-eligible players only).

SHENANDOAH VALLEY LEAGUE

Mailing Address: Route 1, Box 189J, Staunton, VA 24401. **Telephone:** (540) 886-1748. **FAX:** (540) 885-7612.

Year Founded: 1963.

President: David Biery. **Executive Vice President:** Jim Weissenborn. **Director, Public Relations:** Curt Dudley.

1998 Opening Date: May 29. **Closing Date:** Aug. 3.

Regular Season: 40 games.

Playoff Format: Top four meet in best-of-3 semifinal series. Winners meet in best-of-5 series for league championship.

Roster Limit: 25 (college-eligible players only).

FRONT ROYAL CARDINALS

Mailing Address: P.O. Box 995, Front Royal, VA 22630. **Telephone:** (540) 635-6498.

President: Linda Keen. **General Manager:** Danny Wood. **Head Coach:** Dan Albert (Muhlenburg, Pa., College).

HARRISONBURG TURKS

Mailing Address: 1489 South Main St., Harrisonburg, VA 22801. **Telephone/FAX:** (540) 434-5919.

President/General Manager: Bob Wease. **Head Coach:** Cooper Farris (Mississippi Gulf Coast JC).

NEW MARKET REBELS

Mailing Address: P.O. Box 902, New Market, VA 22844. **Telephone:** (540) 740-8727. **FAX:** (540) 740-4186.

General Manager: Tom Linski. **Head Coach:** Aaron Weintraub (U. of Virginia).

STAUNTON BRAVES

Mailing Address: P.O. Box 621, Staunton, VA 24401. **Telephone:** (540) 885-2598. **FAX:** (540) 886-7760.

President: Garland Eutsler. **General Manager:** Tom Chrisman. **Head Coach:** Mike Bocock.

WAYNESBORO GENERALS

Mailing Address: P.O. Box 68, Waynesboro, VA 22980. **Telephone:** (540) 337-1116. **FAX:** (540) 337-2233.

President: F.C. Coyner. **General Manager:** Nancy Frank. **Head Coach:** Terry Rooney (James Madison U.).

WINCHESTER ROYALS

Mailing Address: P.O. Box 2485, Winchester, VA 22601. **Telephone:** (540) 662-4466. **FAX:** (540) 662-3299.

President: Todd Thompson. **Recruiting Coordinator/Head Coach:** Paul O'Neil (Shenandoah, Va., U.).

YOUTH BASEBALL

ALL AMERICAN AMATEUR BASEBALL ASSOCIATION

Mailing Address: 331 Parkway Drive, Zanesville, OH 43701. **Telephone:** (614) 453-8531. **FAX:** (614) 453-3978.

Year Founded: 1944.

President: James McElroy Jr. **Executive Director:** Bob Wolfe.

1998 National Tournament (21 and under): Aug. 8-15 at Johnstown, PA.

AMATEUR ATHLETIC UNION

Mailing Address: The Walt Disney World Resort, P.O. Box 10000, Lake Buena Vista, FL 32830. **Telephone:** (407) 934-7200. **FAX:** (407) 934-7242.

Year Founded: 1982.

Baseball Sports Manager: Sheldon Walker.

Age Classifications, World Series

9 and under	Orlando, FL, July 17-25
10 and under	Kansas City, MO, Aug. 1-8
11 and under	Orlando, FL, July 31-Aug. 8
12 and under	Burnsville, MN, July 31-Aug. 8
13 and under (90 foot)	Lowell, MA, July 31-Aug. 9
13 and under (80 foot)	Riverside, CA, Aug. 7-14
14 and under	Concord, NC, July 31-Aug. 9
15 and under	Sarasota, FL, July 31-Aug. 8
16 and under	Hampton Roads, VA, July 30-Aug. 8
17 and under	Des Moines, IA, July 24-Aug. 1
18 and under	Orlando, FL, July 17-25
20 and under	Fort Myers, FL, July 24-Aug. 1

National Invitation Championships

10 and under	Akron, OH, July 24-Aug. 1
11 and under	Des Moines, IA, July 24-Aug. 1
12 and under	Orlando, FL, Aug. 7-15
13 and under (90 foot)	Winter Haven, FL, July 31-Aug. 8
13 and under (80 foot)	Tulsa, OK, Aug. 1-8
14 and under	Orlando, FL, July 24-Aug. 1
15 and under	Kingsport, TN, July 31-Aug. 8
16 and under	Cocoa, FL, July 31-Aug. 8

AMERICAN AMATEUR BASEBALL CONGRESS

National Headquarters: 118-119 Redfield Plaza, P.O. Box 467, Marshall, MI 49068. **Telephone:** (616) 781-2002. **FAX:** (616) 781-2060.

Year Founded: 1935.

President: Joe Cooper.

Age Classifications, World Series

Roberto Clemente (8 and under)	Wheatridge, CO, July 30-Aug. 2
Willie Mays (10 and under)	Collierville, TN, July 31-Aug. 2
Pee Wee Reese (12 and under)	Toa Baja, PR, Aug. 5-10
Sandy Koufax (14 and under)	Jersey City, NJ, Aug. 7-10
Mickey Mantle (16 and under)	McKinney, TX, Aug. 5-9
Connie Mack (18 and under)	Farmington, NM, Aug. 7-13
Stan Musial (unlimited)	Battle Creek, MI, Aug. 13-17

AMERICAN LEGION BASEBALL

National Headquarters: National Americanism Commission, P.O. Box 1055, Indianapolis, IN 46206. **Telephone:** (317) 630-1213. **FAX:** (317) 630-1369. **Website:** www.legion.org.

Year Founded: 1925.

Program Coordinator: Jim Quinlan.

1998 World Series (19 and under): Aug. 21-25 at Las Vegas, NV.

BABE RUTH BASEBALL

International Headquarters: 1770 Brunswick Pike, P.O. Box 5000, Trenton, NJ 08638. **Telephone:** (609) 695-1434. **FAX:** (609) 695-2505.

Year Founded: 1951.

President/Chief Executive Officer: Ron Tellefsen.

Vice President/Chief Financial Officer: Rosemary Schoellkopf. **Commissioners:** Robert Faherty, Jimmy Stewart, Debra Horn. **Marketing Manager:** Joe Smiegocki.

Age Classifications, World Series

Bambino (11-12)	Vincennes, IN, Aug. 8-15
13-Prep	Cape Coral, FL, Aug. 15-22
13-15	Pine Bluff, AR, Aug. 15-22
16	Loudoun County, VA, Aug. 15-22
16-18	Dare County, NC, Aug. 15-22

CONTINENTAL AMATEUR BASEBALL ASSOCIATION

Mailing Address: 82 University St., Westerville, OH 43081. **Telephone/FAX:** (614) 899-2103.

Year Founded: 1984.

President: Carl Williams. **Commissioner:** John Mocny. **Franchise Director:** Tanya Wilkinson. **Executive Director:** Roger Tremaine.

Age Classifications, World Series

9 and under	Charles City, IA, Aug. 6-16
10 and under	Aurelia, IA, July 23-Aug. 2
11 and under	Tarkio, MO, July 30-Aug. 10
12 and under	Omaha, NE, July 30-Aug. 10
13 and under	Broken Arrow, OK, July 30-Aug. 10
14 and under	Dublin, OH, July 30-Aug. 10
15 and under	Crystal Lake, IL, July 30-Aug. 10
16 and under	Arlington, TX, July 30-Aug. 10
High school age	Cleveland, OH, July 23-Aug. 3
18 and under	Homestead, FL, July 30-Aug. 10
College age	Chicago, IL, July 21-27
Unlimited age	Eau Claire, WI, Aug. 11-17

DIXIE BASEBALL, INC.

Mailing Address: P.O. Box 193, Montgomery, AL 36101. **Telephone:** (334) 241-2300. **FAX:** (334) 241-2301.

Year Founded: 1956.

Executive Director: Jimmy Brown.

Age Classifications, World Series

Dixie Youth (12 and under)	Hattiesburg, MS, Aug. 17-22
Dixie 13	Troy, AL, Aug. 1-6
Dixie Boys (13-14)	Eufaula, AL, Aug. 1-6
Dixie Pre-Majors (15-16)	North Charleston, SC, Aug. 1-6
Dixie Majors (15-18)	Florence, SC, Aug. 1-6

DIZZY DEAN BASEBALL, INC.

Mailing Address: 902 Highway 9 North, Eupora, MS 39744. **Telephone:** (601) 258-7626.

Year Founded: 1962.

Commissioner: Billy Powell.

Age Classifications, World Series

Minor League (9-10)	East Brainerd, TN, July 25-30
Freshman (11-12)	Grenada, MS, July 25-30
Sophomore (13-14)	Ellisville, MS, July 25-30
Junior (15-16)	Site undetermined, July 25-30
Senior (17-18)	Pelham, AL, July 25-30

HAP DUMONT YOUTH BASEBALL

Mailing Address: P.O. Box 17455, Wichita, KS 67217. **Telephone:** (316) 721-1779. **FAX:** (316) 721-8054.

Year Founded: 1978.

National Chairman: Jerry Crowell. **National Vice Chairman:** Jerold Vogt.

Age Classifications, World Series

10 and under	Harrison, AR, July 31-Aug. 5
11 and under	Russell, KS, July 31-Aug. 5
12 and under	Houston, TX, July 31-Aug. 5
13 and under	Casper, WY, July 31-Aug. 5
14 and under	Norman, OK, July 31-Aug. 5
16 and under	Brainerd, MN, July 31-Aug. 5

PAN AM and WORLD BASEBALL PROGRAM

Mailing Address: P.O. Box 72711, Roselle, IL 60172. **Telephone:** (630) 893-6273. **FAX:** (630) 893-5549.

Year Founded: 1990.

President, General Manager: Peter Caliendo. **Director, Marketing and Administration:** Jon Wolf. **Public Relations Director:** Mark Madorin. **Fund Raising Director:** Mark Kedziora.

LITTLE LEAGUE BASEBALL, INC.

International Headquarters: P.O. Box 3485, Williamsport, PA 17701. **Telephone:** (717) 326-1921. **FAX:** (717) 326-1074.

Year Founded: 1939.

Chairman: James Whittington. **Chairman Elect:** Ted Reich. **President/Chief Executive Officer:** Steve Keener. **Director, Communications:** Dennis Sullivan. **Director, Media Relations:** Lance Van Auken. **Director, Special Projects:** Scott Rosenberg.

Age Classifications, World Series

Little League (11-12)	Williamsport, PA, Aug. 23-29
Junior League (13)	Taylor, MI, Aug. 17-22
Senior League (13-15)	Kissimmee, FL, Aug. 16-22
Big League (16-18)	Fort Lauderdale, FL, Aug. 14-22

NATIONAL AMATEUR BASEBALL FEDERATION

Mailing Address: P.O. Box 705, Bowie, MD 20718. **Telephone/FAX:** (301) 262-5005.

Year Founded: 1914.

Executive Director: Charles Blackburn.

Rookie (10 and under) .... Cincinnati, OH, July 16-19
Freshman (12 and under) .... Sylvania, OH, July 16-19
Sophomore (14 and under) .... Miamisburg, OH, July 23-26
Junior (16 and under) .... Northville, MI, July 30-Aug. 4
High School (17 and under)........................... Hopkinsville, KY, July 30-Aug. 4
Senior (18 and under) .... Evansville, IN, Aug. 5-9
College (22 and under).. Louisville, KY, Aug. 12-16
Major (unlimited) .... Louisville, KY, Aug. 20-24

NATIONAL ASSOCIATION
OF POLICE ATHLETIC LEAGUES

Mailing Address: 618 North U.S. Highway 1, Suite 201, North Palm Beach, FL 33408. **Telephone:** (561) 844-1823. **FAX:** (561) 863-6120.
Year Founded: 1944
Executive Director: Joseph Wilson. **Director, Member Services:** Nerilda Lugo. **Sports Program Director:** Ashley Bevan.

Age Classifications, World Series

16 and Under .... Fort Myers, FL, Aug. 3-8

PONY BASEBALL, INC.

International Headquarters: P.O. Box 225, Washington, PA 15301. **Telephone:** (724) 225-1060. **FAX:** (724) 225-9852. **E-Mail Address:** pony@pulsenet.com. **Website:** www.pony.org.
Year Founded: 1951.
President: Abraham Key. **Director, Baseball Operations:** Don Clawson.

Age Classifications, World Series

Shetland (5-6)... No National Tournament
Pinto (7-8).. No National Tournament
Mustang (9-10) .... Irving, TX, Aug. 5-8
Bronco (11-12) .... Monterey, CA, Aug. 6-12
Pony (13-14) .... Washington, PA, Aug. 15-22
Colt (15-16) .... Lafayette, IN, Aug. 4-11
Palomino (17-18)..................................... Greensboro, NC, Aug. 12-15

REVIVING BASEBALL IN INNER CITIES (RBI)

Mailing Address: 350 Park Ave., New York, NY 10022. **Telephone:** (212) 339-7800. **FAX:** (212) 888-8632.
Year Founded: 1989.
Founder: John Young. **Executive Director, Market Development:** Kathleen Francis. **National Manager:** Tom Brasuell (212-339-7844).

Age Classifications, World Series

Junior Boys (13-15) .... Lake Buena Vista, FL, Aug. 12-17
Senior Boys (16-18) .... Lake Buena Vista, FL, Aug. 12-17

T-BALL USA ASSOCIATION, INC.

Office Address: 915 Broadway, Suite 607, New York, NY 10010. **Telephone:** (212) 254-7911, (800) 741-0845. **FAX:** (212) 254-8042.
Year Founded: 1993.
President: Bing Broido. **Vice President:** Lois Richards.

U.S. AMATEUR BASEBALL ASSOCIATION

Mailing Address: 7101 Lake Ballinger Way, Edmonds, WA 98026. **Telephone/FAX:** (425) 776-7130. **Website:** www.usaba.com.
Year Founded: 1969.
Executive Director: Al Rutledge.

Age Classifications, World Series

11 and under .... Unavailable
12 and under .... Unavailable
13 and under.. West Covina, CA, Aug. 5-15
14 and under .... Fresno, CA, Aug. 6-15
15 and under .... Victoria, B.C., Aug. 4-15
16 and under .... Salt Lake City, UT, Aug. 6-15
17 and under .... Los Angeles, CA, July 23-Aug. 1
18 and under .... Unavailable
19 and under .... Unavailable

U.S. JUNIOR OLYMPIC
BASEBALL CHAMPIONSHIP

Mailing Address: 3400 East Camino Campestre, Tucson, AZ 85716. **Telephone:** (520) 327-9700. **FAX:** (520) 327-9221.
Coordinator, Youth Baseball: Ray Darwin.

Age Classifications, Championships

16 and Under .... Tucson, AZ, June 19-28

SERVICE DIRECTORY

ACCESSORIES

American Athletic, Inc.
800-247-3978
Fax: 515-386-4566

R.C. Manufacturing Company
11961 31st Court North
St. Petersburg, FL 33716
888-726-3488
Fax: 813-572-4162

Tuff Toe
726 W. Angus Ave., Suite B
Orange, CA 92868
800-888-0802
Fax: 714-997-9594

ACCOUNTANTS/CONSULTANTS

Resnick Amsterdam Leshner P.C.
653 Skippack Pike, Suite 300
Blue Bell, PA 19422
215-628-8080
Fax: 215-628-4752

AGENTS

Panco Sports Enterprises
800-644-3380/213-876-5984
Fax: 213-876-5076

StrongHold Athletic Management, Inc.
120 E. Parrish Street, Suite 300
Durham, NC 27701
919-688-6335/919-682-8092
Fax: 919-682-5091

APPAREL

Joy Athletic, Inc
3555 East 11 Avenue
Hialeah, FL 33013
305-691-7240
Fax: 305-691-7247

Minor Leagues, Major Dreams
P.O. Box 6098
Anaheim, CA 92816
800-345-2421 Fax: 714-939-0655
www.minorleagues.com

Rawlings Sporting Goods
1-800-RAWLINGS
www.rawlings.com

Seven Sons
864-574-7660
Fax: 864-574-7611

Star Struck, Inc.
8 F.J. Clarke Circle
Bethel, CT 06801
800-908-4637 Fax: 800-962-8345
www.starstruck.com

Wilson Sporting Goods
773-714-6800

Fax: 800-642-4600

AWARDS/TROPHIES

American Special Promotions
800-501-2257
Fax: 770-271-4006

Barnstable Bat Company
508-362-8046/888-549-8046
Fax: 508-362-3983

Sigma Glass Studio
2318 16th Avenue North
St. Petersburg, FL 33713
813-525-5384
Fax: 813-522-5211

STIX Baseball
800-533-STIX 407-425-3360
Fax: 407-425-3560

BAGS

Irwin Sports/Cooper Baseball
800-268-1732
Fax: 800-268-6399

Louisville Slugger
800-282-2287 502-585-5226
Fax: 502-585-1179

Markwort Sporting Goods
314-652-3757
Fax: 314-652-6241

Rawlings Sporting Goods
1-800-RAWLINGS
www.rawlings.com

BASEBALL CARDS

GrandStand Cards
818-992-5642
Fax: 818-348-9122

Minford's Minors
704-733-1145
Fax: 704-733-1145

STB Sports/Minor League Team Sets
310-325-4331
Fax: 310-325-1584

BASEBALLS

American Athletic, Inc.
800-247-3978
Fax: 515-386-4566

The Jugs Company
800-547-6843
Fax: 503-691-1100

Markwort Sporting Goods
314-652-3757
Fax: 314-652-6241

Master Pitching Machine, Inc.
800-878-8228
Fax: 816-452-7581

Rawlings Sporting Goods
1-800-RAWLINGS
www.rawlings.com

SSK America
800-421-2674
Fax: 310-549-2904

BASES

Adams USA/Neumann Gloves
931-526-2109
Fax: 931-372-8510

Beacon Ballfields/Lodestar L.L.C.
P.O. Box 45557
Madison, WI 53744-5557
800-747-5985
Fax: 608-274-6072

BATS

Barnstable Bat Company
508-362-8046/888-549-8046
Fax: 508-362-3983

Glomar Enterprises
116 W. Walnut Avenue
Fullerton, CA 92832
714-871-5956 Fax: 714-871-5958
www.glomarbats.com

Irwin Sports/Cooper Baseball
800-268-1732
Fax: 800-268-6399

Louisville Slugger
P.O. Box 35700
Louisville, KY 40232
800-282-2287 502-585-5226
Fax: 502-585-1179

The Original Maple Bat Co.
Maker of SamBat™ & S. Holman Bat
93 Bayswater Avenue
Ottawa, Ontario K1Y 2G2
613-724-2421 Fax: 613-725-3299

Professional Diamond Clubs Inc.
336-248-5537
Fax: 336-248-5537

Rawlings Sporting Goods
1-800-RAWLINGS
www.rawlings.com

SSK America
800-421-2674
Fax: 310-549-2904

STIX Baseball
800-533-STIX 407-425-3360
Fax: 407-425-3560

Wilson Sporting Goods
773-714-6800
Fax: 800-642-4600

Worth Sports Company
800-423-3714 615-455-0691
Fax: 615-454-9164

Young Bat Company
1449 Ecusta Road
Brevard, NC 28712
888-595-2287
Fax: 704-862-3842

BATTING CAGES

Batting Cages/Grady Lanier
334-222-9189
Fax: 334-222-9189

Beacon Ballfields/Lodestar L.L.C.
800-747-5985

Fax: 608-274-6072

C & H Baseball, Inc.
2215 60th Drive East
Bradenton, FL 34203
800-248-5192
Fax: 941-727-0588

The Jugs Company
11885 S.W. Herman Road
Tualatin, OR 97062
800-547-6843
Fax: 503-691-1100

Master Pitching Machine, Inc.
800-878-8228
Fax: 816-452-7581

Miller Net Company
1674 Getwell Road
Memphis, TN 38181
800-423-6603 Fax: 901-743-6580
home.mem.net/~miller miller@mem.net

National Batting Cages
P.O. Box 250
Forest Grove, OR 97116-0250
800-547-8800
Fax: 503-357-3727

Omni Sports Technologies
P.O. Box 28802
Kansas City, MO 64188
816-880-9170 Fax: 816-880-9172
www.omnisportstech.com

Russell Batting Cages
888-RBC-CAGE
www.groupz.net/RBCCAGE/com

Sterling Net & Twine Co., Inc.
18 Label Street
Montclair, NJ 07042
800-342-0316
Fax: 800-232-6387

BOOKS/VIDEOS

All About Pitching
800-635-2822
www.pitching.com

Global Sports Books
800-350-2665
310-454-6590

MasterPlan Sports
800-282-5254

CAMPS/SCHOOLS

The Baseball Academy
5500 34th Street West
Bradenton, FL 34210
800-872-6425 Fax: 941-756-6891
www.bollettieri.com

Mickey Owen Baseball School
P.O. Box 88
Miller, MO 65707
800-999-8369/417-882-2799
Fax: 417-889-6978

CAPS/HEADWEAR

Minor Leagues, Major Dreams
P.O. Box 6098
Anaheim, CA 92816
800-345-2421 Fax: 714-939-0655
www.minorleagues.com

New ERA Cap Co. Inc.
800-989-0445
Fax: 716-549-5424

Outdoor Cap
501-273-5870
Fax: 501-273-2144

Star Struck, Inc.
8 F.J. Clarke Circle
Bethel, CT 06801
800-908-4637 Fax: 800-962-8345
www.starstruck.com

Twin City Knitting Company, Inc.
704-464-4830
Fax: 704-465-3209

CASES

Anvil Cases
15650 Salt Lake Avenue
City of Industry, CA 91745
800-359-2684 Matt Larson (x120)
Fax: 626-968-1703

CATCHING EQUIPMENT

Rawlings Sporting Goods
1-800-RAWLINGS
www.rawlings.com

SSK America
800-421-2674
Fax: 310-549-2904

Wilson Sporting Goods
312-714-6800
Fax: 800-642-4600

DATABASE SERVICES

Advance Ticket Sales, Inc.
4416 Providence Road, Suite 10
Charlotte, NC 28226
704-365-3274
Fax: 704-365-3749

DIRECT MAIL SERVICES

Advance Ticket Sales, Inc.
4416 Providence Road, Suite 10
Charlotte, NC 28226
704-365-3274
Fax: 704-365-3749

EDUCATION/CONSULTING

Baseball Teaching Ventures, Inc.
888-543-4248/203-661-3012
Fax: 203-869-2629

ENTERTAINMENT

BirdZerk!
P.O. Box 36061
Louisville, KY 40233
502-458-4020 Fax: 502-458-0867
wejam@bellsouth.net

**Bleacher Preacher/
Jerry Pritikin**
150 Maple Street #1307
Chicago, IL 60610
312-664-3231 Fax: 630-543-1215

Morganna c/o SRO Events
"Baseball's Kissing Bandit"
3727 E. 31st Street
Tulsa, OK 74135
918-743-8461 Fax: 918-749-6643

Sports Magic Team
807 S. Orlando Ave., Suite N
Winter Park, FL 32789
407-647-1110 Fax: 407-647-0994
www.sportsmagicteam.com
SportsMagic Team@ worldnet.att.net

FIELD CONSTRUCTION/RENOVATION

Alpine Services, Inc.
5313 Brookeville Road
Gaithersburg, MD 20882
301-963-8833
Fax: 301-963-7901

FIREWORKS

American Promotions of IL.
800-426-8054
Fax: 888-426-8054

FLAGS/BANNERS

Olympus Flag & Banner
414-355-2010
Fax: 414-355-1931

FOOD SERVICE

Concession Solutions, Inc.
16022 - 26th Avenue NE
Shoreline, WA 98155
206-440-9203 Fax: 206-440-9213
concesssol@aol.com

DiGiovanni's Food Service
888-820-4229
Fax: 941-922-8122

Houston's Peanuts
P.O. Box 160
Dublin, NC 28332
910-862-2136 800-334-8383
Fax: 910-862-8076

Lemon Chill & Moore
2376 Culloden Cover
Memphis, TN 38119
901-761-3414
Fax: 901-761-3997

**Marriott Concessions
and Events Services**
90 S. High Street
Dublin, OH 43017
614-761-2330 Fax: 614-761-9903

Slush Puppie Brands
800-543-0860
Fax: 507-257-3285

GLOVE CARE/REPAIR

Bat-Away Glove Relacing Co
24370 Tierra De Oro
Moreno Valley, CA 92553
888-238-1052
Fax: 909-924-2243

Henrys BB Club & Glove Repair
Players 17-30 needed used/new
gloves available 781-891-0621

Louisville Slugger
800-282-2287 502-585-5226
Fax: 502-585-1179

GLOVES

Adams USA/Neumann Gloves
610 South Jefferson Avenue
Cookeville, TN 38501
931-526-2109
Fax: 931-372-8510

**Guerrero Baseball Gloves/
Diamond King Sports**
852 Elmwood Road # 269
Lansing, MI 48917
800-826-1464 Fax: 517-886-8035

Louisville Slugger
P.O. Box 35700
Louisville, KY 40232
800-282-2287 502-585-5226
Fax: 502-585-1179

Markwort Sporting Goods
314-652-3757
Fax: 314-652-6241

Perez Professional Gloves
P.O. Box 786
Dewitt, MI 48820
517-580-8227
Fax: 517-321-1756

Rawlings Sporting Goods
P.O. Box 22000
St. Louis, MO 63126
1-800-RAWLINGS
www.rawlings.com

SSK America
21136 S. Wilmington Ave., Ste 220
Long Beach, CA 90810
800-421-2674
Fax: 310-549-2904
gossk@aol.com

Wilson Sporting Goods
773-714-6800
Fax: 800-642-4600

GRAPHIC DESIGN

Low & Inside Creative
P.O. Box 290228
Minneapolis, MN 55429
612-797-0777 Fax: 612-797-7441
baseball@bitstream.net www.lowandinside.com

HITTING MACHINES

Quic Hands
800-295-8851
Fax: 800-295-8851

INSURANCE

K & K Insurance Group, Inc.
1712 Magna Vox Way
Ft. Wayne, IN 46804
219-459-5662
Fax: 219-459-5120

LOGO DESIGN

Silverman Group, Inc.
700 State Street
New Haven, CT 06511
203-562-6418
Fax: 203-777-9637

MAGNETIC SCHEDULES

Master Marketing International
1776 S. Naperville, Rd., Ste 201-B
Wheaton, IL 60187
800-438-3210
Fax: 630-653-5125

MASCOT COSTUMES

Mascot Masters International, LLC
5830 N.W. Expressway, Suite 354
Oklahoma City, OK 73132
405-722-2922/405-810-8644
Fax: 405-810-8480

Olympus Flag & Banner
414-355-2010
Fax: 414-355-1931

MEMORABILIA

B&J Collectibles
800-388-0912
www.b-j.com

Stan's Sports Memorabilia
14 Washburn Place
Caldwell, NJ 07006
201-228-5257
Fax: 201-228-5257

MLB BENCH TOWELS

McArthur Towels, Inc.
700 Moore Street
Baraboo, WI 53913
800-356-9168
Fax: 608-356-7587

MUSIC/SOUND EFFECTS

Sound Creations
2820 Azalea Place
Nashville, TN 37204
615-460-7330
Fax: 615-460-7331

NATIONAL SHOWCASE EVENTS

Baseball Factory, Inc.
3290 Pine Orchard Lane, Unit D
Ellicott City, MD 21042
800-641-4487
Fax: 410-418-5434

NETTING/POSTS

ATEC
10 Greg Street
Sparks, NV 89431
800-755-5100
Fax: 702-352-2822

C & H Baseball, Inc.
800-248-5192
Fax: 941-727-0588

Master Pitching Machine, Inc.
800-878-8228
Fax: 816-452-7581

Miller Net Company
1674 Getwell Road
Memphis, TN 38181
800-423-6603 Fax: 901-743-6580
home.mem.net/~miller miller@mem.net

Saleen Sportnet
800-382-5399

Sterling Net & Twine Co., Inc.
18 Label Street
Montclair, NJ 07042
800-342-0316
Fax: 800-232-6387

PADDING-FIELD/WALL

Promats, Inc.
P.O. Box 508
Fort Collins, CO 80522
800-678-6287
Fax: 970-482-7740

PHOTOGRAPHY

Wagner Photography
941-277-3100
Fax: 941-275-7029

PITCHING MACHINES

ATEC
800-755-5100
Fax: 702-352-2822

The Jugs Company
800-547-6843
Fax: 503-691-1100

Master Pitching Machine, Inc.
4200 NE Birmingham Road
Kansas City, MO 64117
800-878-8228
Fax: 816-452-7581

Omni Sports Technologies
816-880-9170 Fax: 816-880-9172
www.omnisportstech.com

PLAYING FIELD PRODUCTS

American Athletic, Inc.
800-247-3978
Fax: 515-386-4566

AstroTurf Industries, Inc.
800-233-5714
Fax: 512-259-2952

Beacon Ballfields/Lodestar L.L.C.
800-747-5985
Fax: 608-274-6072

C & H Baseball, Inc.
800-248-5192
Fax: 941-727-0588

Diamond Pro
1341 W. Mockingbird Lane
Dallas, TX 75247
800-228-2987
Fax: 800-640-6735

Midwest Athletic Surfaces
1125 West State Street
Marshfield, WI 54449
715-387-4636 Fax: 715-387-4636
home1.gte.net/lortner/midwest.htm

McArthur Towels, Inc.
800-356-9168
Fax: 608-356-7587

Partac Peat/Beam Clay
Kelsey Park
Great Meadows, NJ 07838
800-247-BEAM/908-637-4191
Fax: 908-637-8421

Promats, Inc.
800-678-6287
Fax: 970-482-7740

Stabilizer, Inc.
2218 E. Magnolia Street
Phoenix, AZ 85034
800-336-2468
Fax: 602-225-5902

PRINTING

Multi-Ad Services
800-348-6485
Fax: 309-692-5444

TradeMark Printing
650-592-9130
Fax: 650-592-2776

PRODUCT DEVELOPMENT

Baseball Teaching Ventures, Inc.
888-543-4248/203-661-3012
Fax: 203-869-2629

PROFESSIONAL SERVICES

Baseball Opportunities
(Franchise Sales)
602-483-8224

Resnick Amsterdam Leshner P.C.
653 Skippack Pike, Suite 300
Blue Bell, PA 19422
215-628-8080
Fax: 215-628-4752

PROMOTIONAL ITEMS

American Promotions of IL., Inc.
800-426-8054
Fax: 888-426-8054

American Special Promotions
800-501-2257
Fax: 770-271-4006

Creative Craze
888-506-0929
Fax: 972-506-7197

HardBall Sports Marketing, Inc.
420 B Wharfside Way
Jacksonville, FL 32207
800-292-1628
Fax: 904-220-1296

K R Industries, Inc.
800-621-6097
Fax: 708-222-1400

Louisville Slugger
800-282-2287 502-585-5226
Fax: 502-585-1179

PROMOTIONS

The Great Gazebo, Inc.
Mike Seddon/National. Sales
1512 Meadowbrook
East Lansing, MI 48823
800-962-2767/517-337-2011
greatgazebo.com info@greatgazebo.com

SCA Promotions, Inc.
8300 Douglas, Ave., Suite 625
Dallas, TX 75225
214-860-3717
Fax: 214-860-3723

PUBLICATIONS

All About Pitching
800-635-2822

The Baseball Scout Newsletter
508-753-8387
Fax: 508-753-8387

**Braunstein's Met/Yankee
Minor League Reporter**
117 West 74th Street #4C
New York, NY 10023
212-258-0026 Fax: 212-307-9518

Low & Inside
P.O. Box 290228
Minneapolis, MN 55429
612-797-0777 Fax: 612-797-7441
baseball@bitstream.net www.lowandinside.com

PUBLIC RELATIONS/PUBLICITY

Sheldon Baker Public Relations
P.O. Box 689
Clovis, CA 93613
800-570-1262
Fax: 209-325-7195

RADAR EQUIPMENT

ATEC
10 Greg Street
Sparks, NV 83431
800-755-5100
Fax: 702-352-2822

Decatur Electronics, Inc.
715 Bright Street
Decatur, IL 62522
800-428-4315 Fax: 217-428-5302
info@decaturradar.com www.decaturradar.com

The Jugs Company
11885 S.W. Herman Road
Tualatin, OR 97062
800-547-6843
Fax: 503-691-1100

Omni Sports Technologies
816-880-9170
Fax: 816-880-9172

Radar Sales
5640 International Parkway
Minneapolis, MN 55428
612-533-1100 888-782-5537
Fax: 612-533-1400

SAFETY EQUIPMENT

GameFace Sports Safety Mask
800-GAMEFACE/301-682-9770
FAX: 301-682-9780

SCOREBOARDS

Fairtron, Division of Trans-Lux
1700 Delaware Avenue
Des Moines, IA 50317
515-265-5305
Fax: 515-265-3364

Nevco Scoreboard Company
301 East Harris Ave., P.O. Box 609
Greenville, IL 62246-0609
800-851-4040
Fax: 618-664-0398

Spectrum Scoreboards
10048 Easthaven
Houston, TX 77075
800-392-5050
Fax: 713-944-1290

SIGNS/TRI-ACTION

Action Graphix
P.O. Box 2337
Jonesboro, AR 72402
501-931-7440
Fax: 501-931-7528

STADIUM ARCHITECTS

Design Exchange Architects, Inc.
Polly Drummond Office Park
Building. 3, Suite 3205
Newark, DE 19711
302-366-1611 Fax: 302-366-1657

Devine deFlon Yaeger Architects, Inc.
3700 Broadway, Suite 300
Kansas City, MO 64111-2507
816-561-2761
Fax: 816-561-9222

DLR Group "Lescher and Mahony"
601 West Swann Avenue
Tampa, FL 33606
813-254-9811 Fax: 813-254-4230
www.dlrgroup.com

Ellerbe Becket
Two Arizona Center
400 North 5th St., Suite 1030
Phoenix, AZ 85004
602-251-0900 Fax: 602-251-0957

Heery International
999 Peachtree Street N.E.
Atlanta, GA 30367-5401
404-881-9880
Fax: 404-875-3273

HNTB Sports Architecture
1201 Walnut, Suite 700
Kansas City, MO 64106
816-472-1201
Fax: 816-472-4060

HOK Sports Facilities Group
323 W. 8th St. Suite 700
Kansas City, MO 64105
816-221-1576
Fax: 816-221-5816

L.D. Astorino & Associates
227 Fort Pitt Blvd.
Pittsburgh, PA 15222
412-765-1700
Fax: 412-765-1711

STADIUM SEATING

American Seating
616-732-6600
Fax: 616-732-6401

Caddy Products
10501 Florida Avenue South
Minneapolis, MN 55438
800-845-0591
Fax: 612-829-0166

Coasters
415-332-5555
Fax: 415-332-5010

GDS Seating/Interkal, Inc.
616-349-1521
Fax: 616-349-5888

Hussey Seating Company
800-341-0401
Fax: 207-676-2222

Irwin Seating Company
616-784-2621
Fax: 616-784-0269

K R Industries, Inc.
800-621-6097
Fax: 708-222-1400

Seating Services, Inc.
P.O. Box 4
Angola, NY 14006
800-552-9470
Fax: 716-549-9011

Southern Bleacher
715 Fifth St., P.O. Box One
Graham, TX 76450
800-433-0912/940-549-0733
Fax: 940-549-1365

Sturdisteel Company
P.O. Box 2655
Waco, TX 76702-2655
800-433-3116
Fax: 254-666-4472

TELEMARKETING SERVICES

Advance Ticket Sales, Inc.
4416 Providence Road, Suite 10
Charlotte, NC 28226
704-365-3274
Fax: 704-365-3749

TRAINING SYSTEMS

Arm Strong™/DH Sports, Inc.
934 Prichard Lane
West Chester, PA 19382
888-321-2720
Fax: 610-692-2398

Quic Hands
800-295-8851
Fax: 800-295-8851

Set Pro
800-890-8803

SoloHitter/Sports Lab USA
800-875-3355

True Sport/Rocket Arm
800-32-ROCKET

TICKETS

Easy Computer Systems
P.O. Box 765
Springfield, MO 65615
417-335-3279
Fax: 417-335-5246

National Ticket Company
P.O. Box 547
Shamokin, PA 17872
800-829-0829
Fax: 800-829-0888

Select Ticketing Systems
344 W. Genesee St., P.P. Box 959
Syracuse, NY 13201
800-944-7277 (x 591)
Fax: 315-471-2715

Sport Productions, Inc.
23775 Commerce Park Road
Cleveland, OH 44122
216-591-2400
Fax: 216-591-2424

Ticket Craft
516-538-6200
516-538-4860
email: ticketcraft!aol.com

TicketStop, Inc.
14042 NE 8th St., Suite 108
Bellevue, WA 98007
800-961-6111
Fax: 425-641-8151

TRAVEL

Broach Baseball Tours
2727 Selwyn Avenue, Suite C
Charlotte, N.C. 28209
800-849-6345
Fax: 704-333-1978

Broach Baseball Tours
2727 Selwyn Avenue, Suite C
Charlotte, N.C. 28209
800-849-6345
Fax: 704-333-1978

Kensport
110 Paladin Place
Cary, NC 27513
919-380-7476
Fax: 919-380-9265

Tour With Us
734-528-0583
734-528-9081

TURFMATS-SYNTHETIC

AstroTurf Industries, Inc.
800-233-5714
Fax: 512-259-2952

TURNSTILE ADVERTISING

Entry Media, Inc.
10151 University Blvd., Suite 204
Orlando, FL 32817
407-678-4446
Fax: 407-679-3590

UNIFORMS

DeLong
515-236-3106
Fax: 515-236-4891

Markwort Sporting Goods
314-652-3757
Fax: 314-652-6241

Rawlings Sporting Goods
P.O. Box 22000
St. Louis, MO 63126
1-800-RAWLINGS
www.rawlings.com

Wilson Sporting Goods
773-714-6800
Fax: 800-642-4600

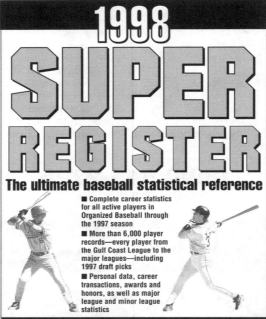

1998DIRECTORYINDEX

MAJOR LEAGUE TEAMS

American League

Page	Club	Phone	FAX
24	Anaheim Angels	714-940-2000	714-940-2205
26	Baltimore Orioles	410-685-9800	410-547-6272
28	Boston Red Sox	617-267-9440	617-375-0944
30	Chicago White Sox	312-674-1000	312-674-5116
32	Cleveland Indians	216-420-4200	216-420-4396
34	Detroit Tigers	313-962-4000	313-965-2138
36	Kansas City Royals	816-921-8000	816-921-5775
38	Minnesota Twins	612-375-1366	612-375-7473
40	New York Yankees	718-293-4300	718-293-8431
42	Oakland Athletics	510-638-4900	510-568-3770
44	Seattle Mariners	206-346-4000	206-346-4050
46	Tampa Bay Devil Rays	813-825-3137	813-825-3111
48	Texas Rangers	817-273-5222	817-273-5206
50	Toronto Blue Jays	416-341-1000	416-341-1250

National League

Page	Club	Phone	FAX
54	Arizona Diamondbacks	602-462-6500	602-462-6600
56	Atlanta Braves	404-522-7630	404-614-1391
58	Chicago Cubs	773-404-2827	773-404-4129
60	Cincinnati Reds	513-421-4510	513-421-7342
62	Colorado Rockies	303-292-0200	303-312-2319
64	Florida Marlins	305-626-7400	305-626-7428
66	Houston Astros	713-799-9500	713-799-9794
68	Los Angeles Dodgers	213-224-1500	213-224-1269
70	Milwaukee Brewers	414-933-4114	414-933-7323
72	Montreal Expos	514-253-3434	514-253-8282
74	New York Mets	718-507-6387	718-565-6395
76	Philadelphia Phillies	215-463-6000	215-389-3050
78	Pittsburgh Pirates	412-323-5000	412-323-9133
80	St. Louis Cardinals	314-421-3060	314-425-0640
82	San Diego Padres	619-881-6500	619-497-5454
84	San Francisco Giants	415-468-3700	415-467-0485

MINOR LEAGUE TEAMS

Page	Club	League	Phone	FAX
148	Akron	Eastern	330-253-5151	330-253-3300
138	Albuquerque	PCL	505-243-1791	505-842-0561
161	Arkansas	Texas	501-664-1555	501-664-1834
193	Asheville	SAL	704-258-0428	704-258-0320
201	Auburn	NYP	315-255-2489	315-255-2675
193	Augusta	SAL	706-736-7889	706-736-1122
166	Bakersfield	Cal	805-322-1363	805-322-6199
201	Batavia	NYP	716-343-5454	716-343-5620
185	Beloit	Midwest	608-362-2272	608-362-0418
220	Billings	Pioneer	406-252-1241	406-252-2968
148	Binghamton	Eastern	607-723-6387	607-723-7779
155	Birmingham	Southern	205-988-3200	205-988-9698
214	Bluefield	Appy	540-326-1326	540-326-1318
209	Boise	Northwest	208-322-5000	208-322-7432
149	Bowie	Eastern	301-805-6007	301-805-6008
177	Brevard County	FSL	407-633-9200	407-633-9210
214	Bristol	Appy	540-645-7275	540-645-7377
129	Buffalo	IL	716-846-2000	716-852-6530
185	Burlington, IA	Midwest	319-754-5705	319-754-5882
214	Burlington, NC	Appy	336-222-0223	336-226-2498
220	Butte	Pioneer	406-723-8206	406-723-3376
138	Calgary	PCL	403-284-1111	403-284-4343
194	Cape Fear	SAL	910-424-6500	910-424-4325
194	Capital City	SAL	803-256-4110	803-256-4338
155	Carolina	Southern	919-269-2287	919-269-4910
186	Cedar Rapids	Midwest	319-363-3887	319-363-5631
195	Charleston, SC	SAL	803-723-7241	803-723-2641
195	Charleston, WV	SAL	304-344-2287	304-344-0083
177	Charlotte, FL	FSL	941-625-9500	941-624-5168
129	Charlotte, NC	IL	704-364-6657	803-548-8055
156	Chattanooga	Southern	423-267-2208	423-267-4258
178	Clearwater	FSL	813-441-8638	813-447-3924
186	Clinton	Midwest	319-242-0727	319-242-1433
139	Colorado Springs	PCL	719-597-1449	719-597-2491
196	Columbus, GA	SAL	706-571-8866	706-571-9107
130	Columbus, OH	IL	614-462-5250	614-462-3271
215	Danville	Appy	804-791-3346	804-791-3347

172	Danville	Carolina	804-791-3346	804-791-3347
178	Daytona	FSL	904-257-3172	904-257-3382
196	Delmarva	SAL	410-219-3112	410-219-9164
179	Dunedin	FSL	813-733-9302	813-734-7661
130	Durham	IL	919-687-6500	919-687-6560
139	Edmonton	PCL	403-414-4450	403-414-4475
215	Elizabethton	Appy	423-543-4395	423-542-1510
161	El Paso	Texas	915-755-2000	915-757-0671
201	Erie	NYP	814-456-1300	814-456-7520
209	Eugene	Northwest	541-342-5367	541-342-6089
210	Everett	Northwest	425-258-3673	425-258-3675
179	Fort Myers	FSL	941-768-4210	941-768-4211
186	Fort Wayne	Midwest	219-482-6400	219-471-4678
172	Frederick	Carolina	301-662-0013	301-662-0018
140	Fresno	PCL	515-243-6111	515-243-5152
220	Great Falls	Pioneer	406-452-5311	406-454-0811
197	Greensboro	SAL	336-333-2287	336-273-7350
156	Greenville	Southern	864-299-3456	864-277-7369
197	Hagerstown	SAL	301-791-6266	301-791-6066
150	Harrisburg	Eastern	717-231-4444	717-231-4445
221	Helena	Pioneer	406-449-7616	406-449-6979
198	Hickory	SAL	704-322-3000	704-322-6137
166	High Desert	Cal	760-246-6287	760-246-3197
202	Hudson Valley	NYP	914-838-0094	914-838-0014
157	Huntsville	Southern	205-882-2562	205-880-0801
221	Idaho Falls	Pioneer	208-522-8363	208-522-9858
140	Indianapolis	IL	317-269-3542	317-269-3541
140	Iowa	PCL	515-243-6111	515-243-5152
162	Jackson	Texas	601-981-4664	601-981-4669
157	Jacksonville	Southern	904-358-2846	904-358-2845
202	Jamestown	NYP	716-664-0915	716-664-4175
216	Johnson City	Appy	423-461-4850	423-461-4864
180	Jupiter	FSL	561-775-1818	561-691-6886
187	Kane County	Midwest	630-232-8811	630-232-8815
216	Kingsport	Appy	423-378-3744	423-392-8538
173	Kinston	Carolina	919-527-9111	919-527-2328
180	Kissimmee	FSL	407-933-5500	407-847-6237
158	Knoxville	Southern	423-637-9494	423-523-9913
167	Lake Elsinore	Cal	909-245-4487	909-245-0305
181	Lakeland	FSL	941-688-7911	941-688-9589
167	Lancaster	Cal	805-726-5400	805-726-5406
187	Lansing	Midwest	517-485-4500	517-485-4518
141	Las Vegas	PCL	702-386-7200	702-386-7214
222	Lethbridge	Pioneer	403-327-7975	403-327-8085
132	Louisville	IL	502-367-9121	502-368-5120
203	Lowell	NYP	978-459-2255	508-459-1674
173	Lynchburg	Carolina	804-528-1144	804-846-0768
198	Macon	SAL	912-745-8943	912-743-5559
217	Martinsville	Appy	540-666-2000	540-666-2139
222	Medicine Hat	Pioneer	403-526-0404	403-526-4000
141	Memphis	PCL	901-721-6000	901-721-6017
188	Michigan	Midwest	616-660-2287	616-660-2288
162	Midland	Texas	915-683-4251	915-683-0994
158	Mobile	Southern	334-479-2327	334-476-1147
168	Modesto	Cal	209-572-4487	209-572-4490
142	Nashville	PCL	615-242-4371	615-256-5684
150	New Britain	Eastern	860-224-8383	203-225-6267
151	New Haven	Eastern	203-782-1666	203-782-3150
203	New Jersey	NYP	973-579-7500	973-579-7502
142	New Orleans	PCL	504-734-5155	504-734-5118
132	Norfolk	IL	757-622-2222	757-624-9090
151	Norwich	Eastern	860-887-7962	860-886-5996
223	Ogden	Pioneer	801-393-2400	801-393-2473
143	Oklahoma	PCL	405-218-1000	405-218-1001
111	Omaha	PCL	402-734-2550	402-734-7166
204	Oneonta	NYP	607-432-6326	607-432-1965
159	Orlando	Southern	407-649-7297	407-649-1637
133	Ottawa	IL	613-747-5969	613-747-0003
133	Pawtucket	IL	401-724-7300	401-724-2140
188	Peoria	Midwest	309-688-1622	309-686-4516
199	Piedmont	SAL	704-932-3267	704-938-7040
204	Pittsfield	NYP	413-499-6387	413-443-7144
152	Portland, ME	Eastern	207-874-9300	207-780-0317
210	Portland, OR	Northwest	503-223-2837	503-223-2948
174	Prince William	Carolina	703-590-2311	703-590-5716
217	Princeton	Appy	304-487-2000	304-487-8762
218	Pulaski	Appy	540-994-8696	540-980-3055
189	Quad City	Midwest	319-324-2032	319-324-3109
168	Rancho Cuca.	Cal	909-481-5000	909-481-5005
152	Reading	Eastern	610-375-8469	610-373-5868
134	Richmond	IL	804-359-4444	804-359-0731
134	Rochester	IL	716-454-1001	716-454-1056

189	Rockford	Midwest	815-962-2827	815-961-2002
205	St. Catharines	NYP	905-641-5297	905-641-3007
181	St. Lucie	FSL	561-871-2100	561-878-9802
182	St. Petersburg	FSL	813-822-3384	813-895-1556
174	Salem	Carolina	540-389-3333	540-389-9710
211	Salem-Keizer	Northwest	503-390-2225	503-390-2227
144	Salt Lake	PCL	801-485-3800	801-485-6818
163	San Antonio	Texas	210-675-7275	210-670-0001
169	San Bernardino	Cal	909-888-9922	909-888-5251
169	San Jose	Cal	408-297-1435	408-297-1453
182	Sarasota	FSL	941-365-4460	941-365-4217
199	Savannah	SAL	912-351-9150	912-352-9722
135	Scranton/W-B	IL	717-963-6556	717-963-6564
163	Shreveport	Texas	318-636-5555	318-636-5670
190	South Bend	Midwest	219-235-9988	219-235-9950
211	So. Oregon	Northwest	541-770-5364	541-772-4466
212	Spokane	Northwest	509-535-2922	509-534-5368
170	Stockton	Cal	209-944-5943	209-463-4937
135	Syracuse	IL	315-474-7833	315-474-2658
183	Tacoma	PCL	253-752-7707	253-752-7135
144	Tampa	FSL	813-875-7753	813-673-3174
136	Toledo	IL	419-893-9483	419-893-5847
153	Trenton	Eastern	609-394-3300	609-394-9666
145	Tucson	PCL	520-325-2621	520-327-2371
164	Tulsa	Texas	918-744-5998	918-747-3267
205	Utica	NYP	315-738-0999	315-738-0992
145	Vancouver	PCL	604-872-5232	604-872-1714
206	Vermont	NYP	802-655-4200	802-655-5660
183	Vero Beach	FSL	561-569-4900	561-567-0819
170	Visalia	Cal	209-625-0480	209-739-7732
206	Watertown	NYP	315-788-8747	315-788-8841
190	West Michigan	Midwest	616-784-4131	616-784-4911
159	West Tenn	Southern	901-664-2020	901-988-5246
164	Wichita	Texas	316-267-3372	316-267-3382
207	Williamsport	NYP	717-326-3389	717-326-3494
175	Wilmington	Carolina	302-888-2015	302-888-2032
175	Winston-Salem	Carolina	910-759-2233	910-759-2042
191	Wisconsin	Midwest	920-733-4152	920-733-8032
212	Yakima	Northwest	509-457-5151	509-457-9909

Phone and FAX numbers for minor league offices can be found on pages 122-23.

OTHER ORGANIZATIONS

Page	Organization	Phone	FAX
320	AAABA	614-453-8531	614-453-3978
314	Alaska Baseball League	907-283-7133	907-283-3390
320	Amateur Athletic Union	407-934-7200	407-934-7242
320	American Amateur BB Congress	616-781-2002	616-781-2060
280	American BB Coaches Assoc.	517-775-3300	517-775-3600
23	American League	212-339-7600	212-593-7138
320	American Legion Baseball	317-630-1213	317-630-1369
312	Area Code Games	707-525-0498	707-525-0214
276	Arizona Fall League	602-496-6700	602-496-6384
315	Arizona Collegiate League	602-965-6085	602-965-9309
113	Associated Press	212-621-1630	212-621-1639
199	Assoc. of Prof. BB Players	714-892-9900	714-897-0233
119	Athletes In Action	813-968-7400	813-968-7515
315	Atlantic Collegiate League	973-702-1755	973-702-1898
277	Australian Baseball League	61-2-9437-4622	61-2-9437-4155
320	Babe Ruth Baseball	609-695-1434	609-695-2505
119	Baseball Assistance Team	212-339-7880	212-888-8632
314	Baseball Canada	613-748-5606	613-748-5767
119	Baseball Chapel	847-438-0978	847-438-6554
114	Baseball Digest	847-491-6440	847-491-0867
119	Baseball Trade Show	813-822-6937	813-821-5819
113	BB Writers Assoc. of America	516-981-7938	516-585-4669
115	Beckett Publications	972-991-6657	972-991-8930
112	CBS Radio	212-975-4321	212-975-3515
112	CTV	416-299-2000	416-299-2076
315	California Coastal League	805-566-1476	—
113	Canadian Press	416-594-2154	—
215	Cape Cod League	508-996-5004	508-996-5004
273	Caribbean BB Confederation	809-562-4737	809-565-4654
316	Central Illinois Collegiate League	309-828-4429	309-827-4652
317	Clark Griffith League	703-536-1729	703-536-1729
317	Coastal Plain League	919-852-1960	919-852-1973
120	Colorado Silver Bullets	404-636-8200	404-636-0530
280	CC League of California	916-444-1600	916-444-2616
115	Coman Publishing	919-688-0218	919-682-1532
320	Continental Amateur BB Assoc.	614-899-2103	614-899-2103
321	Dixie Baseball, Inc.	334-241-2300	334-241-2301
321	Dizzy Dean Baseball	601-258-7626	—
273	Dominican League	809-567-6371	809-567-5720

115	Donruss Trading Cards	972-975-0022	972-975-0077
113	ESPN Radio	860-585-2661	860-589-5523
111	ESPN/ESPN2-TV	860-585-2000	860-585-2400
114	ESPN Magazine	212-515-1000	212-515-1290
111	Elias Sports Bureau	212-869-1530	212-354-0980
115	Fleer/Skybox	609-231-6200	609-727-9460
111	FOX-TV	310-369-6000	310-969-6346
251	Frontier League	614-452-7400	614-452-2999
313	Goodwill Games	404-827-3400	404-827-1394
317	Great Lakes League	440-871-5724	216-871-4221
118	Hall of Fame	607-547-7200	607-547-2044
321	Hap Dumont Youth Baseball	316-721-1779	316-721-8054
278	Hawaii Winter Baseball	808-973-7247	808-973-7117
252	Heartland League	765-474-5341	765-474-6462
111	Howe Sportsdata International	617-951-0070	617-737-9960
114	Inside Sports	847-491-6440	847-491-0867
313	International Baseball Assoc.	41-21-311-1863	41-21-311-1864
114	International Baseball Rundown	630-790-3087	630-790-3182
313	International Olympic Committee	41-21-621-61-11	41-21-621-62-16
268	Japanese Baseball	03-3502-0022	03-3502-0140
318	Jayhawk League	316-755-2361	316-755-1285
115	Krause Publications	715-445-2214	715-445-4087
321	Little League Baseball, Inc.	717-326-1921	717-326-1074
21	MLB International	212-350-8300	212-826-2230
21	MLB Players Alumni Association	719-477-1870	719-477-1875
21	MLB Player Relations Comm.	212-339-7400	212-371-2242
21	MLB Productions	201-807-0888	201-807-0272
15	MLB Properties	212-339-7900	212-339-7628
97	Major League Players Assoc.	212-826-0808	212-752-4378
117	Major League Scouting Bureau	714-458-7600	714-458-9454
118	Major League Umpires Assoc.	215-979-3200	215-979-3201
266	Mexican League	525-557-1007	525-395-2454
273	Mexican Pacific League	52-642-2-3100	52-642-2-7250
280	NAIA	918-494-8828	918-494-8841
112	NBC-TV	212-664-4444	212-664-3602
280	NCAA	913-339-1906	913-339-0043
314	NCAA Summer Baseball	913-339-1906	913-339-0026
280	NJCAA	719-590-9788	719-590-7324
312	National Amateur Baseball Fed.	301-262-5005	301-262-5005
122	National Association	813-822-6937	813-821-5819
322	National Association/PAL	561-844-1823	561-863-6120
314	National Baseball Congress	316-267-3372	316-267-3382
312	Nat'l Classic HS Tournament	714-993-5350	714-524-2458
113	National Collegiate BB Writers	312-553-0483	312-553-0495
312	Nat'l Fed. of State HS Assoc.	816-464-5400	816-464-5571
312	Nat'l HS Baseball Coaches Assoc.	402-457-1962	402-457-1962
53	National League	212-339-7700	212-935-5069
318	New England Collegiate League	860-633-3222	860-633-3222
253	Northeast League	914-436-0411	914-436-6864
282	Northeastern Collegiate League	716-593-3923	716-593-3923
254	Northern League	919-956-8150	919-683-2693
318	Northwest Collegiate League	503-725-5634	503-725-5610
318	Northwoods League	941-644-4022	941-644-1238
21	Office of the Commissioner	212-339-7800	212-355-0007
319	Pacific International League	206-623-8844	602-623-8361
313	Pan American Games	204-985-1999	204-985-1993
115	Pinnacle Brands	214-981-8100	214-981-8200
322	PONY Baseball, Inc.	412-225-1060	412-225-9852
274	Puerto Rican League	787-765-6285	787-767-3028
322	RBI	212-339-7800	212-888-8632
118	SABR	216-575-0500	216-575-0502
319	San Diego Collegiate League	760-438-0347	—
115	Score Board	609-354-9000	609-427-3565
319	Shenandoah Valley League	540-886-1748	540-885-7612
114	Sport Magazine	213-782-2828	213-782-2835
114	The Sporting News	314-997-7111	314-997-0765
114	Sports Illustrated	212-522-1212	212-522-4543
112	The Sports Network	416-494-1212	416-490-7010
101	SportsTicker	201-309-1200	201-860-9742
114	Spring Training BB Yearbook	919-967-2420	919-967-6294
111	STATS, Inc.	847-676-3322	847-676-0821
114	Street and Smith's Baseball	212-880-8698	212-880-4347
313	Sydney Olympic Org. Committee	61-29-297-2000	61-29-287-2020
312	Team One/HS Baseball USA	606-291-4463	606-291-4463
257	Texas-Louisiana League	915-673-7364	915-673-5074
115	Topps	212-376-0300	212-376-0573
114	Total Baseball	212-319-6611	212-310-3820
115	Upper Deck	780-929-6500	780-929-6548
322	US Amateur Baseball Association	425-776-7130	425-776-7130
313	USA Baseball	520-327-9700	520-327-9221
313	US Olympic Committee	719-632-5551	719-578-4654
113	USA Today	703-276-3731	703-558-3988
113	USA Today Baseball Weekly	703-558-5630	703-558-4678
275	Venezuelan League	58-2-751-2079	58-2-751-0891
258	Western League	503-203-8557	503-203-8438

NOTES

NOTES

NOTES